SO-AVD-829

CALIFORNIA
RECREATIONAL
LAKES & RIVERS

FOGHORN OUTDOORS®

CALIFORNIA
RECREATIONAL
LAKES & RIVERS

The Complete Guide to Boating, Fishing, and Water Sports

THIRD EDITION

Tom Stienstra

**AVALON
TRAVEL**

FOGHORN OUTDOORS CALIFORNIA RECREATIONAL LAKES & RIVERS
The Complete Guide to Boating, Fishing, and Water Sports

Third Edition

Tom Stienstra

Text © 2004 by Tom Stienstra.
All rights reserved.
Maps © 2004 by Avalon Travel Publishing.
All rights reserved.

Avalon Travel Publishing is a division of
Avalon Publishing Group, Inc.

Some photos and illustrations are used by permission
and are the property of the original copyright owners.

ISBN: 1-56691-656-9
ISSN: 1538-148X

Please send all feedback about this book to:

ⓕOGHORN OUTDOORS®
California Recreational Lakes & Rivers
Avalon Travel Publishing
1400 65th Street, Suite 250
Emeryville, CA 94608, USA
atpfeedback@avalonpub.com
www.foghorn.com

Printing History
1st edition—1996
3rd edition—March 2004
5 4 3 2 1

Editor: Amy Scott
Series Manager: Marisa Solís
Senior Research Editor: Stephani Cruickshank
Research Editor: Pamela S. Padula
Copy Editor: Jill Metzler
Graphics Coordinator: Deb Dutcher
Production Coordinator: Darren Alessi
Cover and Interior Design: Darren Alessi
Map Editor: Olivia Solís
Cartographers: CHK America, Mike Morgenfeld, Kat Kalamaras, Suzanne Service, Chris Alvarez

Front cover photo: © Mark Gibson, Medicine Lake, CA

Printed in the United States of America by Bang Printing

Foghorn Outdoors and the Foghorn Outdoors logo are the property of Avalon Travel Publishing, a division of Avalon Publishing Group, Inc. All other marks and logos depicted are the property of the original owners.

All rights reserved. No part of this book may be translated or reproduced in any form, except brief extracts by a reviewer for the purpose of a review, without written permission of the copyright owner.

Although every effort was made to ensure that the information was correct at the time of going to press, the author and publisher do not assume and hereby disclaim any liability to any party for any loss or damage caused by errors, omissions, or any potential travel disruption due to labor or financial difficulty, whether such errors or omissions result from negligence, accident, or any other cause.

About the Author

GARY TODOROFF

Tom Stienstra has made it his life's work to explore the West—boating, fishing, camping, hiking, biking, and flying—searching for the best of the outdoors and then writing about it.

His trips include several epic expeditions on rivers and lakes. He has rafted the entire 200-mile Klamath River from its headwaters in Oregon to the Pacific Ocean, and canoed the Sacramento River its 400-mile length from Redding to San Francisco. He has also canoed the remote Owhyee River from the Jarbridge Mountains in northwest Nevada through Idaho and into Oregon, and completed the 75-mile Bowron Lake canoe circuit in British Columbia.

For this book, he visited hundreds of Lakes and Rivers with his inflatables, canoe, and powerboats.

Tom is the nation's top-selling author of outdoor guidebooks. In 2003, he was inducted into the California Outdoor Hall of Fame and has twice been awarded National Outdoor Writer of the Year, newspaper division, by the Outdoor Writers Association of America. He has also been named California Outdoor Writer of the Year four times. Tom is the outdoors columnist for the *San Francisco Chronicle,* and his articles appear on www.SFGate.com and in newspapers around the country.

Tom lives with his family in Northern California. His wife, Stephani Stienstra, has co-authored two books with him and their boys, Jeremy and Kris, have recently been promoted to the rank of captain in "The Stienstra Navy."

You can contact Tom directly via the website www.TomStienstra.com. His other books are also available on his website, including:

Foghorn Outdoors California Camping
Foghorn Outdoors California Fishing
Foghorn Outdoors California Hiking (with Ann Marie Brown)
Foghorn Outdoors California Wildlife (with illustrator Paul Johnson)
Foghorn Outdoors Northern California Cabins & Cottages (with Stephani Stienstra)
Foghorn Outdoors Oregon Camping
Foghorn Outdoors Pacific Northwest Camping
Foghorn Outdoors Tom Stienstra's Bay Area Recreation
Foghorn Outdoors Washington Camping (with Stephani Stienstra)

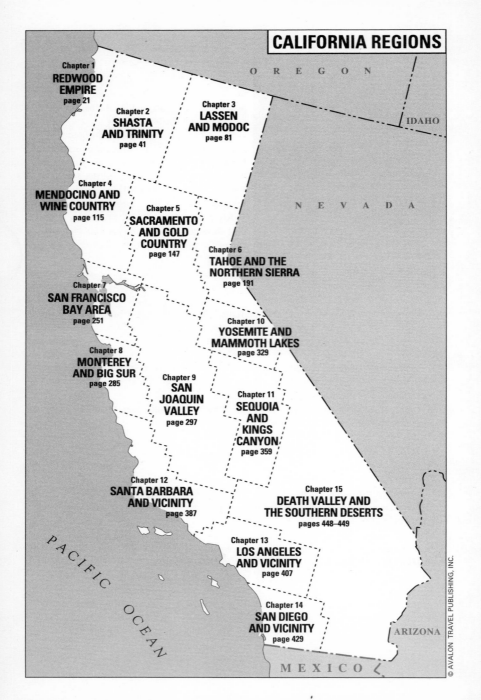

CALIFORNIA REGIONS

OREGON

IDAHO

Chapter 1
REDWOOD EMPIRE
page 21

Chapter 2
SHASTA AND TRINITY
page 41

Chapter 3
LASSEN AND MODOC
page 81

Chapter 4
MENDOCINO AND WINE COUNTRY
page 115

Chapter 5
SACRAMENTO AND GOLD COUNTRY
page 147

NEVADA

Chapter 6
TAHOE AND THE NORTHERN SIERRA
page 191

Chapter 7
SAN FRANCISCO BAY AREA
page 251

Chapter 10
YOSEMITE AND MAMMOTH LAKES
page 329

Chapter 8
MONTEREY AND BIG SUR
page 285

Chapter 9
SAN JOAQUIN VALLEY
page 297

Chapter 11
SEQUOIA AND KINGS CANYON
page 359

Chapter 12
SANTA BARBARA AND VICINITY
page 387

Chapter 15
DEATH VALLEY AND THE SOUTHERN DESERTS
pages 448–449

Chapter 13
LOS ANGELES AND VICINITY
page 407

Chapter 14
SAN DIEGO AND VICINITY
page 429

ARIZONA

PACIFIC OCEAN

MEXICO

© AVALON TRAVEL PUBLISHING, INC.

Contents

Preface

This book puts the best of California's lakes and rivers right in your hands. It was written with the intent that it will become your bible for boating, fishing, and water sports across California. *Foghorn Outdoors California Recreational Lakes & Rivers* is the most accurate, up-to-date guidebook of its kind. I have detailed every lake, every river—nearly 400 listings—and the water sports popular at each, as well as precise directions to each area's boat ramps.

This includes:

—180 areas with boat ramps.
—122 areas for water-skiing and wake boarding.
—272 places for swimming.
—172 areas for sailboarding.
—107 places for personal watercraft.
—67 places for rafting, canoeing, or kayaking.

Activity icons show which activities can be enjoyed at every locale. Boating rules, speed limits, and safety zones are also described to make your trip as safe and fun as possible, and to help you select the best destination for your adventure. As an added bonus, we've included an adaptation of the State of California Department of Boating and Waterways' *ABCs of the California Boating Law,* a must-read for every boat owner in the state.

Beyond the scope of lakes, rivers, streams, bays, and coastal areas in California, I discovered a much more important lesson in writing this book: For anybody who desires adventure, excitement, fun, and a chance at true freedom, the fastest way to get it is with a boat. In a boat, there is nothing but open space, often for miles . . . no stoplights, no traffic jams . . . and in the outdoors, I have learned firsthand that heading out in a boat is the fastest and easiest way to put a giant smile on your face.

See you out there!

—Tom Stienstra

Our Commitment

We are committed to making *Foghorn Outdoors California Recreational Lakes & Rivers* the most accurate, thorough, and enjoyable boating, fishing, and water sports guide to the state. With this third edition you can rest assured that every lake and river in this book has been carefully reviewed and accompanied by the most up-to-date information. Be aware that with the passing of time some of the fees listed herein may have changed, and some parks may have closed unexpectedly. If you have a specific need or concern, it's best to call the location ahead of time.

If you would like to comment on the book, whether it's to suggest a lake or river we overlooked, or to let us know about any noteworthy experience—good or bad—that occurred while using *Foghorn Outdoors California Recreational Lakes & Rivers* as your guide, we would appreciate hearing from you. Please address correspondence to:

> *Foghorn Outdoors California Recreational Lakes & Rivers*, 3rd edition
> Avalon Travel Publishing
> 1400 65th Street, Suite 250
> Emeryville, CA 94608
> email: atpfeedback@avalonpub.com

If you send us an email, please put "Foghorn Outdoors California Recreational Lakes & Rivers" in the subject line.

MAP SYMBOLS

═══ Superhighway	★ Point of Interest	Ranger Station
══ Primary Road	• Accommodation	ᵮ Picnic Area
══ Secondary Road	▪ Other Location	State Park
------- Trail	∧ Campground	Golf Course
○ City/Town	☑ Marina	Waterfall
✕ Airfield/Airstrip	▬ Boat Ramp	▲ Mountain
	▬ Dam	// Mountain Pass

© AVALON TRAVEL PUBLISHING, INC.

How to Use This Book

You can search for your ideal boating, fishing, or water sports spot in two ways:

1) If you know the name of the lake or river you'd like to visit, or the name of the surrounding geographical area or nearby feature (town, national or state park, forest, mountain, etc.), look it up in the index and turn to the corresponding page.

2) If you know the general area you want to visit, turn to the map at the beginning of the chapter that covers that area. Each chapter map is broken down into detail maps, which show by number all the lakes and rivers in that chapter. You can then determine which lakes and rivers are near your destination by their corresponding numbers. Lakes and rivers are listed sequentially in each chapter so you can turn to the page with the corresponding map number for the site you're interested in.

About the Ratings

Every listing in this book is rated on a scale of 1 to 10. The ratings are based on three factors: the quality of the boating, the diversity of the water sports, and scenic beauty. Because water conditions can fluctuate wildly from year to year, so can the validity of the ratings. Many destinations rated a 4 or 5 can still provide a great experience when conditions are ideal.

About the Profiles

Each site in this book is listed in a consistent, easy-to-read format to help you choose the ideal boating, fishing, or water sports spot. From a general overview of the setting to detailed driving directions, the profile will provide all the information you need. Here is an example:

Map number and site name → **❶ SOMEWHERE USA RIVER**

Icons noting activities and facilities at or nearby the site

Rating: 10 ← Overall rating, on a scale of 1–10

General location of the site named by its proximity to the nearest major town or landmark →

south of Somewhere USA Park

Map 1.2, page 4 ← Map the site can be found on and page number the map can be found on

Each site in this book begins with a brief overview of its setting. The description typically covers ambience, information about the attractions, and activities popular at the site. **Access:** This section notes the type of boat ramps available at the site and their location. Put-ins and hand launching spots are also described. **Facilities, fees:** This section describes the facilities available at or near the site, such as restrooms, picnic areas, snack bars, restaurants, lodges, marinas, boat rental outlets, campgrounds, and where to buy supplies like groceries and gas. Whether access is free or day-use and other fees are charged is also noted here. **Water sports, restrictions:** This section provides details on boating rules, speed limits, and safety zones, as well as information on what activities can be enjoyed at the site. Also refer to the *ABCs of the California Boating Law* in the Resource section in the back of the book. **Directions:** This section provides mile-by-mile driving directions to the site from the nearest major town. **Contact:** This section provides an address, phone number, and email address and website, if available, for each site.

About the Icons

The icons in this book are designed to provide at-a-glance information on activities, facilities, and services provided that are available on-site or within walking distance of each site. The icons are not meant to represent every activity or service, but rather those that are most significant.

— Boating opportunities are available. Various types of vessels apply under this umbrella activity, including motorboats and personal watercrafts (Jet Skis). Refer to the text for that site for more details, including mph restrictions and boat ramp availability.

— Canoeing, kayaking, and/or rafting opportunities are available.

— Jet Skiing (referred to in this book as personal watercraft riding) opportunities are available.

— Water-skiing opportunities are available.

— Sailboarding opportunities are available.

— Fishing opportunities are available.

— Hiking trails are available.

— Biking trails or routes are available.

— Swimming opportunities are available.

— Hot or cold springs are located nearby. Refer to the text for that listing for more information.

— Pets are permitted. Sites that allow pets may require an additional fee or that pets be leashed. Refer to the text for specific instructions or call in advance.

— A playground is available.

— Wheelchair access is provided. However, concerned persons are advised to call the contact number to be certain that their specific needs will be met.

— RV camping sites are available.

— Tent camping sites are available.

About the Maps

This book is divided into chapters based on regions; an overview map of these regions precedes the table of contents. At the start of each chapter, you'll find a map of the entire region, enhanced by a grid that divides the region into smaller sections. These sections are then enlarged into individual detail maps. Sites are noted on the detail map by number.

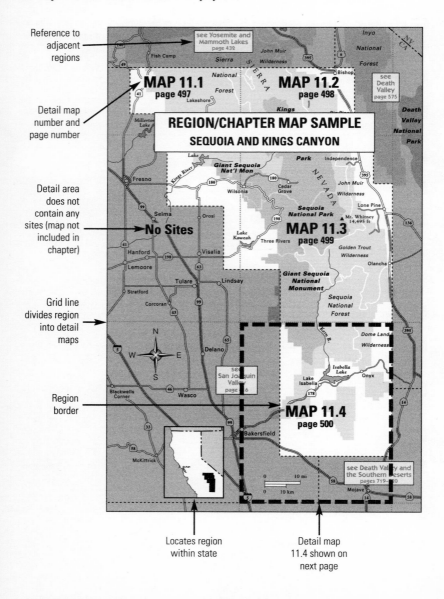

Reference to adjacent regions

Detail map number and page number

Detail area does not contain any sites (map not included in chapter)

Grid line divides region into detail maps

Region border

Locates region within state

Detail map 11.4 shown on next page

REGION/CHAPTER MAP SAMPLE
SEQUOIA AND KINGS CANYON

No Sites

MAP 11.1 page 497

MAP 11.2 page 498

MAP 11.3 page 499

MAP 11.4 page 500

see Yosemite and Mammoth Lakes page 432

see Death Valley page 575

see San Joaquin Valley page 6

see Death Valley and the Southern Deserts pages 719-760

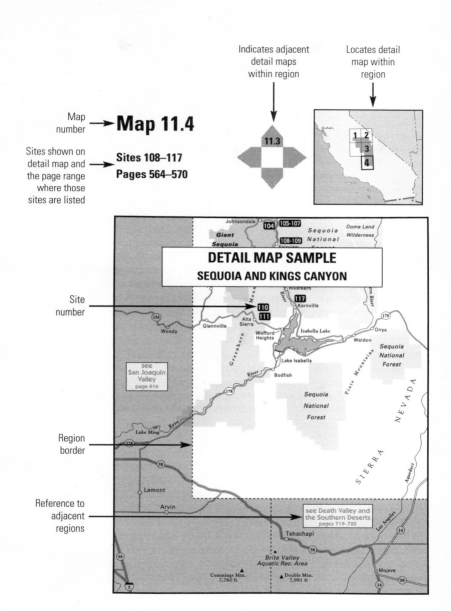

Indicates adjacent
detail maps
within region

Locates detail
map within
region

Map
number → **Map 11.4**

Sites shown on
detail map and → **Sites 108–117**
the page range
where those
sites are listed **Pages 564–570**

11.3

DETAIL MAP SAMPLE
SEQUOIA AND KINGS CANYON

Site
number →

Region
border →

Reference to
adjacent
regions →

FOGHORN OUTDOORS®

© ROBERT HOLMES/CALTOUR

Introduction

Introduction

Let Your Ship Come In

Do you feel useless, unhappy, and have a lousy sex life?

Join the club, eh? Just kidding . . . but one answer to a better life, according to a national survey, is to get a boat, any boat (well, almost any boat) and get out there and have some fun.

Maybe that's why the sales of boats and motors have remained steady across the nation even during years when there are economic downturns, when there is little money available for most people to buy goodies.

Because according to a survey conducted by the Impulse Research Corp., if you want to harbor health, then let your ship come in. By margins of roughly 10 percent, the survey concludes that boaters have better health, self-esteem, the ability to enjoy life, and a better sex life than non-boaters. Conversely, by margins of 4 to 8 percent, non-boaters are more prone to feeling useless, lonely, unhappy, and fatigued. These margins would probably be larger except there are some boaters who own old outboards that won't start at the boat ramp, and that not only skews the results, but increases the homicide level (man shoots motor to death).

The latter may be why the sales of outboards have gone up in recent years when just about every industry on the planet went down. It also is a fact that boaters new and old are equally entranced with the new generation of four-cycle engines. It used to be that trolling with a smoky two-cycle felt something like mowing the lawn. Those days are a nightmare of the past with the development of clean-running, quiet four-strokes.

The other areas with big increases are car-top boats, primarily canoes and kayaks. The reasons are money, SUVs, and reality afield.

Canoes and kayaks are the cheapest way to get in the game. And SUVs are the easiest way to make a trip work, that is, where you throw a canoe on top of your rig, then venture off to a lake to claim it for your own. Since California has 190 recreation lakes, reachable by vehicle, that do not have boat ramps (yet most have campgrounds), this can be the best summer gig in the state.

But once you discover the charm of a canoe or kayak on flat water, you will eventually desire an upgrade, and thus the addiction begins. It started for me with a small raft, floating around ranch ponds, casting for bass. It graduated to a canoe, a 17-foot Old Town Tripper, which I took everywhere imaginable, from San Francisco Bay to mountain lakes to the Canadian wilderness. Then it was on to a flat-water kayak and an inflatable kayak. Then to a small skiff, and eventually to a 20-foot fiberglass cruiser that didn't run right (tried to get in on the cheap; bad move). Finally, I caved and bought something expensive, a new 19-foot, aluminum, do-it-all boat with a bullet-proof 115-horse four-stroke.

Note that this process started innocently with the purchase of a $79 raft with $10 plastic paddles.

What You'll Find Inside This Book

My first intent in writing this book was to capture what I've seen and learned in 25 years of roaming around as a full-time outdoors writer, covering nearly one million miles in California alone. I've explored all 58 counties, logged 20,000 hiking miles, and experienced 1,000 lakes, the entire coast, 20 national forests, 50 wilderness areas, and 250 state, national, regional, and county parks. I'm always looking for another place to explore and capture the outdoor experience, and there always seems to be another place to discover.

I also want the book to steer you in the right direction. Imprecise directions have always bugged me. So for this edition, I rewrote directions with a new master style. All directions have been carefully reviewed and have been written as if the passenger is reading it to the driver. In many cases, the accuracy is now to .10 mile.

"No Place Left to Go?"

The way this book came about is filled with irony. It started when I kept hearing people complaining that, "there is nowhere left to go in California." I used to think that myself. In the 1980s, I even started planning to move to Alaska or the Northwest Territories to be a bush plane pilot and guide. In the process of being certified as a pilot, I looked down on the vast California landscape and started seeing another world out there, a world outside the tunnel of freeway traffic, where all things great and wonderful seemed possible. My mission suddenly changed. I wanted to explore all of these beautiful places that were being unveiled to me from the air.

This book largely details that lifelong adventure.

The Best Time to Go Is Now

As you may have realized, this is not a hobby for me, as it is for some part-time writers who publish books. Between my job as outdoors columnist for the *San Francisco Chronicle* and putting together guidebooks, this is my full-time job—and has been for 25 years. I spend 200 days a year in the field, traveling an average of 30,000 to 40,000 miles per year; it works because I often fly to cut time, and I don't commute to a job or watch TV. This has given me years' worth of extra time in the outdoors. In the process, I see first-hand how seriously people take their fun, what they need to know to make their trip work, and how their underlying fears of getting stuck without a spot for the night can take the life out of what should be a rejuvenating experience. Sound familiar?

Solve these problems by taking my advice. Never go anywhere without this book on your front seat!

The outdoors is good for the soul, especially when shared with the people you care for most. If you don't think you have enough time to be outdoors enjoying what nature has to offer, do what I do and schedule time for outdoor activities. It's a great way to beat the time trap. If you schedule it, you'll do it, and there's no better time than right now to enjoy the outdoors.

Tom Stienstra, March 2004
website: www.tomstienstra.com

Buying the Perfect Boat

The First Commandment of buying the perfect boat is to "define the boat's mission."

"No boat is perfect for all families or all uses," advises Frank Sargeant, a longtime comrade in the outdoor writing business, the author of *The Complete Idiot's Guide to Boating,* and a former charter boat skipper. "Choose a boat that suits most of your needs, but be aware that it has limitations."

That is where nearly everybody gets stuck. Nobody wants limits. We want a boat to do everything, no matter where we take it. So right off, we violate the First Commandment.

Thus starts the paradox for every person looking to buy a boat, and why it can take years to find the right fit. At the San Francisco Sports & Boat Show at the Cow Palace, there are typically nearly 1,000 boats from 250 dealers, most designed for specific uses. At the International Sportsmen's Exposition at Cal Expo in Sacramento, there are another 125 boats from 17 different dealers.

It took me three years and advice from a half-dozen experts and a broker to find the new addition to The Stienstra Navy—a boat that would satisfy every need, including what is acknowledged in the industry as "The Wife Factor."

"What you want is pretty much impossible," said Galen Onizuka, a former boat salesman and licensed skipper. "Boats are built to do one thing well. It's about impossible to find one that will do it all. That's the first rule of buying a boat."

George Seifert, the retired coach of the San Francisco 49ers and Carolina Panthers, advised me once that it can take years to find the ideal boat.

"I read the Sportsmen's Corner every morning just to see what's happening in the boat market," he said.

After Seifert flipped a skiff in the surf off the San Francisco beach and almost drowned, former 49er owner Eddie DeBartolo gave Seifert a bigger boat, a 23-foot Grady White powered by giant twin outboards. It's ideal for fishing the ocean, Seifert's passion.

"It took years of looking, but I picked it out at the Boat Show," Seifert said. "Eddie gave it to me as a present for winning my first Super Bowl."

If you want guacamole, I've learned, you better get an avocado, so the first thing I did was sit down with my pal Bob Simms, owner of six boats, and then hire him as a broker who would represent me as an anonymous buyer.

Like every buyer, we started by detailing my family's needs: "The boat needs to do everything." Heh, heh, heh.

"That's impossible, of course," Simms responded with a laugh. "Actually, it's just difficult, but we'll find it."

"How much money should I put aside?" I asked.

"All of it," he answered with a hearty laugh.

So like every family buying a boat, we made our list. The first question, with every boat, is this: Where do you plan on using it?

The answer, well, was "everywhere."

That's right, big enough to handle the bays, even the ocean on a flat-calm day, and the big lakes in the region.

Yet at the same time, it needed to be down-sized enough for the smaller lakes with speed limits, and 100 other small, often pristine lakes sprinkled across the mountain country. The boat also needed to be light enough to trailer easily in urban traffic as well as into the mountains, and to also maneuver and back up with scarcely a second thought, and to load on a trailer quickly at the boat ramps.

"OK," Bob explained, "that makes it an 18- to 19-footer, aluminum hull. What else?"

The boat needs to be stable, so it won't rock when used as a family swimming platform or broach when several people are leaning over on one side, and be able to handle a wind chop at cruise—that is, where the hull doesn't slam the water over and over again like a teeter-totter.

"That means an 8-foot beam amidship for stability," I was told, "with a 15-degree V-hull at the bow to smooth out wind chop."

It needs to be fast enough to cover big water, even at high-elevation lakes (where engines lose power), with enough zip out of the hole for tubing, and easy access for swimmers.

That translates to a 115-horsepower outboard engine, a fast, removable ski tow bar, and a built-in swim step and ladder off the stern.

Yet not only does the boat need to be fast, but it also has to have the ability to run at a slow walk, that is, so it can be used for slow-trolling techniques for giant trout. The impossible dream, especially with a big engine, right?

Wrong. "We'll add a transom-mount, 76-pound thrust electric motor," I was told, not only ideal for slow-trolling, but whisper quiet. "For conditions where typical trolling speeds are acceptable, add a trolling plate on the outboard."

Of course, the outboard engine must be environmentally clean and quiet, with the best technology available, legal for Lake Tahoe and other lakes requiring the EPA's 2006 standards.

That makes it a four-cycle engine, and in this case, a Honda that absolutely purrs, so quiet it is stunning, so clean there is no smell at all, and aces the most stringent environmental tests. A Honda 115 can also troll all day without missing a beat.

Now this boat was actually beginning to take shape.

Since it would be needed for so many uses—fishing, water recreation, camping, picnics on the water, for both family and professional use—I needed to be able to have different seating configurations, depending on how many people were aboard.

No problem, came the answer. "That means removable seats."

Lots of bells and whistles required, adding to the list: Built-in live well, Scotty Depthpower downriggers, Lowrance X-65 fishfinder, stand-up removable fishing top with canvas and windshield for bad weather, Tonneau cover for protection when stored or when towed, and built-in compartments for fishing rods, safety equipment, drinks.

"No problem again," Bob explained, "just add it to the list."

But what about the electrical system, I asked. With the electric trolling motor and all this gear, would it drain the batteries? After all, got to listen to the baseball games on the radio in the summer, right?

Absolutely, came the answer, especially Giants vs. Dodgers, and hence on the spot, we created a special four-battery electrical system: two marine batteries dedicated to the trolling motor alone—with an external plug pre-wired for easy re-charging—and two others to power the engine and other components.

Well, that was pretty much it. After a significant search, it turned out that such a boat didn't actually exist. But almost.

I saw a boat up at Lake Tahoe being run by State Parks that looked about perfect, and told the broker about it.

It turned out it was built by a shop in Chico called Design Concepts that will take one of its base models, then customize it for individual needs. I did some homework, and discovered that the California Department of Parks and Recreation and many sheriff departments have bought more than 100 boats here, custom designed for their needs, just as I wanted.

The broker gave them the list, negotiated a price, and I then emerged from anonymity and had the words "The Stienstra Navy" painted on the engine.

In one of the first voyages, a trip to Lake Berryessa with Dusty Baker and pals, Dusty gave the boat a critical lookover, then was astonished at the quietness of the engine, and later, the with the boat's stability when a fish was caught and five of us all looked over the side to see how big it was.

Later in the day, he was casting for bass at the bow, and I asked him, "Well, Dusty, what would you change with this boat?"

"Nothing," he answered. "I wouldn't change a thing. Everything is just right. Now if we can just get the fish to bite."

The Old Green Canoe

A stranger at the boat ramp laughed, then shook his head as I hoisted my old canoe from the top of my truck, then set it in the lake.

"That's a pretty old, worn-out looking boat," the stranger said. "Tippy looking, too. I'm surprised you don't have something better."

I looked at the old canoe, and noticed that the outer green hull was chipped in about a dozen spots on each end, where the white inner layer was showing through, from so many landings on rocky shores. The gunwale was bent from where a houseboat hit it. A seat was partially cracked, yeah, just old, the yoke was discolored from portages, and the inside was stained from fish, dirt, and 25 years of living—the past 15 with me.

After looking at the canoe for a minute, I turned back to the stranger. "You know, I don't like to brag, but this is quite a boat and I really love this old green canoe." He moved closer to hear why, a mix of a little bit of logic and a lot of heart.

You know, I bought it for $175 in 1981, a 17-foot Old Town Tripper, and it's been through five trucks, thousands of miles, and hundreds of adventures. For paddling, it is stable enough to handle big lakes, and slippery enough for Class II whitewater rivers. For camping, it will hold 1,100 pounds of people and gear. For fishing, I bolt a two-horsepower engine on a sidemount, which allows perfect approaches for a cast at a secret spot or precise control over trolling speed, and have installed backrests for comfort. For the wilderness, it weighs 81 pounds and I've carried that old green canoe on my shoulders for miles on portages between lakes.

I've also learned that California has 190 lakes you can reach by vehicle where there are no boat ramps—lakes that are perfect for canoes and other car-top boats. In a state with 840,000 registered boats and 34 million residents, you can often count on having these places to yourself, even on a warm evening when the trout are jumping, right in the middle of summer. And at lakes with boat ramps, more than a hundred have speed limits that protect low-speed boats such as canoes.

But while logic gives you what you need, logic has nothing to do with what really drives people. What drives people are the things they crave and must have, things that go to the heart of passions, memories, and the chance of fulfilling dreams in the days to come.

Anybody who has almost lost their life knows this to be true, and so it was with me on a dark, icy day at a lake in the Cascades, when I misloaded that old green canoe—no weight in the front—and was paddling solo when it flipped because of the weight imbalance and dumped me into chilling waters.

The canoe wouldn't turn upright and float, so I kept it upside down as a paddle board and tried to kick my way back to shore. After 15 minutes, my brother, Bob, judged from shore that I wasn't going to make it. He stripped, jumped in, grabbed the front of that capsized boat, and together, we managed to struggle for another 15 minutes and make our way to land, ice-cold, too cold to shiver, our legs so numb that we couldn't stand up. But we were alive.

Later when we turned the canoe over, everything was lost except, lodged under a seat, one paddle and a fishing rod, the one my grandfather gave me when I turned 12.

"I think this is a message," I remember my brother saying. "You are supposed to paddle and fish a lot more in this boat."

And so it has been. I have adventured across the West, seeing the best of America and western Canada, from diving ospreys and eagles, to deer and moose swimming across lakes, to giant trout I have given names like Luther, Jargo, Horgon, and Herganon.

Crazy stuff has happened. My old friend Ed Ow accidentally plowed right over the top of "Old Green" in a houseboat, but it survived with a battle scar. Another time, amid a late-night poker game at a Redding hotel with other outdoors writers, I poked my head outside and saw that my beloved canoe was gone from the top of my truck, apparently stolen. I was distraught beyond imagination, but then I heard a happy shriek, looked down, and there in the hotel swimming pool were two women in evening gowns paddling around in the canoe—and then they tipped over.

I had always wanted a canoe, and back in 1977 I was offered an Old Town Tripper by a camping pal, Tom Bullock of Redwood City, a photographer.

"I want you to have this boat, and I want you to go to the Bowron Lakes," Bullock said, his eye alive with the vision of paddling Canada's 75-mile canoe circuit.

"I just can't right now, just can't afford it," I answered. At the time, I was quitting my job as a columnist to write books, and was saving every penny I could. He tried to convince me to take it, but to no avail.

Three years passed, my articles started selling, and I realized how bad I still wanted that boat, so I called Tom Bullock and told him the time was right for me to buy it. "It's not available," he said, flecked with chagrin. "I just don't want to part with it right now." Turns out he had terminal cancer and died a few days later.

Another year passed and I started looking for a canoe, but couldn't find the right model. Another friend, John Reginato of Redding, said he knew of an old green one that had been sitting for months in a yard at a house about 10 miles outside of town. He thought it was an Old Town, maybe even a Tripper.

Two weeks later I made the trip, and yes, it was an Old Town Tripper, and after a short negotiation with the owner, John Morrill, I bought it for $175. Just as I was hoisting it on my truck, Morrill stopped me.

"Before you take it away, you should know who really owned this canoe," Morrill said. "It actually belonged to my wife's dad, who was quite a guy. He was a great outdoorsman, canoed the Bowron Lakes, a real character, a great photographer. His name was Tom Bullock."

As I put the boat in the lake this week, I remembered that incident as if it had happened the previous day, about how the turns of destiny had brought this canoe to my life, and the pleasure I have had from it. Sometimes at dusk, when the swallows are catching bugs and the eagle comes out for the rising trout, I swear that I can feel the angel of my old friend, Tom Bullock, watching over me.

Then I looked at the stranger at the boat ramp, who was inspecting the bent gunwale.

"You know, on second thought, I do like to brag," I told him, "because I'm pretty proud of this old, green canoe."

Author's Picks

Top 5 Places for Houseboating

1. Shasta Lake, Shasta and Trinity, page 68. This is the boating capital of the West. Giant Shasta Lake has 370 miles of shoreline, 400 houseboat rentals, 12 marinas, 14 boat ramps, 12 campgrounds, lakeshore lodging, and 22 species of sport fish. From a houseboat, it takes about five or six days to see the whole thing. With all the houseboaters on the water, it can seem like one big party of happy people. If you want peace and quiet, just head into one of the coves.

2. South/East Delta, San Joaquin Valley, page 306. What a great spot for houseboating, here on the threshold of 1,000 miles of waterways. Some of the houseboats on the delta are host to floating parties that kick off on a Friday evening and go nonstop through Sunday. If you want to experience complete insanity—the fun type—head out here for a three-day weekend.

3. Lake Oroville, Sacramento and Gold Country, page 157. Lake Oroville has it all: houseboats, campgrounds, enough water for all kinds of boating, a fish for every angler, and accommodations tailor-made for boaters/campers, including floating campsites, floating toilets (no kidding), boat-in campgrounds, and two excellent marinas. This huge, man-made reservoir has extensive lake arms and a large central body of water, covering more than 15,000 acres, with 165 miles of shoreline.

4. Lake Don Pedro, San Joaquin Valley, page 315. A giant lake with many extended arms, Don Pedro is one of the best boating and water sports destinations in California during high water years. Giant? When full, it covers nearly 13,000 surface acres and has 160 miles of shoreline. The lake arms provide zillions of hidden coves where you can park your boat, camp, swim, play, and fish.

5. Trinity Lake, Shasta and Trinity, page 66. Many houseboaters consider Trinity Lake the ideal destination. The lake is set at an elevation of 2,300 feet at the eastern foot of the Trinity Alps. It covers 17,000 acres, ample room for all types of water sports, including water-skiing, personal watercraft, sailboarding, and fishing, yet is distant enough that it rarely attracts hordes of boaters. By August the lake feels like a huge bathtub, making it great for swimming; the best swimming is at the day-use areas and campgrounds operated by the Forest Service.

Top 10 Prettiest Lakes

1. Emerald Bay (Lake Tahoe), Tahoe and the Northern Sierra, page 225. Along with the Yosemite Valley and Oregon's Crater Lake, Lake Tahoe is one of those rare natural wonders that make you feel something special just by looking at it. One of the premier outdoor experiences in the world is boating in Emerald Bay, which brings you right into the heart of Tahoe's incomparable scenic beauty. No matter where you go in the bay, you'll be floating on clear, cobalt blue waters and surrounded by a mountain rim that is topped in early summer with bright white snow. The sight is always remarkable, always breathtaking.

2. Donnells Reservoir, Tahoe and the Northern Sierra, page 245. Donnells is set in a remote gorge in the Stanislaus River Canyon in the central Sierra and resembles a hidden Yosemite. It has steep granite walls, cobalt-blue water, and a massive rock dome that resembles a miniature Half Dome plunging into the lake on the south shore. In the spring, melting snow feeds Little Niagara Falls, which pours over the southern canyon rim to create a 500-foot, two-tiered freefall, a replica of Yosemite Falls, visible only from the north shore and headwaters. With access difficult to impossible, to paddle a kayak across this lake becomes a world-class experience.

3. Tenaya Lake, Yosemite and Mammoth Lakes, page 341. There may be no prettier lake anywhere than Tenaya Lake on a warm, windless evening. It is set in a natural rock basin in the pristine, high granite country of Yosemite. It has an elevation of 8,141 feet and covers 150 acres. The atmosphere feels almost sacred, like a mountain temple.

4. Sardine Lake (Lower), Tahoe and the Northern Sierra, page 201. Sometimes there just is no substitute for spectacular natural beauty. Sardine Lake is set in a rock bowl, with the Sierra Buttes towering above, an eye-popping spectacle. To paddle a canoe across this lake on a quiet dawn or dusk is like dipping your paddle in magic waters. No visit to the Plumas area is complete without a trip to take in the beauty of Sardine Lake.

5. Lake Sabrina, Sequoia and Kings Canyon, page 371. From Bishop, you can see the deep canyon rising west to the Sierra crest. This canyon is a contrast in color, a sea of aspens against the rising backdrop of glacial-carved, steel-gray granite with 12,000-foot peaks. Sabrina is big, gorgeous and comes with a dramatic Sierra backdrop, so beautiful that some can feel overwhelmed when it first comes into sight. On that first visit, many people simply stare in wonder, lost in the moment. This is the prettiest lake in the Eastern Sierra.

6. Independence Lake, Tahoe and the Northern Sierra, page 211. On calm days when the wind doesn't blow (and that can be rare here), Independence Lake is drop-dead beautiful, colored deep azure blue, set in a canyon bordered by timbered slopes. This is California's mystery lake. It is difficult to find, difficult to get a boat in, and difficult to fish. The lake is set at an elevation of 6,949 feet, north of Truckee, and its secrets include a resident ghost as well as some of the biggest (and most elusive) cutthroat and brown trout around.

7. Donner Lake, Tahoe and the Northern Sierra, page 216. The first glimpse of Donner Lake is always a stirring one, and many vacationers cruising past on I-80 stop to look at the sparkling blue waters. The remarkable beauty evokes a heartfelt response in all who witness it. This is a big oblong lake, three miles long, three-quarters of a mile wide, with 7.5 miles of shoreline, and is set near the Sierra crest at an elevation of 5,900 feet.

8. Lake Siskiyou, Shasta and Trinity, page 59. This lake sits at the base of giant Mount Shasta, which towers above at 14,162 feet, giving it one of the loveliest settings for a man-made lake in America. Recreation—not water storage for farming—was the sole reason Siskiyou was built. Thus, while reservoirs in the foothills of California are drained when water is needed, Siskiyou remains full, often having a jewel-like quality. That is why people come here—to visit the most beautiful lake along the entire I-5 corridor.

9. Convict Lake, Yosemite and Mammoth Lakes, page 352. People who worship untouched natural beauty can practice their religion at this mountain shrine. The lake is framed by a back wall of wilderness mountain peaks and is fronted by a shoreline dotted with giant rocks and a few scattered pines. Although it is set at 7,583 feet and bordered by the John Muir Wilderness to the west, it is easily accessed off U.S. 395 to the east.

10. Hell Hole Reservoir, Tahoe and the Northern Sierra, page 220. Sapphire-blue water fills this lake in a massive granite gorge backed by the Granite Chief Wilderness. The water is pure and is fed by the most remote stretches of the pristine Rubicon River. At dawn, the water is cobalt blue, as blue as Tahoe. It's a long drive to get here. But few things worth remembering come easy.

Top 10 Boat-In Camping Sites

1. Emerald Bay (Lake Tahoe), Tahoe and the Northern Sierra, page 225. If you are looking for one of the best outdoor experiences on the planet, try boating in Emerald Bay followed by a stay at one of its boat-in campsites. With a boat you can do more than just stare in awe at the clear, cobalt blue waters and the nearby mountain rim; you can surround yourself with this incomparable beauty. And with a boat-in camp, you can wake up in the middle of it all, too.

2. Shasta Lake, Shasta and Trinity, page 68. When Shasta fills in the early summer, it is a stunning sight, with 370 miles of shoreline and ringed by budding vegetation and blooming dogwood and redbud. A highlight is four developed boat-in camps (Gooseneck, Greens Creek, Arbuckle Flat, Ski Island), and hundreds of flat spots deep inside coves where you can beach your boat and camp do-it-yourself style.

3. Bullards Bar Reservoir, Sacramento and Gold Country, page 160. Bullards Bar Reservoir stands out like a silver dollar in a field of pennies when compared to the other reservoirs in the Central Valley foothills. Not only are there two boat-in campgrounds, but boaters are allowed to create their own primitive campsites anywhere along the lakeshore.

4. Lake Sonoma, Mendocino and Wine Country, page 136. Lake Sonoma is often the first major lake to fill in California each year, often topping out at 100 percent before Christmas. By March, it usually settles, clears, and greens up, creating a gem in the foothills, and looks to stay that way well into June. There are 109 primitive boat-in sites, along with two developed campgrounds and a few hike-in sites.

5. Union Valley Reservoir, Tahoe and the Northern Sierra, page 229. Set at 4,900 feet in the Crystal Basin, Union Valley is the prettiest of the many lakes in this region of the Sierra. The lake fills every spring, and is kept at higher levels than other lakes in the region. A personal favorite is the Azalea Cove boat-in camp.

6. Silverwood Lake, Los Angeles and Vicinity, page 412. When full, Silverwood covers 1,000 acres and has 13 miles of shoreline. It is set at an elevation of 3,378 feet, and is bordered by San

Bernardino makes this place very popular with boaters, especially during hot summers. Boat-in and hike-in campsites are a great bonus.

7. Englebright Lake, Sacramento and Gold Country, page 163. Boaters have access to a rare bonanza here: 17 boat-in campsites that provide both privacy and beautiful views. The reservoir, which covers just 815 acres yet offers 24 miles of shoreline, looks something like a water snake winding its way through the Yuba River Canyon. It is set in the Yuba County foothills at about a 500-foot elevation.

8. Klamath River (Sarah Totten Campground to Happy Camp), Shasta and Trinity, page 51. One spring week in March, I rafted the entire river at flood stage, from its headwaters in Oregon all the way to the Pacific Ocean. The 36-mile downstream stretch from Sarah Totten Campground is ideal for rafting, and there are private beaches where you are permitted to camp.

9. Stone Lagoon, Redwood Empire, page 29. Stone Lagoon covers 521 acres and has a visitors center and a primitive boat ramp located at the parking area along the west side of U.S. 101. From here you plunk into your canoe, wide-bodied kayak, or dinghy, then paddle or sail over to Ryan's Cove, which is straight across the lake and out of sight of the highway. There you will find a great, secluded boat-in campground with sites dispersed along 300 yards of shoreline.

10. Trinity Lake, Shasta and Trinity, page 66. Several good boat-in camps are available, including one at Captain's Point on the west shore of the Trinity River Arm. The lake is set at a 2,300-foot elevation at the eastern foot of the Trinity Alps and covers 17,000 acres, huge enough to accommodate all types of water sports, including water-skiing, personal watercraft, sailboarding, and fishing, yet distant enough that it rarely attracts large numbers of boaters.

Top 10 Places for Rafting

1. Main Stem Tuolumne River, Yosemite and Mammoth Lakes, page 339. Many rafters are baptized by the cool, clear, pounding waters of the Tuolumne, commonly known as "The T." Here you'll find one of California's most thrilling rapids, Pinball, and one of the most terrorizing, Clavey Falls. The 18-mile run, from Meral Pool downstream to Ward's Ferry, is rated Class IV+. Anybody who runs it will have experienced the true essence of exhilaration.

2. Salmon River, Shasta and Trinity, page 49. Most of the rapids on the Cal Salmon, as the Salmon River is affectionately known, alternate between Class IV and V, and only experienced paddlers who don't mind living on the edge need apply. Highlights include Bloomer Falls (Class IV), The Maze (Class IV), Whirling Dervish (Class IV+), and Last Chance (Class V). The latter is a mind-bender of a drop that will send your heart out of your body for what seems like an eternity. In fact, among rafters there is a clear-cut division between those who have run the Cal Salmon and those who have not.

3. Forks of the Kern River, Sequoia and Kings Canyon, page 378. You have to be a little crazy to raft the Forks of the Kern, and that's exactly why we like it. This is expert-only territory, and attempting to run it can be a death-defying act even for the best. The run is rated Class V, just a bit saner than a suicidal Class VI. It is renowned for three things: heart-pumping rapids in quick succession, the stunning canyon setting, and its extremely difficult access.

4. Upper Klamath River, Shasta and Trinity, page 51. Rafting Hell's Corner on the Upper Klamath is kind of like putting a saddle on the space shuttle and riding off into orbit. The worst stretch is Satan's Gate (Class IV), Hell's Corner (Class IV+), and Ambush (Class IV)—one right after the other. This is where boating turns into an act of faith. And it just keeps going. The last big rapids you'll encounter are Snag Islands Falls (Class III+) and Stateline Falls (Class III), providing two final chances to dump.

5. South Fork American River, Sacramento and Gold Country, page 179. Here you have it: the most popular rafting river in America. For newcomers to the sport, the South Fork American is the best choice, offering easy access, enough of a white-water challenge to add some sizzle, and a huge array of guided trips to choose from. This is a Class III run, considered the perfect introduction to rafting, and there are plenty of takers. The white-water highlights include Meatgrinder (Class III), Troublemaker (Class III+), and Satan's Cesspool (Class III+), which can challenge even experienced paddlers and give most novices the opportunity to see if their heart can pound a hole through their chest.

6. Upper Kings River, Sequoia and Kings Canyon, page 374. The Upper Kings is a scintillating stretch of water suitable only for daredevil experts. It features a Class V+ rating, incredible views, and near-death drops. The reward is unequaled wilderness scenery, including a breathtaking view of 640-foot Garlic Falls (on the right at mile 5). Note: There is no trail access to much of this stretch of river, except for the two-mile trail to the put-in. This means there is no chance of rescue.

7. Merced River, Yosemite and Mammoth Lakes, page 347. The Merced features an extraordinarily long (29 miles) stretch of river that can be run from the put-in at Red Bud to the takeout at Bagby. It is rated Class IV+ for the first 9 miles and the last 13 miles, and is rated Class II for the 7 miles in between. The scenery is attractive and the run has a remote feel, even though much of it is paralleled by the highway. The first 2.5 miles contain some Class IV white water, most notably Chipped Tooth and Nightmare Island.

8. Klamath River (Happy Camp to Green Riffle), Shasta and Trinity, page 46. Nature's artwork can seem perfect here. The Klamath River tumbles around boulders and into gorges, then flattens into slicks, all the while framed by a high, tree-lined canyon rim and an azure blue sky. From Happy Camp to Green Riffle it's 37.5 miles, and highlights include Kanaka Falls (Class III) and Dragon's Tooth (Class III+). To sum it up, this is a very pretty run with lots of birdlife, pretty river bends, and a good number of easy runs interspersed by slicks, making it a kick for all comers.

9. Middle Fork American River, Tahoe and the Northern Sierra, page 218. The scenery is exquisite, remote, and lush. The water is cold and clear. Historical sites from the Gold Rush days abound. And the white-water rafting runs bear such names as Texas Chainsaw Mama and Murderer's Bar. Need more be said? Texas Chainsaw Mama? Hey, where do they get these names, anyway? Right, this is the Middle Fork American, the challenging alternative to the popular South Fork American.

10. Lower Kern River, Sequoia and Kings Canyon, page 383. A challenging intermediate-advanced section is featured on this run. Most of the white water is rated Class III+, though there are a few Class IVs sprinkled along the route, including White Maiden's Walkway, Dead Man's Curve, Hari-Kari, Horseshoe Falls, and Pinball. Here's an insider's note: You'll find hot springs at the Miracle Hot Springs camping area. The area is not maintained, but you can still find hot pools if you search around a bit.

Top 10 Fishing Sites

1. San Joaquin Delta, San Francisco Bay Area, page 259. The San Joaquin Delta provides the most consistent catches for largemouth bass and is a great year-round fishery. Even in summer on the hottest days, you can search out the thickest weed beds, cast weedless frogs and rats, and the big bass will explode through the weed mat to take the lure. Add the chance for migratory striped bass, salmon, and sturgeon, and you've got the No. 1 fishing spot in California.

2. Lake Barrett, San Diego and Vicinity, page 444. An exit survey showed that under the lottery system, the average catch here was 19 bass per angler, and because some people came only for the giant bluegill and crappie, the survey meant in reality that the average bass catch was far higher. In fact, talented anglers on good days have caught more than 100 bass. Even in slow periods, the average catch is 10 bass per day.

3. Lake San Antonio, Santa Barbara and Vicinity, page 392. Can you imagine catching 100 bass in a day? At San Antonio, that fantasy occasionally can even become a reality. This lake is one of the best in California for high catch rates of largemouth bass, which makes the whole San Antonio experience very special. Lake San Antonio is a long and narrow lake, covering 5,500 surface acres and offering 60 miles of shoreline.

4. Lake Cachuma, Santa Barbara and Vicinity, page 397. Cachuma has become one of the hottest bass lakes in America, for both largemouth and smallmouth bass. About 48,500 trout are stocked here yearly, and they are like growing pills for the bass. When full, the lake is lovely and big, covering 3,200 acres.

5. Smith River, Redwood Empire, page 27. Smith River is unforgettable, thanks to its great natural beauty, redwoods, firs, pines, granite-lined gorges, and the free-flowing water. There's no place like it. There's also no place else in California with bigger steelhead in the winter, and the best chance at a 40- or 50-pound salmon in the fall.

6. Shasta Lake, Shasta and Trinity, page 68. Shasta Lake is the outdoor recreation capital of Northern California. The lake has 22 species of fish with trout, bass, salmon, and catfish providing the best results. On my top day fishing for trout, we caught 58, including several over 18 inches. In the spring, bass practically shout "Catch me!" On one trip with my brother, Rambob, we tried to keep track of the number of fish we caught but lost the figure at around 73 when we had a series of doubles; the hookups were just coming too fast to count.

7. Lake Almanor, Lassen and Modoc, page 105. Lake Almanor is big and beautiful, featuring sapphire-blue waters and views of snowcapped Mount Lassen to the northwest. In the spring and fall, fishing for trout and salmon is often excellent, not so much for the number of fish, but rather for their size. Excellent, that is, providing you can handle them. Once you figure out this lake, trout and salmon in the four- and five-pound class might be your average catch.

8. El Capitan Lake, San Diego and Vicinity, page 440. The bassers call this place "El Cap," usually with a hint of reverence in their voices. While you might hear stories about the bass at other lakes, El Cap is the one that produces them. The water clarity is typically only fair here, which makes the bass far less spooky than at most lakes. Compared to other bass lakes in Southern California, catch rates are often quite high.

9. Convict Lake, Yosemite and Mammoth Lakes, page 352. Although this lake features spectacular high mountain scenery, it is known primarily for fishing, particularly for the good catch rates of rainbow trout and the rare but huge brown trout. I've even named some of the fish I've lost at this lake.

10. San Pablo Reservoir, San Francisco Bay Area, page 263. Daybreak at San Pablo Reservoir is one of the prettiest boating scenes in the Bay Area, highlighted by blues and greens, placid water, and fishing boats trailing fresh, white wakes. Trout fishing serves as the main attraction here. The lake gets the highest trout stocks of any lake in California, with a large number of 12- to 15-inchers and a sprinkling of 8- to 15-pounders.

Top 10 Places for Water-Skiing

1. Lake Havasu, Death Valley and the Southern Deserts, page 462. Giant Lake Havasu stands out like a lone sapphire in a pile of coal. Only the Colorado River breaks up a measureless expanse of desert, and when the Parker Dam was set across the river, Havasu was born. It is 45 miles long and covers 19,300 acres at the low elevation of 482 feet. This is one of the most popular boating destinations in the southwestern United States, and its size, weather, warm water, and proximity to Las Vegas make it one of the top vacation and water-skiing hot spots in the West. Most boaters do their own thing, heading off on this great stretch of water in search of wild fun and frolic. And most find it. Over the course of a year, enough suntan oil is used at Lake Havasu to flood the California Aqueduct.

2. San Joaquin Delta, San Francisco Bay Area, page 259. Yeah, it gets insane here, and that's exactly why so many people like the San Joaquin Delta. There are boats, boats, boats everywhere, not to mention boat owners who are on weekend vacations trying to completely escape the reality of their Monday-to-Friday lives. And the water-skiing? You've never seen so many boats ripping up and down, with happy (and somewhat insane) folks aboard and bright white wakes trailing behind. By early Saturday afternoon on the typical hot summer weekend, so much beer has been consumed that the scene deteriorates from crazed to maniacal.

3. Colorado River, Death Valley and the Southern Deserts, pages 460, 464, 469. Hot weather and cool, calm water make this one of the water-ski capitals of America. Bring your suntan lotion and a beach towel. There are plenty of hot bodies and hot boats, and water-skiing is the dominant activity in the summer. The roar of the big V8s in the jet boats can be unbelievable, along with the bright wakes spewing from boats and skiers alike. It gets extremely crowded in the summer with happy boaters, skiers, swimmers, and general tourist traffic. Then there are the speedboat racers who show up every year for various competitions.

4. Shasta Lake, Shasta and Trinity, page 68. Shasta has four lake arms—the Sacramento Arm, McCloud Arm, Pit Arm, and Squaw Creek Arm—and each arm is like a separate lake. That's in addition to the main lake near the dam. Add to that the thousands of little coves and secret inlets, and you've got a body of water that's so big no boater can ever fully explore it. In other words, this is one place that has plenty of room for everybody. With all the houseboaters and water-skiers, the scene resembles a giant party. Everybody's happy, and there's lots of sun, skin, oil, and liquid refreshments.

5. San Vicente Lake, San Diego and Vicinity, page 439. San Vicente is located in the arid San Diego foothills at an elevation of 659 feet, and when it's full it covers 1,070 acres and offers 14 miles of shoreline. An island completes the picture. To prevent conflicts, water-skiing is prohibited on fishing day (Friday), and fishing is prohibited on water-skiing days (Thursday, Saturday, and Sunday). Many people think this is an ideal setup.

6. Lake Nacimiento, Santa Barbara and Vicinity, page 393. This big lake is set in the coastal foothill country of southern Monterey County. When full of water, it covers more than 5,000 acres with 165 miles of shoreline, plus there are a remarkable number of lake arms and coves. That combination—an enormous surface area and many private coves—provides the ideal conditions for high-speed boating, water-skiing, and personal watercraft, as well as for low-speed boating, canoeing, and fishing. In the main lake, there is even a slalom course for expert water-skiers.

7. Lake Perris, Los Angeles and Vicinity, page 421. In the summer and fall, the weather out here can make you feel like you're standing in a fire pit. That's why water-skiing and swimming are such big hits at Lake Perris. The lake is set in the Moreno Valley at an elevation of 1,500 feet, just southwest of the Badlands foothills. There are large ski beaches on the northeast and southeast shores, and this can be a great place to go water-skiing or ride personal watercraft.

8. Lake Piru, Santa Barbara and Vicinity, page 402. Things can get crazy at Piru. Fortunately, it's usually a happy crazy, not an insane crazy. You see, this lake is pretty close to the Los Angeles Basin and it attracts quite a few people who come for the boating, water-skiing, fishing, sunbathing, and swimming. Temperatures are warm, and the water often seems to feel just right. And get this: No areas are off-limits to water-skiers.

9. Lake Elsinore, Los Angeles and Vicinity, page 423. Whoosh! Whoosh! What's faster than a speeding bullet? Whoosh! Whoosh! If you're at Lake Elsinore, then the answer is a water-skier being towed by a jet boat. The place is loaded with them. And why not? With day after day of barn-burner weather throughout summer and into fall, and few anglers to get in the way, it's the perfect place. Lake Elsinore is set at 1,239 feet in an area that gets hot enough to make the water here more valuable to water-skiers than gold. The lake is big enough to accommodate all kinds of boaters, too. It's a winner, and lots of people take advantage of it.

10. Pyramid Lake, Santa Barbara and Vicinity, page 400. Although Pyramid Lake (elevation 2,600 feet) is surrounded by Angeles National Forest, I-5 is routed right past several lake arms.

This makes it one of the more easily accessed bodies of water in California. Because it's a show-piece, the water masters tend to keep it fuller than other lakes on line with the California Aqueduct. That makes it a favorite for powerboaters, especially water-skiers (a 35-mph speed limit is enforced).

Top 10 Family Destinations

1. Lake Siskiyou, Shasta and Trinity, page 59. Giant Mount Shasta rises 14,162 feet above Siskiyou, creating the prettiest setting of any lake along Interstate 5. The 10-mph speed limit ensures quiet waters, and the nearby campground makes the place ideal for family vacations. Children often play in the swimming area, which has a great swimming beach, or pedal around in paddleboats. The lake provides an excellent campground (clean and patrolled), cabin rentals, great swimming, decent trout fishing, and good leisure boating opportunities.

2. Big Bear Lake, Los Angeles and Vicinity, page 416. Talk about a place that has it all: Big Bear offers good trout fishing, quality boating opportunities, many campgrounds, a few resorts, and excellent swimming; and it is located near the highest regions of the San Bernardino National Forest, at 6,738 feet. Among all the bodies of water in the region, this lake has an unmatched beauty, particularly in the spring when the snow is melting. The lake covers more than 3,000 acres with 22 miles of shoreline, and has a faithful vacation following.

3. Convict Lake, Yosemite and Mammoth Lakes, page 352. We're talking simply spectacular beauty. And even if that weren't enough, consider that the adjacent facilities include a boat ramp, boat rentals, cabin rentals, Forest Service campground, small store, fine restaurant, horse rentals, and a wilderness trailhead. In addition, maps detailing the location of several hot springs in the area are available at the Convict Lake Store.

4. Shaver Lake, Sequoia and Kings Canyon, page 368. Shaver is set in the Sierra foothills at 5,370 feet, a great family getaway. Water-skiing and wake boarding are extremely popular, with family campers taking center stage. The lake is also well stocked with trout and kokanee salmon. The best area for swimming and playing in the water is on the lake's east side. Though more difficult to reach, this part of the lake offers sandy beaches rather than the rocky drop-offs so common on the west side.

5. Klamath River, Shasta and Trinity, pages 46, 51. The rafting run from Sarah Totten Campground to Happy Camp is probably the best trip in California for families. Beautiful scenery and lots of birds and wildlife can be seen along the way. The run is lively enough to make the trip memorable, yet easy enough that it's doable for the whole family. White-water highlights are Upper Savage and Otter's Play Pen (both Class III-). There are plenty of thrills to get your blood pumping and lots of flat water so you can calm down or beach the boat and go swimming.

6. June Lake, Yosemite and Mammoth Lakes, page 346. Sierra peaks that are often edged with snow tower above June Lake, a 160-acre mountain lake set at a 7,600-foot elevation. Amenities? If you need something, you can get it here. There are campsites near the shore, nearby cabins, a good boat ramp, and stores within a mile. June Lake is easily accessed off Highway 158. It is very beautiful, and it has the best fishing, best camping sites, best swimming, and best sailboarding. Even when there are many people here, the 10-mph speed limit guarantees at least a semblance of serenity.

7. Silver Lake, Tahoe and the Northern Sierra, page 234. Beautiful and inviting, Silver Lake is set at an elevation of 7,200 feet in a classic granite cirque just below the Sierra ridgeline in Eldorado National Forest. Visitors have access to cabin rentals, a campground, boat rentals, decent trout fishing, great hiking trails, horseback riding campgrounds, and several other nearby lakes. Most people congregate on the north side of the lake, where the campgrounds, picnic areas, and marina are located.

8. Zaca Lake, Santa Barbara and Vicinity, page 396. Very few people know about Zaca, a small lake that makes the perfect family retreat, complete with cabin rentals. Covering just 25 acres, it is set at an elevation of 2,400 feet in Los Padres National Forest, about 40 miles north of Santa Barbara. Swimming is popular, and a buoy line designates a swimming area and rocky beach at the south end of the lake. Side trip options include hiking and horseback riding; good trails through National Forest land start just north of here.

9. Lake Alpine, Tahoe and the Northern Sierra, page 242. In many people's minds, Lake Alpine fits the exact image of what a mountain lake is supposed to look like. For example, on a typical early summer evening, the surface of the lake is calm and emerald green, with little ripples made by hatching bugs and rising trout. The shoreline is well wooded (including some giant ponderosa pines), the smell of pine duff is in the air, and campsites are located within a short distance of the lake.

10. Rancho Seco Lake, Sacramento and Gold Country, page 178. For the ideal family picnic spot in the Sacramento/San Joaquin Valley, give this place a try. The 160-acre lake is part of the 400-acre Rancho Seco Recreation Area, which has a boat ramp (no motors permitted) and several docks. There is a large, sandy swimming area, a pleasant picnic site, and a campground for tents or RVs. There are also trails for hiking, horseback riding, and bicycling, as well as several fishing docks along the shore.

© TOM STIENSTRA

Chapter 1

Redwood Empire

Chapter 1—Redwood Empire

Visitors come from around the world to the Redwood Empire for one reason: to see the groves of giant redwoods, the tallest trees in the world. On a perfect day in the redwoods here, refracted sunlight beams through the forest canopy, creating a solemn, cathedral-like effect. It feels as if you are standing in the center of the earth's pure magic.

But the redwood forests are only one of the attractions to this area. The Smith River canyon, Del Norte and Humboldt coasts, and the remote edge of the Siskiyou Wilderness in Six Rivers National Forest all make this region like none other in the world.

The Smith River is the crown jewel of California rivers. It is one of the last major free-flowing rivers in America. Wild, pristine, and beautiful, it's set in a series of gorges and bordered by national forest. It features three forks: the Middle Fork along Highway 199, the South Fork along South Fork Road out of Hiouchi, and the remote, wild, and scenic North Fork, which runs north of Gasquet. Because there are no dams on the Smith, this river is run by rafters and kayakers in late winter when flows are ideal. In summer, it is too low—yet still good for swimming in many deep holes located upriver.

The centerpiece of the Smith is Jedediah Smith State Park and its grove of monster-sized redwoods. South Fork Road provides an extended tour into Six Rivers National Forest along the South Fork Smith River to Big Flat. The Smith River also provides the opportunity for the state's biggest steelhead all winter long, and in the fall it attracts a run of giant-sized salmon.

There are several other rivers and streams that make for do-it-yourself trips: Klamath River, Mad River, Eel River, Van Duzen River, South Fork Eel, and Mattole.

Several one-of-a-kind lagoons and small lakes also highlight the Redwood Empire.

North of Trinidad, three coastal lagoons provide unique boating opportunities: Freshwater Lagoon, Stone Lagoon, and Big Lagoon. Highway 101 provides easy access to all three.

Hidden lakes include Lake Earl and Dead Lake near Crescent City, and Muslatt Lake and Dry Lake in Six Rivers National Forest east of Crescent City. None of these are classic recreation lakes. They are rather out-of-the-way destinations where campers with a canoe on their rigs can head out and create their own little hideaway.

The Lost Coast is often overlooked by visitors because of the difficulty in reaching it; your only access is via a slow, curvy road through the Mattole River Valley, past Petrolia, and out to a piece of coast. The experience is like being in suspended animation—your surroundings peaceful and pristine, with a striking lack of people.

The Del Norte coast, Smith River canyons, and groves of giant redwood trees at Jedediah Smith State Park make this area one of the most beautiful spots in America.

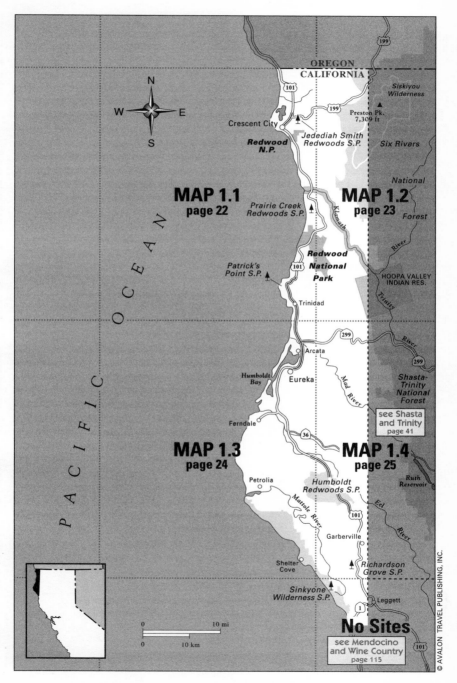

MAP 1.1
page 22

MAP 1.2
page 23

MAP 1.3
page 24

MAP 1.4
page 25

OREGON
CALIFORNIA

Siskiyou
Wilderness

Preston Pk.
7,309 ft

Crescent City

Jedediah Smith
Redwoods S.P.

Six Rivers

Redwood
N.P.

National

Prairie Creek
Redwoods S.P.

Forest

Klamath

Patrick's
Point S.P.

Redwood
National
Park

HOOPA VALLEY
INDIAN RES.

Trinidad

Trinity

Arcata

Humboldt
Bay

Eureka

Mad River

Shasta-
Trinity
National
Forest

see Shasta
and Trinity
page 41

Ferndale

Petrolia

Humboldt
Redwoods S.P.

Mattole River

Ruth
Reservoir

Garberville

Eel River

Shelter
Cove

Richardson
Grove S.P.

Sinkyone
Wilderness S.P.

Leggett

No Sites

see Mendocino
and Wine Country
page 115

OCEAN

PACIFIC

N
W   E
S

0   10 mi
0   10 km

© AVALON TRAVEL PUBLISHING, INC.

Map 1.1

Sites 1–6
Pages 26–31

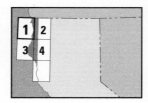

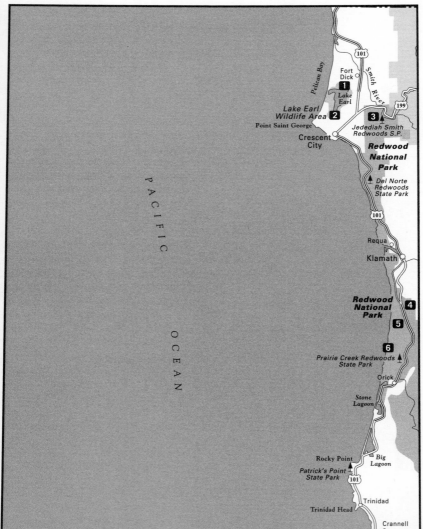

Map 1.2

Sites 7–9
Pages 31–33

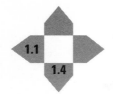

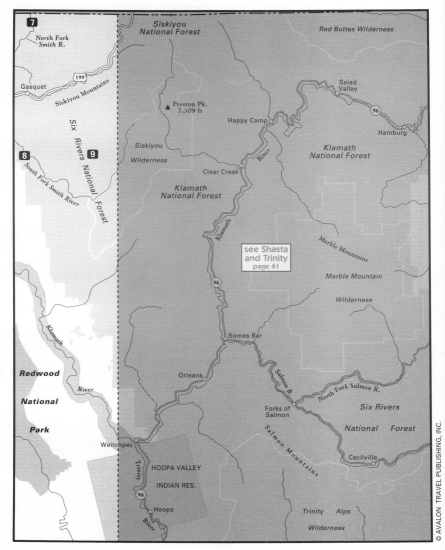

7
North Fork
Smith R.

Siskiyou
National Forest

Red Buttes Wilderness

Gasquet

199

Siskiyou Mountains

Seiad
Valley

96

▲ Preston Pk.
7,309 ft

Happy Camp

Hamburg

Six Rivers National Forest

Klamath
National Forest

8

9

Siskiyou
Wilderness

South Fork Smith River

Clear Creek

Klamath River

Klamath
National Forest

Marble Mountains

Klamath

see Shasta
and Trinity
page 41

Marble Mountain

96

Wilderness

Klamath

Somes Bar

Redwood

Orleans

National

River

Forks of
Salmon

North Fork Salmon R.

Salmon R.

Six Rivers

Park

National   Forest

Weitchpec

Salmon Mountains

Cecilville

Trinity

HOOPA VALLEY

INDIAN RES.

96

Trinity   Alps

Hoopa

River

Wilderness

© AVALON TRAVEL PUBLISHING, INC.

Map 1.3

Sites 10–12
Pages 33–36

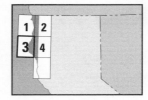

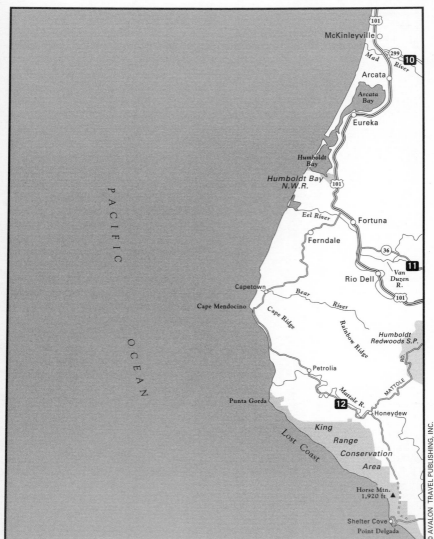

© AVALON TRAVEL PUBLISHING, INC.

Map 1.4

Sites 13–14
Pages 36–38

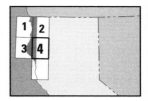

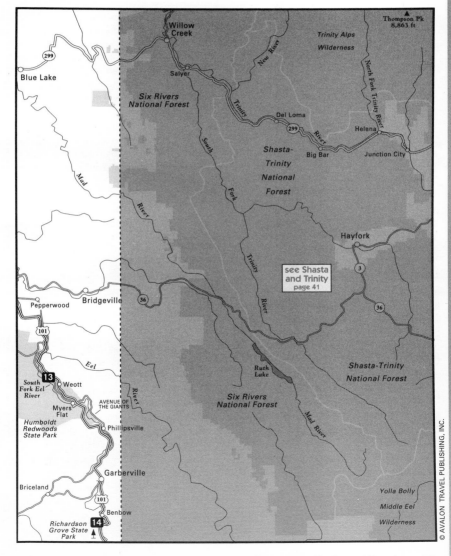

1 LAKE EARL

Rating: 6

near Crescent City

Map 1.1, page 22

Although Lake Earl is by far the largest lake in Del Norte County, it attracts very little attention. One reason is that motorists can't see it from U.S. 101; another is that there are limited recreational opportunities here. Lake Earl is uniquely situated, near sea level less than a mile from the Pacific Ocean. Its neighbor to the west, Lake Tolowa, is connected to Lake Earl by a short, narrow curve of water and borders coastal sand dunes.

After heavy rains, the lake can get so full with water that it breaches to the ocean. Sometime rangers will help this along by building a ditch to the ocean to help drain the overflow, which prevents adjacent roads from being flooded.

The lake is large, approximately 2,500 surface acres, but alas, it is both shallow and marshy. A boat ramp is available; however, boats rarely venture out on the water. If you just like to float around without a care, Lake Earl can provide peace and solitude. On the rare clear day, sunset watching from the eastern shore can be spectacular, with the light reflecting off the lake in a solitary beam. This is the perfect way to cap a day of camping in one of the little-known primitive campsites here, a world apart from the summer vacation traffic on U.S. 101.

When you first arrive, Lake Earl looks like a great spot for fishing. Nope. Once in a while sea-run cutthroat trout and flounder are caught at the Narrows, the stretch of water that connects Earl and Tolowa Lakes. Most anglers don't catch anything, which is why the locals tend to stay away.

Access: An unpaved boat ramp is provided.

Facilities, fees: No facilities are provided at the boat ramp. At the walk-in campsites, vault toilets and drinking water is available. Access to Lake Earl is free. A fee is charged for camping.

Water sports, restrictions: No motors are allowed during the waterfowl season, generally October through early January. Otherwise there are no restrictions; the lake is generally considered too marshy to be used for anything except bird watching, duck hunting, and fishing.

Directions: For the Lake Earl boat launch: In Crescent City, turn northwest on Northcrest Drive and drive about 3.5 miles to Lake View Road. At Lake View Road, turn left and drive a mile to the road's end at Lake Earl.

For walk-in campsites: In Crescent City, drive on U.S. 101 to the lighted intersection at Northcrest Drive. Turn left (northwest) and drive about five miles (Northcrest becomes Lake Earl Drive) to Lower Lake Road. Turn left and drive 2.5 miles to Kellogg Road. Turn left on Kellogg Road and drive .5 mile. A small metal gate, for which the combination is given at registration, and parking area large enough for a few cars is the access point on the right side of the road.

Contact: Tolowa Dunes State Park, California State Parks, North Coast Redwoods District, 707/464-6101, ext. 5151, website: www.parks .ca.gov (click on Find A Park); Lunker Fish, 707/458-4704.

2 DEAD LAKE

Rating: 5

near Crescent City

Map 1.1, page 22

If you like secret fishing spots, file this one away in the back of your mind and then make sure you try it out when you are in the area. This little lake provides good bass fishing, is easy to reach, and is missed by virtually everyone who passes through the area. Unfortunately, it is small, narrow, and marshy, and has no paved boat ramp—just a primitive dirt launching area—making it extremely poor for other water sports. But that helps keep Dead Lake a secret for the few who know of it.

Access: There is no boat ramp. A primitive dirt launching area is available.

Facilities, fees: No facilities are provided at the lake. However, full services and lodging are available two miles away in Crescent City. Access is free.

Water sports, restrictions: Rowboats, canoes, and kayaks are permitted. No motors. The lake is too marshy for swimming and sailboarding.

Directions: From U.S. 101 in Crescent City, turn west on Washington Boulevard and drive 1.5 miles (almost to the airport) to Riverside Road. Turn right (north) on Riverside Road and drive to the lake.

Contact: California State Parks, North Coast Redwoods District, Redwood Coast Sector, 707/464-6101, ext. 5151.

3 SMITH RIVER

Rating: 10

east of Crescent City in Six Rivers National Forest

Map 1.1, page 22

The crown jewel of the nation's streams, the Smith River is a fountain of pure water, undammed and unbridled, running free through sapphire-blue serpentine canyons.

When you first see the Smith, you will probably exclaim: "Look how beautiful the water is!" Even after heavy winter rains, which can turn most rivers into brown muck, the Smith is usually pretty, blue, and clear. The river's hard granite base, combined with the large volume of water drained from a huge mountain acreage, gives the river a unique ability to cleanse itself.

In the winter and spring, from November through May, this river is great for expert kayakers and fair for rafting and canoeing. In the summer it's decent for people heading far upstream looking for a swimming hole. The North Fork Smith (see listing in this chapter) provides a stellar opportunity for rafting and kayaking. Few commercial trips run the Smith, because of its remote location. The Smith is best known as the number one producer of large steelhead in California (mid-December through mid-March).

The most tantalizing section of the river for kayakers and rafters is a six-mile stretch near Gasquet, rated as Class II+, with an additional one mile of Class V water directly below in the Oregon Hole Gorge. Only experts run the gorge, and doing so is a kind of rite of passage for kayakers ready to take the daredevil test. In the winter I have occasionally seen master kayakers giving lessons to small groups of people who want to conquer the Gorge.

Canoeists should forget about the Gorge or any other stretch of upstream water. Instead put in at Ruby Van Deventer County Park for a 10-mile Class I paddle down to the public boat ramp, a good easy day trip.

The best swimming holes in the Smith River drainage are well up the South Fork Smith River (see listing in this chapter), accessible on South Fork Road, though a deep, calm spot is available in the summer at the Forks, the confluence of the Middle Fork and South Fork. Access is available just downstream from the bridge north of Hiouchi; to get there, take U.S. 199 west to Hiouchi and drive over the bridge, continue .25 mile, and then turn right at the unsigned cutoff. This is also a good put-in spot for a canoe trip.

In summer, there are several good swimming holes on the Middle Fork just off U.S. 199. The best spots include near the Panther Flat Picnic Area, the Forks (the confluence of the South Fork and Middle Fork in Gasquet), and Mary Adams Peacock Bridge. All are signed and located just off U.S. 199.

As with any river, weather is the key variable, and the Smith gets more of the wet kind than any other place in the Lower 48. My pal Michael Furniss, one of the top hydrologists in America, set up a rain gauge at nearby Camp Six and documented 256 inches of rain in 1983, still a national record. Heavy rains mean the river can rise quickly and turn what would otherwise be a wild trip down The Gorge into an act of insanity.

But what you will remember best is the great natural beauty of the river; the redwoods, firs, and pines; beautiful rock-lined gorges; and the pristine free-flowing water. There's no place like it.

Access: No boat ramps are available.

Facilities, fees: Several campgrounds are available nearby, including at Jedediah Smith Redwoods State Park and a few low-cost Forest Service camps. Lodging is available in Hiouchi. No boat rentals are available. Access is free. Rafting permits are not required.

Water sports, restrictions: Rafting, kayaking, drift boats, and swimming are permitted. A designated personal watercraft area is available near the mouth of the Smith River off U.S. 101.

Directions: To Jedediah Smith State Park: From Crescent City, drive north on U.S. 101 for three miles to the junction with U.S. 199. Turn east at U.S. 199 and drive about five miles. Turn right at the well-signed entrance station.

To Ruby Take-Out: From Crescent City, drive north on U.S. 101 for three miles to the junction with U.S. 199. Turn east at U.S. 199 and drive four miles to Highway 197 (just over the Smith River Bridge). Turn left on Highway 197 and drive one mile to the Ruby take-out on your left.

To the Forks: From Crescent City, drive north on U.S. 101 for three miles to U.S. 199. Turn east (right) on U.S. 199 and drive about seven miles (just past the entrance to Jedediah Smith State Park) to the town of Hiouchi. In Hiouchi, continue for one mile to South Fork Road. Turn right and look for the dirt road down to the river bank. Turn right and drive to the put-in.

To South Fork: From Crescent City, drive three miles north on U.S. 101 for three miles to U.S. 199. Turn east (right) on U.S. 199 and drive about seven miles (just past the entrance to Jedediah Smith State Park) to the town of Hiouchi. In Hiouchi, continue for one mile to

South Fork Road. Turn right and drive .5 mile to a junction with South Fork Road. Turn left on South Fork Road and drive 14 miles to Big Flat Road/County Road 405. At Big Flat Road, turn left and drive .25 mile to the campground entrance road (Forest Road 15N59) on the left. Turn left and drive a short distance to the camp on the left. Access is available here for expert kayakers.

Contact: Six Rivers National Forest, Gasquet Ranger District, 707/457-3131, website: www.fs.fed.us/r5/sixrivers; Jedediah Smith Redwoods State Park, c/o Redwoods National and State Parks, 707/464-6101, ext. 5112 or 5064, website: www.parks.ca.gov (click on Find A Park). For guided trips contact Aurora River Adventures, 707/677-3494 or 800/562-8475, website: www.rafting4fun.com; Bigfoot Rafting Company, 530/629-2263 or 800/722-2223, website: www.bigfootrafting.com; Tributary Whitewater Tours, 530/346-6812 or 800/672-3846, website: www.whitewatertours.com; Smith River Outfitters, 707/487-0935; Lunker Fish Trips, 707/458-4704.

◢ FRESHWATER LAGOON
🏕️ ⛰️ 🛶 🎣 🏊 🌊 🚐

Rating: 7

north of Trinidad in Humboldt Lagoons State Park

Map 1.1, page 22

The lagoon's name gives it all away. From that alone all the vacationers cruising U.S. 101 figure out that this is freshwater, not salt water. Of the three lagoons in the immediate area, this is the only one on the east side of the highway. Right, another tip-off.

That is why visitor traffic pours into this spot, while Stone Lagoon and Big Lagoon to the south get a relative trickle. And people galore are what you find here. The water is a lot warmer here than at the other two lagoons, so it attracts more of everything, more sailboarders, personal watercraft, water-skiers, swimmers, and yes, because it is stocked with rainbow trout, more anglers. Even scuba divers practice here.

At 241 acres, this is the smallest of the three lagoons, yet it has the best boat ramp of the three, located at the north end.

The trout fishing is often good, courtesy of regular stocks by the Department of Fish and Game. There's a small boat ramp, which opens it to easy access for those towing boats.

There is unlimited RV parking ($10 a night) along the Freshwater Spit, where the RVs can be lined up for three miles on the wide shoulder of the highway. The current plan is to phase out RV parking here by 2005, but the truth is that there is no end in sight.

In the summer, when you first drive up, the number of motor homes and trailers parked in the extended shoulder along the highway can be unbelievable. Some days it looks like the Winnebago capital of the world, with vehicles lined up one after another, sometimes double-parked for miles.

All these people couldn't be wrong, could they? Nope. They've got it right. With the clear fresh water, easy access, and all those parking spaces for motor homes, this spot provides just what they want.

Access: A dirt launching area is located on the north end of the lagoon.

Facilities, fees: A visitor center, restrooms with flush toilets, and boat ramp are available. A large, flat area on the west side of the highway is available to RVs (on three-day weekends they are sometimes lined up for miles). Campgrounds are available nearby at Stone Lagoon. Boat launching and day-use access are free.

Water sports, restrictions: Boats with motors, personal watercraft, wake boarding, water-skiing, sailing, sailboarding, and swimming are permitted. A recreation area on the north end is popular with swimmers and sailboarders. There are several good swimming access points around the lagoon.

Directions: From Eureka, drive 22 miles north on U.S. 101 to Trinidad. At Trinidad, continue north on U.S. 101 for eight miles to Big

Lagoon Park Road. Continue eight miles to Freshwater Lagoon on the right.

Contact: Humboldt Lagoons State Park, Visitor Center, 707/488-2041, website: www.parks .ca.gov (click on Find A Park); Humboldt County Parks, 707/445-7651; North Coast Adventures, 707/677-3124; Department of Fish and Game, 707/445-6499.

5 STONE LAGOON

Rating: 8

north of Trinidad in Humboldt Lagoons
State Park

Map 1.1, page 22

This lagoon covers 521 acres, far smaller than Big Lagoon, yet has even more unique qualities than its big brother. The features here are fish and wildlife.

The lake has sea-run cutthroat trout (check Department of Fish and Game regulations), best caught using a Jake's wobbler (gold with red spots). The surrounding habitat supports a growing herd of Roosevelt elk. A great adventure is to paddle along the western shoreline, looking for elk or game trails, then landing and tracking. Of course, bring binoculars for close-up views, and maintain considerable distance.

Since the visitor center is located along the highway at Stone Lagoon, many vacationers will stop and look, and then depart. What they don't see is that just across the lake in a protected cove is a boat-in campground, one of the few camps in the state set up primarily for canoes and kayaks.

Once your base camp is established, you can paddle and explore. Features include the pretty inlet stream, the open/shut sandbar "dam" along the ocean that bursts open during heavy rains, an occasional elk sighting, and a chance to fish for sea-run cutthroat trout. Like Big Lagoon to the south, this is also a good spot for sailboarding.

In addition, you can land your craft on the far shore and gain access to a remote section of the Coastal Trail as well as the sand spit that separates this lagoon from the ocean. Most of those people zooming by on nearby U.S. 101 don't have a clue that this pretty spot exists.

Access: A primitive boat ramp is located near the visitor center.

Facilities, fees: A visitor center, drinking water, restroom with flush toilets are available. Three campgrounds are available: Dry Lagoon, a walk-in camp; Big Lagoon; and the best, Stone Lagoon, a boat-in at Ryan's Cove, located on the western shoreline across the lagoon. Supplies are available in Trinidad. A fee is charged for camping. Day use is free.

Water sports, restrictions: Powerboats, canoeing, kayaking, sailing, sailboarding, and swimming are permitted. No water-skiing or personal watercraft are allowed. A 10-mph speed limit is strictly enforced. Swimming is permitted, but most swimmers prefer the clearer water of nearby Freshwater Lagoon.

Directions: From Eureka, drive 41 miles north on U.S. 101 (15 miles north of Trinidad) to Stone Lagoon. At Stone Lagoon, turn left at the visitor information center and boat access. The boat-in campground is in a cove directly across the lagoon from the visitor center. The campsites are dispersed in an area covering about 300 yards in the landing area.

Contact: Humboldt Lagoons State Park, Visitor Center, 707/488-2041, website: www.parks.ca.gov (click on Find A Park); Humboldt County Parks, 707/445-7651; North Coast Adventures, 707/677-3124; Department of Fish and Game, 707/445-6499.

6 BIG LAGOON

Rating: 7

north of Trinidad in Humboldt Lagoons State Park

Map 1.1, page 22

A series of three lagoons lies on California's northern coast, midway between Eureka and Crescent City along U.S. 101. They look similar, but each has a distinct character and unique attractions.

Traveling north on U.S. 101 from Eureka, you come to Big Lagoon, the first of the three lagoons, which covers 1,740 acres. The lagoon has brackish water, a mixture of fresh water and salt water, and is bordered on the west by a sand spit and the ocean, and on the east by second-growth forest.

This place is great for those who like to sailboard or sail small boats since it frequently gets winds out of the north, especially on spring and summer afternoons, and from the south during the winter. The water is cold, typically about 50 to 60 degrees, so most sailboarders will need to put on their wet suits.

On days when the wind is down, you can take advantage of an excellent beach walk out of Patrick's Point State Park. From the parking area for the Octopus Trees Trail, a staircase is routed down to a large beach. From here walk north all the way to the sand spit that borders the western edge of the lagoon, an extremely isolated setting.

Big Lagoon is by far the largest of the three lagoons, and it offers the best opportunity for extensive paddling and the chance for creating a secluded beach picnic site, boat-in style. That is because its western shore consists of a three-mile long sand spit. It is here where you can beach your boat, walk over the top and have a huge expanse of beach all to yourself.

Another great paddle here is on the east side of the highway, where you can explore a shallow-water marsh and wetlands. Blue herons, egrets, and many waterfowl migrants can be found here, and even with the proximity of the highway, it feels like a secret world.

Despite these qualities, Big Lagoon is the least used of the three lagoons. That is because its open expanses make it vulnerable to wind, particularly in the afternoon. It seems ideal for sailing small boats or sailboarding, but few take advantage of the conditions. The water is brackish, so there is little fishing.

Access: A paved boat ramp is located on the east side of the lagoon off U.S. 101.

Facilities, fees: A boat ramp, drinking water, and restrooms with flush toilets are available. Trinidad has two tackle shops: Salty's and Bob's Boat Basin. Campgrounds are available at Patrick's Point State Park in Trinidad and at Stone Lagoon to the immediate north. There is a camping fee. Access is free.

Water sports, restrictions: Canoeing, kayaking, sailing, sailboarding, and swimming are permitted. No water-skiing or personal watercraft are allowed.

Directions: From Eureka, drive 22 miles north on U.S. 101 to Trinidad. At Trinidad, continue north on U.S. 101 for eight miles to Big Lagoon Park Road. Turn left (west) at Big Lagoon Park Road and drive two miles to the park. The boat ramp is located on the east side of the lagoon off U.S. 101.

Contact: Humboldt Lagoons State Park, Visitor Center, 707/488-2041, website: www.parks.ca.gov (click on Find A Park); Humboldt County Parks, 707/445-7651; North Coast Adventures, 707/677-3124.

7 NORTH FORK SMITH RIVER

Rating: 10

east of Crescent City in Six Rivers National Forest

Map 1.2, page 23

This is California's most remote river trip, all of it sheltered by a V-wedge canyon, with no sign anywhere of human impact. It is inaccessible by foot in winter and spring, and telephone and radio contact is impossible.

In the process, you traverse a Class IV river with dozens of gorges, chutes, rock gardens, and falls, all of it interspersed with dramatic serpentine formations, a gallery of waterfalls, insect-eating plants, and a chance to see giant spawning steelhead. The run: 14.6 miles, Low Divide Bridge to Gasquet, Class IV, typically 400 to 2,000 cubic feet per second, start to finish.

With no dams anywhere, this is one of the last free-flowing river systems in America. But that also means that the river is low and unrunnable in summer, when rafting is popular. So to run it, you have to go in the rain season. Since no rafting companies advertise the trip, you have to wildcat it—that is, talk a pro into leading the way or shoot the moon on your own in a kayak.

In the first 10 miles, not only are there a series of Class III and IV rapids that define the exhilaration of white-water sports, but you pass a series of natural phenomenons that make up a setting unlike anywhere else. At one point, on a curving left turn, on the far right bank, there is a sheet-like waterfall created from the overhang of an eroded cliff. We guided our raft right through the waterfall and under the overhang, so we could look out through the sheet of water and back to the river, a euphoric moment. The waterfall occurs during and after heavy rains.

The pristine clarity of the water creates a sensation that kayakers call "floating on air," a feeling that is simply ecstatic. At several different spots, there are stands of pitcher plants, strange plants that trap and eat insects. Because of the dozens of waterfalls, there may be no other river with more water ouzels, the remarkable little birds that can fly, swim and walk on river bottoms to feed, and which nest along the interior of falls. The river is closed to fishing in winter, and at the heads of riffles, giant steelhead can be spotted spawning.

Throughout the river's course, there is a series of serpentine and peridotite-based rock formations, massive outcrops and miniature rock islands. From this, along with the high volume of pure water, rises a white-water experience unique in America.

Of course, it comes with a price. It is cold and wet, with no relief anywhere. Dry suits, neoprene gloves and boots, and waterproof hats are a must. And then there is always the chance you will screw up.

This isn't the kind of trip where you punch

in the numbers and roll up the miles, placing the round pegs in the round holes, and put the raft on automatic pilot. You figure it out as you go.

Access: This run is accessible for only hand-launched kayaks and rafts.

Facilities, fees: A chemical toilet is available at the put-in. There is a store near the take-out in Gasquet. Lodging and restaurants are available in Hiouchi. Campgrounds are available along Highway 199. Access to the river is free.

Water sports, restrictions: Kayaks and rafts are permitted. No motors allowed.

Directions: From Crescent City, drive north on U.S. 101 to the town of Smith River and Rowdy Creek Road. Turn right and drive 35 miles (roughly 1 hour, 15 minutes) to Low Divide Bridge and the put-in. The take-out is in the town of Gasquet on Highway 199.

Contact: Smith River National Recreation Area, 707/457-3131, website: www.delnorte.org/srnra.html; Six Rivers National Forest, 707/442-1721, website: www.fs.fed.us/r5/sixrivers. For a map, ask for Six Rivers and send $6 to U.S. Forest Service, Map Sales, P.O. Box 587, Camino, CA 95709, 530/647-5390.

8 SOUTH FORK SMITH RIVER

Rating: 10

east of Crescent City in Six Rivers National Forest

Map 1.2, page 23

The hallmarks of the South Fork Smith include beautiful scenery, good access, excellent white water for kayaking, pretty campsites, and decent swimming holes.

South Fork Road, a paved two laner, follows the river well up to its headwaters. On the way, you will pass one of the prettiest undammed streams you can see without having to hike, set deep in Six Rivers National Forest, with clear, emerald green water flowing free over a pristine granite base. There are frequent turnouts along the road, each with

primitive, steep trails that anglers in search of steelhead use to reach prime river holes during the winter. These same routes provide access in the summer to the best swimming holes, especially far upstream.

The highlight of the South Fork Smith is an 11.5-mile stretch of Class III white water, all of it in virtual solitude, making this a great destination for skilled kayakers. The run features many short pool-and-drops feeding into rapids, with lots of breaks in moving flat water. That gives paddlers plenty of action, as well as a sufficient number of short breaks to let them catch their breath.

Newcomers should be warned about South Fork Gorge, which is located about a mile upstream from the confluence with the Middle Fork. The gorge starts with a set of falls, actually a fast-dropping rapid. If you dump here there's no way out and you'll have to float/swim the entire gorge. It is rated Class V and can be suicide for all but the best.

The prime kayaking season is fall, often mid-October through mid-June, when the river is pumped up from Del Norte County's legendary rains. The South Fork gets significantly less use than the Middle Fork.

Access: There is no boat ramp. To reach the put-in, follow the previous directions, driving south on South Fork Road for 13 miles. The put-in is at the fourth bridge (Steven Bridge) over the river. You may also put in at the second and third bridges. Take out at a turnout on South Fork Road approximately one mile above the first South Fork Bridge (Craigs Creek Access). Unless you're an expert kayaker, make sure you take out here, because the next section, South Fork Gorge, offers only difficult Class V rapids. Big Flat Camp, a primitive Forest Service campground, is located adjacent to where Hurdy Gurdy Creek enters the South Fork Smith. There is no drinking water. Vault toilets are available. The nearest facilities are available in Hiouchi. A fee is charged for camping. River access is free. Rafting permits are not required.

Water sports, restrictions: There are several good swimming holes off South Fork Road; the best is located at the second bridge.

Directions: From Crescent City, drive north on U.S. 101 for three miles to U.S. 199. Turn east (right) on U.S. 199 and drive about seven miles (just past the entrance to Jedediah Smith State Park) to the town of Hiouchi. In Hiouchi, continue for one mile to South Fork Road. Turn right and drive .5 mile to a junction with South Fork Road. Turn left on South Fork Road and drive 14 miles to Big Flat Road/County Road 405. At Big Flat Road, turn left and drive .25 mile to the campground entrance road (Forest Road 15N59) on the left. Turn left and drive a short distance to the camp on the left. Access is available here for expert kayakers.

Contact: Six Rivers National Forest, Gasquet Ranger District, 707/457-3131, website: www.fs .fed.us/r5/sixrivers; Jedediah Smith Redwoods State Park, c/o Redwoods National and State Parks, 707/464-6101, ext. 5112 or 5064, website: www.parks.ca.gov (click on Find A Park).

Guided rafting trips: Aurora River Adventures, 707/677-3494 or 800/562-8475, website: www.rafting4fun.com; Bigfoot Rafting Company, 530/629-2263 or 800/722-2223, website: www.bigfootrafting.com; Tributary Whitewater Tours, 530/346-6812 or 800/672-3846, website: www.whitewatertours.com; Smith River Outfitters, 707/487-0935; Lunker Fish Trips, 707/458-4704.

9 DRY LAKE

Rating: 6

near Crescent City in Six Rivers
National Forest

Map 1.2, page 23

Dry Lake is a tiny, bowl-like lake situated in national forestland that even the locals don't venture into. The area is pretty, set at an elevation of 2,000 feet near the headwaters of Hurdy Gurdy Creek. This is a decent spot for paddling a raft or a canoe in complete seclusion because Dry Lake is small and shallow.

This small lake has become popular for the few locals who know of it. After being stocked with trout by the Department of Fish and Game, fishing is good for several days.

Note: If you continue north on the Forest Service road over Gordon Mountain (4,153 feet) and down the other side to Camp Six, about a 10-mile drive from the lake, you will reach the rainiest place in the Lower 48. In 1983 it rained 256 inches, the highest amount ever recorded in the contiguous United States. Dry Lake? As the locals say, "Dry it ain't."

Access: There is no boat ramp.

Facilities, fees: The lake has one small, primitive campsite with a vault toilet that is available in summer months. No drinking water or other facilities are provided. Access is free.

Water sports, restrictions: No motors are permitted on the lake. The lake is too small and muddy for swimming and other water/body contact sports.

Directions: From Crescent City, drive three miles north on U.S. 101 for three miles to U.S. 199. Turn east (right) on U.S. 199 and drive about seven miles (just past the entrance to Jedediah Smith State Park) to the town of Hiouchi. In Hiouchi, continue for one mile to South Fork Road. Turn right and drive .5 mile to a junction with South Fork Road. Turn left on South Fork Road and drive 14 miles to Big Flat Ranger Station and County Road 405/French Hill Road. Turn left on County Road 405/French Hill Road, and then drive five miles to Dry Lake.

Contact: Six Rivers National Forest, Gasquet Ranger District, 707/457-3131, website: www.fs .fed.us/r5/sixrivers.

10 MAD RIVER

Rating: 6

near Arcata

Map 1.3, page 24

This short coastal stream is viewed each year

by thousands upon thousands who cross it on the bridge near McKinleyville. They give it a brief look, usually note the color and the flow, and then soon forget about it. Except for in the winter when anglers come in search of steelhead, the Mad River does not attract large numbers of recreational users. In addition, the water often runs brown in the winter and a shade of milky green the rest of the year.

Regardless, some locals have discovered a few good swimming holes upstream near the fish hatchery. To access them, you must park at the hatchery and walk up or downstream. The water isn't too cold during the summer, but that's not the reason swimmers stay away from here; it's the fact that there are so many cold, foggy days. If you don't want to get your feet wet, you might just come for a picnic, another popular pastime near the hatchery.

Access: There is no boat ramp.

Facilities, fees: A picnic area with restrooms and drinking water are provided at the hatchery. RV camping is available nearby. Access is free.

Water sports, restrictions: Kayaking, canoeing, inflatables, and drift boats are permitted. Several good swimming holes are located up and downstream of the hatchery.

Directions: From Eureka, drive north on U.S. 101 for 12 miles to Highway 290. Turn east on Highway 299 and drive six miles to the town of Blue Lake. From Blue Lake Boulevard, turn right on Greenwood Boulevard and drive to the four-way stop. Bear right (Greenwood turns into Hatchery Road) on Hatchery Road and drive 1.5 miles to the Mad River Fish Hatchery. To access the best swimming holes, hike up or downstream of the hatchery.

To mouth of the Mad River: From Eureka, drive north on U.S. 101 to the Giuntoli Lane exit. Turn west and drive .5 mile north on Janes Road to Miller Lane. Turn left on Miller Lane and drive one mile west to Mad River Road. Turn north on Mad River Road and drive to the river mouth.

Contact: Mad River Fish Hatchery, 707/822-

0592; stream conditions, Department of Fish and Game, 707/442-4502.

11 VAN DUZEN RIVER

Rating: 7

near Eureka

Map 1.3, page 24

The Van Duzen is known almost exclusively by two groups of people: the local expert kayakers who thrive on the short, difficult, and beautiful run available here, and the few anglers who come to fish for steelhead in the winter.

The most compelling feature is the four-mile run from Pepperwood Falls on down to Grizzly Creek Redwoods State Park, a decent stretch for kayaks and canoes. Although it is beautiful, bordered in part by lush forest, few rafters travel on this run. Unfortunately, the flow levels on the Van Duzen go up and down like crazy, ranging from extremely low in the summer, making it unrunnable by mid-May, to extremely high in the winter, when it's more like a flood. So you need to hit it when the flows are just right. That is why you typically see only locals on the water, since they have the luxury of being able to schedule their trips practically at a moment's notice. Because of the hit-and-miss nature of the river, commercial rafting trips are not offered.

Ambitious rafters had better have their act together if they decide to continue beyond Grizzly Creek Redwoods State Park. There is a difficult stretch here that practically comes with a guarantee that river-runners will dump during late winter and early spring, which is when the river is most popular. Grizzly Creek Redwoods State Park attracts many visitors in the summer months.

The Van Duzen River is subject to emergency fishing closures if flows are below the prescribed levels needed to protect migrating salmon and steelhead. For a recorded message detailing the status of coastal streams, call the Department of Fish and Game at 707/442-4502.

Access: There is no boat ramp. A put-in is located at Pepperwood Falls, four miles east of Grizzly Creek Redwoods State Park on Highway 36. Boaters can take out at Grizzly Creek Redwoods State Park; if you choose to continue, be aware of the difficult, unnamed Class IV-V run located just a few miles downstream. Be sure to scout the river from the road before proceeding.

Facilities, fees: You can camp at Grizzly Creek Redwoods State Park. Supplies can be obtained in Bridgeville or Carlotta. There is a day-use fee at Grizzly Creek Park.

Water sports, restrictions: Rafting, kayaking, canoeing, and swimming are permitted. A good swimming hole is located at Grizzly Creek Redwoods State Park.

Directions: From Eureka, drive south on U.S. 101 to the junction of Highway 36 at Alton. Turn east on Highway 36 and drive about 17 miles to Grizzly Creek Redwoods. River access points are located along Highway 36.

Contact: Grizzly Creek Redwoods State Park, 707/777-3683; Van Duzen County Park, 707/768-3898; Humboats, 707/443-5157, website: www.humboats.com; Bucksport Sporting Goods, 707/442-1832, website: www.reninet .com/bucksport.

12 MATTOLE RIVER

Rating: 8

near Eureka

Map 1.3, page 24

The Honeydew Valley is one of Northern California's little paradises that most people know nothing about. It is set on the Lost Coast, bordered by mountains and oceans. Ah, but then there is the Mattole River, which cuts a charmed path down the center of the valley, a pretty, winding ribbon that is capable of handling a tremendous volume of water in the monsoon winter months.

Most people come either to explore the surrounding area in the summer or to go steel-head fishing during the late winter when the bite is on. But another option is to take a trip down a fairly benign stretch of water in a raft, canoe, or kayak. You put in at the Honeydew Store and then float and paddle your way for 13 miles to A.W. Way County Park. Note that in the drier months, particularly late summer and fall, the river can be too low to run. It is usually runnable through June, sometimes well into July.

Visitors who make the trip here in the summer are treated to a demure stream and a county park that offers excellent picnicking, camping, and good swimming. Little do they know what a beast this river can be in the winter, when it can rain as much as anywhere in the Lower 48, sometimes getting pounded with up to an inch an hour. That is when the nice, sweet Mattole is transformed into a powerful torrent that inspires both trepidation and respect, and leaves an image in your mind that you will never forget.

The Mattole River is subject to emergency fishing closures if flows are below the prescribed levels needed to protect migrating salmon and steelhead. For a recorded message detailing the status of coastal streams, call the Department of Fish and Game at 707/442-4502.

Access: There is no boat ramp. Canoeists and kayakers can put in at the Honeydew Store, located approximately 20 miles east of Petrolia on Mattole Road, and take out at the Fire Station, or farther downstream at A.W. Way County Park.

Facilities, fees: Campgrounds with restrooms, showers, flush toilets, and drinking water are nearby. Supplies can be obtained in Petrolia and at the Honeydew Store. There is a fee for camping and a day-use fee is charged at the county park.

Water sports, restrictions: Drift boats, rafting, canoeing, kayaking, and swimming are permitted. There are two popular swimming holes. One spot is called the Fire Station and is located just west of Honeydew on Mattole Road (off a dirt road across the street from the fire station). The other is located at A.W. Way County Park, located 7.5 miles east of Petrolia on Mattole Road.

Directions: From Eureka take U.S. 101 to the South Fork Road turnoff (just north of Weott), head west on the somewhat winding road (it turns to gravel) to Honeydew.

To mouth of Mattole: From U.S. 101 north of Garberville, take the South Fork-Honeydew exit and drive west to Honeydew. At Honeydew, turn right on Mattole Road and drive toward Petrolia. At the second bridge over the Mattole River, one mile before Petrolia, turn west on Lighthouse Road and drive five miles to the campground at the end of the road.

Contact: Honeydew Store, 707/629-3310; A.W. Way County Park, 707/629-3659; Humboats, 707/443-5157, website: www.humboats.com; Tsunami Surf and Sport, 707/923-1965, website: www.tsunamisurfandsport.com.

13 SOUTH FORK EEL RIVER

Rating: 7

north of Leggett

Map 1.4, page 25

The South Fork Eel is like a chameleon, always changing, both in color and character. The shifts tend to be even more dramatic in rating its appeal to the public.

Most visitors see the South Fork Eel in the summer while vacationing in the Redwood Empire. They cruise on U.S. 101 right alongside the river as it runs north from Leggett, through Cooks Valley, past Benbow, and into Richardson Grove State Park. At this time of year, the river slows to a warm trickle, interrupted with the occasional deep pool that's ideal for swimming. A bottom scraper all the way, this river is really out of the question for canoeing, kayaking, and rafting. Instead, a favorite activity here is a picnic along the rock-strewn banks, possibly followed by a dip in one of the swimming holes. The best and most easily accessible holes are found near Richardson

Grove State Park and Standish-Hickey State Recreation Area.

As you motor down U.S. 101 in this area, you will eventually spot one of the "High Water Mark" signs along the roadside. Trying to imagine the river running that high, way over the highway, is inconceivable to most people. But it did indeed swell that high in the winter of 1964, which should tell you everything you need to know about how much the character of this river can change. Remember the chameleon.

To understand how such changes can be wrought, you must know that in the winter it doesn't just rain here, it pours and can just keep on pouring. Hey, how do you think the trees grow so tall? Well, before long the ground becomes saturated and the storm runoff streams right into the South Fork Eel. After a day or two of nonstop rain, the river becomes very muddy, then starts to rise. As the deluge continues, the river keeps on climbing, swelling bank to bank with cold, brown water that is running high, fast, and powerful on its northward course to the Pacific Ocean.

Even expert kayakers shudder to think what would happen if their little plastic boats were to get wrapped around a boulder in such conditions. Right, this is no river to tangle with.

The best time to run this river is when the high water is receding and the green color is beginning to return. This occurs primarily in late winter and early spring, when there are significant breaks in the storm pattern and rain. Even then, beginners need not apply.

To get the most out of the run, use the put-in at Wilderness Lodge (see Access), and meander down the 10-mile Class II run to the South Fork Gorge. This, however, is only a warm-up. Once you head downstream, there are no take-outs above the gorge, which means you are committed to going all the way. In high water this would be suicide. Even in moderate water flows, kayakers are right out there on the edge of life and death. That's what Class V is all about. There are so many tricks and turns, suckholes and boulders, chutes and swallows, and its makeup changes so often according to river height, that few attempt the run.

The skilled and ambitious souls who do take the risk will find themselves guided downstream surrounded by forest and vegetation, and with it a sense of lush isolation. The stretch from Wilderness Lodge at Branscomb is particularly beautiful. Once you hit the gorge, though, you will no longer notice your surroundings. You won't have time. Also, enjoying the Class II portion is difficult, knowing that the overbearing shadow of the Class V gorge looms ahead.

The South Fork Eel may be subject to emergency fishing closures if flows are below prescribed levels needed to protect migrating salmon and steelhead. For a recorded message detailing the status of coastal streams, phone the Department of Fish and Game, 707/442-4502.
Access: No boat ramp is available. There are two standard put-ins:
• **Wilderness Lodge:** Take U.S. 101 to Laytonville and Branscomb Road. Turn west on Branscomb Road and drive 17 miles (through Branscomb) to Wilderness Lodge Road. Turn north and continue to the lodge at the end of the road. The put-in is adjacent to the lodge. Note: The first 10 miles of this run is rated Class II, but at the confluence with Tenmile Creek, boaters will run into South Fork Gorge, a Class V, experts-only run. There is no feasible take-out upstream of the gorge.
• **Black Oak Ranch:** This put-in is actually on Tenmile Creek, on which you can descend to meet the South Fork Eel. To get there: Take U.S. 101 to Laytonville and then continue north and look for the sign for Black Oak Ranch on the west side of the highway. The creek is directly off the highway, and parking is limited to a wide spot on the side of the road. Parking here is risky, and shuttling is highly recommended (see Contact below). Note: This run, from the put-in through South Fork Gorge, is Class V and for experts only.
Facilities, fees: Several campgrounds are located nearby with restrooms with flush toilets and drinking water. Supplies can be obtained in Leggett, Laytonville, and Piercy. State parks charge a day-use fee and a camping fee. Rafting permits are not required.
Water sports, restrictions: Drift boats, rafting, kayaking, and swimming are available. Excellent swimming holes and riverside beaches can be found at Richardson Grove State Park and Standish-Hickey State Recreation Area.
Directions: To Standish-Hickey: From the junction of U.S. 101 and Highway 1 in Leggett, drive north on U.S. 101 for one mile to the park entrance. North of Standish-Hickey, access is also good at Smithe Redwoods State Reserve at Bridges Creek and Dora Creek (off the South Leggett exit), and off the Highway 271 exit (four-wheel drive is advisable here).
Contact: Richardson Grove State Park, 707/247-3318; Standish-Hickey State Recreation Area, 707/925-6482; River's Run Lodge, 707/984-6321; Redwood River Resort, 707/925-6249.

Guided river trips: Aurora River Adventures, 707/677-3494 or 800/562-8475, website: www.rafting4fun.com; Redwoods and Rivers, 530/629-4947 or 800/429-0090, website: www.redwoods-rivers.com; Rubicon Whitewater Adventures, 707/887-2452, website: www.rubiconadventures.com; Tributary Whitewater Tours, 530/346-6812 or 800/672-3846, website: www.whitewatertours.com. For a small fee the folks at River's Run Lodge will sometimes provide shuttles to the Tenmile Creek put-in.

14 BENBOW LAKE

Rating: 6

near Garberville in Benbow Lake State Recreation Area

Map 1.4, page 25

"Benbow Lake? Where's Benbow Lake? I can't find it anywhere on the map!" That's a typical remark for newcomers. You can look all you want and never find it on most maps.

In theory, Benbow Lake is created each

summer when the South Fork Eel River is dammed on a temporary basis, creating a 1,000-acre lake for swimming and light boating. This seasonal dam is usually installed in mid-June and kept in place until mid-September. However, there is no guarantee this will occur. There was no lake in 2000 or 2002, due to dam repairs and ensuring downstream passage of steelhead smolts. If you're making a vacation planned around lake recreation, always call first.

The lake is long and narrow, of course, covering 230 acres. It makes a popular spot for sunbathing and nonmotorized boating. Only boats without motors are allowed on the lake. This is an ideal setting for canoeing, floating around on rafts, inner tubes and air cushions, and swimming. Temperatures are quite warm in the summer, and there is a beach that is perfect for people who want to take advantage of it by doing absolutely nothing. Picnickers will be happy to find a picnic area nearby.

There is rarely enough wind for sailboarding or sailing, but that's fine with the folks floating around in a lovely summer daze.

Access: A gravel boat launch is located near the day-use area; it is available only in the summer.

Facilities, fees: A state campground is provided, and a private RV park and golf course are located across the highway. Supplies can be obtained in Garberville. Fees are charged for day use and camping. There is an additional fee to use the boat ramp. Pedal boats and other small craft can be rented at the concessionaire. **Water sports, restrictions:** Rowboats, canoes, kayaks, inflatables, and swimming are permitted. No motors. A swimming beach is available near the picnic area.

Directions: From the junction of U.S. 101 and Highway 1 in Leggett, drive north on U.S. 101 past Richardson Grove State Park to the Benbow exit (two miles south of Garberville). Take that exit and drive 2.7 miles to the park entrance. The lake is located just inside Benbow Lake State Recreation Area.

Contact: Benbow Lake State Recreation Area, 707/923-3238, website: www.parks.ca.gov (click on Find A Park); Benbow Valley RV Resort & Golf, 707/923-2777, website: www.BenbowRV.com; for fishing information or tackle, contact Brown's Sporting Goods in Garberville, 707/923-2533.

© ROBERT HOLMES/CALTOUR

Chapter 2

Shasta and Trinity

Chapter 2—Shasta and Trinity

A t 14,162 feet, Mount Shasta rises like a diamond in a field of coal. Its sphere of influence spans a radius of 125 miles, and its shadow is felt everywhere in the region. This area has much to offer, highlighted by giant Shasta Lake, the Sacramento River above and below the lake, and the wonderful Trinity Divide country with its dozens of pretty backcountry lakes and several wilderness areas. This is one of the best regions anywhere for an outdoor adventure—especially hiking, fishing, powerboating, rafting, and exploring.

There are hundreds of destinations, but the most popular are Shasta Lake; the Trinity Alps and their surrounding lakes and streams; and the Klamath Mountains, known as "Bigfoot Country" by the locals.

Shasta Lake is one of America's top recreation lakes. It is the one destination that is big enough to handle all who love it. The massive reservoir boasts 370 miles of shoreline, 1,200 campsites, 21 boat launches, 11 marinas, 35 resorts, and numerous houseboat and cabin rentals. A remarkable 22 species of fish live in the lake. Many of the campgrounds feature lake views. In addition, getting here is easy—a straight shot off I-5.

At the geographic center of this beautiful region are the Trinity Alps, where lakes are sprinkled everywhere. This area is also home to the headwaters for feeder streams to the Trinity River, Klamath River, New River, Wooley Creek, and others.

Trinity Lake provides outstanding boating and fishing, and just downstream, smaller Lewiston Lake offers a quiet alternative. One advantage to Lewiston Lake is that it is always full of water, even all summer long, making for a very pretty scene. Downstream of Lewiston, the Trinity River provides low-cost rafting and outstanding shoreline access along Highway 299 for fishing for salmon and steelhead.

The neighboring Klamath Mountains are well known as Bigfoot Country. If you drive up the Forest Service road at Bluff Creek, just off Highway 96 upstream of Weitchpec, you can even find the spot where the famous Bigfoot movie was shot in the 1960s. Well, we haven't seen Bigfoot, but we have discovered tons of outdoor recreation.

This remote region features miles of the Klamath and Salmon Rivers, as well as the Marble Mountain Wilderness. Options include canoeing, rafting, and fishing for steelhead on the Klamath River, or hiking to your choice of more than 100 wilderness lakes.

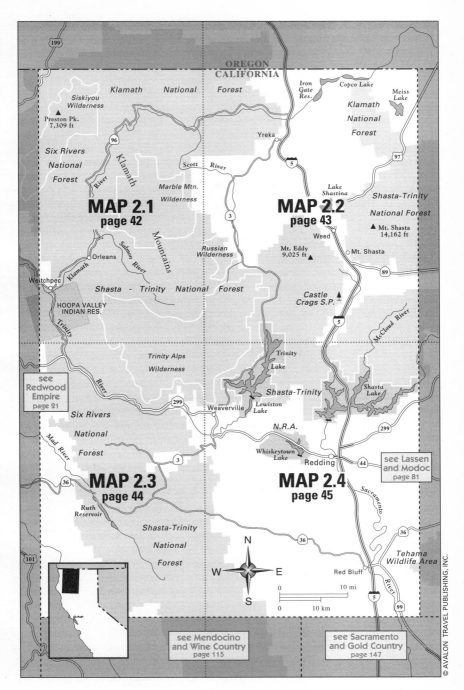

Map 2.1

Sites 1–5
Pages 46–51

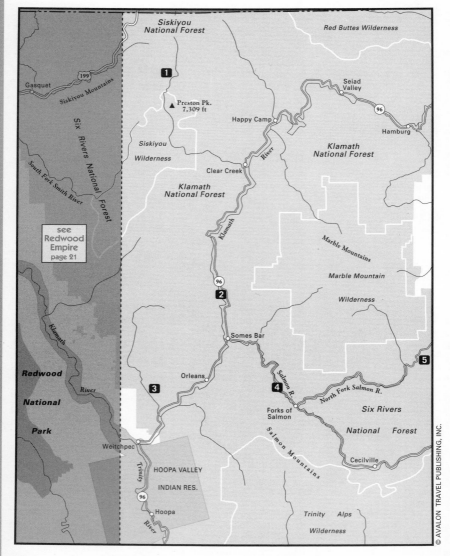

Map 2.2

Sites 6–20
Pages 51–64

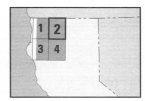

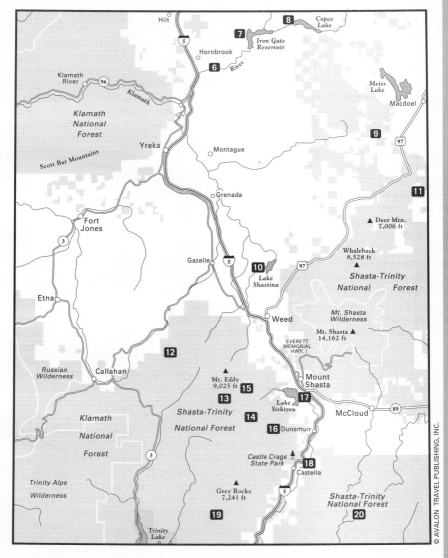

© AVALON TRAVEL PUBLISHING, INC.

Map 2.3

Sites 21–22
Pages 64–66

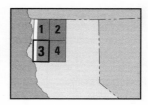

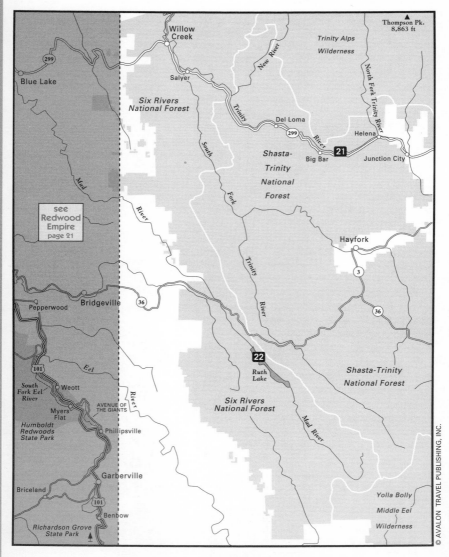

Map 2.4

Sites 23–29
Pages 66–77

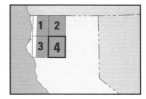

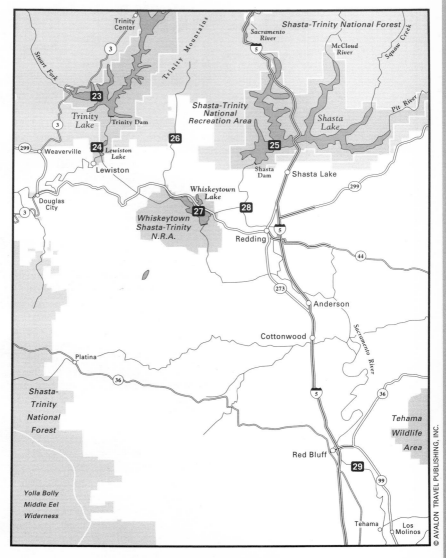

© AVALON TRAVEL PUBLISHING, INC.

1 SANGER LAKE

🍴 🛶 〰️ ⛺

Rating: 6

near Gasquet in Six Rivers National Forest

Map 2.1, page 42

Little Sanger Lake is a small, out-of-the-way, cold-water pond that provides peace, quiet, and a chance to catch tiny brook trout. Set just below Sanger Peak (5,862 feet) to the north, the lake is reached via a long drive on dirt roads, a trip that is daunting enough to keep most folks away—far away. Long? It seems to go on forever. From Eureka it takes two hours to reach the turnoff on U.S. 199, and from there it's more than an hour to the lake.

When you finally arrive, you find six-acre Sanger Lake, set at an elevation of 5,100 feet on the edge of the Siskiyou Wilderness. The water is clear and cold, reaching a maximum depth of 25 feet. This is the kind of place where you can plop a raft or canoe in the water and just float around, enjoying the serenity. It is also good for swimming, especially in late summer after a hike. The trailhead for Young's Valley Trail, which is routed along Clear Creek, is located near here at the end of the access road that passes Sanger Lake.

For the most part, the lake gets light use because it is small and it takes so long to get here. But that is exactly what some people are looking for.

Access: Small boats can be hand launched. No boat ramp is available.

Facilities, fees: There are no on-site facilities. A small, primitive campsite is available. No restroom or drinking water is available. Trash must be packed out.

Water sports, restrictions: Rowboats, canoeing, kayaking, and swimming are permitted. The lake is too small for other uses.

Directions: From Crescent City, drive north on U.S. 101 for three miles to U.S. 199. Bear right (east) on U.S. 199 and drive 32 miles to Forest Road 18N07/Knopki Road. Turn right and drive five miles to Forest Road 18N07.

Continue on Forest Road 18N07 for 10 miles (twisty) to Sanger Lake.

Contact: Smith River National Recreation Area, P.O. Box 228, Gasquet, CA 95543, 707/457-3131; Klamath National Forest, Happy Camp Ranger District, 530/493-2243.

2 KLAMATH RIVER (FROM HAMBURG TO WEITCHPEC)

Rating: 9

in Six Rivers National Forest

Map 2.1, page 42

This is one place where nature's artwork can seem flawless. The Klamath River tumbles around boulders, into gorges, and then flattens into slicks, all framed by a high, tree-lined canyon rim and an azure sky.

Rafters find prime territory here because the water runs at ideal flows throughout summer, courtesy of releases from Iron Gate Dam way up east of Hornbrook near the Oregon border.

One year when the river was near flood stage in March, I rafted the entire river, from its headwaters in Oregon all the way to the Pacific Ocean. We completed the trip in five and a half days, the first documented descent of the entire river, covering more than 1,000 rapids.

On that great adventure we discovered that the Klamath is abundant with not only fish, but with many species of birds and wildlife. They say this is the home of Bigfoot; there have been many sightings of the elusive creature in the Bluff Creek area, and that famous film of the Sasquatch strolling along the creek bank was shot along the Klamath in the 1960s.

The three most popular rafting runs on the Klamath are:

• Sarah Totten Campground to Happy Camp: 36 miles; Class III for the first 15 miles, then Class I+ until Happy Camp. Highlights: Upper Savage and Otter's Play Pen (both Class III-). Synopsis: Lively and doable in an inflatable kayak, this is also a good run for first-time rafters, with just enough excitement to get your heart pounding, yet plenty of flat water to catch your breath or beach the boat and go swimming.

• Happy Camp to Green Riffle: 37.5 miles; Class III; take out above Ishi Pishi Falls. Highlights: Kanaka Falls (Class III), Dragon's Tooth (Class IV). Synopsis: A gorgeous run, with lots of birdlife, pretty river bends, and a good number of easy runs interspersed by slicks, making it a kick for all comers.

Warning: Green Riffle is the last take-out before Ishi Pishi Falls. Do not attempt to run Ishi Pishi, which has only been run once by a rafting crew without loss of life. Many people have perished here. In addition, take special note of the sacred Native American ceremonial grounds along the banks of the Klamath eight miles past the put-in, where Clear Creek enters the river. For about a month in the summer, camping and stopping on the banks are banned.

• Salmon River to Weitchpec (aka Ike's Run): 24 miles; Class III-IV. Highlights: The Ikes (Little Ike, Class III-; Big Ike, Class IV; and Super Ike, Class III+). Synopsis: The Ikes are a fantastic series of big rollers, and the key for every rafter is to make sure you do not dump at the first one, which can have you swimming for your life as the current sweeps you through the other two sections. Once you pass the Ikes, the river rolls through one of its most beautiful sections—deep, emotive, and green, framed by granite walls.

The three featured runs offer stunning scenery, lots of wildlife, and solitude, despite the fact that Highway 96 runs alongside the river.

While the water is warm in the summer and fall, there are few clear, slow-moving deep pools for swimming. The nearby Salmon River is much better for swimming, as are Dillon and Elk Creeks.

There are several Forest Service campgrounds located along the Klamath River. A few cabin and lodging business are also available.

If you prefer a do-it-yourself adventure and want to rent your own raft, Bigfoot Rafting Company is the only game in town.

Access: No boat ramps are available, but there are several primitive access spots. A popular spot is Green Riffle just north of Somes Bar on Highway 96. Rafters can put in at the following locations:

• Sarah Totten Campground to Happy Camp: Put in at Sarah Totten Campground, located .5 mile east of Hamburg on Highway 96. Take out at the bridge in Happy Camp or at one of several access points just upstream.

• Happy Camp to Green Riffle: Put in at the bridge in the town of Happy Camp. Take out at Green Riffle, 3.5 miles upstream of Ishi Pishi Falls, or at one of several access points upstream. Note: Unless you're an expert, be sure to take out above Ishi Pishi Falls, an extremely difficult Class VI run.

• Salmon River to Weitchpec: Put in at a bridge where the Salmon River enters the Klamath, just south of Somes Bar on Highway 96. You can also put in farther upstream on the Salmon. Take out about .5 mile west of Weitchpec, just below the confluence of the Trinity and Klamath Rivers.

Facilities, fees: Several campgrounds with drinking water and vault toilets are located along Highway 96. Supplies can be obtained in the towns of Klamath River, Weitchpec, Somes Bar, Happy Camp, Seiad Valley, Horse Creek, and Orleans. Raft rentals and gear are available from Bigfoot Rafting Company. A fee is charged for camping. Access is free and rafting permits are not required.

Water sports, restrictions: Several swimming holes are located along Highway 96. One beauty is at Dillon Creek Campground, 15 miles north of Somes Bar on Highway 96.

Directions: From the junction of U.S. 101 and Highway 299 near Arcata, turn east on Highway 299 and drive to Willow Creek. In Willow Creek, turn north on Highway 96 and drive to Weitchpec, continuing on Highway 96 for five miles to the Aikens Creek West campground on the right side of the road. Access is available from here on upstream along Highway 96.

From Yreka, drive north on I-5 to the junction with Highway 96. At Highway 96, turn west and drive to Horse Creek, continuing west for five miles to Sarah Totten Campground on the right side of the road. If you reach the town of Hamburg, you have gone .5 mile too far. Access is available from here on downstream along Highway 96.

Contact: Klamath National Forest, Orleans Ranger District, 530/627-3291; Happy Camp Ranger District, 530/493-2243.

Guided rafting trips: Aurora River Adventures, 707/677-3494 or 800/562-8475, website: www.rafting4fun.com; Bigfoot Rafting Company, 530/629-2263 or 800/722-2223, website: www.bigfootrafting.com; Environmental Traveling Companions, 415/474-7662, website: www.etctrips.org/index.html; Klamath River Outfitters, 530/469-3349 or 800/748-3735, website: www.klamathriveroutfitters.com; Living Waters Recreation, 530/926-5446 or 800/994-7238, website: www.livingwatersrec.com; Marble Mountain Ranch, 530/469-3322 or 800/552-6284, website: www.marblemountainranch.com; Osprey Outdoors Kayak School, 530/926-6310, website: www.ospreykayak.com; Redwoods and Rivers, 530/629-4947 or 800/429-0090, website: www.redwoods-rivers.com; River Dancers, 530/926-3517 or 800/926-5002; website: www.riverdancers.com; Rubicon Whitewater Adventures, 707/887-2452, website: www.rubiconadventures.com; Tributary Whitewater Tours, 530/346-6812 or 800/672-3846, website: www.whitewatertours.com; Trinity River Rafting, 530/623-3033 or 800/307-4837, website: www.trinityriverrafting.com; Turtle River Rafting, 530/926-3223 or 800/726-3223, website: www.turtleriver.com; Whitewater Voyages, 510/222-5994 or 800/400-7238, website: www.whitewatervoyages.com; Wilderness Adventures, 530/926-6282 or 800/323-7238, website: www.trinityadventures.com.

Fishing supplies or information: Somes Bar Store, 530/493-2243; Klamath River Outfitters (listed above).

❸ FISH LAKE

Rating: 7

southwest of Orleans in Six Rivers National Forest

Map 2.1, page 42

In many ways this lake provides the ideal summer camping/fishing destination. The key is in the out-of-the-way location: almost everybody misses it, yet it really isn't that difficult to reach.

Upon arrival, you discover that Fish Lake is quite pretty, set in the woods with a Forest Service road going right around it. You get a lakeside camp that is practically within casting distance of the water. The lake covers 22 acres and is set at an elevation of 1,800 feet on the Six Rivers National Forest's eastern edge.

During peak summer months, the lake and the adjoining campsites get what is best termed as "medium use," with most people coming for the scenery, tranquility, and good trout fishing. Because there is no boat ramp, some people bypass the place. But that makes it ideal for those with car-top boats, such as canoes or inflatable rafts. Fish Lake is pretty and intimate, and on warm summer days, this is a great place to just float around without a care in the world.

Access: A primitive area for hand-launching small boats is located on the lake's east side.

Facilities, fees: A campground, drinking water, and vault toilets are available. A fee is charged for camping. Access is free.

Water sports, restrictions: Rowboats, prams, canoes, kayaks, and inflatables are permitted. Swimming is permitted. Motors are not permitted on the lake.

Directions: From I-5 in Redding, turn west on Highway 299 and drive to Willow Creek. At Willow Creek, turn north on Highway 96 and drive to Weitchpec, continuing seven miles north on Highway 96 to Fish Lake Road. Turn left on Fish Lake Road and drive five miles (stay to the right at the Y) to Fish Lake.

Contact: Six Rivers National Forest, Orleans Ranger District, 530/627-3291.

4 SALMON RIVER

Rating: 8

near Orleans in Klamath National Forest

Map 2.1, page 42

The Salmon River is one of California's greatest hidden treasures. It flows from the snowmelt in the nearby Trinity Alps, then runs through deep canyons en route to its confluence with the famous Klamath River. In the process it offers outstanding prospects for rafting, much of it suitable for advanced paddlers, as well as a wealth of great swimming holes.

Don't make the mistake of thinking that the Cal Salmon, as it is commonly called, is anything like its big brother, the Klamath. It isn't. The Salmon is clear, clean, and cold, set in a beautiful and remote deep canyon, and it gets far less use by the general public than the Klamath.

The main activity here is rafting. The best put-in spot is near the town of Forks of Salmon. From here the first five miles are Class II+, which makes a good run for beginners in inflatable kayaks. After that, however, the river really sizzles.

The rapids alternate between Class IV and V, and only experienced paddlers who don't mind living on the edge need apply. Highlights include Bloomer Falls (Class IV), the Maze (Class IV), Whirling Dervish (Class IV+), and Last Chance (Class V). The latter is a mind-bender of a drop that will have your heart leaving your body for what seems like an eternity. Another rapid that is something of a legend is called Freight Train (Class V).

The Butler Run starts just downstream of these rapids. This too is a very exciting Class IV run, featuring rapids named Contusion and Gaping Man.

Among rafters, there is an unspoken division between those who have run the Cal Salmon and those who have not—once you have run this river, the pros figure you have captured one of the ultimate experiences in the outdoors.

The Otter Bar Lodge Kayak School, which is based in Forks of Salmon, offers week-long instructional packages that include food, lodging, and gear—a great way to learn the sport. Several commercial rafting companies lead trips on the Salmon, most lasting from one to four days.

Although the water is cold in early summer, this is the best stream in the Klamath river system for swimming. Trails that access pools begin from a number of pullouts on the gravel road along the river. One of the better spots is near the confluence of Wooley Creek, located at mile 14 on the access road. Smaller pools are located farther upstream.

Access: There is no boat ramp. Put-ins are available upriver of Forks of Salmon at Methodist Creek, and at the Nordheimer Access below Forks of Salmon. Look for a large gravel beach a little downstream of the schoolhouse in town. Beginners should take out at one of several points before mile five; the following 14 miles are Class IV-V. If you choose to continue through the rest of the run, take out at Oak Bottom Campground at mile 16.

Facilities, fees: Campgrounds with drinking water and vault toilets are available nearby. Supplies can be obtained in Orleans, Somes Bar, Cecilville, and Callahan. A fee is charged for camping. Access is free. Rafting permits are not required.

Water sports, restrictions: There are several good swimming spots along the river; keep an eye out for the "River Access" signs as you drive on Salmon River Road. Two popular places are Blue Hole and Hogie's.

Directions: From Redding, drive north on I-5 just past Weed and take the Edgewood turnoff. At the stop sign, turn left and drive a short distance to the stop sign at Old Stage Road. Turn right on Old Stage Road and drive six miles to Gazelle. In Gazelle, turn left at Gazelle-Callahan Road and drive over the summit.

From the summit, continue west to Callahan and the junction with Cecilville-Callahan Road (Salmon River Road). Turn left and drive to Cecilville and Forks of Salmon. Access is available on Salmon River Road from the forks on downstream.

From Eureka, drive north on U.S. 101 for 12 miles to Arcata and Highway 299. Turn east on Highway 299 and drive 42 miles to Willow Creek and Highway 96. Turn left on Highway 96 turnoff and drive 40 miles to Orleans, and then continue seven miles to the town of Somes Bar and Salmon River Road. Turn right. Access is available along Salmon River Road.

Contact: Klamath National Forest, Scott and Salmon River Ranger District, 530/468-5351.

Guided trips: Aurora River Adventures, 707/677-3494 or 800/562-8475, website: www.rafting4fun.com; Bigfoot Rafting Company, 530/629-2263 or 800/722-2223, website: www.bigfootrafting.com; Klamath River Outfitters, 530/469-3349 or 800/748-3735, website: www.klamathriveroutfitters.com; Living Waters Recreation, 530/926-5446 or 800/994-7238, website: www.livingwatersrec.com; Marble Mountain Ranch, 530/469-3322 or 800/552-6284 or website: www.marblemountainranch.com; Redwoods and Rivers, 530/629-4947 or 800/429-0090, website: www.redwoods-rivers.com; River Dancers, 530/926-3517 or 800/926-5002; website: www.riverdancers.com; Rubicon Whitewater Adventures, 707/887-2452, website: www.rubiconadventures.com; Tributary Whitewater Tours, 530/346-6812 or 800/672-3846, website: www.whitewatertours.com; Trinity River Rafting, 530/623-3033 or 800/307-4837, website: www.trinityriverrafting.com; Turtle River Rafting, 530/926-3223 or 800/726-3223, website: www.turtleriver.com; Whitewater Voyages, 510/222-5994 or 800/400-7238, website: www.whitewatervoyages.com; Wilderness Adventures, 530/926-6282 or 800/323-7238, website: www.trinityadventures.com.

Kayak instruction: Otter Bar Lodge Kayak School, 530/462-4772, website: www.otterbar.com.

Supplies and fishing information: Orleans Market, 530/627-3326 or Somes Bar General Store, 530/469-3350.

5 TAYLOR LAKE

Rating: 7

southwest of Etna in the Russian Wilderness

Map 2.1, page 42

If you want the wilderness experience without having to endure a serious overnight hike, you've come to the right place.

Because Taylor Lake is located just inside a wilderness-area boundary, many people looking at a map mistakenly believe it is very difficult to reach. Not true. The walk in takes less than 20 minutes.

Taylor Lake is at an elevation of 6,500 feet, covers 12 acres, and reaches a depth of 35 feet. None of the lakes in the Russian Wilderness are very sizable, but this is one of the biggest, shaped kind of like a kidney bean, with the outlet creek set along the access trail. It is a destination for hikers, campers, anglers, and swimmers.

For those people making their first overnight trek into a wild area, this lake provides what may be an ideal experience: a short hike to a remote area with good trout fishing.

Nothing is perfect, however, and that includes Taylor Lake. Because there is plenty of feed, horse traffic can be common, as packers prepare for trips on the nearby Pacific Crest Trail. In addition, even though this is wilderness, there are occasional bovine intrusions. Yep, cows, as hard as it may be to believe, are allowed to graze the immediate region.

Access: There is no boat ramp.

Facilities, fees: A primitive campground is provided, but there are no other facilities. There is a wheelchair-accessible path around the lake. Access is free.

Water sports, restrictions: Swimming is permitted. Boats and inflatables that can be carried and hand launched are permitted.

Directions: From I-5 at Yreka take the Highway 3/Fort Jones exit and drive 28 miles southwest to Etna. Turn west on Etna-Somes Bar Road (Main Street in town) and drive 10.25 miles just past Etna Summit to Forest Road 41N18 (signed access road). Turn left and continue to the parking area. Park and walk a short distance to the lake.

Contact: Klamath National Forest, Scott and Salmon River Ranger District, 530/468-5351. For a map, send $6 to U.S. Forest Service, Attn: Map Sales, P.O. Box 587, Camino, CA 95709, 530/647-5390, fax 530/647-5389, website: www.fs.fed.us/r5/forests. Major credit cards accepted.

6 KLAMATH RIVER (IRON GATE DAM TO ORLEANS)

Rating: 10

in Klamath National Forest

Map 2.2, page 43

Rafting Hell's Corner is kind of like putting a saddle on the space shuttle and riding off into the stratosphere. This series of big water rapids is the highlight of the Upper Klamath and one of the most exciting runs in the western US. The put-in is in Oregon just below John Boyle Powerhouse (a good spot for trout fishing). From here the descent downstream is more like an assault, warming up with a series of Class III rapids for the first five miles.

Then things get exciting—and more difficult. The first big rapid is Caldera (Class V), a long siege of rollers. I dumped here my first time down and ended up swimming most of it. Here, though, "swimming" means being pulled under by the hydraulics of the river until the force of your life jacket pops you back up. You grab a quick breath, and a moment later the river pulls you right back down. Wild, wet, and crazy.

This is only the start. The worst stretch is Satan's Gate (Class IV), Hell's Corner (Class V), and Ambush (Class IV), one right after another. Boating here is an act of faith. Go only with an experienced guide in an oar boat, not a small paddle boat or inflatable kayak. The guy who taught me how to raft big water, former guide Dean Munroe, lost an eye here when he tried to rescue a boatload of rafters who were pinned against a rock and the lead rope snapped, hurling a metal clasp into his face.

The challenges just keep coming. The final big rapids are Snag Islands Falls (Class III+) and Stateline Falls (Class III), providing two more chances to dump. But hey, a lot of people like dumping here. It feels like winning a merit badge, and survivors can say, "Yeah, I dumped at Ambush, but I made it anyway."

The run is 11 miles long, a hell of a day, though some rafting companies split the outing into two days over a weekend and make the 17-mile trip all the way to Copco Lake. This option requires a good deal of paddling in slow water at the head of the lake. Rafting season is April to October, and water released from John Boyle Dam keeps the run optimum even through warm, dry summers.

A few words of caution: Be aware of sharp volcanic rocks, and if you dump, keep your feet in front of you while you are floating downstream. In addition, pack in your own drinking water. The Klamath is often warm and tinged with algae.

If you're looking for something easy, try the stretch of river from Iron Gate Dam past the I-5 bridge to the Tree of Heaven Campground. This is Class I all the way, technically not even a run, but it is great for inner tubing and canoeing, and for beginners in inflatable kayaks. Although many commercial companies run Hell's Corner, only one—River Dancers—offers commercial trips on this piece of river below Iron Gate Dam. But if you have your own craft and want a fun, stress-free day on the Klamath, this is the place.

Access: Primitive boat ramps are available at the John Boyle Powerhouse, Copco Lake, below Iron Gate Dam, and at Tree of Heaven Campground.

Facilities, fees: Several private and Forest Service campgrounds are located along the river. Drinking water and vault toilets are available. Full services and facilities are available in Yreka. Boat rentals are not offered. Access is free. Rafting permits are not required.

Water sports, restrictions: Rafting, kayaking, canoeing, and swimming are permitted. No powerboats. There are several good swimming holes along Highway 96; look for the "River Access" signs. Swimming in the Upper Klamath is not recommended due to the algae-laden water and sharp volcanic rocks.

Directions: To Hell's Corner put-in: Take I-5 north across the Oregon border to the town of Ashland and Exit 14. Take that exit and drive east on Highway 66 for 45 miles to John Boyle Reservoir. Just before you cross the reservoir, you will see a dirt road on the right. Turn right and drive about five miles to John Boyle Powerhouse. The signed put-in is just downstream of the powerhouse. Take out below Stateline Falls (just below the Oregon/California border) or farther downstream at Copco Lake.

To Iron Gate Reservoir put-in: From Redding, drive north on I-5 to Yreka and the Highway 3/Montague exit in Central Yreka. Turn right on Highway 3 and drive to Montague and the intersection with Montague/Ager Road. Turn left and drive north on Montague/Ager Road for eight miles (over the Klamath River bridge) to Highway 96. Turn right and drive to Iron Gate Reservoir (signed turnoff on the right).

To Tree of Heaven take-out: From Redding, drive north on I-5 to Highway 96. Turn west on Highway 96 and drive seven miles to the Tree of Heaven campground entrance on the left side of the road.

Contact: Klamath National Forest, Scott River Ranger District, 530/468-5351.

Guided trips: Aurora River Adventures, 707/677-3494 or 800/562-8475, website: www.rafting4fun.com; Bigfoot Rafting Company, 530/629-2263 or 800/722-2223, website: www.bigfootrafting.com; Environmental Trav-

eling Companions, 415/474-7662, website: www.etctrips.org/index.html; Klamath River Outfitters, 530/469-3349 or 800/748-3735, website: www.klamathriveroutfitters.com; Living Waters Recreation, 530/926-5446 or 800/994-7238, website: www.livingwatersrec.com; Marble Mountain Ranch, 530/469-3322 or 800/552-6284, website: www.marblemountainranch.com; Osprey Outdoors Kayak School, 530/926-6310, website: www.ospreykayak.com; Redwoods and Rivers, 530/629-4947 or 800/429-0090, website: www.redwoods-rivers.com; River Dancers, 530/926-3517 or 800/926-5002; website: www.riverdancers.com; Rubicon Whitewater Adventures, 707/887-2452, website: www.rubiconadventures.com; Tributary Whitewater Tours, 530/346-6812 or 800/672-3846, website: www.whitewatertours.com; Trinity River Rafting, 530/623-3033 or 800/307-4837, website: www.trinityriverrafting.com; Turtle River Rafting, 530/926-3223 or 800/726-3223, website: www.turtleriver.com; Whitewater Voyages, 510/222-5994 or 800/400-7238, website: www.whitewatervoyages.com; Wilderness Adventures, 530/926-6282 or 800/323-7238, website: www.trinityadventures.com.

Fishing information: Quigley's General Store, 530/465-2224; Klamath River Outfitters (listed above).

7 IRON GATE RESERVOIR

Rating: 7

north of Yreka near Klamath National Forest

Map 2.2, page 43

This summertime vacation spot gets a fair amount of use, but most people overlook the place because of its remote location near the Oregon border.

Set at an elevation of 2,400 feet, east of I-5, the reservoir is nearly seven miles long and covers 825 surface acres. In early summer waterskiing and swimming are popular activities, but when the warm weather arrives, the water begins to develop an overabundance of algae.

In fact, if you fall in while water-skiing, you will find yourself coated with green bits. Nobody appreciates this experience.

Iron Gate is more popular with those who enjoy catching bass and perch in good numbers.

Access: There are three boat ramps located on the west side of the reservoir off Copco Road.

Facilities, fees: Primitive campsites with vault toilets and drinking water (summer only) are available. Supplies can be obtained in Hornbrook. Access is free.

Water sports, restrictions: Powerboating, water-skiing, wake boarding, sailing, sailboarding, canoeing, and kayaking are permitted. A 10-mph speed limit is enforced in designated areas. Swimming beaches are located around the reservoir.

Directions: From Redding, drive north on I-5 to Yreka and the Highway 3/Montague exit in Central Yreka. Turn right on Highway 3 and drive to Montague and the intersection with Montague/Ager Road. Turn left and drive north on Montague/Ager Road for eight miles (over the Klamath River bridge) to Highway 96. Turn right and drive to Iron Gate Reservoir (signed turnoff on the right).

Contact: Pacific Power, 888/221-7070, website: www.pacificpower.net (click on Recreation).

8 COPCO LAKE

Rating: 6

north of Yreka near Klamath National Forest

Map 2.2, page 43

If you swim in Copco Lake in the summer, you'll emerge looking like you've got some kind of disease, or as if you have been exposed to radioactive material. You will practically glow with a fresh coating of green algae mire. Are we having fun yet?

No, we are not. But it can get very hot out here, and some people finally give in and take the plunge. Boat traffic is very light, and though water-skiing is permitted, nobody likes getting doused with all the green stuff.

Copco Lake is set at an elevation of 2,613 feet, is five miles long, and covers 1,000 acres. In addition to the surplus algae, it offers something that no other lake can: fantastic opportunities in the summer to catch yellow perch. Imagine a scenario where families catch 40 or 50 (there's no limit) of the little buggers (seven to nine inches long) with little effort. I guess yellow perch don't mind all the algae.

Copco gets far less use than neighboring Iron Gate Reservoir, and in turn, the atmosphere is more remote. The boat ramp, by the way, is steep and somewhat primitive, and the adjacent parking area is small, but that's the price you pay for all the yellow perch you can catch.

Access: A paved boat ramp is located at Mallard Cove, which can be accessed on Ager Beswick Road.

Facilities, fees: A primitive campground is located at Mallard Cove. Vault toilets are available. The Copco Store has supplies. Access is free.

Water sports, restrictions: Powerboating, water-skiing, wake boarding, sailing, sailboarding, canoeing, and kayaking are permitted. A 10-mph speed limit is enforced in designated areas. Swimming beaches are located around the reservoir, best at Mallard Cove.

Directions: From Redding, drive north on I-5 to Yreka and the Highway 3/Montague exit in Central Yreka. Turn right on Highway 3 and drive to Montague and the intersection with Montague/Ager Road. Turn left and drive north on Montague/Ager Road for about five miles to Ager/Bestick Road. Turn right (signed for Copco Lake) on Ager/Bestick Road and drive 13 miles to Copco Lake. Note: Copco Lake can be also reached from Iron Gate Reservoir by driving east on Copco Road. As you leave Iron Gate, the road becomes gravel, bumpy, and narrow, and most arriving from the south prefer the suggested route on Ager/Bestick Road.

Contact: Copco Lake Store, 530/459-3655, website: www.copcolakestore.com; Copco Vacation Rentals, 530/459-3051.

9 JUANITA LAKE

Rating: 6

near Macdoel in Klamath National Forest

Map 2.2, page 43

Juanita Lake is a perfect example of the kind of place that gets overlooked by so many Californians who hunger for exactly what it has to offer. It is small. It is out of the way, yet is accessible by car. It has lakeside camping and decent trout fishing. But you've probably never heard the name, right? Don't feel bad. Not many folks have, and the same goes for hundreds of similar lakes in the more remote areas of California.

The lake is surrounded by high desert at an elevation of 5,100 feet in Klamath National Forest. A mountain known as the Goosenest, a volcanic peak north of Mount Shasta Juanita, overlooks the lake.

The cold water, which is a little on the mucky side, and a rocky shore inhibit swimming, so Juanita Lake gets very light use. One of the highlights: the lake is ringed by a 1.5-mile paved, barrier-free hiking trail that is wheelchair-accessible (the campground is also wheelchair-accessible).

Access: A primitive boat ramp is located on the north end of the lake.

Facilities, fees: A campground with vault toilets and drinking water is available. Supplies can be obtained in Macdoel. There is a charge for camping Day use access is free.

Water sports, restrictions: Rowboats, canoes, kayaks, inflatables, sailboats, and sailboards are permitted. No motors. The water is usually too cold for swimming and other water-contact sports.

Directions: From Redding, drive north on I-5 to Weed and the exit for Highway 97. Take that exit, turn right, and drive one mile (through town) to a lighted intersection with Highway 97. Turn right and drive 37 miles to Ball Mountain Road. Turn left on Ball Mountain Road and drive 2.5 miles (bear

right at the fork) and continue a short distance to the lake.

Contact: Klamath National Forest, Goosenest Ranger District, 530/398-4391.

10 LAKE SHASTINA

Rating: 7

near Weed and Klamath National Forest

Map 2.2, page 43

It seems as if it's always windy at Lake Shastina. The wind blows, blows, blows, and people just learn to put up with it. Yet I've also seen it on calm days, where the surface glasses out and reflects Mount Shasta, a moment of seeming perfection.

This is one of the few lakes in the northern part of California where condo/house rentals are available. Shastina is located near Weed (named after a man, Abner, not a plant), set at 3,000 feet in elevation within close range of the north slopes of Mount Shasta. The country here is arid and desertlike, making Shastina sparkle and glow, especially when full in the spring and early summer.

This is a great lake for water-skiing and wake boarding, especially in early summer, when the cool, clean water is high, and the temperatures warm.

In the spring, even though the water is cold, this is a good lake for sailboarding, but the sport has not caught on big time as it has in areas with warmer spring climates. Water-skiing and personal watercraft are more popular, especially when the warm weather sets in and the wind isn't blowing too much. For the most part, fishing for trout and bass are the favored activities and lure the bulk of the visitors.

The surrounding land, including the Lake Shastina Golf Course, is privately owned. Condo rentals can be arranged by calling the golf course. Be aware that, while it is a good-size lake, by autumn it can be reduced to a large puddle thanks to irrigation demands by hay farmers located downstream. The water level can get so low that some locals dub the lake "River Shastina."

Access: A paved boat ramp is located off Jackson Ranch Road at the signed public fishing access; the boat ramp is nonfunctional when the lake level drops below the concrete ramp.

Facilities, fees: A primitive campground with chemical toilets is available. No drinking water. Supplies can be obtained in Weed. Access is free.

Water sports, restrictions: Powerboats, personal watercraft, water-skiing, wake boarding, sailing, and sailboarding are permitted. A portable toilet is available. No swimming at fishing dock or boat ramp. Boat rentals are not available.

Directions: From Redding, drive north on I-5 to Weed and the exit for Highway 97. Take that exit, turn right, and drive one mile (through town) to a lighted intersection with Highway 97. Turn right and drive north on U.S. 97 for five miles to Big Springs Road. Turn left (west) on Big Springs Road and drive about one mile to Jackson Ranch Road. Turn left (west) on Jackson Ranch Road and drive .5 mile to Emerald Isle Road (watch for the signed turnoff). Turn right and drive two miles to the lake and boat ramp.

Contact: Siskiyou County Public Works, 530/842-8250; Siskiyou County Visitors Bureau, 530/926-3850, website: www.visitsiskiyou.org. For lodging, call Lake Shastina Golf Course, 530/938-3201, website: www.shastinagolf.com.

11 ORR LAKE

Rating: 6

near Macdoel in Klamath National Forest

Map 2.2, page 43

The road in is in terrible shape, the larger fish can be very elusive, and in the hot summer months, visitors—especially those with kids—should be extremely careful about crossing paths with rattlesnakes. So drive a vehicle that can take the bumps, bring along your angling

smarts, and keep your eyes on the ground. That accomplished, you're in for a treat.

The setting, in the high plateau country of northern Siskiyou County, affords a great view of Mt. Shasta. Although the lake is quite small, unsuitable for boats with motors, it is ideal for relaxing and floating around in a canoe, raft, or car-top boat. No matter what you do, you will keep gazing northward to Shasta, a silver dollar in a field of pennies.

The land here is privately held, but the owners allow public access to the lake. Regardless, it gets light use. One reason is that the water tends to be cold and a bit murky, sometimes even mucky, making swimming and other contact water sports undesirable. Still, kids can have a good time splashing around, and they usually don't notice the difference.

Access: There is a gravel boat ramp.

Facilities, fees: A campground offering drinking water and restrooms with flush toilets is available nearby. A fee is charged for camping. Access to the lake is free.

Water sports, restrictions: Small boats, canoes, kayaks, sailing, sailboarding, and swimming are permitted. The lake is too small for large boats with motors, and is usually too cold for swimming and other sports involving water contact.

Directions: From Redding, drive north on I-5 to Weed and the exit for Highway 97. Take that exit, turn right at the stop sign, drive through Weed and bear right (north) on Highway 97 and drive 40 miles to Ball Mountain Road. Turn right at Ball Mountain Road and drive 2.5 miles to a T with Old State Highway 97. Turn right and drive 4.25 miles (crossing railroad tracks) to the Shafter Campground (on the right side of the road) and continue to the lake.

Contact: Klamath National Forest, Goosenest Ranger District, 530/398-4391.

12 KANGAROO LAKE

Rating: 8

near Callahan in Klamath National Forest

Map 2.2, page 43

Little Kangaroo Lake is nestled in the Scott Mountains, a perfect hideaway for campers and anglers who want to get away from it all. The road in is quite pretty, especially below Scott Mountain, where there are scenic valleys filled with greenery and edged by forestland and mountains.

This small (25 acres) but deep (100 feet) alpine water is situated in a mountain bowl at an elevation of 6,500 feet. The campsites are reached via a short walk from the parking area, and the lake is just a few minutes from the campground. There's good shoreline fishing for large brook trout and decent-sized rainbow trout. And here's a rare plus: a wheelchair-accessible ramp. The water is cold, so only members of the Polar Bear Club try swimming here.

At the camp, hikers will find a trailhead for the Pacific Crest Trail, which provides a route for an invigorating day hike up to a peak that has great views of the lake.

Access: There is no boat ramp. A short walk on a paved, wheelchair-accessible trail is required to reach the lake.

Facilities, fees: A walk-in campground and a fishing pier are available. Some facilities are wheelchair-accessible. A fee is charged for camping; day use is free.

Water sports, restrictions: Inflatables, canoes, prams and kayaks are permitted but must be carried in and hand launched. Swimming is permitted but the water is often cold. No motors. No sailboarding.

Directions: From Redding, drive north on I-5 just past Weed and take the Edgewood turnoff. At the stop sign, turn left and drive a short distance to the stop sign at Old Stage Road. Turn right on Old Stage Road and drive six miles to Gazelle. In Gazelle, turn left at Gazelle-Callahan Road and drive over the summit.

From the summit, continue about five miles to Rail Creek Road. Turn left at Rail Creek Road and drive approximately five miles to where the road dead-ends at Kangaroo Lake Walk-In.

Contact: Klamath National Forest, Scott and Salmon River Ranger District, 530/468-5351.

13 PICAYUNE LAKE

Rating: 7

near Mt. Shasta in Shasta-Trinity National Forest

Map 2.2, page 43

This is one of the prettiest alpine lakes in the Trinity-Divide country—almost always full, lined by firs, pines, and cedars, and bordered on the western side by a steep facing. It gets very little traffic because a gate blocks the access road's last half mile, and most people just don't want to hike in, and also because camping is prohibited. The lake is bordered by land owned by the Roseburg Lumber Company, not the US Forest Service, and while public access is permitted, the gate is there to discourage it.

Picayune is set at an elevation of 6,100 feet, covers 11.5 acres, and is 27 feet deep. Despite its beauty, it receives very light use, primarily by day hikers having picnics. It is too cold for swimming until midsummer, and the trout fishing is just fair. A few ambitious souls will carry in inner tubes or rubber rafts and float around in the center of Picayune Lake to take in all this great beauty.

Roseburg Lumber has built a nice cabin and dock at the lake, but they are strictly off-limits to visitors.

Access: There is no boat ramp.

Facilities, fees: Vault toilets are available. A small dock and cabin have been built, but they are off-limits to the public. No drinking water. Supplies can be obtained in Mount Shasta. Access is free.

Water sports, restrictions: Canoeing, kayaking, and inflatables are permitted, but must be carried in and hand launched. No motors. Swimming is permitted.

Directions: From the town of Mount Shasta on I-5, take the Central Mount Shasta exit and drive to the stop sign. Turn west and continue a short distance to Old Stage Road. Turn left and drive .25 mile to a Y at W. A. Barr Road. Bear right on W. A. Barr Road and drive past Box Canyon Dam and the Lake Siskiyou Campground entrance. Continue 10 miles to a fork (left goes to Gumboot). Stay right at the fork and continue one mile to Bear Creek Road/Forest Road 40N4s. Turn right and drive along the ridge (the lake will be below you to the left) for one mile to an unsigned junction. Turn left and drive to the gate. Park and hike the last .5 mile to the lake.

Contact: Shasta-Trinity National Forest, Mt. Shasta Ranger Station, 530/926-4511; Mt. Shasta Visitor Center, 530/926-4865 or 800/926-4865.

14 GUMBOOT LAKE

Rating: 7

near Mt. Shasta in Shasta-Trinity
National Forest

Map 2.2, page 43

Gumboot is quite pretty, bordered on its far side by a meadow and a steep mountain face, and well forested on the other. A pool of emerald green water that's only 15 feet deep, the lake is set at an elevation of 6,050 feet and covers just seven acres.

Easy access makes this a popular stop for shoreline anglers and car-top boaters who haul in canoes, prams, and inflatable rafts. The water is chilly, too cold to swim in for very long. Yet there are many summer evenings when it is ideal to float around in an inflatable.

Fishing for trout is often good here. So is hiking.

If you're in the mood for a picnic and a hike, this is an excellent destination. My favorite is to scramble up the mountain behind the lake to the ridgeline, hit the Pacific Crest Trail, then

turn left, and claim the peak that is set just above the lake. This is a great vantage point, with a stellar view of Gumboot and Mt. Shasta in the distance.

Another option is hiking about 10 minutes through forest to Upper Gumboot Lake, a small lake that is well hidden.

Access: No boat ramp is available. Car-top boats may be hand launched.

Facilities, fees: Dispersed campsites at the lake with a vault toilet are available. No drinking water. Garbage must be packed out. Access is free.

Water sports, restrictions: Canoeing, kayaking, inflatables, sailboarding, sailing, and swimming are permitted. No motors. No trailered boats are permitted.

Directions: From the town of Mount Shasta on I-5, take the Central Mount Shasta exit and drive to the stop sign. Turn west and continue a short distance to Old Stage Road. Turn left and drive .25 mile to a Y at W. A. Barr Road. Bear right on W. A. Barr Road and drive past Box Canyon Dam and the Lake Siskiyou Campground entrance. Continue 10 miles to a fork, signed for Gumboot Lake. Bear left and drive .5 mile to the lake and campsites.

Contact: Shasta-Trinity National Forest, Mount Shasta Ranger District, 530/926-4511. For kayak tours or instruction: Osprey Outdoors Kayak School, 530/926-6310, website: www.ospreykayak.com.

15 TOAD LAKE

Rating: 7

near Mt. Shasta in Shasta-Trinity
National Forest

Map 2.2, page 43

This is a pretty hike-in lake that sits on the edge of wilderness, providing good camping, swimming, hiking, and fair fishing—and you can be here after an easy 15-minute walk.

A lot of people stay clear of the lake because the road in is long and rough, particularly a terribly bumpy spot about .5 mile from the parking area. At least you'll be rewarded for your efforts with a little solitude—solitude and a 23.5-acre, 40-foot-deep lake in an attractive setting at an elevation of 6,950 feet.

Swimming? Although the lake freezes over in winter, by midspring it is refreshing and not too cold, and by summer it is excellent for swimming. Camping? Outstanding, with all the elements of a wilderness trip without a long tromp, allowing you to make repeat trips to carry in lots of bonus items. Hiking? A half-hour hike, starting by looping around the lake in a counterclockwise direction, will take you to a trail that is routed above the rock bowl and on to the Pacific Crest Trail. Another 15 minutes on foot will get you to Porcupine Lake, an absolutely pristine setting. Mountain climbing? An all-day, leg-straining grunt will help you reach the top of Mount Eddy, which peaks at 9,025 feet, making it the highest mountain in the local range.

Add it all up and put it in your mental cash register: Right, Toad Lake is quite a place to visit.

Access: There is no boat ramp.

Facilities, fees: Dispersed, primitive campsites and a vault toilet are available. Drinking water is not available. All garbage must be packed out. Supplies can be obtained in Mount Shasta. Access is free.

Water sports, restrictions: Swimming is permitted. Inflatables, canoes, and kayaks are permitted, but must be carried in and hand launched.

Directions: From the town of Mount Shasta on I-5, take the Central Mount Shasta exit and drive to the stop sign. Turn west and drive a short distance to Old Stage Road. Turn left and drive .25 mile to a Y at W. A. Barr Road. Bear right and drive past Box Canyon Dam and the entrance to Lake Siskiyou, and continue up the mountain (the road becomes Forest Road 26). Just past a concrete bridge, turn right at the sign for Toad Lake, drive .2 mile, then turn left on a dirt Forest Service road and

continue for 11 miles to the parking area. The road is extremely bumpy and twisty, and the final .5 mile to the trailhead is rocky and rough. High-clearance, four-wheel-drive vehicles are recommended. Walk in about .5 mile to the lake and campsites.

Contact: Shasta-Trinity National Forest, Mt. Shasta Ranger District, 530/926-4511. For a map of Shasta-Trinity National Forest, send $6 to U.S. Forest Service, Attn: Map Sales, P.O. Box 587, Camino, CA 95709, 530/647-5390, fax 530/647-5389, website: www.fs.fed.us/r5/forests. Major credit cards accepted.

16 CASTLE LAKE

Rating: 8

near Mt. Shasta in Shasta-Trinity National Forest

Map 2.2, page 43

Bring your camera. No, not to take pictures of big fish, because there are very few of those, but rather to take pictures from some of California's most scenic lookouts.

The view of Mt. Shasta from the road in, just .5 mile below the lake, is absolutely spectacular. More magazine pictures of the magic mountain are taken here than from any other lookout.

Set at an elevation of 5,400 feet, the lake covers 47 acres and is 120 feet deep. Extremely pure water that is low in nitrogen (similar to Lake Tahoe) has resulted in a color that is deeper blue than any lake in the Trinity-Divide country and has been the focus of a study by UC Davis scientists for years. The depth of the lake keeps the water cold, even in summer, but some brave souls claim that if you take the plunge, you will be rejuvenated by the lake's magical properties.

Hand-launch boats, including canoes, kayaks, and inflatables, are well suited for Castle Lake, especially for exploring the unusual rock face on the lake's back wall. It is a beautiful spot, set in a granite bowl with a spectacular wall on the far side.

Castle Lake is easy to reach, with a paved road all the way in. Although in winter it provides one of the few good spots for ice fishing (and ice skating) in Northern California, the views are what visitors find unforgettable.

But for an even better photo opportunity, hike in from Castle Lake to Heart Lake and then take a snapshot of Shasta with that little lake in the foreground. Unless you are careful, you might win an award for that one, it's that beautiful. To get to Heart Lake, take the trail that starts on the left side of Castle Lake and hike for .5 mile up to the saddle. Then continue to the right and up for another .5 mile. Heart Lake is nestled in an upper ledge along the back wall of the rock basin.

Access: There is no boat ramp.

Facilities, fees: No facilities at the lake. A small campground with vault toilets is available nearby. No drinking water. Supplies can be obtained in the town of Mount Shasta. Access to the lake is free.

Water sports, restrictions: Inflatables, canoes, prams, and kayaks are permitted but must be carried in and hand launched. Swimming is permitted but the water is often cold. No motors. Sailboarding is also allowed, but no one sailboards here.

Directions: From the town of Mount Shasta on I-5, take the Central Mount Shasta exit and drive to the stop sign. Turn west and drive a short distance to Old Stage Road. Turn left and drive .25 mile to a Y at W. A. Barr Road. Bear right on W. A. Barr Road and drive past Box Canyon Dam. Turn left at Castle Lake Road and drive seven miles to the campground access road on the left. Turn left and drive a short distance to the campground. Note: Castle Lake is another .25 mile up the road; there are no legal campsites along the lake's shoreline.

Contact: Shasta-Trinity National Forest, Mt. Shasta Ranger District, 530/926-4511.

17 LAKE SISKIYOU

Rating: 8

near Mt. Shasta in Shasta-Trinity
National Forest

Map 2.2, page 43

This lake sits at the base of giant Mt. Shasta, which towers above at 14,162 feet, giving it one of the loveliest settings for a man-made lake in America. Recreation—not water storage for farming—was the sole reason Siskiyou was built. Thus, while reservoirs in the foothills of California are drained when water is needed, Siskiyou remains full, often having a jewel-like quality. That is why people come here—to visit the most beautiful lake along the entire I-5 corridor.

Lake Siskiyou covers 435 acres and is set at an elevation of 3,181 feet. In the summer months the lake gets a lot of traffic from RV campers, sunbathers, and anglers. In the winter the shore is snowbound, but the lake does not freeze over. Favorite activities include fishing in the spring, and swimming and leisure boating in the summer, a time when many families take weeklong camping trips here. The campground is huge, yet it can fill up on summer weekends and reservations are advised. Camping season at the lake kicks off on Memorial Day weekend, and this spot is popular well into mid-September.

The 10-mph speed limit ensures quiet waters, and the nearby campground with easy access off I-5 makes it ideal for family vacationers. Children often play in the swimming area and tool around in pedal boats. On hot summer weekends when the campground is full, Lake Siskiyou's beach can get pretty crowded. Sailboarding, which is usually fair on windy afternoons in May and early June, is practiced primarily near the north shore.

In spring, fishing is good for trout. Then, as the water warms with summer temperatures, it is good for smallmouth bass.

This place is so wonderful that you can just stretch out on a beach blanket, gaze across the water at Mt. Shasta, and be thankful to witness such a beautiful scene.

Access: A two-lane boat ramp with a dock is provided. To get there, drive past the entrance kiosk and continue straight for .5 mile.

Facilities, fees: A small marina, dock, boat ramp, snack bar, and tackle shop are located at the boat dock. Fishing boats, pontoon boats, pedal boats, canoes, and kayaks can be rented. A campground, lodging units, RV cabins, restrooms with showers, coin laundry, fish-cleaning station, playground, RV dump station, convenience store, and restaurant with bar are available. North shore access is limited to day use only; vault toilets are available. Fees are charged for day use, boat launching and camping. Access to the north shore is free.

Water sports, restrictions: Powerboating, canoeing, kayaking, sailboarding, sailboating, and swimming are permitted. A 10-mph speed limit is strictly enforced. A sandy beach is located on the western shore of the lake, a five-minute walk from the marina. The adjacent swimming area is protected from boats by a line of buoys.

Directions: From the town of Mount Shasta on I-5, take the Central Mount Shasta exit and drive to the stop sign. Turn west and drive a short distance to Old Stage Road. Turn left and drive .25 mile to a Y at W. A. Barr Road. Bear right on W. A. Barr Road and drive past Box Canyon Dam. Two miles farther, turn right at the entrance road for Lake Siskiyou Campground and Marina and drive a short distance to the entrance station.

Contact: Lake Siskiyou Campground, 530/926-2618 or 888/926-2618, website: www.lakesis.com; Lake Siskiyou Marina, 530/926-2617; Osprey Outdoor Kayak School, 530/926-6310, website: www.ospreykayak.com; River Skills Center, 530/926-4657, website: www.riverskills.com.

18 UPPER SACRAMENTO RIVER

Rating: 7

near Mt. Shasta upstream of Shasta Lake

Map 2.2, page 43

The best way to see mother nature at work is as a skilled kayaker, either in a hard shell or an inflatable, running the river. Rafting in oar boats is usually limited to spring and early summer; after that the reduced stream flows can cause bottom scraping on too much of the route.

Skilled kayakers have two popular runs to choose from:

Cantara Loop through Dunsmuir: This very demanding run is filled with Class IV rapids and requires a lot of technical paddling through pocket water sprinkled with boulders and quick turns. Although very pretty, with riparian vegetation again flourishing on the riverbanks, it is not secluded, especially right through Dunsmuir. In addition, the Southern Pacific railroad parallels the river all the way through Dunsmuir, and it is common to hear the cacophonous roar of passing trains. A technical highlight of this run is Mears Creek Falls, which is rated Class V and is located below Dunsmuir at Mile 21. It's the largest rapid on the river, and during high flows it should be portaged.

Sims Flat to Dog Creek: This is a more popular run than the previously detailed stretch of water. Its Class III and IV rapids and abundance of technical, quick turns around boulders and eddies renders it challenging and exciting. More so than most rivers, this section of stream varies wildly in character from spring through summer according to river flows. Even though you will be heading south as you venture downstream, be sure to pull over at clearings and look to the north for spectacular views of Mt. Shasta.

A key piece of insider knowledge for the Upper Sacramento River is to match up the level of river flows with your approach for fishing or rafting. Because rivers fluctuate according to weather, snowmelt, season, feeder streams and dam releases, this can make or break a trip.

To get current river flows, go to the Department of Water Resources website at: http://cdec.water.ca.gov/cgi-progs/queryDaily?s (click on DLT—Sacramento River at Delta). This will provide you with the river flows measured in cubic feet per second, known as CFS, at the state's water gauge at the town of Delta (located at signed turnoff for Vollmers).

With the CFS data, you can use the following info as a guide for your trip:

—1,800 to 2,000 CFS and up: High, fast and turbid. Too high to fish. For rafting, Class IIIs become Class IV rapids, dangerous for novices.

—1,400 to 1,800 CFS: High and fast. Marginal fishing conditions, extremely difficult fly-fishing, nymphing edges of eddies and behind boulders. Excellent rafting.

—1,000 to 1,400 CFS: Moderate and clear. Superb levels for rafting and fishing. Good nymphing during the day, with some mayfly and caddis hatches when shade is on the water (or on overcast days).

—700 to 1,000 CFS: Medium-speed flows, with pockets behind rocks and boulders better defined. Outstanding flyfishing, good hatches after 6 P.M. for dry fly fishing. Good for rafting.

—500 to 700 CFS: Low to medium flows. Superb flyfishing, both nymphing during the day and surface hatches at dawn and dusk. Marginal rafting, "bony" with some bottom skidding.

—300 to 500 CFS: Low and very clear. Easy to wade, delicate presentations a must for fly-fishers, lots of pocket water, great caddis hatch common late in the season. No rafting.

In 1991 I was on the scene when a Southern Pacific freighter derailed and dumped a tanker wheels-up into the river, spilling 19,000 gallons of an all-purpose herbicide. That seems so long ago, now that the entire aquatic food chain is again healthy and full, with trout filling the river from Box Canyon to Shasta Lake.

After Southern Pacific killed the river, few people would dare dream of such a recovery.

All anybody could do was pray for a fresh start. Those prayers have been answered, and today the fish are back and this place offers the chance to experience nature in her prime.

Access: No boat ramps are available.

Facilities, fees: Several campgrounds and RV parks are located nearby. Restrooms with flush toilets, vault toilets, and drinking water are available. Supplies can be obtained in Mount Shasta, Dunsmuir, Castella, Lakehead, and Redding. Access is free. Rafting permits are not required.

Water sports, restrictions: Rafting, kayaking, and swimming are permitted. The best swimming holes with the easiest access are at Sims Flat Campground, at the end of Prospect Street in Dunsmuir, and at the Sweetbrier Bridge south of Castle Crags.

Directions: To Cal Trout/Mt. Shasta **Access:** Take I-5 to Mount Shasta and the exit for Central Mount Shasta. Take that exit to the stop sign. Turn west and drive one mile to W.A. Barr Road. Turn left, drive for a mile to a Y junction with Old Stage Road. Bear left on Old Stage Road and drive to Cantara Road. Turn right and continue down to the river. The put-in is at the Cal Trout fishing access above the Cantara Loop Railroad Bridge.

To Sims Road **Access:** Take I-5 to the exit for north Dunsmuir. Take that exit to the stop sign. Turn west and drive a short distance to Dunsmuir Avenue, and then continue a short distance to Prospect Avenue. Turn right and drive one mile to the river access (well signed in Dunsmuir).

To Prospect Ave./Dunsmuir **Access:** Take I-5 to the exit for Sims Road (12 miles south of Dunsmuir). Take that exit and take Sims Road east to Sims Flat Campground and access.

To Dog Creek **Access:** Take I-5 to the exit for Vollmers/Dog Creek. Take that exit and drive west a short distance to the river access.

Contact: Shasta-Trinity National Forest, Mount Shasta Ranger District, 530/926-4511. River flow information, website: http://cdec.water.ca.gov.

Guided trips: Aurora River Adventures,

707/677-3494 or 800/562-8475, website: www.rafting4fun.com; Living Waters Recreation, 530/926-5446 or 800/994-7238, website: www.livingwatersrec.com; Osprey Outdoors Kayak School, 530/926-6310, website: www.ospreykayak.com; River Dancers, 530/926-3517 or 800/926-5002; website: www.river-dancers.com; Tributary Whitewater Tours, 530/346-6812 or 800/672-3846, website: www.whitewatertours.com; Trinity River Rafting, 530/623-3033 or 800/307-4837, website: www.trinityriverrafting.com; Turtle River Rafting, 530/926-3223 or 800/726-3223, website: www.turtleriver.com; Wilderness Adventures, 530/926-6282 or 800/323-7238, website: www.trinityadventures.com.

19 TAMARACK LAKE

Rating: 7

near Castella in Shasta-Trinity
National Forest

Map 2.2, page 43

Tamarack makes a good base camp for people who have a taste for exploring. Of course if you just want to sit back and gaze at it, that's okay, too. This is one of the prettiest lakes in the Trinity-Divide country.

The lake is set at an elevation of 5,900 feet, covers 21 acres, and is 16 feet deep. To drive all the way in, you need a four-wheel-drive vehicle. Many people stop short where the access road gets rough and hike in the last .5 mile. Some four-wheelers bring canoes or rafts and enjoy the spectacular beauty from the water. Fishing for small trout is only fair here, and the water is often too cold for swimming until midsummer. The best fishing spot is at the south end of the lake.

Side trips include a hike to the foot of Gray Butte, that craggy mountaintop to the northeast, and visits to nearby Twin Lakes and Lily Pad Lake. This is a great place for four-wheel-drive adventure.

Access: There is no boat ramp.

Facilities, fees: No facilities are available on site. Primitive, do-it-yourself campsites are available. Supplies can be obtained in Castella. Access is free.

Water sports, restrictions: Swimming, inflatables, canoes, and kayaks are permitted. The lake is too small for most water sports.

Directions: From Redding, drive north on I-5 to the town of Castella (near Castle Crags) and Castle Creek Road. Take that exit, turn west, and drive 11 miles west on Road 25 (Castle Creek Road) to Twin Lakes Road. Turn left (south) and drive three miles. Bear left where the road forks and proceed one mile to the lake. (The last four miles of road are very rough, suitable only for high-clearance, four-wheel-drive vehicles.)

Contact: Shasta-Trinity National, Mt. Shasta Ranger District, 530/926-4511. For a map, send $6 to U.S. Forest Service, Attn: Map Sales, P.O. Box 587, Camino, CA 95709, 530/647-5390, fax 530/647-5389, website: www.fs.fed.us/r5/forests. Major credit cards accepted.

20 MCCLOUD RIVER

Rating: 10

near McCloud in Shasta-Trinity
National Forest

Map 2.2, page 43

A visit to the McCloud River is about as close as you can get to an adventure in a time machine. Here, just walking, hiking, kayaking, or fishing can make you feel as if you have turned back the clock two centuries.

On the Upper McCloud out of Fowler's Camp, a great 20-minute walk will take you to Lower Falls and to one of the prettiest waterfalls in Northern California: spectacular Middle Falls, a wide and tall silvery cascade that pounds into a deep pool. On the Lower McCloud, starting at the Nature Conservancy, another wonderful hike is routed along the river, where you need to boulder-hop some of the way. Everything is pristine and untouched;

the Nature Conservancy keeps it that way and I hope they always will.

The river is too cold for swimming in the Lower McCloud, painful even for a quick dunk. However, there is a nice hole in the Upper McCloud near Cattle Camp, and there are always lots of folks jumping off Lower Falls and playing in the deep hole below. A ladder runs up from this swimming hole to a flat, rocky area where people like to sunbathe and picnic. Please do not litter there (or anywhere)!

The Lower McCloud is too shallow and technical most of the year for kayakers or rafters and always presents a challenge for fly fishers. Regardless, the river gets the top rating for its dramatic scenery and challenging terrain for paddlers and anglers.

There are two primary runs for rafts and kayaks:

• Upper McCloud, from Lower Falls to Lake McCloud: This Class III, 10-mile stretch includes three miles on the lake, a real drag. But the river passes the Hearst's Wyntoon Estate, complete with castles (look, but don't stop or touch). The first two miles of the run is typically shallow with a lot of bottom scraping, and then the flows pick up and make for a good, yet technical, run. By July it's all over. The run gets bony and it is a long and tedious exercise in frustration. Even in good conditions, it takes all day and into the early evening to reach the Lake McCloud boat ramp.

Former rafting guide Diane Strachan told me that when she made the run, she stopped at a rock to look at the Hearst castles, then spotted this mean-looking gardener, who appeared to be glaring at her.

"Is it okay if I get out and look at the paintings on the walls of the castles?" she asked.

"Okay," the gardener answered, "but only for a moment."

Well, Diane looked closer and noticed the "gardener" was familiar. Could it be? It was. Turned out to be Clint Eastwood.

• Lower McCloud, from Ash Camp to Gilman Road at Shasta Lake: With many of the rapids

rated at Class IV and V, this is for expert kayakers only. Extremely technical work is required around shallow riffles sprinkled with boulders and pocket water. The season is extremely short, usually over by mid-May, and few try it. This is a long, exhausting, and grueling stretch of river for even the most skilled paddlers.

A few notes: No commercial trips are permitted on the McCloud; this is do-it-yourself only.

Access: There is no boat ramp. Boats must be hand launched.

Facilities, fees: Campgrounds with chemical toilets and drinking water are available. A picnic area is located at Lower Falls. Supplies can be obtained in McCloud. Access is free. Rafting permits are not required.

Water sports, restrictions: Although the water is very cold, you can swim near Cattle Camp and at Lower Falls.

Directions: To Upper McCloud at Fowler's Camp: From Redding, drive north on I-5 and continue just past Dunsmuir to the junction with Highway 89. Turn east on Highway 89 and drive 12 miles to McCloud. From McCloud, drive five miles southeast on Highway 89 to the campground entrance road on the right. Turn right and drive a short distance to a Y. For the put-in below Lower Falls (kayaks only), turn right and drive to the parking area. For the put-in at Lakim Dam (flat water, canoes OK), turn left and drive to the parking area adjacent to the dam.

To Lower McCloud at Ah-Di-Na: From Redding, drive north on I-5 past Dunsmuir to the junction with Highway 89. Turn right and drive nine miles to McCloud and Squaw Valley Road. Turn right on Squaw Valley Road and drive to Lake McCloud. Turn right at Lake McCloud and continue along the lake to a signed turnoff on the right side of the road (at a deep cove in the lake). Turn right (the road turns to dirt) and drive four miles to the campground entrance on the left side of the road. Turn left and drive a short distance to the campground (kayaks only). The take-out is at Gilman Road on the

McCloud Arm of Shasta Lake. This Class IV-V run is for experts only.

Contact: Shasta-Trinity National Forest, McCloud Ranger District, 530/964-2184.

21 TRINITY RIVER

Rating: 9

in Shasta-Trinity National Forest

Map 2.3, page 44

The Trinity River runs clear and blue green, tumbling around boulders and into deep holes, all the while framed by a high, tree-lined canyon.

Located in Northern California west of Redding, the Trinity starts as a trickle in the Trinity Alps and then flows westward for 100 miles, eventually joining with the Klamath River in its journey to the sea. It is a fountain of beauty, rolling pure through granite gorges and abounding with birds and wildlife. Because flows are controlled by upstream dam releases, white-water rafting levels are guaranteed throughout summer.

This is a rafter's river and is especially suited to beginners for several reasons: Trips here are the lowest priced anywhere in California; the setting for rafters is a classic pool-and-drop, with most rapids in the Class II range; and the summer weather is often perfect. Shuttle rides are available, and guided oar-boat trips also are available at a higher price. Another bonus at Big Flat is the Steelhead Cabins for lodging, as well as nearby campgrounds.

The best trip for newcomers is near Big Flat, where the river has long, deep pools interspersed with sudden riffles and drops. Class II and III rapids such as Hell Hole, the Slot, Zig-Zag, Fishtail, Pinball, and others arrive every five minutes or so, providing bursts of pure thrill and then short rests that allow you to regain your composure. The commercial rafting company at Big Flat provides gear rentals, and a survey we made revealed this was the lowest-cost rafting trip in California.

The Trinity has two additional runs:

• Lewiston Bridge to Douglas City: This is an easy paddle with Class I and II rapids, nothing difficult. The best put-in spots are at Lewiston Bridge and Trinity River Lodge RV Resort. Inner tubers looking for a great trip should plop in at Lewiston Bridge, float a few miles downstream, and take out at Trinity Lodge Resort. The entire 37 miles of river here is easy and manageable for longer trips. The surrounding vegetation is pretty, but the heavy traffic on adjacent Highway 299 is a common reminder that civilization is close at hand.

• Pigeon Point to Cedar Flat: Pigeon Point, along with a Forest Service campground, is located just downstream of where the North Fork Trinity enters the main stem Trinity. This is the most popular put-in spot on the river, although there are a few other campgrounds upstream that also offer river access. The best bet here is to make the 12-mile run, taking out above Burnt Ranch Gorge, a mostly pristine river section that features deep pools and beautiful giant boulders. Burnt Ranch Gorge is rated Class V, clearly for experts in oar boats who like living on the edge and don't mind a little danger.

As for guided trips, only Trinity River Rafting and Wilderness Adventures run Burnt Ranch Gorge. Meanwhile, many other companies run other stretches of the river.

One of Northern California's greatest swimming areas is here at Tish-Tang Campground, located just upstream from the Hoopa Valley. In mid to late summer, it is the perfect place to laze around in an inner tube or to simply put on a life jacket and slowly float down the river in the warm, benign water.

Access: A primitive boat ramp (small, flat-bottomed boats and rafts only) is available at Trinity River Lodge RV Resort, located south of Lewiston off Trinity Dam Boulevard. Rafters can put in at the bridge in the town of Lewiston and take out at one of several points north of Douglas City.

There are no boat ramps on the lower stretch of the river. Rafters can put in near Pigeon

Point Campground (access is located just upriver of North Fork); take out five miles down near Big Flat Campground (access is located .25 mile downstream from Big Flat Store); those who want a longer run can take out 24 miles downstream at the highway bridge at Cedar Flat. Note: Unless you're an expert, take out at Cedar Flat or upstream. Downstream of Cedar Flat lies Burnt Ranch Gorge, a difficult eight-mile, Class IV-V run.

Facilities, fees: Several campgrounds are located along Highway 299 and off Trinity Dam Boulevard. Drinking water and vault toilets are available at most campgrounds. Limited boat rentals are available at Lewiston Lake; you can rent rafts and inflatable kayaks at Bigfoot Rafting Company, located in Willow Creek and also at Big Flat on Highway 299. Supplies can be obtained in Lewiston. A fee is charged for camping. Access is free. Rafting permits are not required.

Water sports, restrictions: Rafts, kayaks, and drift boats are permitted. Both stretches of the river offer excellent swimming holes; two of the best are at Pigeon Point Campground on Highway 299 and at the bridge in the town of Helena.

Directions: To upper Trinity River: From Redding, go west on Highway 299, drive over Buckhorn Summit, and continue for five miles to Trinity Dam Boulevard. Turn right on Trinity Dam Boulevard and drive four miles to Lewiston. Continue on Trinity Dam Boulevard to Rush Creek Road. Turn left on Rush Creek Road and drive 2.3 miles to Trinity River Lodge RV Resort on the left.

To Steiner Flat: From Redding, go west on Highway 299 and continue over the bridge at the Trinity River near Douglas City to Steiner Flat Road. Turn left on Steiner Flat Road and drive .5 mile to Douglas City campground on the left. To reach Steiner Flat, continue two more miles and look for the campground on the left and nearby river access.

To Pigeon Point: From Redding, head west on Highway 299 and drive to Weaverville.

Continue west on Highway 299 to Helena and continue .5 mile to the campground on the left (south) side of the road and nearby river access.

Contact: Shasta-Trinity National Forest, Big Bar Ranger Station, 530/623-6106; Trinity River Lodge RV Resort, Lewiston, 530/778-3791; Steelhead Cabins, 530/623-6325. For guided trips: Aurora River Adventures, 707/677-3494 or 800/562-8475, website: www.rafting4fun.com; Bigfoot Rafting Company, 530/629-2263 or 800/722-2223, website: www.bigfootrafting.com; California Canoe and Kayak School, 916/353-1880 or 800/366-9804, website: www.www.calkayak.com; Environmental Traveling Companions, 415/474-7662, website: www.etctrips.org; Living Waters Recreation, 530/926-5446 or 800/994-7238, website: www.livingwatersrec.com; Marble Mountain Ranch, 530/469-3322 or 800/552-6284, website: www.marblemountainranch.com; Redwoods and Rivers, 530/629-4947 or 800/429-0090, website: www.redwoods-rivers.com; River Dancers, 530/926-3517 or 800/926-5002; website: www.riverdancers.com; Rubicon Whitewater Adventures, 707/887-2452, website: www.rubiconadventures.com; Tributary Whitewater Tours, 530/346-6812 or 800/672-3846, website: www.whitewatertours.com; Trinity River Rafting, 530/623-3033 or 800/307-4837, website: www.trinityriverrafting.com; Turtle River Rafting, 530/926-3223 or 800/726-3223, website: www.turtleriver.com; Wilderness Adventures, 530/926-6282 or 800/323-7238, website: www.trinityadventures.com.

22 RUTH LAKE

Rating: 7

near Mad River in Six Rivers National Forest

Map 2.3, page 44

California's northwest corner is known for its great rivers—the Smith, Klamath, Trinity, Mad, Mattole, Eel, and Van Duzen to name just a few—but the entire region has scarcely any lakes.

Ruth Lake, in fact, is the only major lake that offers significant recreational opportunities within a decent driving distance of Eureka.

Even then it requires a long drive on twisty Highway 36. But in the summer, when the Humboldt coastline is fogged in, the hot climate here makes Ruth an attractive destination. The lake, really a reservoir that covers 1,200 acres, is located at an elevation of 2,600 feet on the western edge of Trinity County, remote by almost anyone's standards.

In the summer, the warm water makes this an ideal place for families to spend some time swimming. Most water sports are permitted on the lake, including water-skiing and riding personal watercraft, but houseboats are not allowed (pontoon boats are okay). Fishing is decent for rainbow trout in the spring and for bass in the summer.

Access: Three boat ramps are available at Ruth Lake.

Facilities, fees: Ruth Lake Marina has full marina services and rents out fishing boats, ski boats, and pontoon boats. Picnic areas and an RV dump station are also provided. Several campgrounds with drinking water and vault toilets are nearby. Littlefield Ranch has cabins for rent. Supplies can be obtained in Mad River. Access is free.

Water sports, restrictions: Power boats, water-skiing, wake boarding, riding personal watercraft, sailing, and sailboarding are permitted. Swimming beaches are available at Sheriff's Cove Day-Use Area, Ruth Recreation Area, Old Ruth Day-Use Area, and at a small gravel bar adjacent to Ruth Lake Marina.

Directions: To Bailey Canyon: From Eureka, drive south on U.S. 101 to Alton and the junction with Highway 36. Turn east on Highway 36 and drive about 50 miles to the town of Mad River. Turn right at the sign for Ruth Lake/Lower Mad River Road and drive 13 miles to the campground on the right side of the road (on the east side of the lake).

Contact: Six Rivers National Forest, Mad River Ranger District, 707/574-6233; Ruth Lake

Marina, 707/574-6524; Littlefield Ranch, 707/574-6689; Ruth Recreation (campgrounds), 707/574-6152 or 800/500-0285; Ruth Lake Community Services District, 707/574-6332, website: www.saber.net/~ruthlakecsd.

23 TRINITY LAKE

Rating: 8

near Weaverville in Shasta-Trinity National Forest

Map 2.4, page 45

Trinity is a big lake with full-service marinas. You can rent a houseboat, stay in a cabin at Cedar Stock Resort, or head out and pitch a tent at a boat-in camp (there are several good camps, including one at Captain's Point on the west shore of the Trinity River Arm). The lake boasts a wide variety of fishing, including smallmouth bass and rainbow trout. Even when the water level is down, there is still plenty of lake to explore and fish.

Nestled at the eastern foot of the Trinity Alps, the lake is set at an elevation of 2,300 feet and covers 17,000 acres. This is big enough to provide plenty of room for all types of water sports, including water-skiing, personal watercraft, sailboarding, and fishing; yet it's sufficiently remote that large numbers of boaters rarely descend on the place. Most of the people who visit the area end up spending some time in Trinity Center, a big-time family resort destination.

The lake's surface temperature fluctuates greatly throughout the year, dipping to freezing cold in winter and only becoming tolerable for swimming by July. By August, however, the lake is practically a giant bathtub, great for swimming, with the best access at the day-use areas and campgrounds operated by the Forest Service.

If only Trinity Lake were a real lake and not a reservoir, it would be a virtual mountain paradise for fishing, boating, and camping. But it is a reservoir, and as such is subject to severe drawdowns because water is diverted and sent to the Sacramento River for farming. That means less water is around for Trinity Lake, particularly by late summer.

For a major lake with significant facilities, marinas, and lodging, it is somewhat remote. For many, that is perfect. It has all the qualities of Shasta Lake, Northern California's No. 1 recreation lake, yet without the crowds on the water.

Access: Eight boat ramps are located on Trinity Lake.

Facilities, fees: Paved boat ramps, boat docks, rentals for houseboats, fishing boats, ski boats, personal watercraft, and pontoon boats are available at full-service marinas. Lodging, campgrounds with restrooms, drinking water, showers, flush toilets and vault toilets, gas, and stores are available nearby. Resorts include: Trinity Center Marina, Estrellita Marina, Pinewood Cove Resort, and Trinity Lake Resort and Marina (see Contact, below). Many campgrounds are available, including boat-in sites. There are fees for boat launching and lodging. Some resorts charge day-use fees or require rentals.

Water sports, restrictions: Powerboats, waterskiing, wake boarding, personal watercraft, sailing, sailboarding, and swimming are permitted. A 5-mph speed limit is enforced near the marinas and in coves. There are several swimming spots here; the Clark Springs and Stoney Creek day-use areas have large beaches.

Directions: To Tannery Gulch: From Redding, take Highway 299 west and drive to Weaverville at Highway 3. Turn north on Highway 3 and drive 13.5 miles to County Road 172. Turn right on County Road 172 and drive 1.5 miles to the campground and nearby boat ramp.

To Stuarts Fork Boat Ramp: From Redding, take Highway 299 west and drive to Weaverville at Highway 3. Turn north on Highway 3 and drive seven miles to the Stuarts Fork arm of Trinity Lake.

To Bowerman Boat Ramp: From Redding, take Highway 299 west and drive to Weaver-

ville at Highway 3. Turn north on Highway 3 and drive to Covington Mill (six miles south of Trinity Center). Turn right (south) on Guy Covington Road and drive two miles to the boat ramp entrance.

To Pinewood Resort: From Redding, take Highway 299 west and drive to Weaverville at Highway 3. Turn north on Highway 3 and drive 14 miles to the resort entrance on the right.

To Wyntoon Resort: From Redding, take Highway 299 west and drive to Weaverville at Highway 3. Turn north on Highway 3 and drive to Trinity Lake and continue to Trinity Center. At Trinity Center, continue .5 mile north on Highway 3 to the resort on the right.

Contact: Shasta-Trinity National Forest, Weaverville Ranger Station, 530/623-2121; Shasta Cascade Wonderland Association, 530/365-7500 or 800/474-2782, website: www.shastacascade.org; Trinity Lake Resort and Marina, 530/286-2215, 530/286-2225, or 800/255-5561 website: www.foreverresorts.com; Estrellita Marina, 800/747-2215, website: www.estrellitamarina.com; Wyntoon Resort, 530/266-3337 or 800/715-3337, website: www.wyntoonresort.com; Pinewood Cove Resort, reservations only at 800/988-5253, or 530/286-2201, website: www.pinewoodcove.com.

24 LEWISTON LAKE

Rating: 9

near Lewiston in Shasta-Trinity National Forest

Map 2.4, page 45

This is one of the prettiest reservoirs in California, always full to the brim and ringed by conifers, with the Trinity Alps to the northwest providing a beautiful backdrop. Features include a campground in a gorgeous lakeside setting (Mary Smith), a small, friendly resort with cabin rentals (Lakeview Terrace), and good trout fishing.

Long and narrow, Lewiston is set at 1,900 feet in elevation, spanning a length of nine miles and 750 acres, with 15 miles of shoreline. People often overlook this lake in favor of its big brother, nearby Trinity Lake, which covers 17,000 acres. When viewed from the air, it is easy to see how Lewiston Lake is actually the afterbay for Trinity, with the flows from Trinity Dam forming the headwaters of Lewiston. When those flows are running through the powerhouse, the trout fishing is outstanding anywhere from Lakeview Terrace on upstream, but it is usually best just below Trinity Dam.

For owners of small boats, the best thing about Lewiston Lake is the strictly enforced speed limit, 10 miles per hour, which keeps the lake quiet and calm. These are ideal conditions for canoes and small aluminum boats because all the powerboaters go to Trinity Lake. Also, the water here is quite cold, great for trout fishing but poor for swimming.

So despite Lewiston's beauty, it gets relatively light use. Water-skiers, personal watercraft, and powerboaters avoid Lewiston, but people looking for a quiet day on a pretty lake treasure it.

Access: A paved ramp is located at Pine Cove Marina. A primitive launch is provided at Lakeview Terrace Resort for resort guests only.

Facilities, fees: Fishing boats and houseboats can be rented at Lakeview Terrace. Pine Cove Marina offers full marina services and rents out fishing boats. Campgrounds with drinking water and vault toilets are available. Supplies can be obtained in Lewiston. Fees are charged for camping, day use, and boat launching.

Water sports, restrictions: Fishing boats, rowboats, canoes, kayaks, inflatables, sailing, and sailboarding are permitted. A 10-mph speed limit is strictly enforced. Water-skiing, wake boarding, and personal watercraft are not permitted. The water is generally too cold for swimming and other water/body contact sports.

Directions: To Lakeview Terrace: From Redding, take Highway 299 west and drive to Buckhorn Summit, and continue for five miles to Trinity Dam Boulevard. Turn right on Trinity Dam Boulevard and drive 10 miles (five miles past Lewiston) to the resort on the left side of the road. To reach Pine Cove Marina, continue .5 mile on Trinity Dam Boulevard.

Contact: Shasta-Trinity National Forest, Weaverville Ranger Station, 530/623-2121 website: www.fs.fed.us/r5/shastatrinity; Shasta Cascade Wonderland Association, 530/365-7500 or 800/474-2782; Lakeview Terrace Resort, 530/778-3803, website: www.lakeviewterraceresort.com.

25 SHASTA LAKE

Rating: 10

near Redding in Shasta-Trinity
National Forest

Map 2.4, page 45

This is the boating capital of the west. This giant lake has 370 miles of shoreline, 400 houseboat rentals, 11 marinas, 15 boat ramps, 13 campgrounds, lakeshore lodging, and 22 species of sport fish. No matter what the season, Shasta is so big that there is plenty of room for everybody—water-skiers, wake boarders, personal watercraft riders, houseboaters, anglers, swimmers, sailboarders. You name it, Shasta can accommodate them all.

Shasta is really five bodies of water in one, with each lake arm forming a separate lake: Sacramento Arm, McCloud Arm, Pit Arm, Squaw Creek Arm, and the central lake body (Sacramento) near the dam. Add in the thousands of little coves and secret inlets, and you have the equivalent of a mansion that is so big you could never fully explore it.

It is easy to get accustomed to the large number of boaters at Shasta Lake. In the summer there are hundreds of houseboats here, plus quite a few water-skiers and wake boarders. But this is one place where there is plenty of room for all comers. With all the houseboaters on the water, it can seem like a giant party, with everybody happy, and you can bet on lots of sun, skin, lotion, and potent liquids. If you want to escape the festivities, just head into one of the quiet coves.

Shasta Lake is located just north of Redding, in the foothill country at an elevation of 1,000 feet. Covering 29,500 surface acres, this is the biggest reservoir in California, with 370 miles of shoreline. In a houseboat it takes about five or six days to tour the whole thing. Most people, however, develop an affinity for one section of the lake and return to it year after year, just like going to a second home.

Houseboating has become so popular that virtually every houseboat available for rent on the lake is booked the entire summer, Memorial Day through Labor Day. That makes planning and reserving far in advance a necessity. After a short instructional and safety lesson on how to operate the boat, you are set free to roam and play on your own.

Because surface water temperatures at Shasta range from the 70s to the low 80s in the summer, the lake can feel like a giant bathtub, ideal for water-skiing and personal watercraft. Swimming is only fair, primarily because most of the shoreline areas have steep drop-offs, as do most reservoirs. Two of the better spots to jump in for a swim are at Jones Valley and Gregory Creek, where the lake bottom contours are more gradually sloped. No matter where you take the plunge, children should always be supervised in the water.

Campgrounds never completely fill up, and boaters can take advantage of the additional boat-in sites, the best of which is at Ski Island. One problem at the drive-in campgrounds is the distance between the campsites and the water. Because the big reservoir is drawn down in late summer as water is shipped to points south, campgrounds located on the upper arms of the lake can end up being a steep hike from the water, with a wheezer of a climb up on the way back.

A few side notes: In the spring, bass fishers can have 30-fish days using plastic worms along the shoreline of the Squaw Creek Arm, Sacramento Arm, and McCloud Arm. Trolling for trout and salmon is often excellent at the Dry Creek Arm, and fishing for spotted bass with live minnows or Senko worms is sensational from late March through early June. The best hiking is on the Centimudi Trail near Jones Valley, and the Shasta Caverns offers a great tour of the limestone caves on the McCloud Arm. The lake has several full-time sheriff's patrol boats. Competitions for wake boarding, water-skiing, and kneeboarding are held here through late spring and summer. In recent years, wake boarding, in particular, has become extremely popular. Water-skiing and wake boarding lessons are available.

When you put it all together, no place provides more boating recreation opportunities, diversity, and quality than Shasta Lake.

Access: There are many boat ramps:

• Antlers Resort: From Redding, drive north on I-5 for 24 miles to the Lakeshore-Antlers Road exit in Lakehead. Take that exit, turn right at the stop sign, and drive a short distance to Antlers Road. At Antlers Road, turn right and drive one mile south to the campground and nearby boat ramp. A paved ramp is available, along with a full-service marina, campground, convenience store, and picnic area. Houseboats, pontoon boats, aluminum fishing boats, personal watercraft, ski boats, and canoes can be rented. For more information call 530/238-2553 or 800/238-3924. A campground and paved boat ramp are available nearby at Antlers RV Park and Campground, 530/238-2322 or 800/642-6849.

• Bridge Bay Resort & Marina: From Redding, take I-5 north for eight miles to the Bridge Bay exit. Take that exit and continue one mile to the office. Pay for boat launching, then drive south 100 yards to the boat ramp. A paved ramp, full-service marina, boat store, motel, convenience store, restaurant, and picnic area are available. Houseboats, ski boats, personal watercraft, pontoon boats, and aluminum fishing boats are available for rent. For more information call 530/275-3021 or 800/752-9669.

• Digger Bay Marina: From I-5 in Redding, drive north for three miles to the exit for the town of Shasta Lake City and Shasta Dam

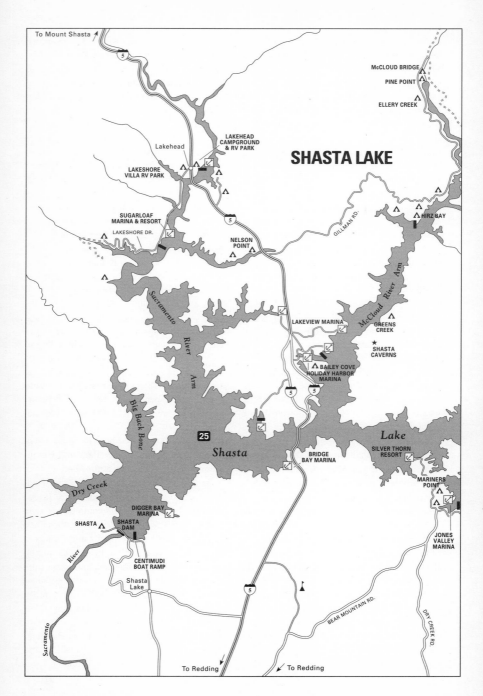

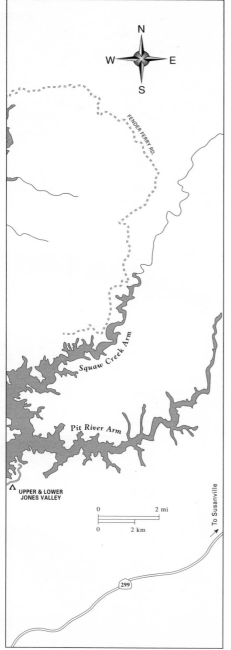

Boulevard. Take that exit and bear west on Shasta Dam Boulevard and drive about three miles to Shasta Park Drive. Turn right on Shasta Park Drive (which becomes Digger Bay Road) and drive about four miles to the marina and boat ramp. A paved ramp, a full-service marina, gas, and store are available. Houseboats, ski boats, personal watercraft, and aluminum fishing boats can be rented. For more information call 530/275-3072 or 800/752-9669.

• Holiday Harbor: From Redding, drive north for 18 miles on I-5 to the O'Brien/Shasta Caverns Road exit. Turn right (east) at Shasta Caverns Road and drive about one mile to the marina entrance on the right. A two-laned paved ramp, full-service marina, RV park, snack bar, convenience store, gas, picnic area, and playground are available. Houseboats, ski boats, pontoon boats, personal watercraft, aluminum fishing boats, and canoes can be rented. For more information call 530/238-2383 or 800/752-9669.

• Jones Valley Resort: From Redding, turn east on Highway 299 and drive 7.5 miles (just past the town of Bella Vista) to Dry Creek Road. Turn left and drive nine miles to a Y in the road. For Jones Valley public ramp or Jones Valley Resort, bear right at the Y. For Silverthorn Resort, bear left at the Y. A boat ramp, full-service marina, and convenience store are available. Houseboats, fishing boats, ski boats, pontoon boats, personal watercraft, rowboats, canoes, and kayaks are available for rent. Parasailing is available. For more information call 530/275-7950.

• Lakeview Marina Resort: From Redding, drive north for 18 miles on I-5 to the O'Brien/Shasta Caverns Road exit. Turn right (east) at Shasta Caverns Road and drive to the marina road entrance (just past mailboxes) on the left. Turn left and drive to the marina and boat ramp. A full-service marina and convenience store are available. Houseboats, ski boats, personal watercraft, pontoon boats, fishing boats, kayaks, and canoes are available for rent.

Only marina customers can use the paved boat ramp. For more information call 530/238-2442 or 877/474-2782.

• Packers Bay: From Redding, drive north for 18 miles on I-5 to the Shasta Caverns Road exit. Take that exit to the stop sign, turn left, drive a short distance, and then turn left and drive south on I-5 a short distance to the exit for Packer's Bay. Take that exit and drive two miles to the marina and boat ramp. A boat ramp, marina, dock, fuel, and convenience store are available. Houseboats are available for rent. For more information call 530/275-5570 or 800/331-3137.

• Shasta Marina: From Redding, drive north for 18 miles on I-5 to the O'Brien/Shasta Caverns Road exit. Take that exit to the stop sign. Turn west on O'Brien Inlet Road and drive one mile to the entrance to the marina and boat ramp. A marina, gas, and convenience store are available. Houseboats are available for rent. For more information call 530/238-2284 or 800/959-3359.

• Silverthorn Resort: From Redding, turn east on Highway 299 and drive 7.5 miles (just past the town of Bella Vista) to Dry Creek Road. Bear left at the Y. A paved ramp, full-service marina, cabins, mooring, gas, pizza parlor (summer only) and a store are available. Houseboats, pontoon boats, ski boats, aluminum fishing boats, canoes, and personal watercraft are available for rent. For more information call 530/275-1571 or 800/332-3044.

• Sugarloaf Marina: From Redding, drive north on I-5 for 24 miles to the Antlers-Lakeshore Drive exit. Take that exit and turn left on Lakeshore Drive. Drive three miles (look for the "Loaf on Inn" sign) and turn left and drive to the entrance for Sugarloaf. Turn left and drive to the marina and boat ramp. A two-lane paved ramp, full-service marina, campground, and convenience store are available. Houseboats, ski boats, pontoon boats, aluminum fishing boats, and kayaks are available for rent. For more information call 530/238-2711 or 800/223-7950.

Facilities, fees: Lodging, cabins, campgrounds, restrooms with showers and flush toilets, drinking water, and convenience stores are available. Many marinas (see below) have fishing boats, ski boats, personal watercraft, and accessories available for rent. Fees are charged for boat launching, day use and camping.

Water sports, restrictions: All boating and water sports are permitted. Water-skiing, wake boarding and personal watercraft are permitted. A 5-mph speed limit is strictly enforced around the coves and marinas and a sheriff's boat patrol enforces no-ski zones and speed limits. Swimming is excellent, best from a boat well up any lake arm. Two of the better spots are Gregory Creek and Jones Valley. Sailboarding is best on the McCloud Arm of the lake, where there is more wind on summer afternoons; two good jump-off points are Bailey Cove and Hirz Bay.

Directions: Follow directions to Access points, above.

To Hirz Bay: From Redding, drive north on I-5 for about 20 miles to the Salt Creek/Gilman exit. Turn right on Gilman Road/County Road 7H009 and drive northeast for 10 miles to the campground/boat launch access road. Turn right and drive .5 mile to the boat ramp.

To Lakeshore Marina: From Redding, drive north on I-5 for 24 miles to the Antlers-Lakeshore Drive exit. Take that exit to the stop sign. Turn left and drive a short distance to Lakeshore Drive. Turn left on Lakeshore Drive and drive one mile to the marina and boat ramp.

To Bailey Cove: From Redding, drive north on I-5 over the Pit River Bridge at Shasta Lake to O'Brien Road/Shasta Caverns Road exit. Turn east (right) on Shasta Caverns Road and drive .25 mile to a signed turnoff for Bailey Cove. Turn right and drive one mile to Bailey Cove Boat Ramp.

To Centimudi/Shasta Dam: From I-5 in Redding, drive north for three miles to the exit for the town of Shasta Lake City and Shasta Dam Boulevard. Take that exit and bear west on Shasta Dam Boulevard and drive three miles to Lake Boulevard. Turn right on Lake Boulevard and drive two miles to a fork. Turn right and drive .5 mile to the boat launch.

Contact: Shasta Lake Visitor Information Center, 530/275-1589, website: www.fs.fed.us/r5/shastatrinity; Shasta Cascade Wonderland Association, 530/365-7500 or 800/474-2782, website: www.shastacascade.org. Water sports and marinas: John Steiner's Water Sports Center, 530/275-6744; Ensane Wakeboarding, 530/275-6744, website: www.ensanewakeboarding.com; Holiday Harbor Resort and Marina, 800/776-2628, 530/238 2383, website: www.lakeshasta.com.General information websites: www.shastalake.com, www.shastalake resorts.com.

26 CLEAR CREEK

Rating: 6

west of Redding

Map 2.4, page 45

"Pssssst. Want to hear a secret? Just don't tell anybody about it."

That is how people talk about Clear Creek. You see, everybody in this area goes to nearby Whiskeytown Lake. They don't know that Clear Creek, along with the little campground here, exists. But it does.

Clear Creek is pretty, with beautiful riparian habitat bordering the water, yet it's far enough off the beaten path that it gets light use. So if you visit Whiskeytown Lake during the peak early summer season and are seeking a quiet alternative, little Clear Creek just might suit your needs.

Several excellent swimming holes, along with a couple of nice sandy bars, are available right off the access road. They are favorite retreats for a few locals. Fishing for small trout here is fair.

Whiskeytown Lake (see the next listing) is a National Recreation Area that offers full facilities, most water sports, hiking, biking, and camping. Despite all these attractions, Clear Creek has a special charm that is just as compelling.

Access: There is no boat ramp.

Facilities, fees: A small primitive campground is provided north of French Gulch. Vault toilets are available. No drinking water. Garbage must be packed out. Other campsites are located at Whiskeytown Lake. Supplies can be obtained in Redding. Access is free.

Water sports, restrictions: Several good swimming holes are located off Trinity Mountain Road; look for the access roads.

Directions: From Redding, turn west on Highway 299 and drive 17 miles to Trinity Lake Road (just west of Whiskeytown Lake). Turn north on Trinity Lake Road and continue past the town of French Gulch for about 12 miles to the Trinity Mountain Ranger Station. Turn right on County Road 106/East Side Road (gravel) and drive north for about 11 miles to the campground access road (dirt) on right. Turn right on the access road. Access is available off short roads that junction with Trinity Mountain Road, which parallels the creek.

Contact: Shasta-Trinity National Forest, Weaverville Ranger District, 530/623-2121, website: www.fs.fed.us/r5/shastatrinity.

27 WHISKEYTOWN LAKE

Rating: 8

near Redding in Shasta-Trinity National Forest

Map 2.4, page 45

Whiskeytown is easy to reach, is sizable enough that you can spend a lot of time exploring, and has decent camping accommodations. Year-round this is a good place for boating, but the highlights here are excellent sailing in the spring, great hiking and biking, and typically high water levels. Is there any downside? Well, the wind can really kick up during the spring, but, hey, that is why this is the hands-down favorite in the area for sailboarders and sailboaters.

The good-sized lake covers 3,220 acres with 36 miles of shoreline and is just a short drive west of Redding at an elevation of 1,200 feet.

In the summer the water is clear and warm, and with a few large sandy beaches, it is ideal for youngsters to kick around in. The popular picnic areas at Oak Bottom and Brandy Creek are exceptional, and the operators of both marinas are extremely helpful and friendly. Fishing is good for kokanee salmon and rainbow trout, although to be successful you'll need to be skilled in trolling techniques. But Whiskeytown really shines in the spring when west winds typically reach 10 to 15 knots, making it perfect for sailing and sailboarding.

The federal ban on personal watercraft at national parks took effect at Whiskeytown in 2003.

Just beyond the western end of the lake at Mill Creek, a pretty hiking trail is routed along the stream for several miles. Covered by a canopy of oak woodlands, Mill Creek runs gin-clear in the summer and strong in the spring, with lots of miniature waterfalls, pools, and drops. The trail parallels this pretty ribbon of water, crossing and recrossing the creek many times. The only sounds to accompany your thoughts are the twittering of birds, rushing water, and perhaps a light breeze rustling the leaves, always gorgeous in the fall.

Upon arrival, your first stop should be the visitor center, an outstanding facility located just off the highway. Free brochures and flyers are available, as is a staff of professionals who can answer any recreation questions.

Access: There are three boat ramps:

• Brandy Creek Marina: From Redding, drive west on Highway 299 for eight miles to the park visitor center. Turn left at the visitor center (Kennedy Memorial Drive) and drive five miles to the campground entrance road on the right. Turn right and drive a short distance to the camp. A paved launch ramp, swimming beach, snack bar and convenience store are available.

• Oak Bottom Marina: From Redding, drive west on Highway 299 for 15 miles (past the visitors center) to the campground entrance road on the left. Turn left and drive a short distance to the campground. A paved launch

ramp, full-service marina, convenience store, and a snack bar are available. Pontoon boats, ski boats, sailboats, fishing boats, canoes, and pedal boats can be rented.

• Whiskey Creek: From Redding, drive west on Highway 299 for eight miles to the visitor center. Turn left at the visitor center (Kennedy Memorial Drive) and drive six miles to the campground on the right side of the road. A paved launch ramp is available. A convenience store is nearby.

Facilities, fees: There are three campgrounds with drinking water and vault toilets. Picnic areas are available. Snacks are sold at Brandy Creek and Oak Bottom; full supplies can be obtained in Redding. Access and boat launching are free. Fees are charged for day use, boat launching, and camping. Annual passes available.

Water sports, restrictions: Powerboats, waterskiing, wake boarding, sailing, sailboarding, and swimming are allowed. No personal watercraft. Several sandy swimming beaches are located around the lake for swimming. The best are at the day-use areas at Brandy Creek and Oak Bottom.

Directions: See directions to Access points, above.

Contact: Whiskeytown National Recreation Area, 530/246-1225, website: www.nps.gov/whis; Brandy Creek Marina, 530/243-2733; Oak Bottom Marina, 530/359-2269; Shasta Cascade Wonderland Association, 530/365-7500 or 800/474-2782, website: www.shastacascade.org; Shasta-Trinity National Forest, Weaverville Ranger District, 530/623-2121, website: www.fs .fed.us/r5/shastatrinity.

28 KESWICK LAKE

Rating: 4

near Redding in Shasta-Trinity National Forest

Map 2.4, page 45

This long, narrow reservoir is situated directly below giant Shasta Lake, and with Shasta getting such heavy use, you might think Keswick would make a great, less-crowded alternative.

Well, there are indeed fewer people here. In fact, the lake is used by practically no one except for a few anglers. But great? Sorry.

The water entering 630-acre Keswick comes from the bottom of Shasta Dam, making this lake extremely cold, even in summer. The result is limited opportunities for water sports, including water-skiing and swimming. It is doubly poor for swimming, because not only is the water painfully chilly, but the shoreline is rough and blocky with not a beach in sight.

Almost everybody in search of a good lake in the Redding area heads northbound on I-5 to Shasta or west on Highway 299 to Whiskeytown, giving nary a thought to Keswick Lake. Everybody, that is, except a handful of anglers who have learned that there is a chance that giant rainbow trout will bite when the powerhouse is running at the head of the lake. Alas, when the powerhouse is down, fishing opportunities go kaput as well. When that happens you can head up here and never encounter another soul, even in summer.

Access: A paved boat ramp is located off Iron Mountain Road on the east side of the lake.

Facilities, fees: Vault toilets are available at a day-use area. No drinking water. Access is free.

Water sports, restrictions: Water-skiing, wake boarding, sailing, sailboarding, and personal watercraft are permitted, but rarely seen. Swimming is allowed, but there are no beaches and the water is quite cold even in summer.

Directions: From I-5 at Redding, take the Highway 299 West exit. Drive four miles west to Iron Mountain Road. Turn right (north) on Iron Mountain Road and drive four miles to the lake. Follow the signs to the boat ramp.

Contact: U.S. Department of Interior, Bureau of Reclamation, 530/275-1554.

29 LOWER SACRAMENTO RIVER

Rating: 7

near Redding

Map 2.4, page 45

Nothing captivates in the spring and early summer quite like a river adventure through woods and water, paddling by day in a canoe (or kayak), and then camping along the river by night. I've done several multi-day trips like this in Northern California on the lower Klamath, Eel, and Sacramento Rivers, and elsewhere. The best all-around easy trip with a few thrills in the mix is the Sac, paddling from Redding to Woodson Bridge State Recreation Area near Corning.

This trip runs about 70 miles, best done in four days and three nights, includes a Class II gorge, several Class I runs, with excellent camping on sand bars. The trip can also be shortened by putting in or taking out at other access points along the way. The most notable of these are at Balls Ferry in Anderson (to avoid the rapids) and at the Red Bluff Diversion Dam. The Diversion Dam starts operations on May 15; before that you can paddle right on through, after that, you must portage. If you don't have a canoe, rentals are available in San Francisco, Oakland, and Sacramento.

The best put-in is at the Posse Grounds in Redding, which is adjacent to the Redding Convention Center. This provides the most scenic trip. From here, the first 20 miles down to Balls Ferry is pretty and easy, with no surprises. The river runs emerald green and is bordered by cottonwoods and alders, a gorgeous upland riparian zone. Wildlife is abundant, especially blue herons and wood ducks, and paddlers will also see turtles sunning on logs or rocks, with deer and wild turkey common along the shore.

This is also the best stretch of river for trout fishing. The best prospects are anchoring just above riffles and slicks, and then running a nightcrawler, Hot Shot, or Glo Bug downstream on the edges of these spots, near the bottom.

Another great fishing spot is at the Tehama Riffle for shad, best from late May through mid-June.

But you know what happens? At the starting point, most are eager to paddle, and also become concerned about covering enough water, so many rush through the early stages of the trip, where the fishing is best and wildlife sightings are highest.

About 10 miles past Balls Ferry, the trip's biggest challenge awaits: China Rapids, rated Class II. This is a chute in a short, rocky gorge, where your canoe will rock like a teeter-totter as you are propelled forward. Paddlers can add to their safety margin by rocking their paddles back and forth in the current. That will slow the boat down, making it far easier to pick your way through the rough stuff. If you paddle hard, on the other hand (as if in a raft), you can be propelled out of control. If you broach, you'll flip.

There are a few other Class I rapids that can be dealt with by taking "an inside line," as it is called, away from the white water.

The evening camping is sensational, with a choice of many large sand bars set on the inside of pretzel turns on the river. With a canoe, you can bring plenty of supplies, so each evening is a celebration of the day, not a recovery.

River flows are based on releases from Keswick Dam. By late May, releases are typically 12,500 to 15,000 CFS, which makes for a faster ride—but a required portage around the Red Bluff Diversion Dam. To avoid that portage, some will shorten the trip by using Red Bluff as either the ending point or starting point.

This stretch of the Sacramento is also very popular for fishing, with plenty of trout from spring through early summer, and salmon from mid-August through October. Powerboaters should be aware of fluctuating water levels and shallow spots, which is why most boaters remove their propellers and switch to jet drives, despite the reduction in speed. Potentially dangerous obstacles include downed trees, floating debris, and, rarely, rebar from concrete blocks from failed riprap projects.

Some people try inner tubing on the river, but conditions are extremely poor, primarily because the water is so cold that it numbs the feet and because there are few places to stop along the bank. If these things don't bother you, be aware that, according to the law, inner tubers must wear life jackets. County sheriffs patrol the river and will issue citations.

Access: There are four public boat ramps:

• Posse Grounds put-in: Take I-5 to Redding and the exit for Highway 299 West/Central Redding. Take that exit and drive one mile (over the Sacramento River) to Auditorium Drive. Turn right and drive .5 mile (Convention Center on your right) to the parking lot and boat access.

• Lake Redding Park: Take I-5 to Redding and the exit for Lake Boulevard exit. Take that exit west and drive to North Market Street. Turn south (left) on North Market Street and drive .5 mile to Quartz Hill Road. Turn west (right) on Quartz Hill Road and continue to the second entrance on the left into the park and look for signs for the boat ramp.

• Bonnyview: Take I-5 to south Redding and the exit for Bonnyview-Bechelli Lane/Churn Creek. Take that exit to Bonnyview and turn west and drive (across the river) to the first left after the bridge. Turn left to the parking area and boat ramp.

• Woodson Bridge take-out: Take I-5 to Corning and the exit for South Ave. Take that exit east and drive six miles to the entrance on the right (immediately after crossing the river).

Facilities, fees: Several campgrounds and RV parks are nearby. Access to the river and the public ramps is free.

Water sports, restrictions: Powerboats, driftboats, canoes, kayaks, and rafts are permitted. The river is too cold for swimming and other water/body contact sports. Those floating in rafts or inner tubes must be wearing life jackets or face arrest by the Shasta County Sheriff Boat Patrol.

Directions: Take I-5 to Shasta County. Access is available from exits for Riverside, Balls Ferry/Anderson, and Jellys Ferry, and elsewhere. In Redding, access is also available at the Posse Grounds near the Redding Civic Auditorium.

Contact: Shasta Cascade Wonderland Association, 530/365-7500 or 800/474-2782; website: www.shastacascade.org; U.S. Forest Service, Lake Red Bluff Recreation Area, 530/527-2813, website: www.fs.fed.us/r5/shastatrinity; Woodson Bridge State Recreation Area, 530/839-2112. River flows, website: http://cdec.water.ca.gov.

Canoe & kayak rentals: California Canoe & Kayak in Oakland 510/893-7833, Sacramento 916/353-5171, website: www.calkayak.com; Outdoors Unlimited in San Francisco, 415/476-2078, website: www.outdoors.ucsf.edu/ou. Canoe instruction: Canoe West, 530/242-6765, website: www.snowcrest.net/canoewest; Shasta Climbing and Paddle Sports, 530/222-4606; Marina RV Park, 530/241-7275; Balls Ferry Resort, 530/365-8708.

FOGHORN OUTDOORS®

© TOM STIENSTRA

Chapter 3

Lassen and Modoc

Chapter 3—Lassen and Modoc

Mount Lassen and its awesome volcanic past seem to cast a shadow everywhere you go in this region. At 10,457 feet, the mountain's domed summit is visible for more than 100 miles in all directions. It blew its top in 1914, with continuing eruptions through 1918. Although now dormant, the volcanic-based geology dominates the landscape everywhere you look.

The most famous destinations are Lassen Volcanic National Park, Lake Almanor, Eagle Lake and Burney Falls State Park, and adjoining Lake Britton. But that's only a start.

A highlight, for instance, is the best still-water canoeing and fly fishing at Fall River, Big Lake, and Ahjumawi State Park. Access to Ahjumawi is by canoe or powerboat only; it's got a great boat-in campground with access to a matrix of clear, cold waters with giant trout.

Nearby is Burney Falls State Park, along with the Pit River and Lake Britton, which together make up one of Northern California's best recreation destinations for families. This is also one of the best areas for fly fishing, especially at Hat Creek, Pit River, Burney Creek, and Manzanita Lake.

If you prefer major recreation lakes, Lake Almanor and Eagle Lake provide lakeside campgrounds and excellent fishing and boating recreation.

And there's more. In remote Modoc County, Lava Beds National Monument and the South Warner Wilderness provide unusual getaways.

Lava Beds is a stark, pretty, and often lonely place. It's sprinkled with small lakes full of trout, is home to large-antlered deer that migrate in after the first snow (and after the hunting season has closed), and features a unique volcanic habitat with huge flows of obsidian (dark, smooth, natural glass formed by the cooling of molten lava) and dacite (gray, craggy volcanic flow).

Lava Beds National Monument features 445 caves and lava tubes, including the 6,000-foot Catacomb tunnel. Nearby is pretty Medicine Lake, formed in a caldera, which provides good trout fishing, hiking, and exploring.

Of all the areas covered in this book, this region has the least number of romantic getaway spots. It caters instead primarily to outdoors enthusiasts.

It's often off the radar scope of vacationers, making it one of the few national parks where you can enjoy the wilderness in relative solitude. Yet no matter where you go, there are so many small lakes, streams and campgrounds that you can always find a match for your desires.

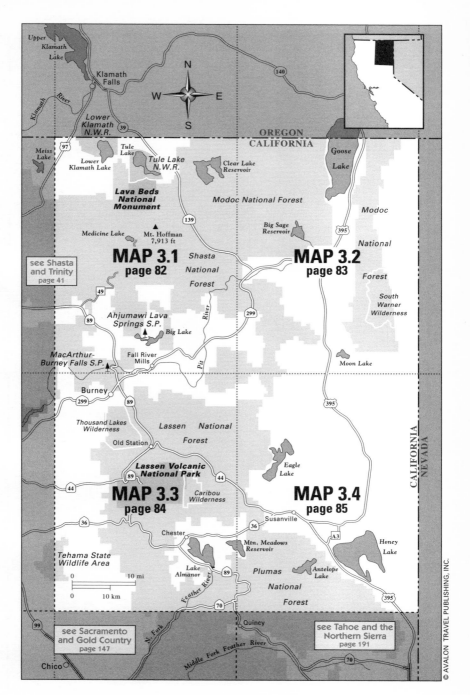

Upper Klamath Lake

Klamath Falls

Klamath River

Lower Klamath N.W.R.

39

Meiss Lake

97

Lower Klamath Lake

Tule Lake

Tule Lake N.W.R.

Lava Beds National Monument

Medicine Lake

Mt. Hoffman 7,913 ft

140

OREGON

CALIFORNIA

Clear Lake Reservoir

Modoc National Forest

Goose Lake

Modoc

Big Sage Reservoir

395

MAP 3.1
page 82

Shasta National Forest

see Shasta and Trinity page 41

MAP 3.2
page 83

National

Forest

South Warner Wilderness

49

89

Ahjumawi Lava Springs S.P.

Big Lake

299

MacArthur-Burney Falls S.P.

Fall River Mills

Pit River

Moon Lake

Burney

299

89

Thousand Lakes Wilderness

Old Station

Lassen National

Forest

395

Eagle Lake

Lassen Volcanic National Park

89

44

44

MAP 3.3
page 84

Caribou Wilderness

MAP 3.4
page 85

36

36

Susanville

A3

Chester

Mtn. Meadows Reservoir

Honey Lake

Tehama State Wildlife Area

0   10 mi

0   10 km

Lake Almanor

89

Antelope Lake

Plumas

National

Forest

395

CALIFORNIA
NEVADA

70

99

see Sacramento and Gold Country page 147

N. Fork

Quincy

Middle Fork Feather River

Feather River

see Tahoe and the Northern Sierra page 191

70

Chico

© AVALON TRAVEL PUBLISHING, INC.

Map 3.1

Sites 1–6
Pages 86–91

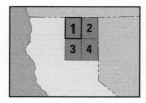

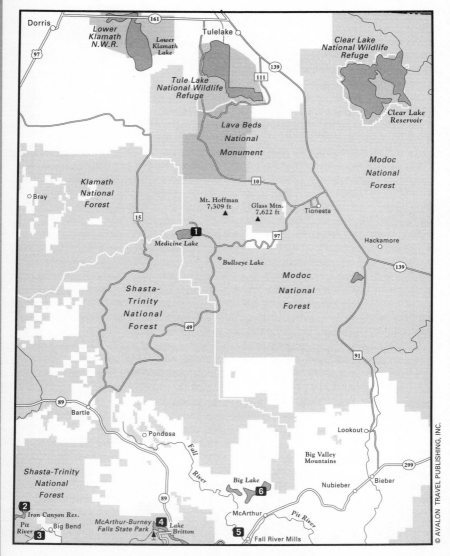

© AVALON TRAVEL PUBLISHING, INC.

Map 3.2

Sites 7–16
Pages 91–97

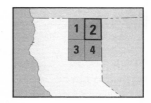

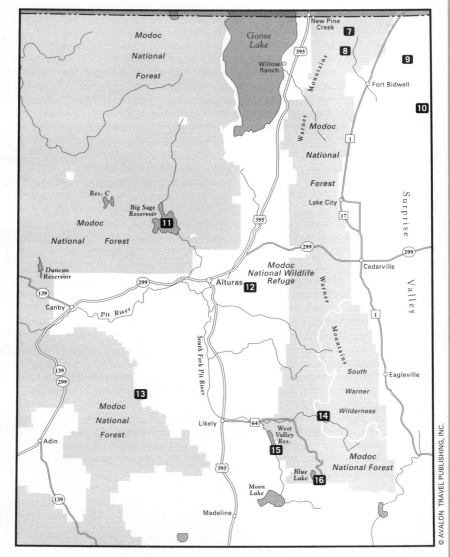

© AVALON TRAVEL PUBLISHING, INC.

Map 3.3

Sites 17–33
Pages 97–109

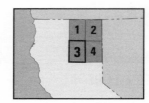

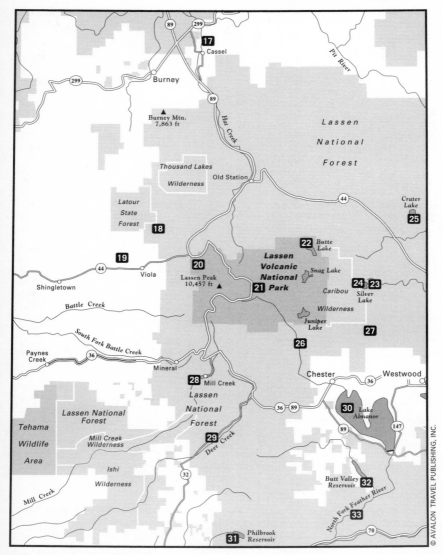

Map 3.4

Sites 34–37
Pages 109–112

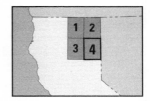

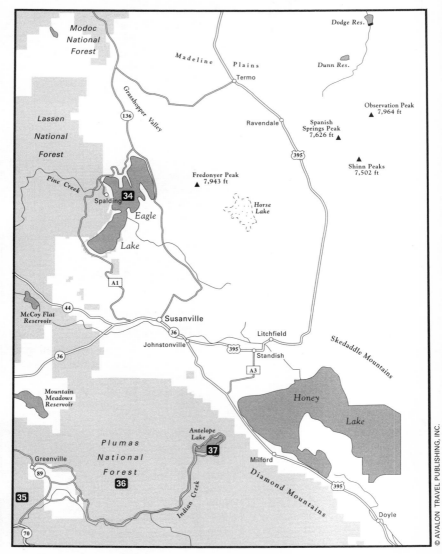

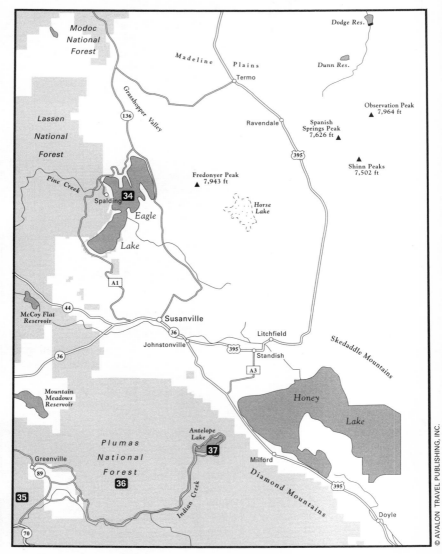

Modoc National Forest

Dodge Res.

Madeline Plains

Termo

Dunn Res.

Observation Peak
▲ 7,964 ft

Grasshopper Valley

Lassen National Forest

136

Ravendale

Spanish Springs Peak
7,626 ft ▲

395

Shinn Peaks
▲ 7,502 ft

Pine Creek

Fredonyer Peak
▲ 7,943 ft

Horse Lake

Spalding

34

Eagle Lake

A1

McCoy Flat Reservoir

44

Susanville

36

Johnstonville

36

Litchfield

395

Standish

Skedaddle Mountains

36

Mountain Meadows Reservoir

A3

Honey Lake

Plumas National Forest

Antelope Lake

37

Milford

Diamond Mountains

395

Greenville

36

89

35

Indian Creek

Doyle

70

© AVALON TRAVEL PUBLISHING, INC.

■ MEDICINE LAKE

Rating: 9

near McCloud in Modoc National Forest

Map 3.1, page 82

A place of mystery, Medicine Lake has capti-
vated many. The mystery is that the lake was
originally a caldera, that is, the mouth of a volcano. It draws a natural comparison to Crater
Lake in Oregon, although it's not as deep and
not as blue. Nevertheless, the lake has a sense
of history, unlike most lakes in California. It is
beautiful here, with lakeside campsites and a
paved road all the way in; the snow is cleared
by June, sometimes earlier, and sometimes later.

Undiscovered, however, Medicine Lake is
not. The unique setting—at 6,700 feet in elevation in remote Modoc National Forest near
the Lava Beds National Monument—attracts
people from near and far.

The lake is oval, covers 640 acres, and reaches 150 feet at its deepest point. There is a good
boat ramp, and all water sports are popular,
including water-skiing, personal watercraft riding, sailboarding, and sailing. But most visitors come for the fishing and camping, and
they usually leave surprised at the number of
large brook trout they've caught. This area
often gets buried in snow during the winter,
and as a result, the water remains quite cold
well into summer.

As this lake has become popular, rangers
here have been very strict about enforcing rules.
Their pet peeve is dogs. There is a leash law,
and dogs are banned from the beach. You are
hereby warned not to test them on how seriously they feel about this.

On a lighter note there are several exciting
side-trip destinations in the area, including ice
caves (created by glacial action), a restored
Forest Service lookout on top of Little Mount
Hoffman (jaw-dropping views featuring Mt.
Shasta), nearby Bullseye and Blanche Lakes
(quite tiny but pretty), and Lava Beds National Monument (geologic phenomena). You can

spend several days exploring the area, using
Medicine Lake as your base camp.

Access: A paved boat ramp and a dock are
available near the picnic area on the east side
of the lake.

Facilities, fees: Four campgrounds with drinking water and vault toilets are available. Supplies can be obtained in McCloud; Bartle Lodge
has a bar and café. A fee is charged for camping. Access and boat launching are free.

Water sports, restrictions: Powerboats, water-
skiing, wake boarding, personal watercraft, sailing, sailboarding, and swimming are permitted.
There are several sandy beaches for swimmers.
The best ones are located near the campgrounds.

Directions: From Redding, drive north on I-5
past Dunsmuir to Highway 89. Bear right (east)
on Highway 89 and drive 28 miles to Forest
Road 15/Harris Springs Road (just past Bartle). Turn left on Forest Road 15/Harris Springs
Road and drive five miles to a fork with Forest Road 49/Medicine Lake Road. Bear right
at the fork at Medicine Lake Road and drive
26 miles to the lake access road on the left.
From Bartle, the route is signed.

Contact: Modoc National Forest, Doublehead
Ranger District, 530/667-2246; Shasta-Trinity
National Forest, McCloud Ranger District,
530/964-2184.

■ IRON CANYON RESERVOIR

Rating: 7

near Big Bend in Shasta-Trinity
National Forest

Map 3.1, page 82

When the lake is at its fullest in the spring, this
is a very pretty place, set in national forest land
just above the elevation line where nature grows
conifers instead of deciduous trees. Iron Canyon
is set at 2,700 feet in elevation and covers 500
acres with 15 miles of shoreline.

Most people come here to camp, fish, and
enjoy the remote, quiet setting and beautiful
landscape. The water is a striking emerald

green, and during a windless sunset, it appears to glow. Some come to swim, others to see the osprey and bald eagles.

In winter, the water masters drop the water levels down to almost nothing, rendering an unbelievable sight. Spring rains then make the shoreline extremely muddy, and since the water never fills the reservoir, all water sports are out of the question except for fishing and swimming. It is just too stumpy for water-skiing, personal watercraft, or sailboarding. Because the place doesn't have a beach, only exposed lake bottom, the swimming is just so-so.

I was told that they screwed up when they built Iron Canyon Reservoir. Apparently the intake and dam are set up so the lake never fills. The result is this perpetual moonscape on the upper end of the lake, dotted with what's left of the trees that were once here, a kind of stump graveyard. It also means Deadlun Camp is too far away from the water.

Access: A paved launch ramp is available at Hawkins Landing. Small boats are recommended.
Facilities, fees: Campgrounds, drinking water, and vault toilets are available. Supplies can be obtained in Big Bend or Burney. A fee is charged for camping. Day use and boat launching are free.
Water sports, restrictions: Powerboats, canoeing, kayaking, sailing, sailboarding, and swimming are permitted.
Directions: To Hawkins Landing access/boat ramp: From Redding, drive east on Highway 299 for 37 miles to Big Bend Road. At Big Bend Road turn left and drive 15.2 miles to the town of Big Bend. Continue for 2.1 miles to Forest Road 38N11. Turn left and drive 3.3 miles to the Iron Canyon Reservoir Spillway. Turn right and drive 1.1 miles to a dirt road. Turn left and drive .3 miles to the campground and boat ramp.

To Deadlun access: From Redding, drive east on Highway 299 for 37 miles to Big Bend Road. At Big Bend Road, turn left and drive 15.2 miles to the town of Big Bend. Continue for five miles to the lake, bearing right at the

T intersection, and continue for two miles (past the boat launch turnoff) to the campground turnoff on the left side of the road. Turn left and drive one mile to the campground.
Contact: Shasta-Trinity National Forest, Big Bend Ranger Station, 530/337-6502; PG&E Land Projects, 916/386-5164, website: www .pge.com/recreation.

3 PIT RIVER

Rating: 7

northeast of Redding in Shasta-Trinity National Forest

Map 3.1, page 82

What makes the Pit great for most visitors is the natural hot spring pool that's bubbling away just a short distance from the river. This provides the rare opportunity to get heated up in the hot spring, then cooled down in the river, alternating between the two. The spring is located just downstream from the Pit River Bridge in the town of Big Bend, with access at Big Bend Hot Springs. The latter also has a series of concrete tubs perched on a bluff above the river, and the hot spring water pours in a series of miniature waterfalls from one tub to the next. This experience is not so much swimming as it is taking a dunk.

The river is strikingly pretty; it's a freestone stream—that is, where the water tumbles over boulders and into pools. Trout fishing is excellent. Flocks of bandtail pigeons course up and down the waterway, and the occasional bald eagle soars overhead. The best fishing spots are below Lake Britton Dam (near McArthur-Burney Falls State Park) and at the Big Bend Bridge. Other spots have difficult access and are extremely challenging for anglers to wade in. Many people take a tumble here, with slippery boulders and no obvious routes.

Big Bend Hot Springs has become well known to hippies heading over to Mount Shasta during the annual weeklong summer pilgrimage when they harmonically converge, or whatever it is they say they are doing.

Access: There is no boat ramp.

Facilities, fees: Several campgrounds with drinking water and vault toilets are in the area. Supplies are available in Big Bend and Burney. Access is free.

Water sports, restrictions: Swimming is permitted. You can swim at Fender's Flat (at the end of Fender's Ferry Road) and near the town of Big Bend. A natural hot spring is located just west of Big Bend. Note: Much of the shoreline is rugged and treacherous, with steep drop-offs into the river and deep pools below. Use care when walking. No boating is advised.

Directions: To Fender Ferry's section: From Redding, take Highway 299 East and drive 30 miles to Fender's Ferry Road. Turn left on Fender's Ferry Road and drive four miles. Access is available on the left side of the river, below the dam. The river can also be accessed off several roads that intersect Big Bend Road, about 35 miles east of Redding. These roads are unimproved, and high-clearance vehicles are recommended.

To Big Bend section: From Redding, take Highway 299 east and drive 34 miles to Big Bend Road. Turn left on Big Bend Road and drive to the town of Big Bend and Hagen Flat Road. Turn east on Hagen Flat Road. Access is available directly off this road near Powerhouses No. 3 and 4 and at several spots in between. Access is also available below the Lake Britton Dam, east of Lake Britton: At the junction of Highways 299 and 89, drive about seven miles north on Highway 299 to Powerhouse No. 1.

Contact: Shasta-Trinity National Forest, Shasta Lake Ranger District, 530/275-1587; Shasta Lake Visitor Center, 530/275-1589.

4 LAKE BRITTON

Rating: 9

near Fall River Mills in Shasta-Trinity National Forest

Map 3.1, page 82

Do you want the ideal camping/fishing/boating vacation for a family? Lake Britton may be the answer to your prayers. Campgrounds are available on the north shore of the lake, as well as at nearby McArthur-Burney Falls Memorial State Park. Boat ramps provide easy access, and the lake is host to a wide variety of fish species.

Lake Britton is set at an elevation of 2,700 feet, covering 1,600 acres with 18 miles of shoreline. Its proximity to McArthur-Burney Falls State Park guarantees heavy use during the summer. Adjacent to the park's boat launch is a top-notch rental service where visitors can rent canoes, kayaks, small fishing boats with motors, and pedal boats.

The water is warm and surrounded by lush forestland, making this a prime spot for water-skiing and swimming. Because getting here requires a long drive, water-skier use is not high, yet it provides a great alternative for boaters who want something more forested and intimate than the giant lakes in the Central Valley foothills. All water sports are permitted. In the spring, when runoff is high, be on the lookout for floating debris.

With emerald green water set in a high-walled granite gorge, the lake headwaters are very pretty. The surrounding landscape is well forested with many giant ponderosa pines, which are best known for their impressive, mosaic-like bark.

Fishing is often good here, for trout in late winter, for smallmouth bass in spring, and for crappie in summer.

Unlike so many lakes, this reservoir is easily accessible. Highway 89 runs right across it, and many people first learn of Lake Britton as they drive over the bridge on their way to or from McArthur-Burney Falls State Park. Burney Falls—a virtual freshwater fountain, 129 feet high—makes an excellent side trip. The peak offers outstanding viewing areas and hiking trails near the falls.

The hiking trails in this area are excellent. The Pacific Crest Trail runs along Burney Creek, through the park, and then past the dam on its 2,700-mile course to Canada. If you enjoy fishing, take note: The lake has fair prospects for trout and is sometimes excellent for crappie.

Access: There are boat ramps at McArthur-Burney Falls State Park and North Shore.

Facilities, fees: The state park's small marina has rowboats, boats with motors, canoes, kayaks, and pedal boats available for rent. Campgrounds, restrooms with coin showers, flush toilets, vault toilets, and picnic areas are available nearby. Fees are charged for day use, boat launching, and camping.

Water sports, restrictions: Powerboats, water-skiing, wake boarding, personal watercraft, canoes, kayaks, sailing, sailboarding, and swimming are permitted. A sandy swimming beach is available at McArthur-Burney Falls Memorial State Park; this is also a popular starting point for sailboarders.

Directions: To McArthur-Burney Falls State Park: From Redding, drive east on Highway 299 to Burney and then continue for five miles to the junction with Highway 89. At Highway 89, turn north (left) and drive six miles to the park entrance on the left side of the road. Turn left, stop at the kioask, and then continue one mile to the launch ramp and small marina.

To North Shore: From Redding, drive east on Highway 299 to Burney and then continue for five miles to Highway 89. Turn left (north) and drive 9.7 miles (past the state park entrance and over the Lake Britton Bridge) to Clark Creek Road. Turn left (west) and drive about a mile to North Shore access road. Turn left and drive one mile to the North Shore campground and launch ramp.

Contact: McArthur-Burney Falls State Park, 530/335-2777, website: www.parks.ca.gov (click on Find A Park); PG&E Land Services, 530/386-5164, website: www.pge.com/recreation; Burney Falls Store, 530/335-4214.

5 FALL RIVER LAKE

Rating: 5

near Fall River Mills

Map 3.1, page 82

Most out-of-towners overlook this little reservoir set behind the town of Fall River Mills. It's relatively small, but locals come here to water-ski. They know that the water is warm and conditions are excellent for water-skiing and swimming.

A lakeside picnic area with a few tables and grills is provided adjacent to a beach that makes a good spot for sunbathing and swimming. Again, these are popular hangouts with locals, their secret from the outside world. Fishing here is typically poor; instead, you should just plunk in a canoe and paddle around without a care. The nearest campgrounds are at Crystal Lake and Lake Britton.

Access: A paved launch ramp is located on the southwest side of the lake, adjacent to the picnic area.

Facilities, fees: A picnic area is available. No drinking water is available. Garbage must be packed out. Supplies can be obtained in Fall River Mills. Access is free.

Water sports, restrictions: Powerboats, water-skiing, wake boarding, personal watercraft, sailing, sailboarding, and swimming are permitted. A sandy beach for swimming is available by the day-use area.

Directions: From Redding, drive east on Highway 299 for 69 miles to the town of Fall River Mills and continue to Long Street. Turn left on Long Street and drive to the lake.

Contact: Fall River Valley Chamber of Commerce, 530/336-5840; Vaughn's Sporting Goods, 530/335-2381.

6 BIG LAKE

Rating: 10

near McArthur

Map 3.1, page 82

Here in the Fall River Valley, located in eastern Shasta County, is a place that the Pit River Native Americans named "Ahjumawi." It means "where the waters come together." It is one of the most extraordinary freshwater habitats in North America, a fantastic getaway for fly-fishing for giant trout, canoeing, and bird-watching, while staying in a waterfront lodge or boat-in camping.

Ahjumawi and Big Lake are accessible only by boat, launching from a small public access point called Rat Farm, or through Lava Creek Lodge, a private resort. Otherwise it is walled off by private property, with no public shore access.

What makes this habitat unique is a series of huge freshwater springs from underground lava tubes. They produce a tremendous volume of pure water that create a matrix of clear, slow-moving waterways: Fall River, Lava Creek, Rising River, Tule River, Ja-She-Creek, Eastman Lake, Horr Pond, and Big Lake.

Together these waters form one of the largest freshwater, spring-fed waterways in the world. It is clear and slow-flowing, perfect for dry-fly fishing for giant native rainbow trout—or canoeing while bald eagles are perched nearby on pines.

What you'll see here is a valley floor with primeval beauty where springs are flowing from the lava along the shoreline. Much of the land is covered by lava flows, including large areas of jagged black basalt, along with spattercone and conic depressions. Eastman Lake and Big Lake are brilliant aqua in some shallow areas, and the place is so quiet that you can hear the trout rising from 50 yards away.

The canoeing is world-class, yet it is very little known. From Lava Creek or the Rat Farm, you can paddle across these pristine waters to Big Lake or Horr Pond to a series of 11 boat-in campsites. It can be euphoric to paddle a canoe here, like living in suspended animation. There are tons of waterfowl in the area, especially grebes, mallards, and Canada geese, along with snipe everywhere and great numbers of raptors: bald eagles, golden eagles, red-tailed hawks, and great horned owls.

At dusk, though, it is the call of those big trout that many anglers must answer with a delicately-presented dry fly. In a few hours, my partner, Ed Rice, and I must have had 75 strikes. Our catches included several trout in the 16- to 20-inch class, hooked, brought to the boat, and released to fight again another day. If you stay with it, you have a genuine opportunity to entice a six-pounder. Whether or not you land it can be up to the fish.

How big is Big Lake? About 150 acres. This is intimate enough for a canoe, yet large enough for a powerboat, though a 10-mph speed limit keeps things relaxing and calm. That's right, no fast boats, no water-skiing, no personal watercraft, just a small, quiet lake with warm water, decent fishing, and lakeside camping.

Access: No access to Big Lake at Ahjumawi State Park is available by car or trail. Access is by boat only, launching from Lava Creek Lodge or Rat Farm. From Rat Ranch Road turn right across a canal to reach the unpaved boat ramp.

Facilities, fees: A picnic area is provided. A boat-in campground is available at Big Lake at Ahjumawi Lava Springs State Park. Lava Creek Lodge has a boat ramp, canoe rentals, guided flyfishing trips with boats, lodging, restaurant, and a bar available. Supplies can be obtained in Fall River Mills and McArthur. There are fees for boat launching and camping.

Water sports, restrictions: Powerboats, canoes, kayaks, sailboarding, sailing, and swimming are permitted. No personal watercraft, wake boarding, or water-skiing. There is a 10-mph speed limit on the lake. You can swim near the picnic area.

Directions: To Rat Farm boat launch: From Redding, drive east on Highway 299 for 73 miles to McArthur and Main Street. Turn left on Main Street and drive 3.5 miles (becomes a dirt road) to the Rat Farm boat launch at Big Lake. Launch boat and paddle or row 1 to 2.5 miles to one of the nine boat-in campsites.

To Lava Creek Lodge: From Redding, drive east on Highway 299 to Burney and continue for 17 miles to Glenburn Road. Turn left and drive five miles to McArthur Road. Turn right and drive .2 mile to the church. Bear left at the church (still is McArthur Road) and drive 1.9 miles to Island Road. Turn right and drive three miles to the lodge at the end of the road. **Contact:** Ahjumawi Lava Springs State Park, 530/225-2065 or 530/335-2777, website: www.parks.ca.gov (click on Find A Park); Lava Creek Lodge, 530/336-6288, website: www.lava creeklodge.com; Burney Chamber of Commerce, 530/335-2111, website: www.burney-chamber.com.

◪ CAVE LAKE

Rating: 7

in Modoc National Forest

Map 3.2, page 83

Two lakes are located here at the same destination, Cave Lake and Lily Lake (see the next listing). Together they make a nice set. Both are very quiet, get light traffic, and offer decent fishing for trout in the foot-long class. Cave Lake has very little surrounding vegetation, which makes Lily Lake the more attractive of the pair.

Tiny Cave Lake is set at 6,600 feet in elevation in remote Modoc County, far enough away from most people that it attracts little attention. It's the rare day when someone goes to the trouble of hauling a car-top boat, such as a canoe or johnboat, this far just to go trout fishing, even though you can camp overnight here. When people do venture this way, they usually go to neighboring Lily Lake, which is far prettier (but there is no campground at Lily Lake).

Though sailboarding is permitted, conditions are usually poor for sailboards. It is a much better spot to visit with canoe.
Access: There is a primitive boat ramp suitable for small boats.
Facilities, fees: A campground with vault toilets is available nearby. No drinking water. Supplies can be obtained in New Pine Creek. Access is free.
Water sports, restrictions: Rowboats, canoes, kayaks, sailing, and swimming are permitted. No motors are allowed.
Directions: From Redding, drive east on Highway 299 and for 146 miles to Alturas and U.S. 395. Turn north on U.S. 395 and drive 40 miles to Forest Road 2 (if you reach the town of New Pine Creek on the Oregon/California border, you have driven a mile too far). Turn right on Forest Road 2 (a steep dirt road—trailers are not recommended) and drive six miles to the campground entrance on the left side of the road, just beyond the Lily Lake picnic area.
Contact: Modoc National Forest, Warner Mountain Ranger District, 530/279-6116.

◪ LILY LAKE

Rating: 8

in Modoc National Forest

Map 3.2, page 83

Little Lily is way out there in no-man's-land, but it is well worth the trip. People drive to this remote but premium destination for a day or two of camping (at neighboring Cave Lake, see previous listing), fishing, and solitude. Because there are some conifers sprinkled around the lake, Lily Lake is a lot prettier than Cave. Its remoteness makes it a treasured destination for the few people who venture here.

There is a gravel boat ramp for small boats, and light car-top boats such as canoes and kayaks can be hand launched. Some people bring float tubes so they can float around and fish. This is a remote, pretty spot that is ideal for a cool dip on a hot day. Due to the location, it gets light use even in peak summer months.

Access: There is a gravel boat ramp.

Facilities, fees: A picnic area with a vault toilet is available. A campground with vault toilets is available at nearby Cave Lake. Supplies can be obtained in New Pine Creek. Access is free.

Water sports, restrictions: Rowboats, canoes, kayaks, sailing, and swimming are permitted. No motors.

Directions: From Redding, drive east on Highway 299 and for 146 miles to Alturas and U.S. 395. Turn north on U.S. 395 and drive 40 miles to Forest Road 2 (if you reach the town of New Pine Creek on the Oregon/California border, you have driven a mile too far). Turn right on Forest Road 2 (a steep dirt road—trailers are not recommended) and drive six miles to the Lily Lake picnic area.

Contact: Modoc National Forest, Warner Mountain Ranger District, 530/279-6116.

9 LAKE ANNIE

Rating: 6

near Fort Bidwell

Map 3.2, page 83

Lake Annie is the backyard fishing hole for the folks who live in Fort Bidwell, a unique community that time seems to have passed by. The small town is an anachronism. Just west of town, there is a natural hot spring.

To the east of the lake is Annie Mountain, from which it gets its name. Bordering Lake Annie to the west are the Warner Mountains, a lonely, quiet place. The surrounding country is fairly sparse, and one thing is for sure: nobody arrives here by accident.

Lake Annie covers 30 acres and is situated at 4,700 feet in elevation, with a rocky shoreline surrounded by sagebrush and grassy hills. That's right: There are no trees. It's also right that the lake is too small for anything but cartop boats. The water can be on the cloudy side,

but it is passable for swimming. Most of the few people who do visit this lake come primarily to fish for trout.

Access: There is no boat ramp. Car-top boats may be hand launched.

Facilities, fees: Lake Annie has no facilities. Supplies can be obtained in Cedarville. Access is free.

Water sports, restrictions: Swimming is permitted, but there are no beaches.

Directions: From Redding, drive 146 miles east on Highway 299 to Alturas. From Alturas, continue east on Highway 299 to Cedarville and Surprise Valley Road. Turn north on Surprise Valley Road and continue (the road becomes Highway 17, Highway 13, and then Highway 1) to the town of Fort Bidwell and Lake Annie Road/Highway 4. In Fort Bidwell, turn north on Lake Annie Road and drive 2.5 miles to the lake.

Contact: Bureau of Land Management, Surprise Field Office, 530/279-6101.

10 FEE RESERVOIR

Rating: 6

near Fort Bidwell

Map 3.2, page 83

What's the price of a stunning high desert sunset? There's no monetary fee at Fee Reservoir—just the time it takes to get here.

The setting is typical of Modoc County's high desert country. You get a chance to see that special orange glow at dawn and dusk, and in early summer the variety of wildflowers makes a normally stark landscape come alive with a multiplicity of colors.

It is set at 5,329 feet in elevation on the Modoc Plateau. When full, Fee Reservoir covers 337 acres, but because the water is used for irrigation, it is subject to major summer drawdowns and erratic level fluctuations based on water demand.

For this reason not many people come here for water-skiing, personal watercraft use, or sailboarding, although these sports are permitted. In the future, the Bureau of Land Management hopes to build a paved launch ramp. For now, boaters hoping to catch some trout just launch from the dirt road that heads down to the shore.

The water is often cloudy, and it's rare to see people on the lake.

Access: There is a paved boat ramp and parking area.

Facilities, fees: A small campground with vault toilets and drinking water is available. There are no fees for camping, boat launching, or day use.

Water sports, restrictions: Powerboating, water-skiing, wake boarding, personal watercraft, sailing, sailboarding, and swimming are permitted. All water sports should be exercised with caution due to debris commonly on the lake surface.

Directions: From Redding, drive east on Highway 299 for 146 miles to Alturas. From Alturas, continue east on Highway 299 for 21 miles to Cedarville and County Road 1. Turn north on County Road 1 and drive 30 miles to Fort Bidwell and Fee Reservoir Road. Turn right on Fee Reservoir Road (good gravel road) and drive 7.5 miles to the reservoir.

Contact: Public Works, County of Modoc, 530/233-6403; Bureau of Land Management, Surprise Field Office, 530/279-6101.

11 BIG SAGE RESERVOIR

Rating: 5

near Alturas in Modoc National Forest

Map 3.2, page 83

Don't be scared off by the dirt road that provides access to this lake. It's smooth enough to trailer a boat over, and it leads to a decent boat ramp and a campground.

The highlight of this reservoir is that there are no restrictions on powerboating (except for a ban on personal watercraft), so if you have a fast boat, you can really let it rip. Despite

Big Sage's considerable size, there are typically very few people here. On many days, you might have the place all to yourself. The water gets nice and warm by late summer, and a few islands dotting the waterscape provide habitat for largemouth bass.

Upon arriving in the sparse sagebrush country at elevation 5,100 feet, you will find that Big Sage makes a pretty sight. When you consider that this is the biggest recreational lake in Modoc County, covering 5,000 surface acres, you might think you've really found something special. Well, that's what you get for thinking.

The shoreline is made of clay and mud, and the water is often very murky. Algae growth is usually a problem in midsummer, and by late summer, anybody who tries water-skiing or swimming here will most likely emerge coated in green muck. See ya.

The water level can fluctuate greatly from year to year here, dropping way down during drought years. This is one of the better bass lakes in Modoc County. Catfish and crappie can also be caught in the summer.

Access: A paved boat ramp is located near the picnic area.

Facilities, fees: A campground with vault toilets is available. No drinking water. Garbage must be packed out. Access, boat launching, and camping are free.

Water sports, restrictions: Powerboating, water-skiing, wake boarding, sailing, sailboarding, and swimming are permitted. No personal watercraft allowed.

Directions: From Alturas, drive west on Highway 299 for three miles to Crowder Flat Road/County Road 73. Turn right on Crowder Flat Road and drive about five miles to County Road 180. Turn right on County Road 180 and drive four miles. Turn left at the access road for the campground and boat ramp and drive a short distance to the camp on the left side of the road.

Contact: Modoc National Forest, Devil's Garden Ranger District, 530/233-5811.

12 DORRIS RESERVOIR

Rating: 6

near Alturas in Modoc National Wildlife Refuge

Map 3.2, page 83

Drive a short way out of Alturas and you will find Dorris Reservoir in the Modoc National Wildlife Refuge, which provides a safe habitat for ducks, geese, and other waterfowl.

The lake is big enough for water-skiing, but boaters should be wary of submerged stumps, which pose serious hazards, especially when the lake is not full. As with many lakes in Modoc County, this one has some problems with water clarity, although you won't encounter anything like the slimy green mess you will find elsewhere. Water-skiing, swimming, and other sports involving water contact are legal, but they're not very popular due to the fairly turbid water.

The lake's shoreline is composed more of gravel and sand than mud, which makes the place somewhat appealing for sunbathers and swimmers. Dorris Reservoir is open for day use only—that is, no camping is allowed here—and it closes at 8 P.M. during the summer.

Access: Two primitive boat launches are located on the northwest side of the lake. Note: Due to fluctuating water levels, boating is permitted only from April through September.

Facilities, fees: Vault toilets are available. No drinking water. A campground is located near Cedar Pass. Supplies can be obtained in Alturas. Access is free.

Water sports, restrictions: Powerboating, sailing, sailboarding, and swimming are permitted. Water-skiing and wake boarding permitted from June through September. No personal watercraft allowed.

Directions: From the south end of Alturas, turn east on Parker Creek Road (County Road 56) and drive three miles until the road forks with County Road 57. Bear right on County Road 57 and travel a short distance to the boat ramp, or bear left and continue to the north end of the reservoir.

Contact: Modoc National Wildlife Refuge, 530/233-3572.

13 BAYLEY RESERVOIR

Rating: 2

south of Alturas

Map 3.2, page 83

This lake is way out in the middle of nowhere. What makes it worth seeing? Mainly that it is far away from anything. In fact, the first time I stopped in nearby Likely, which consists of a gas station/store and a cemetery, I asked this old fella at the gas pump why, of all things, they named the town Likely.

"Because you are likely not to get there," he answered. That's the way they are in Modoc. You're in cow country now, and if you want to have a lake all to yourself, this is the one. The trees are small, there is plenty of chaparral, and there are more trout than people.

But be forewarned that the only thing this lake is good for is paddling around in a boat (no motors allowed) and fishing for trout. Speaking of trout, this lake is stocked with more of 'em than any other in the region.

When you arrive, it's likely that you will not find what you were looking for, just like the man said, because this lake is very small and is often yucky and smelly. A ranger we spoke to told us about the time when, while doing some research work, he waded into the lake for a short time, then later on the trip home discovered a terrible rash had broken out all over his legs. No thanks!

Access: A primitive boat launch is available for car-top boats only.

Facilities, fees: A few primitive campsites are available. No other facilities. No drinking water. Garbage must be packed out. Supplies can be obtained in Alturas. Access is free.

Water sports, restrictions: Motors are not allowed on the water. No water sports are permitted here.

Directions: From the south end of Alturas, turn south on Centerville Road and drive two miles to Westside Road/County Road 60. Turn left and drive 6.5 miles to Bayley Reservoir Road/County Road 62. Turn right on Bayley Reservoir Road/County Road 62 and drive 5.5 miles to the reservoir.

Contact: Bureau of Land Management, Eagle Lake Field Office, 530/257-0456.

14 MILL CREEK (MODOC NATIONAL FOREST)

Rating: 5

near Likely in Modoc National Forest

Map 3.2, page 83

Mill Creek emerges right out of the South Warner Wilderness, those lonely mountains of the northeast. The best strategy for a good trip is to go sightseeing at Mill Creek Falls, then head onward, park at Soup Springs Camp, and hike into the South Warner Wilderness along the creek's pretty headwaters.

The waterfall is beautiful, and it has far more power than most people realize. Do not try to swim there or explore too closely on the adjacent rocks, which are slippery. Enjoy the view, move on, and get ready for more fun.

And you will have fun when you follow the trail over the hill and into the valley floor, where Mill Creek awaits. The product of snowmelt, the creek water is cold, making swimming (actually more like taking a dunk) impossible until late in the summer, when the water flows are slower and and it warms up a bit. Early in the summer, it is so cold that all you can do is have contests with your friends to see who can keep their feet in the stream the longest.

Pretty, pristine, and calm, Mill Creek is primarily a wilderness fishing stream, a great place to take a relaxing hike. When you're ready to rest a spell, dunk your feet in the water and enjoy the quiet paradise.

Access: There is no boat ramp.

Facilities, fees: A campground with drinking water and vault toilets is available. Supplies can be obtained in Likely. Access is free. A fee is charged for camping.

Water sports, restrictions: No boating. Swimming is available downstream of Mill Creek Falls.

Directions: From Alturas drive 17 miles south on U.S. 395 to the town of Likely and Jess Valley Road. Turn left on Jess Valley Road/County Road 64 and drive nine miles to the fork. Bear left on West Warner Road/Forest Road 5 and drive 2.5 miles to Forest Road 40N46. Turn right on Forest Road 40N46 and drive two miles to the campground entrance at the end of the road. Access is available off Forest Service roads near the campground, and also along trails that lead into the South Warner Wilderness.

Contact: Modoc National Forest, Warner Mountain Ranger District, 530/279-6116.

15 WEST VALLEY RESERVOIR

Rating: 7

near Likely

Map 3.2, page 83

Nothing is perfect, but in Modoc County, West Valley Reservoir will have to do.

If you come on a calm, warm day, this is one of the better choices in the entire region. West Valley Reservoir provides good access, has a quality boat ramp, and usually fills up during the winter with runoff from the South Fork Pit River.

In the hot summer months, the place is ideal for swimming, with warm water and a gravelly shore. Summers are also great for sailboarding, good for water-skiing and personal watercraft, and fair for trout fishing.

The lake is set at 4,770 feet, covers 970 surface acres, and has seven miles of shoreline. A great bonus is that boat-in camping is permitted anywhere along the shore, a do-it-yourself affair with no resorts, marinas, or facilities of any kind.

This lack of facilities, as well as the long drive most people have to undertake to get here, keeps most boaters away. Those who do come find that West Valley makes a good alternative destination with plenty of room, few boats, and warm water.

Sailboarders will be thrilled to find that the lake is exceptionally suited to their sport. Perched on the edge of the great basin and the high desert, the location is perfect for catching prevailing winds in the spring and early summer.

Unfortunately, sometimes it is too perfect. In the spring, whipping winds can churn the lake into a froth, making conditions extremely hazardous for boaters; there have been several accidents. Some boaters claim that ghosts of past accident victims hover overhead.

Other problems to be aware of: By late summer it is advised that you call ahead and check the water level at the reservoir. During that time of year, the reservoir is often drained to very low levels to supply local ranchers with water. Finally, it gets really cold in the winter. Up here on the Modoc Plateau, temperatures often dip to around zero degrees Fahrenheit for several weeks starting in mid-December, and this lake freezes hard.

Access: To reach the paved boat ramp, turn right at the sign for West Valley Reservoir and drive four miles south.

Facilities, fees: A few unimproved campsites with drinking water and vault toilets are available. Supplies can be obtained in Likely. Access, boat launching, and camping are free.

Water sports, restrictions: Powerboating, water-skiing, wake boarding, personal watercraft, sailing, sailboarding, and swimming are permitted.

Directions: From Alturas, drive south on U.S. 395 for 17 miles to the town of Likely and Jess Valley Road. Turn east on Jess Valley Road (County Road 64) and drive two miles to the sign for West Valley Reservoir. Turn right and drive four miles to the boat ramp at West Valley Reservoir (the north end of the lake can be accessed via a short road off Jess Valley Road).

Contact: County of Modoc, Public Works, 530/233-6403; Bureau of Land Management, Alturas Field Office, 530/233-4666; website: www.ca.blm.gov/alturas.

16 BLUE LAKE

Rating: 8

near Likely in Modoc National Forest

Map 3.2, page 83

Shaped like an egg and rimmed by trees, this is one pretty lake. Bordering on pristine, it is one of the most attractive lakes you can reach on a paved road in northeastern California, and makes an ideal vacation site for campers, boaters, hikers, and anglers. It covers 160 surface acres, set at an elevation of 6,000 feet.

Despite being located so near to the South Warner Wilderness, Blue Lake's access is quite good, with a paved road that leads all the way to the northeast shore. The campground has an attractive setting, will accommodate RVs, and is close to a good boat ramp.

With the surrounding landscape and clear water, the lake has great appeal for all water sports enthusiasts, although it is typically on the cold side until mid-July. Of the lakes in Modoc County that are decent for water-skiing, this one edges out West Valley as the best. The shoreline is a gravel/sand mix, not mud, which makes it good for wading or just horsing around.

A good hiking trail is routed around the lake and takes less than an hour to complete. A wheelchair-accessible fishing platform is a nice touch. Trout fishing is often good, and the fish here are often larger than at other lakes in the region. Brown trout in the 30-inch class are occasionally hooked, sometimes landed. In addition, you have the chance to make a great side trip to nearby Mill Creek Falls, which most local campers consider a must-see destination.

A pair of nesting bald eagles live here; over the last several years there have been three fledged chicks. Although their presence negates year-round use of six campsites otherwise available, the trade-off is an unprecedented opportunity to view the national bird.

Access: A paved boat ramp is located next to the picnic area on the north end of the lake.

Facilities, fees: A campground with drinking water and vault toilets is available. A boat ramp, picnic area, and fishing pier are wheelchair-accessible. Supplies can be obtained in Likely. Access and boat launching are free. There is a fee for camping.

Water sports, restrictions: Powerboating and swimming are permitted. There is a 5-mph speed limit. Sailboarding and sailing are allowed, but conditions are only occasionally good.

Directions: From Alturas, drive south on U.S. 395 for 17 miles to the town of Likely and Jess Valley Road. Turn left on Jess Valley Road/County Road 64 and drive nine miles to the fork with Forest Service Road 64. At the fork, bear right on Forest Service Road 64 and drive seven miles to Forest Service Road 38N60. Turn right on Forest Service Road 38N60 and drive two miles to the campground at the lake.

Contact: Modoc National Forest, Warner Mountain Ranger District, 530/279-6116.

⓱ BAUM & CRYSTAL LAKES

Rating: 6

near Burney

Map 3.3, page 84

Baum (90 acres) and Crystal Lakes (60 acres) are adjoining bodies on Hat Creek that offer extremely limited boating opportunities. In fact, this water is used almost entirely for trout fishing.

Powerboats are prohibited here, which limits watercraft to car-top, hand-powered boats, such as canoes and rowboats. Yet there are few of either on the water. Instead, what you will see are a number of people fishing from the shore (never swimming, an illegal activity here). For a good side trip, visit the adjacent Crys-

tal Fish Hatchery, which is operated by the Department of Fish and Game.

Special note: Some readers will wonder why this book does not contain a listing for Hat Creek. That is because swimming was banned following several drownings in the river section along Highway 89, where there are several campgrounds. If caught swimming you can be cited and evicted from your campsite.

Access: A primitive boat ramp is located off Cassel Road.

Facilities, fees: Vault toilets are available at Baum Lake. There are no facilities at Crystal Lake. No drinking water is available. Drinking water is available at the powerhouse and fish hatchery. Campgrounds are nearby. Supplies can be obtained in Burney. Access is free.

Water sports, restrictions: Canoes, kayaks, sailboats, and inflatables are permitted. No motors. No swimming or sailboarding.

Directions: From Redding, drive east on Highway 299 to Burney and continue for five miles to the junction with Highway 89. At the junction, continue straight on Highway 299 for two miles to Cassel Road. Turn right at Cassel Road, and drive 3.6 miles to the campground entrance on the left (or turn left on Hat Creek-Powerhouse Road and continue to Baum Lake and the adjoining Crystal Lake).

Contact: PG&E Land Projects, 916/386-5164, website: www.pge.com/recreation; Vaughn's Sporting Goods, Burney, 530/335-2381, website: www.vaughnfly.com.

⓲ NORTH BATTLE CREEK RESERVOIR

Rating: 6

near Viola

Map 3.3, page 84

A lot of folks bypass this lake. They're too busy and excited to get to Lassen Park on Highway 44. If they just slowed down, they might notice the turnoff for North Battle Creek Reservoir and discover a much less-used spot than the nearby national park.

If the campgrounds are crowded at Lassen, what the heck, just roll on over to North Battle Creek Reservoir. The place appeals to vacationing families who are looking for a quiet spot to set up camp near the water.

Swimming is permitted, but there is no formal beach, and the water stays pretty cold through early summer. It's a good choice for car-top boaters, folks who haul in a canoe or rowboat. Most of them bring along a fishing rod and a few dreams of landing a couple of trout while they are here.

Access: A primitive boat ramp is available for car-top boats only.

Facilities, fees: A campground with drinking water and vault toilets is available. Access is free. A fee is charged for camping.

Water sports, restrictions: Rowboats, boats with electric motors, canoes, and kayaks are permitted on the reservoir. No gas motors. Sailing, sailboarding, and swimming are allowed.

Directions: From Redding, drive east on Highway 44 to Viola. From Viola, continue east for 3.5 miles to Forest Road 32N17. Turn left on Forest Road 32N17 and drive five miles to Forest Road 32N31. Turn left and drive four miles to Forest Road 32N18. Turn right and drive .5 mile to the reservoir and the campground on the right side of the road.

Contact: PG&E Land Projects, 916/386-5164, website: www.pge.com/recreation.

19 MACUMBER RESERVOIR

Rating: 6

east of Redding

Map 3.3, page 84

Lots of folks bypass this little lake, so easy to reach from Redding. They just whiz by in their cars and never take notice. Whoa there. If you put your foot to the brake you'll discover little Macumber Reservoir, elevation 3,500 feet.

Macumber was created when a dam was

placed across the North Fork of Battle Creek. It is a PG&E-run facility that is open to the public. This is a prime spot for small electric-powered boats, prams, and canoes; gas-powered motors are not permitted.

Swimming is allowed, but there are no beaches. Although the shoreline is pretty muddy, once you get out in the lake the water is clear. All these factors make it ideal for floating around in a raft and enjoying a warm summer day.

Access: There is a primitive boat launch for car-top boats.

Facilities, fees: A small campground with vault toilets and drinking water is available. Day use is free. A fee is charged for camping.

Water sports, restrictions: Rowboats, boats with electric motors, canoes, kayaks and inflatables, sailboats, sailboarding, and swimming are allowed. No gas motors.

Directions: In Redding, turn east on Highway 44 and drive toward Viola to Lake Macumber Road (if you reach Viola, you have gone four miles too far). Turn left at Lake Macumber Road and drive two miles to the reservoir and campground.

Contact: PG&E Land Projects, 916/386-5164, website: www.pge.com/recreation.

20 MANZANITA LAKE

Rating: 8

in Lassen Volcanic National Park

Map 3.3, page 84

The centerpiece of Lassen Volcanic National Park is, of course, the old Lassen Peak volcano, and the climb up that beauty is one of the best two-hour (one-way) hikes in California. But Manzanita Lake and its idyllic surroundings also rate high among the park's attractions. In many ways the lake makes an ideal vacation destination.

Because it offers great natural beauty, a location with easy access from Highways 89 or 44, and a large, easily accessible campground, Manzanita is the most popular lake in the park. On weekdays, when campground use is low, this place really shines. On busy weekends, though, when it is overrun with campers, it takes on quite a different character. Ah, but with a small boat, canoe, or pram, you can flee to the safety and sanity of the water and soak in the surroundings until you don't have a care in the world.

Manzanita is small but quite beautiful. Powerboats are not permitted on the lake, making it perfect for a canoe, raft, or pram. The pristine body of water is set at an elevation of 5,890 feet and covers 53 acres.

With 179 sites, the campground adjacent to the lake is Lassen's largest, and yet it fills up during many summer weekends. It is also the easiest to reach, being so near a major entrance to the park.

The lake's prime attraction is trout fishing. There are restrictions mandating catch-and-release and the use of artificials with single barbless hooks. Show up with salmon eggs and Power Bait and you'll get strung up on the yardarm. There is very little shoreline access for fishing. Angles will need a pram or other small boat.

Swimming is permitted, but the lake lacks a swimming beach area, and the water is typically very cold until August. Although there are no restrictions on sailboarding, you'll rarely see anyone doing this here; there is heavy fishing traffic and most sailboarders don't want to deal with user conflicts. Park rangers, too, want to keep this place serene and pristine.

Access: A primitive boat ramp that's suitable only for car-top boats is provided near the campground.

Facilities, fees: A campground with drinking water and flush toilets is available. A picnic area, convenience store, museum, visitor center, RV dump station, coin showers, and coin laundry are nearby. There is a park entrance fee and camping fee.

Water sports, restrictions: Rowboats, canoes, and kayaks are permitted. No motors. Swimming is allowed.

Directions: From Redding, drive east on Highway 44 to the junction with Highway 89. Turn right (south) on Highway 89 and drive one mile to the entrance station to Lassen Volcanic National Park (the state highway becomes Lassen Park Highway/Main Park Road). Continue a short distance on Lassen Park Highway/Main Park Road to the campground entrance road. Turn right and drive .5 mile to the campground.

Contact: Lassen Volcanic National Park, 530/595-4444, website: www.nps.gov/lavo; Manzanita Lake Camper Store, 530/335-7557.

21 SUMMIT LAKE

Rating: 5

in Lassen Volcanic National Park

Map 3.3, page 84

The lake covers just 15 acres, set high in Lassen Volcanic National Park, at 6,695 feet in elevation. Summit Lake is the most popular lake for swimming in the park. The water is cold in June, but usually warms up by mid to late July. There is no boat launch, and if you hand-launch a canoe or other car-top boat, you must carry the craft some distance to reach the water.

One of the best things about this lake is the large campground that's near the water that offers campers their pick of pretty sites on the north and south shores. Campers often get a special treat when deer arrive at sunset to explore the meadow near the southeastern shore.

The water is cold in early summer because it freezes over solid every winter. But because the lake is so small, the water temperature rises more quickly, and despite the high elevation, taking a dip here can be tolerable by midsummer. If your goal is to catch your dinner, forget it; ever since trout plants were suspended in the park, this lake has been largely fished out.

For an easy evening hike, just amble around the lake, making sure to keep an eye out for deer. There's a good chance you'll spot one of these beautiful creatures emerging from the trees to browse.

Access: There is no boat ramp. Car-top boats may be hand launched.

Facilities, fees: A campground with drinking water and vault toilets is available. A convenience store is available near the park entrance station at Manzanita Lake. There is a park entrance fee and camping fee.

Water sports, restrictions: Swimming, sailboarding, and hand-launched boats are permitted. No motors.

Directions: From Redding, drive east on Highway 44 to the junction with Highway 89. Turn right (south) on Highway 89 and drive one mile to the entrance station to Lassen Volcanic National Park (the state highway becomes Lassen Park Highway/Main Park Road). Continue 12 miles to the Summit Lake Campground entrance road on the left.

Contact: Lassen Volcanic National Park, 530/595-4444, website: www.nps.gov/lavo; Manzanita Lake Camper Store, 530/335-7557.

22 BUTTE LAKE

Rating: 6

south of Burney in Lassen Volcanic National Park

Map 3.3, page 84

It is large (212 acres), has a high-mountain setting (6,100 feet elevation), and is beautiful. But because you must access it via an extremely obscure entrance to Lassen Volcanic National Park, most people overlook Butte Lake.

It is one of the most remote drive-to lakes in the park and also one of the largest. Butte is very appealing to car-top boaters, especially canoeists, who enjoy paddling around amid the unusual, spectacular scenery.

Hikers are not excluded from the fun. The trailhead for the Cinder Cone Trail is near the boat launch area. This is a strenuous hike, involving a climb of 800 feet over the course of two miles to the top of the Cinder Cone for

spectacular views. There are also trails leading to Snag Lake to the south and Prospect Peak to the west. Another good side trip is the day hike to Bathtub Lake, a fetching little spot.

Butte's size, along with the spring winds that come out of the northwest, makes it a wild card for sailboarding. This can be quite a place to practice the sport, providing you don't mind the long drive in.

The campground is set in an open volcanic setting with a sprinkling of lodgepole pine. The contrast of the volcanics against the emerald greens of the lake is beautiful and memorable.

Access: A primitive boat ramp near the picnic area is available for car-top boats only.

Facilities, fees: A campground with drinking water and vault toilets is available. There is a park entrance fee and a camping fee.

Water sports, restrictions: Car-top boats, canoes, kayaks, sailboarding, and swimming are permitted. No motors.

Directions: From Redding, drive east on Highway 44 to the junction with Highway 89. Bear north on Highway 89/44 and drive 13 miles to Old Station. Just past Old Station, turn right (east) on Highway 44 and drive 10 miles to Forest Road 32N21/Butte Lake Road. Turn right and drive six miles to the campground.

Contact: Lassen Volcanic National Park, 530/595-4444.

23 SILVER LAKE

Rating: 6

near Westwood in Lassen National Forest

Map 3.3, page 84

Although Silver Lake is the largest of the little alpine lakes in the region, it is completely dwarfed by Lake Almanor, Mountain Meadows Reservoir, and Butt Valley Reservoir to the south. For that reason, many vacationers overlook the place.

It is a small and pretty lake, set at 6,400 feet in elevation. That translates to cold water that freezes over in winter, with ice-out usually occurring by June. By then, warm summer temperatures make the trout hungry, and the surface water is at least less frigid. With no boat ramp and motors banned from the lake, this is the kind of place where you can haul in a canoe on your rig and have the time of your life, paddling around, fishing for trout, enjoying the scenery, and maybe going for a midday swim. Although the lake has no swimming beach, much of the shore slopes gradually. By August the water is warm enough for a dip.

The campgrounds are excellent, and so are the nearby hiking trails. In addition, Caribou Lake (see next listing) provides a close alternative if you want to hit two lakes in one trip.

Silver Lake makes a good first-night camp for an expedition into the adjoining Caribou Wilderness. From here, hikers can access routes that will take them to Emerald Lake to the northwest and to Betty, Trail, and Shotoverin Lakes nearby to the southeast. That's right, this lake is primarily used as a jumping-off point for a backpacking trip into the wilderness, though it's lovely enough in its own right to warrant a visit.

Access: An unimproved boat ramp is located near the picnic area. Only car-top boats are permitted.

Facilities, fees: Two campgrounds are provided: Silver Bowl and Rocky Knoll, with drinking water and vault toilets available. Supplies can be obtained in Westwood. Access is free. A fee is charged for camping.

Water sports, restrictions: Rowboats, canoes, and kayaks are allowed. No motors. Sailboarding and swimming are permitted.

Directions: From Red Bluff, drive east on Highway 36 to the junction with Highway 89. Continue east on Highway 89/36 past Lake Almanor to Westwood. In Westwood, turn left on County Road A21 and drive 12.5 miles to Silver Lake Road. Turn left on Silver Lake Road/County Road 110 and drive 8.5 miles north to Silver Lake. At Silver Lake, turn right and drive a short distance to the campground.

Contact: Lassen National Forest, Almanor Ranger District, 530/258-2141.

24 CARIBOU LAKE

Rating: 6

near Westwood in Lassen National Forest

Map 3.3, page 84

Everyone should fly in an airplane over this area at least once to appreciate it. There are literally dozens of lakes here, most of them pristine little spots that are so quiet you can practically hear the flowers bloom.

Caribou is one you can reach by car rather than by parachute. Because it is set on the edge of the wilderness, it provides a jumping-off point for hikes to several other small lakes. These include Jewel, Eleanor, Black, Turnaround, Twin, and Triangle Lakes, which you hit in that order as you venture into the wilderness interior.

Small and intimate, Caribou is set at 6,400 feet in elevation, and is similar to nearby Silver Lake (see previous listing) except without campgrounds—a real shame. Like Silver Lake, this is a good spot for car-top boaters because there is no boat ramp and motors aren't allowed, meaning you can typically have the place all to yourself. The water is cold year-round except for a few weeks from late July through mid-August, the only time when swimming is not just tolerable but exceptional.

Access: There is no boat ramp. Car-top boats may be hand launched.

Facilities, fees: Vault toilets are available. No drinking water. Garbage must be packed out. Campgrounds are available nearby at Silver Lake. Access to the lake is free.

Water sports, restrictions: Rowboats, canoes, and kayaks are allowed. No motors. Sailboarding and swimming are permitted.

Directions: From Red Bluff, drive east on Highway 36 to the junction with Highway 89. Continue east on Highway 89/36 past Lake Almanor to Westwood. In Westwood, turn left on County Road A21 and drive 12.5 miles to Silver Lake Road. Turn left on Silver Lake Road/County Road 110 and drive 8.5 miles north to Silver Lake. Continue past Silver Lake a short distance to Caribou Lake.

Contact: Lassen National Forest, Almanor Ranger District, 530/258-2141.

25 CRATER LAKE

Rating: 5

near Susanville in Lassen National Forest

Map 3.3, page 84

Crater Lake Mountain rises just above little Crater Lake, an obscure spot that is set at an elevation of 6,800 feet within Lassen National Forest.

This is a small lake, just 27 acres. A primitive boat ramp and campground is a nice plus. Not only is Crater Lake remote, but the access road is quite rough. A lot of people don't want to tangle with the drive just for the opportunity to fish for some small rainbow trout planted by the Department of Fish and Game.

The lake freezes over when winter sets in, and the water stays cold almost year-round. Very few people swim here, even in late summer after days of hot temperatures have made the surface layer at least tolerable.

Those brave souls who don't mind the bumpy access road to the lake are rewarded with a good side-trip option: take the Forest Service road that leads to the top of Crater Lake Mountain and loops around near the summit. From this vantage point you will have a great lookout to the east across a huge expanse of wildlands.

Access: A dirt boat ramp is located on the lake's east side.

Facilities, fees: A campground with drinking water and vault toilets is available. Supplies can be obtained in Susanville. Access is free. A fee is charged for camping.

Water sports, restrictions: Rowboats, canoes, and kayaks are allowed. No motors. Sailboarding and swimming are permitted.

Directions: From Redding, drive east on Highway 44 to the junction with Highway 89 (near the entrance to Lassen Volcanic National Park). Turn north on Highway 89 and drive to Highway 44. Turn east on Highway 44 (left) and drive to the Bogard Work Center and adjacent rest stop. Turn left at Forest Road 32N08 (signed Crater Lake) and drive one mile to a T intersection. Bear right and continue on Forest Road 32N08 for six miles (including two hairpin left turns) to the campground on the left side of the road.

Contact: Lassen National Forest, Eagle Lake Ranger District, 530/257-4188.

26 WILLOW LAKE

Rating: 4

near Chester in Lassen National Forest

Map 3.3, page 84

This little egg-shaped lake always comes as a surprise. Although located near some of California's top vacation destinations, it is so far off the ol' beaten path that it gets missed by out-of-towners every time.

Willow Lake is located in national forestland just west of Kelly Mountain, only three miles from the southeastern border of Lassen Volcanic National Park at Drakesbad, and 10 miles northwest of giant Lake Almanor. Still, it manages to provide an intimate, quiet atmosphere.

Set at an elevation of approximately 6,500 feet, the lake is tiny, and marshy in some places. It is too small for any boating other than car-top or inflatable craft, and gets very light use. The water is too cold for swimming until midsummer; swimmers who do come when things warm up are treated to a small shoreline clearing (more dirt than sand) where they can sunbathe.

Nearby Drakesbad at Lassen Park provides a great side trip for hikers, with destinations such as Devil's Kitchen and several alpine lakes within an hour's walk.

Access: There is no boat ramp. Car-top boats may be hand launched.

Facilities, fees: Dispersed campsites with vault toilets and drinking water are available. Garbage must be packed out. Supplies can be obtained in Chester. Access and camping are free.

Water sports, restrictions: Car-top boats, canoes, kayaks, and inflatables are permitted. Motors are permitted, but the lake is too small for anything but very small engines or electric motors. Swimming is permitted; a small stretch of shoreline near the campground is available for sunbathing.

Directions: From Red Bluff, turn east on Highway 36 and drive to Chester (at Lake Almanor) and Feather River Drive. Turn left on Feather River Drive and drive .75 mile to County Road 312. Bear left on County Road 312 and drive five miles to the fork with County Road 311 and 312. Bear left on County Road 311 and drive one mile to Forest Service Road 29N14 (a dirt road). Turn right and drive to Willow Lake.

Contact: Lassen National Forest, Almanor Ranger District, 530/258-2141, fax 530/258-5194. For a map, send $6 to U.S. Forest Service, Attn: Map Sales, P.O. Box 587, Camino, CA 95709, 530/647-5390, fax 530/647-5389, website: www.fs.fed.us/r5/forests. Major credit cards accepted.

27 ECHO LAKE

Rating: 5

near Chester in Lassen National Forest

Map 3.3, page 84

Obscure? Hard to reach? Primitive camping? Trout fishing? Not many people around? That is what most people want on a vacation, and that is exactly what Echo Lake provides. The one drawback is its small size, but that's only a problem on extended trips.

This lake is set at an elevation of about 6,500 feet. A highlight is the small, primitive campground that provides seclusion and a very pretty setting. Almost too small for hand launching boats, the lake is better suited for rafts, tubes,

and prams. Swimming conditions are fair once the water warms up by midsummer, but you can expect the bottom to be mushy.

The Caribou Wilderness is located less than a mile to the northwest. With a national forest map to help you find your way, it can be easy to make a short trek into the nearby wilderness and hit a lake loop. Hidden Lakes, Long Lake, Posey Lake, and Beauty Lake are all on the same loop trail.

Access: There is no boat ramp. Car-top boats may be hand launched.

Facilities, fees: A primitive campground, drinking water, and vault toilets are available. Garbage must be packed out. Supplies can be obtained in Chester. Access is free.

Water sports, restrictions: Car-top boats, canoes, kayaks, and inflatables are permitted. Swimming is allowed.

Directions: From Red Bluff, take Highway 36 east to Chester. Continue east on Highway 36 for eight miles to Chester Dump Road. Turn left on Chester Dump Road and drive west a short distance on a connector road, then continue north for 9.5 miles to Echo Lake.

Contact: Lassen National Forest, Almanor Ranger District, 530/258-2141; Sports Nut, Chester, 530/258-3327. For a map, send $6 to U.S. Forest Service, Attn: Map Sales, P.O. Box 587, Camino, CA 95709, 530/647-5390, fax 530/647-5389, website: www.fs.fed.us/r5/forests. Major credit cards accepted.

28 MILL CREEK (LASSEN NATIONAL FOREST)

Rating: 5

near Mineral in Lassen National Forest

Map 3.3, page 84

Mill Creek is a pretty little trout stream running through national forestland, complete with streamside trail. It is the kind of place where you go for a walk in the summer, maybe stopping at a swimming hole on a hot day or casting for trout on a cool evening.

With Lassen National Forest surrounding the lake, which is set at 4,500 feet in elevation, this is a heavily forested, picturesque area. Mill Creek is a popular destination for vacationers staying in the area. The prime time here is from mid-July on through summer; with the snowmelt over, the stream drops and the water warms up.

Highlights here include good hiking and two developed campgrounds. Mill Creek is too small for any rafting or boating. Instead, after parking you hit the trail for access to several swimming holes. Do not think of wandering from the trail; some of the land bordering this stream is privately owned.

Access: No boat ramps are available.

Facilities, fees: Two campgrounds with vault toilets and drinking water are available nearby. Supplies can be obtained in Mineral. Access is free. A fee is charged for camping.

Water sports, restrictions: No boating. Several excellent swimming holes are located along the Mill Creek Trail.

Directions: From Red Bluff, take Highway 36 east and drive 43 miles to the town of Mineral and the junction with Highway 172. Turn right on Highway 172 and drive six miles to the town of Mill Creek and a Forest Service road signed Mill Creek/Hole in the Ground. Turn right and drive three miles to a parking area and trailhead, or continue five miles to the campground access road. Turn left and drive .25 mile to the camp. A hiking trail follows Mill Creek for several miles.

Contact: Lassen National Forest, Almanor Ranger District, 530/258-2141; Mill Creek Resort, 530/595-4449. For a map, send $6 to U.S. Forest Service, Attn: Map Sales, P.O. Box 587, Camino, CA 95709, 530/647-5390, fax 530/647-5389, website: www.fs.fed.us/r5/forests. Major credit cards accepted.

29 DEER CREEK

Rating: 6

near Mineral in Lassen National Forest

Map 3.3, page 84

From its headwaters on downstream, Highway 32 parallels Deer Creek, providing easy stream-side access at three campgrounds, a series of roadside pullouts, and a hiking trail.

Don't think the proximity to Highway 32 means that the drive here is painless. Just the opposite. Highway 32 is not even close to being an actual highway and is very twisty, extremely narrow in spots, and far away for most visitors. That is why we advised accessing the road from the junction with Highway 36 and then driving downhill, the easiest route by far.

Deer Creek, at an elevation of 4,000 feet, is primarily a trout stream, with large numbers of trout stocked here each summer, mainly near the three campgrounds. A trail that is routed right along the stream provides good hiking and takes you to a hidden waterfall. The water, fed from snowmelt, is cold until late in the summer.

The traffic ranges from very light early and late in the season, to medium in early summer, then heavy in midsummer when the trout plants are high, the weather is warm and clear, and the stream flows are perfect. Regardless, Deer Creek makes a good alternative to the oft-crowded scene at nearby Lake Almanor (see next listing).

Access: There is no boat ramp.

Facilities, fees: Campgrounds with vault toilets and drinking water are nearby. Supplies are available in Mineral. Access is free. A fee is charged for camping.

Water sports, restrictions: Several good swimming holes are located along Highway 32, including near Potato Patch, Elam Creek, and Alder Creek Campgrounds.

Directions: From Chico, take Highway 32 northeast for 40 miles. Just after crossing a small red metal bridge (locals call it the "Red Bridge") that crosses Deer Creek, park on the south side of the road where there's a dirt pullout. The trailhead is located just up from the bridge on the north side of the road. This section is good for flyfishing for trout. There are also several good swimming holes.

From Red Bluff, take Highway 36 east for 44 miles to the junction with Highway 89. Continue east on Highway 36/89 to the junction with Highway 32. Turn south on Highway 32 and drive eight miles to the campground on the right side of the road. Trailers are not recommended. Direct access to the creek is available off Highway 32 at pullouts.

Contact: Lassen National Forest, Almanor Ranger District, 530/258-2141. For a map, send $6 to U.S. Forest Service, Attn: Map Sales, P.O. Box 587, Camino, CA 95709, 530/647-5390, fax 530/647-5389, website: www.fs.fed.us/r5/forests. Major credit cards accepted.

30 LAKE ALMANOR

Rating: 10

east of Red Bluff in Lassen National Forest

Map 3.3, page 84

Lake Almanor is a jewel ringed by conifers. It's a big lake, about 13 miles long with 28,000 surface acres, set at an elevation of 4,500 feet. Although Almanor is a reservoir built by PG&E, it looks more like a natural lake because it is kept full most of the year and much of the shoreline is wooded. Big and beautiful, Almanor has sapphire blue water and views of snow-capped Mount Lassen to the northwest.

People have figured out that there are precious few lakes in California where it is possible to build a vacation home, and that Almanor is one of these few. There are also opportunities to stay in a lakeside vacation home or rent a cabin here.

The water is clear, ideal for all kinds of boating and water sports, and a large number of vacationers take advantage of it every summer. Water-skiing, wake boarding, and using personal watercraft are excellent in July and August. The best spots for swimming and sailboarding are located almost exclusively along the east shore, but like most reservoirs, the beaches here are few.

This is one of the best lakes in the state for large rainbow trout, brown trout, and lake-raised salmon. Smallmouth bass also live in these waters, and they come to life at midsummer, right when the cold-water species go into a short lull. In the spring and fall, fishing for trout and salmon is often excellent, not so much for the number of fish you can land, but rather for their size. Natural springs keep the water cold and circulating, and along with the penetrating rays of sunlight, help get the aquatic food chain in motion. The lake is so big that many newcomers are unsure where to try their luck. To get the lowdown, always call Lassen View Resort at 530/596-3437; fishing guides are also available there.

Spring winds and a long winter will always prevent this place from turning into a year-round vacation paradise. Wind? Yow, it can really howl. For instance, in May it can be as calm as a small pond at daybreak; then it starts to blow by 9 A.M., and by 10 A.M., the white-caps start churning and continue for the rest of the day. This occurs in the spring, from April through early June, and while not a daily event, it happens plenty enough to keep owners of small boats especially wary. Winter is long and cold here, often with tremendous amounts of snow. Sometimes the lake even freezes over, an amazing sight on such a large body of water.

Regardless, Almanor is a jewel. It's one of the best recreation lakes in California, and an excellent destination for boaters, campers, and anglers.

Access: Many boat ramps are available at resorts and campgrounds around the lake:
• Big Cove Resort: Two paved ramp, docks, and a full-service marina with water sports equipment are available. Fishing boats, water

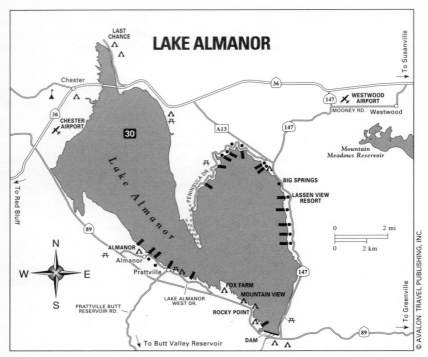

bikes, and pontoon boats are available for rent. For more information call 530/596-3349.

• Wilson's Camp Prattville: A dirt ramp, docks, and limited marina services are available. For more information call 530/259-2464.

• Knotty Pine Resort: A paved ramp, docks, and a full-service marina are available. Fishing boats, ski boats, personal watercraft, kayaks, canoes, pontoon boats, and pedal boats are available for rent. For more information call 530/596-3348, website: www.knottypine.net.

• Lake Almanor Resort: From Red Bluff, take Highway 36 east for 44 miles to the junction with Highway 89. Continue east on Highway 36/89 to Lake Almanor and the next junction with Highway 89 (two miles before reaching Chester). Turn right on Highway 89 and drive six miles to County Road 310. Turn left on County Road 310 and drive one mile to the campground. There is a paved ramp and docks. For more information call 530/596-3337.

• Lake Cove Resort and Marina: A paved ramp and dock are provided. Fishing boats and pontoon boats are available for rent. For more information call 530/284-7697, website: www.lakecove-rv-resort.com.

• Lake Haven Resort: A paved ramp, docks, and limited marina services are available. For more information call 530/596-3249.

• Lassen View Resort: From Red Bluff, take Highway 36 east for 44 miles to the junction with Highway 89. Continue east on Highway 36/89 to Chester and drive through Chester to the junction with County Road A13. Turn right (south) and drive about four miles to the junction with Highway 147. Turn right on Highway 147 and drive .9 mile to the well-signed camp entrance on the right. A three-lane paved ramp and docks are provided. Cabins, fishing boats, and pontoon boats are available for rent. For more information call 530/596-3437.

• Little Norway Resort: There is a paved ramp

and a full-service marina. Fishing boats, ski boats, pontoon boats, and personal watercraft are available for rent. For more information call 530/596-3225, website: www.littlenorway.net.
• Plumas Pines Resort/Major's Outpost: Fishing boats, ski boats, personal watercraft, and pontoon boats are available for rent. For more information call 530/259-2727.
• Northshore Campground: From Red Bluff, take Highway 36 east for 44 miles to the junction with Highway 89. Drive east on Highway 36/89; the camp and boat ramp are two miles past Chester on the right. A paved ramp and dock are available. For more information call 530/258-3376.

Facilities, fees: Several campgrounds, restrooms with flush toilets, drinking water, and in some cases, vault toilets, are available. Lodging, cabins, restaurants, laundry facilities, showers, groceries, and gas are available. Access is free. A fee is charged for boat launching.

Water sports, restrictions: Powerboats, waterskiing, wake boarding, personal watercraft, sailing, sailboarding, and swimming are permitted. Swimming beaches are located at Canyon Dam Picnic Area, Eastshore Picnic Area, and Camp Conery Group Camp on the lake's southeast end. Sailboarding is best at these areas.

Directions: See directions to Access points, above, or call individual resorts listed under Access.

Contact: Lassen National Forest, Almanor Ranger District, 530/258-2141; PG&E Land Projects, 916/386-5164, website: www.pge.com/recreation.

31 PHILBROOK RESERVOIR

Rating: 6

near Paradise in Lassen National Forest

Map 3.3, page 84

Maybe they got the name wrong. Paradise Lake is located very near to the southwest. After getting a glimpse of the two lakes, you might think Philbrook Reservoir deserves to have the name Paradise more than the original does.

That is because after traversing a very rough

access road, you discover a pretty alpine lake at elevation 5,000 feet, with forest campsites, swimming beaches, and a picnic area. All in all, it's the ideal spot for car-top boats and inflatables, especially canoes and rafts.

Getting here is just difficult enough to keep most folks away. Or many people just plain don't know the place exists. The road is jarring at times, very rough on vehicles not built to handle unpaved roads.

Once here, the hardy few tend to set up camp and then fish for trout or plunk their canoe or raft in and paddle around, submersing themselves in the rapture of this pretty alpine setting.

Access: A car-top boat ramp is provided.

Facilities, fees: A campground, vault toilets, drinking water, and a picnic area are available. Access is free. A fee is charged for camping.

Water sports, restrictions: Car-top boats are permitted. Swimming and sailboarding are allowed; the best spots are at the campground or the picnic area.

Directions: At Orland on I-5, take the Highway 32/Chico exit and drive to Chico and the junction with Highway 99. Turn south on Highway 99 and drive to Skyway Road/Paradise (in south Chico). Turn east on Skyway Road, drive through Paradise, and continue for 27 miles to Humbug Summit Road. Turn right and drive two miles to Philbrook Road. Turn right and drive 3.1 miles to the campground entrance road. Turn right and drive .5 mile to the campground.

Contact: PG&E Land Projects, 916/386-5164, website: www.pge.com/recreation; Lassen National Forest, Almanor Ranger District, 530/258-2141.

32 BUTT VALLEY RESERVOIR

Rating: 6

near Chester

Map 3.3, page 84

While the official name of this place is Butt Valley Reservoir, nobody calls it that. The reservoir goes by Butt Lake, and it is a peculiar place, despite having lakeside campgrounds and the occasional giant rainbow trout. What is so peculiar is that it has the potential for greatness but usually falls just a bit short.

A PG&E-run lake that receives its water via a tunnel coming from nearby Lake Almanor, Butt Lake is set at an elevation of 4,100 feet and is five miles long. In water plumbing terminology, this is the afterbay for Almanor. When full, Butt Lake is very pretty, with campsites set within view of the water and a boat ramp for launching small trailered boats, mainly used by people fishing for trout. When the powerhouse runs at the head of the lake, pond smelt from Lake Almanor get poured right into the water, which can inspire every big resident trout to go on a feeding frenzy.

In the spring and early summer, a predictable wind plows right down the Feather River Canyon, making conditions good for expert sailboarders. The water, which can be cold, warms up enough by summer for short swims.

As a collective vision this seems just right, eh? Unfortunately, it rarely lives up to the expectations.

The biggest problem is that the lake is often quite low, with lots of stumps on the bare lake bed. Even though there is no speed limit, water-skiing is not permitted because of the underwater hazards, and drivers of fast boats who stray from the channel run the risk of hitting one of those stumps. Another minus is that the trout have grown so fat from feeding on the pond smelt pumped in from Almanor that they usually bite only when the powerhouse is running, an unpredictable event. Also, other than the boat ramp and the campgrounds, the place lacks facilities and a marina.

Hence, what you have here is a lake that's got tons of potential. Curiosity about Butt Lake causes many vacationers from nearby Almanor to at least swing by to take a look-see at the possibilities.

Access: A paved boat ramp is located near Cool Springs Campground on the east shore of the lake.

Facilities, fees: Two campgrounds, vault toilets, drinking water, and a picnic area are provided on the eastern shoreline. Supplies can be obtained in Chester. Access is free. A fee is charged for camping.

Water sports, restrictions: Boats with motors, canoes, kayaks, inflatables, sailing, and sailboarding are permitted. No water-skiing, wake boarding, or personal watercraft are allowed. Swimming areas are available near the campgrounds and picnic area.

Directions: From Red Bluff, take Highway 36 east for 44 miles to the junction with Highway 89. Continue east on Highway 36/89 to Lake Almanor and the next junction with Highway 89 (two miles before reaching Chester). Turn right on Highway 89 and drive about seven miles to Butt Valley Road. Turn right on Butt Valley Road and drive 5.7 miles to the campground and boat ramp on the right.

Contact: PG&E Land Projects, 916/386-5164, website: www.pge.com/recreation; Lassen National Forest, Almanor Ranger District, 530/258-2141.

33 NORTH FORK FEATHER RIVER

Rating: 6

south of Belden Forebay in Plumas National Forest

Map 3.3, page 84

The highlight at the North Fork Feather is a series of campgrounds and an access road that is routed up to Belden Forebay. The campgrounds have become very popular for their pretty settings along the stream, and the road that parallels the river provides easy access to swimming holes and trout fishing spots.

When water flows are right, this is a great stream for kayaking, particularly in inflatable kayaks. The problem is that when flows are wrong, it is a dud, often a bony proposition with a lot of butt-dragging. Starting in 2003, a program was put in place to provide visitors with water flow information to maximize water sports. Call 530/283-0555 for updates.

Early in the year, the water is often swift and cold from snowmelt, and only an otter would dare swim here. By summer the flows are greatly reduced, temperatures have warmed considerably, and a few swimming holes near the campgrounds are usually passable for taking a dunk.

Most of the people you see around here are fishing for trout. Stocks are made at each of the campgrounds, as well as upstream at Belden.
Access: There is no boat ramp.
Facilities, fees: Campgrounds, restrooms with flush toilets, drinking water, and vault toilets are available. Three campgrounds are set on the river, with access off Caribou Road. Others are provided off Highway 70. Access is free. A fee is charged for camping.
Water sports, restrictions: Rafting and kayaking are permitted when flows are safe; call ranger district for status at 530/283-0555. The best swimming spots are at Queen Lily, North Fork, and Gansner Bar Campgrounds, all located on Caribou Road.
Directions: To Gansner Bar camp and access: From Oroville, drive north on Highway 70 to Caribou Road (two miles past Belden). Turn left on Caribou Road and drive a short distance to the campground on the left side of the road.
Contact: Plumas National Forest, Mount Hough Ranger District, 530/283-0555; Sportsmen's Den, Quincy, 530/283-2733.

34 EAGLE LAKE

Rating: 9

near Susanville in Lassen National Forest

Map 3.4, page 85

How does a huge lake with massive trout, hot summer temperatures, and lakeside campsites sound to you? Perfect? To some, it is. To others, well . . . (and we'll get to that).

Eagle Lake is set at 5,100 feet in elevation on the edge of high desert country in northeastern California (hence all the wind, which comes roaring across the plateau). The lake is huge, 27,000 acres with 100 miles of shoreline, yet relatively shallow; it's depth of just 10 to 15 feet in many areas helps the wind quickly whip the water to a froth.

Excellent campgrounds, large trout, and the proximity to Susanville guarantee heavy use all summer. Most visitors tend to congregate around the marina, where there are a beach, Forest Service campgrounds, and picnic areas. As a recreational facility it makes an ideal vacation destination.

Sooner or later, the trout become the most compelling attraction. The strain of Eagle Lake trout averages 18 to 22 inches; that's right, and they'll take a nightcrawler under a bobber. Fishing is best late in the year just outside the tules at the north end of the lake.

If you hit the lake when it is calm, you might want to move here—it is that pretty. But don't pack your bags quite yet. You see, the wind can really howl at Eagle Lake in the spring and early summer, which quickly results in waves and whitecaps that make boating unpleasant at the least, very dangerous at the worst.

Every Memorial Day weekend, the lake opens with great excitement and hope, and then windy and often foul weather usually sets in. If you're here in the early summer, the solution is to get out on the lake very early—an hour before dawn—and expect the wind to kick up by 10 to 11 A.M. I've had openers here where I'd caught my limit before the sun peeked out over the eastern horizon. Either that or schedule your visit for early fall when conditions are much calmer.

Because of the wind, this is an excellent place for sailboarding and sailing. Just be wary. When the whitecaps are too big to deal with and surface conditions become choppy, cold, and extremely uncomfortable, get off the water. If you hit it during moderate winds, however, you will think you've finally found nirvana.

The lake is so big that there is plenty of room for powerboaters and skiers. Cold water means that only the hardy can stay out for long, however. When the chips are down, you will usually only find a good number of hard-core fishermen in pursuit of their dream trout.

Access: In addition to the ramps at Aspen Grove Campground and Spaulding (see Directions), there are two other boat ramps:

• Eagle Lake Marina: Head north on Eagle Lake Road and follow the signs to the marina, which has a three-lane paved boat ramp.

• Stones Landing: Head north on Eagle Lake Road, past the signs for the marina, to Stones Landing on the north end of the lake. There is a paved ramp.

Facilities, fees: Lodging, cabin rentals, and campgrounds with drinking water and flush toilets are available. Eagle Lake Marina has fishing boat rentals, convenience store, coin showers, and coin laundry. There are fees for launching, docking, and camping.

Water sports, restrictions: Powerboating, water-skiing, wake boarding, and riding personal watercraft are permitted. Sailing, sailboarding, and swimming are allowed. Gallatin Beach, a developed area near the marina, offers a large, sandy swimming area roped off with buoys for protection.

Directions: To Aspen Grove Campground and boat ramp: From Red Bluff, drive east on Highway 36 toward Susanville. Three miles before Susanville, turn left on Eagle Lake Road/County Road A1 and drive 15.5 miles to County Road 231. Turn right on County Road 231 and drive two miles to the campground on the left side of the road.

To west shore, Spaulding boat ramp: From Red Bluff, drive east on Highway 36 toward Susanville. Just before reaching Susanville, turn left on County Road A1 and drive (staying left at the junction with County Road 231) to the lake's west shore at Spaulding Tract and County Road 518. Turn right on County Road 518

and drive through a small neighborhood to Strand Way (the lake frontage road). Turn right on Strand Way and drive about eight blocks (the boat ramp is on the left) to Palmetto Way and the entrance to the store and the RV park entrance at 687-125 Palmetto Way. Register at the store.

Contact: Lassen National Forest, Eagle Lake Ranger District, 530/257-4188, website: www .ca.blm.gov/eaglelake; Eagle Lake Marina, 530/825-3454; Mariner's Resort, Stones Landing, 530/825-3333; Spaulding Tract General Store, 916/825-2191.

35 ROUND VALLEY RESERVOIR

Rating: 4

near Greenville in Plumas National Forest

Map 3.4, page 85

Considering that Round Valley Reservoir is set at an elevation of 4,500 feet, you might wonder why it's got all those weeds and lily pads. Well, the answer is that this is one of the few warm-water lakes in California's mountain country. If you've never visited here before, it's bound to pleasantly surprise you.

The area surrounding the lake is quite pretty, with trails for hiking and horseback riding nearby.

But there are rules restricting most boating and water sport opportunities. Because the lake is used as a domestic water supply. No swimming or water contact is permitted, and no motors over 7.5 horsepower are allowed. What you end up with is a rare mountain lake where anglers can try for bass and catfish (not trout) without having to worry about fast boats or swimmers.

Some may remember a small resort here that once rented boats and provided a small campground. The operation is gone.

Access: A gravel boat ramp is located on the east side of the lake.

Facilities, fees: A picnic area and vault toilets

are available. No drinking water. Supplies can be obtained in Greenville. Access is free.

Water sports, restrictions: Boats with small motors, canoes, kayaks, and inflatables are permitted. No motors larger than 7.5 horsepower are allowed. No swimming or water-contact sports.

Directions: From Red Bluff, take Highway 36 east and drive 44 miles to the junction with Highway 89. Continue east on Highway 36/89 to Lake Almanor and the next junction with Highway 89 (two miles before reaching Chester). Turn right on Highway 89 and drive about 25 miles to the town of Greenville and Greenville Road. Turn right (south) on Greenville Road and drive three miles to the signed turnoff for Round Valley Reservoir. Turn left and continue to the lake.

Contact: Plumas National Forest, Mount Hough Ranger District, 530/283-0555; Sportsmen's Den, 530/283-2733.

36 TAYLOR LAKE

Rating: 4

near Taylorsville in Plumas National Forest

Map 3.4, page 85

Very few boaters pay attention to this small and obscure mountain lake located at an elevation of 5,000 feet. It is too small for most boats, but large enough for a float tube or a raft; visitors occasionally use one of those little float boats to fish for brook trout.

The water is clear and very cold in early summer, but quite tolerable by midsummer. Although there are no beaches, there are swimming access spots all around the lakeshore. The surrounding region of Plumas National Forest is well forested, with a network of jeep roads in the area just waiting to be explored.

This is a primitive spot. Those with SUVs and a raft or canoe might claim it and stake it out for their own.

Access: There is no boat ramp. Small car-top boats may be hand launched.

Facilities, fees: A few primitive campsites are available. No drinking water or vault toilets. Garbage must be packed out. Supplies can be obtained in Taylorsville. Access is free.

Water sports, restrictions: Rowboats, canoes, kayaks, inflatables, and swimming is permitted. The lake is too small for sailboarding and other water sports.

Directions: From Oroville, drive east on Highway 70 to the junction with Highway 89. Turn left on Highway 89 and drive seven miles to County Road 22. Turn right and drive five miles east to Taylorsville and County Road 214. Turn north on County Road 214 and drive about two miles to County Road 214. Turn right on Forest Service Road 27N10 and drive about 10 miles east (stay to the left). Turn left on Forest Service Road 27N57 and travel one mile to the lake.

Contact: Plumas National Forest, Mount Hough Ranger District, 530/283-0555; Sportsmen's Den, 530/283-2733. For a map, send $6 to U.S. Forest Service, Attn: Map Sales, P.O. Box 587, Camino, CA 95709, 530/647-5390, fax 530/647-5389, website: www.fs.fed.us/r5/forests. Major credit cards accepted.

37 ANTELOPE LAKE

Rating: 8

near Taylorsville in Plumas National Forest

Map 3.4, page 85

Mountain lake circled by conifers with campsites, good boating, and trout fishing.

Some people might want to put an advertisement in the newspaper to find such a place, but that isn't necessary for in-the-know visitors to northern Plumas County. They'll direct you to Antelope Lake, which is ringed by forestland, provides campgrounds at each end of the lake, and has a boat ramp conveniently located just a few miles from each camp.

Antelope Lake is just about perfect for a boating/camping vacation. Seclusion is practically guaranteed—the lake is located approximately

100 miles from Oroville by our estimate—and the road in is accessible to trailered boats. Although not huge, Antelope Lake is big enough, with 15 miles of shoreline and plenty of little islands, coves, and peninsulas to create an intimate atmosphere.

The lake is set at 5,000 feet elevation and covers 930 surface acres. Even though the shoreline is heavily forested, there are good swimming areas adjacent to the campgrounds. Sailboarders will find the prime spots for their sport on the west side near the boat ramp and at Long Point Campground (both offer more wide-open access).

What makes Antelope Lake special is that the drive here is too daunting for most visitors. If it were any closer to civilization, the place would be loaded with vacationers every day throughout summer. Still, it is by no means unknown. On summer weekends it can even get crowded. Hey, it makes sense. After all, a description of this lake reads like an advertisement for a good time.

Access: A two-lane paved ramp is available on the north shore.

Facilities, fees: Campgrounds, vault toilets, and drinking water are available. A convenience store and RV dump station are nearby. Supplies can be obtained in Taylorsville. Access is free.

Water sports, restrictions: Powerboating, waterskiing, wake boarding, personal watercraft, sailing, sailboarding, and swimming are permitted. Swimming access is best near the campgrounds.

Directions: To Long Point Campground from Red Bluff, drive east on Highway 36 to Susanville and U.S. 395. Go south on U.S. 395 and drive about 10 miles (one mile past Janesville) to County Road 208. Turn right on County Road 208 (signed Antelope Lake) and drive about 15 miles to a Y (one mile before Antelope Lake). Turn right at the Y and drive one mile to the campground entrance on the left side of the road. The boat ramp is at Lost Cove, a three-mile drive on Indian Creek Road on the lake north shore.

Contact: Plumas National Forest, Mount Hough Ranger District, 530/283-2050.

FOGHORN OUTDOORS®

COURTESY OF U.S. ARMY CORPS OF ENGINEERS

Chapter 4

Mendocino and Wine Country

Chapter 4—Mendocino and Wine Country

For many people, this region offers the best possible combination of geography, weather, and outdoor activities around. It offers year-round recreation in a wide spectrum of settings. That alone sets it apart.

Recreation lakes include major destinations such as Clear Lake, Lake Berryessa, and Lake Sonoma. If the shoe fits—and for many, it does—you can have a great time boating, water-skiing, fishing, and camping. These are big lakes with a myriad of possibilities. And even though they're crowded on summer weekends, I've often had them virtually to myself on weekday mornings.

Other recreation lakes in this region include Lake Pillsbury, East Park Reservoir, Indian Valley Reservoir, Lake Mendocino, and Spring Lake.

The coast features a series of romantic hideaways and excellent adventuring and hiking. The Fort Bragg area alone has three state parks, all with outstanding recreation, including several easy hikes, many amid redwoods and along pretty streams.

Navarro Redwoods provides a destination for an easy do-it-yourself canoe or kayak trip on the lower Navarro River. A rare coastal lake is available at MacKerricher State Park near Fort Bragg, a good spot for youngsters.

Inland, Cache Creek near Rumsey provides the closest white-water rafting experience to the Bay Area.

The region is more famous for other attractions, of course. The Mendocino coast is dramatic and remote, with several stellar state parks for hiking, while Sonoma Valley, in the heart of wine country, produces some of the most popular wines in the world. For many, this area is where people go for romance, fine cuisine, great wine, mineral springs, and anything else that comes to mind spur-of-the-moment. Such is a vacation in the Napa-Sonoma wine country, or the beautiful Sonoma and Mendocino coast.

What a region: Geography that spans from a rocky coast to a foothill landscape spliced with streams feeding major lakes, weather that allows year-round recreation, and a full scope of outdoor activities that could please nearly anybody.

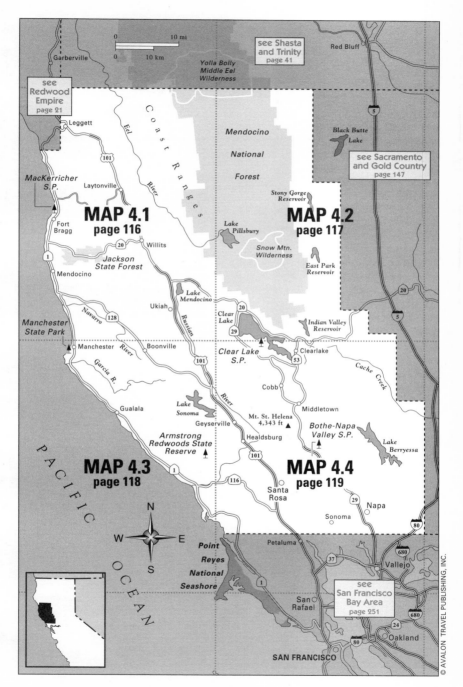

© AVALON TRAVEL PUBLISHING, INC.

Map 4.1

Sites 1–8
Pages 120–125

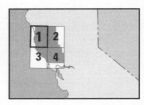

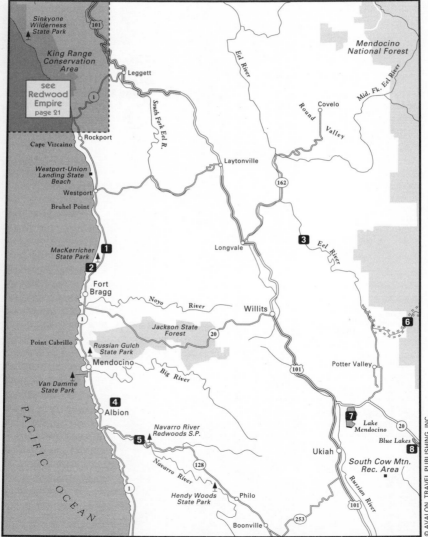

Sinkyone Wilderness State Park

King Range Conservation Area

see Redwood Empire page 21

Leggett

Eel River

Mendocino National Forest

Mid. Fk. Eel River

Round Valley

Covelo

Rockport

Cape Vizcaino

South Fork Eel R.

Laytonville

Westport-Union Landing State Beach

Westport

Bruhel Point

MacKerricher State Park

1

2

Fort Bragg

Noyo River

Longvale

3 Eel River

Willits

Jackson State Forest

20

6

Point Cabrillo

Russian Gulch State Park

Mendocino

Big River

101

Potter Valley

Van Damme State Park

4 Albion

Navarro River Redwoods S.P.

5

Lake Mendocino

7

20

Blue Lakes

8

Ukiah

South Cow Mtn. Rec. Area

Navarro River

128

Russian River

Hendy Woods State Park

Philo

Boonville

253

101

PACIFIC OCEAN

© AVALON TRAVEL PUBLISHING, INC.

Map 4.2

Sites 9–18
Pages 126–135

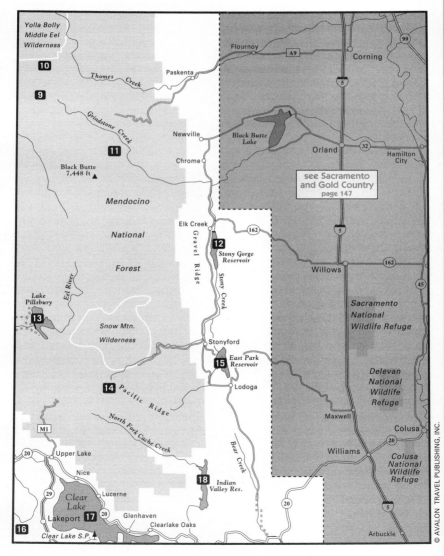

Yolla Bolly Middle Eel Wilderness

10

9

Thomes Creek

Grindstone Creek

Paskenta

Flournoy

A9

Corning

99

5

Newville

Black Butte Lake

Orland

32

Hamilton City

11

Chrome

Black Butte 7,448 ft ▲

Mendocino

National

Forest

see Sacramento and Gold Country page 147

Elk Creek

162

12

Stony Gorge Reservoir

Gravel Ridge

Stony Creek

Willows

162

5

45

Ed River

Lake Pillsbury

13

Snow Mtn. Wilderness

Sacramento National Wildlife Refuge

Stonyford

15

East Park Reservoir

Delevan National Wildlife Refuge

14

Pacific Ridge

Lodoga

North Fork Cache Creek

Bear Creek

Maxwell

Colusa

20

M1

20

Upper Lake

Nice

29

Lucerne

Clear Lake

Lakeport

16

17

20

Glenhaven

Clearlake Oaks

Clear Lake S.P. ▲

18

Indian Valley Res.

20

Williams

Colusa National Wildlife Refuge

5

Arbuckle

© AVALON TRAVEL PUBLISHING, INC.

Map 4.3

Sites 19–20
Pages 135–137

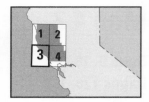

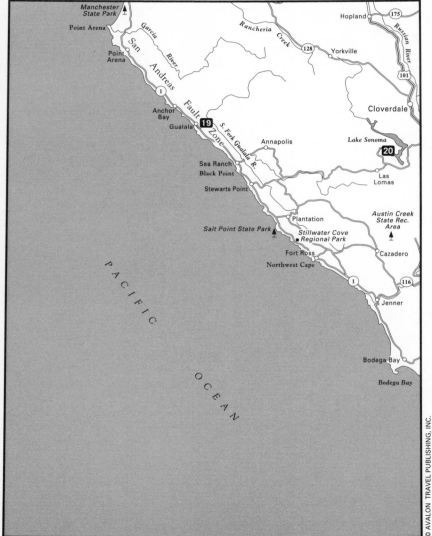

© AVALON TRAVEL PUBLISHING, INC.

Map 4.4

Sites 21–27
Pages 137–143

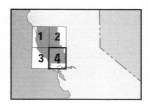

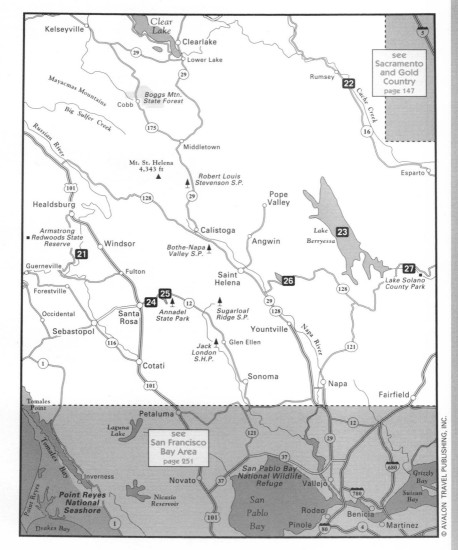

1 TEN MILE RIVER

Rating: 3

north of MacKerricher State Park

Map 4.1, page 116

Little Ten Mile River starts in the mountains just north of Bucha Ridge and tumbles some 20 miles on its short journey to the Pacific Ocean. In the winter, when fierce coastal squalls pound the ridge, water rushes down the canyon, forming this stream.

Only a tiny stretch of the river, from the mouth and on upstream for a few miles, is appropriate for canoeing or kayaking and swimming. The river narrows here and runs slowly most of the year, creating conditions that are suitable only for canoes and kayaks. Easy access is the big plus. Farther upstream the Ten Mile cuts through private property, and the riverbanks are smothered by thick brush.

Most people playing in the lower river are doing so as a side trip from another destination, usually MacKerricher State Park. MacKerricher is a great park, boasting a beautiful beach, outstanding walks, lookout for viewing harbor seals, small freshwater lake (Cleone Lake—see next listing) with trout fishing, and excellent campgrounds, including great walk-in campsites. Day-use access is free at MacKerricher, which is an extreme rarity for a state park.

Access: No boat ramp is available. There is no standard put-in, but boaters with small craft (canoes or kayaks) may park at the bridge and put in at the beach at the river's mouth.

Facilities, fees: Campgrounds are provided at MacKerricher State Park. Supplies can be obtained in Fort Bragg. Access is free. Rafting permits are not required.

Water sports, restrictions: Kayaks, canoes, inflatables, and swimming are permitted. Swimming is best at the beach or at the lagoon inside the river's mouth.

Directions: From Fort Bragg, take Highway 1 north for three miles to MacKerricher State Park (on the left). Ten Mile River is located at the park's north end, and is accessible by driving east on Camp 1 Ten Mile Road or south on Camp 2 Ten Mile Road.

Contact: MacKerricher State Park, 707/964-9112; Noyo Pacific Outfitters, 707/961-0559, website: www.noyopacific.com.

2 CLEONE LAKE

Rating: 6

north of Fort Bragg in MacKerricher State Park

Map 4.1, page 116

Cleone Lake is one of the few lakes in the state that is actually located west of Highway 1, nestled in a little pocket between the highway and Laguna Point. Along with the surrounding MacKerricher State Park, the lake makes an ideal destination for a weekend vacation.

Although small, the lake is gorgeous, bordered by tules on one side and forest on another, and opening to the coast on the west (the ocean is about 100 yards away). A parking area and restroom are available right next to the lake. This is where visitors can hand launch their car-top boats; canoes, rafts, prams, and the like are recommended. From the shoreline, anglers fish for trout, which are stocked by the Department of Fish and Game.

The grassy shoreline on the northwest side makes getting in and out of the water a snap, but few people swim here. The water is too cold most of the year because summers are foggy and the lake never gets a chance to heat up.

Cleone Lake holds more appeal for hikers, offering a great short trail around its circumference, much of it on a raised wooden walkway that passes in some spots like a tunnel through the lush greenery. Other great hikes at MacKerricher include one that leads to a harbor seal viewing area and tidepools. Camping is also excellent here, especially at the walk-in campsites.

Access: There is no boat ramp, but car-top boats may be hand launched.

Facilities, fees: A campground with drinking water, flush toilets, coin-operated showers, and RV dump station are available. Supplies can be obtained in Fort Bragg. Day use is free. There is a fee for camping.

Water sports, restrictions: Rowboats, canoes, kayaks, prams, and inflatables are allowed. No motors. Swimming is permitted.

Directions: From Fort Bragg, take Highway 1 north for three miles to MacKerricher State Park (on the left). Turn left and drive .5 mile to the lake.

Contact: MacKerricher State Park, 707/964-9112; Noyo Pacific Outfitters, 707/961-0559.

❸ EEL RIVER (MIDDLE FORK)

Rating: 8

Longvale to Alderpoint

Map 4.1, page 116

A handful of rafters and campers are going to cringe when they read this. They are going to be filled with worry that all will know a stellar run that was once secret. But fear not, because this place is too remote. It requires skills in wilderness camping and intermediate boating, and most people just don't have the time, equipment, and talent to make the trip.

Those that do, get what they deserve—a 45-mile run from Dos Rios to Alderpoint. The run has everything going for it: seclusion (there are practically no access roads along the route), beauty (set in a gorgeous canyon that's forested on both sides), great camping (at several good beaches on the banks), and a stretch of water just challenging enough to keep things interesting.

With a Class II-III rating, the run is doable in an inflatable kayak as well as rafts and hardshell kayaks. Canoeists must be skilled and experienced, as there are many trick eddies that can turn and flip a canoe. In any case, make sure that all your gear is waterproof and

strapped in tight—you'll most likely need your warm, dry clothes at the end of the day.

Unpredictable water flows and weather are the biggest problems on the Middle Fork Eel. For the most part, the best time to run is in March, although cold temperatures (for the Humboldt coast) can sap the energy from some boaters, particularly if you get wet weather on your trip. By April this run is largely a goner, and by May and June the flows become more like a dribble, rendering the river unrunnable. If you try to make the trip before March, downpours can be a problem; it can rain, rain, and keep on raining to the point that you might consider boarding an ark instead of an inflatable.

The Eel River is subject to emergency fishing closures if flows are below the prescribed levels needed to protect migrating salmon and steelhead. For a recorded message detailing the status of coastal streams, phone the Department of Fish and Game, 707/442-4502. Also note that the Main Stem Eel is subject to special regulations, which may be changed on a yearly basis.

Access: There is no boat ramp. The put-in is at the small town of Dos Rios. From the south: Take U.S. 101 to Laytonville and Laytonville-Dos Rios Road. Turn east and drive 15 miles to Dos Rios (the road is narrow and curvy). From the north: Take U.S. 101 to Longvale and Highway 162. Turn east and drive to Dos Rios. Put in below the Eel River Bridge. Take out 45 miles downstream at Alderpoint.

Facilities, fees: Several campgrounds with drinking water, restrooms, flush toilets, and RV dump stations are available. State parks charge day-use fees. There is a fee for camping. River access is free. Rafting permits are not required.

Water sports, restrictions: A few swimming holes are located off Highway 162, but they can be difficult to access. Several sandbars north of Dos Rios provide opportunities for sunbathing and swimming. They are accessible only by raft or boat.

Directions: To Main Eel: From Eureka, drive

south on U.S. 101. The river largely parallels the highway, and access is available off almost every spur road, as well as through several small towns along the river, including Fortuna, Rio Dell, Shively, and Holmes.

To South Fork Eel: U.S. 101 parallels much of the South Fork Eel, starting in Leggett (84 miles south of Eureka) and running downstream (north) past Benbow, Garberville, Miranda, and Myers Flat on to its confluence with the main stem of the Eel.

Contact: Bureau of Land Management, Arcata Field Office, 707/825-2300. For guided river trips: Aurora River Adventures, 707/677-3494 or 800/562-8475, website: www.rafting4fun.com; Redwoods and Rivers, 530/629-4947 or 800/429-0090, website: www.redwoods-rivers.com; Rubicon Whitewater Adventures, 707/887-2452, website: www.rubiconadventures.com; Tributary Whitewater Tours, 530/346-6812 or 800/672-3846, website: www.whitewatertours.com.

4 ALBION RIVER

Rating: 6

south of Mendocino

Map 4.1, page 116

Many people who trailer their boats bypass this area. They do not realize that there is a boat ramp. Well, there is. If you are touring along the coast, a stop here can add the missing piece to your vacation puzzle.

The area in the vicinity of Schooner's Landing is well protected, making it a good launch site for trailered boats. With campgrounds on grassy sites and full hookups available for RVs, this is an ideal base camp for a multiday trip.

A great plus is the short cruise to the fishing grounds. Most boaters head around Albion Head to the north, then make a left turn, and cruise around Salmon Point to the south. There are good chances you'll catch rockfish here, and salmon often school in this area in midsummer.

If you do not wish to venture to the ocean, another option is to canoe in the lower river. It is more like a lagoon, with the tidal forces extending about three miles upstream, providing a great little day paddle.

Because this is a coastal environment, temperatures stay in the 50s throughout the year. It is too cold for water sports unless you don a wet suit. However, this stretch of the Mendocino coast is exceptional for snorkeling and abalone diving. There are dozens of secluded spots along the coast that have giant rocks set in sheltered tidal lagoons, perfect grounds for snorkeling.

The ocean is within walking distance of Schooner's Landing, which has a good beach for beachcombing. Wear heavy or layered clothing because the weather is typically foggy or windy.

Access: A paved boat ramp is located at Schooner's Landing.

Facilities, fees: A campground, restrooms with flush toilets and coin showers, and drinking water is available. Canoe and kayak rentals, boat ramp, and dock are available at Schooner's Landing. Supplies are available nearby. Access is free. Fees are charged for boat launching and camping. Access is free. No rafting permits are necessary. Canoeists may put in at the boat ramp and paddle upstream.

Water sports, restrictions: The water is too cold for swimming and other water sports.

Directions: From Mendocino, drive south on Highway 1 for 5.5 miles to the town of Albion and Albion River Road (just before the bridge, north side of river). Turn left on Albion River Road and drive .25 mile to the bottom of the hill, take another left, and drive to the harbor. A boat ramp is available at Schooner's Landing, just north of the Albion Bridge.

Contact: Schooner's Landing, 707/937-5707; Noyo Pacific Outfitters, 707/961-0559, website: www.noyopacific.com; Noyo Harbor District, 707/964-4719; general information website: www.mendocinocoast.com.

5 NAVARRO RIVER

Rating: 6

south of Mendocino

Map 4.1, page 116

Highway 128 follows the river all the way to the ocean, providing visitors easy access and a good look at conditions.

In the spring and summer months, this river gets very heavy use. It is excellent for swimming in the summer, when the water heats up a little and the rafters have departed for the season. Many pullouts along Highway 128 offer access to short trails routed to the river, with dozens of great picnic spots along the way.

While the river is too narrow and brushy for large rafts, it is great for beginners in canoes, inflatable kayaks, and hard-shell kayaks. Class I+ all the way, you'll have a relatively easy paddle no matter what stretch of water you choose.

One favorite stretch starts at Hendy Woods State Park, from whence it takes four hours to get downstream to Paul Dimmick State Park and another two to reach the mouth of the river. Time it so you hit an outgoing tide on the lower river and you'll have an easy ride all the way. The route is very pretty, graced with a variety of riparian vegetation throughout; some stretches feature redwood forest.

Access: There is no boat ramp. Canoeists and kayakers can put in at the junction of Highway 128 and Mountain View Road in Boonville, which is about eight miles east of Hendy Woods State Park on Highway 128. You can boat all the way to the mouth of the river, but standard take-outs are located at Hendy Woods State Park and Paul Dimmick State Park.

Facilities, fees: Campgrounds, restrooms with flush toilets, and drinking water are available. There is a fee for day use at state parks. A fee is charged for camping. Rafting permits are not required.

Water sports, restrictions: Several good swimming spots are located along Highway 128; one of the best is at at Iron Bridge, located at mile marker 3.66, with a sandy beach and deep swimming hole.

Directions: To Hendy Woods: From Cloverdale on U.S. 101, turn northwest on Highway 128 and drive about 35 miles to Philo Greenwood Road. Turn left on Philo Greenwood Road and drive .5 mile to the park entrance.

To Navarro Redwoods: From Cloverdale on U.S. 101, drive north for two miles to Highway 128. Turn west on Highway 128 and drive 49 miles. Look for the signed campground entrance on the left side of the road. The highway parallels the lower river.

Contact: Hendy Woods State Park, 707/895-3141; Mendocino District, 707/937-5804; Fort Bragg-Mendocino Coast Chamber of Commerce, 707/961-6300.

6 EEL RIVER (PILLSBURY RUN)

Rating: 9

Scott Dam to Van Arsdale Reservoir

Map 4.1, page 116

Of all the rafting runs on the main stem Eel River, the Pillsbury Run is the most popular. One reason might be that the area is so close to the campgrounds at Lake Pillsbury, a great bonus.

The nine-mile run to the final take-out above Van Arsdale Reservoir makes a doable day trip. You can shorten the trip by using one of several other take-outs available upstream.

With a Class III+ rating, the run has a few technical rapids and is an excellent choice for those whose skills are at the intermediate level. Along the way, rafters are treated to beautiful scenery. The river is bordered for the most part by dense forest, and the setting makes you feel far removed from civilization.

When it comes to rafting, the Eel River is hardly a star attraction. But of all the available runs, this stretch is the best.

Access: There is no boat ramp. The put-in is just below Scott Dam, southwest of Lake Pillsbury off Potter Valley Road (M-8/Eel River

Road). Take out at your choice of several points above Van Arsdale Reservoir, located approximately 15 miles north of Highway 20 off Potter Valley Road.

Facilities, fees: Campgrounds, lodging, restrooms, a resort, and facilities are available at Lake Pillsbury. A fee is charged for camping. Access is free. Rafting permits are not required.

Water sports, restrictions: Rafting and kayaking are permitted. Swimming is possible, but the river can be difficult to access. When driving on Potter Valley Road, look for spots where you can turn off and park.

Directions: To Fuller Grove: From Ukiah on U.S. 101, drive north to the junction with Highway 20. Turn east (right) on Highway 20 and drive five miles to East Potter Valley Road (M-8/Eel River Road). Turn northwest on East Potter Valley Road toward Lake Pillsbury and drive 5.9 miles to the town of Potter Valley. Continue on East Potter Valley Road to Eel River Road. Turn right and drive 15 miles to the Eel River Information Kiosk at Lake Pillsbury. Continue for 2.2 miles to the campground access road. Turn right and drive .25 mile to the campground. Or continue to Scott Dam. Limited access is available along Potter Valley Road and below the Scott Dam.

Contact: Mendocino National Forest, Upper Lake Ranger District, 707/275-2361. For guided rafting trips contact Aurora River Adventures, 530/629-3843 or 800/562-8475, website: www.rafting4fun.com.

⑦ LAKE MENDOCINO

Rating: 7

near Ukiah

Map 4.1, page 116

Quite a transformation has occurred at Lake Mendocino. At one time this was a quiet place, with little boating traffic and few campers, lost in the shadow of Clear Lake to the east. Apparently more and more boaters are becoming enamored with it each year, and now the campgrounds sometimes fill up, the lake is abuzz with ski boats, and the swimming beach is sprinkled with lots of happy folks.

The lake is set at 750 feet in elevation in the foothill country east of Ukiah, covers 1,750 acres, and has 15 miles of shoreline. It is a major destination point for boaters and campers, especially families who appreciate the warm, clear water, and the easy driving access (compared to Clear Lake). One bonus is an excellent swimming beach set adjacent to restrooms.

Another bonus is that there are excellent opportunities to sailboard, especially in May and June, when the weather is warm, yet the wind is coming out of the northwest—the perfect combination. Once school is out in June, water-skiing activity picks up, especially on weekends, and sailboarders have to be on a constant lookout.

In 2003, a marina that once rented all styles of boats closed shop for good.

Access: There are two boat ramps.

Facilities, fees: Campgrounds, restrooms with flush toilets, vault toilets, and drinking water are available. Three boat-in campgrounds are located on the east side of the lake. Supplies are available in Ukiah. Access is free. There are fees for camping and boat launching.

Water sports, restrictions: Powerboats, water-skiing, wake boarding, personal watercraft, sailing, and sailboarding are permitted. A sandy swimming area roped off with buoys for protection is available in the Pomo Day-Use Area.

Directions: To Che-Ka-Ka: From Ukiah, drive north on U.S. 101 to Lake Mendocino Drive. Exit right on Lake Mendocino Drive and continue to the first stoplight. Turn left on North State Street and drive to the next stoplight. Turn right (which will put you back on Lake Mendocino Drive) and drive about one mile to the signed entrance to the campground and boat ramp at Coyote Dam.

To Kyen: From Ukiah, drive north on U.S. 101 for five miles to the Highway 20 turnoff. Drive east on Highway 20 to Marina Drive.

Turn right and drive 200 yards to the boat ramp (and campground).

Contact: U.S. Army Corps of Engineers, Lake Mendocino, 707/462-7581.

8 BLUE LAKES

Rating: 7

near Upper Lake

Map 4.1, page 116

Lake County is home to these Blue Lakes, which are not to be confused with several other Blue Lakes elsewhere in the state. There are Blue Lakes in Toiyabe-National Forest, Modoc National Forest, Inyo National Forest, Tahoe National Forest, and Hoover Wilderness. There's even a town called Blue Lake near Arcata, where there are no lakes at all, and then there is Big Blue Lake in the Russian Wilderness.

Located along Highway 20 north of Clear Lake, these two lakes feature quiet water, low-speed boating, trout fishing, and a lakeside resort with rental units. The lakes are long and narrow, created from the flows of Cold Creek, which eventually meets up with the East Fork Russian River and empties into Lake Mendocino. The upper lake is by far the better of the pair.

The calm, cool, and clean water, combined with the opportunity to catch trout, is very compelling in this region, and Blue Lakes gets heavy use. As for that 5-mph speed limit, don't ignore it or your vacation will end abruptly; they're very strict about enforcing it.

This foothill setting (an elevation of 1,400 feet) is very pretty, with a forested shoreline and a fair number of sandy beaches. You can swim just about anywhere here. Of course most sailboarders don't give Blue Lakes the time of day because the speed limit is more like a stop sign. But beginners will find a good spot on the west shore near Pine Acres Resort, which gets a fair wind out of the north in the spring.

If you end up loving this place and worry that other people will make the same discovery, hey, just tell 'em you're going to Blue Lakes. They won't have a clue.

Access: There are four private boat ramps:
• Le Trianon Resort: Located on the north end of the lake off Highway 20 with a paved launch ramp, this resort has a dock and rowboats, with kayaks and pedal boats available for rent, 707/275-2262.
• Blue Lakes Lodge: Located on the east side of the lake off Highway 20, Blue Lakes has a paved launch ramp and a dock, 707/275-2181, website: www.bluelakeslodge.com.
• Narrows Lodge: On the west side of the lake off Blue Lakes Road, this lodge has a paved launch ramp, dock, rowboats, boats with motors, kayaks, canoes, pontoon boats, and pedal boats available for rent, 707/275-2718, website: www.thenarrowsresort.com.
• Pine Acres Resort: Located on the west side of the lake off Blue Lakes Road, Pine Acres offers a paved launch ramp, pier, and rowboats, kayaks, and pedal boats for rent, 707/275-2811, website: www.bluelakepineacres.com.

Facilities, fees: Cabins, lodging, campgrounds, restrooms with showers, flush toilets, limited marina facilities, restaurants, convenience stores, and gas are available. There are fees for camping and boat launching (inclusive for guests at Blue Lakes Lodge).

Water sports, restrictions: Powerboats, rowboats, canoes, kayaks, and inflatables are permitted. A 5 mph speed limit is strictly enforced. Swimming and sailboarding are permitted. Protected, sandy swimming beaches are located near the lakeside resorts. The best sailboarding spot is near Pine Acres Resort.

Directions: To Le Trianon Resort: From Ukiah, drive north on U.S. 101 for five miles to the junction with Highway 20. Turn east on Highway 20 and drive 12 miles to the resort on the right (5845 W. Hwy. 20).

Contact: Lake County Visitor Information Center, 707/274-5652 or 800/525-3743, website: www.lakecounty.com.

9 HOWARD LAKE

Rating: 5

near Covelo in Mendocino National Forest

Map 4.2, page 117

Little Howard Lake is tucked deep in the interior of Mendocino National Forest between Espee Ridge to the south and Little Doe Ridge to the north. For a drive-to lake, it is surprisingly remote and provides good fishing and primitive camping.

Set at an elevation of 3,600 feet, it covers about 15 or 20 acres. As you might have guessed, this is not a big water-recreation destination. Instead, this is a pretty, remote spot that you can paddle your canoe around in, perhaps trying to catch a trout now and then. By early June the water is usually warm enough for swimming, but the shoreline is a little muddy and it is rare to see people taking a dip.

Hammerhorn Lake is located about six miles away.

Access: A primitive boat ramp for car-top boats only is located on the northwest side of the lake.

Facilities, fees: A campground, vault toilets and drinking water is available. Pack out your garbage. Supplies can be obtained in Covelo. Access is free. A fee is charged for camping.

Water sports, restrictions: Rowboats, boats with electric motors, canoes, and kayaks are permitted. No gas motors. Swimming is allowed.

Directions: From Willits, drive north on U.S. 101 for 13 miles to Longvale and the junction with Highway 162. Turn northeast on Highway 162 and drive to Covelo. Continue east on Highway 162 to the Eel River Bridge. Turn left at the bridge on Forest Road M1 and drive about 11 miles to the lake and campground.

Contact: Mendocino National Forest, Covelo Ranger District, 707/983-6118, fax 707/983-8004.

10 HAMMERHORN LAKE

Rating: 4

near Covelo in Mendocino National Forest

Map 4.2, page 117

A veritable dot of a lake at just two acres, Hammerhorn is more like a mountain pond set at an elevation of 3,500 feet in remote Mendocino National Forest. Despite the small size there are a few factors that make the place special: The lake is quite pretty, there is a campground, and the location is near the border of the Yolla-Bolly Wilderness.

There is no boat ramp, of course (after all, it's only two acres), but small car-top boats and inflatables can be launched by hand. That is exactly what some campers do, possibly tossing out a line for trout, though the lake's population of hardhead shiners has cut into fishing success. The lake is warm enough for swimming by mid-June, but few people make it out here just to take a dip.

The place typically attracts the hiking crowd. Backpackers will make the drive into the Mendocino wildlands and camp here before heading off the next day for a trip into the Yolla-Bolly Wilderness; a trailhead is located nearby to the northeast.

Access: There is no boat ramp. Car-top boats may be hand launched.

Facilities, fees: A small, primitive campground, vault toilets, and drinking water are available. No drinking water in fall and winter. Garbage must be packed out. Supplies can be obtained in Covelo. The lake has two wheelchair-accessible piers. Access is free. A fee is charged for camping.

Water sports, restrictions: Rowboats, canoes, and kayaks are permitted. No motors. Swimming is allowed.

Directions: From Willits, drive north on U.S. 101 for 13 miles to Longvale and the junction with Highway 162. Turn northeast on Highway 162 and drive to Covelo. Continue east on Highway 162 to the Eel River Bridge. Turn left at the bridge on Forest Road M1 and drive about 17 miles to Forest Road M21. Turn right and drive one mile to the campground entrance and lake.

Contact: Mendocino National Forest, Covelo Ranger District, 707/983-6118.

11 PLASKETT LAKES

Rating: 4

northwest of Willows in Mendocino National Forest

Map 4.2, page 117

Plaskett Lakes are a pair of connected, dot-size mountain lakes that form the headwaters of little Plaskett Creek. They are difficult to reach, located at the end of a rough road, out in the middle of nowhere.

The lakes are set at an elevation of 6,000 feet. They cover just three and four acres and get very light use. You'll typically find just a few people out here floating around in rafts and fishing for trout. Swimming is not recommended because the lake bottoms are mucky and your feet will sink into the ooze when you enter and leave the water.

But the area is pretty, gets little traffic, and is remote—the nearest town is 35 miles away. There are good opportunities for hiking (one trail is routed along Plaskett Creek), including a number of Forest Service roads (the best in the area is routed up Chimney Rock).

Trout fishing is best at the westernmost of the two lakes. No motors are permitted in the lakes and swimming is not recommended. Note that Plaskett Lakes were drained to kill weeds and were first restocked with trout in summer of 2002.

Access: There is no boat ramp. Car-top boats may be hand launched.

Facilities, fees: Campgrounds, drinking water, vault toilets, and a picnic area are available. Supplies can be obtained in Elk Creek. Access is free. A fee is charged for camping.

Water sports, restrictions: Rowboats, canoes, and kayaks are permitted. No motors. Swimming is allowed.

Directions: In Willows on I-5, turn west on Highway 162 and drive toward the town of Elk Creek. Just after crossing the Stony Creek Bridge, turn north on County Road 306 and drive four miles. Turn left on Alder Springs Road/Forest Highway 7 and drive 31 miles to the lake entrance road (and campground) on the left. Turn left and drive a short distace to the lake.

Contact: Mendocino National Forest, Grindstone Ranger District, 530/934-3316, fax 530/934-1212.

12 STONY GORGE RESERVOIR

Rating: 6

near Elk Creek

Map 4.2, page 117

If only the Bureau of Reclamation made recreation a top priority at Stony Gorge Reservoir, this place would have a chance of being something special.

This is a long, narrow lake set in a canyon, at an elevation of 800 feet, with 1,300 surface acres and 25 miles of shoreline. A classic foothill reservoir, it gets hot weather and experiences summer water drawdowns. The setting is fairly pretty, and all boating and water sports are permitted. In the spring when the lake is full, the water is starting to warm up, and the surrounding hills are green, you might think you've really found something.

Other than the boat ramp and vault toilets, there are no developed facilities of any kind, not even potable water. A marina? Gas? A bait shop? You've got to be kidding.

In the late spring, conditions are excellent for water-skiing and swimming, with swimmers congregating at a beach near the boat ramp. Then summer arrives and puts an end to all the festivities.

By June, the lake level starts dropping rapidly. Most years the launch ramp is unusable by summer, and even if you do manage to get a boat in the water, you will have to negotiate lots of underwater hazards and deal with the day-to-day fluctuations in the water level.

Access: A paved boat ramp is located on the northeast side of the lake at Skipper's Point.

Facilities, fees: Campgrounds, vault toilets, and picnic areas are available. No drinking water. Limited supplies can be obtained in Elk Creek. Access is free.

Water sports, restrictions: Powerboats, water-skiing, wake boarding, personal watercraft, sailing, sailboarding, and swimming are permitted. A beach is available at Skipper's Point.

Directions: From Sacramento, drive 90 miles north on I-5 to Willows. Turn west on Highway 162 and continue for about 19 miles; turn left at the signed entrance and travel two miles to the reservoir.

Contact: Bureau of Reclamation, 530/275-1554 or 530/934-7066.

13 LAKE PILLSBURY

Rating: 8

near Ukiah in Mendocino National Forest

Map 4.2, page 117

Bit by bit, Lake Pillsbury is growing more popular every year. At one time not so long ago, this was just a mountain lake that had good weather, plenty of water, few people, and lots of trout. Well, with all those attractions, it isn't surprising that more vacationers than ever before are heading here.

Covering some 2,000 acres, Pillsbury is by far the largest lake in the Mendocino National Forest. Besides the surrounding forestland, highlights include lakeside camping and good boat ramps. Groceries and gas are also available.

Set at an elevation of 1,800 feet, Pillsbury is big and pretty when full, with 65 miles of shoreline. It is becoming a popular vacation destination with Bay Area folks, who tend to congregate at the north end of the lake, where

beaches, Forest Service camps, and a boat ramp are located.

Most visitors will fish a little and water-ski a little, enjoy the sun, and maybe take a dunk in the cool green waters. Though conditions are decent for sailboarding in the early summer, few sailboarders are willing to make the circuitous drive for less than great prospects. Interestingly, you are more apt to see hang gliders here.

The lake remains just difficult enough to reach that it probably will never get inundated with people, as occasionally occurs at Clear Lake. If you're staying at Pillsbury, one great side trip is a rafting run down the nearby Eel River (see the Eel River listings in this chapter).

The fishing is often good for trout in the spring, and then bass in the warmer months. There is an advisory for eating fish caught from Pillsbury.

Access: There are three paved boat ramps: one at Fuller Grove Campground on the lake's northwest end, one just past Sunset Campground on the northeast end, and one at Lake Pillsbury Resort on the west end. The boat ramp at Fuller Grove is wheelchair-accessible.

Facilities, fees: Campgrounds, vault toilets, and drinking water are available. Lodging, marina, boat rentals, gas, and convenience store are available at Lake Pillsbury Resort. Access is free. There are fees for boat launching and camping.

Water sports, restrictions: Powerboats, water-skiing, wake boarding, personal watercraft, sailing, sailboarding, and swimming are permitted. Sailboarding and swimming are best on the lake's north end, which has large, sandy beaches.

Directions: To Lake Pillsbury Resort: From Ukiah on U.S. 101, drive north to the junction with Highway 20. Turn east (right) on Highway 20 and drive five miles to East Potter Valley Road (toward Lake Pillsbury). Turn northwest on East Potter Valley Road and drive 5.9 miles to the town of Potter Valley. Continue on East Potter Valley Road to Eel River Road. Turn right and drive 15 miles to Lake Pillsbury and

Forest Road 301F. Turn right at Forest Road 301F and drive two miles to the resort.

To Sunset: From Ukiah on U.S. 101, drive north to the junction with Highway 20. Turn east (right) on Highway 20 and drive five miles. Turn northwest on East Potter Valley Road toward Lake Pillsbury. Drive 5.9 miles to the town of Potter Valley. Continue on East Potter Valley Road to Eel River Road. Turn right and drive 15 miles to the Eel River Information Kiosk at Lake Pillsbury. Continue east for 4.1 miles to Lake Pillsbury and the junction with Hall Mountain Road. Turn right and drive three miles to the camp entrance. A boat ramp is available .25 mile to the south.

To Fuller Grove: Continue as above to the Eel River Information Kiosk at Lake Pillsbury. Continue for 2.2 miles to the campground access road. Turn right and drive .25 mile to the campground.

Contact: Lake Pillsbury Resort, 707/743-1581; Mendocino National Forest, Upper Lake Ranger District, 707/275-2361; Lake County, 707/263-2222.

14 LETTS LAKE

Rating: 6

west of Maxwell in Mendocino National Forest

Map 4.2, page 117

Okay, c'mon now, admit it: You've never seen directions like the ones provided in the Directions field (below) for Letts Lake, right? If you think they are confusing, imagine how difficult it would be to find the lake without this book. Result? Advantage, you.

When you eventually get here, you find a small lake (35 acres) set at 4,500 feet in elevation just within Mendocino National Forest, along with a few campgrounds on the north shore.

Because boats with motors are not allowed and the access road is quite circuitous, people with car-top rowboats, canoes, and rafts will fare well at Letts Lake. Swimming prospects

are good; although there is no sandy beach area, there is a rocky shoreline.

The surrounding area is pretty, with excellent views and good hiking. You can turn a hike into a fortune hunt by trying to discover one of several natural springs in the area: Fir Rock Springs, Summit Springs, Cold Springs, Freezeout Springs, Board Camp Springs, Young's Corral Springs, and Sylar Springs.

Access: A primitive boat ramp that's suitable for car-top boats is located on the east side of the lake.

Facilities, fees: Campgrounds, vault toilets, drinking water, and a wheelchair-accessible fishing pier is available. Supplies can be obtained in Stonyford. Access is free.

Water sports, restrictions: Rowboats, canoes, and kayaks are permitted. No motors. Swimming is allowed.

Directions: From I-5 at Maxwell, turn west on Maxwell-Sites Road and drive to Sites and Sites-Lodoga Road. Turn left on Sites-Lodoga Road and continue to Lodoga and Lodoga-Stonyford Road. Turn right on Lodoga-Stonyford Road and loop around East Park Reservoir to reach Stonyford and Fouts Spring Road. Turn west on Fouts Springs Road/County Road M10 and drive about 17 miles into national forest (where the road becomes Forest Service 17N02) to the campground on the east side of Letts Lake.

Contact: Mendocino National Forest, Grindstone Ranger District, 530/963-3128. For a map of Mendocino National Forest, send $6 to U.S. Forest Service, Attn: Map Sales, P.O. Box 587, Camino, CA 95709, 530/647-5390, fax 530/647-5389, website: www.fs.fed.us/r5/forests. Major credit cards accepted.

15 EAST PARK RESERVOIR

Rating: 7

near Stonyford in Mendocino National Forest

Map 4.2, page 117

It can get hot here, absolutely sizzling. In midsummer, temperatures in the 90s and 100s are common, and some summers the area is hit with a string of 100-degree days that seems to go on forever. The water levels drop a bit almost daily, and by August, East Park Reservoir has been transformed into a bathtub, complete with the ring.

But until that happens, this is a great lake for powerboating, water-skiing, and swimming. Although the place is primitive, the foothill setting is pretty, launching and access are free, and all water sports are permitted. The best swimming areas are near the campgrounds.

In low rain years and after late July, powerboaters should check water levels before heading out. The dropping levels result in navigational hazards, and tree stumps are often just beneath the surface.

One of the great secrets of this lake is that the crappie fishing can be sensational. It is best at night, with live minnows or crappie jigs tossed under a bright light. There are also big bass in this lake, including in the 10-pound class.

Access: A primitive boat ramp is located on the lake's northwest side at the end of the access road.

Facilities, fees: Primitive campsites, and vault and chemical toilets are available. No drinking water. Supplies can be obtained in Stonyford and Lodoga. Camping (except for groups), boat launching, and day use are free.

Water sports, restrictions: Powerboats, water-skiing, wake boarding, personal watercraft, sailing, sailboarding, and swimming are permitted. A 5-mph speed limit is enforced anywhere within 100 feet of the shoreline and near swimming areas. Swimming beaches are located near the campgrounds.

Directions: Take I-5 to Maxwell (67 miles north of Sacramento) and Maxwell-Sites Road. Turn west on Maxwell-Sites Road and drive to Sites. Turn left on Sites-Lodoga Road and continue to Lodoga. Turn right on Lodoga-Stonyford Road and drive to East Park Reservoir and the boat ramp.

Contact: East Park Reservoir, 530/968-5267; Bureau of Reclamation, 530/275-1554; Stonyford General Store, 530/963-3235.

16 HIGHLAND SPRINGS RESERVOIR

Rating: 6

west of Clear Lake

Map 4.2, page 117

People can drive to giant Clear Lake many times over a lifetime and never learn about nearby Highland Springs Reservoir or the adjacent Adobe Creek Reservoir. Yet these two lakes are so close, only about 10 miles west of Clear Lake, and between them they fulfill many needs.

Highland Springs Reservoir is located in the foothills just southwest of Big Valley, about a mile west of Adobe Creek Reservoir. Created when a dam was built on Highland Creek, a tributary of Adobe Creek, it covers about 150 acres.

Because no gas-powered motors are allowed on the lake, Highland Springs offers a perfect alternative for people with small, hand-powered boats, such as canoes, rafts, or prams. Boaters are guaranteed calm water, even on three-day weekends when nearby Clear Lake just about gets plowed under by all the hot jet boats.

This is a nice, quiet, day-use only lake that's ideal for a few hours of picnicking and splashing or wading around. With warm, fairly clear water and no motorized boats to disturb the peace, the swimming here is decent and sailboarding is excellent. The lake gets moderate use, and most of the visitors are anglers. A golf course is available next to the lake.

Access: A primitive boat ramp is located on the lake's east side adjacent to the picnic area.

Facilities, fees: Restrooms with flush toilets, a grassy picnic area, horseshoe pits, and basketball court are provided. Access is free.

Water sports, restrictions: Small boats, canoes, kayaks, inflatables, sailing, sailboarding, and

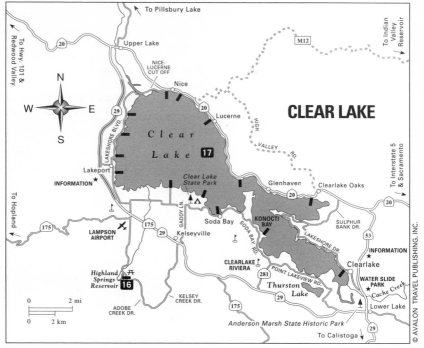

CLEAR LAKE

To Pillsbury Lake

To Hwy. 101 & Redwood Valley

Upper Lake

NICE-LUCERNE CUT OFF

Nice

Lucerne

Clear Lake

17

Lakeport

INFORMATION ★

To Hopland

LAKESHORE BLVD

Clear Lake State Park

Glenhaven

Clearlake Oaks

To Interstate 5 & Sacramento

GADDY LN.

Soda Bay

KONOCTI BAY

SODA BAY RD.

SULPHUR BANK DR.

LAKESHORE DR.

Kelseyville

LAMPSON AIRPORT

Highland Springs Reservoir

16

ADOBE CREEK DR.

KELSEY CREEK DR.

CLEARLAKE RIVIERA

POINT LAKEVIEW RD.

Thurston Lake

INFORMATION ★

Clearlake

WATER SLIDE PARK

Cache Creek

Lower Lake

Anderson Marsh State Historic Park

To Calistoga

To Indian Valley Reservoir

M12

HIGH VALLEY RD.

0   2 mi

0   2 km

© AVALON TRAVEL PUBLISHING, INC.

swimming are permitted. No gas motors allowed. Swimming is best at the picnic area. **Directions:** From Vallejo, drive north on Highway 29 and proceed to the town of Lower Lake. Bear left on Highway 29 and drive to Kelseyville, then continue on Highway 29 four miles to Highland Springs Road. Turn left on Highland Springs Road and drive four miles to the reservoir.

Contact: Lake County Flood Control, 707/263-2341; Tackle It, 707/262-1233; general information website: www.lakecounty.com/lakes.html.

17 CLEAR LAKE

Rating: 9

north of Calistoga

Map 4.2, page 117

Clear Lake is a remarkable vision the first time you drive over the hills and lay your eyes on

it: so big, so full, perhaps a few cumulus clouds sprinkled in the sky over nearby Mount Konocti. It is one of the prettiest sights in California, particularly in the spring when the surrounding hills are green and everything is so fresh and clean.

This is one of those rare places where reality can equal the vision. There is just something about Clear Lake that makes a visit here a special experience. Maybe it's the knowledge that this is a true lake fashioned entirely by the forces of nature rather than a reservoir created by humans to serve humans.

For one thing, the body of water is vast, covering more than 40,000 surface acres amid the foothills of Lake County; it's the largest natural freshwater lake within California's borders. It often seems full right to the brim, and with Highway 20 running alongside the eastern shore, there is a sense of intimacy that large reservoirs just can't claim, where the water levels can be low and roads far from the water. With dozens of resorts and private campgrounds sprinkled along the 100 miles of shoreline, the lake can accommodate huge numbers of visitors without making one feel crowded. In addition, there are almost 100 boat ramps (including 10 free ramps). That makes Clear Lake ideal for boater/camper weekends.

Every imaginable water sport—even parasailing—can be enjoyed here, and just about every kind of watercraft is available for rent. Add to that staying at a resort, camping, fishing, hiking, horseback riding, bicycling, rockhounding, golfing, touring wineries, taking glider flights, exploring Native America village archaeological sites, and well, you've got it all.

The lake is shaped somewhat like an hourglass, with the northern section much larger and rounder than its southern counterpart. These two sections are somewhat divided by an extended peninsula. Water-skiing is best on calm summer days on the lake's northern part. Note that the shoreline along the north and west shores, and along the southern half of the lake, is very popular for bass fishing, so waterskiers should avoid the shoreline, particularly in the coves. To ensure that water-skiers stay where they're supposed to, a sheriff's boat patrols the lake full time.

The water is very warm in summer, with surface temperatures often approaching 80 degrees—ideal for all water sports. The Nor-Cal Boat & Ski races are held here each summer, along with the annual Splash In, an event for seaplane owners.

Clear Lake is the bass capital of the west. It can be the most rewarding lake in California. Yet in the turnaround of a day, it can also be the most humbling. More times than not, however, it rewards, not humbles. There may be no better place in America to catch a big bass. The average angler is going to catch one five pounds or better 80 percent of the time. There are also wads of 12- and 14-inch bass in the lake, and you can catch and release 30 or 40 of them. But the big ones are the appeal.

If you target the bigger fish, you hope for five bites. Some days you get lucky and get 10 bites. Of those bites, you hope to catch them all.

The lakes also has excellent numbers of catfish, crappie, and bluegill.

The lake's marinas are complete and well staffed, and the marinas that have lodging and docking facilities are extremely popular all summer long. Reservations are always advised and often needed at the higher quality spots. The same is true at Clear Lake State Park, which provides campgrounds, as well as boater access to an adjacent section of tule-edged shoreline that is especially good for fishing for bluegill and bass.

Dozens of mom-and-pop operations are located around the lake. They vary greatly in quality, but virtually all have their own boat ramps or are situated very close to a public ramp. The most developed operation is at Konocti Harbor Resort & Spa, which has condo-style units, a restaurant, full marina, and a small concert hall.

Sailboarding is possible just about anywhere there's a beach. The best time for the sport is in the spring, when the wind is up, of course.

There are several beaches around the lake. The Lake County Visitor Information Center provides a free map that details all the public boat ramps and beach access points.

Access: Clear Lake has 10 free boat launches, along with dozens at private resorts and a launch at the state park. For a complete list, contact the Lake County Visitor Information Center at the phone number given in the Contact section below.

• Holiday Harbor near Nice: From north of Ukiah on U.S. 101, drive north to the junction with Highway 20. Turn east on Highway 20 and drive to the town of Nice and Howard Avenue. Turn left on Howard Avenue and drive 200 feet to the park and boat launch at the end of the road. For more information call 707/274-1136.

• Arrow Park RV near Lucerne: From north of Ukiah on U.S. 101, or from Williams on

I-5, turn on Highway 20 and drive to the town of Lucerne. Continue on Highway 20 to the east side of Lucerne and the campground and boat launch at 6720 East Highway 20. For more information call 707/274-7715.

• Glenhaven Beach at Glenhaven: From north of Ukiah on U.S. 101, or I-5 at Williams, turn on Highway 20 and drive to Clear Lake and the town of Glenhaven (four miles northwest of Clearlake Oaks). In Glenhaven, continue on Highway 20 to the camp and boat ramp at 9625 East Highway 20. For more information call 707/998-3406.

• Clear Lake State Park near Kelseyville: From Vallejo, drive north on Highway 29 to Lower Lake. Turn left on Highway 29 and drive seven miles to Soda Bay Road. Turn right on Soda Bay Road and drive 11 miles to the park entrance on the right side of the road. For more information call 707/279-4293.

From Kelseyville on Highway 29, take the Kelseyville exit and turn north on Main Street. Drive a short distance to State Street. Turn right and drive .25 mile to Gaddy Lane. Turn right on Gaddy Lane and drive about two miles to Soda Bay Road. Turn right and drive one mile to the park entrance on the left.

• Edgewater Resort at Soda Bay: In Kelseyville on Highway 29, take the Merritt Road exit and drive on Merritt Road for two miles (it becomes Gaddy Lane) to Soda Bay Road. Turn right on Soda Bay Road and drive three miles to the park entrance and boat ramp on the left. For more information call 707/279-0208.

There are also the following free public ramps:
• Lake County Park: On Highway 29 south of Kelseyville, turn north on Soda Bay Road/Highway 281 and drive to Park Drive. Turn north on Park Drive drive to the paved ramp at 1985 Park Drive.

• Redbud City Park: In the town of Clearlake, look for the park entrance at 14655 Lakeshore Drive. A four-lane paved ramp is available.

• First Street Ramp: From Main Street in the town of Lakeport, turn east on First Street and continue to the two-lane paved ramp.

• Third Street Ramp: From Main Street in the town of Lakeport, take Third Street east to the two-lane paved ramp.

• Fifth Street Ramp: From Main Street in the town of Lakeport, turn east on Fifth Street and drive to the two-lane paved ramp.

• Clear Lake Avenue: From Main Street in the town of Lakeport, take Clear Lake Avenue east and head to the paved ramp located at the lake's edge.

• Lakeshore Drive and Crystal Lake Way: From Main Street in the town of Lakeport, turn west on Clear Lake Avenue and continue to High Street. Turn north, drive to Lakeshore Drive, turn right and continue to the paved ramp at the junction with Crystal Lake Way.

• Lucerne Harbor County Park: A paved ramp is available in the town of Lucerne at 6225 East Highway 20.

• H. V. Keeling County Park: This park is located in the town of Nice at 3000 Lakeshore Boulevard and has a paved ramp.

• Hudson Avenue: From Highway 20 in Nice, turn south on Hudson Boulevard and continue to the two-lane paved ramp at the lake's edge.

Facilities, fees: Full marina services are available at Ferndale Marina in Kelseyville, 707/279-4866; Glenhaven Marina in Glenhaven, 707/998-3406; Will-O-Point Resort in Lakeport, 707/262-5896, and others. Boat rentals, bait and tackle, and supplies are available. Camping and cabins are available. Boat launching is free at most public ramps. Fees are charged for camping and boat launching at private marinas.

Water sports, restrictions: Powerboats, water-skiing, wake boarding, personal watercraft, sailing, sailboarding, and swimming are permitted. Swimming beaches are located at Clear Lake State Park in Kelseyville, Redbud City Park in Clearlake, Star Beach in Lucerne, H.V. Keeling Park in Nice, and at 16th Street in Lakeport.

Directions: From San Francisco, cross the Golden Gate Bridge and drive north on U.S. 101 past San Rafael to Highway 37. Drive east on Highway 37 for 23 miles to Vallejo and Highway 29.

Turn north on Highway 29 and drive 70 miles to the town of Lower Lake.

From Sacramento, take I-5 north to Williams and Highway 20. Turn west on Highway 20 and drive to the town of Clearlake.

From the North Coast, take U.S. 101 south to Calpella (17 miles south of Willits) and Highway 20. Turn east on Highway 20 and drive to the town of Nice.

Contact: Lake County Visitor Information Center, 707/274-5652 or 800/525-3743 (in California only), website: www.lakecounty.com; Greater Lakeport Chamber of Commerce, 707/263-5092, website: www.lakeportchamber.com; Konocti Harbor Resort & Spa, Kelseyville, 707/279-4281, website: www.konoctiharbor.com.

Boat rentals: Funtime RV Park, Clearlake (pontoon boats, fishing boats, and ski boats), 707/994-6267; Blue Fish Cove Resort, Clearlake Oaks (fishing boats, pedal boats, and personal watercraft), 707/998-1769; Lake Marina Resort, Clearlake Oaks (pontoon boats and canoes), 707/998-3787; Konocti Harbor Resort Marina, Konocti Bay (pontoon boats, ski boats, fishing boats, pedal boats, kayaks, and personal watercraft), 707/279-6628; Disney's Water Sports, Lakeport (fishing boats, ski boats, pontoon boats, pedal boats, kayaks, and personal watercraft), 707/263-0969, website: www.disneyswatersports.com; Shaw's Shady Acres, Lower Lake (fishing boats), 707/994-2236; Edgewater Resort, Soda Bay (fishing boats and kayaks), 707/279-0208 or 800/396-6224.

Boat cruises & tours: Clear Lake Queen (tri-level paddlewheel), Lucerne, 707-994-5432; Konocti Harbor Resort Marina (75-passenger charter boat), Konocti Bay, 707/279-6628.

18 INDIAN VALLEY RESERVOIR
🚤 🔪 ⛷ 🛶 🏊 ⛺

Rating: 5

near Clear Lake

Map 4.2, page 117

Imagine a lake so ugly that it is beautiful. Such is the case at Indian Valley Reservoir.

Ugly? To some people it is one downright ugly dog. The water level is often very low, turning the lake into a long, narrow strip with miles of exposed shore. For most of the year, the surrounding hills are brown and barren. The road in from either side is a twisted nightmare.

But after a while Indian Valley Reservoir becomes more like a homely dog that you love more than anything in the world, because inside beats a heart that will never betray you.

Indian Valley is a long, narrow reservoir set at 1,500 feet elevation. When full, the lake covers about 4,000 acres and has 41 miles of shoreline. The water harbors many submerged trees, which provide an excellent habitat for bass, kokanee salmon, and catfish. This is some of the best bass fishing territory in Northern California.

A 10-mph speed limit, clear water, and hot days create a quiet setting for fishing and make for good swimming all summer long. There are no sandy beaches, but the clear, warm water is good for swimming, and those who want to take the plunge can jump in wherever and whenever they desire. After all, it is fairly remote and primitive out here. Rental boats are not available.

The saving graces are the little Indian Valley Store at the lake's south end and the boat ramps located at the north and south ends. Boater traffic is low, consisting primarily of people who come to fish for bass and kokanee salmon. Relatively few know about this place, and of those who do, the long twisty drive, ugly surroundings, and enforced speed limit keep most of them away.

But for anglers that makes it just beautiful.

Access: There are two boat ramps.

Facilities, fees: Campgrounds, vault toilets, drinking water, and a convenience store are available. Fees are charged for day use (boat launching included) and camping.

Water sports, restrictions: Powerboats, canoes, kayaks, inflatables, sailing, sailboarding, and swimming are permitted. A 10-mph speed limit is strictly enforced. No water-skiing, wake boarding, or personal watercraft. Although there are no designated beaches, you can swim all along the shoreline; the most popular swimming spots are near the campgrounds.

Directions: From Williams on I-5, turn west on Highway 20 and drive 25 miles into the foothills to Walker Ridge Road. Turn north (right) on Walker Ridge Road (a dirt road) and drive north for about four miles to a major intersection of two dirt roads. Turn left and drive five miles (you will pass Blue Oak Campground to your right) to the Indian Valley Store and boat ramp at the south end of the lake near the dam. Note that the access road is dirt and washboarded.

Or, from the north end of Clear Lake at the town of Nice, drive one mile east on Highway 20, then turn left on Bartlett Springs Road. The twisty road is routed to the north end of the lake, where there's a boat launch.

Contact: Indian Valley Store, 530/662-0607; Yolo County (water level info), 530/662-0265, website: www.ycfcwcd.org; Bureau of Land Management, Ukiah Field Office, 707/468-4000, website: www.ca.blm.gov/ukiah.

19 GUALALA RIVER

Rating: 6

south of Point Arena

Map 4.3, page 118

Remote and pretty, the Gualala River is the best of the smaller rivers flowing along the Sonoma and Mendocino coastline. Families and novice rafters find that it makes a great place to enjoy an easy float in a canoe or a kayak. The water is clean and warm in the summer, and the lower river is good for swimming.

Because the river's upper stretches are often too shallow in the summer, the lower section gets pretty heavy recreational use. The run down in a kayak or canoe is an easy Class I affair that gets a lot of traffic in the summer months. About 50 kayaks are available for rent, and customers are provided with all of the nec-

essary accessories and shuttle service. Bikes and canoes are also available.

The river is very scenic, and boaters should be able to see lots of wildlife and a variety of bird species. Swimming is good all along the lower river, which has deep swimming holes and even rope swings in a couple of places. One word of warning: Don't try to find swimming spots upstream because that river section is bordered by private property.

The season here is a two-part affair. Part One is during relatively higher flows, when the river runs into the ocean. Part Two is when flows drop and a sand bar closes the mouth of river. Both provide boating opportunities—the first for down-the-river technical kayaking, the second for flat-water, family-style opportunities.

Access: There is no boat ramp. To reach the standard put-in (called Switchvale), follow the directions below for access to the lower river; once on the Old State Highway, drive three miles to a parking area. Park and carry your gear a short distance down to the beach. An alternate put-in is located about six miles upstream (at an access known as Hot Spot), but it is generally only boatable very early in the season.

Facilities, fees: Campgrounds, restrooms with flush toilets, drinking water, and vault toilets are available nearby. Kayak rentals, shuttle service, and boating supplies can be obtained at Adventure Rents. Full facilities are available in Gualala. Access is free. Rafting permits are not required. A fee is charged for camping.

Water sports, restrictions: Driftboats, kayaks, canoes, and inflatables are permitted. Several swimming holes are located off the roads mentioned above.

Directions: To access the lower river from the town of Gualala, turn east on Old Stage Road (County Road 501) and drive less than one mile to Old State Road (County Road 502). Turn right on Old State Road, where access is available on the road. To reach the upper river from Gualala, drive south on Highway 1 to Annapolis Road. Turn left (east) on

Annapolis Road and travel to the twin bridges. The bridges cross the Gualala.

Contact: Adventure Rents, 707/884-4386, website: www.adventurerents.com; general information website: www.redwoodcoastchamber.com.

20 LAKE SONOMA

Rating: 10

north of Santa Rosa

Map 4.3, page 118

Nestled in the rich foothill country of Sonoma County, Lake Sonoma offers one of the best boater/camper experiences around. A 5-mph speed limit and no-wake zones have been established in many areas of the lake, along with 109 boat-in campsites and two group boat-in campgrounds. This guarantees peace, quiet, and excellent swimming and fishing opportunities; yet there's still a huge section of water available for water sports.

There's plenty of room for everybody. The lake is set at an elevation of 450 feet and covers 2,500 surface acres, with 53 miles of shoreline and hundreds of hidden coves. In addition, the lake is adjacent to an 8,000-acre wildlife area that has 40 miles of hiking trails. From the dam, the lake extends nine miles north on the Dry Creek Arm and four miles west on Warm Springs Creek. Each of the lake arms has several fingers and miles of quiet and secluded shore. One of the great things about this lake is that boat rentals, including houseboat rentals, are available at the marina.

Any potential conflict between high-speed operators and anglers has been resolved by setting aside a large area in the main lake for water-skiing, wake boarding, and personal watercraft use.

Water-skiers usually stick to the Warm Springs Arm, which gets less wind than the Dry Creek Arm. Swimmers and beginning sailboarders will find the best conditions near Yorty Creek, although speed-loving sailboarders can venture into the water-skiing area on the Dry Creek

Arm. How is the water? Well, after the winter storm runoff turns it a bit off-color, the lake quickly turns green in the spring, and by summer surface temperatures are in the high 70s.

The lake attracts heavy use, with most visitors staying at the Liberty Glen Campground. Boaters have the advantage of being able to access the boat-in camps, which are great if you're looking for a personal, secluded site. These are primitive sites without drinking water, but they provide chemical toilets, garbage cans, tent sites, picnic tables, fire rings, and lantern poles (you can hang your food on them). Be sure to bring some kind of sunscreen, even if it's just a light tarp rigged with poles and ropes.

To get the most out of a stay here, stop at the visitor center below the dam to pick up maps, brochures, and other information, and ask about boat-in campsite availability.

All in all, Lake Sonoma provides the perfect example of how to do something right.

Access: A five-lane paved boat ramp is located on the lake's west side. A primitive, hand-launch area is available at Yorty Creek.

Facilities, fees: A full-service marina and boat slips are available. Ski boats, houseboats, fishing boats, personal watercraft, canoes, and pedal boats are available for rent. There are 109 primitive boat-in campsites around the lake, several hike-in sites, four group sites (two of which are boat-in), and 95 tent sites and two group sites at Liberty Glen Campground 2.5 miles from the lake. Restrooms with flush toilets and solar showers and an RV dump station are provided. Vault toilets are provided at the primitive sites. No drinking water. Supplies can be obtained at the Dry Creek Store on Dry Creek Road near Healdsburg. Fees are charged for day use, boat launching, and camping.

Water sports, restrictions: Powerboats, water-skiing, wake boarding, and personal watercraft are allowed in designated areas; a large area is set aside in the main lake body. Other designated areas have a posted 5-mph speed limit. The best area for swimming and sailboarding is from the Yorty Creek access.

Directions: To primary ramp: From Santa Rosa, drive north on U.S. 101 to Healdsburg. In Healdsburg, take the Dry Creek Road exit, turn left, and drive northwest for 11 miles. After crossing a small bridge, you will see the visitor center on your right. To reach the boat ramp, continue past the visitor center for about three miles. Follow the signs to the public launch ramp across the ridge or to the ramp at Lake Sonoma Marina.

To Yorty Creek access: Car-top boats can be launched at the Yorty Creek access. From Santa Rosa, drive north on U.S. 101 to Cloverdale. Take the first Cloverdale exit and turn left at the stop sign, driving over U.S. 101 to South Cloverdale Boulevard. Turn right and drive to West Brookside Road. Turn left and drive to Foothill Drive/Hot Springs Road. Turn left and follow the narrow, winding road several miles to the lake.

Contact: U.S. Army Corps of Engineers, Lake Sonoma, 707/433-9483, website: www.spn.usace .army.mil/lakesonoma; Lake Sonoma Marina, 707/433-2200; Dry Creek Store, 707/433-4171.

21 RUSSIAN RIVER

Rating: 8

northwest of Santa Rosa

Map 4.4, page 119

Want to find out just how well you get along with somebody? Try paddling a canoe with them down the Russian River. By the end of the day, you either will have bonded with your companion or will want to jam a paddle down their throat.

Rest assured that this is a great place for such an experiment because the results are likely to be positive. Most of the year, the river is fresh and rolling green, with a prime 10-mile stretch between Forestville and Guerneville that is routed through redwoods. All this makes for a great first-time paddle.

The most popular launching spot for canoeists is Burke's Canoes. From here, you take your time

floating lazily down to their private beach in Guerneville, where you can catch a shuttle ride back (it's included in the price). Without guides, you set the pace of your trip. It's an easy paddle along one of the prettiest sections of the entire river, winding through the heart of the redwoods. The area is green and lush, yet also has many sunny beaches where you can picnic. And whereas other river sections have temporary dams to retain water, here there are no dams to cross.

Burke's is the long-established canoe rental service and campground on the Russian River. The favorite trip is the 10-miler from Burke's in Forestville to Guerneville, which is routed right through the heart of the area's redwoods, about a 3.5-hour paddle trip with plenty of time in the day for sunbathing, swimming, or anything else you can think of. The cost is $45, including a return by shuttle. Many other trips are available.

There are several other places to put in downstream, however, and it's an easy float nearly all the way to the ocean. Casini's is another popular put-in, the beginning of a six-mile paddle trip.

In the summer, the river gets heavy use, with lots of boaters and swimmers at every imaginable access point. There are large, sandy beaches all along the highway. The best are at Johnson's Beach and Monte Rio, which offer full-facility beaches with lifeguards.

Way upstream on the Russian River, between Cloverdale and Hopland, is a challenging bend and rapid at Squaw Rock where kayakers like to practice. You'll sometimes see people taking kayaking lessons here.

From Cloverdale on downstream past Geyserville, it's an easy paddle. The river is more sedate, and there are far fewer people than at the stretch downstream of Forestville. With only a handful of short, unrated rapids, this is the kind of place where you can enjoy being close to the water as it helps to propel you downstream, and you gain a sense of exhilaration from the freedom of riding a river. Regardless of which section you pick, the Russian River is an ideal first-time destination for canoeing or kayaking.

Access: Paved boat ramps are provided at Burke's put-in, Casini's put-in, and Monte Rio Fishing Access.

Facilities, fees: Lodging, cabins, campgrounds, restrooms, showers, canoe and kayak rentals, and shuttles are available. Public beaches with restrooms, picnic facilities, and snack bars are available as well. Day use is free in most areas. Fees are charged for camping and boat launching at private campgrounds.

Water sports, restrictions: Several excellent swimming beaches are available along Highway 116. They include Johnson's Beach in Guerneville, the public beach at Monte Rio, and the beach at Casini Ranch Campground.

Directions: To Burke's put-in: From the Bay Area, drive north on U.S. 101 to the junction with Highway 116 West (just north of Petaluma). Take Highway 116 West and drive 15 miles to Forestville and Mirabel Road (at the gas station). Turn right and drive 1.5 miles until it dead-ends at Burke's and the Russian River.

To Casini's put-in: On U.S. 101 north of Santa Rosa, turn west on River Road and drive 16 miles to Guerneville and Highway 116. Continue west on Highway 116 and drive seven miles to Duncan Mills and Moscow Road. Turn left (southeast) on Moscow Road and drive .7 miles to the campground on the left.

To Monte Rio Fishing Access: In the town of Monte Rio, turn south on Church Street and continue down to the ramp.

Contact: Burke's Canoes, 707/887-1222, website: www.burkescanoetrips.com; Trowbridge Canoe Trips, 707/433-7247 or 800/640-1386; Casini Ranch Family Campground, 707/865-2255 or 800/451-8400, website: www.casiniranch.com.

22 CACHE CREEK

Rating: 7

southeast of Clear Lake

Map 4.4, page 119

Cache Creek is best known as the closest place to go white-water rafting by people who live in the San Francisco Bay Area.

From San Francisco it is 110 miles away, and for residents of Napa in the northern Bay Area, it is only 65 miles away. The most accessible area is right along Highway 16, the little two-laner that links tiny towns such as Guinda and Rumsey and eventually connects with Highway 20 near the Cache Creek Wildlife Area.

This is an ideal river for inflatable kayaks, a first-time white-water experience, or an easy overnight trip.

For one-day trips the best put-in spot is about 10 miles north of Rumsey. You can cover about eight miles of river, including shooting three Class II rapids, and use adjacent Highway 16 as your shuttle road. The best take-out is at Camp Haswell, which has a good picnic area that closes at dusk.

The warm water is ideal for swimming, and many rafters fall in on purpose. Although the scenery is not spectacular, the rural foothill country setting is quiet. There is a good deal of traffic here in the summer, mostly Bay Area people taking a quick trip. But if you leave enough room between boats when you get on the river, you can go a full day and not see anyone anyway.

An insider's note: The upper reach of Cache Creek, just south of Clear Lake, is largely inaccessible. However, few people know that a two-mile stretch of water can be reached on the obscure road that runs out of Anderson Flat.

Access: Rafters may put in along Highway 16 just before the point where the highway and the creek split off into different directions (this is roughly 10 miles north of the town of Rumsey, near the county line). Take out about six miles downstream at Camp Haswell.

Facilities, fees: Campgrounds, restrooms with flush toilets, drinking water, and vault toilets are nearby. Access to the river is free. A fee is charged for camping.

Water sports, restrictions: Swimming access is available at most of the campgrounds and picnic areas along Highway 16.

Directions: From Vacaville on I-80, turn north on I-505 and drive 21 miles to Madison and the junction with Highway 16 West. Turn northwest on Highway 16 and drive northwest for about 45 miles to the town of Rumsey. From Rumsey, continue west on Highway 16 for five miles to the park entrance on the left. Direct access is available here near the confluence of Bear Creek. Note that the creek is largely bordered by private property south of Rumsey.

Contact: Cache Creek Canyon Regional Park, 530/666-8115. Rafting trips: Whitewater Adventures, 707/257-444 or 800/977-4837, website www.gotwhitewater.com; Cache Canyon River Trips, 530/796-3091 or 800/796-3091, website: www.CacheCanyon.com. General information website: www.yolocounty.org.

23 LAKE BERRYESSA

Rating: 9

north of Vallejo

Map 4.4, page 119

This is a big lake, covering some 21,000 acres with 165 miles of shoreline, complete with secret coves, islands, and an expanse of untouched shore on the eastern side.

Berryessa is the Bay Area's backyard boating headquarters, often a wild scene on hot weekends with lots of fast boats, water-skiers, suntan oil, and flowing liquid refreshment of various origins. During the week the place is more peaceful and the natural beauty really shines; this is the best time for fishing and family recreation.

All water sports are permitted, but the focus is on powerboaters, wake boarding, water-skiing, and tubing. Enthusiasts have a field day on summer weekends in the warm, clear water.

Berryessa does not provide free public boat ramps. Instead, there are several resorts, all of which have ramps, marinas of varying size, small stores, and campgrounds. The largest is Steele Park Resort, which has waterside condo units, motel, marina, boat rentals, RV park, cottages,

pool, tennis courts, and a water-skiing school. Most of the marinas offer boat rentals.

The main body of Berryessa is upstream of the Narrows. To the north is a wide expanse of water that is so roomy that jet boats and personal watercraft can go crazy and have all the space anybody could dream of. To the south of the Narrows, where fishing is more popular, the lake is much smaller and more intimate.

Fishing is excellent at Berryessa. Fishing for trout and salmon can provide spectacular numbers of fish for those on the water early and trolling the proper depth, typically 25 to 40 feet deep. Bass fishing is also great in late winter through early summer, with counts of 30 and 40, catch-and-release, for know-hows. There is a sprinkling of giant bass and catfish, usually caught by surprise.

Another unique element of Berryessa is at the far northern end of the lake, well up the Putah Creek Arm. A buoy line there marks the point where powerboats aren't permitted upstream, making it ideal for canoeists to paddle into this rarely traveled lake section, bordered on the west by a dramatic granite wall and on the east by a meadow where deer often graze. You will never forget it.

Access: There are seven boat ramps on Lake Berryessa:

• Putah Creek Resort: From Vallejo, drive north on I-80 to the Suisun Valley Road exit. Take Suisun Valley Road and drive north to Highway 121. Turn north on Highway 121 and drive five miles to Highway 128. Turn left on Highway 128, drive five miles to Berryessa-Knoxville Road, and continue 13 miles to 7600 Knoxville Road.

A paved boat ramp, marina, motel, restaurant, bar, campground, restrooms, showers, coin laundry, and convenience store are available. For more information call 707/966-2116.

• Rancho Monticello Resort: From Vallejo, drive north on I-80 to the Suisun Valley Road exit. Take Suisun Valley Road and drive north to Highway 121. Turn north on Highway 121 and drive five miles to Highway 128. Turn left on Highway 128, drive five miles to Berryessa-Knoxville Road. Turn right, and drive 12.5 miles to 5800 Knoxville Road.

A paved boat ramp, boat rentals, full-service marina, gas, campground with restrooms and showers, coin laundry, convenience store, and snack bar are available. 707/966-2188; marina, 707/966-9803.

• Lake Berryessa Marina Resort: From Vallejo, drive north on I-80 to the Suisun Valley Road exit. Take Suisun Valley Road and drive north to Highway 121. Turn north on Highway 121 and drive five miles to Highway 128. Turn left on Highway 128, drive five miles to Berryessa-Knoxville Road, turn right, and continue nine miles to 5800 Knoxville Road.

A paved boat ramp, full-service marina, houseboat and boat rentals, cabins, campground, flush toilets, showers, RV dump station, coin laundry, snack bar, RV supplies, and convenience store are available. For more information call 707/966-2161, website: www.lakeberryessa.com.

• Spanish Flat Resort: From Vallejo, drive north on I-80 to the Suisun Valley Road exit. Take Suisun Valley Road and drive north to Highway 121. Turn north on Highway 121 and drive five miles to Highway 128. Turn north on Highway 128 and drive five miles to Berryessa-Knoxville Road. Turn right on Berryessa-Knoxville Road and continue four miles to 4290 Knoxville Road.

A paved boat ramp, full-service marina, boat rentals, park-model cabins, campground, restrooms, drinking water, flush toilets, showers, and convenience store are available. A deli and grill is open on summer weekends. Coin laundry, restaurant, and RV supplies are available within 1.5 miles. For more information call 707/966-7700, marina 707/966-7708, website: www.spanishflatresort.com.

• Steele Park Resort: From Vallejo, drive north on I-80 about 10 miles to the Suisun Valley Road exit. Take Suisun Valley Road and drive north another 10 miles to Highway 121. Turn north right on Highway 121 and drive about eight miles to the end of Highway 121 and the junction with Highway 128. Turn left (west) on Highway 128 and drive a short distance to Steele Canyon Road. Turn right and drive miles to the resort.

A paved boat ramp, full-service marina, gas, covered and open berths, dry storage, boat rentals, water-ski school, RV park, motel, cottages, two restaurants, bar, convenience store, and picnic area are available. For more information call 707/966-2123 or 800/522-2123, website: www.steelepark.com.

• Pleasure Cove Resort: From Vallejo, drive north on I-80 about 10 miles to the Suisun Valley Road exit. Take Suisun Valley Road and drive north another 10 miles to Highway 121. Turn north (right) on Highway 121 and drive about eight miles to the end of Highway 121 and the junction with Highway 128. Bear right (southeast) on Highway 128 and proceed four miles to Wragg Canyon Road. Turn left and continue three miles to the resort entrance at the end of the road.

A paved boat ramp, full-service marina, boat rentals, gas, park-model cabins, campground, restrooms, showers, ice, restaurant, bar, bait & tackle, propane gas, RV dump station, and convenience store are available. For more information call 707/966-2172.

• Markley Cove Resort: From Vallejo, drive north on I-80 about 10 miles to the Suisun Valley Road exit. Take Suisun Valley Road and drive north another 10 miles to Highway 121. Turn north (right) on Highway 121 and drive about eight miles to the end of Highway 121 and the junction with Highway 128. Bear right (southeast) on Highway 128 and drive eight miles to the resort on the left.

A paved boat ramp, marina, gas, pumphoue, fishing boat rentals, houseboat moorings, bait, convenience store, and snack bar are available. For more information call 707/966-2134.

Facilities, fees: All resorts have boat ramps and marinas. Most have campgrounds and/or lodging. Fees are charged at resorts for day use, boat launching, and camping.

Water sports, restrictions: Powerboats, water-skiing, wake boarding, personal watercraft, sailing, and sailboarding are permitted. A public swimming beach is available at Oak Shores, about three miles south of Lake Berryessa Marina on Knoxville Road. Beaches are also available at Lake Berryessa Marina, Spanish Flat Resort, and Steele Park Resort, and are for guests only. No-wake zones are signed and strictly enforced in the vicinity of all marinas. High-speed users are advised to avoid the shoreline. No motors are permitted past the signed entrance of the northern Putah Creek arm of the lake.

Directions: From Sacramento, take I-80 east to Davis and the exit for Highway 113. Take that exit and drive north on Highway 116 to Covell Boulevard. Turn west on Covell Boulevard and drive to Winters (where the road becomes Highway 128), and then continue up Putah Creek and past Monticello Dam. See access directions for specific boat ramps, marinas, and resorts.

From the Bay Area, take I-80 east to Cordelia and the exit for Suisun Valley Road. Take that exit, turn north and drive 17 miles to Highway 121. Turn right on Highway 121 and drive seven miles to Moskowite Corners and the junction of Highway 128. See access directions for specific boat ramps, marinas, and resorts.

Contact: Contact any of the resorts listed above or Napa Chamber of Commerce, 707/226-7455, website: www.napachamber.com; Willi's Water-ski Center, Steele Park Resort, 707/966-5502.

Boat rentals: Spanish Flat Resort, 707/966-7708; Wet Dawg Watersports, 707/966-5701; Wet Pleasure and Jet Ski Rentals, 707/966-4204; Berryessa Marina Resort, 707/966-2827, website: www.lakeberryessa.com; American Watercraft Rentals, 707/966-1000; Rancho Monticello Resort, 707/966-9803.

Fishing guides: Jim Munk Fishing Guide & Instruction, 707/987-3734; Larry Hemphill Guide & Instruction, 530/674-0276.

24 LAKE RALPHINE

Rating: 5

in Santa Rosa at Howarth Park

Map 4.4, page 119

Little Lake Ralphine is located within Santa Rosa's Howarth Park. It is available for day use only and is used primarily for fishing, paddling, and rowing small boats, or for enjoying a picnic on the shore.

Some even come here just to watch the water and feed the ducks. On the lake's edge are a snack bar and a boathouse where you can rent a small boat. In early spring Ralphine is stocked with trout twice a month. There is also a trail that connects this park with nearby Spring Lake.

The surrounding Howarth Park is an ideal destination for families with young children, with pony rides, petting barn, carousel, and miniature steam train.

Access: A boat ramp is adjacent to the picnic area.

Facilities, fees: Rowboat, canoe, and sailboat rentals are available. A picnic area is nearby. Access to the lake is free.

Water sports, restrictions: Rowboats, canoes, and sailboats are permitted. No motors. No swimming or water-contact sports. All boaters must wear life jackets.

Directions: In the North Bay, take U.S. 101 to Santa Rosa and the junction with Highway 12. Turn east on Highway 12 (it will become Hoen Avenue) and continue to Summerfield Road. Turn left and drive to Howarth Park.

Contact: Santa Rosa Parks Department, 707/543-3282, website: www.santarosarec.com.

25 SPRING LAKE

Rating: 6

in Santa Rosa in Spring Lake County Park

Map 4.4, page 119

A precious handful of parks in the San Francisco Bay Area have both campgrounds and lakes, and this is one of them. The others are Del Valle Reservoir, Lake Chabot, Uvas Reservoir, Coyote Reservoir, and Pinto Lake.

Spring Lake covers 75 acres and is set within 320 acres of parkland. It is pretty, with tules on one side of the water, an exceptional sight in the spring when the surrounding hills have greened up.

This is the kind of place where you hand launch a car-top boat, then float around and enjoy the sun, watch the resident ducks, and maybe have a picnic. Some people come here to fish for trout, which are stocked in spring and early summer, or bass, which occasionally reach large sizes.

Sailboarding is a wild card at Spring Lake, best from April through early June when there are good winds in the afternoon. There are occasionally demonstrations available to the public of small sailboats. Swimming is permitted only in the lagoon area.

Spring Lake County Park offers many recreational opportunities, with hiking, biking, fishing, horseback riding trails, and picnic areas available.

Access: A two-lane paved boat ramp is located on the lake's south end, just west of the dam.

Facilities, fees: A campground, restrooms with flush toilets, drinking water, showers, and picnic areas are available. Fees are charged for day use and camping.

Water sports, restrictions: Rowboats, boats with electric motors, canoes, kayaks, and inflatables are permitted. No gas motors. All boaters must wear life jackets. Swimming is allowed only at the swimming lagoon on the lake's east side, near the visitor center. Sailboarding is permitted (sailboarders must wear life jackets), with the best access on the south end near the boat ramp.

Directions: In the North Bay, take U.S. 101 to Santa Rosa and the junction with Highway 12. Turn east on Highway 12 (it will become Hoen Avenue) and continue about .5 mile to Newanga Avenue. Turn left and drive .25 mile to the park and boat ramp at the end of the road.

Contact: Spring Lake County Park, 707/539-8092; Sonoma County Parks, 707/565-2041, website: www.sonoma-county.org/parks.

26 LAKE HENNESSEY/CONN DAM

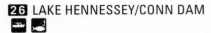

Rating: 5

north of Napa in Lake Hennessey City Recreation Area

Map 4.4, page 119

The City of Napa owns Lake Hennessey, and it does a good job of keeping quiet about it. Most people from elsewhere in the Bay Area have never heard of the place. Many call it "Conn Dam."

The lake is quite small and is used almost exclusively for fishing. The fish population is supplemented with light doses of trout plants from winter through spring.

Even in the summer Hennessey receives very little recreational traffic other than anglers. The main reason is that body contact with the water is not allowed, and that rules out swimming and sailboarding.

In addition, only boats with small engines are permitted, which at least makes for a nice, quiet visit. The shoreline is rough and covered with oak trees. A picnic area is available off the highway.

Access: An unpaved boat ramp is located on the lake's south side, just off the highway.

Facilities, fees: A picnic area is provided near the dam. Drinking water and vault toilets are available. Supplies can be obtained in Napa. Day use is free. Fees are charged for boat launching and fishing permits.

Water sports, restrictions: Boats with small motors and rowboats are permitted. No engines over 10 horsepower are permitted. Swimming, kayaking, and water-contact sports are not allowed.

Directions: Take Highway 128/29 to Napa and Trancas Street. Turn east (right if coming from the south) on Trancas and drive to the Silverado Trail. Turn north on Silverado Trail and drive about 15 miles to Highway 128 East. Turn right and drive three miles to the boat launch and recreation area.

Contact: Lake Hennessey, 707/257-9521; City of Napa, Public Works & Water, 707/257-9521.

27 LAKE SOLANO

Rating: 5

near Lake Berryessa in Lake Solano County Park

Map 4.4, page 119

Sometimes a lake is not a lake at all. That is the case with Lake Solano, which is actually Putah Creek with a small dam on it.

Whatever you call it, it does provide a quiet alternative to nearby Lake Berryessa, located immediately upstream. The water entering Lake Solano comes from Lake Berryessa's Monticello Dam, cold and clean.

Because motorized boats are prohibited from the water, this lake is a good bet for folks with canoes, rowboats, or other small people-powered craft. When Berryessa is teeming with too many people and too many fast boats, you can escape to Lake Solano to enjoy a much quieter day.

Fed by water that comes straight down from the dam, Solano is usually too cold (around 50 degrees) for swimming. That often makes it good for trout fishing. It is the closest trout stream to the Bay Area. As for sailboarding and sailing, the winds aren't strong enough for those sports. Instead, the place appeals to those who are looking for some quiet trout fishing and overflow camping when Berryessa is crowded.

Access: There is a boat ramp near the campground.

Facilities, fees: A campground, restrooms with flush toilets, showers, drinking water, RV dump station, and picnic areas are provided. Pedal boats and canoes are available for rent. Supplies can be obtained nearby. A fee is charged for day use, which includes boat launching.

Water sports, restrictions: Canoes, kayaks, inflatables, and sailboarding are permitted. No motors. Swimming is permitted, but water is often cold, sometimes weedy, and many swimmers end up wading instead.

Directions: From Sacramento, take I-80 east to Davis and the exit for Highway 113. Take that exit and drive north on Highway 116 to Russell Boulevard. Turn west on Russell Boulevard and drive to Winters (the road becomes Highway 128) and then continue up Putah Creek to the signed entrance to the park.

From the Bay Area, take I-80 east to Vacaville and I-505. Bear north on I-505 and drive to Winters and Highway 128. Turn west on Highway 128 and continue up Putah Creek to the signed entrance to the park.

Contact: Lake Solano County Park, 530/795-2990, website: www.solanocounty.com.

FOGHORN OUTDOORS®

© JOHN POIMIROO/CALTOUR

Chapter 5

Sacramento and Gold Country

Chapter 5—Sacramento and Gold Country

From a distance, this section of the Sacramento Valley looks like flat farmland extending into infinity, with a sprinkling of cities and towns. But a closer look reveals a landscape filled with Northern California's most significant rivers—the Sacramento, Feather, Yuba, American, and Mokelumne. All of these provide water recreation, in both lakes and rivers, as well as serve as the lifeblood for a series of wildlife refuges.

The highlight of the foothill country for lake recreation are the series of great lakes for water sports and fishing. These include Camanche, Rollins, Oroville, and many others. Note that the mapping we use for this region extends up to Bucks Lake, set high in Plumas National Forest, the northern start to the Gold Country.

Timing is everything in love and the great outdoors, and so it is in the Sacramento Valley and the nearby foothills. Spring and fall are gorgeous here, along with many summer evenings. But there are always periods of 100-plus temperatures in the summer.

That's what gives the lakes and rivers such appeal, and in turn, why they are treasured. Take your pick: Lake Oroville in the northern Sierra, Folsom Lake outside Sacramento . . . the list goes on. On a hot day, jumping into a cool lake makes water more valuable than gold, a cold drink on ice worth more than silver. These have become top sites for boating-based recreation and fantastic areas for water sports and fishing.

In the Mother Lode country, three other lakes—Camanche, Amador, and Pardee—are outstanding for fishing. I rank three of this chapter's lakes among the best lakes for fishing in the state—Lake Oroville and Lake Camanche make the list for bass and Lake Amador makes it for bluegill and catfish—no small feat considering the 385 other lakes they were up against.

Rafting trips are among the best in California, featuring the American (and its distinct forks), the Feather, the Yuba, and Mokelumne. These are ideal for those seeking guided trips, with dozens of outfitters available, or for experts as well.

The Sacramento River runs right through the center of the valley, north to south. I've canoed all 400 miles of it, from Redding to Fisherman's Wharf in San Francisco. The stretch from Redding to Chico is outstanding; from Red Bluff to Woodson Bridge State Recreation Area is best for first-timers; those with at least a bit of experience should check out the stretch from Redding to Red Bluff.

This region is a favorite for California history buffs, with Malakoff Diggins State Historic Park and Auburn State Recreation Area in the center of some of the state's most extraordinary history: the gold rush era.

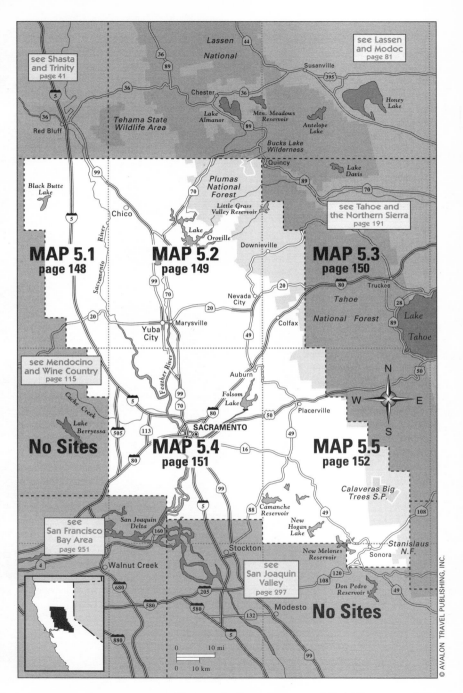

Map 5.1

Sites 1–2
Pages 153–155

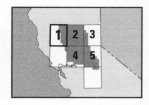

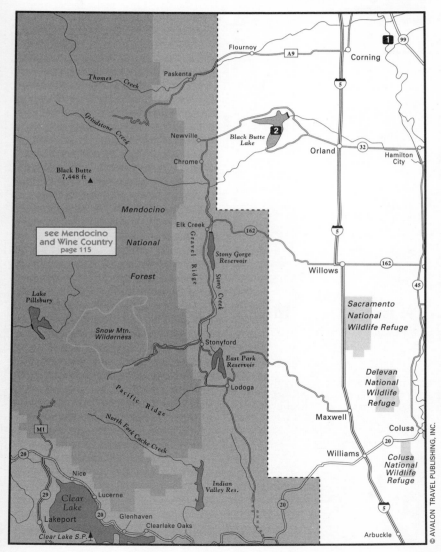

Flournoy

Corning

A9

99

5

Paskenta

Thomes Creek

Grindstone Creek

Newville

Black Butte Lake

2

Orland

32

Hamilton City

Chrome

Black Butte
7,448 ft

Mendocino

see Mendocino
and Wine Country
page 115

Elk Creek

162

5

National

Gravel Ridge

Stony Gorge
Reservoir

Willows

162

Forest

Stony Creek

45

Lake
Pillsbury

Sacramento
National
Wildlife Refuge

Snow Mtn.
Wilderness

Stonyford

East Park
Reservoir

Delevan
National
Wildlife
Refuge

Pacific Ridge

Lodoga

North Fork Cache Creek

Maxwell

Colusa

M1

20

Nice

Indian
Valley Res.

Williams

Colusa
National
Wildlife
Refuge

20

Lucerne

29

Clear
Lake

20

Glenhaven

Lakeport

Clearlake Oaks

Clear Lake S.P.

Arbuckle

5

© AVALON TRAVEL PUBLISHING, INC.

Map 5.2

Sites 3–14
Pages 155–166

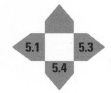

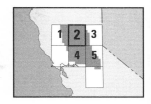

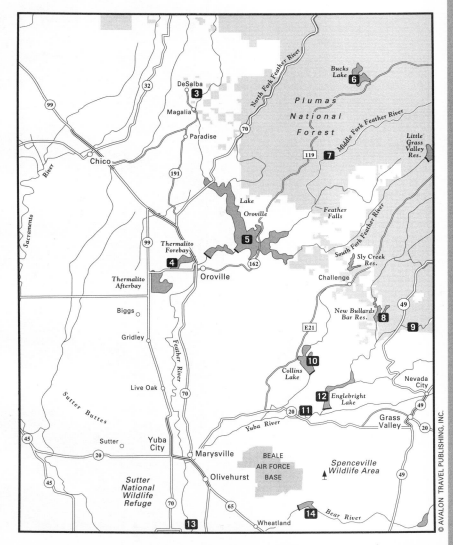

© AVALON TRAVEL PUBLISHING, INC.

Map 5.3

Sites 15–21
Pages 166–172

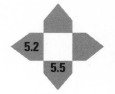

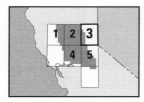

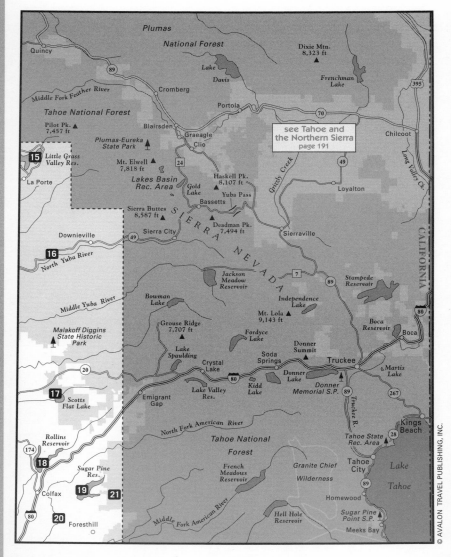

© AVALON TRAVEL PUBLISHING, INC.

Map 5.4

Sites 22–26
Pages 172–179

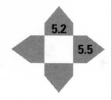

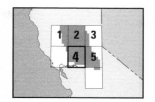

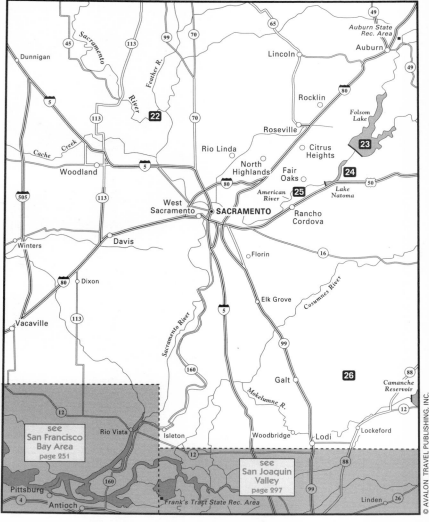

© AVALON TRAVEL PUBLISHING, INC.

Map 5.5

Sites 27–36
Pages 179–187

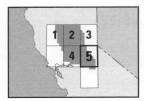

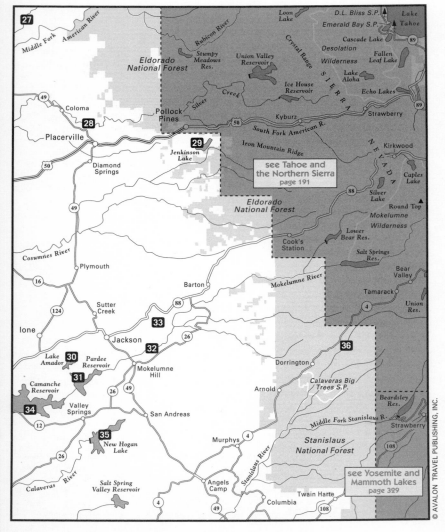

see Tahoe and the Northern Sierra page 191

see Yosemite and Mammoth Lakes page 329

© AVALON TRAVEL PUBLISHING, INC.

❶ SACRAMENTO RIVER (RED BLUFF TO COLUSA)

🚣 🎣 ⛴ 🛶 🐟 🏊 🌊 ⛺

Rating: 9

in the Sacramento Valley

Map 5.1, page 148

The old river is an emerald green fountain, the lifeblood of Northern California, and a living, pulsing vein in the heart of the state. But to phrase it a little more directly, this section of the river from Red Bluff downstream to Colusa is the prettiest part of California's Sacramento Valley, a place filled with beauty and power.

What a shame that most people never see this. The river's most visible aspect is the variety of recreation offered at Lake Red Bluff, created by a fish-killing atrocity called the Red Bluff Diversion Dam. Lake Red Bluff has calm water for ski boats, wake boards, and personal watercraft, and some areas for swimming. Conditions are often perfect in the spring and early summer for sailboarding, with a strong wind, calm water surface, and warm temperatures, yet it is extremely rare to see anyone practicing the sport. Although there are no beaches at Lake Red Bluff, there is a large grassy area on the west bank where people sunbathe and swim. This is the only practical spot for wading and swimming because water temperatures are much colder out on the main lake body.

Below the Red Bluff Diversion Dam, there is a great stretch of easy canoeing water, Class I all the way. Woodson Bridge State Recreation Area is the most popular take-out. The river is wide, cool, and bordered by riparian habitat. This is an outstanding opportunity to cool off on a typical hot summer day in the north valley.

Commercial outfitters do not offer rafting trips here. Instead, this is a do-it-yourself special; just plop in and enjoy the scenery and the wildlife. When giant blue herons lift off before your eyes, they look almost prehistoric. Other common sights are turtles sunning on rocks, hawks soaring overhead, and deer venturing out to the riverbanks. If you're lucky, you might see an eagle or even a wild turkey.

Water flows often run at 14,000 to 16,000 cubic feet per second in the summer months, a good, strong rate that makes your paddle strokes seem quite powerful. Most people take their time, with more floating than paddling, but those aboard eventually end up paddling a bit anyway. Either way you go, you gain a personal glimpse of one of the valley's least-visited paradises.

There are a few other Class I rapids that can be dealt with by taking "an inside line," as it is called, away from the white water. The evening camping is sensational on multi-day canoe and kayak trips, with a choice of many large sand bars set on the inside of pretzel turns on the river. With a canoe, you can bring plenty of supplies, so each evening is a celebration of the day, not a recovery.

Access: There are four boat ramps. Rafters should put in at the Red Bluff Diversion Dam and float down to Woodson Bridge State Recreation Area.

• Bend Bridge Public Ramp: Take I-5 to the exit for Jellys Ferry Road (north of Red Bluff.) Take that exit and turn east on Jellys Ferry Road. Continue to the signed turn off for Bend RV Park. A two-lane paved ramp is located just behind the park.

• Red Bluff Diversion Dam: Take I-5 to Red Bluff and the exit for Susanville-Highway 36. Take that exit and drive east a short distance to Sale Lane. Turn right and drive to the end of the road. A paved ramp is available that provides access downstream of the Diversion Dam.

• Red Bluff River Park: Take I-5 to Red Bluff and the exit for central Red Bluff. Take that exit west and drive to Main Street. Turn left on Main Street and drive four blocks to the Red Bluff River Park entrance. Turn left into the park and continue through the parking area to the paved ramp. Restrooms are available.

• Woodson Bridge State Recreation Area: Take I-5 to Corning and the exit for South

Avenue. Take that exit and turn east and drive six miles to the entrance on the right (immediately after crossing the river). Turn right and follow the signs to the paved boat ramp.

Facilities, fees: Several campgrounds and RV parks are located nearby. They include Bend RV Park near Red Bluff, Hidden Harbor RV Park near Los Molinos, and Woodson Bridge State Recreation Area near Corning. Lodging and supplies can be obtained in Red Bluff, Corning, and other towns. Access is free. Rafting permits are not required. A fee is charged for camping.

Water sports, restrictions: Powerboats, waterskiing, wake boarding, personal watercraft, canoes, kayaks, inflatables, and sailboarding are permitted. Swimming is permitted at Lake Red Bluff. Life preservers are required for all users with inflatables.

Directions: The river is accessible off roads that join with I-5 near Red Bluff, Corning, and Orland. Highway 45 parallels the river southeast of Orland, and direct access is available to Colusa.

Contact: Lake Red Bluff Recreation Area, 530/527-2813; Woodson Bridge State Recreation Area, 530/839-2112, website: www.parks .ca.gov (click on Find A Park); Shasta Cascade Wonderland Association, 530/365-7500 or 800/474-2782, website: www.shastacascade.org; Kittle's Outdoor Sport Company (kayak rentals/shuttles), 530/458-4868, website: www.kit-tlesoutdoor.com; Driftwood RV (rentals, shuttles, camping), 530/384-2851, website: www .campdriftwoodrvpark.com; Hidden Harbor RV, 530/384-1800.

2 BLACK BUTTE LAKE

Rating: 6

near Orland

Map 5.1, page 148

Hit this lake at the wrong time and you'll get the vacation from hell. Hit it right and you'll wonder why more people aren't taking advantage of paradise on earth. The reality here is that there is rarely an in-between.

If you come in late March, April, or May, you will find a pretty lake amid freshly greened foothills, with some 40 miles of shoreline and lakeside camps.

But arrive in late July or August and you will find a low water level, brown and mostly barren hillsides, and camps like sweat pits. Let there be no doubt as to when you should plan your trip.

Black Butte is set at 500 feet in elevation in the west valley foothills and covers 4,500 surface acres. Just a short jog off I-5, the lake is easily accessible, making it very attractive to people with trailered boats. It gets heavy use during the prime season, when warm temperatures set in and spring gives way to summer.

This is the best time for water-skiing, wake boarding, and powerboating, as well as for fishing for crappie, a prize that attracts many anglers.

The best launch points for sailboarding as well as for wading or swimming are near the Orland Buttes Campground and at the Buckhorn Day-Use Area.

The water is warm at Black Butte and, as mentioned previously, the lake is best visited in spring and early summer. By fall not only do the surroundings turn brown, hot, and dusty, but the water levels drop, creating a number of boating hazards just under the surface.

Access: There are boat ramps at Buckhorn, Orland Buttes, and Eagle Pass.

Facilities, fees: Campgrounds, restrooms with flush toilets and coin showers, and drinking water is available. An RV dump station, convenience store, and propane gas are available. Access is free. Fees are charged for boat launching and camping.

Water sports, restrictions: Powerboats, waterskiing, wake boarding, personal watercraft, sailing, and sailboarding are permitted. Swimming areas are available near Buckhorn Picnic Area and at Eagle Pass Day-Use Area, near the dam.

Directions: To Buckhorn: From I-5 in Orland, take the Black Butte Lake exit. Drive about

12 miles west on Road 200/Newville Road to Buckhorn Road. Turn left and drive a short distance to the campground and boat ramp on the north shore of the lake.

To Orland Buttes: From I-5 in Orland, take the Black Butte Lake exit. Drive west on Road 200/Newville Road for eight miles to Road 206. Turn left and drive three miles to the camp entrance and boat ramp on the left.

To Eagle Pass: Drive as above to the fork with Buckhorn Road and Road 206. Bear right (signed for the dam) and drive to the turn on the left for the Eagle Pass Picnic Area and boat ramp. Turn left and continue to the paved boat ramp.

Contact: U.S. Army Corps of Engineers, Black Butte Lake, 530/865-4781.

3 PARADISE LAKE

Rating: 5

near Paradise

Map 5.2, page 149

There are a lot of things you can't do at Paradise Lake. You can't have a motor on your boat. You can't swim. You can't sailboard. There's no campground, yet they charge a day-use fee. Car-top boats are strictly regulated by lake officials; only "approved" craft (that is, approved by them) are permitted. Kayaks cannot be completely self-enclosed, inflatables must have two outside air chambers, and all boaters must wear life jackets at all times.

Despite all the can'ts, Paradise Lake has earned a fair rating. Set at 3,000 feet in the Mount Lassen foothills, the pretty lake is in the transition zone where the valley woodlands give way to alpine country. With all the boating restrictions, the lake is primarily visited by trout fishermen. There is also a pretty picnic area, and you can plunk in a car-top boat.

You get quiet water that is ideal for small paddle-powered boats. In early summer this can be the perfect place to bring your canoe and spend a few calm, relaxing hours.

Access: A paved boat ramp is located across from the picnic area on North Lake Road.

Facilities, fees: A day-use picnic area is provided. Supplies can be obtained in Paradise. Fees are charged for day use and boat launching.

Water sports, restrictions: Rowboats, canoes, kayaks (no self-enclosed kayaks), and inflatables (must have at least two air chambers) are permitted. No motors. No swimming, sailboarding, or water-contact sports. Life jackets must be worn at all times when on water. No dogs.

Directions: From Chico, drive south on Highway 99 to Skyway Road. Turn east on Skyway Road and drive 10 miles to Paradise and Coutolenc Road. Turn right on Coutolenc Road and drive 3.5 miles to the lake entrance.

Contact: Paradise Lake Irrigation District, 530/873-1040, website: www.paradiseirrigation.com.

4 THERMALITO FOREBAY

Rating: 6

near Oroville in Lake Oroville State Recreation Area

Map 5.2, page 149

With so many boaters, campers, and anglers heading to nearby Lake Oroville (see next listing), Thermalito Forebay is becoming a surprisingly attractive option to those who prefer quiet water and freedom from motorized boats. Although small compared to the giant Lake Oroville, the Forebay is not exactly pint-sized, covering 300 acres in the Oroville foothills at an elevation of 900 feet.

The North Forebay is the prettiest area here and makes the best spot for swimming and sailboarding. Only non-motorized boats are allowed, so you get quiet water and don't have to keep looking over your shoulder. There is also a swimming beach and a picnic area with drinking water, shaded shelters, and lots of trees. What a concept.

The South Forebay, on the other hand, is visited almost entirely by people hoping to land

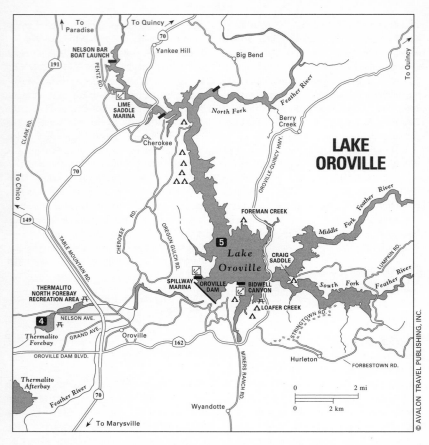

a few fish. It is much more primitive, offering only vault toilets and not a tree (or a fire hydrant) in sight. Dogs have it tough.

At less than 1,000 feet in elevation, this area gets hit with blowtorch heat day after day once midsummer arrives. Visit then and you might as well camp in the caldera of a volcano.

Access: The North Forebay has a two-lane paved ramp, and the South Forebay has a four-lane paved ramp.

Facilities, fees: A day-use picnic area is provided at the North Forebay. Restrooms with drinking water and flush toilets are available. Supplies can be obtained in Oroville. Fees are charged for day use and boat launching.

Water sports, restrictions: Motors are not permitted on the North Forebay. A sandy beach is available for swimming, and sailboarding and sailing are allowed. The South Forebay is open to all boating. There is a 5-mph speed limit within 100 yards of the shoreline. Swimming access is available along the shore.

Directions: To North Forebay: Take Highway 70 to Oroville and continue two miles to Garden Drive. Turn left on Garden Drive and drive .5 mile to the picnic area.

To South Forebay: Take Grand Avenue west and drive three miles to the parking area.

Contact: North Thermalito Forebay, 530/538-2221; Lake Oroville State Recreation Area,

530/538-2200; Huntington's Sportsman's Store, 530/534-8000, website: www.huntingtons.com.

⑤ LAKE OROVILLE

Rating: 9

near Oroville

Map 5.2, page 149

Lake Oroville is a huge, man-made reservoir with extensive lake arms and a large central body of water. When full, it covers more than 15,000 acres and offers 165 miles of shoreline. Throughout much of the year, Oroville has it all: campgrounds, enough water for all kinds of boating, a fish for every angler, and accommodations that are tailor-made for the boater/camper, including boat-in floating campsites, floating toilets (no kidding), and an excellent marina.

You will find this beauty in the Sacramento foothills set at an elevation of 900 feet. The fully developed recreation sites make it a favorite family destination. Most newcomers head to the Bidwell Canyon area, where the primary marina, boat ramp, and most of the campgrounds are located. But there are many alternatives.

Fishing has improved in recent years at Oroville. Anglers seek out the quiet water in the lake coves, where there is fantastic underwater cover for spotted bass; 30- and 40-fish days are common in May and June.

In the summer the water in the main lake warms up, making it ideal for water-skiing. Water temperatures in June can be 5 to 10 degrees colder up in the lake arms. Most skiers prefer the warm water, and anglers tend to prefer the cold water. By mid-July, though, even the water up in the lake arms begins to warm significantly. When the water levels are high, it creates a dramatic setting, especially for water-skiing in the old Feather River Canyon.

Several problems at Lake Oroville prevent its being awarded a perfect 10 rating. First, in years with light rains, so much water is drained out of the lake for farmers that the place can look like the Grand Canyon of Oroville by September, with acres and acres of exposed lake bottom. That makes the hike up to the boat-in campsites long and steep. After heavy winters, however, the problem isn't nearly as severe. Another dilemma is the weather. At an elevation of 900 feet in foothill country, the lake gets some very hot temperatures in the summer. Anybody who isn't prepared for it will shrivel like a prune. Creating shade, whether on your boat or at your camp, is critical.

Major advances in bass fishing here are the result of habitat improvement projects and the success of spotted bass. At reservoirs in the foothills, the Department of Fish and Game planted spotted bass, which solved a 50-year problem of lake drawdowns leaving the spawns of largemouth bass high and dry. Spotted bass spawn deep, so reproduction is very high, even with drawdowns. That is why Oroville, Berryessa, Camanche, Folsom, Shasta, and many others are now loaded with bass.

The DFG has advanced this success at Oroville by creating a slot limit, that is, that all bass 12 to 15 inches must be released. That is why there are more big spotted bass at Oroville than any other lake in Northern California; it has the Northern California record: 14 pounds, 11 ounces.

Improvements at Lake Oroville, including upgraded boat-in campsites, make this big lake an ideal destination for an overnight boating/camping trip.

Access: Four paved boat ramps are available:
• Bidwell Canyon Marina: From Highway 70 in Oroville, take the Oro Dam Boulevard exit, turn right, and drive 1.5 miles to Highway 162/Olive Highway. Turn right and drive approximately seven miles to Kelly Ridge Road. Turn left and continue to Arroyo Road. Turn right and continue to the marina and the paved boat ramp. Houseboats, ski boats, fishing boats, and pontoon boats are available for rent.
• Lime Saddle: From Oroville, take Highway 70 and drive nine miles north to Pentz Road.

Turn left on Pentz Road and drive three miles; look for signs indicating the marina. A multi-lane paved boat ramp and a dock are provided.
• Loafer Creek: From Highway 70 in Oroville, take the Oro Dam Boulevard exit, turn right, and drive 1.5 miles to Highway 162/Olive Highway. Turn right and drive eight miles to the turnoff for Loafer Creek Campground. A paved launch ramp is adjacent to the campground.
• Spillway: From Highway 70 in Oroville, take the Oro Dam Boulevard exit and follow the signs heading to the dam and the adjacent multilane paved boat ramp.
Facilities, fees: Campgrounds, restrooms with flush toilets and coin showers, and RV dump station are available. Floating campsites and restrooms are available on the lake. Marinas with boat accessories and convenience stores are available. Fees are charged for day use, boat launching, and camping. Day use and boat launching fees are charged.
Water sports, restrictions: Powerboat, water-skiing, wake boarding, personal watercraft, sailing, sailboarding, and swimming are permitted. Swimming beaches are located near Loafer Creek and Bidwell Canyon Campgrounds.
Directions: To State Recreation Area: From the Sacramento area, drive north on I-5 and to the junction with Highway 99/70. Turn north on Highway 99/70 and continue on Highway 70 into Oroville to Highway 162. Turn east and drive eight miles to Kelly Ridge Road. Turn north (left) and drive 1.5 miles to Arroyo Drive. Turn right and drive to the state park entrance.
Contact: Lake Oroville Visitor Center (open weekends), 530/538-2219; Lake Oroville State Recreation Area, 530/538-2200, website: www.parks.ca.gov (click on Find A Park); Oroville Chamber of Commerce, 530/538-2542 or 800/655-4653; Bidwell Canyon Marina, 530/589-3165, website: www.gobidwell.com.
Fishing guides: Cash Colby, 530/533-1510; Larry Hemphill, 530/674-0276; Huntington Sportsman's Store, 530/534-8000, website: www.huntingtons.com.

6 BUCKS LAKE

Rating: 10

near Quincy in Plumas National Forest

Map 5.2, page 149

Here's one of the perfect boating/camping/fishing spots if only—if only it attracted fewer people.

Bucks Lake is set at an elevation of 5,200 feet in Plumas National Forest, about a 25-minute drive out of Quincy. That's remote enough to make you feel like you're on the edge of wilderness and high enough to give you a full dose of the four seasons. It's an ideal destination for a family on a camping trip with a boat.

At 1,800 acres the lake is big enough for all water sports. Campers tend to congregate on the lake's northwest side, where the less expensive Forest Service campgrounds are located; the marina, cabins, and developed facilities are all on the east side. The campsites are pretty and wooded, some with views of the lake, and provide excellent shoreline access. Trout fishing is outstanding here; it's one of the state's top mountain lakes for trout. In addition to good numbers of rainbow trout, there are also occasionally huge rainbow, brown, and mackinaw trout.

When the water levels are high, the lake has a gemlike beauty, its deep blue-green surface contrasted with a forested backdrop and an azure summer sky. But even when the water is low, there are benefits, as several beaches become accessible. In high water, only the beach at the Sandy Point Day-Use Area is available.

The lake freezes over every winter, and snow buries the access road. The road is usually plowed by the end of April or very early in May, and even with snow still on the ground at the campgrounds, fishing is usually outstanding. By late June, the surface waters start to warm and powerboaters and skiers come out to take advantage of the warm midday temperatures. The combination of clear water and frequent afternoon winds makes Bucks Lake by far the best in the region for sailboarding, a fact that is not well known.

What is well known, however, is that this lake is just about the perfect destination for families who are hauling their boats along in search of some camping fun. That fact keeps the place full of happy folks.

Access: There are three paved boat ramps, all on the east side of the lake. When you're driving in on Bucks Lake Road, look for the signs for Lakeshore Resort, Bucks Lake Lodge, and Haskins Valley Inn.

Facilities, fees: Lodging, marinas, boat rentals, cabins, campgrounds with drinking water, and a picnic area are available. Convenience stores and a restaurant are available. Access is free. Fees are charged for camping and boat launching.

Water sports, restrictions: Powerboats, waterskiing, wake boarding, and personal watercraft are permitted. Swimming and sailboarding are allowed; the best beach is at the Sandy Point Day-Use Area on the northwest end of the lake.

Directions: From Oroville, drive north on Highway 70 to the junction with Highway 89. Turn south on Highway 89/70 and drive 11 miles to Quincy. In Quincy, turn right at Bucks Lake Road and drive 16.5 miles to the lake and the resort on the right.

Contact: Plumas National Forest, Mount Hough Ranger District, 530/283-0555; Bucks Lake Lodge, 530/283-2262 or 800/481-2825; Bucks Lake Marina, 530/283-4243; Bucks Lakeshore Resort, 530/283-6900, website: www.bucks lake.com; Timberline Inn, 530/283-9667 or 800/481-28925.

7 MIDDLE FORK FEATHER RIVER

Rating: 4

northeast of Oroville in Plumas National Forest

Map 5.2, page 149

The Middle Fork Feather River is one of the wildest streams in Northern California. Cut-

ting through the bottom of a deep canyon, it is beautiful and free-flowing, remote and untamed. Most people who venture here are hikers and backpackers taking steep, butt-kicking trails in and out of the canyon, some crossing the river on the Pacific Crest Trail. There are a number of pools for fishing and swimming, though the water is cold.

Only a handful of expert rafters will try conquering the Middle Fork Gorge, a wild and woolly run that can be terrifying. A series of Class IV and V rapids, as well as some unrunnable suicide portions, must be portaged. These include several waterfalls, even the dramatic Granite Dome Falls. Newcomers should have at least one person in their party who knows the river well, and they should attempt running the river only during low water. The season when this river is runnable is very short. Flows cannot be too high, nor too low. No commercial rafting companies are permitted to offer trips on this section of river.

That said and done, you have a 32-mile run at the bottom of a canyon in beautiful, extremely remote country. It is a virtual wilderness, where rafters are commonly treated to wildlife sightings and lush vegetation borders much of the river. Once you embark on this run, there is no way out of the canyon, so you are committed to heading downstream all the way to the take-out. Rescues are nearly impossible.

Access: There is no boat ramp. Rafters may put in at the following locations:

• Upper put-in: From Quincy, drive southeast on Highway 70/89 for three miles to La Porte Road. Turn south and drive seven miles. The put-in is on the left bank, just past the bridge. Note: This Class V+ run is considered one of the most difficult in the state. Only highly skilled and experienced boaters should attempt it, and then only in kayaks or self-bailing rafts.

• Milsap Bar: In Oroville, drive to the junction of Highway 70 and 162. Turn north on Highway 162 (Olive Highway) and drive 26 miles to the town of Brush Creek and Bald Rock Road. Turn right (south) on Bald Rock Road and drive .5 mile to Forest Service Road 22N62 (Milsap Bar Road). Turn left and drive (steep and rough) to Middle Fork Feather and the Middle Fork Bridge. Access is available directly off the road. Other sections of the Middle Fork Feather are also available by hiking or driving to other trailheads and access points.

• Blairsden: Drive north on Highway 70/89. Access is available off the highway between the towns of Blairsden and Sloat, and off trails that junction with it.

Facilities, fees: Primitive campgrounds with vault toilets are available nearby. No drinking water. Garbage must be packed out. Supplies can be obtained in Oroville and Blairsden. Access is free. Rafting permits are not required.

Water sports, restrictions: Rafting, kayaking, and swimming are allowed. No commercial rafting companies are permitted to offer trips on this section of river. Various swimming holes are available off the access roads mentioned above. Reaching some spots requires hiking; consult a map of Plumas National Forest for specifics.

Directions: See directions to put-ins in Access, above.

Contact: Plumas National Forest, Feather River Ranger District, 530/534-6500; Sportsmen's Den, 530/283-2733. For a map, send $6 to U.S. Forest Service, Attn: Map Sales, P.O. Box 587, Camino, CA 95709, 530/647-5390, fax 530/647-5389, website: www.fs.fed.us/r5/forests. Major credit cards accepted.

8 BULLARDS BAR RESERVOIR

Rating: 10

near Camptonville in Tahoe National Forest

Map 5.2, page 149

Bullards Bar Reservoir shines like a silver dollar in a field of pennies when compared to the other reservoirs in the Central Valley foothills.

The lake is set at an elevation of 2,300 feet, and with 4,700 surface acres and 55 miles of shoreline, it covers a lot of territory. Not only are there two boat-in campgrounds, but boaters are allowed to create their own primitive campsites anywhere along the lakeshore (a chemical toilet is required). This is a great breakthrough for boater/campers, and the combination of boat-in campgrounds and do-it-yourself sites make this one of the best bets in California.

There's more, too. The average surface temperature in the summer is 78 degrees, ideal for all water sports. The steep shoreline makes this a poor place for children to go wading, but most people here have boats, and the warm water makes it great for boats towing just about anything—skiers, wake boarders, and tubers. It is a kick just to strap on a life preserver and float around for an hour on a hot summer afternoon.

The fishing runs hot and cold here. Prospects are best when trolling for kokanee salmon, a growing fishery. Rainbow trout are also caught.

Many of the 155 major reservoirs in California are just water-storage facilities, drawn down at the whims of the water brokers regardless of the effects on recreation and fisheries. But the folks who control the plumbing at Bullards Bar somehow manage to keep this lake nearly full through July, even in low-water years when other reservoirs have been turned into dust bowls. So right off, you get good lakeside camping, boating, and general beauty along with a lot of water.

Access: Two paved ramps are available, one at Dark Day Day-Use Area on the west side of the lake, and one at Emerald Cove Marina on the south end of the lake.

Facilities, fees: A full-service marina is available at Emerald Cove with fishing boat, ski boat, pontoon boat, and houseboat rentals. A snack bar and convenience store are also available. Boat-in camping includes two developed boat-in campgrounds, with vault toilets available, and many primitive boat-in sites with no drinking water where boaters are required to bring portable chemical toilets. Garbage must be packed out. Full supplies can be obtained in Marysville, Camptonville, and Dobbins. Access is free.

Water sports, restrictions: Powerboats, water-skiing, wake boarding, personal watercraft, sailing, sailboarding, and swimming are permitted. The best swimming areas are in coves accessible only by boat.

Directions: To Emerald Cove Marina: From Marysville, drive northeast on Highway 20 to Marysville Road. Turn north at Marysville Road (signed Bullards Bar Reservoir) and drive about 10 miles to Old Marysville Road. Turn right and drive 14 miles to reach the entrance road for Cottage Creek Launch Ramp and the marina (turn left just before the dam).

To reach the Dark Day boat ramp, continue over the dam and drive four miles, turn left on Dark Day Road, and continue to the ramp.

Contact: Emerald Cove Resort and Marina, 530/692-3200; Yuba County Water Agency, 530/741-6278; Tahoe National Forest, North Yuba Ranger Station, 530/288-3231. General information website: www.bullardsbar.com.

9 SOUTH FORK YUBA RIVER

Rating: 6

east of Nevada City in Tahoe National Forest

Map 5.2, page 149

With beautiful, clear blue water and forested banks flanked by granite boulders and walls, this is a particularly scenic river. Recreational options include swimming and sunbathing, as well as hiking, fishing, and panning for gold.

Although swimming in the river can be excellent, things sometimes turn dangerous. On hot days the pools look cool and inviting, but swimmers who are new to the river may not recognize how cold and swift the water can be or just how quickly they can get into trouble. The risk is heightened greatly when swimmers down a lot of beer and their judgment is impaired. Despite the river's fun nature, several people drown here each year, usually during a period of high snowmelt.

Explorers will discover a number of spots along the river that are ideal for picnicking and

sunbathing. The prettiest one is at Purdon Crossing, which has become notorious for nude bathing; if that isn't what you have in mind, head in the other direction to Edwards Crossing.

This river is generally too shallow and rocky for rafting, but early in the season and at high water it is possible for expert kayakers to have a go at it. A 12-foot waterfall below Humbug Creek must be portaged. Again, this is rafted by experts only, usually in the company of at least one or two others who have experience on the river and can recognize the portage spot before everyone goes sailing over the waterfall.

Access: There is no boat ramp. Three of the best swimming holes are available north of Nevada City:

• Edwards Crossing: From Highway 49 in Nevada City, drive to North Bloomfield Road. Turn north on North Bloomfield Road and drive up a hill until you come to a Y intersection. Bear right and continue about five miles to the parking area at Edwards Crossing.

• Highway 49 Bridge: From Nevada City, drive north on Highway 49 for 6.5 miles to the Highway 49 bridge.

• Purdon Crossing: From Highway 49 in Nevada City, drive to North Bloomfield Road. Turn north on North Bloomfield Road and drive up a hill until you come to a Y intersection. Bear left at the sign for Lake Vera-Purdon Crossing and continue about five miles on a dirt road to the river at Purdon Crossing.

Facilities, fees: Campgrounds are available off I-80; there is also a campground just over the river from Purdon Crossing. Restrooms are provided at Edwards Crossing. Supplies can be obtained in Nevada City and off I-80. Access is free.

Water sports, restrictions: See directions for swimming areas above.

Directions: From Sacramento, take I-80 east to Emigrant Gap to Indian Springs Road and continue to the exits for Eagle Lakes or Big Bend/Rainbow Road. Access to this section of the Yuba is available from either road. Much of the land bordering the South Yuba is private; be on the lookout for signs.

Contact: Tahoe National Forest, Nevada City Ranger District, 530/265-4531, fax 530/478-6109; Bureau of Land Management, Folsom Field Office, 916/985-4474.

10 COLLINS LAKE

Rating: 9

north of Marysville in Collins Lake Recreation Area

Map 5.2, page 149

The boating rules have resolved most of the potential user conflicts at Collins Lake, setting an example for lakes across the rest of the state.

Conflicts between water-skiers and anglers are kept to a minimum because each group has a separate area to roam in the summer. In addition, skiing is not allowed after September 30, when the water-skier crowds tend to dwindle anyway, and cool water attracts more people who want to fish at the lake.

Set at 1,200 feet in the foothill country of Yuba County, Collins Lake is a pretty spot that's ideal for the camper/boater. The lake covers 1,000 acres and has 12 miles of shoreline. Temperatures are warm from March through October, and in the summer visitors enjoy day after day of hot weather and cool water. In late spring, when the foothills are green and the lake sparkles, the area can almost appear to be glowing.

A recreation area has been developed to accommodate hordes of summer visitors. It includes a huge swimming beach with restrooms, showers, and snack bar, and well-maintained picnic and camping facilities. Many folks use the swimming beach as a jumping-off point for sailboarding; conditions for this sport are fair here. Sailing is not popular.

If you see someone pulling into the campground towing a trailer with a personal watercraft, don't panic; personal watercraft users will often camp here, then drive 20 minutes up the road to Bullards Bar for the day.

Are you starting to think that this quality operation must attract a good number of people? Well, you got that right. On weekends from Memorial Day through Labor Day, the campgrounds are almost always filled to capacity.

This lake is known among serious anglers as an outstanding destination for trophy-size trout, especially in spring. Bass fishing is also good.

Access: A paved boat ramp is located between the picnic area and the southernmost campground.

Facilities, fees: A full-service marina is available with rentals for fishing boats, rowboats, kayaks, pedal boats, and pontoon boats. Campgrounds, restrooms, drinking water, flush toilets, RV dump station, coin-operated showers, volleyball, three group picnic areas, convenience store, coin laundry, wood, ice, and propane gas are available. Fees are charged for day use, boat launching, and camping.

Water sports, restrictions: Powerboats, canoes, kayaks, inflatables, sailing, and sailboarding are permitted. Water-skiing and wake boarding are permitted from May 15 through September 30 only. No personal watercraft permitted. Designated areas reserved solely for fishing with a 5-mph speed limit. A large, sandy swimming beach is available near the picnic area.

Directions: From Marysville, drive east on Highway 20 for about 12 miles to Marysville Road. Turn north and drive approximately eight miles to the recreation area entrance road on the right. Turn right, drive a mile to the entrance station, and then continue to the campground.

Contact: Collins Lake Recreation Area, 530/692-1600 or 800/286-0576, website: www.collins lake.com.

11 YUBA RIVER

Rating: 5

from Browns Valley to Marysville

Map 5.2, page 149

The Yuba is one of California's great rivers

for inner tubing. Unfortunately, that means that it is not so great for other water sports.

Throughout the Sacramento and San Joaquin Valleys, the condition of many rivers depends on water releases from the reservoirs located upstream. In this case, the fact that Bullards Bar Reservoir is always so full of water means that the Yuba River is often quite low.

That makes it perfect for inner tubing. Tubers should be aware that they are advised to wear life jackets, that access here is difficult, and that if you hit the river on a rare day when water releases are up out of Bullards Bar, the flows of the Yuba can be swift. Several sandbars along the river make the best spots for swimming, but they are inaccessible by car. Some tubers will float to these spots, set up a day camp and picnic site, then enjoy themselves and jump into the river now and then. Camping is not permitted on the river.

The Yuba is usually too shallow for boats larger than canoes or kayaks, and even kayakers must occasionally get out and portage their boats to deeper water. Another pain is that it is necessary to take out above Daguerra Dam, where you portage, and then put in below the dam and continue downstream to Marysville.

The Yuba is used mostly by locals. Upstream, difficult access is a perennial problem, with the river bordered for many miles by private property—the landowners treat it as their personal river to be used as they see fit, not a public resource available to all.

Access: There is no boat ramp. Canoeists and kayakers can put in at Parks Bar, located at the bridge where Highway 20 crosses the river, approximately 20 miles east of Marysville. Note: Boaters must take out above Daguerra Dam (there are warning signs for boats). Another put-in is available just below the dam. From here, boaters can continue all the way to Marysville.

Facilities, fees: Lodging and supplies can be obtained in Marysville or Yuba City. No commercial rafting trips. Access is free.

Water sports, restrictions: Rafting, canoe-

ing, and kayaking are permitted. Swimming is best at eddies adjacent to extended sandbars. Swimming is not recommended in the main river channel.

Directions: Take I-5 to Williams and junction with Highway 20. Take Highway 20 east and drive about 30 miles to Marysville. Access is available at the Simpson Lane Bridge in Marysville and at the E Street Bridge on Highway 20. Much of the Yuba upstream is bordered by private property and public access is very difficult.

Contact: Marysville Parks and Recreation, Yuba County, 530/741-6666, website: www.marysville.ca.us; Yuba City, website: www.yubacity.net; Johnson's Tackle, Yuba City, 530/674-1912. River Guide Service, 530/673-5716, website: http://cdec.water.ca.gov.

12 ENGLEBRIGHT LAKE

Rating: 10

northeast of Marysville

Map 5.2, page 149

This lake resembles a huge water snake winding its way through the Yuba River Canyon. Although Englebright covers just 815 acres, it has 24 miles of shoreline.

Englebright Lake is set at an elevation of 520 feet in the Yuba County foothills, so it gets hot here in the summer, ideal for sun-loving water enthusiasts. It is a water-skiing mecca, with warm and calm water (south of Upper Boston). A bonus is that the nearby shoreline gives skiers an illusion of greater speed—something you don't get on a wide-open lake.

But the real bonanza here is for boaters. There are 100 boat-in campsites, more than any other lake in California. These campsites rarely fill up, even in summer when the lake can get crowded on weekends with day-use water-skiers.

As with any narrow lake where high-speed water-skiers run the risk of rounding a point and plowing into a low-speed fishing boat, crowded conditions can present major conflicts. But rules have been enacted to resolve that problem: All boating is permitted up to Upper Boston, yet fast boating is restricted from Upper Boston upstream to the North Fork Yuba. So you find people happily waterskiing below Upper Boston, and people contentedly fishing above Upper Boston where the trout fishing is good.

Because Englebright Lake is set in a river canyon, the shoreline drops abruptly and is quite rocky. Hence most of the lake provides poor swimming access, but there are still a few sandy stretches adjacent to the campgrounds.

The water level is fairly stable, but boaters should be aware of underwater hazards. With a boat at Englebright Lake, you can enjoy water sports to your heart's desire and still have the luxury of a pretty campsite.

Access: Two paved ramps are available, one just east of the dam, adjacent to the picnic area, and one at the marina at Skipper's Cove. There are signs for each on the entrance road.

Facilities, fees: Boat-in campsites, group camp, vault toilets, full-service marinas, moorings, convenience store, fuel dock, and houseboat, pontoon boat, ski boat, fishing boat, canoe, and pedal boat rentals are available. Drinking water is available at the marina. Day use is free. Fees are charged for day use, boat launching, and camping.

Water sports, restrictions: Powerboats, waterskiing, wake boarding, personal watercraft, sailing, and sailboarding are permitted only below the lake's Upper Boston area. Sandy beach areas are located near several of the boat-in campgrounds.

Directions: From Auburn, drive north on Highway 49 to Grass Valley and the junction with Highway 20. Turn west on Highway 20 and drive to Mooney Flat Road (if you reach Smartville, you have gone a mile too far). Turn right on Mooney Flat and drive three miles to a fork. Turn left at the fork and drive a mile to park headquarters and the boat ramp just east of the dam.

Contact: U.S. Army Corps of Engineers, Sacramento District, Englebright Lake, 530/639-2342, website: www.englebrightlake.com; Skipper's Cove, 530/639-2272.

13 FEATHER RIVER

Rating: 6

from Marysville to Sacramento

Map 5.2, page 149

The placid appearance of the Feather River often belies its true nature. Actually, the river has quite a strong current, and anyone thinking of getting into the water should be prepared to wear a life jacket. This goes for swimmers, sailboarders, water-skiers, and personal watercraft riders.

Many of the people on the river, however, are in powerboats whose engines have been converted to jet drives. As you might guess, most of them are here to bring in a few fish. The river attracts striped bass in the spring, shad in the early summer (best at Shanghai Bend), and salmon in late summer and fall (best at Verona).

The most popular general recreation area, complete with boat ramp, is at Riverfront Park near Marysville. Another boat ramp is at Verona Marina, located near where the Feather feeds into the Sacramento River; this is primarily a boat-access point used by anglers.

Access: River access is limited. Paved boat ramps are available at Riverfront Park and Verona Marina.

Facilities, fees: Boating services are available at Verona Marina. Riverfront Park has picnic facilities, drinking water, and restrooms with flush toilets. Campgrounds and lodging are available nearby. Supplies can be obtained in Yuba City and Marysville. Day use is free. Private marinas charge a fee for boat launching.

Water sports, restrictions: Powerboats, waterskiing, personal watercraft, drift boats, canoes, kayaks, sailboarding, and swimming are permitted. Swimming is not recommended in most areas. No swimming at banks or boat dock at Riverfront Park.

Directions: To Shanghai Bend: Take I-5 to Williams and the junction with Highway 20. Turn east on Highway 20 and drive 30 miles to Yuba City and the Garden Highway. Turn south on Garden Highway and drive four miles to Shanghai Bend Road. Turn left and continue on a dirt road to the parking area.

To Verona: At the junction of I-5 and Highway 99 (north of Sacramento), take Highway 99 north and drive eight miles to Sankey Road. Turn left and drive two miles west to the Verona Marina.

To Riverfront Park: From Yuba City, drive east on Highway 20 into Marysville, cross the bridge and continue to the second stoplight, turn left and continue to a stop sign. Continue straight to a second stop sign. Turn left, continuing over a levee, and follow the signs to Riverfront Park.

Contact: Yuba City Parks and Recreation, 530/822-4650, website: www.yubacity.net; Verona Marina, 916/927-8387; City of Marysville, 530/741-6666, website: www.marysville.ca.us; River Guide Service, 530/673-5716, website: http://cdec.water.ca.gov.

14 CAMP FAR WEST RESERVOIR

Rating: 9

east of Marysville

Map 5.2, page 149

Camp Far West is one of the best lakes for bass fishing in the Sacramento Valley. It is set at an elevation of 320 feet in the foothill country, getting an early spring followed by a hot summer. The lake covers 2,000 surface acres with 29 miles of shoreline, and is an outstanding destination for boating and water sports, with warm water, hot weather, and plenty of room for everybody.

For the most part, users split the lake into two areas. Most powerboaters and water-skiers head to the lake's southern side. It can get out-

rageous on the weekends when a few impromptu boater parties get under way with lots of liquids and suntan lotion flowing almost as fast as the jet boats. In fact, jet boat races are held here during the summer.

The northern side of the lake, on the other hand, tends to be quieter, a setting for more family-oriented activities. This is also where the lake's best day-use area is located. Waterskiers should note that there is a large rocky area on the northwest side of the lake that should be avoided when the water level drops.

Because the lake is used to store water for agricultural use, by late summer the levels can fall quite a bit. In fact, in low rain years the change can be quite drastic. By late August it is recommended that visitors call ahead for conditions. The lake typically drops up to 36 feet by fall. When full in spring, the lake can be 200 feet deeper than in early winter.

Use is moderate on summer weekends, high on three-day holidays, and light during the week.

Access: There are two paved boat ramps, one on the north side and one on the south side. Clearly marked signs for both boat ramps are posted on the entrance road.

Facilities, fees: Campgrounds, flush toilets, drinking water, and picnic areas are available. On the north shore, a boat dock with fishing boats, personal watercraft, and pedal boat rentals is available. Convenience store, bait and tackle, and snack bars are nearby. On the south shore, gas, boat dock, and limited facilities are available. Fees are charged for day use (including boat launching) and camping.

Water sports, restrictions: Powerboats, waterskiing, wake boarding, personal watercraft, sailing, and sailboarding are permitted. A large day-use and swimming area is provided on the north side near the campground; a smaller swimming area is available on the lake's south side.

Directions: From I-80 in Sacramento, drive east toward Roseville to Highway 65. Turn north on Highway 65 and drive to the town of Sheridan and Rio Oso Road. Turn right on Rio Oso Road and drive about five miles to McCourtney Road. Turn left on McCourtney Road and drive to the lake. The road circles the lake and provides access to campgrounds and launching ramps at the north and south shores.

Contact: Camp Far West, North Shore, 530/633-0803; South Shore, 916/645-0484; boat rentals, 530/742-6277.

15 LITTLE GRASS VALLEY RESERVOIR

Rating: 8

near La Porte in Plumas National Forest

Map 5.3, page 150

This lake has become quite popular, and why not? It has a little bit of everything, and most of it is high quality. The lake is set at an elevation of 5,000 feet in Plumas National Forest and covers 1,600 acres, so you get alpine beauty plus plenty of room for people to enjoy all water sports.

Boat launching is free, a nice perk. The water is clear and, by midsummer, has warmed up. Lake levels are usually quite good. A program establishing kokanee salmon has given the fishery a boost, too.

The best places for sailboarding and swimming are near the campgrounds on the east side of the lake. This is a great spot for recreation, with hiking trails (the Pacific Crest Trail runs nearby) and a number of Forest Service roads in the area.

But it is the camper/boater who benefits most. You name it, you can get it here. Except for solitude, that is. A growing number of summer visitors are becoming quite enamored with the place, so expect company.

Access: Three paved boat ramps are available.
Facilities, fees: Campgrounds, restrooms with flush toilets, drinking water, and an RV dump station are available. Supplies can be obtained in La Porte. Access and boat launching are free. A fee is charged for camping.
Water sports, restrictions: Powerboats, water-

skiing, wake boarding, personal watercraft, sailing, sailboarding, and swimming are permitted. Swimming beaches are available at Running Deer and Little Beaver Campgrounds.

Directions: To Wyandotte: From Oroville, drive east on Highway 162 for about eight miles to the junction signed Challenge/LaPorte. Bear right (to LaPorte) and drive east past Challenge and Strawberry Valley to LaPorte. Continue two miles past LaPorte to the junction with County Road 514/Little Grass Valley Road. Turn left and drive one mile to a junction. Turn left and drive one mile to the campground entrance road on the right.

To Black Rock: Drive as above to LaPorte. Continue two miles past LaPorte to the junction with County Road 514/Little Grass Valley Road. Turn left and drive about five miles to the campground access road on the west side of the lake. Turn right on the access road and drive .25 mile to the campground and nearby boat ramp.

To Peninsula Tent: Drive as above to County Road 512 (which becomes County Road 514/Little Grass Valley Road) for three miles to Forest Road 22N57. Continue on Forest Road 514 for one mile to the campground entrance on the right. Turn right and drive .25 mile to the campground.

Contact: Plumas National Forest, Feather River Ranger District, 530/534-6500.

16 NORTH YUBA RIVER

Rating: 9

near Sierra City in Tahoe National Forest

Map 5.3, page 150

The North Fork Yuba is one of the prettiest streams to flow westward out of the Sierra Nevada. The stretch of river near Downieville is especially gorgeous; it is fed by the melting snow from the Sierra crest, has deep pools and miniature waterfalls, and is in places edged by slabs of granite and punctuated with boulders.

In the spring, this can be a wild and cold

force of water, running blue-white during peak snowmelt. In the summer and fall, it greens up, warms considerably, and takes on a more benign demeanor in its routed canyon course.

Highway 49, which is shaped more like a pretzel than a highway, parallels much of the river, providing access not only to the stream but to a series of campgrounds operated by the Forest Service. Along the road are many good swimming holes that are accessible from the camps. One of the best is six miles east of Downieville near Quartz Point at Union Flat Campground.

Rafting season generally lasts from April through June here, and the river offers several great runs. The two best are the Downieville Run and the Goodyears Bar Run. Spanning 19 miles, Downieville Run features white water rated Class IV-V. The Class V highlights include Moss Canyon and Rossasco Ravine. This is a tight canyon with lush vegetation and cold water. Wet suits or dry suits are necessary; they are available for rent from Whitewater Voyages.

Goodyears Bar Run is one of the prime one-day rafting trip runs in California. It covers eight miles with a series of Class III-IV rapids and one monster Class V called Maytag, which rafters who are unfamiliar with the river may choose to portage. The trip can be extended farther downstream to Bullards Bar Reservoir, and the reward for doing so is a six-mile stretch with Class IV-IV+ white water. You pay for this encounter, however, by having to paddle 12 slow miles across flat water at the reservoir to the nearest take-out, Dark Day Boat Ramp. It would be wise to make advance arrangements for a tow.

Access: No boat ramp is available. Put-ins for the two popular rafting runs described above:
• Downieville Run: To reach the put-in, from Downieville, drive east on Highway 49 for six miles to Union Flat Campground. Take out 10 miles downstream at the Goodyears Bar Bridge or continue through the Goodyears Bar Run. Note: This run is Class IV-V with

some very difficult sections and should be run by experts only.
• Goodyears Bar Run: From Downieville, drive west on Highway 49 for about five miles to Goodyears Bar. Take out downstream at Fiddle Creek Campground or continue an additional eight miles to Bullards Bar Reservoir (which requires a long paddle on flat water).
Facilities, fees: Campgrounds with drinking water and vault toilets are available nearby. Supplies can be obtained in Bassetts, Sierra City, Downieville, and Camptonville. Access is free. A fee is charged for camping.
Water sports, restrictions: Rafting and kayaking are permitted. There are several excellent swimming holes along Highway 49, with the best at the Forest Service campgrounds.
Directions: From Auburn, take Highway 49 north to Nevada City and continue (the road jogs left, then narrows) to Camptonville. Drive 9.5 miles to the campground entrance on the right. This is a good starting spot. Access is available at pullouts along Highway 49 up past Sierra City.
Contact: Tahoe National Forest, Nevada City Ranger District, 530/265-4531.

Guided rafting trips: Whitewater Voyages, 510/222-5994 or 800/488-7238, website: www.whitewatervoyages.com; Beyond Limits Adventures, 209/869-6060 or 800/234-7238, website: www.rivertrip.com; Tributary Whitewater Tours, 530/346-6812 or 800/672-3846, website: www.whitewatertours.com.

17 SCOTTS FLAT LAKE

Rating: 8

east of Nevada City in Scotts Flat Recreation Area

Map 5.3, page 150

Scotts Flat Lake is one of the prettier lakes in the Sierra Nevada foothills. The reservoir is shaped like a teardrop, with 7.5 miles of shoreline circled by forestland at an elevation of 3,100 feet. With a campground located close to the water's edge and a nearby boat launch, it makes for an ideal family camping destination.

The lake covers 850 surface acres. The primary activities are camping and fishing, but there are also some surprisingly outstanding sailing and sailboarding conditions from a predictable afternoon breeze. The best places to sailboard are at Scotts Flat Marina and on the other side of the lake at Cascade Shores. All boating (except for personal watercraft) is permitted.

Visitor use is high on summer weekends, when the campgrounds almost always fill up. The lake's developed area is called Gate 2, which has a store, boat ramp, and large campground, set on the lake's north side. A more primitive campground, called Gate 1, is available on the undeveloped, southern shore.

The surrounding scenery is beautiful and heavily forested, and there are lots of hiking trails nearby. Trout fishing is good in the spring and early summer.

Access: There are two boat ramps:
• Cascade Shores: On Highway 49 in Nevada City, drive to Red Dog Road. Turn south on Red Dog Road and drive three miles to Quaker Hill Road. Turn left on Quaker Hill Road and drive east to the sign for the Cascade Shores Day-Use Area.
• Scotts Flat Marina: From Auburn, drive north on Highway 49 to Nevada City and the junction with Highway 20. Turn right on Highway 20 and drive five miles (east) to Scotts Flat Road. Turn right and drive four miles to the entrance road on the right (on the north shore of the lake).

Facilities, fees: A full-service marina with fishing boat and pedal boat rentals are available. Two campgrounds and a picnic area are located on the lake's northwest side. A day-use area is provided on the southeast side. Restrooms, coin showers, coin laundry, RV dump station, general store, bait and tackle shop, and a playground are also available. A restaurant is four miles away. Fees are charged for day use, boat launching, and camping.

Water sports, restrictions: Powerboats, water-skiing, wake boarding, sailing, and sailboarding are permitted. No personal watercraft are allowed. Sandy beaches with roped-off swimming areas are located at the day-use area at Scotts Flat Marina and at Cascade Shores Day-Use Area. No horses or motorcycles are allowed in the recreation area.

Directions: From Auburn, drive north on Highway 49 to Nevada City and the junction with Highway 20. Turn right on Highway 20 and drive five miles (east) to Scotts Flat Road. Turn right and drive four miles to the entrance road on the right (on the north shore of the lake).

Contact: Scotts Flat Recreation Area, 530/265-8861; Scotts Flat Marina, 530/265-0413.

18 ROLLINS LAKE

Rating: 8

southeast of Grass Valley

Map 5.3, page 150

Just a short drive north from Colfax brings you to Rollins Lake, set at an elevation of 2,100 feet at the point where the foothill country becomes forest. The result is a mix of pine, cedar and oak trees. In late winter the snow line is somewhere around here as well. The result is a lake that crosses the spectrum as a trout lake and bass lake, water-ski lake, and a swimming lake.

Rollins extends far up two lake arms, covering 825 acres with 26 miles of shoreline. It can get quite hot in summer, which makes this place attractive for swimming and water-skiing. The latter is very popular, with boaters drawn to the warm summer weather and water ranging 75 to 80 degrees. Sunny weather, good campgrounds, cabin rentals, and the opportunity for all water sports make Rollins Lake a winner in the summer.

Another plus is that boat ramps and large, sandy swimming beaches are available near all four campgrounds. With all this to offer, it's no surprise that the lake draws fairly large crowds throughout the summer. Your best bet for snagging a remote campsite is at Peninsula Campground (reached via Highway 174 and You Bet Road); although it's developed and has full facilities, it gets less traffic than Orchard Springs or Long Ravine. Long Ravine is by far the most popular area because it is located next to the marina and restaurant. This is also the best put-in spot for sailboarding, though this sport (as well as sailing) is not popular at Rollins Lake.

Access: There are four paved boat ramps (see Directions, below).

Facilities, fees: A full-service marina with powerboat, fishing boat, canoe, kayak, and pontoon boat rentals is available. Lodging, cabins, campgrounds, restrooms with showers, convenience stores, RV dump station, a restaurant, floating gas dock, dock rentals, and swimming beach with water slide are available. Supplies can be obtained in Colfax. Fees are charged for day use, boat launching, and camping.

Water sports, restrictions: Powerboats, waterskiing, wake boarding, personal watercraft, sailing, and sailboarding are allowed. Beaches with roped-off swimming areas are available at each of the four campgrounds.

Directions: To Long Ravine: From Auburn, drive northeast on I-80 for about 20 miles to Colfax/Highway 174. Turn north on Highway 174 (a winding, two-lane road) and drive about two miles to Rollins Lake Road. Turn right on Rollins Lake Road and drive 1.5 miles to the campground and boat ramp at 26909 Rollins Lake Road.

To Orchard Springs/Rollins Lakeside Inn: From Auburn, drive northeast on I-80 for about 20 miles to Colfax and Highway 174. Turn north on Highway 174 (a winding, two-lane road) and drive 3.7 miles (bear left at Giovanni's Restaurant) to Orchard Springs Road. Turn right on Orchard Springs Road and drive .5 mile to the road's end. Turn right at the gatehouse and continue to the campground and boat ramp.

To Peninsula: From Auburn, drive north-

east on I-80 for about 20 miles to Colfax and Highway 174. Turn north on Highway 174 and drive about eight miles (a winding, two-lane road) to You Bet Road. Turn right and drive 4.3 miles (turning right again to stay on You Bet Road), and continue another 3.1 miles to the campground entrance and boat ramp at the end of the road.

To Greenhorn: From Auburn, drive northeast on I-80 for about 20 miles to Colfax and Highway 174. Turn north on Highway 174 and drive (a winding, two-lane road) to Greenhorn Road. Turn right and drive to the boat ramp.

Contact: Rollins Lake Resort/Long Ravine Campground, 530/346-6166, website: www.long ravineresort.com; Orchard Springs Campground, 530/346-2837; Greenhorn Campground, 530/272-6100; Peninsula Campground, 530/477-9413 or 866/469-2267, website: www.penresort.com. Wake boarding lessons, 530/272-6100.

19 SUGAR PINE RESERVOIR

Rating: 7

northeast of Auburn in Tahoe National Forest

Map 5.3, page 150

Lakeside campgrounds make Sugar Pine Reservoir a popular summer vacation spot. Covering 160 acres, the lake is set at 3,600 feet in the lower alpine region of the Sierra Nevada. The surrounding area is heavily forested, the lake is quite scenic, and for the most part, access is not difficult. A paved trail circles the lake.

The 10-mph speed limit ensures that activities are subdued and the water remains calm. Fishing, canoeing, swimming, and sailboarding appeal to most visitors. The recreation area is fully developed, and the campgrounds can fill up. There are nice areas for swimming, sailboarding, and with the water always calm and quiet, canoeing.

The trout fishing at Sugar Pine is fair—that is, not great, not bad.

A bonus is that some facilities are wheelchair-accessible.

Access: A paved boat ramp is available on the south shore.

Facilities, fees: Campgrounds, vault toilets, drinking water, and a picnic area are available. An RV dump station is located near the boat ramp. Supplies can be obtained in Foresthill. Fees are charged for day use and camping.

Water sports, restrictions: Powerboats, canoes, kayaks, inflatables, sailboarding, and sailing are permitted. A 10-mph speed limit is strictly enforced. Swimming is available near the campgrounds and picnic areas on the north side of the lake.

Directions: From Sacramento, drive east on I-80 to the north end of Auburn and the Foresthill Road exit. Take that exit and drive east for 20 miles to Foresthill. Drive through Foresthill (road changes to Foresthill Divide Road) and continue for eight miles to Sugar Pine Road/Forest Road 10. Turn left and drive five miles to the lake and campground.

Contact: Tahoe National Forest, Foresthill Ranger District, 530/367-2224.

20 NORTH FORK AMERICAN RIVER

Rating: 10

near Auburn

Map 5.3, page 150

The scenery is superb here, with impressive canyons, lush vegetation, clear and cold water, and a wilderness-like feel to the entire canyon. Of the three forks of the American River, the North Fork is the most difficult to run in a raft. Anybody who makes it through Locomotive Falls, Dominator, and Nutcracker Chute is bound to feel lucky to be alive and may even want to kiss the nearest available rock rooted firmly in solid ground.

The rafting season generally runs from April to June; in high water years, it starts a bit later and lasts into the beginning of July. Although access is limited, there are plenty of campsites along the river below the Giant Gap Run.

Although the water's clear and cold, you must always purify it before drinking. The water is cold enough that most rafting outfitters require all participants to wear wet suits or dry suits on guided trips.

Here are the breakdowns on the available runs:

Big Bend and Clementine Runs is a nine-mile stretch of all Class I and II water—a nice, scenic traverse where you can catch your breath and congratulate yourself on making it out alive if you cascaded through the upper river.

Chamberlain Falls Run is a very popular run, a particular favorite with commercial rafting companies. It is named after Chamberlain Falls, rated Class IV+, but includes a heart-thumping vertical drop of eight feet. You'll never forget it. Other highlights include Slaughter's Sluice (Class IV), Zig-Zag (Class IV), Bogus Thunder (Class IV), and Devil's Staircase (Class IV+).

Giant Gap Run is the most difficult run on the North Fork, and it is very popular. It is rated Class V, experts only. Rafters who are new to the river should be in rafts guided by experts. The run cuts through a very narrow, scenic gorge. Just to reach the put-in requires a downhill two-mile hike (an easy descent), which means boats and gear must be carried in. For this reason, most commercial trips start farther downstream at the Colfax-Iowa Hill Road bridge access.

For those willing to pay the price, encounters with some of the most daredevil white water imaginable await. You will meet Nutcracker Chute (Class V), then Locomotive Falls (Class V-V+ with a vertical drop), and Dominatrix (Class V) and Dominator (Class V). All four may be portaged. Of the four, Locomotive Falls is the run most often portaged. Everybody has a hell of a time. Heaven or hell? You decide.

The proposed Auburn Dam project would eliminate the possibility of rafting on both the Chamberlain Falls and Big Bend Runs of the North Fork, as well as the entire stretch of the

Middle Fork. An alternate proposal seeks to turn these areas into a protected National Recreation Area, an idea that's much more appealing to rafters for obvious reasons. Many of the rafting companies listed below have information on how individuals can support this effort.

Access: There are four well-known put-ins:

• Giant Gap Run: From Auburn, take I-80 east past Colfax to the exit for Alta. Take that exit to Casa Loma Road. Turn southeast on Casa Loma Road and drive three miles to the Euchre Bar Trailhead. A two-mile hike is required to reach the river. The put-in is just past a small bridge that crosses the America River. Take out 14 miles downstream at the bridge at Colfax-Iowa Hill Road, or continue through the Chamberlain Falls Run. Note: Giant Gap run is Class V; experts only.

• Chamberlain Falls Run: From Auburn, take I-80 east to Colfax to the exit for Canyon Way. Take that exit and turn south (right) on Canyon Way and drive .5 mile to Colfax-Iowa Hill Road. Turn left (east) and drive to the bridge that crosses the river. Take out five miles downstream at the Shirttail Canyon access or continue through the Big Bend Run. Note: Chamberlain Falls Run is Class IV-V+; experienced paddlers only.

• Big Bend Run: From Auburn, take I-80 east to Colfax to the exit for Canyon Way. Take that exit and turn south and drive to Yankee Jim's Road (watch for the sign for Foresthill). Turn left and drive east to the put-in (located slightly upstream from the bridge on the left). Take out 4.5 miles downstream at Ponderosa Way or continue through the Clementine Run, another 4.5 miles.

• Clementine Run: From Auburn, take I-80 east to the exit for Weimar Crossroad. Take that exit to Canyon Way. Turn south and drive 5.5 miles (the road turns to dirt) to a bridge that crosses the American River. Put in on the right bank, just below the bridge. Take out 4.5 miles downstream at Clementine Lake, where Upper Clementine Road intersects on the left bank. Most of this run is a mild Class I-II.

Facilities, fees: Campgrounds with vault toilets and drinking water are available nearby. Supplies can be obtained in Auburn. Access is free. Rafting permits are not required. Fees are charged for camping.

Water sports, restrictions: Rafting, kayaks, and inflatables are permitted. Swimming is available at the Highway 49 bridge and near the rafting put-ins for the Big Bend and Clementine Runs (see Access, above).

Directions: From Sacramento, drive east on I-80 to Auburn. From Auburn drive south on Highway 49. Access is available at the confluence of the North Fork and Middle Fork of the American River where the bridge crosses the river.

Contact: Bureau of Land Management, Folsom Field Office, 916/985-4474; Auburn State Recreation Area, 530/885-4527.

Guided rafting trips: Action Whitewater Adventures, 800/453-1482 or 801/375-4111 (international), website: www.riverguide.com; Adventure Connection, 530/626-7385 or 800/556-6060, website: www.raftcalifornia.com; All Outdoors Whitewater Rafting, 925/932-8993 or 800/247-2387, website: www.aorafting.com; American River Recreation, 530/622-6802 or 800/333-7238, website: www.arrafting.com; American Whitewater Expeditions, 818/352-3205 or 800/825-3205, website: www.americanwhitewater.com; Chili Bar Outdoor Center, 530/621-1236 or 800/356-2262, website: www.cbocwhitewater.com; Earthtrek Expeditions, 530/642-1900 or 800/229-8735, website: www.earthtrekexpeditions.com; Mariah Wilderness Expeditions, 510/233-2303 or 800/462-7424, website: www.mariahwe.com; Motherlode River Trips, 530/626-4187 or 800/427-2387, website: www.malode.com; Outdoor Adventure River Specialists (OARS), 209/736-4677 or 800/346-6277, website: www.oars.com; Rapid Descent Adventures, 530/659-7800; River and Rock Adventures, 916/965-6262; Tributary Whitewater Tours, 530/346-6812 or 800/672-3846, website: www.whitewatertours.com; Whitewater

Connection, 530/622-6446 or 800/336-7238, website: www.whitewaterconnection.com; Whitewater Excitement, 530/888-6515 or 800/750-2386, website: www.whitewaterexcitement.com; Whitewater Voyages, 510/222-5994 or 800/488-7238, website: www.whitewatervoyages.com; Wilderness Adventures, 530/926-6282 or 800/323-7238, website: www.wildrivertrips.com; Whitewater Expedition & Tours (WET), 916/451-3241, website: www.raftwet.com.

Rentals: California Canoe & Kayak, Rancho Cordova, 916/353-1880; Sierra Outdoor Center, Auburn, 530/885-1844. Rentals are not available in El Dorado County because of county ordinance.

21 BIG RESERVOIR/MORNING STAR LAKE

Rating: 6

northeast of Auburn in Tahoe
National Forest

Map 5.3, page 150

Beautiful Big Reservoir—also called Morning Star Lake—is a 70-acre freshwater pocket surrounded by forest and set at an elevation of 4,100 feet. In addition to being quite pretty, it is also quiet because no gas-powered motors are permitted.

A picnic area is provided at the lake's edge, and a campground is available nearby. With all these features, this little lake is becoming a favorite for families. Many families find that the lake is easily accessible, located a relatively short distance from Sacramento.

Another wonderful aspect of Big Reservoir is that conditions are about perfect for sailboarding. A breeze kicks in around 9 A.M. and continues into the late afternoon, only to pick up again around 7 P.M. In addition, you can swim anywhere on the lake because the entire shoreline is sandy and gently sloped. The lake is stocked with rainbow trout.

Morning Star Resort offers a developed camp-

ground with showers. The lake is very popular on summer weekends and the campground fills quickly for Friday and Saturday nights.

Access: A primitive boat ramp is available next to the picnic area.

Facilities, fees: A campground, vault toilets, drinking water, and picnic area are available. Restrooms with showers, a small store, and pedal boat rentals are available at Morning Star Lake Resort. Supplies can be obtained in Foresthill. A day-use parking fee is charged.

Water sports, restrictions: Gas-powered motors are not permitted on the lake. Sailboarding is allowed. Swimming beaches are provided, but you can swim anywhere along the shoreline.

Directions: From Sacramento, drive east on I-80 to the north end of Auburn and the Foresthill Road exit. Take that exit and drive east for 20 miles to Foresthill. Drive through Foresthill (road changes to Foresthill Divide Road) and continue for eight miles to Sugar Pine Road. Turn left and drive about 4.5 miles to Forest Road 24 (signed Big Reservoir). Bear right on Forest Road 24 and drive about 1.5 miles to the campground and lake entrance road on the right.

Contact: Tahoe National Forest, Foresthill Ranger District, 530/367-2224, fax 530/367-2992; Morning Star Lake Resort, 530/367-2129.

22 SACRAMENTO RIVER (COLUSA TO SACRAMENTO)

Rating: 7

in the Sacramento Valley

Map 5.4, page 151

When I canoed the entire Sacramento River, this particular section left the most lasting memories, both good and bad.

Near Colusa the river is quite beautiful as it winds its way southward. The banks are lined with trees, and there are some deep holes, gravel bars, and good fishing for salmon in the fall and for striped bass in the spring. Most of the boaters are there to go fishing. You will occasionally see a water-skier or personal water-craft rider, as well as a few power cruisers out for a scenic river drive.

The bulk of the recreational traffic is near the Feather River mouth at Verona and the American River mouth in Sacramento near Discovery Park. In fact, the latter is sometimes inundated with people on warm summer weekend afternoons.

After all, nearby Sacramento is the state's capital and the largest city in the valley, and this beautiful river represents to a lot of people the best chance to enjoy freedom and fun.

The scenery is dramatic in Sacramento. In addition to the riparian zone along the river, you see some old bridges, the occasional ship, and a wide variety of boats, from runabouts to yachts. Both water-skiing and personal watercraft have become quite popular, along with power cruising and pontoon boating. Fishing is generally fair at the mouths of the American and Feather Rivers, with the best prospects for salmon in the fall and for striped bass in the winter and spring.

The river is quite benign in the summer months when it has a decent flow, green water, and a predictable nature. Such is not the case, however, the rest of the year. Runoff causes the water to turn murky and run swiftly, and is highest in the spring and early summer. After big storms, all manner of debris is sent floating down the river, even trees, creating dangerous boating hazards. In addition, dead fog is common from mid-December through early February.

For the most part, the Sacramento River is a great recreational resource, made even more important by the number of people living nearby.

Fishing is often excellent during peak migrations, with the best section of river from Sacramento to Freeport. In the spring, striped bass fishing can be outstanding near Colusa. In the fall, salmon fishing takes on the entire river.

Many people have never seen the river section between Colusa and Verona, largely a nightmare. Many long segments have been converted into a virtual canal by the U.S. Army Corps of Engineers; they have turned the riverbanks into rip-rapped levees, complete with beveled edges and 90-degree turns. These parts of the river are treeless, virtually birdless, and the fish simply use it as a highway, migrating straight upriver without pausing. There are a few river holes near Grimes, but that's about it. The best reason to venture to this stretch of water south of Colusa is outstanding fishing for crawdads. Commercial crawdad traps are found all along the rocky, rip-rapped banks.

Access: Boat ramps are available at several locations. Canoeists and kayakers can also put in at these boat ramps:

• Colusa/Sacramento River State Recreation Area: From I-5 in Williams, turn east on Highway 20 and drive to Colusa and 10th Street. Turn north on 10th Street and continue to the park entrance. There is a paved ramp. For more information call 530/458-4927.

• Ward's Boat Landing: From I-5 at Williams, turn east on Highway 20 and drive to Colusa and Market Street. Turn right on Market Street to the road's end. Turn left (still on Market), drive over the bridge to Butte Slough Road. Turn right on Butte Slough Road and drive five miles to the marina. There is a paved ramp. For more information call 530/696-2672.

• Verona Marina: At the junction of I-5 and Highway 99, take Highway 99 north and drive eight miles to Sankey Road. Turn left and drive two miles west to Verona Marina. Or: From I-5 north of Sacramento, take the Garden Highway north and drive approximately nine miles to Verona. Full services and a paved ramp. For more information call 916/927-8387.

• Alamar Marina: From I-5 north of Sacramento, take the Garden Highway north and continue to Alamar Marina, where there is a paved ramp. For more information call 916/922-0200. Pontoon boats, ski boats, and fishing boats are available for rent next door at Metro Marina, 916/920-8088.

• Discovery Park: From I-5 at Sacramento,

take the Garden Highway exit and turn left and drive to Natomas Park Drive. Turn right and drive to the traffic signal, and follow the signs into Discovery Park. Sacramento County Parks, 916/875-6672.

• Miller Park: From I-5 at Sacramento, turn east on I-80 and drive to Sixth Street. Take the Sixth Street exit and drive south to Broadway. Turn right and continue to Miller Park. A paved ramp and a marina are provided. City of Sacramento Marina, 916/264-5712.

• Freeport Marina: From I-5 south of Sacramento, take the Pocket Road exit. Turn left on Pocket Road and drive to Freeport Boulevard. Turn right and drive .74 miles to the marina, 916/665-1555.

• Clarksburg Flat: From I-5 south of Sacramento, take the Pocket Road exit. Turn left on Pocket Road and drive to Freeport Boulevard. Turn right and drive about one mile (until you come to a bridge). Turn right, cross the bridge, make an immediate left, and follow the road through Clarksburg. The paved ramp is located about 2.5 miles south of Clarksburg on the left side.

Facilities, fees: Discovery Park has picnic facilities available. Campgrounds, lodging, and supplies are available in the Sacramento area. Fees for day use and camping are at state parks. Boat launching fees charged at all private marinas.

Water sports, restrictions: Powerboats, water-skiing, wake boarding, and personal watercraft are permitted. Sailboarding and swimming are allowed, but due to the river's murky water and steep drop-offs, swimming is generally not recommended along this section's northern reaches. Sandy beaches are available at the Colusa-Sacramento River State Recreation Area, and along the Garden Highway north of Sacramento at Discovery Park, and south of Sacramento near Clarksburg. No-wake zones are posted near boat ramps and marinas.

Directions: Access is available off roads that junction with I-5.

Contact: Sacramento Chamber of Commerce, 916/552-6800; Sacramento County Department

of Regional Parks, Recreation & Open Space, 916/875-6961, website: www.sacparks.net.

Services: Sherwood Harbor Marina, 916/371-3471, website: www.sherwoodharbor.com; Freeport Bait, Sacramento, 916/665-1935; Broadway Bait, Sacramento, 916/448-6338; Kittle's Outdoor Sport Company, 530/458-4868, website: www.kittlesoutdoor.com.

Boat rentals: Houseboats, pontoon boats, ski boats, personal watercraft, and fishing boats at Alamar Marina, Sacramento, 916/922-0200; personal watercraft and ski boats at Mikk's Jet Ski and Boat Rentals, Metro Marina, Sacramento, 916/923-2466; canoes and kayaks at California Canoe & Kayak, Rancho Cordova, 916/353-1880.

Boat charters and tours: Riverboat Cruises, two paddlewheeler boats that accommodate 150 to 400 people each, 916/552-2933 or 800/433-0263, website: www.spiritofsacramento.com; River City Queen, Sacramento, 916/921-1111; River Otter Water Taxi, Sacramento, 916/446-7704, website: www.riverotter.com; Delta Expeditions, 37-foot yacht, Rio Vista, 916/600-2420, website: www.deltaexpeditions.com.

23 FOLSOM LAKE

Rating: 9

northeast of Sacramento in Folsom Lake State Recreation Area

Map 5.4, page 151

Folsom Lake State Recreation Area is Sacramento's backyard vacation spot, a huge lake covering some 18,000 acres with 75 miles of shoreline, which means plenty of room for boating, water-skiing, fishing, and suntanning.

Because of the lake's shallow arms, water levels can fluctuate dramatically from winter to spring. This lake can look almost empty before the rains start in winter, then in spring seem to fill overnight.

This is an extremely popular (and populated) spot in summer. Families, college students, and anyone in Sacramento with a yearning for some lake-oriented fun seem to flock here, sometimes at the same time. Some come for the water-skiing, some for the fishing, and some for the camping.

Visitors have the use of attractive swimming beaches with lifeguards and buoys, several boat ramps, boat rentals, and nice campgrounds and day-use areas. Fishing is available for trout, bass, catfish, and perch. The adjoining recreation area has a network of trails for jogging, hiking, and horseback riding.

Temperatures get extremely hot here in the summer. One-hundred-degree days are common, and as early as May the mercury often hits the 90s. If you stick around long enough, you'll witness just about every imaginable stunt that is borne of the combination of hot sun, cold suds, and lots of people.

There are opportunities for hiking, biking, running, picnics, and horseback riding. A 32-mile long trail connects Folsom Lake with many Sacramento County parks before reaching Old Sacramento. This trail is outstanding for family biking and in-line skating.

Access: There are five paved boat ramps:
• Folsom Point: From Sacramento, take U.S. 50 east to the exit for Folsom. Take that exit to Folsom Boulevard and drive to Blue Ravine Road. Turn right on Blue Ravine Road and drive four miles to East Natoma Road. Turn right and drive to the boat ramp adjacent to a picnic area. A multi-lane paved ramp is available.
• Folsom Lake Marina: From Sacramento, take U.S. 50 east to the exit for Folsom. Take that exit to Folsom Boulevard and drive to Blue Ravine Road. Turn right on Blue Ravine Road and drive four miles to Green Valley Road (road name changes from Blue Ravine to Green Valley). Continue straight for approximately two miles to the signed turn for Folsom Lake Marina on the left. Take that turn and drive to marina. A multi-lane paved boat ramp is available.
• Granite Bay: Take I-80 east of Sacramento

to the exit for Douglas Boulevard. Take that exit to Douglas Boulevard East and drive to where it dead-ends at Granite Bay. A multi-lane paved ramp is available.
• Peninsula: Take I-80 east of Sacramento to Auburn and the exit for Maple Street. Take that exit, stay right on Maple Street and drive south (it turns into Auburn-Folsom Road) four miles to Rattlesnake Bar Road. Turn right on Rattlesnake Bar Road and drive 2.5 miles to the entrance. A paved ramp is available.
• Rattlesnake Bar: From Placerville, drive north on Highway 49 (toward the town of Coloma) for 8.3 miles into the town of Pilot Hill and Rattlesnake Bar Road. Turn left on Rattlesnake Bar Road and drive nine miles to the end of the road and the park entrance.

Facilities, fees: Campgrounds, picnic areas, restrooms with flush toilets and showers, drinking water, mooring, ice, bait and tackle, and a snack bar (summer only) are available. Folsom Lake Marina has full boating services and rents out fishing boats in summer. Rentals of pontoon boats, ski boats, fishing boats, and personal watercraft are also available near the Granite Bay boat launch. Supplies can be obtained in Folsom. Fees are charged for day use, boat launching, and camping.

Water sports, restrictions: Powerboats, water-skiing, wake boarding, personal watercraft, sailing, and sailboarding are permitted. Designated swimming beaches are available at Granite Bay and Beals Point. Swimming is permitted anywhere along the shoreline except at boat launching areas. For boat-in camping, boats must be registered at either the marina off Green Valley Road or Granite Bay.

Directions: From Sacramento, drive east on U.S. 50 to the Folsom Boulevard exit. Turn left at the stop sign and continue on Folsom Boulevard for 3.5 miles, following the road as it curves onto Leidesdorff Street. Head east on Leidesdorff Street for .5 mile, dead-ending into Riley Street. Turn left onto Riley Street and proceed over the bridge to Folsom-Auburn Road. Turn right on Folsom-Auburn Road and drive north for 3.5 miles to the park entrance on the right.

Contact: Folsom Lake State Recreation Area, 916/988-0205; Folsom Lake Marina, 916/933-1300; Fran and Eddy's Sports Den, Rancho Cordova, 916/363-6885; Folsom Lake Boat Rentals, 916/223-8129, website: www.folsom-lakerentals.com.

24 LAKE NATOMA

Rating: 6

east of Sacramento at Nimbus Dam

Map 5.4, page 151

Below every major reservoir is usually a small lake called an afterbay, and Lake Natoma is just that for big Folsom Lake to the east. Natoma provides water-sports enthusiasts in the area with a decent alternate destination for sailboarding, sailing, fishing, and low-speed boating.

This narrow lake covers 500 acres with 13 miles of shoreline. Because it gets its water from the bottom of Folsom Dam, Natoma tends to be colder than big brother Folsom.

The real plus here is quiet and calm water. Water-skiing is prohibited and a 5-mph speed limit is enforced, so visitors never have to compete with personal watercraft and speedboats.

The CSUS Aquatic Center draws a college-age crowd who come to learn about sailboarding and sailing. Sailing and rowing are the two most popular activities on the lake. Recreation is concentrated at two points: the Aquatic Center for boaters, and Negro Bar for campers, swimmers, and picnickers. Use is fairly heavy in the summer.

Access: Boat ramps for launching small boats are located at the California State University System (CSUS) Aquatic Center on the lake's south end, and at Negro Bar on the west end.

Facilities, fees: Restrooms with flush toilets and drinking water are available. Rowboats, sailboats, and sailboards are available for rent. CSUS Aquatic Center offers sailing and sail-boarding classes. Fees are charged for day use and boat launching.

Water sports, restrictions: Boats with small motors, canoes, kayaks, inflatables, sailing, and sailboarding are permitted. A 5-mph speed limit is strictly enforced. A sandy swimming beach is available at Negro Bar. You can also swim at Nimbus Flat, but there is no beach.

Directions: From I-80 north of Sacramento, take the Douglas Boulevard exit and head east for five miles to Auburn-Folsom Road. Turn right on Auburn-Folsom Road and drive south for six miles until the road dead-ends into Greenback Lane. Turn right on Greenback Lane and merge immediately into the left lane. The park entrance is approximately .2 mile on the left.

Contact: Folsom Lake State Recreation Area, 916/988-0205, website: www.ca.parks.gov (click on Find A Park); CSUS Aquatic Center, 916/985-7239, website: www.csusaquaticcenter.com; Fran & Eddy's, 916/363-6885.

25 LOWER AMERICAN RIVER

Rating: 8

from Nimbus Dam to Sacramento

Map 5.4, page 151

The American River is the site of some of the biggest water parties in California, starting Memorial Day weekend and ranging well into summer. Just about anybody can get into a raft here and go for a float on a hot summer day, and that is exactly what a lot of folks do.

It's great fun, even though there are many people on the river, some of them absolutely ripped from the combination of too much beer and too much sun. There are a few drownings every year, and the typical victim is someone who got drunk, didn't wear a life jacket, then fell overboard. Don't drink alcohol and do keep your life jacket on, and you'll surely enjoy the float (and stay afloat).

This section of the American flows from the outlet at Nimbus Basin on downstream, past Fair Oaks and Rancho Cordova before entering the Sacramento River at Discovery Park. The entire run is 23 miles. Within that span are several excellent access points. In addition, the Sacramento River Parkway provides a 23-mile trail that runs parallel to the American River on downstream to the Sacramento River.

This is an easy rafting river, rated Class I. A couple of Class II rapids are thrown in: Suicide Bend, located about three miles downstream of the dam; San Juan Rapids, one mile farther; and Arden Rapids, another five miles past that. These rapids are not difficult, but newcomers may want to scout them from the shore. Portaging is easy at all the runs.

One great bonus is that American River Recreation rents out kayaks and rafts of all sizes. When renting, you always put in at their shop on Sunrise Boulevard, then enjoy the 2.5-hour float down to Goethe Park. For a small fee they will give you a shuttle ride back.

The only outfitter offering guided trips is California Canoe & Kayak. But this is an easy float, and novice boaters can do most of it alone.

Though temperatures around here get hot, the water is often cold, which can come as a big surprise. Rafters sometimes discard their life jackets to enjoy the sunny weather, then are stunned by the cold water when they fall in. After big winters, the river can be quite high and cold on Memorial Day weekend, the traditional kickoff of the party/rafting season on the American River.

Access: By boat, the best and most easily accessible spot is at the confluence of the Sacramento and American Rivers at Discovery Park in Sacramento. Several boat ramps and rafting put-ins and take-outs are available:

• Ancil Hoffman Park: From I-80 at Sacramento, drive to the exit for Arden Way. Take that exit east and drive 4.5 miles to Fair Oaks Boulevard. Turn left on Fair Oaks Boulevard and drive 1.5 miles to Oak Avenue. Turn right and drive to California Avenue. Turn left and drive .5 mile to Tarshes Drive. Turn right and drive west into Ancil Hoffman Park. No boat

ramp. Hand-launching is difficult, and the former put-in area is washed out.

• Discovery Park: From I-5 at Sacramento, drive to the exit for the Garden Highway. Take that exit, turn left, and drive to Natomas Park Drive. Turn right and drive to the signed park entrance. A paved ramp is available.

• Goethe Park: From Sacramento, take U.S. 50 east to the exit for Bradshaw Road. Take that exit, turn north, and drive to Folsom Boulevard. Turn right on Folsom Boulevard and drive about one mile to Rod Beaudry Drive. Turn left on Rod Beaudry Drive and continue to Goethe Park. No boat ramp. Hand-launching only.

• Harrington Way: From I-80 in Sacramento, take the Arden Way exit. Turn west on Arden Way and drive 4.5 miles to Kingsford Drive. Turn right on Kingsford Drive (which turns into Harrington Way) and continue to the access. No boat ramp. Hand-launching only.

• Howe Avenue: From Sacramento, take U.S. 50 east to the exit for Howe Avenue. Take that exit, turn north, and drive to La Riviera Drive. Turn right on La Riviera Drive and drive to the sign for the river access.

• Mira Del Rio: From Sacramento, take U.S. 50 east to the exit for Bradshaw Road. Take that exit, turn north, and drive to Folsom Boulevard. Turn left and drive a short distance west to Butterfield Way. Turn right and drive to Stoughton Way. Turn right and drive to Mira Del Rio Drive. Turn left on Mira Del Rio, and then immediately turn right for river access. No boat ramp is available. Some boats are launched from the gravel bar, but difficult for two-wheel drive vehicles or four-wheel-drive vehicles without significant tires.

• Rossmoor Drive: From Sacramento, take U.S. 50 east to the exit for Sunrise Boulevard. Take that exit, turn north and drive .5 mile to Coloma Road. Turn left turn on Coloma Road and drive 1.5 miles west to Rossmoor Drive. Turn right on Rossmoor Drive and continue into the park to the car-top boat ramp at the end of the road.

• Sailor Bar: From Sacramento, take U.S. 50 east to the exit for Hazel Avenue exit. Take that exit, turn north and drive 1.5 miles to Winding Way. Turn left and drive about .5 mile to Illinois Avenue. Turn left on Illinois Avenue and continue to the end of the road. A paved boat ramp was installed in 2002.

• Upper Sunrise: From Sacramento, take U.S. 50 east to the exit for Sunrise Boulevard. Take that exit, turn north, and drive 1.5 miles to South Bridge Street. Turn right and drive to the car-top boat ramp. A paved launch for hand-launched boats was installed in 2003.

• Watt Avenue South: From Sacramento, take U.S. 50 east to the exit for Watt Avenue. Take that exit and drive about .5 mile to the sign for the launching area. A paved ramp is available for launching small boats.

• Lower Sunrise: From Sacramento, take U.S. 50 east to the exit for Sunrise Boulevard. Take that exit, turn north and drive 1.5 miles to South Bridge Street. Turn right on South Bridge Street and drive past the Upper Sunrise turnoff and continue (looping around) to Lower Sunrise (located just past the bridge). No ramp is available.

• Sacramento Bar: From Sacramento, take U.S. 50 east to the exit for Sunrise Boulevard. Take that exit, turn north and drive two miles to Fair Oaks Boulevard. Turn left and drive a short distance to Pennsylvania Avenue. Turn left on Pennsylvania Avenue and drive .5 mile to the river. No ramp is available.

Facilities, fees: Campgrounds, lodging, and supplies are available in the Sacramento area. Restrooms with flush toilets, drinking water, picnic areas, and barbecues are provided at many river access points. Fees are charged for day use, boat launching, and camping. Rafting permits are not required.

Water sports, restrictions: Powerboats (not advised), drift boats, rafts, canoes, kayaks, and inflatables are permitted. A 5-mph speed limit is strictly enforced. Boating, swimming, and rafting are prohibited from Nimbus Dam to 150 feet downstream. Swimming is allowed at most of the parks listed above and at several other access points along the river.

Directions: From Sacramento, take U.S. 50 to Rancho Cordova or Fair Oaks. More specific directions are listed for specific access areas above.

Contact: Sacramento Chamber of Commerce, 916/552-6800, website: www.sacramentocvb.org; Sacramento County Parks, 916/875-6961, park rangers 916/875-6672, website: www.sacparks.net; U.S. Bureau of Reclamation, 800/742-9474, website: www.mp.usbr.gov.

Guided rafting trips: California Canoe & Kayak, 916/353-1880 or 800/366-9804. Raft or kayak rentals: American River Recreation, 916/635-6400, website: www.raftrentals.com; River Rat, 916/966-6777, website: www.river-rat.com.

Flyfishing: Specialities, Citrus Heights, 916/722-1055.

26 RANCHO SECO LAKE

Rating: 5

southeast of Sacramento in Rancho Seco Recreation Area

Map 5.4, page 151

Looking for the ideal spot for a family picnic? Here it is. Rancho Seco Lake (160 acres) is part of the 400-acre Rancho Seco Recreation Area and offers a boat ramp (no motors permitted), picnic area, and several docks. Because no motors are allowed, you get quiet water, fair fishing, and good access and picnic sites. Bring the family.

There is a large, sandy swimming area, a pleasant picnic site, and a campground for tents or RVs. In addition there are trails for hiking, horseback riding, and bicycling, as well as several fishing docks along the shore.

This lake is also popular with sailboarders. Every afternoon from spring through summer, you will usually see about a dozen people on sailboards catching the afternoon breeze.

Access: A boat ramp is located near the picnic area.

Facilities, fees: A campground and a picnic area are provided. Lodging and supplies can be obtained in Sacramento. A fee is charged for day use.

Water sports, restrictions: Gas-powered motors and live bait are not allowed on the lake. Sailboarding is permitted. A large swimming beach is available near the picnic area. The park is open for day use only, closing each day at sunset.

Directions: From Sacramento drive about 12 miles south on Highway 99. Take the Highway 104 exit and drive 12 miles east on Highway 104/Twin Cities Road. Turn right at the signed entrance for Rancho Seco Recreation Area and continue to the lake.

Contact: Rancho Seco Recreation Area, 209/748-2318.

27 CLEMENTINE LAKE

Rating: 10

northeast of Auburn on the American River

Map 5.5, page 152

Some places you just plain need a boat. When you visit Clementine Lake, you will discover that this is one of those places.

Clementine Lake is 3.5 miles long and quite narrow, set in a dammed-up gorge on the North Fork American River at an elevation of 1,200 feet. It is ideal for the boater, with boat-in campsites, great boat-in swimming beaches, and a 25-boat limit. The water is warm in summer, great for water sports.

Highlights include very pretty scenery, easy access from Auburn, and the boat-in campgrounds, which provide visitors with a wilderness-like atmosphere. It is extremely popular with water-skiers and locals from the Auburn area. Although no stocking program is in effect, there's fishing for trout and smallmouth bass in season.

It is critical to understand the ramifications of the 25-boat quota implemented by the Auburn State Recreation Area. What it all boils

down to is that boaters who are camping at the lake get priority, and if you're coming on a weekend to spend the day, you run the risk of being shut out. Arriving during the week is a better bet for day use; if you're scheduling a trip for a summer weekend, you should reserve a campsite.

The lake is not stocked. It instead provides a self-perpetuating fishery for trout in spring and smallmouth bass in the summer.

No services are offered at the lake, except for gasoline, a plus.

Shoreline access is virtually impossible without a boat. But with a boat? Heh, heh, what a payoff!

Access: There's a paved ramp at the end of the access road.

Facilities, fees: Boat-in campgrounds, floating chemical toilets, picnic areas, and gas are available. No drinking water. Garbage must be packed out. Supplies can be obtained in Auburn. Access to the lake is free. Fees are charged for boat launching and camping.

Water sports, restrictions: Powerboats, waterskiing, wake boarding, and personal watercraft are permitted. The lake is too small for sailing and sailboarding. Swimming areas are available in front of the campgrounds; access is limited to boats only.

Directions: To boat-in camps: From I-80 at Auburn, take the Foresthill exit on to Foresthill Road. Continue northeast on Foresthill Road for three miles to Lake Clementine Road. Turn left and drive 2.5 miles to the boat launch.

Contact: Auburn State Recreation Area, 530/885-4527.

28 SOUTH FORK AMERICAN RIVER

Rating: 10

near Placerville in Eldorado National Forest

Map 5.5, page 152

Behold, the most popular rafting river in the Western United States. For newcomers to the sport, the South Fork American is the choice, with easy access, enough white-water challenge to add some sizzle, and a huge array of trips offered by rafting outfitters. No experience needed; just hop on for the ride.

The run begins at Chili Bar, the somewhat legendary put-in, and is a 20-mile trip to completing the entire run. Half-day trips are extremely popular.

This is a Class III run, considered a perfect introduction to rafting, and there are plenty of takers. River traffic is very heavy starting on Memorial Day weekend, especially on weekends, and anybody desiring any semblance of solitude should go elsewhere.

The river can usually be run from April through early October, but there are no guarantees, as flows are determined from upstream hydro releases. The scenery is pleasant, not sensational, but there's an open, rugged feel and lots of Gold Rush historical sites along the way.

White-water highlights include Meatgrinder (Class III), Troublemaker (Class III+, the most dramatic drop on the river), and Satan's Cesspool (Class III+), which can challenge even experienced paddlers and give most any beginner the opportunity to see if their heart can pound a hole through their chest. After Meatgrinder, there are 10 sets of rapids until reaching Troublemaker. This stretch covers nine miles and takes you to Coloma. The second half of the trip covers 11 miles from Coloma to Salmon Falls, referred to as The Gorge. The run starts off lazy enough before abruptly dropping into The Gorge. Here you will encounter back-to-back rapids, including Satan's Cesspool, Haystack Canyon, Bouncing Rock, and Hospital Bar.

Guides always point out to the occupants in the raft that there is a seven-mile stretch running past several private homes and campgrounds that boaters are asked to treat as a quiet zone. That means rafters have to try to not act like lunatics for about two hours, no mean feat for some people.

Many rafting companies offer an array of specialty trips on this river. These include family trips, youth trips, theme trips, and half-day trips.

Access: There is no boat ramp. You can put in at Chili Bar (see Directions, below). Take out 20 miles downstream from Chili Bar just above the Salmon Falls Bridge (above Folsom Lake) or farther upstream at one of several other access points: The Highway 49 bridge in Coloma, Henningsen-Lotus County Park, or Camp Lotus (Highway 49 in Coloma to Lotus Road, then to Bassi Road). Access is available at Marshall Gold Discovery State Park, but only put-ins are allowed, no take-outs.

Facilities, fees: Private campgrounds are available on Highway 49 near Coloma and Lotus. No camping at the state park or the county park. Supplies available in Placerville. A private concession charges a fee to put in at Chili Bar. Access fees are charged at Marshall Gold Discovery State Park, Henningsen-Lotus County Park, and Camp Lotus.

Water sports, restrictions: Rafting and kayaking is permitted. Swimming is available at all the parks listed.

Directions: To Chili Bar Run: Take U.S. 50 to Placerville and the exit for Highway 49. Take that exit and drive north on Highway 49 to Highway 193. Turn right and drive three miles down to the bridge at Chili Bar.

Contact: Bureau of Land Management, 916/985-4474; El Dorado National Forest, Visitor Center, 530/644-6048; Marshall Gold Discovery State Park, 530/622-3470; El Dorado County, Parks and Recreation Department, 530/621-5353; Camp Lotus, 530/622-8672.

Boat rentals: California Canoe & Kayak in Rancho Cordova, 916/353-1880; Sierra Outdoor Center in Auburn, 530/885-1844; River Rat Rentals in Fair Oaks, 916/966-6777. No rentals are available in El Dorado County because of ordinance prohibiting them.

Guided rafting trips: California Canoe & Kayak, 510/893-7833 or 800/366-9804, website: www.calkayak.com; Current Adventures

Kayaking, 530/333-9115, website: www.kayaking.com; WET River Trips (Whitewater Expeditions & Tours), 888/723-8938 or 916/451-3241, website: www.raftwet.com; Disabled Sports USA, 530/581-4161; Whitewater Connection, 530/622-6446 or 800/336-7238, website: www.whitewaterconnection.com; Tributary Whitewater Tours, 530/346-6812 or 800/672-3846, website: www.whitewatertours.com; Outdoor Adventure River Specialists (OARS), 209/736-4677 or 800/346-6277, website: www.oars.com; Rapid Descent Adventures, 530/659-7800; Beyond Limits, 209/869-6060 or 800/234-7238, website: www.rivertrip.com; ARTA (America River Touring Association), 209/962-7873 or 800/323-2782, website: www.arta.org; Chili Bar Outdoor Center, 530/621-1236 or 800/356-2262, website: www.cbocwhitewater.com; All Outdoors Whitewater Rafting, 925/932-8993 or 800/247-2387, website: www.aorafting.com; Rock-N-Water, 530/621-3918; Motherlode River Trips, 530/626-4187 or 800/427-2387, website: www.malode.com; Whitewater Voyages, 510/222-5994 or 800/488-7238, website: www.whitewater-voyages.com.

29 JENKINSON LAKE/SLY PARK

Rating: 10

east of Placerville in Sly Park
Recreation Area

Map 5.5, page 152

The only thing wrong with Jenkinson Lake is that it's hardly a secret. In fact, it may just be the ideal vacation destination.

The lake is set at 3,500 feet elevation, covering 640 acres with eight miles of forested shoreline. All water sports are permitted, and rules that separate high-speed users from low-speed users help to resolve potential conflicts and set the stage for first-class water recreation.

The 5-mph zone covers 80 acres of the lake north of Sierra Point; of course, water-skiers and wake boarders should stay clear of there.

The Stonebraker launch ramp lies within this zone and is used primarily by anglers. Visitors with ski boats and other fast craft should launch instead at the other ramp.

Swimming is available all along the shoreline, but swimmers are cautioned to stay within 50 feet of the shore to avoid any chance of getting in the way of fast boats. Sailboarding is also good here, usually best from 11 A.M. to 3 P.M., when a steady wind courses over the lake.

Anglers often head upstream into the Hazel Creek arm of the lake for trout in the spring and for bass in the summer. In addition, this is one of the better lakes in the Sierra for brown trout.

A bonus at Sly Park is the variety of campgrounds, with campsites available for individuals, youths, families, and equestrians. No pets or babies in diapers are permitted in the lake.

Access: Two paved boat ramps are available:
• **Stonebraker:** On the entrance road, continue straight past Pine Cone Campground to the Stonebraker Campground and launch ramp.
• **West Shore:** Once inside the lake entrance, drive 50 feet past the kiosk to the boat ramp access road on the right. Turn right and drive .25 mile to the ramp.

Facilities, fees: A small marina with docks, campgrounds, vault toilets, drinking water, and picnic areas, RV dump station, snack bar, bait and tackle, and a convenience store are available. Full supplies can be obtained in Pollock Pines. Fees are charged for day use, boat launching, and camping.

Water sports, restrictions: Powerboats, water-skiing, wake boarding, sailing, and sailboarding are permitted. No personal watercraft. A 5-mph speed limit is enforced north of Sierra Point (on the north side of the lake).

Directions: From Sacramento, drive east on U.S. 50 to Pollock Pines and take the exit for Sly Park Road. Drive south for five miles to Jenkinson Lake and the campground access road. Turn left and drive one mile to the campground.

Contact: Sly Park Recreation Area, El Dorado Irrigation District, 530/644-2545, website: www.eid.org.

30 LAKE AMADOR

Rating: 5

northeast of Stockton

Map 5.5, page 152

Yeah, this lake seems like it was planted on Earth for one reason: fishing.

Although there is a campground and swimming pond nearby, Amador is better known for providing excellent fishing for trout and bass, with good catch rates for rainbow trout and a fair number of giant Florida bass. The lake is set at an elevation of 485 feet in the foothill country east of Stockton, covering 425 acres with 13.5 miles of shoreline. Of the four lakes in the immediate area—Camanche, Pardee, New Hogan, and Amador—it is Amador and Pardee that have enacted the most restrictive boating rules to guarantee that anglers have quiet water and the best chances for success.

That means no water-skiing, personal watercraft, or sailboarding. And while swimming is not prohibited, much of the shoreline is rocky, swimming access is poor, and hey, with a one-acre pond specifically designated for swimming near the campground, you never see people taking a dunk in the lake. The pond is family oriented, with a playground, water slide, and gently sloping sandy beaches. Use is high year-round, the campground is often full in early summer, and reservations are suggested. There also are hiking and mountain biking trails in the area.

Among the fishing highlights: Trout are stocked weekly . . . the largest two-man bass limit was caught here, at 80.4 pounds, and the lake-record bass was 17 pounds, 1 ounce . . . catfish up to 40 pounds are caught in summer . . . a special strain of cross-bred trout called cutbow are stocked here.

Access: A paved boat ramp is available at Lake Amador Marina, located just off Lake Amador Drive.

Facilities, fees: A small marina rents fishing boats. Campgrounds, picnic area, drinking water, restrooms, showers, RV dump station, fishing supplies (including bait and tackle), snack bar, convenience store, propane gas, swimming pond, and a playground are available. Fees are charged for day use, fishing permits, boat launching, and camping.

Water sports, restrictions: Powerboats, canoes, kayaks, inflatables, sailing, and sailboarding are permitted. A 5-mph speed limit is enforced within the coves and around the marina. No water-skiing, wake boarding, or personal watercraft. A swimming pond is available near the campgrounds.

Directions: From Stockton, turn east on Highway 88 and drive 24 miles to Clements. Just east of Clements, bear left on Highway 88 and drive 11 miles to Jackson Valley Road. Turn right (well signed) and drive four miles to Lake Amador Drive. Turn right and drive over the dam to the campground office.

Contact: Lake Amador Recreation Area, 209/274-4739, website: www.lakeamador.com.

31 PARDEE LAKE

Rating: 5

northeast of Stockton

Map 5.5, page 152

Of all the lakes in the Mother Lode country, Pardee is the prettiest, covering more than 2,000 acres with 37 miles of shoreline. The lake, which has a T-shape configuration, is most beautiful in early spring, when the lake is full, the hills are green, and the wildflowers are blooming. And one other thing: The trout are biting then, too.

Like Amador, this lake was designed exclusively for fishing. Water-skiing, swimming, and sailboarding are prohibited. There is a 25-mph speed limit and most boaters heed a "common courtesy" rule, making the lake safe and comfortable. That includes for those with small, low-speed craft, such as canoes or small fishing boats. Pardee has full facilities for boating, even a marina, and in spring this is the ideal destination for the camper/boater/angler.

The lake opens each year in February, often kicking right off with good trolling for trout and kokanee salmon. It is stocked with trout weekly. With good fishing and good weather, it doesn't take long before the campground can get quite crowded. During hot weather, attentions turns to bass, both smallmouth and largemouth, as well as catfish. The lake closes in the fall in late October during the migratory bird season.

Many families take advantage of the swimming pool near the campground, which tends to be deluged with throngs of youngsters and their parents.

Access: A 10-lane paved ramp is available at Pardee Recreation Area, located on the northeastern arm of the lake.

Facilities, fees: A full-service marina has fishing boats and pontoon boats for rent, boat moorings, and boat storage. A campground, drinking water, restrooms, showers (in the RV section of the campground), RV dump station, fish-cleaning station, coin laundry, convenience store, propane gas, RV storage, wading pool, and a seasonal swimming pool are available. Fees are charged for day use, camping, fishing permits, boat launching, and float tubes.

Water sports, restrictions: Powerboats, canoes, and float tubes are permitted. No body contact with the water is permitted. No water-skiing, wake boarding, personal watercraft, and swimming. Those with float tubes must wear waders. A large swimming pool is available at the campground.

Directions: From Stockton, drive east on Highway 88 for 24 miles to the town of Clements. Just east of Clements, bear left on Highway 88 and drive 11 miles to Jackson Valley Road. Turn right and drive to a four-way stop sign at Buena Vista. Turn right and drive for three miles to Stony Creek Road on the left. Turn

left and drive a mile to the campground on the right.

Contact: Pardee Recreation Area, 209/772-1472, website: www.lakepardee.com.

32 MOKELUMNE RIVER

Rating: 7

northeast of Stockton

Map 5.5, page 152

This short, three-mile stretch of the Mokelumne River provides a window to the way the entire river once was. It's a great spot for inner tubing and easy kayaking and is decent for swimming.

The rafting season is a long one here, from March to September, when the river features warm water and good scenery. It's an easy river to kayak, mostly Class I with a couple of Class II rapids, ideal for beginning and practicing kayakers (especially in inflatable kayaks), as well as for inner tubers.

The three-mile-long run cuts through the Gold Rush towns of Jackson and Mokelumne Hill, and there are many historic sites in the area. By far the best spot for swimming is at Electra Picnic Area. Although use is moderate, and no guided trips are available, there can be lots of inner tubers here on hot summer weekends, and kayaking is extremely popular in the spring and early summer.

But there is a major problem. The river is a prisoner of water releases, which means that flows can fluctuate wildly according to the whims of the water master, not rainfall and snowmelt. You should always call the Bureau of Land Management to check flow levels before scheduling a trip on the Mokelumne.

Access: There is no boat ramp. Kayakers, canoeists, and inner tubers can put in just below Electra Powerhouse (see Directions below). Take out three miles downstream at the Highway 49 bridge.

Facilities, fees: A picnic area is provided on Electra Road. Access to the river is free.

Water sports, restrictions: Rafting, canoeing,

kayaking, and tubing are available. Swimming access is available at Electra Picnic Area.

Directions: From Stockton, drive east on Highway 88/12 for 24 miles to the town of Clements. Continue on Highway 88 past Lake Camanche and Pardee Lake to Martell and Highway 49/88. Turn south on Highway 49/88 and drive through Jackson and continue to Electra Road. Turn left on Electra Road and drive east. The river is accessible off this road for four miles upstream to the Electra powerhouse.

Contact: Bureau of Land Management, Folsom Field Office, 916/985-4474; PG&E Land Projects, 916/386-5164, website: www.pge.com/recreation.

33 LAKE TABEAUD

Rating: 4

near Jackson

Map 5.5, page 152

It is always funny to hear people try to pronounce the name of this lake on their first visit. People who commonly mangle names sometimes call it Lake "Tay-Be-A-Ud." It's pronounced "Tah-Bow." Just like it looks.

This lake is an hour's drive east of Stockton, set at an elevation of 2,000 feet, just high enough to keep the water cool into early summer. The lake gets light use, primarily by anglers.

The surrounding area is pretty and attracts a small amount of vacation traffic. No motors are permitted, which limits boating to rowboats, canoes, and inflatables. Swimming and sailboarding are also not allowed—just paddling, fishing, and picnicking. That's about it. And sometimes that's just plenty.

Access: No boat ramp is available. Car-top boats may be hand launched.

Facilities, fees: A picnic area is available. Supplies can be obtained in Jackson. Access to the lake is free.

Water sports, restrictions: Rowboats, canoes, kayaks, and inflatables are permitted. No

motors. No swimming. The lake is too small for sailing and sailboarding.

Directions: From Stockton, drive east on Highway 88 to Highway 49. Turn south on Highway 49 and drive to Jackson. From Jackson, continue south on Highway 49 for .5 mile to Clinton Road. Turn left on Clinton Road and drive east for 5.1 miles to Tabeaud Road. Bear right on Tabeaud Road and continue two miles to the lake.

Contact: PG&E Land Projects, 916/386-5164, website: www.pge.com/recreation.

34 LAKE CAMANCHE

Rating: 10

northeast of Stockton

Map 5.5, page 152

Camanche is a large, multifaceted facility that covers 7,700 acres and has 53 miles of shoreline. It is set in the foothills east of Lodi at an elevation of 325 feet. Here you will find the best of everything—boating, camping, fishing, water-skiing, swimming, and sailboarding—with enough space for everyone and rules to keep user conflicts to a minimum.

The water is clear and warm, resorts and campgrounds are available at both the north and south ends of the lake, and as you might expect, visitor turnout is high, especially during the peak months in late spring and early summer. There are few trees here, with shoreline largely exposed.

All boating is allowed on the lake, but fast boats and personal watercraft are prohibited in the narrows on the northern end.

Sailboarding conditions at Lake Camanche are excellent because the afternoons are breezy just about every day. Yet there is hardly any sailboarding activity.

The swimming is also good here. Most people sunbathe for a spell, then jump into the lake to cool off and have a little fun. Although there are no designated swimming beaches, much of the shoreline has suitable access; the two most popular spots are at Campers Cove on the north shore and the area near the snack bar on the south shore.

More than anything, though, this is a lake for fishing. In the spring and summer, it provides outstanding fishing for trout, bass, king salmon, crappie, bluegill, and catfish. Because of extensive structure in the lake, it is well known as a premier bass lake.

Access: Multilane paved boat ramps are available at both recreation areas (see Directions, below).

Facilities, fees: Full-service marinas offer fishing boat and pontoon boat rentals, mooring and boat storage. Lodging, campgrounds, restrooms, showers, RV dump station, trout pond, coin laundry, snack bar, and a convenience store are available. Restaurants are available nearby. Fees are charged for day use, boat launching, fishing permit, and camping.

Water sports, restrictions: Powerboats, water-skiing, wake boarding, personal watercraft, canoeing, kayaks, and inflatables are permitted. No water-skiing, wake boarding, or personal watercraft permitted in the narrows on the northern end of the lake. Sailboarding, sailing, and swimming are permitted. There are no designated beach areas, but almost all of the shoreline is rocky and sandy and gradually sloped.

Directions: To North Shore: From Stockton, drive east on Highway 88 for 24 miles to Clements. Just east of Clements, bear left on Highway 88 and drive six miles to Camanche Parkway. Turn right and drive seven miles to the Camanche North Shore entrance gate.

To South Shore: From Stockton, drive east on Highway 88 for 24 miles to Clements. Just east of Clements continue east on Highway 12 and drive six miles to South Camanche Parkway. Turn left and drive six miles to the entrance gate.

Contact: Lake Camanche North Shore, 209/763-5121; North Shore marina, 209/763-5166; Lake Camanche South Shore, 209/763-5178; South Shore marina, 209/763-5915; general information website: www.camancherecreation.com.

35 NEW HOGAN LAKE

Rating: 8

east of Stockton

Map 5.5, page 152

New Hogan is a big lake, covering 4,400 acres with 50 miles of shoreline. There are many good spots along the eastern shore at Deer Flat that are suitable for boat-in camping. It's that last factor that makes this a tremendous vacation spot for anglers who have boats and want to camp overnight.

All water sports are popular here. Since the water is quite warm in the summer, swimming, water-skiing, and sailboarding are extremely popular. The place gets heavy use on weekends from Memorial Day to Labor Day. Note that as of 2003, no marina operator or boat rentals were available for the third straight year. The U.S. Army Corps of Engineers is hoping for a replacement in 2004. If this is of concern, call prior to making your trip.

Numerous sandy areas are available all along the shoreline for swimming, although none is designated specifically for that activity. Some boaters will pull up at one of these spots for a picnic, and the youngsters aboard will jump out and cavort in the shallows. In a few of these areas, the underwater drop-off is steep, so kids should always wear life jackets.

New Hogan Lake is a decent lake for fishing, with a unique opportunity for striped bass, and it's OK for largemouth bass. Of the four lakes in the immediate area, Amador attracts anglers who are looking for bass and trout, Camanche gets those who want bass and crappie, Pardee lures anglers seeking trout and kokanee salmon, while New Hogan gets those who are in search of stripers and largemouth bass. New Hogan also has crappie, bluegill, and catfish.

From December through March, this lake is a wintering area for bald eagles, and sightings are a common highlight. In late fall, this lake provides limited hunting opportunities for waterfowl, usually on the southern side of the lake.

A 5-mph speed limit in the coves keeps the atmosphere decent enough for fishing. That leaves the rest of this big lake wide open for fast boats, and on hot summer days, they really let it rip out here.

Access: Paved boat ramps are available, a four-lane ramp at the Fiddleneck Day-Use Area, and one two-lane ramp adjacent to Acorn East Campground. Ramps can be accessed from the entrance road; watch for signs.

Facilities, fees: Drive-in campgrounds, drinking water, restrooms with flush toilets, showers, pay telephones, fish-cleaning station, and RV dump station are available. Boat-in campsites, picnic area, gas, and golf course are nearby. Fees are charged for day use, camping, and boat launching.

Water sports, restrictions: Powerboating, waterskiing, wake boarding, personal watercraft, sailing, and sailboarding are permitted on the lake's main body. A 5-mph speed limit is enforced around the coves, and a 15-mph speed limit is enforced across the lake after sunset. Swimming access is available all along the shoreline; a popular spot is at Wrinkle Cove, located off the lake's entrance road.

Directions: From Stockton, drive east on Highway 26 for about 35 miles to Valley Springs and Hogan Dam Road. Turn right and drive 1.5 miles to Hogan Parkway. Turn left and drive one mile to South Petersburg Road. Turn left and drive .25 mile to the campground at the lake on the right.

Contact: U.S. Army Corps of Engineers, Sacramento District, 209/772-1343.

36 NORTH FORK STANISLAUS RIVER

⚔️ 🏕️ 🏊 ♿ ⛰️

Rating: 9

near Arnold in Stanislaus National Forest

Map 5.5, page 152

Beautiful, wild, and exciting—this stretch of river has everything going for it but length. Only the rafting run's relatively short length, a mere five miles, keeps the North Fork Stanislaus from snagging the highest rating.

This river is rated as Class IV and is ideal for most rafters, difficult enough for plenty of excitement, yet with only one truly mind-bending piece of white water. That stretch, Sourgrass Ravine, will launch you to the edge and beyond, then release you back to your senses, as well as to the seat of your raft. The scenery is beautiful, with big granite boulders peppered about the river, and pines and sequoias lining much of the adjacent shore, plus a sprinkling of fragrant azaleas.

Not only is the run short, but right out of the starting gate you encounter the big one, Sourgrass Ravine. After conquering that (or not), you face a number of challenging Class IV rapids and drops, including Beginner's Luck, Sierra Gate, The Claw, Convulsion, Wallet Slot, and Emerald Falls. You couldn't demand more from a five-miler.

The water is clear, cold, and beautiful. How cold? In the spring dry suits or wet suits are mandatory, but they become optional by summer, when temperatures are considerably warmer. In most years the season runs from April through August, though it can be shortened due to a low snowpack and the resultant minimal melt-off.

Only a few commercial companies are permitted to raft here, so the water is significantly less crowded than the main stem Stanislaus. Regardless, it is becoming increasingly popular, especially among non-guided experts who want a trip that can be completed in a day.

The North Fork Stanislaus is a real favorite for swimming and sunbathing, with the most popular spot being at Candy Rock. Note that this is an infamous spot for nudists, not a typical hangout for families from Stockton. There are natural and man-made rock slides here, as well as several large, deep pools, and the water is warmer than at places farther upstream.

Families are better off heading to the series

of pools located about a mile upstream past Sourgrass Campground; there's a parking area there and a short hiking trail down to the swimming hole.

Trout are stocked monthly near Wa Ka Luu Hep Yoo Campground, and fishing is good for rainbow, brook, and brown trout.

Access: There is no boat ramp. To reach the rafting put-in from Angels Camp, drive east on Highway 4, past Arnold to Dorrington and Boards Crossing Road, and then continue driving four miles to Sourgrass Campground. Put in on the left bank above the bridge.

Note: A difficult Class V drop is located immediately downstream of the put-in; boaters who wish to avoid it can put in below the rapid (on the right bank). When you reach Calaveras Big Trees State Park, take out just downstream of the bridge

Facilities, fees: Campgrounds are available on Boards Crossing Road and at Calaveras Big Trees State Park. Restrooms, drinking water, showers, and flush and vault toilets are available. Picnic areas are nearby. A wheelchair-accessible river trail is available at Wa Ka Luu Hep Yoo Campground. Supplies can be obtained in Dorrington and Arnold. Fees are charged for camping and for day use. Rafting permits are not required.

Water sports, restrictions: Rafting and kayaking are permitted. Good swimming areas are available near Sourgrass Campground, Wa Ka Luu Hep Yoo Campground, and at Calaveras Big Trees State Park. Farther downstream is a popular area called Candy Rock, which is accessed by taking Hunter Dam Road south off Highway 4 (just east of Hathaway Pines) for five miles to the river. Several large pools and rock slides are available.

Directions: From Angels Camp, drive east on Highway 4, past Arnold to Dorrington and Boards Crossing Road. Turn right and drive four miles to the forest service campground on the left (just before the bridge that crosses the Stanislaus River). Access is also available at Calaveras Big Trees State Park on Highway 4.

Contact: Stanislaus National Forest, Calaveras Ranger District, 209/795-1381; Calaveras Big Trees State Park, 209/795-2334.

Guided rafting trips: All-Outdoors Whitewater Rafting, 925/932-8993 or 800/247-2387, website: www.aorafting.com; Outdoor Adventure River Specialists (OARS), 209/736-4677 or 800/346-6277, website: www.oars.com; Beyond Limits, 209/869-6060 or 800/234-7238, website: www.rivertrip.com.

FOGHORN OUTDOORS®

© ROBERT HOLMES/CALTOUR

Chapter 6

Tahoe and the Northern Sierra

Chapter 6—Tahoe and the Northern Sierra

L ake Tahoe is one of the few places on earth where people feel an emotional response just by looking at it, scanning across a cobalt blue expanse of water bordered by mountains that span miles of Sierra wildlands. The beauty strikes a deep chord.

This area has the widest range and number of campgrounds in California—a stunning 193 different campgrounds, with most all of them at lake and river settings.

"What about all the people?" you ask. It's true that people come here in droves. But I've found many spots that I've shared only with the chipmunks. You can enjoy these spots, too—this book puts every spot in the palm of your hands—if you hunt a bit, and most importantly, time your trip to span Monday through Thursday.

Tahoe and the northern Sierra feature hundreds of lakes, including dozens you can drive to. The best for scenic beauty are Echo Lakes, Donner, Fallen Leaf, Sardine, Caples, Loon, Union Valley . . . well, you could go on and on. It is one of the most beautiful regions anywhere on earth.

To make it easier for you to find the spots, we included special, more detailed inset maps that show many of the hidden lakes.

The north end of the Sierra starts near Bucks Lake, a great lake for trout fishing. Each canyon features a major river that feeds a series of beautiful lakes on the slopes of the Sierra Nevada.

These include the Lakes Basin Recreation Area (containing Gold, Sardine, Packer, and other lakes) in southern Plumas County, the Crystal Basin (featuring Union Valley Reservoir and Loon Lake, among others) in the Sierra foothills west of Tahoe, Lake Davis (with the highest catch rates for trout) near Portola, and the Carson River Canyon and Hope Valley south of Tahoe, and extends to Bear River Canyon (and Caples Lake, Silver Lake, and Bear River Reservoir).

Major rivers include the Yuba, American, Truckee, Mokelumne, and Carson, each with a full spectrum of adventures available.

You could spend weeks exploring any of these places, having the time of your life, and still not get to Tahoe's magic. But it is Tahoe where the adventure starts for many, especially in the surrounding Tahoe National Forest and Desolation Wilderness.

With so many places and so little time, this region offers what can be the ultimate adventureland.

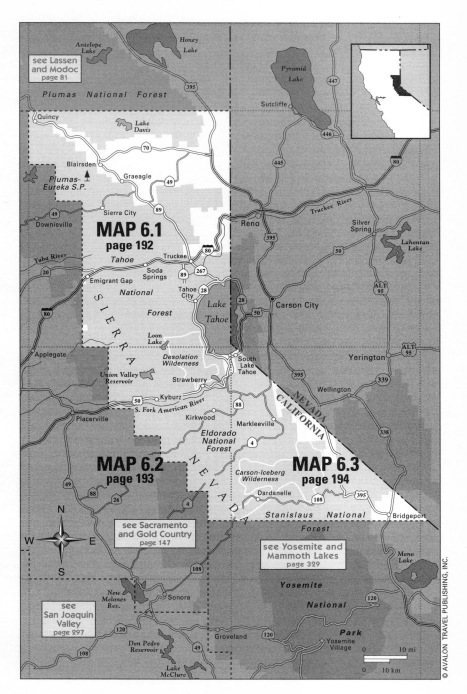

see Lassen and Modoc
page 81

Antelope Lake
Honey Lake
Pyramid Lake
Sutcliffe
395
447
446
445
Plumas National Forest
Quincy
Lake Davis
80
70
Blairsden
Graeagle
49
Plumas-Eureka S.P.
89
Sierra City
Reno
Truckee River
Silver Spring
Lahontan Lake
49
Downieville
MAP 6.1
page 192
Yuba River
Tahoe
Truckee
80
395
20
National
Soda Springs
89
267
Emigrant Gap
Tahoe City
28
Carson City
ALT 95
80
Forest
Lake Tahoe
28
50
Loon Lake
50
Applegate
Desolation Wilderness
South Lake Tahoe
Yerington
ALT 95
Union Valley Reservoir
Strawberry
395
50
Kyburz
Wellington
339
Placerville
S. Fork American River
88
Kirkwood
Markleeville
338
Eldorado National Forest
4
MAP 6.2
page 193
NEVADA
CALIFORNIA
MAP 6.3
page 194
49
88
26
Carson-Iceberg Wilderness
N
4
Dardanelle
108
395
W E
S
see Sacramento and Gold Country
page 147
Stanislaus National Forest
Bridgeport
see Yosemite and Mammoth Lakes
page 329
Mono Lake
108
New Melones Res.
Sonora
Yosemite
120
see San Joaquin Valley
page 297
National
120
Groveland
120
Park
Yosemite Village
0   10 mi
0   10 km
108
Don Pedro Reservoir
49
Lake McClure

© AVALON TRAVEL PUBLISHING, INC.

Chapter 6 • Tahoe and the Northern Sierra   191

Map 6.1

Sites 1–35
Pages 195–224

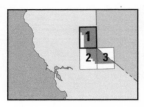

6.2

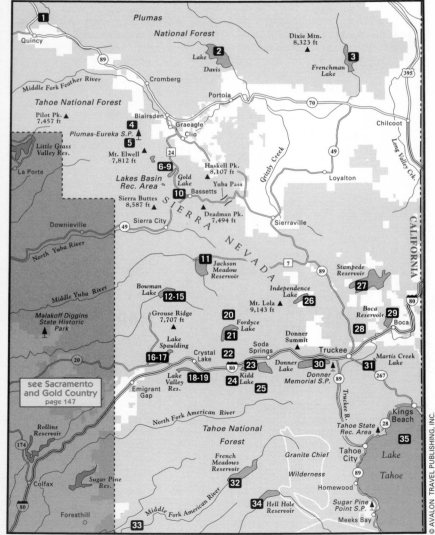

Plumas

National Forest

Quincy

Dixie Mtn.
8,323 ft ▲

89

Lake
Davis

2

Cromberg

Frenchman
Lake

3

395

Middle Fork Feather River

Portola

70

Tahoe National Forest

Blairsden

Graeagle

Chilcoot

Pilot Pk. ▲
7,457 ft

Plumas-Eureka S.P. ▲

4

Clio

Little Grass
Valley Res.

5

24

49

Loyalton

La Porte

Mt. Elwell
7,812 ft ▲

6-9

Haskell Pk.
8,107 ft ▲

Grizzly Creek

Long Valley Ck.

Lakes Basin
Rec. Area

Gold
Lake

Yuba Pass

Bassetts

Sierra Buttes
8,587 ft ▲

10

Deadman Pk.
7,494 ft ▲

Sierraville

CALIFORNIA

Downieville

49

Sierra City

7

North Yuba River

Jackson
Meadow
Reservoir

11

Stampede
Reservoir

27

Middle Yuba River

Bowman
Lake

12-15

Independence
Lake

89

Mt. Lola ▲
9,143 ft

26

80

Malakoff Diggins
State Historic
Park

Grouse Ridge
7,707 ft ▲

20

Boca
Reservoir

29

Boca

Lake
Spaulding

21

Fordyce
Lake

28

20

16-17

Crystal
Lake

22

Soda
Springs

Donner
Summit ▲

Truckee

Martis Creek
Lake

see Sacramento
and Gold Country
page 147

18-19

Lake
Valley Res.

23

24

Kidd
Lake

25

Donner
Lake

30

31

267

Emigrant
Gap

Donner
Memorial S.P.

89

Rollins
Reservoir

174

North Fork American River

Tahoe National

Forest

Truckee R.

Tahoe State
Rec. Area

28

Kings
Beach

35

Colfax

Sugar Pine
Res.

French
Meadows
Reservoir

Granite Chief

Tahoe
City

Lake

Wilderness

32

89

Tahoe

Foresthill

80

34

Hell Hole
Reservoir

Homewood

Sugar Pine
Point S.P. ▲

33

Middle Fork American River

Meeks Bay

© AVALON TRAVEL PUBLISHING, INC.

SIERRA NEVADA

Map 6.2

Sites 36–51
Pages 225–238

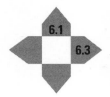

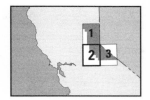

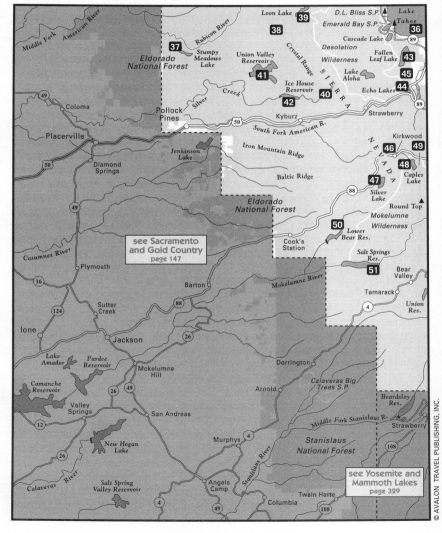

© AVALON TRAVEL PUBLISHING, INC.

Map 6.3

Sites 52–64
Pages 238–248

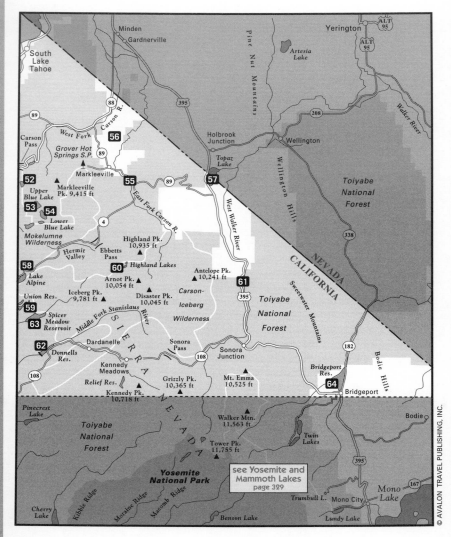

© AVALON TRAVEL PUBLISHING, INC.

1 SPANISH CREEK

Rating: 3

northwest of Quincy in Plumas
National Forest

Map 6.1, page 192

Little Spanish Creek is known primarily by the local residents who fish for trout here, but a handful of people are aware that this is also a good spot for swimming on hot summer days.

Although there are no designated swimming areas, there is excellent access right off the road. Visitors can simply look for a wide spot in the road, pull over, and wade into a good swimming hole. The place gets a fair amount of use, mostly by local folks.

Access: There is no boat ramp.

Facilities, fees: Lodging, campgrounds with vault toilets and drinking, and other facilities are available nearby at Bucks Lake. Supplies can be obtained in Quincy. Access is free.

Water sports, restrictions: Swimming access points are found at several spots along the roads mentioned above.

Directions: From Oroville, drive north on Highway 70 to the junction with Highway 89. Turn south on Highway 89/70 and drive 11 miles to Quincy and Bucks Lake Road. Access is available from a campground on Highway 70 about 10 miles north of Quincy. Access is also available from Bucks Lake Road. See a map of Plumas National Forest.

Contact: Plumas National Forest, Mount Hough Ranger District, 530/283-0555; Sportsmen's Den, 530/283-2733. For a map, send $6 to U.S. Forest Service, Attn: Map Sales, P.O. Box 587, Camino, CA 95709, 530/647-5390, fax 530/647-5389, website: www.fs.fed.us/r5/forests. Major credit cards accepted.

2 LAKE DAVIS

Rating: 7

near Portola in Plumas National Forest

Map 6.1, page 192

Lake Davis has become known across the nation for its continuing pike problems. But it has always been a centerpiece for recreation, fishing, and boating.

It is located in the southern reaches of Plumas National Forest just 50 miles from Reno. Set high in the northern Sierra at 5,775 feet in elevation, this is a good-size lake that covers 4,000 acres and has 30 miles of shoreline.

Lake Davis is one of the top mountain lakes for fishing in California, with large rainbow trout in the early summer and fall. The campgrounds are perfectly situated for a fishing trip. One of the best spots for big trout is at Lightning Tree Point on the lake's remote northeast shore, directly across the lake from Freeman Creek.

This lake is famous for the botched poisoning job by the Department of Fish and Game when it was trying to rid the lake of pike in the 1990s. Then in turn, it received the biggest trout plants to take place at a single lake in California history: more than 1 million trout were planted! Since pike have reappeared, the future of this lake is one of the biggest environmental timebombs in California; if pike escape downstream, they could invade the Delta and wipe out salmon and other species.

The character of the lake undergoes great changes according to the season. In the spring, after ice-out, winds are often ideal for sailing and sailboarding (a thick wet suit is essential). At times in late winter and early spring, the winds can even be dangerous for small boats, and only extremely experienced boaters in appropriate craft should be on the water.

Then spring and summer suddenly arrive, along with warming weather and plenty of campers. Many campers bring small boats, which they use to go fishing for trout and bass.

Water-skiing and personal watercraft use are prohibited, a rule that ensures that the water remains calm. That is a bonus for anglers as well as for swimmers. Although there are no beaches, several coves provide good swimming areas. As summer progresses, camper use increases greatly.

A summer's worth of hot weather spurs the growth of a rich aquatic food chain, and much of the lake can become quite weedy by the end of August. Fouled propellers can be a problem in some spots. Then, after the first cold nights of October, the trout go on a feeding binge. This results in outstanding trolling for large rainbow trout, which often reach lengths of 16 to 22 inches, and sometimes even bigger.

One of the byproducts of pike in the lake is that the lake level is often kept low, to keep pike from escaping over the top of the spillway from flood levels.

Because of the elevation, the area gets a lot of snow dumped on it in the winter. This lake can freeze over, despite the fact that it is large. By winter, just about everything is shut down, except for the cabins that are rented by people who want to play in the snow or go cross-country skiing. Say, how far away is Reno?

Access: There are four boat ramps:

• Honker Cove: From Grasshopper Flat, a paved ramp is located just north of the campground at Honker Cove.

• Mallard Cove: Continue north on Grizzly Road (passing Honker Cove) and drive to Mallard Cove. There is an unpaved ramp for car-top boats.

• Lightning Tree: Continue north on Grizzly Road to Lightning Tree Campground, the northernmost site on the lake to a paved ramp.

• Old Camp Five: At the south end of the lake, turn left on Davis Lake Road and drive west past the dam to a paved boat ramp.

Facilities, fees: The Grizzly Store rents out fishing boats and sells limited supplies. Campgrounds, vault toilets, and drinking water are available nearby. A fee is charged for boat launching.

Water sports, restrictions: Powerboats, canoes, kayaks, inflatables, sailing, sailboarding, and swimming are permitted. Water-skiing, wake boarding, and personal watercraft are not allowed. Swimming is best at the cove at Grasshopper Flat Campground.

Directions: To Lightning Tree: From Truckee, turn north on Highway 89 and drive to Sattley and County Road A23. Turn right on County Road A23 and drive 13 miles to Highway 70. Turn left on Highway 70 and drive one mile to Grizzly Road. Turn right on Grizzly Road and drive about six miles to Lake Davis. Continue north on Lake Davis Road along the lake's east shore and drive about five miles to the campground entrance on the left side of the road.

Contact: Plumas National Forest, Beckwourth Ranger District, 530/836-2575; Grizzly Store, 530/832-0270.

❸ FRENCHMAN LAKE

🛶 🚤 🎣 🧗 🐟 🏊 ⛺

Rating: 6

near Portola in Plumas National Forest

Map 6.1, page 192

High desert borders the east side of Frenchman Lake. A game refuge and Plumas National Forest lie to the west. So visitors to this lake get a piece of two different worlds, as well as the opportunity for good boating, fishing, and camping throughout much of the summer.

Frenchman is set in fairly high country, at an elevation of 5,500 feet, which means things get cold and windy in the spring and fall as wind sails over the Sierra crest and plunges eastward toward the Nevada desert. In addition, due to water demands, the lake level often drops substantially in late summer and fall. During this time of the year, you are advised to phone the Forest Service before planning a boating trip to make sure the water level isn't below the ramp.

That leaves a relatively short period, mid-June through early August, when the temperatures are warm, the wind is down, and the lake level is up. At that time, boating and camping are good, the trout bite, and the swimming is decent. A number of people have figured this out, so the place can be bustling in midsummer and then seem as deserted as a ghost lake a month later.

The lake is surrounded by a mix of sage and pines and has 21 miles of shoreline, including a few deep, secluded coves on the west side that are protected from the early summer winds. The best sailboarding spots are near the ramp at Frenchman Campground and at Big Cove Campground.

The lake provides good fishing for stocked rainbow trout. The best spots are in the cove near the campgrounds, and the two inlets, one along the west shore and one at the head of the lake.

Frenchman Lake can be used as a base camp for two good excursions. Dixie Mountain State Game Refuge is just to the northwest. Reno is only 35 miles away.

Access: A paved boat ramp is located at Frenchman Campground, just east of the dam. Another is located on the west side of the lake at Lunker Point.

Facilities, fees: Campgrounds, restrooms with flush toilets, vault toilets, and drinking water are available. Supplies are available seven miles away in Chilcoot. Access is free. A fee is charged for camping.

Water sports, restrictions: Powerboats, waterskiing, wake boarding, personal watercraft, sailing, sailboarding, and swimming are permitted.

Directions: From Reno, drive north on U.S. 395 to the junction with Highway 70. Turn west on Highway 70 and drive to Chilcoot and the junction with Frenchman Lake Road. Turn right on Frenchman Lake Road and drive nine miles to the lake and to a Y. At the Y, turn right and drive 1.5 miles to the campground on the left side of the road. The boat ramp is nearby.

Contact: Plumas National Forest, Beckwourth Ranger District, 530/836-2570.

4 EUREKA LAKE

Rating: 6

near Graeagle in Plumas-Eureka State Park

Map 6.1, page 192

The centerpiece of Plumas-Eureka State Park is Eureka Lake. Set at an elevation of 6,300 feet, the small lake is nestled below Eureka Peak (7,447 feet) and is surrounded by a mix of forest and meadow, with a good wildflower bloom in early summer.

The lake is used mostly for fishing and picnicking and as a jumping-off point for the great hike to Eureka Peak. There is no boat ramp, but car-top boats are well suited for the lake because they can be hand launched. Although the surrounding parkland gets heavy use, the lake itself does not, and boaters can enjoy a day free from competition with motorized boats.

A beach is available on the northern shore, and some visitors will swim or bob around a bit late in the summer when the water warms up a bit. However, after big snow years result in heavy runoff, the beach is often submerged.

This is a gorgeous state park with great recreation opportunities, a pretty lake, a fantastic hike to Eureka Peak, and usually available campsites.

Access: There is no boat ramp at the lake. You may launch car-top boats by hand.

Facilities, fees: No facilities at the lake. A campground, restrooms with flush toilets, coin showers, and drinking water are available nearby. Supplies can be obtained in Graeagle. A dayuse fee is charged at the park.

Water sports, restrictions: Rowboats, canoes, kayaks, and inflatables are permitted. No motors. No sailboarding. There is a swimming beach on the north side of the lake.

Directions: In Truckee, drive north on Highway 89 to Graeagle. Just after passing Graeagle (one mile from the junction of Highway 70) turn left on County Road A14/Graeagle-Johnsville Road and drive west for about five miles to the park entrance on the left. Continue a short distance to the lake.

Contact: Plumas-Eureka State Park, 530/836-2380, website: www.parks.ca.gov (click on Find A Park).

5 JAMISON CREEK

🛶 🚣 ⛰️

Rating: 4

near Graeagle in Plumas-Eureka State Park

Map 6.1, page 192

Little Jamison Creek is a prime spot for families with youngsters who want to cool off on a hot summer day. Several excellent swimming holes can be found along the creek and are easily accessible. The best time to swim here is from mid- to late summer, when the water is not only warmer but the flows are low and calm.

Though out-of-towners have no idea that this little creek exists, it is a favorite with the locals. The elevation is approximately 5,000 feet.

Access: No boat ramp is available.

Facilities, fees: No facilities at the creek. A campground, restrooms with flush toilets, coin showers, and drinking water are available nearby. Supplies can be obtained in Graeagle. A day-use fee is charged at the park. A fee is charged for camping.

Water sports, restrictions: Several swimming holes are available along the creek, which runs directly through the park's campground. Start at the campground and follow the stream to access the various spots.

Directions: From Truckee, drive north on Highway 89 to Graeagle. Just after passing Graeagle (one mile from the junction of Highway 70) turn left on County Road A14/Graeagle-Johnsville Road and drive west for about five miles to the park entrance. Access to the creek is available off the road near the campground.

Contact: Plumas-Eureka State Park, 530/836-2380, website: www.parks.ca.gov (click on Find A Park).

6 GOLD LAKE

🚐 🏕️ 🚣 🛶 🎣 🛶 🚤 ⛰️

Rating: 8

near Sierraville on the border of Tahoe and Plumas national forests

Map 6.1, page 192

Imagine a beautiful, sky blue lake set in a rock basin in the northern Sierra, the kind of place where you might want to hide out in a cabin and plan on never leaving.

That is how a visit to Gold Lake can make you feel. It is set near the Sierra crest at an elevation of 6,400 feet, and because it is a natural lake, not a reservoir, it is always full of water—a beautiful sight. On the whole this place makes a great vacation destination, with one disclaimer.

The lone drawback, alas, is the wind, which can really blow here, particularly during the afternoons throughout the summer. But that is why sailboarders love the place. The wind is predictable from Memorial Day through early July, from 2 P.M. to 6 P.M.

The lake is stocked with rainbow trout. Most of the fish are caught from boats, especially the occasional giant mackinaw trout. It is difficult to catch fish from shore here.

The water is very cold until late in summer, and sometimes the snow and ice aren't gone until late June, but lots of people swim anyway during the vacation season. There's a swimming beach at the resort. The heart of the lake is Gold Lake Lodge, where cabins are typically booked solid in July and August. Gold Lake Lodge is located about .5 mile north of Gold Lake.

Access: A paved ramp is located on the north side of the lake.

Facilities, fees: Primitive campsites and chemicals toilets are nearby. No drinking water. Garbage must be packed out. Cabins, a small store, and a restaurant are nearby at Gold Lake Lodge. Other supplies can be obtained in Graeagle and Bassetts. Access is free.

Water sports, restrictions: Powerboats, water-skiing, wake boarding, personal watercraft, canoes, kayaks, sailboats, and sailboarding are permitted. A swimming beach is available at Gold Lake Beach Resort.

Directions: From Truckee, turn north on Highway 89 and drive 20 miles to Sierraville. At Sierraville, turn left on Highway 49 and drive about 10 miles to the Bassetts Store. Turn right on Gold Lake Highway and drive to the lake access road (well signed) on the left.

Contact: Plumas National Forest, Beckwourth Ranger District, 530/836-2575; Gold Lake Beach Resort, 530/836-2491; Gold Lake Lodge, 530/836-2350, website: www.goldlakelodge.com. For a map, send $6 to U.S. Forest Service, Attn: Map Sales, P.O. Box 587, Camino, CA 95709, 530/647-5390, fax 530/647-5389, website: www.fs.fed.us/r5/forests. Major credit cards accepted.

7 HAVEN LAKE

Rating: 4

near Sierraville on the border of Plumas and Tahoe national forests

Map 6.1, page 192

This small lake is nestled at an elevation of 5,500 feet in the Lakes Basin Recreation Area. It has a forested shoreline, is very pretty, and is always full of water.

Most of the folks you'll see around here have come to fish for brook trout, but there are a handful of people who like to swim in Haven Lake. Fewer yet will plunk in a car-top boat and paddle around a bit. Use is very light, due to the fact that there are so many great destinations nearby.

Access: There is no boat ramp. Car-top boats may be hand launched.

Facilities, fees: A few primitive campsites are available. No drinking water or vault toilets are available. Garbage must be packed out. Supplies can be obtained in Sierra City and Bassetts. Access is free.

Water sports, restrictions: Rowboats, canoes, kayaks, and inflatables that can be hand

launched are permitted. The lake is too small for most boating. Swimming is permitted.

Directions: From Truckee, turn north on Highway 89 and drive 20 miles to Sierraville. At Sierraville, turn left on Highway 49 and drive about 10 miles to the Bassetts Store. Turn right on Gold Lake Highway and drive about five miles. There is no formal access road to the lake; look for dirt roads that lead off the main road to the lake. Forest Service maps are advised.

Contact: Plumas National Forest, Beckwourth Ranger District, 530/836-2575, fax 530/836-0493. For a map, send $6 to U.S. Forest Service, Attn: Map Sales, P.O. Box 587, Camino, CA 95709, 530/647-5390, fax 530/647-5389, website: www.fs.fed.us/r5/forests. Major credit cards accepted.

8 SNAG LAKE

Rating: 4

near the Sierra Buttes in Tahoe National Forest

Map 6.1, page 192

There are better lakes in this area, and then there are worse. So as far as the competition goes, Snag Lake rates in the so-so range. But when you consider how beautiful this section of Tahoe National Forest is, on a larger scale you could do a lot worse. It is set at an elevation of 6,600 feet.

This lake is very small and is used by hardly anyone except a few trout anglers. The shoreline is forested; there's not much beach area, but it is possible to get into the water. The water stays quite cold throughout the summer, but some brave souls do manage to swim around (though their immersion is typically brief).

When you do see a boat in use here, it's almost always a raft or a canoe, with the occupants floating about and enjoying themselves, usually casting a line for rainbow trout.

Access: There is no boat ramp. Car-top boats may be hand launched.

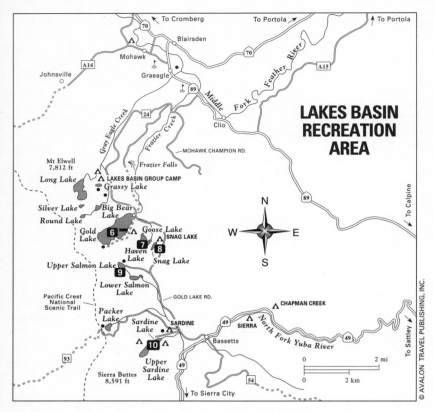

© AVALON TRAVEL PUBLISHING, INC.

Facilities, fees: A primitive campground and vault toilets are available. No drinking water. Garbage must be packed out. Supplies can be obtained in Sierra City and Bassetts. Access is free.

Water sports, restrictions: Small boats, canoes, kayaks, and inflatables that can be hand launched are permitted. Swimming is permitted.

Directions: From Truckee, turn north on Highway 89 and drive 20 miles to Sierraville. At Sierraville, turn left on Highway 49 and drive about 10 miles to the Bassetts Store. Turn right on Gold Lake Highway and drive five miles to the Snag Lake Campground on the left.

Contact: Tahoe National Forest, North Yuba/Downieville Ranger District, 530/288-3231, fax 530/288-0727.

9 SALMON LAKE (UPPER)

Rating: 7

near Sierra Buttes in Tahoe National Forest

Map 6.1, page 192

This is a gorgeous setting, absolutely pristine and beautiful with crystal-clear water and wilderness surroundings. The Salmon Lake Lodge is unpretentious (they don't have a telephone there), but the cabins are among the most difficult to get reservations for anywhere in California.

The lake is excellent for canoeing and kayaking, with rentals available at Salmon Lake Lodge.

Set at an elevation of 6,000 feet, the lake is sheltered from the wind, but the water is typically cold. That doesn't stop kids from jumping off the pier at the lodge, and while they might complain about the cold water, if you listen closely you will learn that they are actually bragging.

Several other hike-to lakes are located nearby, including Lower Salmon Lake, Horse Lake, and Deer Lake. Of these, Deer Lake is the prettiest. But it is difficult to surpass the pristine setting here at Salmon Lake.

Access: There is a small paved boat ramp. Small fishing boats and car-top boats may be hand launched near the dock.

Facilities, fees: Lodging and limited boat rentals are available at Salmon Lake Lodge. A dock and a pier are also provided. Campgrounds are available nearby. Supplies can be obtained in Sierra City and Bassetts. Access is free.

Water sports, restrictions: The lake is too small for sailboarding or large boats. Swimming is permitted.

Directions: From Truckee, turn north on Highway 89 and drive 20 miles to Sierraville. At Sierraville, turn left on Highway 49 and drive about 10 miles to the Bassetts Store. Turn right on Gold Lake Highway and drive about three miles north to a signed turn for Salmon Lake. Turn left and drive one mile to the lake.

Contact: Tahoe National Forest, North Yuba/Downieville District, 530/288-3231, fax 530/288-0727; Salmon Lake Lodge, 530/757-1825.

🔟 SARDINE LAKE (LOWER)

Rating: 10

near Sierra Buttes in Tahoe National Forest

Map 6.1, page 192

This lake is the closest thing to a Golden Pond in California.

The lake is small, but drop-dead gorgeous, blue-green, sheltered with the awesome backdrop of the granite spires of the Sierra Buttes.

Sometimes there is just no substitute for spectacular natural beauty, which is what you'll find when you visit Sardine Lake. Sardine Lake is among the prettiest drive-to lakes in California. It and Upper Sardine Lake are set in a rock bowl beneath the impressive Sierra Buttes and are always full of water, thanks to the melting snow.

Small and intimate, the lake is perfect for low-speed boats, and on the water you are surrounded by this dramatic beauty. Sometimes it feels as if you are literally soaking it up. A primitive boat ramp—accessible to car-top boats and small trailered boats—is provided next to the lodge. There is also a small marina with boat docks where visitors can rent aluminum boats with motors.

Trout fishing is good here, and most boaters bring along a rod. Some visitors rent a boat and venture to the head of the lake, where they can beach and make the short walk to the inlet stream's hidden waterfall.

Nearby Upper Sardine Lake and Sand Pond offer decent swimming opportunities and excellent hiking.

The cabins at Sardine Lake Lodge are small, well kept, and utterly adorable. Getting a reservation to stay in one can require 10 years on a waiting list—really. The only hope here is to sign up on the lodge's cancellation list.

Access: A small, primitive boat launch is available.

Facilities, fees: Lodging, restaurant (reservations required), and rowboat and fishing boat rentals are available at Sardine Lake Lodge. A campground with drinking water and vault toilets is available nearby. Supplies can be obtained in Sierra City and Bassetts. Access is free.

Water sports, restrictions: Small boats with motors, canoes, kayaks, and inflatables are permitted. A 5-mph speed limit is strictly enforced. No swimming, sailboarding, or personal watercraft allowed. Swimming is available nearby at Upper Sardine Lake and Sand Pond.

Directions: From Truckee, drive north on Highway 89 for 20 miles to Sierraville. Turn left on Highway 49 and drive about 10 miles to the

Bassetts Store. Turn right on Gold Lake Road and drive one mile to Sardine Lake Road. Turn left and drive a short distance, then bear left at the fork (signed Sardine Lake) and drive one mile to the lake.

Contact: Sardine Lake Lodge, 530/862-1196 (summer) or 916/645-8882; Tahoe National Forest, North Yuba Ranger Station, 530/288-3231. For a map, send $6 to U.S. Forest Service, Attn: Map Sales, P.O. Box 587, Camino, CA 95709, 530/647-5390, fax 530/647-5389, website: www.fs.fed.us/r5/forests. Major credit cards are accepted.

11 JACKSON MEADOW RESERVOIR

Rating: 9

northwest of Truckee in Tahoe National Forest

Map 6.1, page 192

Jackson Meadow Reservoir is a gorgeous place. There's a reason. Water levels here are often kept higher than at the typical mountain reservoir, which makes the lake quite beautiful and provides for a much wider variety of top-quality boating and recreation than offered by the area's other lakes.

Jackson Meadow is set at an elevation of 6,100 feet, and the surrounding area is just as pretty, featuring forest, meadows, and the trademark granite look of the Sierra Nevada. This is a very popular recreation area, with developed campsites, well-maintained picnic areas, and two large, sandy swimming beaches

Families on vacation and people who just want a quiet spot to bed down will find all they need here. Rangers strictly enforce noise level laws, a courtesy rarely found at Forest Service campgrounds. A bonus is a boat-in campground at Jackson Point, one of the few available in the high Sierra. This is a gorgeous spot set at the end of a peninsula that extends from the east shore.

This is the only lake in the immediate area where all boating is allowed, so it gets heavy use in the summer. Access is fairly easy, just a few miles from Highway 89, and the beautiful forest setting attracts a lot of tourists.

Trout stocks are excellent, with a mix of rainbow and brown trout planted each summer.

Some campers use Jackson Meadow Reservoir as their headquarters for multi-day trips into the surrounding mountain country. Many lakes in the vicinity make good destinations for side trips, and the trailhead for the Pacific Crest Trail is located just east of the lake along the access road.

Access: Two paved boat ramps are provided, located adjacent to Woodcamp and Pass Creek campgrounds.

Facilities, fees: Several campgrounds, including a boat-in campground, two picnic areas, drinking water, vault toilets, and an RV dump station are available. Supplies are available in Truckee. A fee is charged for camping.

Water sports, restrictions: Powerboats, waterskiing, wake boarding, personal watercraft, sailing, and sailboarding are permitted. Two developed swimming beaches are available.

Directions: To Woodcamp: From Truckee, drive north on Highway 89 for 17.5 miles to Forest Road 7. Turn left on Forest Road 7 and drive 16 miles to Jackson Meadow Reservoir. At the lake, continue across the dam around the west shoreline and then turn left at the campground access road. The campground entrance is on the right just before the Woodcamp boat ramp.

To Pass Creek Campground: From Truckee, drive north on Highway 89 for 17.5 miles to Forest Road 7. Turn left on Forest Road 7 and drive 16 miles to Jackson Meadow Reservoir; the campground and boat launch is on the left at the north end of the lake.

Contact: Tahoe National Forest, Sierraville Ranger District, 530/994-3401, fax 530/994-3143; Truckee-Donner Chamber of Commerce, 530/587-2757. For a map, send $6 to U.S. Forest Service, Attn: Map Sales, P.O. Box 587, Camino, CA 95709, 530/647-5390, fax 530/647-5389, website: www.fs.fed.us/r5/forests. Major credit cards accepted.

12 WEAVER LAKE

Rating: 4

north of Emigrant Gap in Tahoe National Forest

Map 6.1, page 192

For the mom and dad who want to get away from it all, but whose family is not ready for the wilderness experience, Weaver Lake provides a rare drive-to alternative.

One of dozens of lakes within a 10-mile radius tucked away in the granite slopes of Sierra Nevada country, Weaver is set at an elevation of 6,000 feet. On the way in you will pass Bowman Lake, with several other small lakes accessible off cutoff routes from the main route in to Weaver.

Most of the visitors to the lake are anglers, but the rough road in makes the place attractive to people who want a wilderness experience without having to hike.

The lake is small, and only car-top boats such as canoes, rowboats, and inflatables are appropriate. Despite the fact that the area can be hit with some hot summer days, the water is chilly, making it quite a feat to jump in and paddle around a bit, even for a short while.

Weaver has a good mix of rainbow trout and brown trout, with a few elusive mackinaw.

Access: There is no boat ramp. Car-top boats may be hand launched.

Facilities, fees: Vault toilets are available. A primitive campground is located at Jackson Creek just east of Bowman Lake. No drinking water is available. Garbage must be packed out. Access to the lake is free.

Water sports, restrictions: Car-top boats, canoes, kayaks, and inflatables are permitted. Small motors are permitted. There is a 10-mph speed limit. Swimming is permitted. The lake is too small for sailboarding or sailing.

Directions: From Auburn, take I-80 east for 45 miles to the exit for Highway 20. Take that exit, turn west and drive four miles to Bowman Lakes Road (Forest Road 18). Turn right and drive 19 miles to Graniteville Road. Turn left and drive one mile to Forest Road 41. Turn right and drive two miles to Weaver Lake. Continue past the private lodge for one mile to the lake access road. Bear right and drive 1.5 miles to the lake.

The road is rough, and although four-wheel-drive vehicles are not required, they are recommended.

Contact: Tahoe National Forest, Nevada City Ranger District, 530/265-4531. For a map, send $6 to U.S. Forest Service, Attn: Map Sales, P.O. Box 587, Camino, CA 95709, 530/647-5390, fax 530/647-5389, website: www.fs.fed.us/r5/forests. Major credit cards accepted.

13 BOWMAN LAKE

Rating: 5

north of Emigrant Gap in Tahoe National Forest

Map 6.1, page 192

Many get their first glimpse of Bowman Lake from the access road, fully intending to drive onward to nearby Weaver Lake to the north or to Jackson Meadow Reservoir six miles to the northeast. But Bowman is so pretty, a sapphire jewel set in granite at an elevation of 5,568 feet, that it is difficult to pass by without wanting to set up camp.

The access road is rough and not conducive to towing trailered boats. In the ideal situation you would have a four-wheel-drive vehicle with a canoe strapped to the top.

This lake is just a bit more popular than its northerly neighbor, Weaver. On the plus side it is larger than Weaver, but when water levels are down in drought years the shoreline can become quite steep and rocky, a minus.

Pine trees surround Bowman Lake, and the shoreline is sprinkled with large granite slabs. Though the water is usually cold, it's decent enough for a quick dunk.

There are lots of small trout, often eager to please during the evening bite. They make this an ideal lake for camping, car-top boating, and fishing.

Access: There is no boat ramp. Car-top boats may be hand launched.

Facilities, fees: A primitive campsite and vault toilets are available. No drinking water and garbage must be packed out. Obtain supplies in Truckee. Access to the lake is free.

Water sports, restrictions: A 10-mph speed limit is enforced. Swimming is permitted.

Directions: From Sacramento, drive east on I-80 past Emigrant Gap to Highway 20. Head west on Highway 20 and drive 4.6 miles to Bowman Road/Forest Road 18. Turn right and drive about 16 miles (much of the road is quite rough) to Bowman Lake and the campground on the right side of the road at the head of the lake.

Contact: Tahoe National Forest, Nevada City Ranger District, 530/265-4531; PG&E Land Projects, 916/386-5164, website: www.pge.com/recreation.

14 SAWMILL LAKE

Rating: 4

north of Emigrant Gap in Tahoe National Forest

Map 6.1, page 192

Tiny Sawmill is the classic "nice little spot." It's very pretty, set at about 6,000 feet amid Sierra granite and pines, but without a campground, boat ramp, or direct access for swimming or launching a car-top boat. So why would you come here? For the beauty, which is sometimes enough.

The lake attracts the curious, mainly people fishing for small trout. Car-top boats (canoes, kayaks) are okay, but you must carry your boat in from wherever you park because, as mentioned, there is limited vehicle access to the shoreline.

The water is cold, and the shoreline is partly rocky, partly weedy, and provides only fair conditions for swimming.

Access: There is a small, primitive boat ramp. Car-top boats may be hand launched.

Facilities, fees: Limited walk-in tent sites are located near the north shore. No facilities. No drinking water. Garbage must be packed out. Access to the lake is free.

Water sports, restrictions: A 10-mph speed limit is enforced. Swimming is permitted.

Directions: From Sacramento, drive east on I-80 past Emigrant Gap to Highway 20. Head west on Highway 20 for 4.6 miles and drive to Bowman Road/Forest Road 18. Turn right and drive about 16 miles (much of the road is quite rough) to Bowman Lake and continue in an easterly direction four miles to a Y at Jackson Creek Campground. Turn south (right) on a forest service road and drive approximately one mile to Sawmill Lake. Road washouts may require four-wheel-drive.

Contact: Tahoe National Forest, Nevada City Ranger District, 530/265-4531. For a map, send $6 to U.S. Forest Service, Attn: Map Sales, P.O. Box 587, Camino, CA 95709, 530/647-5390, fax 530/647-5389, website: www.fs.fed.us/r5/forests. Major credit cards accepted.

15 FAUCHERIE LAKE

Rating: 6

north of Emigrant Gap in Tahoe National Forest

Map 6.1, page 192

It's hard to believe that you can simply drive to beautiful Faucherie Lake. But here it is, a classic alpine lake set in Sierra granite at an elevation of 6,100 feet. The glacier-carved granite bowl is filled with clear, pure water from melting snow.

This is the kind of place that backpackers will hike many miles to reach. Quiet and pristine, it has a completely wilderness feel, a rare quality in a drive-to lake. Imagine arriving at Faucherie Lake on a summer afternoon, plopping in a canoe, then paddling around, and enjoying the natural beauty.

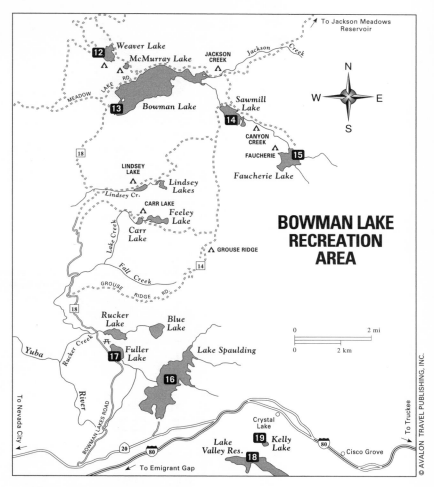

**BOWMAN LAKE
RECREATION
AREA**

© AVALON TRAVEL PUBLISHING, INC.

Not only is it an excellent venue for car-top boating, but there's decent fishing for both rainbow trout and brown trout, with conditions fair for swimming.

This is the most popular lake in the area, mainly because it is the only one with a developed group campground. The entire area to the west of the lake is closed to vehicles, and there is some good hiking available.

Access: There is a concrete boat ramp and limited parking. Car-top boats may be hand launched.

Facilities, fees: A group campground (reser-vations required) and vault toilets are avail-able. No drinking water. Garbage must be packed out. A campground is available one mile away. Access to the lake is free.

Water sports, restrictions: There is a 10-mph speed limit on the lake. Swimming is permitted.

Directions: From Sacramento, drive east on I-80 past Emigrant Gap to Highway 20. Head west on Highway 20 for 4.6 miles and drive to Bowman Road/Forest Road 18. Turn right and drive about 16 miles (much of the road is quite rough) to Bowman Lake and continue in an easterly direction four miles to a Y. Bear right (south) on a forest service road at the Y and drive about three miles to the lake. Road washouts may require four-wheel-drive.

Contact: Tahoe National Forest, Nevada City Ranger District, 530/265-4531. For a map, send $6 to U.S. Forest Service, Attn: Map Sales, P.O. Box 587, Camino, CA 95709, 530/647-5390, fax 530/647-5389, website: www.fs.fed.us/r5/forests. Major credit cards accepted.

16 LAKE SPAULDING

Rating: 10

near Emigrant Gap in Tahoe National Forest

Map 6.1, page 192

Spectacular beauty. Easy to reach. Boat ramp. Campground. Splendid hiking trails in the area.

Lake Spaulding is one of the few lakes that can provide all of these perks. This gorgeous lake covers 698 acres and is set at an elevation of 5,000 feet in the Sierra Nevada. This is classic granite country, and the setting features huge boulders and a sprinkling of conifers around a gray, slab-like shoreline. The entire area looks like it has been cut, chiseled, and smoothed.

The drive here is nearly a straight shot up I-80. If there is one problem, it is the amount of company you'll have at the campground.

The boat ramp is paved, but it is not really intended for large boats. After launching you will enter a beautiful setting that's suitable for most water sports. The water is spectacularly clear and cold; water-skiing is quite popular amid such grandeur and beauty. By August, however, the surface waters become considerably warmer, not too cold for swimming. Sailboarding is popular because winds can be good and this is one of the few large lakes in the area.

Because the lake has a campground and is conveniently located right off I-80, access is extremely easy and the place gets a lot of attention and use.

There's just one word of caution: Water lev-

els tend to drop in late summer, creating visible hazards for boaters.

Fishing for kokanee salmon and rainbow trout is often good. The nearby South Fork Yuba River also offers trout fishing. There are several other lakes set in the mountain country to the immediate north that can make for excellent side trips. These include Bowman, Weaver, and Faucherie Lakes.

Access: A paved boat ramp is available at the end of the access road.

Facilities, fees: A campground, vault toilets, drinking water, and a picnic area are available. Access is free. There is a fee for boat launching.

Water sports, restrictions: Powerboats, waterskiing, wake boarding, sailing, and sailboarding are permitted. No personal watercraft. A swimming area is available near the picnic area.

Directions: From Sacramento, drive east on I-80 past Emigrant Gap to the exit for Highway 20. Take that exit and drive west on Highway 20 for 2.3 miles to Lake Spaulding Road. Turn right and drive .5 mile to the lake.

Contact: Tahoe National Forest, Big Bend Visitor Center, 530/426-3609; PG&E Land Projects, 916/386-5164, website: www.pge.com/recreation.

17 FULLER LAKE

Rating: 5

east of Nevada City in Tahoe National Forest

Map 6.1, page 192

As you drive out on Bowman Road, Fuller Lake is the first lake you'll come to. There are dozens of other lakes set farther back in the mountains. But if you just can't wait any longer, or the lakes nestled deeper in the national forest are inaccessible, stopping here just might prove to be a good idea. The place is ideal for car-top boating, and maybe even a bit of fishing or swimming.

Though there are many lakes in the immediate region, this little lake stands apart because it is relatively easy to reach and has a paved boat ramp; most other lakes around here do not have one.

Fuller is a small lake, best suited for car-top boating, trout fishing, and swimming. The water can remain quite cold through mid-summer, but is clear and pretty. The fishing is better at Fuller Lake than at many of the more remote lakes in the Bowman Lakes Recreation Area.

The setting is at an elevation of 5,400 feet, and the road is usually free of snow by mid-May. Late snowstorms are common in this area, so always phone the Forest Service in advance to get road conditions.

Access: A paved boat ramp and paved parking area are at the lake's day-use area at the northern end of the lake.

Facilities, fees: A day-use area with vault toilets is available. No drinking water. Garbage must be packed out. Access and boat launching are free.

Water sports, restrictions: Rowboats, canoes, kayaks, and inflatables are permitted. The lake is too small for sailboarding, sailing, or power-boating. Swimming is permitted.

Directions: From Sacramento, drive east on I-80 past Emigrant Gap to Highway 20. Head west on Highway 20 and drive 4.6 miles to Bowman Road/Forest Road 18. Turn right and drive four miles to Fuller Lake on the right.

Contact: Tahoe National Forest, Nevada City Ranger District, 530/265-4531. For a map, send $6 to U.S. Forest Service, Attn: Map Sales, P.O. Box 587, Camino, CA 95709, 530/647-5390, fax 530/647-5389, website: www.fs.fed.us/r5/forests. Major credit cards accepted.

18 LAKE VALLEY RESERVOIR

Rating: 7

near Yuba Gap in Tahoe National Forest

Map 6.1, page 192

When full, Lake Valley Reservoir is gorgeous, its shoreline sprinkled with conifers and boulders. It is set at an elevation of 5,786 feet, has a surface area of 300 acres, and offers a decent campground and nearby boat ramp.

Upon arrival you get your first bonus: the very pretty campground, located near the lake but set right in the forest. It is one of the best camps run by PG&E.

Though no powerboating is permitted, the lake earns a pretty high rating anyway because of easy access, scenic beauty, great camping, and outstanding car-top boating conditions. Canoes are perfect for this lake, and paddling about while you fish for trout can be great fun.

Excellent sailboarding is another wonderful aspect of this lake, with a strong west wind on most afternoons. The shoreline is steep and rocky, but there is a suitable swimming area by the picnic area. This is also the best put-in spot for sailboarders.

When you add it all up, Lake Valley Reservoir is a winner. Quite a few vacationers have done the math, too, and they flock here in the summer.

Access: A paved boat ramp is located next to the picnic area on the north side of the lake.

Facilities, fees: A campground, vault toilets, drinking water, and a picnic area are available. Access is free.

Water sports, restrictions: Powerboats, canoes, kayaks, inflatables, sailing, and sailboarding are permitted. No water-skiing, wake boarding, or personal watercraft allowed. A 15-mph speed limit is enforced. Swimming is available at the picnic area.

Directions: Take I-80 to the exit for Yuba Gap. Take that exit and drive south for .4 mile to Lake Valley Road. Turn right on Lake Valley Road and drive for 1.2 mile until the road forks. Bear left and continue for one mile.

Contact: PG&E Land Projects, 916/386-5164, website: www.pge.com/recreation.

19 KELLY LAKE

Rating: 4

east of Nevada City in Tahoe National Forest

Map 6.1, page 192

Kelly is the little brother of nearby Lake Valley Reservoir. It has a similar look, set at an elevation of 5,900 feet and surrounded by granite boulders and conifers, but is just 15 percent of Lake Valley's size.

Many travelers on nearby I-80 take a break here, either for a picnic lunch or to enjoy the pretty scenery. There's usually a handful of people who've hopped over from crowded Lake Valley Reservoir in search of a smaller, more intimate setting.

Before a picnic, some people take a dip in the water. Although there is no designated beach, there is a nice shoreline for swimming.

As no motors are permitted, boating opportunities are only available for car-top boaters. Also, there is no campground or any overnight use facility.

Access: There is no boat ramp. Car-top boats may be hand launched.

Facilities, fees: A picnic area and vault toilets are available. No drinking water. A campground is available nearby at Lake Valley Reservoir. Access is free.

Water sports, restrictions: Rowboats, canoes, kayaks and inflatables are permitted. No motors allowed. Swimming is possible near the picnic area. The lake is too small for sailboarding and sailing.

Directions: Take I-80 to the exit for Yuba Gap. Take that exit and drive south for .4 mile to a fork in the road. Bear left and drive three miles (passing Snowflower private camp) to the lake.

Contact: PG&E Land Projects, 916/386-5164, website: www.pge.com/recreation.

20 MEADOW LAKE

Rating: 5

northwest of Truckee in Tahoe National Forest

Map 6.1, page 192

Few people know about this lake, and most of those few come here to picnic and fish. But what is even less known is that of all the primitive, hard-to-reach lakes in this area, Meadow Lake is among the better ones for swimming. That is because there are some small beach-like areas—stretches of sand/gravel mix along part of the shore—that provide good access and sunbathing territory.

Meadow Lake is set at an elevation of 7,800 feet. It is narrow but pretty good sized, about 1.5 miles long. The water is clear and cold.

Boating is limited to car-top boats. Hikers will find a good side trip by heading south, where a trail is routed to the Meadow Lakes Mine, an old gold mine.

This area is popular with four-wheel-drive enthusiasts. A major wheeling event is held here in mid-August. The old gold mining town of Summit City once occupied the flat on the southwest side of Meadow Lake. In the mid-1800s, it numbered 2,000 people.

Access: There is no boat ramp. Car-top boats may be hand launched.

Facilities, fees: A small campground with vault toilets is available. No drinking water. Garbage must be packed out. Camping is not permitted. Access is free.

Water sports, restrictions: There is a 10-mph speed limit. Swimming is permitted.

Directions: From Auburn, drive east on I-80 for 45 miles to Highway 20. Take the Highway 20 exit and drive 4.6 miles to Bowman Lake Road (Forest Service Road 18). Turn right and drive 19 miles until you reach Meadow Lake Road. Turn right on Meadow Lake Road and drive 10 miles to the lake. Four-wheel-drive vehicles are recommended.

Contact: Tahoe National Forest, Sierraville

Ranger District, 530/994-3401; Truckee-Donner Chamber of Commerce, 530/587-2757. For a map, send $6 to U.S. Forest Service, Attn: Map Sales, P.O. Box 587, Camino, CA 95709, 530/647-5390, fax 530/647-5389, website: www.fs.fed.us/r5/forests. Major credit cards accepted.

21 FORDYCE LAKE

Rating: 4

east of Nevada City in Tahoe National Forest

Map 6.1, page 192

Some strangely shaped lakes were created when dams were built in Sierra gorges, and Fordyce is one of them. This long, curving lake has a very deep southern end near the dam, several coves, and six feeder streams. It is set at an elevation of about 7,000 feet.

It is ideal for four-wheel-drive rigs with car-top boats who can make their way to the lake's narrow west side and then hand launch their craft. Other visitors with less ambition had best pass.

The shoreline is steep and rocky, making it difficult to launch boats or to find access for swimming or sailboarding. It is, however, large, and if you can get your boat or board into it, you can enjoy a private paddle in a wilderness-like setting. You are duly warned that the water does stay quite cold through most of the summer. In addition, the lake often is drawn way down in the late summer.

The fishing is often good in early summer for rainbow and brown trout.

Some good hiking trails are available in the area and are detailed on a Forest Service map. If your vehicle can't handle the access road, you can camp at nearby Lake Sterling to the south and make the short hike to Fordyce on a well-marked trail.

Access: There is no boat ramp. Car-top boats may be hand launched.

Facilities, fees: No facilities. No drinking water. Garbage must be packed out. A primitive camp-ground is available at nearby Lake Sterling. Access is free.

Water sports, restrictions: Rowboats, canoes, kayaks, and inflatables are permitted. No motors allowed. Swimming is allowed.

Directions: From Sacramento, drive east on I-80 to Yuba Gap and continue about four miles to the Cisco Grove exit north. Take that exit, turn left on the frontage road, and drive a short distance onto Rattlesnake Road. Turn right and continue on Rattlesnake Road (gravel, steep, and curvy; trailers not recommended) and drive three miles (look for the campground on the right). When the road forks, bear left and drive three miles (steep, curvy) to the lake. Four-wheel-drive vehicles are recommended.

Contact: PG&E Land Projects, 916/386-5164, website: www.pge.com/recreation; Tahoe National Forest, Nevada City Ranger District, 916/265-4531. For a map, send $6 to U.S. Forest Service, Attn: Map Sales, P.O. Box 587, Camino, CA 95709, 530/647-5390, fax 530/647-5389, website: www.fs.fed.us/r5/forests. Major credit cards accepted.

22 LAKE STERLING

Rating: 6

east of Nevada City in Tahoe National Forest

Map 6.1, page 192

"How high's the water?" Throughout its history, Lake Sterling has been subject to severe water level fluctuations.

This is a small, secluded lake with a primitive but pretty campground and a tree-lined shore. The access road is very rough, which sharply limits the number of visitors and often guarantees that a stay at Lake Sterling will be a private affair, even on summer weekends.

What you get here is the chance to go camping and car-top boating, with some good swimming by day and trout fishing during the early evening.

The water is clear and cold. The surface waters don't start to warm up considerably until late July, when swimming prospects can really shine.

Access: No boat ramp.

Facilities, fees: A small, primitive campground, vault toilets, and drinking water are available. Garbage must be packed out. Access is free.

Water sports, restrictions: Rowboats, canoes, kayaks, and inflatables are permitted. Motors are allowed, but are best confined to small outboards for car-top boats. Swimming is allowed. The lake is too small for sailing, sailboarding, and most water sports.

Directions: From Sacramento, drive east on I-80 to Yuba Gap and continue about four miles to the Cisco Grove exit north. Take that exit, turn left on the frontage road, and drive a short distance onto Rattlesnake Road. Turn right and continue on Rattlesnake Road (gravel, steep, and curvy; trailers not recommended) and drive four miles to Lake Sterling Road. Turn left and drive 2.5 miles (steep, curvy) to the lake. Four-wheel-drive vehicles are recommended.

Contact: Tahoe National Forest, Nevada City Ranger District, 530/265-4531.

23 KIDD LAKE

Rating: 7

west of Truckee in Tahoe National Forest

Map 6.1, page 192

Kidd Lake is one of four lakes sprinkled in a series along the access road, and one of seven in a six-mile radius. The lake is set in the northern Sierra's high country at an elevation of 6,750 feet. It gets loaded with snow every winter. In late spring and early summer, be sure to call ahead to ask about conditions on the access road. Access varies every year in late spring.

Forestland surrounds the small, round lake. The shoreline is somewhat rocky, but there are a couple of good spots that are suitable for swimming. Sailboarding is decent in the afternoon, when the wind picks up. And if you want

a break from the water, you'll find some good hiking trails in the area.

In summer, Kidd Lake gets a lot of traffic from I-80 travelers, mainly anglers who bring small boats and camp overnight. Campsite reservations necessary.

The fishing is often frustrating, consisting of a lot of tiny brook trout.

Access: A primitive boat ramp is available on the lake's west side.

Facilities, fees: A group campground for tents only, restrooms, vault toilets, and drinking water are available. Supplies can be obtained in Truckee. Access to the lake is free. A fee is charged for the group campground.

Water sports, restrictions: Powerboats, canoes, kayaks, and inflatables are permitted. A 10-mph speed limit is enforced. The lake is too small for sailing and sailboarding. Swimming access is available around the lake's edge.

Directions: From Sacramento, drive east on I-80 toward Truckee. Take the Norden/Soda Springs exit, drive a short distance, turn south on Soda Springs Road, and drive .8 mile to Pahatsi Road. Turn right and drive two miles (pavement ends after .3 mile). Bear right at the fork and drive one mile to the entrance on the left for the campground and lake (note that as of 2003, the directions listed on PG&E's website for Kidd Lake are incorrect).

Contact: PG&E Land Projects, 916/386-5164, website: www.pge.com/recreation.

24 CASCADE LAKES

Rating: 4

west of Truckee in Tahoe National Forest

Map 6.1, page 192

A channel connects these two tiny lakes, which are set at an elevation of about 4,000 feet. Both are too small for much boating, though a few die-hard fishermen do haul in their small car-top boats to fish for trout now and then. But close inspection reveals that the brook trout here are perhaps the dinkers of all dinks.

There's no boat ramp, and the shorelines are not conducive to hand-launching. Much of the shore is rocky and steep, which also discourages many swimmers. By midsummer, however, the water is warm and clear, a good place to take a quick dunk on a hot day after driving on I-80, providing you don't mind searching around a bit to find the best access points.

Cascade Lakes are better known among hikers as a good trailhead site and jumping-off point for a backpacking trip. A trailhead that is located at the lake's northwest side is routed south into Tahoe National Forest, up into the drainage to the headwaters of the North Fork American River.

Access: There is no boat ramp.

Facilities, fees: No facilities are provided on-site. A group campground is available nearby at Kidd Lake (reservations required). Supplies can be obtained in Truckee. Access to the lake is free.

Water sports, restrictions: There is a 10-mph speed limit. Swimming and sailboarding are allowed.

Directions: From Sacramento, drive east on I-80 toward Truckee. Take the Norden/Soda Springs exit, drive a short distance, turn south on Soda Springs Road, and drive .8 mile to Pahatsi Road. Turn right and drive two miles (pavement ends after .3 mile). When the road forks, bear right and drive three miles (past Kidd Lake) to Cascade Lakes.

Contact: Tahoe National Forest, Truckee Ranger District, 530/587-3558; Mountain Hardware, 530/587-4844; PG&E Land Projects, 916/386-5164; website: www.pge.com/recreation.

25 SERENE LAKES

Rating: 6

west of Truckee

Map 6.1, page 192

Serene Lakes is actually two connected lakes: Serena and Dulzura. This beautiful setting is too small and shallow for motorized boating

(motors are not allowed), but it is ideal for canoes, kayaks, and other hand-powered boats. Not only is the scenery around Serene Lakes gorgeous, but this is one of the few lakes in California that has adjoining private property where vacation homes have been built. The elevation is 7,000 feet.

An excellent sandy beach is available at the lodge. Another beach nearby is technically reserved for the lake's homeowners.

The lakes are stocked with brook trout and rainbow trout. Fishing is exclusively catch-and-release, occasionally good for flyfishers in float tubes.

Visitor use at Serene Lakes is moderate—pretty much just guests of the lodge and campground. Some good hiking trails are routed through the area.

Access: A boat ramp is located on the lake's east side at Ice Lakes Lodge.

Facilities, fees: A small marina with kayak, canoe, and hydrobike rentals, lodging, restaurant, restrooms, flush toilets, banquet, wedding facilities, and a picnic area are available.

Water sports, restrictions: Rowboats, canoes, kayaks, inflatables, sailing, and sailboarding are permitted. No motors are allowed. A swimming beach is available in front of the lodge.

Directions: From Sacramento, take I-80 east to the exit for Soda Springs/Norden (12 miles west of Truckee). Take that exit and drive to Donner Pass Road. Turn right and drive one mile to Soda Springs Road. Turn right on Soda Springs Road and drive 2.3 miles to the lake.

Contact: Ice Lakes Lodge, 530/426-7660, website: www.icelakeslodge.com.

26 INDEPENDENCE LAKE

Rating: 7

north of Truckee in Tahoe National Forest

Map 6.1, page 192

This is California's mystery lake. It is difficult to find, difficult to get a boat into, and difficult to fish. But on calm days here when

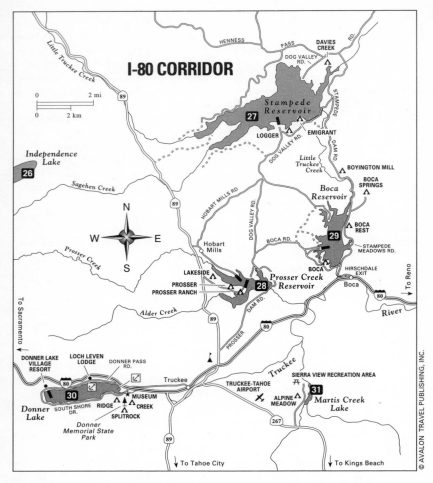

I-80 CORRIDOR

the wind doesn't blow (and that can be rare), it is drop-dead beautiful, a deep azure blue set in a canyon bordered by timbered slopes. The lake is set at an elevation of 6,949 feet, north of Truckee, with unique fishery, rules, and access.

The prize fish here are the 10- to 15-pound cutthroat trout and brown trout in the 20- to 25-pound class. All cutthroat trout must be released. While there are good numbers of kokanee salmon ranging eight to 14 inches and a fair sprinkling of brown trout, there are also

some monster-size browns, including one I've named "Son of Mo."

Yet it can be very difficult. Shore fishing is impossible. You'll never catch a fish. Getting a boat in is very difficult with the access road narrow and rough. In addition, the wind typically howls here, blowing straight up the lake out of the west. Days of white caps can kill a trip.

Even trying to reach this lake can be a real adventure. After turning off from the highway, the road goes quickly from asphalt to dirt, then deteriorates further, with lots of rocks and pot-holes. A high-clearance vehicle is required, and I kept my rig in four-wheel drive the whole route, "walking" it slowly over the rough stuff. On the access road from Jackson Meadow Road (Forest Service Road 7), you even have to cross a creek.

As you drive deeper into forest, you come across a series of unsigned logging road junctions, where wrong turns are easy to make.

An aspen grove along the far end of the lake is drop-dead gorgeous. You can see it by boat, or better yet, land your boat and enjoy one of the most beautiful hideaway picnic sites anywhere in North America, nestled in aspens along a lake like an azure jewel.

Because of that rough access road, most people will not try to trailer in small boats. It can be done, however, at extremely low speeds, taking about an hour to do so after leaving the highway. Most instead put small aluminum boats in the backs of pickup trucks and get boats in that way. A few might bring in car-top boats, such as canoes, but it can get windy here, and boats with more stability are advised.

When you arrive, you pass through a gate to reach a primitive campground, where there are a few rock fire pits, a pit toilet, and a few tables that have been created from the five-foot wooden spools used to load heavy electrical wire. The nearest supplies, gas, and restaurant are about 20 miles away, but most bring everything they need for as long as they plan to stay.

Note that as this book went to press, the property surrounding Independence Lake was being sold by Sierra Pacific Power. Some have feared an unfriendly new owner would take over and lock the gate at the boat ramp, ruining access. But one deal in escrow already fell through because Sierra County wanted to guarantee continued public access, and the new buyer wanted to block it. So the general feeling now is that access will be continued at the lake in some form, no matter who the buyer is. Regardless, always check the status as the first step in planning a trip here.

Access: A primitive boat ramp is available at the end of the road. The ramp is sometimes gated. Call before leaving for your trip.

Facilities, fees: A primitive campground and pit toilets are available. No drinking water. Supplies can be obtained in Truckee. Fees are charged for access, boat launching, and camping.

Water sports, restrictions: Powerboats are permitted; outboard or electric motors only. Speed limit is 10 mph. Canoes, kayaks, and inflatables are permitted, but the wind can be strong here, so their use is not advised. No bait permitted when fishing. Access limited to summer.

Directions: From Truckee, drive north on Highway 89 for 12.5 miles to Forest Service Road 7 (Jackson Meadow Road). Turn left and drive 1.5 miles to Independence Lake Road. Turn left and drive to a fork. Take the middle fork (to the right is a dead-end logging road), cross the creek and drive 6.5 miles to the lake (last unpaved 4.5 miles can be rough). A four-wheel-drive vehicle is recommended. The turns are often unsigned. A map of Tahoe National Forest is advised.

Contact: Sierra Pacific Power, 775/834-3468; Mountain Hardware, Truckee, 530/587-4844.

27 STAMPEDE RESERVOIR

Rating: 8

north of Truckee in Tahoe National Forest

Map 6.1, page 192

Stampede Reservoir is an easy-to-reach, drive-to lake that is hard to beat.

The setting is pretty when full, complete with sage and pine trees. When not full, the lake is rather barren looking.

Stampede is huge, the second largest in the area after Lake Tahoe, covering 3,400 acres with 25 miles of shoreline. It is set at an elevation of 6,000 feet in the Sierra and usually becomes accessible by late May.

There's just one problem. Note the extended launch ramp. Why would a ramp need to be extended? Right, because the water level gets quite low in the late summer and fall, when water is poured out the dam via the Little Truckee River and Boca Reservoir to keep the fish going in the Truckee River along I-80.

Use is high on summer weekends, and the developed campground is usually filled on Friday and Saturday nights. Most of the visitors are campers who are fishing for kokanee salmon or rainbow trout; a number of them bring along small trailered boats. This lake is becoming one of the top fishing lakes in California for kokanee salmon. There are also some large mackinaw trout and a good sprinkling of stocked rainbow trout.

On warm weekends you'll also typically see several fast boats towing water-skiers. During weekdays the scenario is pretty quiet, with relatively few folks out, trolling slowly and hoping to land a big brown trout.

Afternoons bring winds out of the west, shooting right up the I-80 canyon corridor. Wind conditions regularly make sailing and sailboarding quite good. The water, fresh from snowmelt pouring into the lake, is very cold, of course, until midsummer. That prevents most people from swimming here until late July; although there is no designated beach area, you can swim at various spots along the shoreline.

For dramatic effect, there are the occasional classic summer thunderstorms in the late afternoon and stellar starry nights best viewed from a sleeping bag.

Access: From Stampede Road, turn west on Forest Service Road 19N69 and travel toward the dam. Pass the dam and continue past Logger Campground to the paved, three-lane launch ramp on the lake's south side.

Facilities, fees: Campgrounds, restrooms with flush toilets, drinking water, and RV dump station are available. Supplies can be obtained in Truckee. Access is free. A fee is charged for camping.

Water sports, restrictions: Powerboats, water-skiing, wake boarding, personal watercraft, sailing, and sailboarding are permitted. Swimming access is available near the campground.

Directions: From Truckee, drive east on I-80

for seven miles to the Boca-Hirschdale/County Road 270 exit. Take that exit and drive north on County Road 270 for about seven miles (past Boca Reservoir) to the junction with County Road S261 on the left. Turn left and drive 1.5 miles to the campground on the right. The boat ramp is one mile from camp.

Contact: Tahoe National Forest, Truckee Ranger District, 530/587-3558.

28 PROSSER CREEK RESERVOIR

Rating: 7

north of Truckee in Tahoe National Forest

Map 6.1, page 192

This pretty and often serene spot is set at an elevation of 5,741 feet in Tahoe National Forest. Prosser Creek Reservoir covers 740 acres with 11 miles of shoreline. Highlights include good scenery and opportunities for fishing, camping, sailboarding, and swimming.

One of the reasons it is so serene is the 10-mph speed limit that ensures all the fast boats are making waves at other lakes. Access is extremely easy, situated just a few miles off I-80, so the place gets a lot of visitor traffic throughout the summer, especially on weekends.

There are no sandy beaches, but much of the shore is gently sloping, making it easily accessible to sailboarders and swimmers. When the lake is full, the prime jumping-off spot for sailboarding is at the north end, from the campground.

The adjacent shore to campgrounds is decent for hand-launched, car-top boats, providing the lake level is up. Lots of trout are stocked here every year, including 100,000 rainbow trout fingerlings added in an experiment by the Department of Fish and Game to see how fast they will grow.

Access: A paved boat ramp is available near the group campground.

Facilities, fees: Campgrounds, drinking water, vault toilets, and a picnic area are provided. Supplies can be obtained in Truckee. Access to the lake is free.

Water sports, restrictions: Boats with motors, canoes, kayaks, and inflatables are permitted. A 10-mph speed limit is strictly enforced. Sailing and sailboarding are permitted but those exceeding the speed limit are ticketed. Swimming access is available all along the shoreline.

Directions: From Truckee, drive north on Highway 89 for three miles to the campground entrance road on the right. Turn right and drive less than a mile to the campground.

Contact: Tahoe National Forest, Truckee Ranger District, 530/587-3558, fax 530/587-6914; Mountain Hardware, 530/587-4844.

29 BOCA RESERVOIR

Rating: 8

northeast of Truckee in Tahoe
National Forest

Map 6.1, page 192

Accessing this lake is very simple, just a quick hop off I-80. However, a lot of folks miss it because the dam faces the highway, unlike nearby Donner Lake, which is set right along the highway and presents a scenic view to thousands of travelers every day.

Like so many lakes in this region, Boca is extremely pretty. It is set at an elevation of 5,700 feet and covers 980 acres with 14 miles of shoreline. Once on the water, you may find it hard to believe that I-80 is only two miles away. No foolin'.

Still, enough people have discovered this gem, and use is very high all summer. The campgrounds are always full on Friday and Saturday nights, and on hot weekend afternoons there can be a lot of boats zipping around in the water. Sailboarding is also popular here on breezy afternoons in the early summer.

A 5-mph speed limit in all coves and inlets has solved the past conflicts between slow-trolling trout fishermen and fast boats.

Swimming conditions are much like those at Prosser Creek Reservoir (see previous listing),

with access available around most of the shoreline, although there are some steep sections.

In common with other lakes in the area, Boca has no sandy beaches for swimming and sunbathing and no picnic spots. After all, this is the Sierra! Shoreline access, however, is quite good; parts of the lakeshore are grassy and meadowy, with lots of pine trees. These are the prime spots, of course.

In drought years, Boca can be drained so low that the boat ramp is rendered totally unusable. It's a long drive to the boat ramp, so if you are unsure about conditions, call ahead before starting out. In high snow years the lake is usually full by June, a beautiful and inviting sight.

Stocked rainbow trout join the kokanee salmon and a few giant brown trout to make Boca a decent lake for campers who want a chance to catch a fish.

Access: The boat ramp is located on the southwest end of the lake.

Facilities, fees: Campgrounds and vault toilets are available. Drinking water is available at Boca Rest Camp. Supplies can be obtained in Truckee. Access to the lake is free. A fee is charged for camping.

Water sports, restrictions: Water-skiing, wake boarding, personal watercraft, canoes, kayaks, inflatables, sailing, and sailboarding are permitted. A 5-mph speed limit is enforced in all coves and inlets. Swimming access is available all along the shoreline.

Directions: From Truckee, drive east on I-80 for seven miles to the Boca-Hirschdale exit. Take that exit and drive north on County Road 270 about 2.5 miles to the campground on the right side of the road.

Contact: Tahoe National Forest, Truckee Ranger District, 530/587-3558; Mountain Hardware, 530/587-4844.

30 DONNER LAKE

Rating: 10

west of Truckee in Donner Memorial
State Park

Map 6.1, page 192

The first glimpse of Donner Lake is always a stirring one, even though the lake has become a common stop for millions of vacationers cruising past on I-80. Its remarkable beauty evokes a heartfelt response.

Set near the Sierra crest at elevation 5,900 feet, this big, oblong lake—three miles long by .75 mile wide, with 7.5 miles of shoreline—is filled with gem blue water. It is easy to reach and provides a good option for family campers. The area is well developed, with cabins and maintained access roads. A public boat ramp is available at the lake's west end near Donner Village Resort. Those very factors, however, are often cited as the reasons why some people never stay at Donner. They want more seclusion.

If you go by boat, take fair warning that afternoon winds can run you off the lake during the spring and that afternoon thunderstorms can do the same late in the summer. Also note that the lake's spectacular beauty and prominence as a national landmark attract tons of people throughout the summer. All boating and water sports are available, in addition to good hiking, biking, and horseback riding. Note that boaters must be careful of the big, submerged boulders just east of China Cove, located along the south shore.

West winds are common during the afternoon, providing outstanding conditions for sailing and sailboarding. The best put-in spots for sailboarding are at Shoreline Park and Donner State Park. The state park has more than three miles of frontage of Donner Creek and Donner Lake.

Though the water is cold, it heats up by midday. Many people like to swim here. The designated swimming beaches are truly spectacular—large, developed stretches of sand.

Because the lake is such a favorite, reservations are an absolute must if you want to camp at the state park, the only campground at the lake. Also note that there is only one boat ramp, and that boats rented at the state park can be hand launched only.

Fishing is good here, but typically only in the very early morning, trolling for kokanee salmon, big mackinaw trout or brown trout, and rainbow trout.

Access: A paved public ramp is located on the lake's northwest corner, about .5 mile from Donner Lake Resort on Old Highway 40.

Facilities, fees: Campgrounds, vault toilets, drinking water, and picnic areas are available. Lodging is also available. Powerboats, fishing boats, personal watercraft, kayaks, canoes, and pontoon boats can be rented at Donner Lake Village Resort, and pedal boat, canoe, and kayak rentals are available at the state park. Supplies can be obtained in Truckee. A day-use fee is charged at Donner Memorial State Park. Fees are charged for boat launching and camping.

Water sports, restrictions: Boats with motors, water-skiing, wake boarding, personal watercraft, sailing, and sailboarding are permitted. Swimming beaches are available at Donner Memorial State Park (east side), West End Beach (west side), and Shoreline Park (south side). Owners of boats with two-cycle engines should call prior to making the trip. This lake may be restricted to four-cycle engines in the future.

Directions: From Auburn, drive east on I-80 just past Donner Lake to the Donner State Park exit. Take that exit and turn south (right) on Donner Pass Road and drive .5 mile to the park entrance on the left at the southeast end of the lake.

Contact: For boat launching information, 530/582-7720; Donner Memorial State Park, 530/582-7892 or 530/582-7894; Donner Lake Village Resort, 530/587-6081 or 800/621-6664, website: www.donnerlakevillage.com; Truckee-Donner Chamber of Commerce, 530/587-2757, fax 530/587-2439.

31 MARTIS CREEK LAKE

Rating: 4

near Truckee

Map 6.1, page 192

Little Martis, just 70 acres, is well known among a cult of fly fishers for its status as one of the few wild trout lakes in the country. Because the lake is not stocked with trout, you are restricted to catch-and-release fishing, using artificials; most flyfish from float tubes.

The lake is set at the edge of the Martis Valley near the Tahoe-Truckee Airport, and the wind can really howl in the afternoon. The setting is somewhat sparse and open. The elevation is 5,800 feet.

It was originally built to provide flood control and water storage for Truckee, and then was set aside as one of the first wild trout lakes in the state. Motors are prohibited, which keeps things quiet, and most of the visitors are fly fishers in float tubes, casting and retrieving, over and over again, prisoners of hope. There is a reason: Lahontan cutthroat trout reach 25 inches here. There are a sprinkling of equally large brown trout.

The place does lure a few non-anglers, too. It is an excellent destination for sailboarding, or on a calm morning, plunking a canoe in and paddling around a bit. There is a developed recreation area on the west side of the lake where you'll find a beach and picnic spot.

Despite all of the lake's strong points, most folks in the area flock to nearby Lake Tahoe, and Martis gets low to medium use. One problem explains why: The lake level can fluctuate daily, and at times, the lake is extremely low.

Access: No boat ramp is available. Car-top boats may be hand launched.

Facilities, fees: A developed campground is provided near the lake. A picnic and recreation area with drinking water and vault toilets is also available. Supplies can be obtained in Truckee. Fees are charged for day use, boat launching, and camping.

Water sports, restrictions: Canoes, kayaks, prams, and inflatables are permitted. No motors. Sailing, sailboarding, and swimming are also permitted. Fishing is restricted to catch-and-release with single barbless hooks and the use of artificials; no bait is permitted.

Directions: From Truckee, drive south on Highway 267 for about three miles (past the airport) to the entrance road to the lake on the left. Turn left and drive another 2.5 miles to the campground at the end of the road.

Contact: U.S. Army Corps of Engineers, Sacramento District, 530/639-2342, website: www .spk.usace.army.mil.

32 FRENCH MEADOWS RESERVOIR

Rating: 8

northeast of Auburn in Tahoe National Forest

Map 6.1, page 192

If you are searching for a do-it-yourself camping/boating trip in a gorgeous spot, French Meadows just might be the vacation destination you're looking for. Do-it-yourself? Right. Facilities are limited to campgrounds, picnic areas, and two boat ramps. There is no marina, and there are no boats for rent. All the necessary supplies (as well as gas for your boat) must be obtained before you arrive.

What you do get are several sandy areas around the lake that are suitable for sunbathing and swimming; the largest is the designated day-use area at McGuire picnic area on the lake's north side. There's also the chance for some good trout fishing from spring through early summer.

French Meadows Reservoir is set at an elevation of 5,300 feet on a dammed-up section of the Middle Fork American River. When full in the spring, it is big, nearly 2,000 acres. The lake is stocked with rainbow trout, but also is home for huge but elusive brown trout.

In years where there is a good snow pack,

there is enough melt-off to keep the lake high and beautiful through summer. That is often not the case, however, in years following winters with even slightly below normal precipitation.

The water masters who control the dam have a way of turning this big lake into a little lake by fall. That's right, they drain this sucker down until acres and acres of lake bottom are exposed and all kinds of stumps and boulders start poking through the surface. It creates a multitude of navigational hazards and leaves the campgrounds stranded far from the shoreline.

Bears commonly visit the campgrounds on summer nights, searching out the careless who have not properly safeguarded their food.

Access: There are two paved boat ramps, one at the picnic area two miles east of the dam, and one on the opposite side of the lake next to McGuire Picnic Area. Both are directly off the lake's access road and are well signed.

Facilities, fees: Campgrounds, vault toilets, drinking water, and lakeside picnic areas are available. Supplies can be obtained in Foresthill. Access to the lake is free.

Water sports, restrictions: Powerboats, waterskiing, wake boarding, personal watercraft, sailing, and sailboarding are permitted. Low water levels in summer can pose hazards; call ahead to check conditions. A swimming beach is available at McGuire picnic area on the north shore.

Directions: From Sacramento, drive east on I-80 to the north end of Auburn and the Foresthill Road exit. Take that exit and drive east to Foresthill and Mosquito Ridge Road (Forest Road 96). Turn right (east) and drive 40 miles (curvy) to Anderson Dam and to a junction. Turn left (still Mosquito Ridge Road) and then continue along the southern shoreline of French Meadows Reservoir.

Contact: Tahoe National Forest, Foresthill Ranger District, 530/367-2224.

33 MIDDLE FORK AMERICAN RIVER

Rating: 10

near Foresthill

Map 6.1, page 192

The scenery is exquisite, remote, and lush. The water is cold and clear. Historical sites from the Gold Rush days dot the landscape. And the white-water rafting runs have names such as Panic Alley. Need more be said?

Right, this is the Middle Fork American, the challenging alternative to the popular South Fork American. This is the choice for those seeking to step up from the more crowded South Fork American.

The run stretches for 25 miles and has a very long season, typically from May through early October, courtesy of upstream dam releases. The first 17 miles are rated Class III-IV, with one Class IV-V section, Tunnel Chute, a Class V, a narrow 80-foot chasm followed by a water tunnel that is 100 feet long (blasted by miners in the 1850s). After Tunnel Chute, there are numerous Class III-IV rapids, including Last Chance, Submarine Hole, and Kanaka. That is a definite portage for most, unless you have a yearning to make an early visit to the big hydraulic suckhole in the sky. Many rafters take out at Greenwood Bridge.

The last seven miles are referred to as the Lower Middle Fork American River. Continuing downstream from Greenwood Bridge to Mammoth Bar, the run is Class II, pleasant and inspiring most of the way.

Then, just below the entrance of Canyon Creek, arrives the Ruck-A-Chucky Rapids. This stretch includes Ruck-a-Chucky Falls (beautiful but unrunnable, and always portaged), Crystal, Parallel Parking (Class IV), and finally, Catapult (Class IV).

The two-mile section from Mammoth Bar to the North Fork confluence includes the Class V Murders Bar Rapid (not part of the 25-mile Middle Fork Run). The Middle Fork and the

Lower Middle Fork are typically offered as separate trips, or as one overnight two-day trip.

Because river access is difficult and there are several challenging expert sections of water, including some portages, many people opt for the South Fork instead. For those willing to take the challenge, however, rafting here means rewards of considerable solitude and excitement. A word of caution: Do not plan to stop and venture onto the adjoining lands; they are privately owned and the landowners do not take kindly to trespassers, no matter how honorable the intention. Up in the high country, the headwaters for this river start at the trickles of melting snow in both the Granite Chief and Desolation wilderness areas.

The proposed Auburn Dam project would eliminate the possibility of rafting on both the Chamberlain Falls and Big Bend Runs of the North Fork, as well as the entire stretch of the Middle Fork. An alternate proposal seeks to turn these areas into a protected National Recreation Area, an idea that's much more appealing to rafters for obvious reasons.

Access: Access is limited to the rafting put-in downstream of the Oxbow Powerhouse and a few rough dirt roads out of Foresthill. There is no boat ramp.

• Oxbow put-in: Take I-80 east of Auburn to the exit for Foresthill. Take that exit and turn east on Auburn-Foresthill Road and drive 20 miles to Foresthill and Mosquito Ridge Road/Forest Road 96. Turn right on Mosquito Ridge Road and drive to the crossing of the North Fork of the Middle Fork American crossing. Continue for about two miles to the Oxbow Powerhouse on the right. Turn right and drive to the river. The put-in is just downstream of the powerhouse. The take-outs are 16 miles downstream at Greenwood Bridge, and 23 miles downstream at Mammoth Bar.

• Greenwood Bridge take-out: Take I-80 east of Auburn to the exit for Foresthill. Take that exit and turn east on Auburn-Foresthill Road and drive to Drivers Flat Road. Turn on Drivers Flat Road and drive to the river and Greenwood Bridge take-out.

• Mammoth Bar take-out: From Auburn, take Highway 49 to Old Foresthill Road. Turn north and drive to Mammoth Bar Road. Turn on Mammoth Bar Road and drive to the river. Note: You must take out here if you want to avoid the Class V-VI rapid above Murderer's Bar (experts only). Those who wish to continue may take out two miles downstream at the Highway 49 bridge, located at the confluence of the Middle and North Forks of the American. This is the last possible take-out before Folsom Lake.

Facilities, fees: No facilities. Campgrounds with vault toilets and drinking water are nearby. Supplies can be obtained in Auburn and Foresthill. Access is free. Rafting permits are not required.

Water sports, restrictions: Rafts, kayaks, and inflatables are permitted. There are a few excellent swimming holes; the best are reached by boat. You can also swim at Greenwood Bridge and at Ahart Campground on Mosquito Ridge Road.

Directions: See directions to put-in and take-outs in Access, above.

Contact: Tahoe National Forest, Foresthill Ranger District, 530/478-6254. Guided rafting trips: Action Whitewater Adventures, 888/922-8466; Adventure Connection, 530/626-7385 or 800/556-6060, website: www.RaftCalifornia.com; All Outdoors Whitewater Rafting, 925/932-8993 or 800/247-2387, website: www.aorafting.com; American River Recreation, 530/622-6802 or 800/333-7238, website: www.arrafting.com; American Whitewater Expeditions, 818/352-3205 or 800/825-3205, website: www.americanwhitewater.com; ARTA River Trips, 209/962-7873 or 800/232-2782, website: www.arta.org; Beyond Limits, 209/869-6060 or 800/234-7238, website: www.rivertrip.com; Chili Bar Outdoor Center, 530/621-1236 or 800/356-2262, website: www.cboc whitewater.com; Earthtrek Expeditions, 530/642-1900 or 800/229-8735, website: www.earthtrekexpeditions.com; IRIE Rafting, 888/969-4743;

Koolriver Adventure Tours, 562/630-6929; Mariah Wilderness Expeditions, 510/233-2303 or 800/462-7424, website: www.mariahwe.com; Motherlode River Trips, 530/626-4187 or 800/427-2387, website: www.malode.com; Outdoor Adventure River Specialists (OARS), 209/736-4677 or 800/346-6277, website: www.oars.com; Rock-N-Water, 530/621-3918; Rapid Descent Adventures, 530/659-7800; Tahoe Whitewater Tours, 530/581-2441 or 800/442-7238, website: www.gowhitewater.com; Tributary Whitewater Tours, 530/346-6812 or 800/672-3846, website: www.whitewatertours.com; Whitewater Connection, 530/622-6446 or 800/336-7238, website: www.whitewaterconnection.com; Whitewater Excitement, 530/888-6515 or 800/750-2386, website: www.whitewaterexcitement.com; Whitewater Voyages, 510/222-5994 or 800/488-7238, website: www.whitewatervoyages.com; Wilderness Adventures, 530/926-6282 or 800/323-7238, website: www.wildrivertrips.com; Whitewater Expedition & Tours (WET), 916/451-3241, website: www.raftwet.com. For rentals contact California Canoe & Kayak, Rancho Cordova, 916/353-1880; Sierra Outdoor Center, Auburn, 530/885-1844; or River Rat Rentals, Fair Oaks, 916/966-6777. Rentals are not available in El Dorado County because of county ordinance.

34 HELL HOLE RESERVOIR

Rating: 10

northeast of Auburn in Eldorado National Forest

Map 6.1, page 192

Hell Hole Reservoir is more like heaven. The lake elevation is 4,700 feet at the foot of the Granite Chief Wilderness, with mountain country rising off to the west. The water is crystal pure, fed by the most remote stretches of the pristine Rubicon River.

But understand something right off. This lake is extremely remote and access is very poor, requiring a terribly long, slow, twisty drive on mountain back roads to get here. Trailered boats can take a pounding, and so will your nerves. In addition, there are no drive-to campsites on the lake, which means trailering a boat involves a pain-in-the-butt drive back and forth from the nearest campground. Campers are much better served here with a car-top boat equipped to handle a small engine. But even that has some serious drawbacks, since this lake can be subject to strong winds, especially on early-summer afternoons.

The lake covers 1,300 acres and has 15 miles of shoreline. Most of the people you'll see out on the lake are campers/anglers, fishing for brown trout, mackinaw trout, kokanee salmon, and rainbow trout.

Because the long, circuitous drive is so inconvenient, water-skiers are scarce. The handful that make the trip, however, are well rewarded by the scenic beauty.

Sailboarding can be excellent. Afternoon winds are predictable, and on a good day, this is a spectacular setting for such a sport. But note that winds can really howl up here, and sometimes sailboarding, as well as boating, can become dangerous. Lake levels are often dropped significantly in summer.

Despite the grandeur, the long drive to get here keeps use down to moderate levels in summer. The typical visitor is a vacationer who has time to burn.

Access: A paved ramp is located on the access road past Hell Hole Campground.

Facilities, fees: Campgrounds, boat-in campsites, vault toilets, drinking water, and picnic areas are available. Last chance for supplies is in Foresthill. Access is free. A fee is charged for camping.

Water sports, restrictions: Powerboats, water-skiing, wake boarding, and personal watercraft are permitted, although it is a long drive to tow up the twisty access road. Sailing and sailboarding are allowed. Swimming is permitted. The shoreline is rocky and steep in spots.

Directions: From Sacramento, drive east on I-80 to the north end of Auburn. Take the Elm

Avenue exit and turn left at the first stoplight onto Elm Avenue. Drive .1 mile, turn left on High Street, and continue through the signal where High Street merges with Highway 49. Travel on Highway 49 for about 3.5 miles, turn right over the bridge, and drive about 2.5 miles into the town of Cool. Turn left on Georgetown Road/Highway 193 and drive about 14 miles into Georgetown. At the four-way stop turn left on Main Street (which becomes Wentworth Springs/Forest Road 1) and drive about 25 miles. Turn left on Forest Road 2 and drive 22 miles to the campground on the left. Continue one mile to the dam, boat ramp, and parking.

Contact: Eldorado National Forest, Visitor Center, 530/644-6048, fax 530/295-5624; Eldorado National Forest, Georgetown Ranger District, 530/333-4312, fax 530/333-5522.

35 LAKE TAHOE (NORTH)

Rating: 10

east of Sacramento in Lake Tahoe Basin

Map 6.1, page 192

So few places evoke an emotional response at first glance. Lake Tahoe, along with Crater Lake in Oregon and Yosemite Valley, is one of the rare natural wonders that make you feel something special just by looking at it.

Of course it is huge, but there is also an unmatched purity. Huge? Try 22 miles long, 12 miles wide, with 72 miles of shoreline, and 1,645 feet at its deepest point. It is filled with 39 trillion gallons of water, enough to cover California to a depth of 14 inches and (as long as we're speaking hypothetically) enough so that it would require 300 years of severe drought for it to drain significantly.

Pure? Only 99.9 percent pure, similar to the purity of distilled water. It is so clear that on a calm day in late summer, you can see a dinner plate 75 feet or more below the surface.

To capture this essence of purity after you've had your fill of the nearby casinos, you can sit on the ridge above Emerald Bay or take the chairlift to the top of Heavenly Valley and just admire the lake. It conjures one of the greatest feelings ever.

Yet you can take it a giant step further by hopping in a boat. One of the premier outdoor experiences in the world is boating in Emerald Bay, topped off by an overnight stay at one of the boat-in campsites there. The beauty is incomparable. Regardless of where you go by boat, you are out in the middle of clear, cobalt blue waters, surrounded by a mountain rim that's often topped with bright white snow. It is always a remarkable sight, often breathtaking.

This is a place for everyone—and at times it seems that everyone is showing up at once. All boating and water sports are permitted, but it is the roads around the lake that get crowded, not the water. There is always plenty of room on the lake for everybody. Conflicts among users are extremely rare, and hey, just cruise around for five minutes and you'll notice a remarkable phenomenon: suddenly, all the stressed-out people become relaxed and nice.

Other recreational opportunities include bicycling, airplane and hot-air balloon rides, gambling, horseback riding, kayak tours, golfing, hiking, tram rides, musical entertainment, museum tours, and sportfishing charters. Lake Tahoe often provides quality fishing. Mackinaw trout are the resident trophy fish, rainbow trout provide the most predictable results, and kokanee salmon cycle up and down, sometimes furnishing wild sprees in the fall.

To make your visit the best one possible, it is imperative that you make extensive plans for lodging and recreation; reservations are mandatory on weekends. That's true whether you'll be staying in a cabin, campground, or casino. The Lake Tahoe Basin gets more than three million visitors per year. The highest use occurs on winter weekends during the ski season, followed by the summer, from the Fourth of July through early September. There are two periods of relatively light use: after the ski season has ended, in April and early May, and

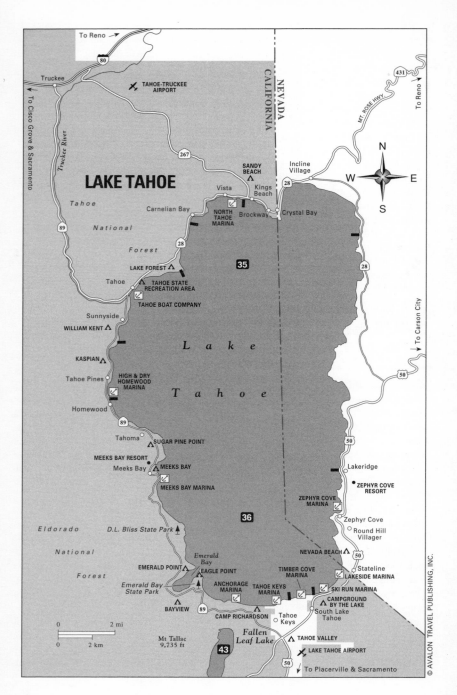

then again in the fall after summer is over, from early September through mid-November.

Despite the teeming masses, Lake Tahoe is always a stellar vacation spot. Traffic and parking difficulties are the main problems. Many vacationers rent condos or cabins and spend their days playing or lounging at the expansive beaches. Only the brave try swimming. Because Tahoe is fed by snowmelt from 63 streams, the water is often cold. The warmest it gets is 68 degrees on the surface, and that only happens after days of hot summer temperatures.

Tahoe was created when the center of three earthquake faults collapsed, forming this giant mountain lacuna, which was then filled with snowmelt. Glaciers carved out Emerald Bay.

The water is so blue because it lacks nutrients. More specifically, there is very little algae. As algal growth increases in a lake, the water becomes greener. Some fear that Lake Tahoe may one day turn green because of increased algae.

The trigger is a synergism of increased nitrogen and phosphorus entering the lake. Only one needs to be stopped in order to keep the lake cobalt blue. Nitrogen enters the lake from car exhaust and fertilizer runoff from golf courses. Phosphorus enters the lake from silt from topsoil damage caused by logging from more than 100 years ago; the lake's ability to screen out the phosphorus in storm runoff was greatly diminished when the Tahoe Keys development at South Lake Tahoe destroyed historic wetlands. A consortium of government agencies is working to reverse this trend, funded by grants, taxes for environmental improvement programs, and the Tahoe License Plate Fund.

Access: Boat ramps can be found at the following locations:

• Kings Beach Recreation Area: Located off Highway 28 in Kings Beach. There is a paved ramp suitable for small boats. Ski boats, sailboats, and personal watercraft can be rented, 530/546-4212.

• North Tahoe Marina: Located on Highway 28 in Tahoe Vista. A paved ramp can only be used by special arrangement; closed to public. A full-service marina with accessories and moorings are available. Powerboats are available for rent. For more information call 530/546-8248.

• Sierra Boat Company: At 5146 North Lake Boulevard in Carnelian Bay. Full-service marina, hoist, and boat storage are available. For more information call 530/546-2551.

• Lake Forest Boat Ramp: Located on North Lake Forest Road, off Highway 28 in Lake Forest. A paved ramp is available. For more information call 530/583-3796, extension 29.

• Tahoe City Marina: On Highway 28 in Tahoe City. Boat lift, full-service marina, moorings, slip rentals, and boat storage are available. Powerboats, fishing boats, and sailboats are available for rent. Parasailing, sailing charters, and fishing charters are available. For more information call 530/583-1039, website: www.tahoecitymarina.com.

• Sunnyside Marina: Located at 1850 West Lake Boulevard (Highway 28), two miles south of Tahoe City. A marina, hoist, and boat storage are available. Water-ski school, 530/583-7417; general information, 530/583-7201.

• Homewood High and Dry Marina: Located on Highway 89 in Homewood. A hoist, full-service marina, moorings, and boat storage are available. Powerboats, ski boats, sailboats, canoes, and kayaks are available for rent. Water-skiing school, 530/583-7417; marina, 530/525-5966.

• Obexers Boat Company: At 5355 West Lake Boulevard in Homewood. A paved ramp, travel lift, boat storage, and limited marina services are available. For more information call 530/525-7962.

• Meeks Bay Resort and Marina: Located on Highway 89, 10 miles south of Tahoe City. A paved ramp and full-service marina are provided. Powerboats, canoes, kayaks, and pedal boats are available for rent. Chartered speedboat available. For more information call 530/525-5588 or 530/525-6946.

• Sand Harbor Ramp: On Highway 28 two miles south of Incline Village. A paved ramp and limited marina facilities are available. For more information call 775/831-0494.

Diving site: Dollar Point Wall, located just off Dollar Point, 1.5 miles east of the Lake Forest Boat Ramp in North Shore.

Beach access: Developed beaches are available at the following locations: Agatam Beach on Highway 28 in Tahoe Vista; D.L. Bliss State Park on Highway 89 south of Meeks Bay; Kaspian Recreation Area on Highway 89 south of Sunnyside; Kings Beach Recreation Area in Kings Beach; Lake Forest Beach one mile east of Tahoe City; Meeks Bay Campground 10 miles south of Tahoe City; Moondunes Beach in Tahoe Vista; North Tahoe Beach Center in Kings Beach; Patton Beach on Highway 28 in Carnelian Bay; Sand Harbor State Park (Nevada) south of Incline Village on Highway 28; Secline Beach on Secline Street in Kings Beach; Tahoe City Commons Beach in Tahoe City; Tahoe State Recreation Area in Tahoe City; William Kent Campground on Highway 89 in Sunnyside; Sugar Pine Point State Park north of Emerald Bay.

Undeveloped beaches: There are undeveloped beaches, including Chimney Beach and Secret Cove, both on the east shore (in Nevada on Highway 28), south of Incline Village. Parking is limited and it's often difficult to find a spot during summer.

Facilities, fees: There are campgrounds and cottages in the area. Fees are charged for parking, boat launching, mooring and camping.

Water sports, restrictions: Powerboats, waterskiing, wake boarding, parasailing, sailing, sailboarding, and swimming are allowed. No carbureted engines are permitted. All four-stroke engines and two-stroke engines with direct fuel injection (DFI) are permitted.

Directions: To North Shore/Kings Beach: From Sacramento, take I-80 east to Truckee, and then continue east three miles to Highway 267. Turn south on Highway 267 and drive to North Shore/Kings Beach and Highway 28. Turn left (east) to access Kings Beach, Crystal Bay, Incline. Turn right (south) to access Tahoe Vista, Agate Bay, Carnelian Bay.

To North Shore/Tahoe City: From Sacramento, take I-80 east to Truckee and Highway 89. Turn south on Highway 89 and drive to Tahoe City and the junction with Highway 89/28. Turn left on Highway 28 to access the North Shore (Tahoe City, Carnelian Bay). Turn right on Highway 89 to access the west shore (Tahoma, Homewood, Meeks Bay).

Contact: Lake Tahoe Basin Management Unit, 530/543-2674; North Lake Tahoe Chamber of Commerce, 530/581-6900 or 800/824-6348, website: www.tahoeinfo.com; Lake Tahoe Central Reservations, website: www.mytahoevacation.com.

Boat rentals: Action Watersports, 530/541-4386 and 775/831-4386; H2O Sports, 775/588-4155; Sun Sports, 530/541-6000; Tahoe Paddle, 530/581-3029; Kings Beach Aqua Sports, 530/546-2782; Tahoe Water Adventures, 530/583-3225; Ski Run Boat Company, 530/544-0200; Lakeview Sports, 530/544-0183.

Parasailing: Action Watersports, 530/544-2942; H20 Sports, 775/588-4155; Ski Run Boat Company, 530/544-0200; Zephyr Cove Marina, 775-589-4908.

Hot-air ballooning: From a boat deck: Balloons over Lake Tahoe, 530/544-7008; Lake Tahoe Balloons, 530/544-1221 or 800/872-9294.

Boat cruises: Lake Tahoe Cruises, 530/541-3364 or 800/238-2463, website: www.laketahoecruises.com; North Tahoe Cruises, 530/583-0141 or 800/218-2464; Woodwind Cruises, 775/588-3000 or 888/867-6394, website: www.tahoeboatcruises.com; M. S. Dixie II, 775/588-3508; Tahoe Thunder, 530/544-2942; Sierra Cloud, 775/832-1234; Kingfish, 530/525-5360 or 800/622-5462; Tahoe Schooner, 530/542-2217 or 888/550-4575; Safari Rose, 888/867-6394; Sierra Cloud and Windsong 530/544-2942; The Party Boat, 530/542-2111 or 888/542-2111.

36 LAKE TAHOE (SOUTH)

Rating: 10

east of Sacramento in Lake Tahoe Basin

Map 6.2, page 193

There is no place on Earth like Lake Tahoe. The South Lake Tahoe's Visitor Authority provided the following facts about the lake:

• It is North America's largest alpine lake.

• The elevation is 6,226 feet, making it the highest lake of its size in the United States.

• With a depth of 1,645 feet (near Crystal Bay), it is the third deepest lake in North America and the 10th deepest in the world (Lake Baikal in Russia is the deepest, at over 4,600 feet). The average depth is 989 feet.

• About 95 percent of the lake's fish live in only 5 percent of the water available.

• If drained, the lake would take 700 years to refill.

• Sixty-three streams flow into Lake Tahoe, but only one, the Truckee River, flows out, running past Reno and into Pyramid Lake.

• The sun shines at Lake Tahoe an average of 274 days per year, but snowfall has been recorded every month and averages 420 inches per year.

• The water is so deep, cold (39 degrees below 700 feet), and devoid of light and oxygen on the bottom, that, according to legend, 1930s mobsters wearing "cement shoes" have been perfectly preserved on the lake bottom, complete with vintage clothing.

Access: Boat ramps can be found at the following locations:

• Camp Richardson Resort and Marina: Located on Highway 89, 2.5 miles north of South Lake Tahoe. A paved ramp and a full-service marina with moorings are available. Powerboats, personal watercraft, kayaks, and pedal boats, are available for rent. Fishing charters, parasailing, and water-ski schools are available. Boat rentals, 530/541-1801 or 800/544-1801; marina, 530/542-6570, website: www.camp richardson.com.

• Lakeside Marina: At the junction of Lakeshore Boulevard and Park Avenue, off Highway 50 in South Lake Tahoe. A paved ramp and a full-service marina and moorings are available. Ski boats, sport boats, and pontoon boats are available for rent. For more information call 530/541-6626.

• Ski Run Marina: At 900 Ski Run Boulevard in South Lake Tahoe, 1.5 miles south of Stateline. Powerboats, personal watercraft, fishing boats, and pontoon boats available for rent. For more information call 530/544-9500.

• South Lake Tahoe Recreation Area/El Dorado Boat Ramp: On Lakeview Avenue off Highway 50 in South Lake Tahoe. A paved ramp is available. For more information call 530/ 542-6056.

• Tahoe Keys Marina: Located on Tahoe Keys Boulevard, off Highway 50. A paved ramp, full-service marina, and fishing and sailing charters are available. Ski boats, personal watercraft, sailboats, kayaks, and canoes are available for rent. Boat rentals, 530/544-8888; marina, 530/541-2155.

• Timber Cove Marina: At 3411 Lake Tahoe Boulevard in South Lake Tahoe. An unimproved boat ramp and limited marina services and moorings are available. Ski boats, personal watercraft, pontoon boats, sailboats, kayaks, pedal boats, and water bikes are available for rent. For more information call 530/544-2942.

• Zephyr Cove Marina: On Highway 50 in Zephyr Cove. An unimproved ramp and full-service marina are available. Ski boats, fishing boats, personal watercraft, canoes, kayaks, pontoon boats, and pedal boats are available for rent. For more information call 775/588-3833.

• Cave Rock Ramp: Located on Highway 50, three miles north of Zephyr Cove. A paved ramp is available. Summer months, 775/588-7975; winter months, 775/831-0494.

Diving sites: Emerald Bay Underwater State Park, located in Emerald Bay near South Shore; Rubicon Point, located two miles north of the entrance to Emerald Bay near South Shore. Sun Sports, South Lake Tahoe, 530/541-6000.

Beach access: Developed beaches are available at the following locations: Baldwin Beach, on Highway 89 four miles north of the junction with Highway 50; Emerald Bay Beach at the base of Emerald Bay; Camp Richardson Beach, on Highway 89, two miles north of the junction with Highway 50; Connolly Beach on Highway 50 at Best Western Timber Cove Lodge; Kiva Beach, on Highway 89, 2.5 miles north of the junction with Highway 50; Nevada Beach, on Elk Point Road off Highway 50 near Roundhill; Pope Beach, on Highway 89 two miles north of the junction with Highway 50; Regan Beach west of Highway 50 on Lakeview and Sacramento Streets in South Lake Tahoe; Zephyr Cove Beach on Highway 50 at Zephyr Cove.

Undeveloped beaches: There are undeveloped beaches, including Chimney Beach and Secret Cove, both on the east shore (in Nevada on Highway 28), south of Incline Village. Parking is limited and it's often difficult to find a spot during summer.

Facilities, fees: There are campgrounds and cottages in the area. Fees are charged for parking, boat launching, mooring and camping.

Water sports, restrictions: Powerboats, waterskiing, wake boarding, parasailing, sailing, sailboarding, and swimming are allowed. No carbureted engines are permitted. All four-stroke engines and two-stroke engines with direct fuel injection (DFI) are permitted.

Directions: From Sacramento, take U.S. 50 east over Echo Summit to Meyers and the junction with Highway 89. Continue straight on U.S. 50/Highway 89 to Four Corners at South Lake Tahoe. Continue straight (north) on Highway 89 to access the southwest shore (Camp Richardson, Emerald Bay, Fallen Leaf Lake). Turn east on U.S. 50 to access the south shore and Nevada (South Lake Tahoe, casino row, Kingsbury Grade).

Contact: Lake Tahoe Basin Management Unit, 530/543-2674; South Lake Tahoe Chamber of Commerce, 530/541-5255; Lake Tahoe Central Reservations, website: www.mytahoevacation.com.

See previous Lake Tahoe (North) listing for information on companies that rent boats, run hot-air balloon rides, boat cruises, and more.

37 STUMPY MEADOWS RESERVOIR

🛥 ✕ 🛶 🎣 ≈ ⛰

Rating: 7

northeast of Placerville in Eldorado National Forest

Map 6.2, page 193

Don't let the name fool you into thinking Stumpy Meadows is a stodgy old place full of algae. Quite the opposite. The water is cold and clear, the lake is surrounded by national forest, and it is an ideal place to camp, fish, and boat.

The only stodgy thing about the place is the 5-mph speed limit for boaters, which keeps the lake quiet—ideal for car-top boats, especially canoes and kayaks.

Stumpy Meadows covers 320 acres and is set at an elevation of 4,400 feet in Eldorado National Forest, up in the snow country. The water is quite cold early in the season, so swimming is only for the brave at heart. However, the lake is perfect for sailboarders who don't have to contend with powerboats and water-skiers.

The lake has both rainbow and brown trout, and in the fall provides good fishing for big browns (they move up into the head of the lake, near where Pilot Creek enters).

Few facilities are available at the lake. Use is moderate on weekdays in the summer, but the campgrounds usually fill up on weekends.

Access: A paved boat ramp is located just south of the dam, off Wentworth Springs Road near Vista picnic area.

Facilities, fees: Campgrounds, vault toilets, drinking water, and a picnic area are provided. Supplies can be obtained in Placerville and Georgetown. Access to the lake is free. A fee is charged for camping.

Water sports, restrictions: Powerboats, canoes,

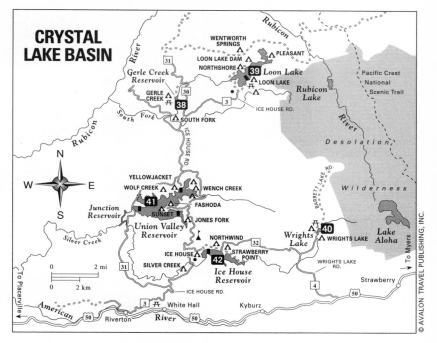

CRYSTAL
LAKE BASIN

WENTWORTH SPRINGS
LOON LAKE DAM
NORTHSHORE
31
Gerle Creek Reservoir
GERLE CREEK
30
38
SOUTH FORK
South Fork
Rubicon
Rubicon River

PLEASANT
39 Loon Lake
LOON LAKE
3
ICE HOUSE RD.

Rubicon Lake

Pacific Crest National Scenic Trail

Desolation

N
W E
S

YELLOWJACKET
WOLF CREEK
41
SUNSET
Junction Reservoir
Union Valley Reservoir
Silver Creek

WENCH CREEK
FASHODA
JONES FORK

NORTHWIND
ICE HOUSE
SILVER CREEK
42
Ice House Reservoir

0   2 mi
0   2 km

31

STRAWBERRY POINT
32

Wrights Lake
40 WRIGHTS LAKE

Wilderness

BARRETT LAKE RD.

Lake Aloha

To Myers

WRIGHTS LAKE RD.

Strawberry

To Placerville

ICE HOUSE RD.
3   White Hall   Kyburz
American
50   Riverton   River   50
4
50

© AVALON TRAVEL PUBLISHING, INC.

kayaks, and inflatables are permitted. No motors larger that 10 horsepower. A 5-mph speed limit is strictly enforced. Sailboarding and sailing are allowed, but the lake is too small and with too low a speed limit for either. Swimming is available at Vista picnic area, near the boat ramp.

Directions: From Sacramento on I-80, drive east to the north end of Auburn. Turn left on Elm Avenue and drive about .1 mile. Turn left on High Street and drive through the signal that marks the continuation of High Street as Highway 49. Drive 3.5 miles on Highway 49, turn right over the bridge, and drive 2.5 miles into the town of Cool. Turn left on Georgetown Road/Highway 193 and drive 14 miles into Georgetown. At the four-way stop, turn left on Main Street, which becomes Georgetown-Wentworth Springs Road/Forest Road 1. Drive about 18 miles to Stumpy Meadows Lake. Continue about a mile and turn right into Stumpy Meadows campground.

Contact: Eldorado National Forest, Visitor Center, 530/644-6048; Eldorado National Forest, Georgetown Ranger District, 530/333-4312.

38 GERLE CREEK RESERVOIR

Rating: 6

west of Lake Tahoe in Eldorado National Forest

Map 6.2, page 193

This is a small, pretty lake, although boating options are somewhat limited. It is set at an elevation of 5,300 feet in Eldorado National Forest.

Small? No boat ramp is provided, making it perfect for people with car-top boats that are easily hand launched, such as canoes. Pretty? Definitely, nestled right in the Gerle Creek Canyon, which feeds into the South Fork Rubicon. Limited? Another affirmative, because here all motors are prohibited.

Among the things this small reservoir does

have are clear water and a scenic campground set in old-growth conifer forest.

As mentioned, boating at Gerle Creek Reservoir is suited only for small, human-powered craft. Sailboarding can be excellent on summer afternoons. The shoreline is grassy and rocky, and some visitors go swimming adjacent to the picnic grounds, where there is a grassy/dirt area that is good for sunbathing.

Traffic is light here. No trout plants are made at this lake and fishing is often poor. A few brown trout provide the only surprise. Most folks head to nearby Loon Lake when they want full-facility boating opportunities.

Access: No boat ramp is available. Car-top boats may be hand launched.

Facilities, fees: A campground, vault toilets, drinking water, a picnic area, and a wheelchair-accessible fishing pier are provided. Supplies can be obtained in Placerville. Access to the lake is free. A fee is charged for camping.

Water sports, restrictions: Motors are not permitted on the lake. Swimming and sailboarding access is available near the picnic area.

Directions: From Sacramento, drive east on U.S. 50 to Riverton and the junction with Ice House Road/Soda Springs-Riverton Road. Turn north and drive 27 miles (past Union Valley Reservoir) to a fork with Forest Road 30. Turn left, drive two miles, bear left on the campground entrance road, and drive a mile to the campground.

Contact: Eldorado National Forest, Visitor Center, 530/644-6048; Eldorado National Forest, Pacific Ranger District, 539/644-2349.

39 LOON LAKE

Rating: 7

south of Lake Tahoe in Eldorado National Forest

Map 6.2, page 193

Loon Lake is a good destination for a weekend camping trip, especially if you have a small boat.

Set near the Sierra crest at 6,400 feet, this is a good-size lake, covering 600 acres and reaching depths of up to 130 feet. It is bordered by Eldorado National Forest and Desolation Wilderness, and a trail from this area is routed out to Winifred Lake, Spider Lake, and Buck Island Lake, all located to the east. If you don't like roughing it, you can opt to stay at Ice House Resort, which you'll pass on the access road about 18 miles from the lake.

Boating is very popular at Loon Lake, where there are no boating restrictions. However, water-contact sports can be dangerous due to heavy use on weekends, very cold water, and the typical high winds in the afternoon. In the early summer these afternoon winds can drive anglers off the lake. But their loss is a boon to sailboarders, who can only cheer.

Water-skiers and sailboarders should always wear wet suits; one dunk in the lake will convince anyone of that. Swimming is not a good idea, and not all that fun, anyway, unless you're a member of the Polar Bear Club (you know—the group of psychos who pride themselves on being the first every year to go swimming in freezing cold lakes). Sailboarders must take into consideration both the cold water and the potentially hazardous winds that can kick up in the afternoon. That is why sailboarders are generally better off heading to Union Valley Reservoir, located to the nearby south.

The lake provides good trout fishing. Once the access road is clear of snow, the lake is usually stocked every week of summer.

It also can make for a jumping-off point for a weeklong backpacking trip (wilderness permits are required through the Forest Service and are not available at the lake).

Access: To reach the paved boat ramp, take the cutoff from Ice House Road to Loon Lake Campground and the picnic area.

Facilities, fees: Campgrounds, vault toilets, drinking water, and a picnic area are available. A primitive campground on the lake's north end can be accessed by boat or trail. Supplies are available at Ice House Resort. Access to the lake is free. A fee is charged for camping. **Water sports, restrictions:** Powerboats, water-skiing, wake boarding, personal watercraft, sailing, and sailboarding are permitted. Wet suits are advised for sailboarders due to the extremely cold water. Swimming is not recommended. **Directions:** From Sacramento, drive east on U.S. 50 to Riverton and the junction with Ice House Road/Soda Springs-Riverton Road on the left. Turn left and drive 34 miles to a fork at the foot of Loon Lake. Turn right and drive one mile to the Loon Lake Picnic Area or boat ramp. **Contact:** Eldorado National Forest, Visitor Center, 530/644-6048; Pacific Ranger District, 530/644-2349; Ice House Resort, 530/293-3321.

40 WRIGHTS LAKE

Rating: 5

southwest of Lake Tahoe in Eldorado National Forest

Map 6.2, page 193

This is your classic alpine lake, small (just 65 acres) and set high in the Sierra Nevada at a 7,000-foot elevation. Wrights Lake is an ideal jumping-off point for a backpacker or day hiker, or a great destination for folks with car-top boats. Note that no motors are allowed on boats.

The primary activity is car-top boating, especially with canoes and kayaks. Most folks head up just to paddle around, and maybe fish a little. Fishing is fair for rainbow trout and brown trout. Swimming is permitted, but the water is pretty cold and the shoreline is mostly rocks and grass, not really suitable for sunbathing.

The beauty of the little lake is the number of side trip options available. You can drive less than a mile to little Dark Lake, and from there hike farther north to the Beauty Lakes or Pearl Lake. For multiday trips, another option is routing a backpack trip to the east in the Crystal Range and the Desolation Wilderness (wilderness permits are required through the Forest Service and are not available at the lake).

The campground and nearby trailhead make this a very popular spot, and it gets a good share of visitor traffic in the summer. **Access:** No boat ramp is available. Car-top boats may be hand launched. **Facilities, fees:** A campground, vault toilets, drinking water, and picnic area are available. Supplies can be obtained in South Lake Tahoe. Access to the lake is free. A fee is charged for camping. **Water sports, restrictions:** Rowboats, canoes, kayaks, and inflatables are permitted. No motors. The lake is not large enough or windy enough for sailing and sailboarding. Swimming is permitted. **Directions:** From Sacramento, drive east on U.S. 50 about 20 miles beyond Placerville. Turn left on Ice House Road and drive north 11.5 miles to Ice House Reservoir. Turn right (east) on Road 32 and drive 10 miles. Turn left on Wrights Lake Road and drive two miles to the campground on the right side of the road. **Contact:** Eldorado National Forest, Visitor Center, 530/644-6048; Pacific Ranger District, 530/644-2349.

41 UNION VALLEY RESERVOIR

Rating: 10

west of Lake Tahoe in Eldorado National Forest

Map 6.2, page 193

The Crystal Basin Recreation Area is one of the most popular backcountry regions for campers from the Sacramento area. Union Valley Reservoir, a big lake covering nearly 3,000 acres, is one of the centerpieces.

The area gets its name from the prominent granite Sierra ridge, which looks like crystal when it is covered with frozen snow. The lake is set at 4,900 feet elevation. Ice House Reservoir to the south and Loon Lake to the north provide nearby options, but this lake is a recreation centerpiece. Ice House gets most of the fishermen and Union Valley gets most of the campers.

Facilities at the lake are limited to eight Forest Service campgrounds and three boat ramps. There is no marina, and no store or supplies available. After all, Union Valley sits right on the edge of wilderness.

All boating and water sports are allowed, and for many this is the perfect destination for camping, boating, and fishing, as well as sailing in small boats and sailboarding. There are additional opportunities for swimming and hiking nearby.

The water is clear and cold, but not too cold for swimming by midsummer. Although there are no true beach-type areas, much of the shoreline is grassy. There is also a swimming area at Fashoda Campground, where the shore is primarily hard-packed soil.

The lake is stocked with rainbow trout, brook trout, and brown trout. This can be a great lake for fishing and camping in spring and early summer. Summer mornings and evening here feature good trout fishing.

By the afternoon, the wind usually comes up, the anglers leave the lake, and out come a few sailboarders, sailboards in hand, and a sprinkling of little sailboats. As they sail across the lake, they often look around as if relishing the sensation of being in the midst of a great paradise.

Access: Three boat ramps are available:

• Fashoda: Follow directions to Riverton in Directions, below. From Riverton, turn left (north) on Ice House Road/Soda Springs-Riverton Road and drive 15 miles to the turnoff for Fashoda and Sunset Campgrounds (one mile past the turn for Jones Fork Camp). Turn left and drive 1.5 miles to the paved boat ramp.

• West Point: From Sacramento, drive east on U.S. 50 to Riverton and the junction with Ice House Road/Soda Springs-Riverton Road. Turn left and drive four miles to Peavine Ridge Road. Turn left and drive three miles to Bryant Springs Road. Turn right and drive five miles north to the paved ramp, located adjacent to the dam.

• Yellowjacket: From Sacramento, drive east on U.S. 50 to Riverton and the junction with Ice House Road/Soda Springs-Riverton Road. Turn left and drive 21 miles to Union Valley Road (at the head of Union Valley Reservoir). Turn left and drive a mile to the campground entrance road. Turn left and drive a mile to the campground. A paved ramp is available.

Facilities, fees: Campgrounds, vault toilets, drinking water, and an RV dump station are available. Supplies can be obtained in Placerville or at the store at Ice House Reservoir (see next listing). Access to the lake is free. A fee is charged for camping.

Water sports, restrictions: Powerboats, waterskiing, wake boarding, personal watercraft, sailing, and sailboarding are permitted. A swimming beach is available at Fashoda Campground, and it is possible to swim at various other spots along the shoreline.

Directions: To Peninsula Recreation Area: From Sacramento, drive east on U.S. 50 to Riverton and the junction with Ice House Road/Soda Springs-Riverton Road. Turn left and drive 15 miles to the campground entrance road (a mile past the turnoff for Jones Fork Camp). Turn left and drive 1.5 miles to the campground at the end of the road (a nearby boat ramp is on the left on the way in).

Contact: Eldorado National Forest, Visitor Center, 530/644-6048, fax 530/295-5624; Eldorado National Forest, Pacific Ranger District, 530/644-2349, fax 530/647-5405.

42 ICE HOUSE RESERVOIR

Rating: 9

west of Lake Tahoe in Eldorado National Forest

Map 6.2, page 193

Of the three major lakes in the beautiful Crystal Lakes Basin, Ice House is the first one you'll drive past. The others are Union Valley Reservoir and farther north, Loon Lake.

Ice House is set at an elevation of 5,500 feet. It was created by a dam on South Fork Silver Creek. When full, it covers about 675 acres, with the deepest spot about 130 feet deep. There are many recreational opportunities here, but the lake is best known for having quality fishing for rainbow trout, brook trout, and brown trout.

All boating is allowed. The best prospects are for sailing and sailboarding on midsummer afternoons. Another good prospect is swimming. The water is quite cold, but there are nice swimming areas at the campgrounds and a gently sloping shoreline all around the lake.

There is one well-developed campground at the lake, Ice House, which has drinking water, wheelchair-accessible sites, a swimming beach, and an adjacent boat ramp. That is the favorite of boater/campers. No dispersed camping is allowed around the shoreline of the lake.

Visitor use at the lake is moderate during the week, but quite heavy on summer weekends.

Access: A paved boat ramp is located next to Ice House Campground.

Facilities, fees: Campgrounds, vault toilets, drinking water, picnic area, and an RV dump station are available. Supplies can be obtained at the Ice House Resort, located a few miles south of the reservoir on Ice House Road. Access to the lake is free. A fee is charged for camping.

Water sports, restrictions: Powerboats, water-skiing, wake boarding, personal watercraft, sailing, and sailboarding are permitted. A swimming beach is available at Ice House Campground. Swimming is also available at the other two campgrounds and at the picnic area west of the dam.

Directions: From Sacramento, drive east on U.S. 50 to Riverton and the junction with Ice House Road/Soda Springs-Riverton Road. Turn left and drive about 11 miles to the junction with Forest Road 3 and Ice House Road. Turn right on Ice House Road and drive two miles to the campground access road on the right.

Contact: Eldorado National Forest, Visitor Center, 530/644-6048, fax 530/295-5624; Eldorado National Forest, Pacific Ranger District, 530/644-2349, fax 530/647-5405; Ice House Resort, 530/293-3321.

43 FALLEN LEAF LAKE

Rating: 8

near South Lake Tahoe in Lake Tahoe Basin

Map 6.2, page 193

Millions of people drive within a mile of this large, beautiful lake and don't even know it's there. It is located just one mile from Highway 89 along Lake Tahoe, only three miles from the town of South Lake Tahoe.

Fallen Leaf Lake, which is set at a 6,400-foot elevation, has water that's almost as deep a shade of blue as nearby Lake Tahoe. It's a big lake, three miles long and three-quarters to one mile wide, and is 430 feet at its deepest point. Because the lake is circled by forest, most of it on private property, shoreline access to the public is poor, and you need a boat to be able to enjoy the lake to its full potential.

This place presents a nice alternative to huge, crowded Lake Tahoe. It gets its share of traffic, too, but has a slightly more wilderness-like feel. Though the water is very cold, the setting is absolutely spectacular for boating. Fishing is best here for kokanee salmon, with some large but elusive mackinaw trout also occasionally caught.

Several pretty swimming beaches are provided around the shore's south and north sides, with the most developed beach located next to the marina. Winds are common in the afternoon, often ideal for sailing and sailboarding, and with the surrounding beauty, either activity can prove to be an extraordinary experience.

Access: The marina and boat ramp are located at the south end of the lake.

Facilities, fees: Lodging, camping, drinking water, vault toilets, small marina, convenience store, and bait and tackle are available. Fishing boats, kayaks, and canoes are available for rent. Access is free. Fees are charged for boat launching and camping.

Water sports, restrictions: Powerboats, water-skiing, wake boarding, sailing, sailboarding, and swimming are allowed. No carbureted two-stroke engines are permitted. All four-stroke engines and two-stroke engines with direct fuel injection (DFI) are permitted. Several small beaches are available around the lake.

Directions: In South Lake Tahoe at the junction of U.S. 50 and Highway 89, turn north on Highway 89 and drive two miles to the Fallen Leaf Lake turnoff. Turn left and drive on Fallen Leaf Lake Road (along the lake) to the signed turn to the marina and boat ramp on the right. Note: The road is very narrow and yet subject to fast oncoming drivers. Use extreme caution and show courtesy. When towing a boat, drive very slowly. RVs are not permitted on this road. There are no turnarounds for trailers.

Contact: Fallen Leaf Lake Marina, 530/544-0787; Fallen Leaf Lake Lodge, 530/541-6330; Fallen Leaf Store, 530/541-4671; Lake Tahoe Basin Management Unit, 530/543-2674.

44 ECHO LAKES

Rating: 9

south of Lake Tahoe in Lake Tahoe Basin

Map 6.2, page 193

Echo Lakes is an exquisite place, a high, azure blue alpine lake set in granite and surrounded by forest. Afternoon sunlight and a light breeze will cover the surface of Echo Lake with slivers of silver. By evening the lake, now calm, takes on a completely different appearance, deep and beautiful, almost foreboding.

Echo Lakes is set in a glacial-carved canyon at 7,500 feet, the gateway to the southern portion of the Desolation Wilderness. The lake is big and blue, covering 300 acres and reaching depths of 200 feet. At one time, it was actually two lakes, but a small dam on Lower Echo Lake raised the water level, and now there is a narrow connecting link to Upper Echo Lake, creating one lake, shaped like an hour glass.

Lower Echo gets most of the traffic, both from water-skiers and anglers. On the main lake, there are water-skiers during the hot summer months. By late summer, though, the cold water

results in the water-skiers giving way to fishermen. The setting is spectacularly beautiful for all boating, and though the water is cold, it gives water-skiers an added incentive not to fall in.

Upper Echo Lake, on the other hand, usually provides quiet water. Use is far less than at Lower Echo, and here you will even see people paddling about in little rowboats and canoes, swimming, and piloting low-speed boats. Underwater obstacles exist in the shallow isthmus that connects the two lakes. Large boats can have difficulty navigating the small channel. The upper land is also sprinkled with small islands, a beautiful setting. We spotted a rock cabin that looks like the setting for a Thomas Kincade mural.

Swimming is permitted anywhere you can find access, and there are lots of rocks and grassy areas, but no beach. The north shore provides the best stretch of shoreline, with a large, fairly flat grassy area and gentle slope.

Fishing is also good for rainbow trout at Echo Lakes. The best prospects are trolling at either dawn or dusk. The clear water makes hopes difficult when the sun is overhead at mid-day.

The Pacific Crest Trail runs right alongside the lake, and this is a main trailhead for the Desolation Wilderness, so the lake gets a lot of traffic, sometimes hordes of hikers. Echo Chalet offers a self-registration box for day-use wilderness permits, and also a hiker's shuttle taxi service by boat for backpackers to the upper end of the lake, which shaves 2.5 miles off the hike. The boat taxi leaves at frequent intervals during the summer. Services are available from Memorial Day weekend to Labor Day weekend and limited services may be provided in the fall.

Many outstanding destinations are accessible along the Pacific Crest Trail, including Tamarack Lake and many other nearby lakes.

Access: A paved boat ramp is located next to Echo Chalet.

Facilities, fees: Drinking water and vault toilets are available. A marina with docks, fishing boat, canoe and kayak rentals, and hiker's shuttle boat taxi are available. Lodging, convenience store, and a snack bar are nearby. Access is free. Fees are charged for boat launching and hiker's shuttle boat.

Water sports, restrictions: Powerboats, waterskiing, wake boarding, personal watercraft, sailing, sailboarding, and swimming are allowed. No carbureted two-stroke engines are permitted. All four-stroke engines and two-stroke engines with direct fuel injection (DFI) are permitted. Swimming is available anywhere along the shore except in the main harbor area; the best spot is on the far end of Upper Echo Lake near the trailhead for the Pacific Crest Trail.

Directions: From South Lake Tahoe, drive south on Highway 89 for five miles to U.S. 50. Drive west on U.S. 50 for 5.5 miles to the signed turnoff for Echo Lakes on the right (located one mile west of Echo Summit). Turn right and drive .5 mile on Johnson Pass Road to Echo Lakes Road. Turn left and drive one mile to a series of parking lots. Continue .25 mile down the hill to the Echo Lake Chalet and marina.

Contact: Echo Lake Chalet, 530/659-7207, website: www.echochalet.com. Lake Tahoe Basin Management Unit, 530/543-2674. For a map, ask for Lake Tahoe Basin Management Unit and send $6 to U.S. Forest Service, Attn: Map Sales, P.O. Box 587, Camino, CA 95709, 530/647-5390, fax 530/647-5389, website: www.fs.fed.us/r5/forests. Major credit cards are accepted.

45 ANGORA LAKES

Rating: 6

south of Lake Tahoe in Lake Tahoe Basin

Map 6.2, page 193

For many visitors to Lake Tahoe, Angora Lakes provides the perfect side trip.

Just a short drive from South Lake Tahoe, followed by a brief walk, lands you at these two small lakes that are set in a bowl below Echo and Angora Peaks.

The quick, uphill hike deters some people, but certainly not all. For many, particularly families with young children, it is the perfect distance to walk, especially at this high elevation. The trek to Upper Angora Lake is a small price to pay for such a beautiful destination, ideal for swimming, renting a rowboat, staying in a cabin (a real long shot getting in), and visiting the legendary lemonade stand.

This is a very popular lake for swimming, with stretches of beach interrupted by large boulders that are excellent for jumping into the drink. After taking this leap of faith, you may have second thoughts in midair about touchdown in the cold water. Many people, children and adults alike, express their reservations with a howl before landing with a splash.

Boating is pretty much restricted to the rowboats that are rented at Angora Lakes Resort, unless you want to carry in your own canoe or inflatable on the .5-mile hike. Few people are willing. Fishing for trout is typically poor.

Cabin rentals are available at the resort, but reservations can be booked years in advance. The only way to get in is to sign up on a waiting list, then wait for years, hoping somebody eventually cancels and leaves their spot open.

The resort has a little store where you can buy sandwiches and lemonade. The woman who provides the latter is somewhat famous here and is known as the "lemonade lady."

If you want to camp, you'll have to head on over to Fallen Leaf Lake, but no matter, this is still a great day-use spot. The Angora Lakes, particularly Upper Angora, is very popular with children's day camps and groups.

Access: There is no boat ramp.

Facilities, fees: Rowboats are available for rent at Upper Angora Lake. Drinking water and restrooms with flush toilets are available at a small convenience store and café. Cabin rentals require signing up on a waiting list that can take several years. Supplies can be obtained in South Lake Tahoe. Access is free.

Water sports, restrictions: Rowboats, canoes, kayaks and inflatables are permitted. No motors. Swimming access is available all along the shoreline.

Directions: From Sacramento, take Highway 50 east to the Highway 50/89 split in South Lake Tahoe. Turn north on Highway 89 to Fallen Leaf Lake Road. Turn left on Fallen Leaf Lake Road and drive up the hill for two miles. When the road forks, bear left for .25 mile to Forest Service Road 12N14. Bear right and drive 2.3 miles (past the Angora Fire Lookout) to the end of the road and a parking lot. A .5-mile shuttle ride to the cabins is available for guests and their gear; otherwise you must make the short hike uphill.

Contact: Angora Lakes Resort, 530/541-2092 (summer) or 805/545-9332 (winter); Lake Tahoe Basin Management Unit, 530/543-2674. For a map, ask for Lake Tahoe Basin Management Unit and send $6 to U.S. Forest Service, Attn: Map Sales, P.O. Box 587, Camino, CA 95709, 530/647-5390, fax 530/647-5389, website: www.fs.fed.us/r5/forests. Major credit cards are accepted.

46 KIRKWOOD LAKE

Rating: 5

south of Lake Tahoe in Eldorado National Forest

Map 6.2, page 193

The Carson Pass area has become a great alternative to crowded Lake Tahoe nearby to the north (it's an hour's drive to the casinos). At the center of it all is Kirkwood Ski Resort, which now offers year-round accommodations, as well as a deluxe base of operations for a hiking trip.

Here, in this beautiful Sierra setting at an elevation of 7,600 feet, you will find little Kirkwood Lake. At this very small, very pretty lake, no motorized boating is allowed, which helps keep things pretty quiet.

Most of the land bordering the lake is private, with summer homes sprinkled about. Public recreation is limited to the west side, where there's a campground that is almost always full during the summer.

Even though the trout fishing here is only fair, most lake users are anglers out in small boats. Some campers do try swimming on hot days, but most of the shoreline is rocky and the water is quite cold. No matter how hot the sun is shining, swimming at Kirkwood usually means taking an in-and-out dunk.

The nearby Kirkwood Ski Area has been transformed into a year-round facility, offering lodging, restaurant, and good opportunities for hiking, horseback riding, and mountain bike rentals.

Access: There is no boat ramp. Car-top boats may be hand launched.

Facilities, fees: A campground, drinking water vault toilets, and picnic area are available. Lodging, a restaurant, restrooms with flush toilets, convenience store, gas station, and horseback riding rentals are nearby. Access to the lake is free. A fee is charged for camping.

Water sports, restrictions: Rowboats, canoes, kayaks, and inflatables are permitted. No motors. Swimming is allowed, but the water is quite cold.

Directions: From Jackson drive east on Highway 88 for approximately 60 miles (four miles past Silver Lake) to the access road entrance on the left (if you reach the sign for Kirkwood Ski Resort, you have gone .5 mile too far). Turn left and drive .25 mile to the campground on the left (the road is very narrow and trailers are prohibited).

Contact: Eldorado National Forest, Amador Ranger District, 209/295-4251; Eldorado National Forest Visitor Center, 530/644-6048; Kirkwood Ski Resort, 209/258-6000.

47 SILVER LAKE

Rating: 8

in Eldorado National Forest

Map 6.2, page 193

Lower Bear River, Silver, and Caples. Of the three, Silver Lake is most often overlooked.

Silver Lake is set at an elevation of 7,200 feet in a classic granite cirque just below the

Sierra ridgeline. The surrounding area is extremely scenic.

The water is quite cold, and unfortunately it stays that way throughout the summer. That doesn't stop people from water-skiing and sailboarding and using personal watercraft, but only the truly brave and/or crazy try it without a wet suit. Sailboarding can be particularly good because winds are often brisk on summer afternoons. Sometimes they're a little too brisk, though, and boaters should take extra care. Swimming is usually a jump-in, jump-out situation, but there are good sunbathing beaches.

Silver Lake also provides decent trout fishing, great nearby hiking trails, horse rentals, campgrounds, and cabins. Full facilities are offered at the three resorts that operate here.

Usually the lake is free of ice by late May or early June, and by summer it's getting quite a lot of use. Most visitors congregate on the lake's north side, where the campgrounds, picnic areas, and marina are located.

Access: A paved ramp is available at Kay's Silver Lake Resort, located on the northwest side of the lake on Highway 88.

Facilities, fees: Kit Carson Lodge rents fishing boats, rowboats, canoes, and kayaks. A small marina at Kay's Silver Lake Resort rents fishing boats. Campgrounds, vault toilets, drinking water, picnic areas, convenience store, restaurants, bar, gas, and a coin laundry are available. Cabins and motels are available. Access to the lake is free. There is a fee for boat launching at Kay's Silver Lake Resort.

Water sports, restrictions: Powerboats, water-skiing, wake boarding, personal watercraft, sailing, and sailboarding are permitted. Wet suits are recommended for sailboarding. Although the water is quite cold for swimming, there are several sandy beach areas for sunbathing; the best are at Sandy Cove and Kit Carson Lodge.

Directions: From Jackson drive east on Highway 88 for 52 miles to the lake entrance road.

Contact: Kit Carson Lodge, 209/258-8500 (summer) or 530/676-1370 (winter), website: www.kit-carsonlodge.com; Kay's Silver Lake Resort,

209/258-8598; Plasse's Resort, 209/258-8814; Eldorado National Forest Visitor Center, 530/644-6048; Eldorado National Forest, Amador Ranger District, 209/295-4251.

48 CAPLES LAKE

Rating: 6

south of Lake Tahoe

Map 6.2, page 193

Caples Lake is surrounded by dramatic scenery and is easily accessed off Highway 88. It is a high mountain lake, set at an elevation of 7,950 feet, covers 600 acres, and provides good trout fishing, low-speed boating (5-mph speed limit), nearby hiking trails, and fair swimming.

This lake is filled by snowmelt, and though the water is cold, people do swim here. Much of the shoreline is rocky and steep in places, but there is a beach area near the resort that is suitable for sunbathing. It is extremely rare to see anyone sailboarding, even though conditions are often ideal—the lake is sizable and wide open, and typically gets good afternoon winds—providing sailboarders wear wet suits.

Use of the lake is moderate on most summer days, primarily attracting anglers who come looking for trout. On weekends use is heavy, with campers showing up in force. Many visitors go hiking. The best opportunity is at the trail that starts just off the highway near the dam at the lake's westernmost portion, and is routed into the Mokelumne Wilderness.

In the spring just pray that the cold wind out of the west doesn't howl. It can go right through you and make you feel like petrified wood.

Access: A boat ramp is available at Caples Lake Resort on Highway 88.

Facilities, fees: Fishing boats, canoes, kayaks, and pedal boats are available for rent at the boat dock and small marina. A lodge, cabins, campground, restrooms with flush toilets, convenience store, horseback riding rentals, bike rentals, and snowshoes (in winter) are available nearby. Access is free. A fee is charged for boat launching.

Water sports, restrictions: Powerboats, rowboats, canoes, kayaks, sailing, and sailboarding are permitted. A 5-mph speed limit is strictly enforced. Swimming is allowed. Wet suits are recommended for sailboarders.

Directions: From Jackson, drive east on Highway 88 for 63 miles (1.5 mile past the entrance to Kirkwood Ski Area) to the lake entrance road on the right.

Contact: Caples Lake Resort, 209/258-8888, website: www.capleslakeresort.com; Eldorado National Forest Visitor Center, 530/644-6048; Eldorado National Forest, Amador Ranger District, 209/295-4251.

49 WOODS LAKE

Rating: 5

in Eldorado National Forest

Map 6.2, page 193

Woods Lake may be located only two miles off Highway 88, yet when you're here, you get the feeling that you are visiting some far-off land.

Set in the high Sierra, elevation 8,200 feet, this small lake comes complete with a campground and an area where you can launch car-top boats. The lake always seems to be full, making a very pretty picture against the granite Sierra backdrop.

Car-top boating in Woods Lake is excellent, as you enjoy beautiful, wilderness scenery, quiet water, and decent trout fishing. Because the water is so cold, swimming is for the brave only.

Despite the backcountry atmosphere, the place is easy to access. Use can be quite high in summer, when the campground is almost always full. Many visitors take advantage of the hiking opportunities in the area, including an outstanding short tromp to nearby Winnemucca Lake.

Access: An unimproved launch ramp is provided.

Facilities, fees: Campground, vault toilets, drinking water (hand-pumped), and a picnic area are available nearby. Supplies can be obtained within five miles. Access to the lake is free.

Water sports, restrictions: Rowboats, canoes, kayaks, and inflatables are permitted. No motors. The lake is too small for sailing and sailboarding. Although the water is quite cold, swimming is permitted.

Directions: From Jackson, drive east on Highway 88 to Caples Lake and continue for a mile to the Woods Lake turnoff on the right (two miles west of Carson Pass). Turn south and drive two miles to the lake (one mile past the campground); trailers and RVs are not recommended.

Contact: Eldorado National Forest Visitor Center, 530/644-6048; Eldorado National Forest, Amador Ranger District, 209/295-4251.

50 BEAR RIVER RESERVOIR

Rating: 8

southwest of Lake Tahoe in Eldorado National Forest

Map 6.2, page 193

As you venture into the mountains on Highway 88, this is the first of three quality mountain lakes you will come to. The others are Silver Lake and Caples Lake (see listings in this chapter).

One advantage at Bear River Reservoir is its lower elevation—5,800 feet. That means the ice melts off far earlier in the year than at its two brothers farther up the line.

The lake is decent sized, at 725 acres. Cold, you say? Well, I might add, it's deep, too.

Even though the location is some distance from Jacksonville on curvy Highway 88, the roads are paved all the way to the boat ramp, and on weekends many people are willing to hitch up their boats and make the trip. So it gets a fair number of boaters, most out for fishing, some for water-skiing. In addition, sailboarding and sailing are excellent, with brisk afternoon winds daily.

On summer weekends, campground reservations are essential. Bear River Resort at the lake also has cabin rentals, and adds trophy-size trout to supplement the little rainbow trout stocked by the Department of Fish and Game. A clean, developed campground and swimming beach are also available at the resort.

Access: A paved ramp is available at Bear River Lake Resort.

Facilities, fees: A boat ramp, a small marina with fishing boat, kayak and canoe rentals, lodging, a grocery store, a restaurant, coin laundry, a lounge, campgrounds, restrooms with flush toilets and showers, a playground, volleyball, beach area, and a game room are available nearby. Fees are charged for parking, boat launching, and camping.

Water sports, restrictions: Powerboats, water-skiing, wake boarding, personal watercraft, sailing, and sailboarding are permitted. A swimming beach is provided at Bear River Resort; swimming is also good near the campgrounds.

Directions: To Bear River Lake Resort: From Stockton, drive east on Highway 88 for about 80 miles to the lake entrance on the right side of the road. Turn right and drive 2.5 miles to a junction (if you pass the dam, you have gone .25 mile too far). Turn left and drive .5 mile to the entrance on the right side of the road.

Contact: Bear River Lake Resort, 209/295-4868, website: www.bearriverlake.com; Eldorado National Forest, Visitor Center, 530/644-6048; Eldorado National Forest, Amador Ranger District 209/295-4251.

51 SALT SPRINGS RESERVOIR

Rating: 9

east of Jackson in Eldorado National Forest

Map 6.2, page 193

Everyone should visit this place at least once in his or her life. You'll find everything here.

Salt Springs Reservoir is a long, narrow lake set in the Mokelumne River Gorge, a dramatic canyon with spectacular surroundings for boaters. It's a good spot for hikers,

too. A trail that is routed into the Mokelumne Wilderness starts just north of the dam. Want more? Got more. A series of small, primitive campgrounds—all very pretty spots—is situated west of the lake, below the dam along the Mokelumne River.

The lake is set at an elevation of 4,000 feet and covers 950 acres. Even though the location is fairly obscure, the scenic beauty attracts vacationers who return year after year.

Swimming access is difficult because the shoreline is steep and rocky. If you can find a good spot to wade in, though, the water is great—fresh, clean, and often just the right temperature.

The surrounding area is particularly scenic, and with the rough road in and a 5-mph speed limit, the lake is often quiet and serene.

The only bugaboo is the high wind that kicks up in the late morning and afternoon and can rudely disrupt the idyllic setting. The safest times to boat are before 10 A.M. and after 4 P.M. If you're planning on boating here, keep this in mind.

Access: A primitive boat launch is located at the north end of the base of the dam.

Facilities, fees: A picnic area and vault toilet are available. No camping at the lake. Primitive campgrounds are available nearby on the Mokelumne River. No drinking water. Garbage must be packed out. Supplies can be obtained in Ham's Station. Access is free.

Water sports, restrictions: Small boats with motors, car-top boats, canoes, kayaks, and inflatables are permitted; boats must be hand carried to the launch. Motors are permitted, but with a 5-mph speed limit. Sailboarding is allowed, but occasional high winds can be hazardous. Swimming is permitted.

Directions: From Jackson, drive east on Highway 88 to Pioneer and then continue for 18 miles to Ellis Road/Forest Road 92 (78 miles from Jackson), at a signed turnoff for Lumberyard Campground. Turn right on Ellis Road and drive 12 miles to Salt Springs Road (Forest Road 9). Turn left, cross the Bear River and continue two miles to the dam. The road is steep, narrow, and curvy in spots, not good for RVs or trailers.

Contact: PG&E Land Projects, 916/386-5164, website: www.pge.com/recreation; Eldorado National Forest, Visitor Center, 530/644-6048; Eldorado National Forest, Amador Ranger District, 209/295-4251. For a map, send $6 to U.S. Forest Service, Attn: Map Sales, P.O. Box 587, Camino, CA 95709, 530/647-5390, fax 530/647-5389, website: www.fs.fed.us/r5/forests. Major credit cards accepted.

52 RED LAKE

Rating: 5

south of Lake Tahoe in Humboldt-Toiyabe National Forest

Map 6.3, page 194

If you have a canoe or any other type of car-top boat or inflatable, Red Lake is an ideal place to come and do your own thing. No motors are permitted, and most boaters just paddle or float around a bit, often with a fishing rod so they can be on the ready for trout.

Red Lake is a high mountain lake set at 8,200 feet elevation just southeast of Carson Pass. It is a fair-sized body of water, about four times bigger than nearby Woods Lake, and is shaped like a lima bean.

Camping is allowed only on the far east end of the lake. Use is light compared to the other lakes in the area, even in midsummer; for the most part only people who want to fish for trout bother to make the trip out. Here a brook trout, there a brook trout, every once in a while, a brook trout.

Vigorous afternoon winds can make this a great lake for sailboarding. Be aware that the water is very cold and wearing a wet suit is highly recommended.

Access: An unimproved boat ramp is located on the lake's northeast corner.

Facilities, fees: No facilities. A few primitive campsites are on the lake's east side. Sup-

plies can be obtained along Highway 88. Access is free.

Water sports, restrictions: Rowboats, canoes, kayaks, inflatables, and sailboarding are permitted. No motors. The lake is too small for sailing. Although the water is quite cold, swimming is permitted.

Directions: From Sacramento, take U.S. 50 to Meyers and the junctions of Highway 89 (two miles south of South Lake Tahoe). Turn right (south) and drive 20 miles to Highway 88. Turn right (west) and drive about six miles southwest to the turnoff for Red Lake. Turn left and continue to the lake.

An optional route from the Sacramento Valley: From Jackson, take Highway 88 east over Carson Pass to the turnoff for Red Lake. Turn right and drive to the lake.

Contact: Humboldt-Toiyabe National Forest, Carson Ranger District, 775/882-2766.

53 UPPER BLUE LAKE

Rating: 6

south of Lake Tahoe in Humboldt-Toiyabe National Forest

Map 6.3, page 194

Upper Blue Lake is one of two lakes that are linked by Middle Blue Creek.

This is the high country, set at 8,200 feet. The landscape is fairly sparse but pristine, featuring sandy soil sprinkled with pines, and bare granite mountains looming above nearby. But it's the good trout fishing and decent campgrounds that provide the true appeal.

The water is cold, with ice-out usually occurring by Memorial Day weekend, later in big snow years. Of the two Blue Lakes here, Upper Blue gets most of the boater traffic—primarily anglers out trolling for trout in small boats.

Other than fishing and low-speed boating, it is extremely rare to see water sports being performed here. Some people swim, but the water is pretty cold and the shoreline fairly rugged.

Of the campgrounds in the area, Upper Blue

Lake, operated by PG&E, is the most remote and private. Hiking is fair here; the best trek is the climb out on the Pacific Crest Trail, which rises on the barren slopes above the lake and awards hikers with scenic views.

Access: Primitive boat launching areas are available on the southern and northern ends of the lake, just off the access road.

Facilities, fees: A campground, vault toilets, and drinking water is available nearby. Access to the lake is free. A fee is charged for boat launching.

Water sports, restrictions: Only small motorized or car-top boats are suitable for the lake. Although the water is quite cold, swimming is permitted.

Directions: From Sacramento, drive east on U.S. 50 to the junction with Highway 89. Turn south on Highway 89 and drive over Luther Pass to the junction with Highway 88. Turn right and drive 2.5 miles to Blue Lakes Road. Turn left and drive 11 miles (the road becomes dirt) to a junction at the south end of Lower Blue Lake. Turn right and drive three miles to Upper Blue Lake on the left side of the road.

From Jackson, drive east on Highway 88 over Carson Pass and continue east for five miles to Blue Lakes Road. Turn right (south) and drive 11 miles (the road becomes dirt) to a junction at the south end of Lower Blue Lake. Turn right and drive three miles to Upper Blue Lake on the left side of the road.

Contact: PG&E Land Projects, 916/386-5164, website: www.pge.com/recreation; Humboldt-Toiyabe National Forest, Carson Ranger District, 775/882-2766.

54 LOWER BLUE LAKE

Rating: 5

south of Lake Tahoe in Humboldt-Toiyabe National Forest

Map 6.3, page 194

This is the smaller of the two Blue Lakes, suitable only for leisurely paddles in a canoe or inflatable. For many that makes for a perfect day.

This is the high country, set at an elevation of 8,100 feet. The terrain is stark and steep and edged by volcanic ridgelines. The deep blue-green color of the lake brightens the landscape.

As the little brother of the pair, Lower Blue receives less traffic, and that means fewer boaters, campers, anglers, and hikers. Yet Lower Blue provides a popular trout fishery with rainbow trout, brook trout, and cutthroat trout all stocked regularly.

Few people swim here, but it is still an option on a hot summer day. The shoreline is rocky and fairly sparse, and you'll need to have footwear to reach the water's edge.

The access road crosses the Pacific Crest Trail, providing a route to a series of nearby hike-to lakes that are small and pretty, just outside the edge of the Mokelumne Wilderness.

Access: A primitive boat launching area is available on the lake's far southern end next to a campground.

Facilities, fees: A campground, vault toilets, and drinking water are available nearby. Access to the lake is free. A fee is charged for boat launching.

Water sports, restrictions: The lake is suitable only for car-top boats. Although the water is quite cold, swimming is permitted.

Directions: From Sacramento, drive east on U.S. 50 to the junction with Highway 89. Turn south on Highway 89 and drive over Luther Pass to the junction with Highway 88. Turn right and drive 2.5 miles to Blue Lakes Road. Turn left and drive 11 miles (the road becomes dirt) to a junction at the south end of Lower Blue Lake.

From Jackson, drive east on Highway 88 over Carson Pass and continue east for five miles to Blue Lakes Road. Turn right (south) and drive 11 miles (the road becomes dirt) to a junction at the south end of Lower Blue Lake.

Contact: PG&E Land Projects, 916/386-5164, website: www.pge.com/recreation; Humboldt-Toiyabe National Forest, Carson Ranger District, 775/882-2766.

55 EAST FORK CARSON RIVER

X 🛶 ⚒ ≋ ⛺

Rating: 7

near Markleeville in Humboldt-Toiyabe National Forest

Map 6.3, page 194

This rafting run is just enough. That is, there's just enough excitement to make it fun, just enough scenic beauty to provide a sense of the natural grace of the great outdoors, and just enough surprises along the way to keep you guessing about what awaits around the next bend.

The best surprise of all on the river is a hot spring, located nine miles downstream of the Hangman's Bridge put-in spot. This hot spot is extremely popular and the Forest Service requests that visitors treat it is as a pristine mountain temple.

The rafting season here tends to be in May and June, when both the weather and the water are cold. Jumping into that hot spring and warming up, then taking a quick dunk in the cold river, then bobbing back into the hot spring—in pretty surroundings with nobody around—well, that can be one of the most exhilarating of life's little experiences.

Pines and high desert make up the streamside scenery. Although it may not be the gorgeous backdrop of granite canyons that you'll find in the western Sierra, the setting does feel remote.

The length of the entire run is 27 miles. The season is usually over in June, though in years with big snowpacks it can extend into July. Because the water is so cold (as well as being very clear), it is essential that rafters wear wet or dry suits.

Note the warning about taking out above the dam; missing the take-out would result in what rafting guides call "disastrous consequences," otherwise known as being dead very quick.

Access: A boat ramp is not available. The standard rafting run on the East Fork is the East Fork Run. From Markleeville, drive two miles south on Highways 89 and 4 to Hangman's Bridge. Take out 20 miles downstream just above the Ruhenstroth Dam. To reach the take-out, start at Markleeville, and then drive seven miles north on Highway 89 to Highway 88. Turn right and drive northeast for 14 miles, crossing into Nevada. At U.S. 395, turn south and drive to Gardnerville, Nevada. Continue five miles south and look for a dirt road on your right. Turn there and drive to a parking area.

Note: It is essential that you take out here because just downstream is a 30-foot vertical drop over a dam.

Upper East Fork Run is rated Class III, and the East Fork Run is Class II.

Facilities, fees: A campground is one mile south of Markleeville. Supplies can be obtained in Markleeville. Access to the river is free. Rafters must register at the put-in.

Water sports, restrictions: Rafting, kayaking, and swimming are permitted. Several swimming holes are available along Highways 89 and 4 and on Wolf Creek Road. Look for turnouts and trails leading to the river. Rafting permits are required.

Directions: From Sacramento, drive east on U.S. 50 to the junction with Highway 89. Turn south on Highway 89 and drive over Luther Pass to the junction with Highway 88. Turn left and drive to Woodfords and Highway 89. Turn right on Highway 89 and drive to Markleeville, then continue six miles. Direct access along the highway is available in this area.

From Stockton, take Highway 4 east over Ebbetts Pass (long, slow, narrow and curvy) to the junction with Highway 89. Turn left. Direct access is available along Highway 89.

Contact: Humboldt-Toiyabe National Forest, Carson Ranger District, 775/882-2766; American River Recreation, 530/622-6802 or 800/333-7238, website: www.arrafting.com; ARTA River Trips, 209/962-7873 or 800/323-2782, website: www.arta.org; Current Adventures, 530/333-9115 or 888/452-9254, website: www.kayaking.com; Tahoe White-water Tours, 530/581-2441 or 800/442-7238, website: www.gowhitewater.com; Tributary Whitewater Tours, 530/346-6812 or 800/672-3846, website: www.whitewatertours.com.

56 INDIAN CREEK RESERVOIR

Rating: 6

near Markleeville in Indian Creek Reservoir Recreation Area

Map 6.3, page 194

This beautiful lake is set amid sparse pines at an elevation of 5,600 feet. This is an excellent lake for trout fishing, and the nearby Carson River is managed as a trophy trout fishery. The lake covers 160 acres, with a maximum speed for boats on the lake set at 10 mph.

In the space of just a few miles, the terrain completely changes in this country. When you cross from the western Sierra over the ridge to the eastern Sierra, the land becomes sparsely forested on the high desert edge, with none of the classic granite-based features of the high Sierra.

Because there are no beaches and the water is cold, swimming is not popular, although it is permitted. Most campers are here in small boats to fish for trout, while others come to hike in the area.

There are several good hikes in the vicinity. The best is a short trek, a one-mile climb to Summit Lake, with scenic views of the Indian Creek area. The trailhead is southwest of the campground area.

Another popular side trip is to nearby Grover Hot Springs, located right outside of Markleeville.

Summers are dry and warm here, with high temperatures typically in the 80s, and nights cool and comfortable. Bears provide an occasional visit. The lake freezes over in winter. It is about 35 miles to Carson City, Nevada, and seven miles to Markleeville.

Like so many lakes set just east of the Sierra, wind is common, particularly in the afternoon. This is due to a katabatic phenomenon, that is, when wind crosses the Sierra ridge then dives down the other side to the east,

picking up speed as it goes. That can make conditions for sailboarding excellent at Indian Creek Reservoir, and it makes sailing pretty popular here, too.

Access: A paved launch ramp is available on the west side of the lake, adjacent to the picnic areas. Another, more primitive launching area is located on the east side, at the end of Airport Road.

Facilities, fees: Campgrounds, restrooms with drinking water, flush toilets, and showers, and picnic areas are available. Supplies can be obtained in Markleeville. Access to the lake is free.

Water sports, restrictions: Small boats, canoes, kayaks, and inflatables are permitted. No large boats permitted. A 10-mph speed limit is enforced. Sailboarding, sailing, and swimming are allowed.

Directions: From Sacramento, drive east on U.S. 50 over Echo Summit to Meyers and Highway 89. Turn south on Highway 89 and drive to Highway 88. Turn left (east) on Highway 88/89 and drive six miles to Woodfords and Highway 89. Turn right (south) on Highway 89 and drive about four miles to Airport Road. Turn left on Airport Road and drive four miles to Indian Creek Reservoir. At the fork, bear left and drive to the campground on the west side of the lake.

From Markleeville, drive north on Highway 89 for about four miles to Airport Road. Turn right on Airport Road and drive about three miles to Indian Creek Reservoir. At the fork, bear left and drive to the campground on the west side of the lake.

Contact: Bureau of Land Management, Carson City Field Office, 775/885-6000.

57 TOPAZ LAKE

Rating: 7

on the California/Nevada border in Humboldt-Toiyabe National Forest

Map 6.3, page 194

Topaz is set at 5,000 feet in the eastern Sierra and is surrounded by high desert country. The

Nevada border runs right through the lake. Some people say the place is cute, as in "cute like an iguana." When the wind kicks up, it can get downright ugly.

In addition to the wind, Topaz is best known for providing premium fishing for rainbow trout, with lots of large rainbow trout for trollers. The surprise is the size of the rainbow trout; the lake boasts one of the highest rates of 15- to 18-inch trout of any lake in the mountain country.

If you fish out of a small aluminum boat, always remember: Safety first. And if the wind starts to come up, then get off the lake, because once it starts it rarely dies, and instead crescendos until the lake is whipped to a froth.

The lake covers 1,800 acres of pretty much wide-open water. All boating and water sports are allowed. In July and August it can be a premium destination for all kinds of water sports enthusiasts, and it does get a lot of stopovers from travelers on adjacent U.S. 395. The RV park, in particular, receives a lot of traffic.

On the typical day anglers are out on the lake early, before the wind comes up, trolling for trout. By 11 A.M. the powerboaters and water-skiers start to appear, but rarely in great numbers. By mid-afternoon there is enough wind for sailboarding, and on most days it can be exceptional.

While swimming is permitted anywhere along the shoreline, there are no designated swimming areas and it is not common to see people in the water. There are several gravel-type beach areas that are suitable for sunbathing; on the rare occasions when someone decides to take a dunk, that's where they go.

Access: There are three boat ramps on Topaz Lake:
• Topaz Lake Park: From U.S. 395 at the California/Nevada border, drive north into Nevada, and then continue one mile to Topaz Park Road. Turn right and drive 1.5 miles to the park entrance. The paved boat ramp is at the end of the access road.
• Topaz Lake RV Park: An unimproved ramp

is available. There is no public access; use is limited to guests of the RV park. It is located a short distance south of Topaz Marina on U.S. 395.
• Topaz Landing Marina: A paved boat ramp is available. It is located on U.S. 395, just south of the California/Nevada border. A 40-boat marina and boat trailer storage is available at lakeside.

Facilities, fees: Fishing boat rentals are provided at Topaz Landing Marina. Campgrounds, restrooms with flush toilets, coin showers, drinking water, coin laundry, propane gas, and convenience store are nearby. A day-use fee is charged at Topaz Lake Park. Fees are charged for boat launching.

Water sports, restrictions: Powerboats, waterskiing, wake boarding, personal watercraft, sailing, and sailboarding are permitted. Swimming access is available at various areas within the county park and along the west shore.

Directions: From Carson City, Nevada, drive south on U.S. 395 for 33 miles to Topaz Lake and the campground/marina on the left side of the road (.3 miles south of the California/Nevada border).

From Bridgeport, California, drive north on U.S. 395 for 45 miles to the campground/marina on the right side of the road.

Contact: Topaz Landing, 775/266-3550; Douglas County Recreation Area (Topaz Lake Park), 775/266-3343; Topaz Lake RV Park, 530/495-2357.

58 LAKE ALPINE

Rating: 7

northeast of Arnold in Stanislaus National Forest

Map 6.3, page 194

For many people, Lake Alpine fits a vision of what a mountain lake is supposed to be. By early evening during the summer, the surface is calm and emerald green, with little pools created by hatching bugs and rising trout. The shoreline is well wooded (and includes some giant ponderosa pines), the smell of pine duff is in the air, and campsites are within a short distance of the lake. Heaven? Almost.

The only problem with this slice of heaven is that a lot of people want to get in. At Alpine that means filled campgrounds, lots of anglers, and on popular weekends, even difficulty renting a boat at the dock.

Lake Alpine covers 180 surface acres and is set at 7,320 feet in the Sierra Nevada, just above the snowplow stopping point. Highway 4 is gated just below the lake. In April, CalTrans opens that gate and plows the highway all the way to the lake.

Most vacationers here are campers who like to hike and fish. Some bring along small boats, either car-top boats, such as canoes or inflatables, or trailered boats. Many others rent a fishing boat, canoe, or kayak at the lake's small marina, and paddle around and bask in the great mountain beauty.

The water is clear and cold, especially early in the season. By July, however, on hot summer days there are always plenty of people jumping in anyway. Most are just taking a dunk, but a few swim around a bit. Although there is no designated swimming beach, there are lots of spots along the entire shoreline suitable for taking the plunge.

Sailboarding can be excellent, with steady winds out of the west kicking up on most afternoons. It is quite a sensation to clip along in the midst of all this supreme mountain lake charm.

But as mentioned, this area gets very crowded, especially on weekends between Memorial Day and Labor Day. The 10-mph speed limit and the long, twisty drive in keep out the fast boats and personal watercraft, but they don't guarantee perfect quiet. Sometimes there are off-road motorcycles in the area, and you can hear their engines in the distance.

The best times to visit and avoid the masses are from late April through May and again in September and October, even though the nights are cold and the weather can be unpredictable.

Access: Just before reaching the lake, look for the signed turn on the right. Turn right and drive .25 mile to the campground and boat ramp on the left.

Facilities, fees: Cabins, restaurant, convenience store, bait and tackle, coin showers, and rentals for fishing boats, rowboats, canoes, and kayaks are available at Lake Alpine. Campgrounds, flush and vault toilets, drinking water, and picnic areas are available. Access to the lake is free. Fees are charged for camping.

Water sports, restrictions: Powerboats, canoes, kayaks, inflatables, sailing, and sailboarding are allowed. A 10-mph speed limit is strictly enforced. Swimming is permitted anywhere along the lake's shoreline.

Directions: From Angels Camp, drive east on Highway 4 to Arnold and continue for 29 miles to Lake Alpine. Alpine Resort is on the left. Campgrounds and the boat ramp are off an access road to the right.

Contact: Stanislaus National Forest, Calaveras Ranger District, 209/795-1381, fax 209/795-6849; Lake Alpine Lodge, 209/753-6358, website: www.lakealpinelodge,com; Ebbetts Pass Sporting Goods, Arnold, 209/795-1686.

59 UNION RESERVOIR

Rating: 4

northeast of Arnold in Stanislaus National Forest

Map 6.3, page 194

For some, just getting here is far enough "out there." But you can get a lot farther "out there" if you want.

Along with the adjoining Utica Reservoir, Union Reservoir is set in Sierra granite at an elevation of 6,850 feet. The surrounding area is very scenic, and this is an excellent spot for kayakers and canoeists. With a canoe or other small boat, you can venture into the center of this exceptionally beautiful mountain setting.

The north end of the lake has a few shallow spots, with some small islands poking through, but the south end is quite deep. The lake is stocked annually with rainbow trout and kokanee salmon.

The water is very cold up here, but Union probably offers the warmest water for swimmers. It's still darn cold, though. Use is heavy from July through early September. Only dispersed camping is allowed, and campers are asked to practice minimum-impact techniques to protect the fragile shoreline.

Access: A boat ramp is available.

Facilities, fees: Walk-in tent campsites and vault toilets are available. No drinking water. Garbage must be packed out. Supplies can be obtained in Tamarack off Highway 4. Access to the lake is free.

Water sports, restrictions: The lake is only suitable for small, car-top boats. Speed limit is 5 mph. Swimming is permitted.

Directions: From Angels Camp, drive east on Highway 4 for about 32 miles to Spicer Reservoir Road (Forest Road 7N01). Turn right (east) and drive for about seven miles to Forest Road 7N75. Turn left and drive three miles to Union Reservoir.

Contact: Stanislaus National Forest, Calaveras Ranger District, 209/795-1381, fax 209/795-6849; Ebbetts Pass Sporting Goods, Arnold, 209/795-1686. For a map, send $6 to U.S. Forest Service, Attn: Map Sales, P.O. Box 587, Camino, CA 95709, 530/647-5390, fax 530/647-5389, website: www.fs.fed.us/r5/forests. Major credit cards accepted.

60 HIGHLAND LAKES

Rating: 7

near Ebbetts Pass in Stanislaus National Forest

Map 6.3, page 194

Highlands Lakes are set high near the Sierra crest at an elevation of 8,200 feet, just below Ebbetts Pass. These are two beautiful alpine ponds that offer good fishing for small brook trout (stocked annually) as well as spectacular panoramic views, with Hiram Peak (9,760 feet) looming to the nearby south.

This getaway is popular with anglers, canoeists, and kayakers, but swimming is only for members of the Polar Bear Club. You can figure out why: the water is frigid, all of it from snowmelt.

On summer weekends the campground is often full, usually with camper/anglers who have small trailered boats. They like the intimacy that you can only find at tiny lakes that have a small campground.

Because the water is so cold, swimming is not popular. For the same reason, sailboarding is also rare.

A bonus here is that it is a good jumping-off spot for hikes, including backpacking trips into the nearby Carson-Iceberg Wilderness. Day hikes up Boulder Creek and Disaster Creek are available. For overnight backpacking, a trail that starts at the north end of Highland Lakes (a parking area is available) is routed east for two miles to Wolf Creek Pass, where it connects with the Pacific Crest Trail; from there, turn left or right—you can't lose.

Access: A primitive boat ramp is available on Upper Highland Lake.

Facilities, fees: A campground, vault toilets, and drinking water is available at Lower Highland Lake. Supplies can be obtained at Lake Alpine Resort on Highway 4. Access is free.

Water sports, restrictions: A 15-mph speed limit is strictly enforced. Swimming and sailboarding are not recommended due to the extremely cold water.

Directions: From Angels Camp, drive east on Highway 4 to Arnold, past Lake Alpine, and continue for 14.5 miles to Forest Road 8N01/Highland Lakes Road (one mile west of Ebbetts Pass). Turn right and drive 7.5 miles to the campground on the right side of the road. High-clearance vehicles are advised. Trailers are not recommended.

Contact: Stanislaus National Forest, Calaveras Ranger District, 209/795-1381. For a map, send

$6 to U.S. Forest Service, Attn: Map Sales, P.O. Box 587, Camino, CA 95709, 530/647-5390, fax 530/647-5389, website: www.fs.fed.us/r5/forests. Major credit cards accepted.

61 WEST WALKER RIVER

Rating: 4

northwest of Bridgeport in Humboldt-Toiyabe National Forest

Map 6.3, page 194

The West Walker is best known as a pretty trout stream on the eastern side of the Sierra where there are a sprinkling of Forest Service campgrounds. What is less known, however, is that for a short period in the early summer, the West Walker provides a challenging rafting run, Class III-IV. Although not well known, the river has a cult-like following among a small group of skilled white-water enthusiasts.

The season is very short, typically from mid-June through mid-July. In spring, the flows are often far too high, cold, and dangerous for anybody. Yet by the end of July, the river is usually too low to try anything but a butt bumper.

Even when the flows are safe, it's considered a somewhat difficult run. From put-in to take-out, you encounter eight miles of steady rapids.

The take-out at China Garden can be a very frustrating experience, to put it nicely. To put it un-nicely, it's a downright pain in the butt. There are no quiet eddies for boats to slip into. That means rafters must crank abruptly into the bank immediately after a rapid, so you must be very alert as well as skilled at paddling.

In years with a low snowpack, the river is unrunnable at all times because of low flows.

The Walker is not exactly a hot spot. And that is exactly why some expert rafters and kayakers love this place—they often have the river to themselves.

It's an attractive river, set mostly in high desert country. One drawback is that after the first few miles, the river directly parallels U.S. 395, not exactly a wilderness atmosphere. But hey, you're going to be navigating Class III-IV rapids, so you probably won't even notice. No foolin' you won't notice.

Access: No boat ramp is available. To get to the put-in: From the junction of U.S. 395 and Highway 108, turn west on Highway 108 and drive three miles to the Sonora Bridge picnic area. The standard take-out is eight miles downstream at China Garden. This take-out is difficult; there are no eddies or pools available. That means you must turn hard into the bank. At high flows the river's rapids are rated Class IV-V. Only skilled paddlers should attempt this run.

Facilities, fees: Camping, drinking water, and vault toilets are available nearby. Supplies can be obtained in Bridgeport. Access is free. Rafting permits are not required.

Water sports, restrictions: Rafting, kayaking, and inflatables are permitted. Swimming is allowed but not recommended.

Directions: From Carson City, drive south on U.S. 395 to Coleville and then continue south for 13 miles to the campground on the west side of the highway (six miles north of the junction of U.S. 395 and Highway 108).

Contact: Humboldt-Toiyabe National Forest, Bridgeport Ranger District, 760/932-7070; Ken's Sporting Goods, Bridgeport, 760/932-7707.

62 DONNELLS RESERVOIR

Rating: 2

near Strawberry in Stanislaus National Forest

Map 6.3, page 194

Donnells is set in a remote gorge in the Stanislaus River Canyon in the central Sierra and resembles a hidden Yosemite. It has steep granite walls, cobalt-blue water, and a massive rock dome that resembles a miniature Half Dome plunging into the lake on the south shore.

In the spring, melting snow feeds Little

Niagara Falls, which pours over the southern canyon rim to create a 500-foot, two-tiered freefall, a replica of Yosemite Falls, visible only from the north shore and headwaters. From the Vista on Highway 108 above the lake, looking straight across the canyon, you can see Fouquet Falls, a wide cascade pouring through a chute, running down a canyon from the Dardanelles—a series of volcanic cones on the west flank on the high Sierra.

It might seem the impossible dream to put a canoe on Donnells Reservoir and then paddle through the center of this magnificent gorge. For most, it is just that: impossible.

This is one of the most beautiful lakes in California. It is also one of the most difficult to get a canoe on.

The options are few. One is to make the 90-minute drive on forest roads to the dam, then try to rope a canoe, kayak, or inflatable into the lake at the dam. The other option is to reach the head of the lake on foot, which requires tracking skills for scrambling on an unsigned route in national forest that mostly resembles a faint game trail. And once you're on the lake you face other perils: High winds with white caps are common in the afternoon, making it dangerous for small craft. Because the lake sits in a gorge, if you capsize, there is often no shore to swim to.

Access is legal for those who want to try to launch a canoe from the dam. But be forewarned. To get access with a canoe or any small boat, you must hoist the boat over the high gates, tipping it like a teeter-totter, and then carrying it up a hill for .5 to the top of the dam. At the dam, you then have to rope the canoe down to the water, which requires strength and stamina. Then, when it's time to leave, it can be extremely difficult, even hopeless for some, to try and rope the canoe back up.

Often the lake is only 10 to 15 percent full, and boulders the size of Volkswagens emerge near the access at the face of the dam. This requires an additional feat: to clamber down the boulders, a difficult and dangerous scram-

ble to reach the water. Again, the return trip can seem nearly impossible to get the boat out.

With such difficult access from the dam at Donnells Reservoir, a handful of trekkers will instead try to hike in to the headwaters of the lake, where there is a resemblance of shore across rounded granite slabs near the inlet.

But this hike is something of an act of faith. From Donnells Vista, you drive up the mountain and turn left for Clark Fork, then continue up a logging road. There are no trailhead signs or signs mentioning Donnells here, either. For newcomers, it can take several wrong turns on spur roads to find the right one, where the route in appears to be little more than an obscure deer trail.

The hike consists of walking, scrambling, and prayer, along with expert use of a topographic map. The route crosses a short ridge, then bears south, down toward the river canyon and the head of the lake. Along the way, the trail often disappears amid fern beds, then reappears as a near-invisible path in forest, with many large sugarpines all about. Do it right and it takes about 90 minutes to reach the head of the lake.

From here, you can take a seat on a granite block with a view of the otherwise hidden southern wall, and the massive ravine that creates Little Niagara Falls. The ambitious few can then launch their hand-carried kayak or inflatable, and paddle out to the center of paradise.

Alongside is the Middle Fork Stanislaus River, fed by Clark Fork and a dozen other smaller tributaries, which enters the lake in a foaming drop and surge. The trout here are huge.

Access: There is no boat ramp.

Facilities, fees: No facilities. No drinking water. Garbage must be packed out. Access is free.

Water sports, restrictions: Canoes, kayaks, and inflatables are permitted. Swimming is permitted.

Directions: To Donnells Dam: From Sonora, drive east on Highway 108 for 31 miles (just past the Dodge Ridge turnoff) to the town of Strawberry. Continue on Highway 108 for four miles to Beardsley Road. Turn left and drive 1 mile to Forest Road 5N95 (Hells Half Acre Road). Turn right and drive 2.1 miles to a fork with Forest Road 5NOX (the "4700 Road"). Bear right at the fork and drive 8.1 miles to the gate. Park and walk .5 mile (passing two gates) to the dam. High-clearance vehicles recommended; roughly 1 hour 15 minutes from Highway 108.

To Donnells Trailhead: From Sonora, drive east on Highway 108 for 31 miles (just past the Dodge Ridge turnoff) to the town of Strawberry. Continue on Highway 108 for 19 miles (three miles past Donnells Overlook) to Clark Fork Road on the left. Turn left and drive one mile to a fork. Bear left at the fork on Forest Road 6N06 and drive about 2.5 miles to an unsigned spur road on the left. Bear left on that spur road, drive a short distance and park. Look for the blue marker ribbons at the trailhead (usually present) and hike 2.5 miles on a faint route to the inlet of Donnells Reservoir. Detailed topo and Forest Service maps and off-trail, mountaineering experience is required. **Contact:** Stanislaus National Forest, Summit Ranger District, No. 1 Pinecrest Lake Road, Pinecrest, CA 95364, 209/965-3434. For a map, ask for Stanislaus National Forest and send $6 to U.S. Forest Service, Map Sales, P.O. Box 587, Camino, CA 95709, 530/647-5390, website: www.fs.fed.us/r5/forests. Major credit cards accepted. For a topographic map, ask for Donnells Lake, California and send $7.50 to U.S. Geologic Survey, Branch of Information Services, Box 25286, Federal Center, Denver, CO 80225, 888/275-8747, website: www.earthexplorer.usgs.gov. Major credit cards accepted.

63 SPICER MEADOW RESERVOIR

Rating: 6

northeast of Arnold in Stanislaus National Forest

Map 6.3, page 194

This lake covers approximately 2,000 acres, and it is quite pretty from a boat, surrounded by canyon walls and set at 6,418 feet. It is nestled below the Pacific Crest Trail near Leavitt Pass.

What you see here are campers with small boats, mostly fishing for trout, and occasionally folks in canoes or kayaks paddling and playing around in the water. Rules ensure a quiet setting for camping and low-speed boating.

The trout fishing is often quite good, and a fishing trail leads around the lake.

The water is very cold, way too cold for swimming—unless, that is, you have a dream of becoming a human Popsicle. And while winds are typically steady from 2 P.M. to 7 P.M., sailboarding is out of the question, too, without a wet suit.

This area can really get hammered with snow in big winters, so in the spring and early summer, always check for access conditions before planning a trip.

This is one of the older reservoirs in the high central Sierra Nevada. Spicer Meadow Reservoir was established in 1929 when a dam was built in the canyon on Highland Creek, creating a short, narrow lake.

Access: A paved boat ramp and parking area is located on the lake's west end, near the campground.

Facilities, fees: A campground, vault toilets, and drinking water are available. Access to the lake is free. A fee is charged for camping.

Water sports, restrictions: Powerboats, canoes, kayaks, inflatables, sailboarding, and sailing are permitted. No motors allowed on the lake's eastern end. A 10-mph speed limit is enforced. Swimming is not recommended due to the extremely cold water. Wet suits advised for sailboarding.

Directions: From Angels Camp, drive east on Highway 4 for about 32 miles to Spicer Reservoir Road/Forest Road 7N01. Turn right, drive seven miles, bear right at a fork with a sharp right turn (Forest Road 7N75), and drive a mile to the campground at the west end of the lake.

Contact: Stanislaus National Forest, Calaveras Ranger District, 209/795-1381. For a map, send $6 to U.S. Forest Service, Attn: Map Sales, P.O. Box 587, Camino, CA 95709, 530/647-5390, fax

530/647-5389, website: www.fs.fed.us/r5/forests. Major credit cards accepted.

64 BRIDGEPORT RESERVOIR

Rating: 6

near Bridgeport

Map 6.3, page 194

Bridgeport Reservoir is set on the high desert edge of the Great Basin, just east of the Sierra Nevada. This is a big lake, covering 4,400 surface acres when full. It is nestled in a valley at an elevation of 6,500 feet and is quite pretty, filled with bright blue water that contrasts with the stark surrounding countryside of the eastern Sierra.

Bridgeport Reservoir has its share of large trout, including some truly monster-sized brown trout. So most of the traffic here is from anglers, along with a few U.S. 395 travelers who are curious about what the lake looks like. Some venture long distances to flyfish here from float tubes.

While there are no restrictions on water sports, it's just not the greatest lake for waterskiing, wake boarding, or swimming. Waterskiers tend to head instead to Twin Lakes. Though winters can be bitter cold here, by summer the water is warm, even sometimes sprinkled with algae by mid-August.

Sailboarding here can be excellent, with brisk afternoon west winds in the summer and a lot of room to really let it rip. A good deal of shoreline is grassy, and as long as water levels are high, the put-ins are clean and not muddy.

Access: There are three boat ramps:
• Bridgeport Marina: From Bridgeport, drive east on Highway 182 for three miles to the marina entrance. A paved ramp and docks are available.
• Paradise Shores RV Park: From Bridgeport, drive east on Highway 182 to the signed turnoff (just past Bridgeport Marina). A dirt launching area is available.
• Bridgeport Public Ramp: From Bridgeport, drive east on Highway 182 for 3.5 miles to the sign for public access. A paved ramp is available.

Facilities, fees: Bridgeport Marina has a full-service marina, boat slips, and fishing boat rentals. Paradise Shores RV Park (no tents) has two rental trailers, restrooms with flush toilets, and coin laundry. The public day-use area has drinking water and restrooms. Picnic areas are provided along the eastern shore. Supplies can be obtained in Bridgeport. Access is free.

Water sports, restrictions: Powerboats, waterskiing, wake boarding, personal watercraft, sailing, and sailboarding are permitted. Although there are no designated beaches, swimming is permitted anywhere along the shoreline.

Directions: From Southern California, take U.S. 395 north to Bishop and onward to Bridgeport. At Bridgeport, turn east on Highway 182 and continue for one mile to the lake. The boat ramps are located directly off the highway.

From Sacramento, take U.S. 50 east to Echo Summit (near South Lake Tahoe). Turn south on Highway 89 and drive to its junction with U.S. 395. Turn south on U.S. 395 and drive through Bridgeport; turn east on Highway 182 and continue one mile to the lake.

Contact: Bridgeport Marina, 760/932-7001, website: www.bridgeportmarina.net; Paradise Shores RV Park, 760/932-7735, website: www.calparadise.com.

FOGHORN OUTDOORS®

COURTESY OF JUSTIN MARLER

Chapter 7

San Francisco Bay Area

Chapter 7—San Francisco Bay Area

The Bay Area has 150 significant parks (including 12 with redwoods), 7,500 miles of hiking and biking trails, 45 lakes, 25 waterfalls, 100 miles of coast, mountains with incredible lookouts, bays with islands, and in all, 1.2 million acres of greenbelt with hundreds of acres being added each year with land bought by money earmarked from property taxes.

The two East Bay counties, Alameda and Contra Costa, provide access to 15 lakes, including six with significant fishing programs (San Pablo Reservoir, Lafayette Reservoir, Lake Chabot, Del Valle Reservoir, Los Vaqueros Reservoir, and Shadow Cliffs Lake), plus 100 miles of bay shoreline, and 10 protected shoreline habitats with extensive wetlands that act as sanctuaries for thousands of waterfowl and marine birds. The habitat is rich across this landscape, highlighted by the highest concentration of wintering golden eagles in the world. The sweeping lookouts from mountaintops often encompass vast areas with stunning views of world-class sights.

Santa Clara County alone has another 14 lakes, including Anderson, Calero, and Coyote, the best in the Bay Area for water-skiing, wake boarding, and powerboating. Yet there is also little hidden Almaden, set high in foothills in Almaden-Quicksilver County Park, where a lone flyfisher in a float tube can cast for bass and bluegill on a weekday morning without another soul in sight.

Because of benign winter weather, access to Bay Area lakes and parks is available 12 months a year for hiking, biking, camping, boating, swimming, fishing, and wildlife watching, a great plus.

Note that proximity to a metropolitan area means that the demand is higher. So plan ahead. One shocker is that in spring and fall, there is a huge drop-off in use on weekdays, Sundays through Thursdays.

There are many world-class landmarks in the Bay Area, of course, which can add texture to any trip.

In fact, instead of going far away for a vacation, residents might consider what so many do from all over the world: Stay and discover the treasures in your own backyard.

It's ironic that many people who have chosen to live in the Bay Area are often the ones who complain the most about it. We've even heard some say, "Some day I'm going to get out of here and start having a good time."

We wish we could take anyone who has ever had these thoughts on a little trip in my airplane and circle the Bay Area at 3,000 feet. What you see is that despite strips of roadways and pockets of cities where people are jammed together, most of the region is wild, unsettled, and beautiful. There is no metropolitan area in the world that offers better and more diverse recreation and open space so close to so many.

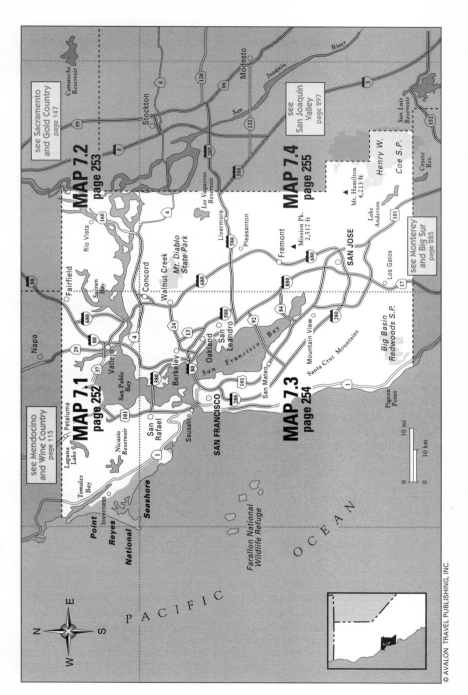

see Sacramento
and Gold Country
page 147

see San Joaquin
Valley
page 297

see Mendocino
and Wine Country
page 115

see Monterey
and Big Sur
page 285

MAP 7.2
page 253

MAP 7.4
page 255

MAP 7.1
page 252

MAP 7.3
page 254

Camanche
Reservoir

Modesto

River

Stockton

San Joaquin

San Luis
Reservoir

Coyote
Res.

*Henry W.
Coe S.P.*

Mt. Hamilton
4,213 ft

Rio Vista

Los Vaqueros
Reservoir

Livermore

Pleasanton

Lake
Anderson

*Mt. Diablo
State Park*

Fremont

Mission Pk.
2,517 ft

SAN JOSE

Concord

Walnut Creek

Los Gatos

Fairfield

Suisun
Bay

Napa

Vallejo

Berkeley

Oakland

San
Leandro

Mountain View

Santa Cruz Mountains

*Big Basin
Redwoods S.P.*

San Pablo
Bay

San Francisco Bay

San Mateo

SAN FRANCISCO

Petaluma

Laguna
Lake

Nicasio
Reservoir

San
Rafael

Sausalito

Pigeon
Point

*Point
Reyes
National
Seashore*

Tomales
Bay

Inverness

Farallon National
Wildlife Refuge

PACIFIC

OCEAN

N
E
W
S

10 mi

10 km

0

0

© AVALON TRAVEL PUBLISHING, INC.

Map 7.1

Sites 1–2
Pages 256–257

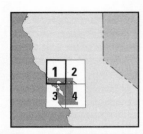

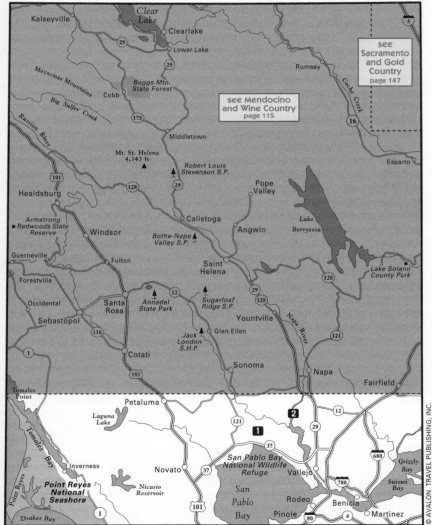

see Sacramento and Gold Country page 147

see Mendocino and Wine Country page 115

Kelseyville

Clear Lake

Clearlake

Lower Lake

Rumsey

Mayacmas Mountains

Cobb

Boggs Mtn. State Forest

Big Sulfer Creek

Russian River

Middletown

Mt. St. Helena 4,343 ft

Robert Louis Stevenson S.P.

Pope Valley

Esparto

Healdsburg

Armstrong Redwoods State Reserve

Windsor

Calistoga

Angwin

Lake Berryessa

Lake Solano County Park

Guerneville

Fulton

Bothe-Napa Valley S.P.

Saint Helena

Forestville

Occidental

Santa Rosa

Annadel State Park

Sugarloaf Ridge S.P.

Yountville

Napa River

Sebastopol

Jack London S.H.P.

Glen Ellen

Cotati

Sonoma

Napa

Fairfield

Tomales Point

Petaluma

Laguna Lake

Novato

Inverness

Nicasio Reservoir

San Pablo Bay National Wildlife Refuge

Vallejo

Grizzly Bay

Point Reyes National Seashore

San Pablo Bay

Rodeo

Benicia

Suisun Bay

Drakes Bay

Pinole

Martinez

Cache Creek

Tomales Bay

Point Reyes

© AVALON TRAVEL PUBLISHING, INC.

Map 7.2

Sites 3–4
Pages 257–261

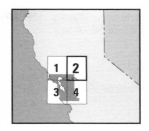

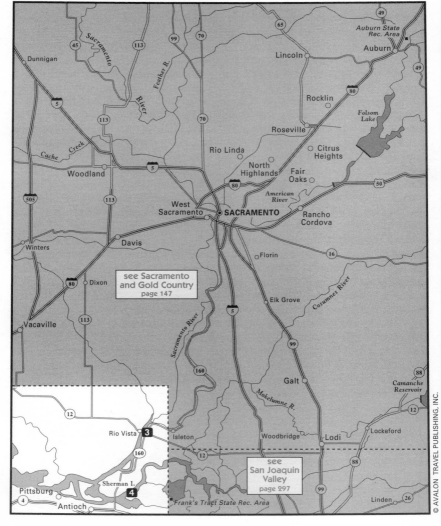

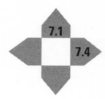

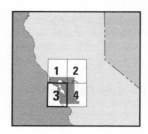

Map 7.3

Sites 5–15
Pages 261–269

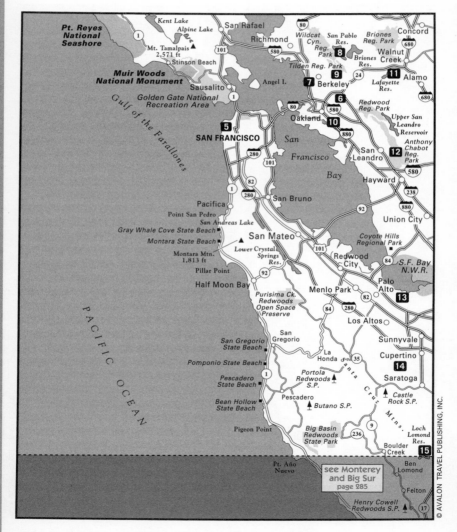

Pt. Reyes
National
Seashore

Kent Lake
Alpine Lake
San Rafael
Richmond
Concord

Wildcat
Cyn.
Reg.
Park
San Pablo
Res.
Briones
Reg. Park

8

Mt. Tamalpais
2,571 ft
Stinson Beach

Briones
Res.
Walnut
Creek

**Muir Woods
National Monument**

Tilden Reg. Park

9

Lafayette
Res.
Alamo

Sausalito

Angel I.

7 Berkeley

Golden Gate National
Recreation Area

6

Redwood
Reg. Park

Gulf of the Farallones

Oakland

5

SAN FRANCISCO

10

Upper San
Leandro
Reservoir

San
Francisco

San
Leandro

Anthony
Chabot
Reg.
Park

12

Bay

Hayward

Pacifica

San Bruno

Point San Pedro
San Andreas Lake
Gray Whale Cove State Beach
Montara State Beach

Union City

Coyote Hills
Regional Park

Montara Mtn.
1,813 ft

San Mateo

Lower Crystal
Springs
Res.

Redwood
City

S.F. Bay
N.W.R.

Pillar Point

Palo
Alto

Half Moon Bay

Purisima Ck.
Redwoods
Open Space
Preserve

Menlo Park

13

Los Altos

Sunnyvale

San Gregorio
State Beach
San
Gregorio

La
Honda

Cupertino

14

Pomponio State Beach

Portola
Redwoods
S.P.

Saratoga

Pescadero
State Beach

Castle
Rock S.P.

Bean Hollow
State Beach

Pescadero

Butano S.P.

Santa Cruz Mtns.

Loch
Lomond
Res.

Pigeon Point

Big Basin
Redwoods
State Park

Boulder
Creek

15

PACIFIC OCEAN

Pt. Año
Nuevo

Ben
Lomond

see Monterey
and Big Sur
page 285

Feiton

Henry Cowell
Redwoods S.P.

© AVALON TRAVEL PUBLISHING, INC.

Map 7.4

Sites 16–31
Pages 269–281

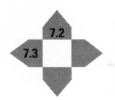

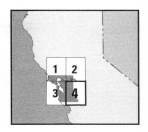

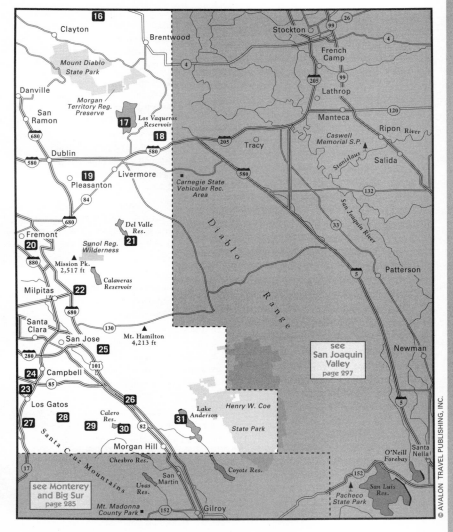

1 NAPA-SONOMA MARSH WILDLIFE AREA

Rating: 10

north of San Pablo Bay

Map 7.1, page 252

The Skaggs Island Boat Ramp is an excellent launch point. From here you can head down Hudeman Slough. Over the space of a mile, you will pass a series of distinct habitats: upland grasslands, tidal salt marsh and mudflats, seasonal wetlands, closed ponds, and open waters.

That variety creates a habitat matrix that provides homes for a fantastic diversity of wildlife. In succession, we saw a marsh harrier, peregrine falcon, and canvasback duck. The latter two are among the fastest birds in the sky; the peregrine is capable of speeds up to 200 mph—the fastest creature alive—and the canvasback is the fastest of all ducks, capable of 70 mph.

There are nearly 50,000 acres of tidal marshes and wetlands here, highlighted by the 14,000-acre Napa-Sonoma Marsh Wildlife Area. It is located just north of Highway 37 along San Pablo Bay, 25 miles from San Francisco, but feels a world apart. With a canoe or kayak, you can explore the mosaic of tidal sloughs, ponds, cuts, and backwaters that provide access to the wildlife area.

From the Skaggs Island Ramp to Hudeman Slough, you can then turn down Devil's Slough, and then to China Slough. From here you can view what is called Pond 2A. As is the case with so much of the area, this was, in the early 1990s, a salt evaporative pond, nearly devoid of native plants and with little wildlife. Tom Huffman of the Department of Fish and Game knocked a hole in the levee here during high water of January, 1995, restoring tidal flows for the first time since the 1950s. The return of native plants, and the aquatic species and bird life they support, has followed.

One key note: While this is a fantastic area for canoeing, kayaking, and exploring by powerboat, be certain to pay careful attention to tides; make sure you have at least 3 feet of water, according to the tide book. In addition, during low tides of 1 foot and lower, particularly minus tides, many of the sloughs can be emptied of water and then turned into mud flats—and there you are, sitting in your boat, stranded on the mud, with a five-hour wait for the incoming tide to free you.

This is a great place for canoeing, kayaking, and low-speed exploring in a powerboat; hiking, jogging, and biking on the levee trails; bird-watching for some 200 species of birds that use the marsh over the course of a year; fishing for striped bass; and for limited duck hunting in winter.

With the tidal, brackish flows restored from San Pablo Bay, more than 1,000 acres in this immediate area have been returned to their native state, with rabbit's foot grass taking over for miles. In turn, the waterway provides habitat for geese, pelican, ducks (especially lots of buffleheads), and a new nursery area in summer and fall for juvenile striped bass. This new habitat could increase the population of striped bass perhaps by 100,000. The Department of Fish and Game has been able to purchase much of this area and offer it for public use as the result of penalties paid by Shell Oil for an oil spill in the mid-1980s near Carquinez Strait.

Access: Five parking areas and two boat ramps. There are few signs indicating these parking areas and boat ramps. Because of this, you need a free map from Fish and Game in order to track down the well-hidden access spots (see Contact information below).

Facilities, fees: No facilities. Access is free.

Water sports, restrictions: Boats with motors, canoes, kayaks, and inflatables are permitted. In waterfowl season, limited duck hunting is allowed. During low tides of 2.5 feet or lower, sloughs will empty of water, grounding boats. Pay careful attention to charts in tide books.

Directions: To Skaggs Island Boat Ramp: From San Rafael, drive north on U.S. 101 to Highway 37. Bear east on Highway 37 and drive to the lighted junction with Highway 121. Turn left on Highway 121 and drive to a fork with Highway 121/Highway 12. Bear right on Highway 121 and drive to Ramal Road. Turn right on Ramal Road and drive to Skaggs Island Road. Turn right on Skaggs Island Road and drive to Hudeman Slough. Turn right and drive a short distance to the boat ramp on the left.

Contact: Napa-Sonoma Marsh Wildlife Area, Department of Fish and Game, 707/226-3641 or 707/944-5500. For a free map that details the five parking areas and trailheads and two boat ramps, write the Department of Fish and Game at P.O. Box 47, Yountville, CA 94599, or pick up in person at the DFG regional office at 7329 Silverado Trail in Napa. General information websites: www.napa-sonoma-marsh.org, www.audubon.org.

2 NAPA RIVER

Rating: 5

near Napa

Map 7.1, page 252

When people embark on a river trip, they usually refer to it as a "float trip." On the Napa River it is just that: a float, along with a good deal of paddling, on water that is dead flat and placid.

After putting in, you drift downstream, paddling to keep moving at a decent pace. You can extend your trip all the way to San Pablo Bay at Mare Island. The surrounding wetlands attract a large number of birds, including herons, egrets, ducks, and the inevitable mud hen.

The Mare Island area offers unlimited adventures for ambitious kayakers; same with the adjacent Napa-Sonoma Marsh Wildlife Area, a paradise for kayaking and canoeing.

This is not the kind of raging river that will tip you over. And you'll be thankful because the water is typically muddy and cold, with the downstream portions of the river within the tidal reach of the bay and the ocean. The Napa River Trail parallels much of the river.

The lower river is wide and quiet, and appeals to people fishing for striped bass and sturgeon,

both long shots. Occasionally, a kayaker or canoeist drifts by.

Access: There are two boat ramps:
• Cuttings Wharf: Once on Cuttings Wharf Road, drive to where the road forks. Bear right and continue to a yield sign. Then bear left and head down to the water. A paved ramp and marina are available (signed).
• Napa Valley Marina: Once on Cuttings Wharf Road, drive to where the road forks. Continue straight to the next intersection. Turn left and follow the signs to the full-service marina. A paved ramp is available.

Kayakers and canoeists may put in at Cuttings Wharf and paddle for several miles to one of numerous take-out spots downstream. There is also access to the Napa-Sonoma Marsh Wildlife Area (see previous listing).

Facilities, fees: A marina is available. Day use is free. A fee is charged for boat launching.

Water sports, restrictions: Powerboats, kayaks, canoes, and inflatables are permitted. Swimming is permitted but not advised.

Directions: From Vallejo, take Highway 29 north (it becomes Highway 121/12) to Cuttings Wharf Road (adjacent to the river). Turn left on Cuttings Wharf Road and follow the directions detailed in Access.

Contact: Napa Valley Marina, 707/252-8011, website: www.napavalleymarina.com; Moore's Landing Restaurant, 707/253-2439; Napa Visitor's Bureau, 707/226-7459, website: www.napavalley.com.

3 SACRAMENTO RIVER DELTA

Rating: 9

near Rio Vista

Map 7.2, page 253

The fabric of the Delta consists of little towns, villages, and marinas that represent the most upscale to the more simple and rustic. Through it all, the Delta is paradise for boaters of all kinds, whether it be for water-skiing, wake boarding, fishing, pleasure touring, or any other activity.

The most popular spot for water-skiing and wake boarding along this stretch of the Sacramento River is in the Rio Vista area. The river is wide here, with plenty of room for all water sports, and the water is warmer here than it is further upstream. There is a good access ramp right at Rio Vista and at nearby marinas. You'll also find beach access in Rio Vista for swimming and sailboarding.

Boating traffic in the Sacramento River Delta is high in the summer. One of the reasons it is so popular is that in a boat you gain access to a network of adjoining waterways, many with excellent sheltered areas suitable for water-skiing. Most boat rentals are booked up on weekends.

One of the best of these areas is known as the Meadows, and is located on Snodgrass Slough near Walnut Grove. It is fed from the Mokelumne River, not the Sacramento River. A boat launch at Walnut Grove Marina provides nearby access.

There's just one problem on the Sacramento River Delta in late spring and early summer: the wind. When temperatures reach the 100-degree range in the Central Valley—yet it is foggy on the San Francisco coast—the wind whistles west, using the river as a passageway. That means rough going for most boating and water sports. These winds tend to come and go in three-day cycles, that is, three days of wind, then three days of calm. Not always, of course, but that is the general pattern.

Boaters can search out the narrow channels adjoining the main river. These channels are not only largely sheltered from the wind, but their very size by nature creates a calmer surface, ideal for water-skiing. Many other such spots are in the adjoining San Joaquin Delta (see next listing).

The Sacramento River is often fantastic for fishing, with striped bass, sturgeon, and salmon caught in excellent numbers during their respective peak migrations. Many of the best spots are in the Rio Vista area, down river near Brannan Island State Recreation Area, and in Montezuma Slough.

Access: Paved boat ramps are available at the following locations:

• B&W Resort, Isleton: Take I-5 to Highway 12 (south of Sacramento, near Lodi). Turn west on Highway 12 and drive 11 miles to Brannan Island Road (after the second bridge). Turn right and drive a very short distance. The resort is on your immediate left. For more information call 916/777-6161, website: www.bandwresort.com.

• Korth's Pirates' Lair Marina, Isleton: Take I-5 to Highway 12 (south of Sacramento, near Lodi). Turn west on Highway 12 and drive 11 miles to Brannan Island Road (after the second bridge). Turn right and drive three miles to the marina. For more information call 916/777-6464, website: www.korthsmarina.com.

• Vieira's Resort, Isleton: Take I-5 to Highway 12 (south of Sacramento, near Lodi). Turn west on Highway 12 and drive approximately 15 miles to the four-way stop at Highway 160 (just before the Rio Vista Bridge). Turn right (northeast) on Highway 160 and drive three miles to the sign for Vieira's on the left. Turn left and drive a short distance into the resort. For more information call 916/777-6661, website: www.vieirasresort.net.

• Brannan Island State Recreation Area, Rio Vista: See Directions below. For more information call 916/777-7701.

• Sandy Beach County Park, Rio Vista: Take I-80 to Fairfield and the exit for Highway 12. Take that exit and drive 14 miles to Rio Vista and the intersection with Main Street. Turn right on Main Street and drive a short distance to Second Street. Turn right and drive .5 mile to Beach Drive. Turn left on Beach Drive and drive .5 mile to the park. Solano County Parks, 707/374-2097, website: www.solanocounty.com.

• Delta Marina Yacht Harbor, Rio Vista: Take I-80 to Fairfield and the exit for Highway 12. Take that exit and drive 14 miles to Rio Vista and the intersection with Main Street. Turn right on Main Street and drive a short distance

to Second Street. Turn right on Second Street and drive to Marina Drive. Turn left on Marina Drive, and continue another short distance to the harbor. For more information call 707/374-2315, website: www.deltamarina.com.
• Snug Harbor Resort, Ryer Island: Take I-80 to Fairfield and Highway 12. Turn east on Highway 12 and drive to Rio Vista and Front Street. Turn left on Front Street and drive under the bridge to River Road. Turn right on River Road and drive two miles to the Real McCoy Ferry (signed Ryer Island). Take the ferry (free) across the Sacramento River to Ryer Island and Levee Road. Turn right and drive 3.5 miles on Levee Road to Snug Harbor on the right. For more information call 916/775-1455, website: www.snugharbor.net.

Facilities, fees: Lodging, cabins, and campgrounds are provided, full-service marinas, and supplies are available at or near many of the boat ramps listed above. Fees are charged at parks and private marinas for day use, boat launching and camping. River access is free along roads.

Water sports, restrictions: Powerboats, waterskiing, wake boarding, personal watercraft, sailing, and sailboarding are permitted. A sandy swimming beach and designated sailboarding area are available at Brannan Island State Recreation Area. Another swimming beach is available at Vieira's Resort in Isleton. Numerous beach access points for swimming, sailboarding, and fishing are available along Highway 160 on Brannan Island.

Directions: To Brannan Island State Recreation Area: From I-80 in Fairfield, take the Highway 12 exit and drive southeast 14 miles to Rio Vista, and continue to Highway 160 (at the signal before the bridge). Turn right on Highway 160 and drive three miles to the park entrance on the left.

From Antioch, take Highway 4 and continue over the Antioch Bridge (where the road becomes Highway 160) and continue to the park on the right.

Contact: Brannan Island State Recreation Area,

916/777-7701; Hal Schell's Delta Map and Guide, $2.99 at stores, $3.75 by mail at P.O. Box 9140, Stockton, CA 95208; California Delta Chamber & Visitor Bureau, 209/367-9840, website: www.californiadelta.org.

Boat rentals: Waterflies (will deliver), 916/777-6431; Herman & Helen's, Stockton, 209/951-4634. Kayak rentals: Big River Kayaks, Bethel Island, 925/684-3095.

Sailing instruction: Martin's Sailing School & Club, 916/369-7700, website: www.lovetosail.com.

Fishing guides: Fish Hooker Charters, 916/777-6498.

Boat charters: Delta Expeditions, 916/600-2420.

4 SAN JOAQUIN DELTA

Rating: 10

near Antioch

Map 7.2, page 253

The network of waterways in the San Joaquin Delta is so vast that you can change the course of your life instantly by simply making another turn—taking you amid the spider web of rivers, sloughs, bays, and estuaries.

The Delta is rimmed by roads perched on the tops of levees, linked by 70 bridges and a few old-time cable ferries. You can explore it for years by boat or car and not see it all. It is among the world's best destinations for boaters.

The best areas for water-skiing and wake boarding are in the sloughs, providing miles of calm water and shelter from the north winds that often affect the Sacramento River side of the Delta.

There are dozens and dozens of sloughs. Middle River, Old River, Grant Line Canal, and Victoria Cut are among the best. The sloughs are better protected from winds than the wide-open areas, such as Frank's Tract and Sherman Lake (where the San Joaquin and Sacramento Rivers join), which means smooth, warm water for water-skiing. Don't underestimate the value of these sheltered areas. At times the wind can be howling 15 miles away on the Sacramento River while False River is being stroked only by a gentle breeze.

Two popular spots for sailboarding are Ski Beach and Swing Beach, both located near Frank's Tract. The best beach access is available in the sloughs, which are reachable by boat only.

In addition, the fishing for largemouth bass is considered among the best in America, especially in the vicinity of Victoria Slough, Old River, and the Grant Line.

The San Joaquin Delta was once a vast marshland. According to Delta historian Hal Schell, Chinese laborers working for 13 cents per cubic yard built the original levees in the Delta. "That work was eventually converted to clamshell dredges, because it was cheaper," Schell said. By 1930, some 700,000 acres had been reclaimed, creating 55 islands.

The Delta levees are lined with tules, cottonwoods, and grass, habitat that supports one of North America's most diverse and abundant arrays of bird life. On any given day, you can see everything from Canada geese to peregrine falcons, mated pairs of mallards to flocks of white pelicans, giant egrets, and marsh hawks.

There is just so much of it. Thus it can be inundated with people and boats in the summer, particularly water-skiers, who descend in unbelievable numbers. The place can get wild.

The problem is that these waterways can be narrow in places, meaning there is sometimes limited forward visibility, yet there are a lot of boats out on weekends. That is one of the reasons the law says you must have a spotter on board to watch the trailing water-skier so that the driver can stay alert to what is going on ahead.

Because water-ski traffic is so heavy on weekends, most sailboarders will head instead to Windy Cove near Brannan Island State Recreation Area (see previous Sacramento River Delta listing). Most beach areas in the San Joaquin Delta are accessible by boat only.

The best time on the Delta (when there are the fewest people on it) is a weekday late September and early October. The best weather of the year arrives in early fall, and on a weekday morning, you can have the whole place—all thousand miles of it—practically to yourself.

Also check out the listing for the South/East Delta in Chapter 9—San Joaquin Valley.

Access: Launching facilities are available at the following locations:

• Emerald Point Marina, Bethel Island: Take Highway 4 to Antioch and continue east to Oakley and Cypress Road. Turn left on Cypress Road and drive three miles (drive over the Bethel Island Bridge and the road name changes to Bethel Island Road) to Stone Road. Turn right on Stone Road and continue 1.5 miles to the sign on the right for the marina entrance. For more information call 925/684-2388.

• Bethel Harbor, Bethel Island: Take Highway 4 to Antioch and continue east to Oakley and Cypress Road. Turn left on Cypress Road and drive three miles (drive over the Bethel Island Bridge and the road name changes to Bethel Island Road) to Harbor Road (on the island's northern side). Turn right and drive to the end of the road. For more information call 925/684-2141.

• Lundborg Landing, Bethel Island: Highway 4 to Antioch and continue east to Oakley and Cypress Road. Turn left on Cypress Road and drive three miles (drive over the Bethel Island Bridge and the road name changes to Bethel Island Road) to Gateway Road. Turn right on Gateway Road and drive two miles to the park entrance on the left (look for the large sign and tugboat). Lundborg Landing, 925/684-9351, website: www.lundborglanding.com.

• Sugar Barge Marina, Bethel Island: Turn left on Cypress Road and drive three miles (drive over the Bethel Island Bridge and the road name changes to Bethel Island Road) to Gateway Road. Turn right on Gateway Road and drive .25 mile to Piper Road. Turn left and drive two miles to Willow Road. Turn right and drive a short distance to the marina. For more information call 925/684-8575 or 800/799-4100, www.sugarbarge.com.

• Eddo's Harbor & RV Park, Sherman Island: Take Highway 4 to Antioch and continue over the Antioch Bridge (where the road becomes Highway 160) and continue to Sherman Island East Levee Road. Turn right and drive three miles to 19530 East Levee Road on the right. For more information call 925/757-5314, website: www.eddosresort.com.

• Lauritzen Yacht Harbor, Antioch: Take Highway 4 to Antioch and the exit for Wilbur Avenue. Take that exit, turn right (east) and drive to Bridgehead Road. Turn left on Bridgehead Road and drive .25 mile to the signed entrance for the yacht club on the right. For more information call 925/757-1916, website: www.lauritzens.com.

Facilities, fees: Lodging, cabins, and campgrounds are provided; full-service marinas and supplies are available at or near many of the boat ramps listed above. River access is free along roads. Fees are charged at parks and private marinas for day use, boat launching, and camping.

Water sports, restrictions: Powerboats, waterskiing, wake boarding, personal watercraft, sailing, and sailboarding are permitted. A sandy swimming beach and designated sailboarding area are available at Brannan Island State Recreation Area. Another swimming beach is available at Vieira's Resort in Isleton. Numerous beach access points for swimming, sailboarding, and fishing are available along Highway 160 on Brannan Island.

Directions: From Antioch, take Highway 4 east and drive to Oakley and Cypress Road. Turn left on Cypress Road, drive over the Bethel Island Bridge, and continue .5 mile to Gateway Road. Turn right and drive on Gateway Road. This route provides access to the interior San Joaquin Delta.

Contact: Brannan Island State Recreation Area, 916/777-7701; Hal Schell's Delta Map and Guide, $2.99 at stores, $3.75 by mail at P.O. Box 9140, Stockton, CA 95208; California Delta Chamber & Visitor Bureau, 209/367-9840, website: www.californiadelta.org.

Boat and houseboat rentals: Waterflies (will deliver), 916/777-6431; Herman & Helen's, Stockton, 209/951-4634; Lundborg Landing, Bethel Island, 925/684-9351, website: www.lundborglanding.com. Kayak rentals: Big River Kayaks, Bethel Island, 925/684-3095.

Sailing instruction: Martin's Sailing School & Club, 916/369-7700, website: www.lovetosail.com.

Fishing guides: Fish Hooker Charters, 916/777-6498.

Boat charters: Delta Expeditions, Rio Vista, 916/600-2420.

5 LAKE MERCED

Rating: 6

in San Francisco

Map 7.3, page 254

There are actually three lakes here: Lake Merced North (105 acres), Lake Merced South (203 acres), and the Merced Impound (17 acres, but typically too low on water for public use).

Lake Merced South is more of a recreation lake for rowers, scullers, and sailboaters. It is larger than most newcomers expect, with a shore almost completely enclosed by tules. Access is restricted to a boat dock behind the restaurant for hand-launched boats only.

Getting afternoon winds off the nearby coast, the South Lake can be good for small sailboats and for novice sailboarders. It is rarely crowded (most of the people fishing are at the North Lake) and is a good place to practice before you head out to a more challenging environment. Beginning classes for sailboarding are even taught here. A small hoist is provided for boats, ideally small sailboats, but the hoist hasn't worked for years, and even if it did, would deposit you amid tules nowadays, not in the lake.

Lake Merced North is surrounded by tules for the most part, except for a beach area for shore fishing on the west shore, and along the Harding Park Golf Course on the south shore. The North Lake has a small paved boat ramp and dock. Rowboats and are docked here, and can be rented at the Merced Boathouse.

If you try sitting in a boat along Lake Merced's tule-lined shore, San Francisco and her 700,000 residents will seem a world apart.

Because the lake is right on the coast, fog is sometimes a problem and temperatures are often cool, even in summer. When the Central Valley is baking in the 100s day after day, Merced can be shrouded in mist from a heavy fog.

The San Francisco Recreation and Parks Department has allowed much of this recreation facility to fall into disrepair. In many ways, the operation is a shipwreck, and the money spent so far by the City of San Francisco at the lake has not addressed any of the defining issues: water levels to maintain a healthy aquatic environment, rampant tule growth that blocks shore access, and maintenance of bathrooms, piers, hoists, and docks.

Access: There is a small paved ramp and dock at the North Lake. A dock for hand-launched boats is available at the South Lake.

Facilities, fees: Rowboats are available for rent at the North Lake. Restrooms, boat launch, dock, restaurant, bar, and fishing pier are available. Fees are charged for fishing and boat launching.

Water sports, restrictions: Gas-powered motors are not permitted on the lake. Swimming and water/body contact are prohibited. Sailing and sailboarding are allowed (sailboarders must wear a wet suit).

Directions: From San Francisco: Take Geary Boulevard west until it ends at the ocean and the Cliff House Restaurant and feeds onto the Great Highway. Bear left on the Great Highway and drive four miles to Lake Merced Boulevard. Turn left and drive 100 yards to the lake entrance on the right.

From Highway 280 in Daly City: Take Highway 280 to the exit for John Daly Boulevard West. Take that exit and drive west to Skyline

Boulevard. Turn right at Skyline Boulevard and drive to Lake Merced Boulevard. Turn right and drive 100 yards to the lake entrance on the right.

From the Peninsula: Take Highway 280 to the exit for Highway 1 in San Bruno. Take that exit and drive west for one mile to Highway 35. Turn right (north) on Highway 35 (becomes Great Highway) and drive five miles to Lake Merced Boulevard. Turn right and drive 100 yards to the lake entrance on the right.

Contact: Lake Merced Boathouse, 415/681-2727; San Francisco Recreation & Parks Department, 415/831-2770; Property Management Unit, 415/831-2773; general information website: www.lakemerced.org.

6 LAKE TEMESCAL

Rating: 5

in the Oakland hills

Map 7.3, page 254

Little Lake Temescal, encompassing only 10 surface acres, is set in the Oakland hills and provides a good retreat for shore fishing and swimming. There is a nice sandy beach and a picnic area for day use.

The swimming area is open spring through fall, with lifeguards on duty during posted periods. A snack stand is nearby, and many facilities are wheelchair-accessible. There are picnic areas at both ends of the lake adjacent to eight acres of lawn. Boats are not permitted on the lake

The lake is used primarily for trout fishing from winter through spring, when the water is cool enough for trout stocks. From May through the summer, it becomes the site of picnics and swimming parties.

Access: Boating is not permitted on the lake.

Facilities, fees: Picnic areas, restrooms, and a snack bar are provided. Most facilities are wheelchair-accessible. Fees are charged for parking and swimming.

Water sports, restrictions: There is a sandy swimming beach. No boating.

Directions: Take Highway 24 to the exit for Broadway. Take that exit and bear left through the intersection, continuing on Broadway (toward Highway 13 southbound). Within .5 mile, look for the signed entrance to the Temescal Regional Recreation Area on the right. Turn right and drive to the park.

Contact: Park headquarters, 510/652-1155; East Bay Regional Parks District, 510/562-7275, website: www.ebparks.org/parks/temescal.htm; group picnic reservations, 510/636-1684.

7 AQUATIC PARK

Rating: 6

near I-80 in Berkeley

Map 7.3, page 254

Many drivers on I-80 spot Aquatic Park off to the east, adjacent to the highway. Most find it curious, and then never give it another thought. Some local workers park here and take their lunch breaks. What you can discover is that Aquatic Park provides a wide range of recreational opportunities, and is a great spot for boating. The park encompasses about 67 acres of water and 32 acres of land.

The public is permitted to use kayaks, canoes, prams, and similar car-top boats and paddle around and enjoy the place, but not the boat ramp—and not powerboats. But hey, you ask, what about the water-skiers and the spectacular jumps they make from ski jump platforms? "If they can do it, why not me?"

The answer is that in order to launch a powerboat and ski at Aquatic Park, you must be a member of the Aquatic Park Water Ski Club. No public access for water-skiing is permitted. Got it? You must be a club member.

Aquatic Park is also a popular destination for competition rowers. The most common are women's rowers from Mills College, who often arrive at daybreak before classes to work out.

There is also a new children's play area called Dream Land, and the wetlands here provide habitat for a wide range of waterfowl and other birds. It is easy to reach for locals in Berkeley, but newcomers have a unique ability of getting lost in the attempt and typically can't find the entrance—even though it can be seen right from the highway.

Access: A boat launch area for hand-launched boats is available.

Facilities, fees: Picnic areas are available. An exercise course and Frisbee golf are available. Access is free.

Water sports, restrictions: Rowboats, kayaks, canoes, and inflatables are permitted. No motors permitted by public. No fishing. Water-skiing and powerboats are permitted only among members of the Aquatic Park Water Ski Club.

Directions: Take I-80 to Berkeley and the exit for University Avenue east. Take that exit and drive to the Second Street off ramp. Take that exit and turn right on Second Street and drive to Addison Street. Turn right on Addison Street and drive a few blocks to the parking area for Aquatic Park.

Contact: Berkeley Parks, Recreation and Waterfront Parks Division, 510/981-5150; Shorebird Nature Center at Berkeley Marina, 510/644-8623; City of Berkeley Parks Administration, 510/981-6700 or 510/644-6530, website: www.ci.berkeley.ca.us; Berkeley Marina Sports Center, 510/849-2727.

8 SAN PABLO RESERVOIR

Rating: 10

near Orinda

Map 7.3, page 254

Daybreak at San Pablo Reservoir highlights one of the prettiest boating scenes in the Bay Area, distinguished by blues and greens, placid water, and boats leaving fresh, white trails. San Pablo is the Bay Area's number one lake, providing a unique combination of beauty, good boating, and good fishing.

The lake is big for one so close to so many people—860 acres. Two major lake arms are featured. The main arm extends south into a waterfowl management area with a 5-mph speed limit, while the Scow Canyon Arm, located across the reservoir from the San Pablo Recreation Area, extends east into the remote foothills of Contra Costa County.

All in all, this is a great destination for boating, big enough to accommodate sizable fiberglass boats, yet small enough to provide intimate settings for tiny aluminum boats and even canoes. The lake supplies drinking water to the Bay Area, so body contact with the water is forbidden; hence, swimming, wading, waterskiing, personal watercraft, and inner tubing are strictly prohibited.

The excellent marina supplies a variety of boat rentals, as well as good over-the-phone reports on wind and fishing conditions. One drawback is that the boat ramp is located some distance from the marina and the recreation area—an odd setup.

Fishing is the main attraction at San Pablo Reservoir, which gets the highest trout stocks of any lake in California. But good conditions for all styles of boating make this lake tops in the Bay Area.

More trout stocks are made here than at any other lake in California, some 7,000 to 10,000 per week in season. The Department of Fish and Game sends 64,000 10- to 12-inch rainbow trout, but the concessionaire outdoes them with 140,000 measuring 12-plus inches. The trout average a foot, with an ample dose of 3- to 5-pounders and a few every year in the 10-pound class.

Lake records: rainbow trout: 21 pounds, 12.8 ounces, by Steve Dwy of San Pablo; largemouth bass: 18 pounds, 11 ounces, by Victor Barfield of Daly City; catfish: 31 pounds, 4.8 ounces, by Dave Edwards of Vallejo; sturgeon: 66 pounds, by Ernesto Nicdao of San Pablo; redear sunfish: three pounds, 6.4 ounces, by Bob Laughlin of San Pablo; crappie: three pounds, 3.2 ounces, by Calvin Warren of Hayward.

Access: A multilane paved launch ramp is located on the east side of the reservoir.

Facilities, fees: Picnic areas, playground, small marina, multilane paved launch ramp, docks, and a snack bar/fishing shop are available. Fishing boats and rowboats can be rented. Fees are charged for parking per vehicle, fishing per person, and boat launching.

Water sports, restrictions: Only four-cycle motors and electric trolling motors are permitted; no two-cycle engines. There is a 5-mph speed limit along the shoreline and in the coves, and a 25-mph limit on the main lake body. Personal watercraft, sailboarding, and swimming are not allowed.

Directions: From the north, take I-80 and exit on San Pablo Dam Road. Turn south (toward Orinda) on San Pablo Dam Road and drive six miles to the main lake entrance on the left. If you have a boat to launch, continue to the second entrance on the left.

From San Jose, take I-680 to Highway 24. Bear west on Highway 24 and drive to Orinda and the exit for Camino Pablo Road. Take Camino Pablo Road north and drive to the lake on the right. The first entrance leads to the boat ramp; the second is the main entrance.

Contact: San Pablo Reservoir, 510/223-1661; fishing report, 925/248-3474; group picnic reservations, 510/223-1661. General information websites: www.ci.san-pablo.ca.us, www.norcalfishing.com/sanpablo.html.

9 LAKE ANZA

Rating: 4

in Berkeley in Tilden Regional Park

Map 7.3, page 254

Don't expect this lake to set your heart a-pumping. It is small, just 11 acres, and the main attraction is the surrounding parkland.

Swimming is permitted at Lake Anza and a sandy beach is available. No boating at Lake Anza. Although Lake Anza does provide an opportunity to take a dunk and swim around a bit, the warm water can turn a bit soupy in mid- to late summer. The fishing isn't all that great either. The surrounding Tilden Regional Park gets quite a lot of use, but few park visitors make a point of visiting Lake Anza.

This is rather a place for a family picnic. Summer evenings and weekend afternoons are popular. Picnic areas are available and can be reserved by groups. For children, the park has pony and carousel rides, and a steam train.

Access: Boating is not permitted on the lake.

Facilities, fees: Picnic areas and restrooms are provided. The facilities are wheelchair-accessible. Fees are charged for swimming and parking.

Water sports, restrictions: There is a sandy swimming beach. Boating is not permitted on the lake.

Directions: Take Highway 24 to just east of the Caldecott Tunnel to the exit for Fish Ranch Road. Take that exit and drive west to Grizzly Peak Boulevard. Turn right, drive up the hill, and turn right on South Park Drive. Drive one mile to Wildcat Canyon Road. Turn left and drive to Central Park Drive. Turn right on Central Park Drive and drive to the entrance to Lake Anza (just before the merry-go-round). Turn right and drive to the right.

Alternate Route: In winter, South Park Drive is closed due to newt migrations. Instead: Take Highway 24 to Orinda and the exit for Camino Pablo. Take that exit and drive north on Camino Pablo for about two miles to Wildcat Canyon Road. Turn left on Wildcat Canyon Road and drive to Central Park Drive; continue as above.

Contact: Tilden Nature Area, 510/525-2233; East Bay Regional Parks District, 510/562-7275, website: www.ebparks.org/parks; group picnic reservations, 510/636-1684; group and equestrian camping information, 510/562-2267.

10 LAKE MERRITT

Rating: 6

in Oakland

Map 7.3, page 254

This is one of the few lakes in the area where boat rentals are available. Lake Merritt has a boat center where you can pick up a canoe, pedal boat, or little sailboat, all ideal for spending a few hours on these waters.

This is an excellent place for beginners to learn how to sail, with winds predictable and steady on spring and summer afternoons, not wild and erratic.

You can also learn how to sailboard here. This is the perfect lake for novices; lessons are available, the water is calm, and the wind is just strong enough most of the time to give you a thrill. You are advised to wear a wet suit. Swimming is prohibited.

This is one of Oakland's prettiest settings and has become a very popular spot for jogging and picnicking.

A small gateway separates Lake Merritt from San Francisco Bay, and though heavy rains turn the lake to fresh water in the winter, it becomes brackish and then salty by summer and fall. That means few fish, because the changing salinity makes the water uninhabitable for freshwater species.

Access: A launch ramp is located on the northeast side of the lake.

Facilities, fees: Restrooms are provided. A boat ramp is available. There are rentals for rowboats, pedal boats, canoes, and sailboats. Boat tours are available on weekends. Sailing lessons are available. There is a fee for boat launching, and an entrance fee is charged on weekends.

Water sports, restrictions: Motors are not permitted on the lake. Sailboarding is allowed, but you are advised to wear a wet suit. Swimming is prohibited.

Directions: Take I-880 into Oakland to Oak Street. Take Oak Street exit and drive north on Oak Street for about seven blocks (Oak becomes Lakeside Drive) to Bellevue Avenue. Turn right on Bellevue and drive into Lakeside Park. Or, take I-580 to Oakland and the exit for Grand Avenue. Take that exit and drive west on Grand Avenue to Bellevue Avenue. Turn left on Bellevue and drive into Lakeside Park.

Contact: Lake Merritt Marina, 510/238-2196.

11 LAFAYETTE RESERVOIR

Rating: 7

near Walnut Creek

Map 7.3, page 254

This 115-acre lake is very pretty, truly a little paradise in the East Bay hills. The surrounding oak-covered hills create a pleasant, quiet setting.

The reservoir is used only for fishing, canoeing, and sailing, and with access restricted to boats that can be hand launched, you are assured peace and lots of space on the water. Gas motors are not permitted, but electric motors are okay, which keeps things quiet. Talk about the ideal spot for canoeing.

There are 135 picnic tables with views of the lake, most located near the dam. Some are accessible only by boat or on foot.

Peak use is in late winter and spring, when the weather begins to warm yet the water temperature is still cool, making for good trout fishing. A small boathouse and a dock are available. Because of its proximity to San Pablo Reservoir, anglers often overlook Lafayette Reservoir. They shouldn't.

The lake was completed in 1933 and provides a back-up water supply for East Bay Municipal Utility District (EBMUD) customers. It was opened to public recreation in 1966.

Access: A primitive launching area (hand launching only) is provided.

Facilities, fees: Rowboats, canoes, kayaks, and sailboats can be hand launched. Rowboats and pedal boats are available for rent. Picnic areas, restrooms with flush toilets, and hiking and bicycling trails are provided. A sailing dock and pedal boat and rowboat rentals are available. A fee is charged for day use.

Water sports, restrictions: Gasoline motors are not permitted on the lake. Swimming, sailboarding, and water/body contact are prohibited.

Directions: Take Highway 24 to Walnut Creek and the exit for Acalanes. Take that exit, which feeds you onto Mount Diablo Boulevard. Drive about a mile on Mount Diablo Boulevard to the signed park entrance located on the right.

Contact: Lafayette Reservoir, 925/284-9669, website: www.lafayettechamber.org; group picnic reservations, 925/284-9669.

12 LAKE CHABOT

Rating: 7

near Castro Valley

Map 7.3, page 254

If you want the world to look like a great place, turn off the TV and take a seat in a canoe or kayak at Lake Chabot. With each paddle stroke comes a sensation of quiet freedom, your boat gliding through peaceful waters.

Though Lake Chabot has many attractions, most special is this opportunity to rent a canoe or kayak and instantly transform your outlook.

Chabot is very pretty in the spring, with emerald water set against green foothills sprinkled with wild radish, blue-eyed grass, and a few golden poppies. The lake covers 315 acres, well hidden in the foothills near San Leandro, featuring a small island and many secluded coves.

Recreation highlights are boat rentals of several styles, improving fishing for trout and bass, and an ambitious bike ride that circles the lake.

If you think you need a change of scenery, my suggestion is to start by changing your perspective by getting yourself in a boat, any boat. The Chabot Marina rents canoes, kayaks, rowboats, a rowboat with an electric motor, and pedal boats. If you own your own canoe, kayak, or float tube, you can hand-launch it. A walk of about 50 yards is required. No inflatable rafts are permitted.

The lake does not have a public boat ramp, and no gas motors are permitted. This provides guaranteed tranquility for hand-powered boaters, often paddling along the shore, venturing into hidden coves, watching the tiny whirlpools that trail from each stroke of the paddle.

A trip in a canoe is also a great first date. You will discover very quickly any long-term prospects with a potential partner. You either work together in a canoe, or you don't work.

Lake Chabot is also often good for fishing. In late winter and spring, it is stocked every Thursday with rainbow trout, providing decent prospects for shoreline baitdunkers, lately best from Indian Cove to Raccoon Point.

The lake is the centerpiece of a 5,000-acre regional park that includes 31 miles of hiking trails, horseback riding rentals, and a campground.

Access: Canoes and kayaks can be hand launched. There is no boat ramp.

Facilities, fees: A small marina, dock, small fishing shop, restrooms with flush toilets and snack bar are available. Rowboats, boats with electric motors, canoes, kayaks, and pedal boats are available for rent. A campground is nearby (but requires separate access). Fees are charged for day use, boat launching, and fishing.

Water sports, restrictions: Electric motors are permitted. No gas motors. Swimming, sailboarding, and all other water/body-contact activities are strictly prohibited.

Directions: From Highway 580 Eastbound, take 580 to San Leandro and the exit for Fairmont Drive. Take that exit and go east for 1.5 miles (Fairmont Drive becomes Lake Chabot Road) and continue to parking area on the left.

From Highway 580 Westbound, take 580 to Castro Valley and the exit for Strobridge. Take that exit and turn right on Strobridge and go a short distance to Castro Valley Boulevard. Turn right and go to Lake Chabot Road. Turn left and go two miles to the marina entrance on the right.

Contact: Chabot Marina, 510/582-2198; Chabot Regional Park, 510/639-4751; website: www.ebparks.org/parks/anchabot.htm; recorded fishing report, 925/248-3474, then press 3; free brochure, East Bay Regional Park District, 510/544-2200—ask for Lake Chabot. General information website: www.norcalfishing.com (click on Lake Chabot).

13 SHORELINE REGIONAL PARK

Rating: 6

Baylands near Mountain View

Map 7.3, page 254

The centerpiece is a 50-acre lake for small boats, sailboats, dinghies, and sailboarding. Shoreline Regional Park is an ideal family destination that is taken advantage of by locals. The park offers a wide variety of activities, including pleasant walks and bike rides on wide, crushed-gravel byways. There is also a small lake (known as Shoreline Sailing Lake) that makes an excellent spot for sailboarding and sailing because of steady winds, as well as many good kite-flying areas on tiny hills, and a golf course.

The park covers 660 acres and is adjacent to additional wetlands and marshlands. Seven miles of trails (primarily service roads) provide access to the best of it. The wetlands include two tidal marshes, two sloughs, a seasonal marsh and storm retention basin, two creeks, and five irrigation reservoirs on the golf course.

This provides habitat for many waterfowl and marsh birds, including pelicans, egrets, great blue herons, coots, ducks, Canada geese, and sandpipers. Jackrabbits and ground squirrels are also common. This park is quite popular with bird-watchers, who can spot everything from egrets to LBJs (Little Brown Jobs). It can be common to see Canada geese on the lawn next to the lake, adjacent to the restaurant.

A concession stand near the lake gets a lot of use from the corn dog-and-Coke crowd, which kind of puts everything in perspective.

Access: A small boat ramp and marina are available next to the restaurant.

Facilities, fees: Restrooms, restaurant, concession stand, and picnic sites are available. Pedalboats, rowboats, canoes, kayaks, sailboards, and sailboats can be rented. Instruction available for sailing and sailboarding. Summer youth camps are held. A fee is charged for day use.

Water sports, restrictions: Canoes, kayaks, inflatables, small sailboats, and sailboarding are permitted. No motors. No swimming or wading. No pets. No camping. Fishing is permitted in designated areas.

Directions: Take U.S. 101 to Mountain View and the exit for Shoreline Boulevard east. Take that exit and drive east (past the Shoreline Amphitheater) to the park entrance station.

Contact: Shoreline Regional Park, 650/903-6392, website: www.ci.mtnview.ca.us.

14 STEVENS CREEK RESERVOIR

⛴ ✗ ⚓ ☞

Rating: 6

near Cupertino

Map 7.3, page 254

When full, Stevens Creek is quite pretty, covering 95 acres. It can fill quickly during a series of heavy rains. In other years, though, the water district largely drains the lake and the place just about dries up by the end of summer.

While sailboarding is permitted, conditions are marginal at best. Only rarely are there sufficient winds to power a sailboard. Most visitors come here to picnic and look at the lake, not to boat on it.

Hit it right and Stevens Creek Reservoir can seem one of the prettiest places in Santa Clara County. The best time is generally in the spring, when the hills are lush and green, the lake is full, and at the lake's headwaters, the creek is flowing through a wooded riparian landscape.

That is when this lake is great for kayaking, canoeing, and other hand-powered boating activities (no motors permitted); when there's a chance for trout fishing (stocked in late winter and early spring); and the hiking, picnicking, and wildlife viewing is exceptional.

The lake is the centerpiece for about 2,000 acres of parkland, with a unit circling the lake, and another set along the creek just above the head of the lake. Kayak rentals (and lessons) are available in season by arrangement. Bird watching is often exceptional. The trail system

here is linked to an adjacent open space preserve. Mountain biking is popular here.

The picnic sites here are a big plus. Six picnic areas are shaded and set about the park. Three others are located along Stevens Creek.

Access: A paved boat ramp is located on the lake's northwest side.

Facilities, fees: Restrooms, picnic areas, and hiking and riding trails are available. Fees are charged for day use and boat launching.

Water sports, restrictions: Electric motors are permitted on the lake, but gas-powered motors are not. Sailboarding is permitted. Float tubes are permitted but fishermen must wear neoprene. Swimming is not allowed.

Directions: Take Highway 280 to the exit for Foothill Boulevard. Take that exit and drive south for four miles on Foothill Boulevard, (which becomes Stevens Canyon Road) and continue to the reservoir.

Contact: Stevens Creek County Park, 408/867-3654; Santa Clara County Parks and Recreation, 408/355-2200, picnic reservations, 408/355-2201, website: www.parkhere.org (click on Find a Park); Midpeninsula Regional Open Space District, 650/691-1200.

15 LOCH LOMOND RESERVOIR

⛴ ✗ ☞

Rating: 8

near Ben Lomond in the Santa Cruz Mountains

Map 7.3, page 254

Just add water and this is one of the prettiest places in the greater Bay Area.

The lake, which was created when Newell Creek was dammed, is nestled in a long, narrow canyon in the Santa Cruz Mountains. It is a beautiful spot, complete with an island, and well forested, with redwoods and firs growing right down to the shoreline.

Although the boat ramp is small, it is big enough to handle similarly small aluminum boats with electric motors, rowboats, and canoes. Boat rentals are available at the adjacent dock.

Unfortunately, swimming, wading, sailboarding, and other water-contact sports are not allowed. Also note that the lake is closed to the public every year from fall through spring.

While most visitors are here for the trout fishing, others do come to row a boat or paddle a canoe for fun. A boat-in picnic site, complete with barbecue, is provided on the island. Imagine that, a boat-in picnic site on an island to call your own.

Loch Lomond is one of the best bass lakes in the Bay Area's nine counties, with good numbers of two- and three-pound bass, best during an early-morning bite in spring for those using white spinnerbaits and Senkos. The trout fishing is also good, with holdovers from each year's plants in the 14 to 18-inch class joining more recent 11-inch planters from the Department of Fish and Game. In addition, the lake has great bluegill fishing on summer evenings, especially flyfishing with woolly worms, or baitdunking a worm under a bobber in sheltered, warm coves.

The surrounding parkland features an excellent hike that parallels the south shore of the lake, then climbs to the small mountain overlooking the water for an incredible view. You gaze down, watch the boats purring around, and realize this is one of the greatest day-trip destinations in the Bay Area.

Access: A paved boat ramp is located on the reservoir's west side.

Facilities, fees: Restrooms, picnic areas, snack bar, and tackle shop are provided. Rowboats and fishing boats with electric motors are available for rent. The park is open from sunrise to sunset seven days a week during open season; the lake is closed from September 15 through February. Fees are charged for day use and boat launching.

Water sports, restrictions: Rowboats, canoes, and kayaks are permitted. Electric motors are permitted. No gas motors. No sailboats or sailboarding. Swimming is not allowed.

Directions: Take Highway 17 south to Scotts Valley and the Mount Hermon Road exit. Take that exit and drive west for 3.5 miles to Graham Hill Road. Turn left and head south for .5 mile to East Zayante Road. Turn left at East Zayante Road and drive 1.5 miles to West Drive. Turn left and drive .75 mile to Sequoia Drive. Turn right at Sequoia Drive and continue to the park entrance.

From Santa Cruz, take Highway 1 to Highway 9. Turn north on Highway 9 and drive to Felton and Graham Hill Road. Turn right and drive (across the railroad tracks) to East Zayante Road. Turn right and drive 2.5 miles to Lompico Road. Turn left and drive 1.5 miles to West Drive. Turn left and drive .75 mile to Sequoia Drive. Turn right and continue to the park entrance. This route is well-signed.

Contact: Loch Lomond Reservoir, 831/420-5320 or 831/335-7424. General information websites: www.ci.santa-cruz.ca.us, www.scc-cvc.org/index.html, www.hwy9.com/site/info/center.html.

16 CONTRA LOMA RESERVOIR

Rating: 7

near Antioch

Map 7.4, page 255

Contra Loma Reservoir is the first stop for water being shipped out of the Delta and bound for points south. It covers 70 acres, is easily accessible to residents of Antioch and nearby towns, and provides a good place for fishing, swimming, and boating. The surrounding parkland is crisscrossed with hiking and horseback riding trails.

One thing to remember is that it gets hot here in the summer, and afternoon winds are common. This makes it ideal for sailboarding and sailing. Both sports are popular here, and the conditions are particularly attractive to beginning sailboarders.

Swimming prospects are also good, with a large beach and play area available for youngsters. Boating rules (no gas-powered motors and no boats more than 17 feet long) ensure that the reservoir remains quiet and peaceful.

Access: There is a paved boat launch.

Facilities, fees: Restrooms with flush toilets, changing rooms, refreshment stand, boat launch, fishing pier, picnic areas, and a snack bar are available. Kayak rentals and sailboarding lessons are available in the summer months. A swimming lagoon with a sandy beach and lifeguard in summer is available. The facilities are wheelchair-accessible. A fee is charged for parking.

Water sports, restrictions: Boats no longer than 17 feet with electric motors are permitted. Gas motors are prohibited. There's a sandy beach suitable for swimming and sailboarding. All sailboarders must shower a minimum of two minutes prior to entering the reservoir and wear at least a short wetsuit; showers are located outside the restrooms and next to the beach used by sailboarders. Fishermen using float tubes must wear waders or other wetsuit material to eliminate body contact with the water in the reservoir. Kayakers with self-bailing kayaks must shower prior to entering the reservoir and wear at least a short wet suit. Dry-type kayaks are permissible, but no rollovers or other activities that cause body contact with the water are permitted.

Directions: Take Highway 4 to Antioch and Contra Loma Boulevard. Turn south on Contra Loma Boulevard and drive to the park entrance.

Contact: Park headquarters, 925/757-9606; East Bay Regional Parks District, 510/562-7275, website: www.ebparks.org/parks; sailboarding lessons, 925/778-6350; recorded fishing information, 510/562-7275.

17 LOS VAQUEROS RESERVOIR

Rating: 7

near Brentwood

Map 7.4, page 255

If you haven't seen Los Vaqueros Reservoir and its surrounding watershed parkland, waiting for you is a sight that will pop your eyes out.

While there have been many questions how Los Vaqueros Reservoir would fit into the Bay Area as a recreation getaway for fishing, boating, biking, and hiking, the answers are in, and most of them are good: The Bay Area's newest lake and parkland has emerged as one of the best of the region's 150 significant parklands.

When you clear the rise and Los Vaqueros first comes into view, you will likely be stunned at the lake's size and beauty. It covers 1,500 acres—twice the size of San Pablo Reservoir near El Sobrante, long the most notable of the Bay Area's 45 lakes. It is also surrounded by 18,500 acres of watershed wildlands, in addition to two regional parks (Morgan Territory and Round Valley), creating roughly 225 square miles of greenbelt.

The lake is set in rolling foothills in the little-known terrain of remote Contra Costa County, well southeast of Mount Diablo, roughly between Livermore to the south and Brentwood to the north.

A marina, boat rentals, and fish plants have jump-started the program. A big focus at the reservoir is the marina at the south end, where there are electric powered boats for rent and two fishing piers.

One big-time downer is that no private boats and no gas engines, not even the clean-burning four-cycle outboards, are permitted on the lake. That creates a safety issue, because the wind can really howl through in May, June, and July. Not having a large enough boat powered by engine could compromise your safety if you got caught in a wind out here.

The south gate (off Vasco Road out of Livermore) is better for hikers and fishermen, with access to both the marina and the Los Vaqueros Trail, which extends about halfway around the lake with sweeping views of the watershed. The watershed covers 18,500 acres and has 55 miles of hiking trails, including 12.5 miles accessible for mountain bikers and equestrians. Los Vaqueros has the chance of providing year-round fisheries, for trout in the cool months, for bass in the summer and fall. Its location and warm weather virtually assures a quality warmwater fishery for bass, bluegill, crappie and catfish, a much-needed opportunity in a region where most lakes are prisoner of trout plants.

So far, the best fishing has been for trout, the result of a high population of minnows and plankton in the lake, 10 times the forage in San Pablo, according to water district scientists. Because of that, many are predicting that the lake will eventually provide the best fishery in the Bay Area for bass and catfish.

Access: There is no boat ramp.

Facilities, fees: Restrooms, boat rentals, small marina, picnic areas, and an interpretive center are available. Fees are charged for day use, fishing, and hiking. It costs $6 to operate the automated entry gate; exact bills required.

Water sports, restrictions: Rental rowboats and boats with electric motors are available at a small marina. No privately owned boats or gas motors are permitted. No swimming or body contact with the water is permitted.

Directions: Take Highway 580 to Livermore and the exit for Vasco Road. Turn north on Vasco Road and drive five miles to Los Vaqueros Road. Turn north and drive to the South Gate entry station. Continue to the marina.

Contact: Los Vaqueros Marina, 925/371-2628; Contra Costa Water District, information hotline at 925/688-8225, website: www.ccwater.com (click on Los Vaqueros).

18 BETHANY RESERVOIR

Rating: 6

near Livermore in Bethany Reservoir State Recreation Area

Map 7.4, page 255

Bethany Reservoir State Recreation Area is best known as the northern hub for the California Aqueduct Bike Path, on which you can ride for hundreds of miles to points south. This reservoir is part of a day-use recreation area, complete with picnic areas, a good boat ramp, and great sailboarding conditions.

Winds can really kick up here in the afternoon, and while the water is a bit choppy, expert sailboarders are able to catch some great rides. Along with fishing, sailboarding is the most popular activity here.

Bethany Reservoir covers 162 acres and, like its cousin to the north, Contra Loma Reservoir, it receives its water via the California Aqueduct. Though there are no restrictions on the size of boats allowed on the lake, a 5-mph speed limit helps keep things quiet.

Fish species in the lake feature rainbow trout, largemouth bass, striped bass, sturgeon, catfish, and bluegill.

Access: A two-lane paved launch ramp is available on the north shore, near a picnic area.

Facilities, fees: Boat mooring, picnic areas, drinking water, and portable toilets are available. Fees are charged for day use and boat launching.

Water sports, restrictions: Powerboats, canoes, kayaks, inflatables, sailing, and sailboarding are permited. A 5-mph speed limit is strictly enforced. No personal watercraft. Swimming is allowed. Open sunrise to sunset.

Directions: Take I-580 to the exit for Grant Line (east of Livermore). Take that exit to Altamont Pass Road. Turn right and drive to Kelso-Christiansen Road. Turn left and drive to the park entrance.

Contact: California State Parks, Four Rivers District, 209/874-2056; Caswell State Park 209/599-3810.

19 SHADOW CLIFFS LAKE

Rating: 7

in Pleasanton

Map 7.4, page 255

Shadow Cliffs is proof that good ideas do work. Once a good-sized water hole for a former rock quarry, this has since been converted into a lake that offers fishing and boating opportunities.

Warm summer temperatures and clear water make for good swimming. A four-flume water slide is available in summer for children. The water slide is open on weekends in the spring and fall, and daily during the hot summer months. Riders must be at least 42 inches tall.

While a steep sloping bank borders much of the lake, the beach area offers a gentle grade and warm water. Afternoon winds are fair for sailboarding, making Shadow Cliffs an ideal place for beginners to practice the sport.

The lake is stocked with trout when the water is cool, from fall through spring, then with catfish in the summer. Most of the boaters you'll see are in hot pursuit of those species.

A key is that the water is high quality and clear, even during the winter. It is not affected by storm runoff, as are most of the 45 lakes with public access in the Bay Area, so it doesn't get muddy.

An outstanding water sports and boating program has been established.

This place started off as nothing but an old gravel quarry with a squarish water hole. When it was donated to the East Bay Regional Park District, its value was assessed at only $250,000.

As a park, it is nearly priceless.

Access: There is a paved launch ramp.

Facilities, fees: Picnic areas, restrooms with flush toilets, docks, small marina, and a snack bar are provided. Picnic areas are available and can be reserved by groups. There is a swimming beach with changing area and refreshment stand, with lifeguards on duty in summer months. A water slide is available for children. Sailboarding lessons and rentals are available. Fees are charged for parking, boat launching, and fishing.

Water sports, restrictions: Boats no longer than 17 feet with electric motors are permitted. Gas motors are prohibited. There's a sandy beach suitable for swimming and sailboarding. Rowboat, canoe, and pedal boat rentals are available. Sailing, sailboarding, and swimming are permitted.

Directions: Take I-580 to Pleasanton and the exit for Santa Rita Road South. Take that exit and drive south for two miles to Valley

Avenue. Turn left on Valley Avenue and drive to Stanley Boulevard. Turn left and drive to the park entrance.

Contact: Park headquarters, 925/846-3000; East Bay Regional Parks District, 510/562-7275, website: www.ebparks.org/parks/shadow.htm; group picnic reservations, 510/636-1684.

20 LAKE ELIZABETH

Rating: 6

in Fremont

Map 7.4, page 255

During the hot summer in the East Bay flats, Lake Elizabeth and the surrounding parkland provide a relatively cool retreat. The lake covers 82 acres amid Central Park's 440 acres.

Strong afternoon winds create excellent sailing conditions. Sailboats are available for rent on the weekend, but you must have your sailing license with you to rent one. A paved launch ramp is located on the lake's west side. Motors are not permitted on the lake. Swimming, sailboarding, and water/body contact are prohibited.

Canoes, pedal boats, and kayaks can also be rented on weekends.

Although your body is not allowed to come into contact with the water at the lake, an adjacent lagoon provides a cool place to take a dip in the summer and is really one of the best swimming spots in the Bay Area. The park offers full recreation facilities, including a jogging/biking trail, baseball fields, tennis courts, grassy lawns, and picnic areas. Use is heavy in summer; during the remainder of the year you'll encounter only a few picnickers and anglers.

The park is bordered by Paseo Padre Parkway, Stevenson Boulevard, and the Union Pacific Railroad.

Access: A paved launch ramp is located on the lake's west side.

Facilities, fees: Picnic areas, snack bars, restrooms, and athletic facilities are provided.

Canoes, pedal boats, kayaks, and sailboats can be rented on weekends. Access is free. There is a fee for boat launching.

Water sports, restrictions: Motors are not permitted on the lake. Swimming, sailboarding, and water/body contact are prohibited, but in the summer months an adjacent swimming lagoon is available.

Directions: Take I-880 to Fremont and the exit for Stevenson Boulevard. Take that exit and drive east for two miles to Paseo Padre Parkway. Turn right on Paseo Padre Parkway and drive about one block to Sailway Drive. Turn left on Sailway Drive and drive a short distance to Central Park.

Contact: City of Fremont, Recreation services at Lake Elizabeth Boathouse, 510/791-4340, website: www.ci.fremont.ca.us/recreation; group picnic reservations, 510/791-4341.

21 DEL VALLE RESERVOIR

Rating: 7

southeast of Livermore in Lake Del Valle State Recreation Area

Map 7.4, page 255

Here is one of the Bay Area's top adventure-lands for fishing, camping, boating, and hiking.

Del Valle Reservoir is set in a long, deep canyon in remote southern Alameda County, about 10 miles south of Livermore. For newcomers, the lake is a shock, covering 750 surface acres with 16 miles of shoreline, ideal for low-speed boating and fishing. This is one of the few lakes in the Bay Area that provides camping, rental boats, and a good ramp for powerboats.

In the summer the weather gets very hot around here and hordes of sunbathers, swimmers, and boaters enjoy the lake. A 10-mph speed limit keeps it tranquil. Despite the speed restriction, almost everybody is having fun; after all, it beats working, and the big lake and adjoining park provide a great place for a respite from the rat race.

Swimming and water sports are permitted year-round, but the water gets cold in the winter and spring, and the water level is dropped in the fall as well. The prime time for swimming is from May to September, when lifeguards are posted at the beaches.

The wind is strong on spring and summer afternoons, making sailboarding here very popular. However, experts may find the speed limit confining.

The park offers boat tours of the natural history and lake ecology of the area.

One great thing about Del Valle is that the trout fishing is often excellent in the late winter and spring. Not only are the catch rates high, but there's a sprinkling of huge rainbow trout in the 8- to 12-pound class, sometimes bigger. In addition, there are also some large striped bass swimming around, providing a wild card challenge for the ambitious few. The lake is stocked with trout and catfish and other species including large- and smallmouth bass and panfish.

Access: A multilane paved boat ramp is available at the end of the entrance road.

Facilities, fees: Fishing boats, rowboats, pontoon boats, pedal boats, and canoes are available for rent at a small marina. Sailboards can be rented at the swimming beach. A campground, drinking water, restrooms with flush toilets and showers, picnic areas, swimming beaches, and RV dump station are available. Fees are charged for day use, fishing, boat launching, and camping.

Water sports, restrictions: Powerboats, canoes, kayaks, sailing, and sailboarding are permitted. A large, sandy beach is available at the day-use area for swimming. No personal watercraft. A 10-mph speed limit is strictly enforced. Rental boats must be returned to marina by 4:30 P.M.

Directions: On I-580, drive to Livermore and the exit for North Livermore Avenue. Take that exit and turn south (right if coming from Bay Area) and drive 1.5 miles (the road becomes Tesla Road) to Mines Road. Turn right on Mines Road and drive 3.5 miles to

Del Valle Road. Turn right on Del Valle Road and drive four miles to the Del Valle Regional Park entrance.

Contact: Park headquarters, 925/373-0332; Del Valle Marina, 925/449-5201; fish line, updated weekly, 925/248-3474 (then press 2); East Bay Regional Parks District, 510/562-7275, website: www.ebparks.org/parks.

22 SANDY WOOL LAKE

Rating: 6

near Milpitas in Ed Levin County Park

Map 7.4, page 255

At just 14 acres this is a small lake, but it is surrounded by parkland with 16 miles of hiking trails. Nonpowered boats are allowed on the water, which makes it a nice spot to paddle around in a raft, canoe, or rowboat. The lake provides opportunities for hand-launched boats (no motors allowed) and also trout fishing (after being stocked in winter months).

Sandy Wool is very popular with families. It is set along a migratory path for waterfowl, so there are always ducks here, including Canada geese in early fall. The youngsters seem to enjoy feeding them. Some kids bring their little remote-controlled model boats and float them around.

There is plenty of wind, and the park attracts hang gliders. Many know the park as a prime destination in the spring and early summer to watch hang gliders or fly kites.

Swimming is not allowed, but you probably wouldn't want to swim anyway, because in summer, the water is algae-laden and quite shallow. This is also why sailboarding is not recommended; only a small area of the lake is deep enough to sailboard in, and the water is mucky enough to keep sailboarders away. There is plenty of wind, though, and the park attracts hang gliders.

Use of the park is moderate, mostly by families in the summer. A sprinkling of people come out to fish during the winter months when the lake is stocked with trout.

Access: There is no boat ramp. Car-top boats may be hand launched.

Facilities, fees: Restrooms, golf course, horseback riding trails, and picnic areas are available. A fee is charged for day use.

Water sports, restrictions: Motors are not permitted on the lake. Swimming is not allowed. Sailboarding is permitted, but not recommended.

Directions: Take I-680 to Milpitas and the exit for Calaveras Road East. Take that exit and drive east for 3.5 miles to Downing Street. Turn left on Downing Street and drive .5 mile to the park entrance (straight ahead). Proceed to the parking area near Sandy Wool Lake.

Contact: Ed R. Levin County Park, 3100 Calaveras Road, Milpitas, CA 95035, 408/262-6980; Santa Clara County Parks and Recreation, 408/355-2200, website: www.parkhere.org (click on Find a Park); Wings of Rogallo, (recorded info. for current conditions), 408/946-9516 or 925/838-9225, website: www.wingsofrogallo.org; group picnic and group camping reservations, 408/355-2201; Spring Valley Golf Course, 408/262-1722, website: www.springvalleygolf-course.com; Calero Ranch Stables, 408/268-2567, website: www.caleroranch.com.

23 VASONA LAKE

Rating: 7

in Los Gatos

Map 7.4, page 255

Vasona is a beautiful city park, with opportunity for kayak rentals, paddling around, and sharing the water with the Vasona Navy—the fleet of Canada geese, ducks, and coots that live here.

This is the kind of place you would visit for a Sunday picnic, maybe get in a good game of softball or volleyball, and perhaps sail around in a dinghy or paddle a canoe or kayak. The 55-acre lake is bordered by large grassy areas and beautiful trails, and is a popular destination for families, especially in the summer.

The best thing going here is the boat rentals.

This is the only lake in the Santa Clara County Parks and Recreation District where you can rent a boat, and kayaking is a lot of fun for families here. Water levels are usually kept high, and the easy accessibility and pretty setting (especially for being so close to so many people) make it quite attractive.

The best opportunities here are for low-speed boating and for biking access to the Los Gatos Creek Trail. When full, the lake is quite pretty, the centerpiece for a city-oriented park. The bike trail is simply a launch point to other places, not an adventure within the park.

The park covers 151 acres and is one of the most popular recreation destinations in the county. The reason is that it attracts families. In addition to the lake, there is a 45-acre turf area, which is used for Frisbee and softball games. There are several picnic areas available on a first-come, first-served basis, including eight group areas that can be reserved.

Access: A paved launch ramp is located on the lake's west side.

Facilities, fees: Picnic areas, restrooms, playground, and fishing pier are provided. Rowboats and pedal boats are available for rent. Fees are charged for parking, lake use, and boat launching.

Water sports, restrictions: Motors are not permitted on the lake. Sailboarding is permitted. Swimming is not allowed.

Directions: Take Highway 17 to Los Gatos to the Lark exit. Turn left on Lark and drive to Los Gatos Boulevard. Turn right on Los Gatos Boulevard and drive to Blossom Hill Road. Turn right on Blossom Hill and drive to the park entrance on the right.

Contact: Lake Vasona, 408/356-2729, website: www.valleywater.org (click on Reservoirs under Short Cuts); Santa Clara County Parks and Recreation, 408/355-2200, website: www.parkhere.org (click on Find a Park); Steven's Creek County Park, 408/867-3654; group picnic reservations, 408/355-2201; City of San Jose Parks and Recreation, 408/277-5561.

24 CAMPBELL PERCOLATION POND

Rating: 5

in Campbell

Map 7.4, page 255

A veritable dot of water, this little pond covers a total of just five acres. In the cooler months the water is stocked with trout, while in the summer it provides opportunities for visitors to go sailboarding or model boating.

In the summer Campbell Percolation Pond provides opportunities for sailboarding or model boating. Sailboarding is permitted at the northernmost pond, and it is quite popular here because on most days the lake gets steady afternoon winds, and conditions are ideal practically every summer afternoon. On weekends, however, it can get crowded.

The middle pond is reserved for model boats, a real rarity. No other boats are permitted on the ponds, and swimming is not allowed.

In the surrounding area you'll also find paths for hiking, biking, and horseback riding. Access is available to the Los Gatos Creek Trail, which extends 14 miles from San Jose to Lexington Reservoir. Flycasting pools are also available.

This dot of water can provide some surprisingly good trout fishing during the winter and spring. The fish aren't big, but stocks from the Department of Fish and Game are decent (16,000 rainbow trout in the 10- to 12-inch class annually) and provide good opportunities for shoreliners.

Access: Boating is not permitted on the ponds.

Facilities, fees: Restrooms, water, and a grassy picnic area are available. A fee is charged for day use from Memorial Day to Labor Day. During the off-season, this fee applies only on weekends.

Water sports, restrictions: Swimming is not allowed. Sailboarding is permitted.

Directions: Take Highway 17 to Campbell and the Camden Avenue/San Tomas exit. Take that exit and drive west on San Tomas Expressway to Winchester Boulevard. Turn south (left) on Winchester Boulevard and drive to Hacienda. Turn left on Hacienda and drive to Dell Avenue. Turn right and drive a short distance to the park entrance.

Contact: Santa Clara County Parks and Recreation, 408/355-2200, website: www.parkhere.org (click on Find a Park).

25 LAKE CUNNINGHAM

Rating: 6

in San Jose

Map 7.4, page 255

Fifty-acre Lake Cunningham is located adjacent to the Raging Waters water slide, which is the best insurance policy for vacation success a family could possibly ask for. If you have a passel of youngsters who are disappointed because the fish just aren't biting, you can always turn them loose at the water slide.

The lake is a popular spot for sailing and sailboarding. The water warms up considerably through April, May, and June, and afternoon winds provide rather good prospects for both.

Several sailing programs are offered in summer. These programs teach new sailors the basics of small boat handling and offer those with experience the opportunity to sharpen skills. Sailing camps run Monday through Friday with both basic and intermediate camps. The sailing classes are offered on selected days in the early evening. An adults-only class is available.

The rules are typical for a small lake: no motors and no swimming allowed, but a swimming lagoon is available at the adjacent Raging Waters.

The lake also provides an urban fishing program. Trout fishing in an urban setting? It doesn't get much more urban than this. However, there are short periods during which prospects are decent in late winter and spring, when every other week the Department of Fish and Game stocks the lake with 16,000 rainbow trout in the 10- to 12-inch range.

Access: A boat launch is available.

Facilities, fees: Restrooms, water, picnic areas, and a small marina are provided. Rowboats, canoes, pedal boats, and sailboats can be rented. Raging Waters is located adjacent to the park. A fee is charged for day use in summer and during the weekend from March to June. Access is free from September through March. There is also a boat-launching fee.

Water sports, restrictions: Motors are not permitted on the lake. Sailboarding is allowed. Swimming in the lake is prohibited, but a swimming lagoon is available at the adjacent Raging Waters park.

Directions: In San Jose, drive south on U.S. 101 to the Tully Road East exit. Take that exit and drive east on Tully Road. After the intersection with Capitol Expressway, look for the park entrance on the left and follow the signs to the lake.

Contact: Lake Cunningham Marina and Ranger Station 408/277-4319; Lake Cunningham Park Headquarters, 408/277-4191; San Jose Parks, Recreation and Neighborhood Services, 408/277-4661 (administration), 408/277-4319 (sailing programs), 408/277-5562 or 408/277-5561 (picnic reservations, recorded information), 408/277-4319 (boat rentals). General information websites: www.ci.san-jose.ca.us, www.sanjose.org.

26 COTTONWOOD LAKE

Rating: 6

in San Jose at Hellyer County Park

Map 7.4, page 255

Calling this place a lake is stretching the truth just a bit. It's more like a pond, eight acres in all, but still it's a pretty spot in the center of Hellyer Park. Access is quite easy, a short hop off U.S. 101. It is a favorite local destination for sailboarders and sailboaters, and for others there are good picnic sites and miles of bike trails.

Like most lakes in Santa Clara County, no motors or swimming are permitted. Those rules make the lake perfect for sailboarding, sailing, and fishing. Fair winds and uncrowded waters are ideal for neophyte sailboarders and sailors in small dinghies. A paved launch ramp is available on the lake's south side.

The Department of Fish and Game plants 16,000 rainbow trout in the 10- to 12-inch class each winter, and if you time it after a plant, you have a chance at good catches. There are two fishing platforms on Cottonwood Lake to accommodate visitors with mobility impairments.

Access: A paved launch ramp is available on the lake's south side.

Facilities, fees: This lake is located in a county park and has restrooms with flush toilets, drinking water, and picnic areas. A fee is charged for day use that includes boat-launching.

Water sports, restrictions: Motors are not permitted on the lake. Sailing and sailboarding are allowed. Swimming is prohibited.

Directions: From San Jose, take U.S. 101 south to the Hellyer exit. Take that exit west and drive a short distance to the entrance for Hellyer County Park.

Contact: Hellyer County Park, 408/225-0225; Santa Clara County Parks and Recreation, 408/355-2200, website: www.parkhere.org (click on Find a Park); City of San Jose Parks Department, 408/277-4573; group picnics, 408/225-0225.

27 LEXINGTON RESERVOIR

Rating: 5

near Los Gatos in the Santa Cruz foothills

Map 7.4, page 255

If you ask questions about Lexington Reservoir, you'll get a few yes's and a lot of no's.

Yes, you can sailboard, and it's the best activity possible here. The reservoir is big, 475 acres when full, and gets a predictable 10- to 20-mph wind out of the northwest, so there is plenty of room, calm water, and enough kick to let it rip with a sailboard. In the summer when conditions are ideal, sailboarding traffic can even

get heavy. Conditions are also good for piloting small sailboats.

Yes also for fishing, with an improving fishery for largemouth bass. Yes for hand-powered boating and the chance to canoe or row in calm water along the quiet western shore and inlet.

Sound good? Unfortunately there are a few no's. No swimming. No motors on boats. And worst of all, sometimes there is no water.

Even when Lexington fills up, creating this big, beautiful lake, the local water agency just drains it anyway some years. They say it is necessary in order to clear silt from the outlet hole, but in the eyes of the public, they're just taking a pretty spot and turning it into a dust bowl.

The big surprise for a few insiders who know of it is the outstanding bass fishing in the spring. From late February through April, you can get an excellent bite on spinnerbaits and shad-type lures along the submerged trees and brush. When the lake is full, the survival rate of planted rainbow trout is very high, making for good trolling (often near the dam) and shoreline fishing (in the coves).

Lexington Reservoir is located adjacent to St. Joseph's Hill Open Space Preserve, a 267-acre preserve that provides a short hike up to a pretty view.

Access: A paved launch ramp is available on the lake's north side.

Facilities, fees: Picnic areas and chemical toilets are available. Fees are charged for day use and boat launching. Lake use fees may be deposited at the self-serve box at the boat launch ramp or Miller Point.

Water sports, restrictions: Motors are not permitted on the lake. Sailboarding is allowed. Swimming is prohibited. Boats must be off the water one half hour before sunset.

Directions: From San Jose, take Highway 17 (to about four miles east of Los Gatos) to the exit for Bear Creek Road. Take that exit, bear right, cross over the freeway, and re-enter Highway 17 and drive a short distance to the exit for Alma Bridge Road. Take that exit and drive east for 1.5 miles (across the Lexington Dam). Parking is available just east of the dam in Lexington Reservoir County Park. The trail starts opposite the boat launching area beyond the dam.

From Santa Cruz, take Highway 17 (to about four miles east of Los Gatos) to the exit for Alma Bridge Road. Take that exit and drive east for 1.5 miles (across the Lexington Dam). Parking is available just east of the dam in Lexington Reservoir County Park. The trail starts opposite the boat launching area beyond the dam.

Contact: Lexington Reservoir, 408/356-2729; Santa Clara County Parks and Recreation, 408/358-3741, fax 408/358-3245, website: www.parkhere.org (click on Find a Park).

28 GUADALUPE RESERVOIR

Rating: 6

near Los Gatos

Map 7.4, page 255

If only looking good beat doing good. Guadalupe Reservoir covers 75 acres in the foothills of the Sierra Azul Range just southeast of Los Gatos. It looks so appealing that in the spring newcomers to the area can practically have heart palpitations upon first glance.

What you get is a small lake for nonpowered boating and poor fishing, with nearby picnic spots and some hiking trails. It's a favored spot for sailing in a small boat, or paddling around in a canoe, kayak, or pedal boat.

Guadalupe is one of two lakes (also see Almaden Lake, next listing) at Almaden Quicksilver County Park. This park covers 3,977 acres and is featured by the evidence of historical mining operations. Almaden was the site of the first quicksilver mine in North America. Mining began in 1845 and continued until 1975.

Because of that mining, the bass and other fish are contaminated with mercury, courtesy of runoff.

Then you learn about the many things that aren't allowed: no motors, water-contact sports, sailboarding, swimming, or wading. There seem to be few fish here, too.

Access: There is no boat ramp. Car-top boats may be hand launched.

Facilities, fees: A picnic area, restrooms, and small marina are available. In the summer months, pedal boats, inflatable canoes, and sailboarding boards can be rented. A fee is charged for day use during the high season months from May to September. Off-season access is free. There is no boat launch fee at Almaden Lake.

Water sports, restrictions: Kayaks, canoes, and small sailboats that can be hand launched are permitted. Motors are not permitted on the reservoir. Swimming and sailboarding are prohibited.

Directions: In San Jose, take Almaden Expressway and drive south to Coleman Road. Turn right at Coleman Road and continue for three miles to Camden Avenue. Turn right on Camden Avenue and drive a very short distance to Hicks Road. Turn left at Hicks and drive to the reservoir entrance (about four miles from Camden Avenue).

Contact: Almaden Quicksilver County Park office (Calero Reservoir County Park), 408/268-3883; Santa Clara County Parks and Recreation, 408/358-3741, fax 408/358-3245, website: www.parkhere.org (click on Find a Park); San Jose Regional Park, 408/277-5562; Almaden Lake Park (City of San Jose), 408/277-5130; nature walks: 408/268-3883.

29 ALMADEN LAKE

Rating: 6

near San Jose

Map 7.4, page 255

Don't confuse Almaden Lake with nearby Almaden Reservoir, which doesn't allow boating or water sports.

Almaden Lake, on the other hand, is a perfect destination for families with kids and for beginning sailboarders. Winds are fairly calm but are consistent enough to power some good sailing. The lake is quite small, so it can get crowded with boards on summer weekends.

Motors are not allowed on the lake, which keeps things quiet.

Almaden was the site of the first quicksilver mine in North America. Because of the mercury mines, there are no fishing programs at the two lakes, a major disappointment for some anglers in Santa Clara County.

A bonus is the adjacent swimming lagoon, an excellent perk in the summer for families.

Almaden Reservoir? No. Almaden Lake? Yes.
Access: A primitive launch ramp is available on the lake's south side.

Facilities, fees: Picnic areas are provided. In the summer months you can rent pedal boats, inflatable canoes, and sailboards. A fee is charged for day use during the high season months from May to September. Off-season is free. There is no boat launch fee.

Water sports, restrictions: Motors are not permitted on the lake. Sailing and sailboarding are allowed. From Memorial Day to Labor Day, an adjacent swimming lagoon is available for swimming.

Directions: Take Highway 85 to the exit for Almaden Expressway. Take that exit and drive south on Almaden Expressway to Almaden Road. Turn right on Almaden Road and drive through New Almaden to the Hacienda park entrance on the right. Continue one mile south to the lake entrance.

Contact: Almaden Quicksilver County Park office, (Calero Reservoir County Park), 408/268-3883; Santa Clara County Parks and Recreation, 408/358-3741, fax 408/358-3245, website: www.parkhere.org (click on Find a Park); San Jose Regional Park, 408/277-5562; Almaden Lake Park (City of San Jose), 408/277-5130; nature walks: 408/268-3883.

30 CALERO RESERVOIR

Rating: 8

near Coyote

Map 7.4, page 255

Calero is the one lake in the Santa Clara County foothills that is often full to the brim, even when other lakes are nearly dry from extended droughts. That makes it very popular for boating, fishing, and all forms of lakeside recreation.

Covering 333 acres, this big lake looks quite pretty in the foothills just west of the south valley, its green water contrasted against the golden hills. Calero is also one of the few lakes in the region that allows powerboating.

Calero is very popular for boating, fishing, and all forms of lakeside recreation. Note that special regulations are in effect, with proof of MTBE-free gas required for all boaters, and that reservations for boat launching are often required. Thus they avoid what would otherwise be a real jam.

The powers that be also have resolved the personal watercraft vs. everybody else conflict by setting aside a special water section just for personal watercraft use, leaving the rest of the reservoir safe for all other boaters.

Fishing for crappie and bass can be quite good at Calero. However, note the health warnings about eating any fish you catch. The fish are contaminated with mercury from metals leeching in from a nearby mine. Almost everybody follows the catch-and-release rule.

Sailboarding conditions are decent on weekdays, but the reservoir gets so crowded on weekends that boarders are generally better off heading to one of the smaller lakes in the area.

The reservoir is the main attraction, but the park covers a 2,421-acre spread in the eastern foothills of the Santa Cruz Mountains. This landscape features foothill grasslands that are peppered with oaks, and some chaparral communities. It produces good displays of wildflowers in the spring, particularly in years when warm temperatures accompany high soil moisture.

Calero has provided the most consistent fishing for bass and crappie of any lake in the Bay Area. Just keep throwing them back and it will stay that way. This is one of the best bass lakes in the Bay Area, and amid the

12-inchers there are some true monsters scaling 10 pounds and up.

Also check out the listings for nearby Chesbro Reservoir, Uvas Reservoir, and Coyote Reservoir in Chapter 8—Monterey and Big Sur.
Access: A paved launch ramp is available on the lake's east side. Launching reservations are required on weekends and holidays.
Facilities, fees: Portable restrooms and a picnic area are provided. Fees are charged for day use and boat launching.
Water sports, restrictions: Powerboating and personal watercraft are permitted. There is a quota set for 20 personal watercraft per day. Sailing and sailboarding are permitted. Swimming is not allowed. A 35-mph speed limit is strictly enforced.
Directions: From San Jose, drive south on U.S. 101 for five miles to Coyote and Bernal Road. Take the Bernal Road exit west and drive a short distance to the Monterey Highway exit. Turn south on Monterey and drive a short way to Bailey Avenue. Turn right and drive to McKean Road. Turn left on McKean Road and drive .5 mile to the park/reservoir entrance.
Contact: Calero Reservoir County Park, 408/268-3883; Santa Clara County Parks, 408/355-2200; boat launching reservations, 408/355-2201; fishing information, Coyote Discount Bait & Tackle, 408/463-0711; group picnic reservations, 408/355-2201; Calero Ranch horse rentals, 408/268-2567.

31 LAKE ANDERSON

Rating: 8

near Morgan Hill

Map 7.4, page 255

Anderson is the boating capital of Santa Clara County. A big lake, it covers nearly 1,000 acres and is set among the oak woodlands and foothills of Mount Hamilton's western slope.

It takes a lot of water to fill the lake, and boating and fishing are only good here when water levels are high. When that occurs, typically after most winters, the place turns into a madhouse on warm weekends.

The lake is long and wide enough for powerboaters to let it rip, and water-skiing is extremely popular on the main lake body. The 35-mph speed limit sets up a kind of game between the jet boaters and the boat patrol, with the speed boaters often gauging just how far they can push it without getting kicked off the lake.

In early summer a midday wind kicks up, making conditions ideal for sailboarding and sailing. Be aware that the wind can really howl here; after all, the lake is set in a canyon. First it gets choppy and uncomfortable, then whitecaps pop up, and then things can get potentially dangerous. When the wind starts to blow, stay alert and don't get caught too far offshore.

On hot weekends and holidays, expect to encounter a lot of people and a lot of boats, including many ski boats. That is the nature of Anderson. If you want quiet water, head over to the section at the lake's south end at the Dunne Avenue Bridge, a popular fishing area where a 5-mph speed limit keeps things sane.

The area near the dam can be especially good for crappie and bass, particularly in the morning. When the lake is full, the best prospects are at the extreme south end of the lake, from the Dunne Bridge on south. This area can be very good for bass, bluegill, and crappie in the early spring before too many anglers have hit it and smartened up the fish.

Also check out the listings for nearby Chesbro Reservoir, Uvas Reservoir, and Coyote Reservoir in Chapter 8—Monterey and Big Sur.
Access: A paved ramp is available. Boat launching reservations are required on weekends and holidays from April through September. Owners of boats with gas motors are required to have proof of using MTBE-free gas.
Facilities, fees: Picnic areas and restrooms are provided. There are fees for day use and boat launching.
Water sports, restrictions: Water-skiing, wakeboarding, sailing, and sailboarding are permitted. A 35-mph speed limit is strictly enforced.

A 5-mph zone is established and signed on the southern end of the lake. Personal watercraft are prohibited. Swimming is not allowed. The use of MTBE-free gas is required.

Directions: From San Jose, drive south on U.S. 101 for seven miles to the exit for Dunne Avenue. Take that exit and turn east on Dunne Avenue and drive through Morgan Hill. Continue to the marina access road (just before Dunne Avenue Bridge) on the left. Turn left and drive to the boat ramp.

Contact: Anderson Lake County Park, 408/779-3634; Santa Clara County Parks and Recreation, 408/355-2200, website: www.parkhere.org (click on Find a Park); boat launching reservations: 408/355-2201; fishing information: Coyote Discount Bait & Tackle, 408/463-0711; group picnic reservations: 408/355-2201.

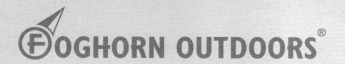

© TOM STIENSTRA

Chapter 8

Monterey and Big Sur

Chapter 8—Monterey and Big Sur

The scenic charm seems to extend to infinity from the seaside towns of Santa Cruz, Monterey, Big Sur, and San Simeon. The primary treasure is the coast, which is rock-strewn and sprinkled with inshore kelp beds, where occasionally you can find sea otters playing. The sea here is a color like no other, often more of a tourmaline than a straight green or blue.

From Carmel to Lucia alone, touring the Big Sur on Highway 1 is one of the most captivating drives anywhere. The inland strip along Highway 1 provides access to state parks, redwoods, coastal streams, Los Padres National Forest, and the Ventana Wilderness. As you explore farther south on the Pacific Coast Highway, you will discover a largely untouched coast. Here also are San Simeon, Hearst Castle, Morro Bay, inland canyons, and three of the most fish-filled lakes anywhere: Lake San Antonio, Lake Nacimiento, and Santa Margarita Lake (the latter two are in the Santa Barbara and Vicinity chapter in this book).

This chapter also includes a few places further north, Uvas and Coyote Lakes, set in southern Santa Clara county in the foothills of the U.S. 101 corridor. Coyote provides an excellent destination for powerboating, with good swimming and water sports possibilities, bluff-top campsites overlooking the lake, and often prospects for bass fishing. There are other surprises. Pinto Lake near Watsonville, for instance, provides RV sites with lake views.

Most vacations to this region include several must-do trips. Most folks head south to Big Sur to take in a few brush strokes of nature's canvas, easily realizing why this area is beloved around the world. However, it's impossible not to want the whole painting.

For those who make the drive to San Simeon, it is amazing how fast the weather and surroundings can change with a short drive inland on a summer day to Nacimiento or San Antonio. Instead of fog, you get heat, and instead of the coast, you get miles of shoreline and unlimited lake-based adventures.

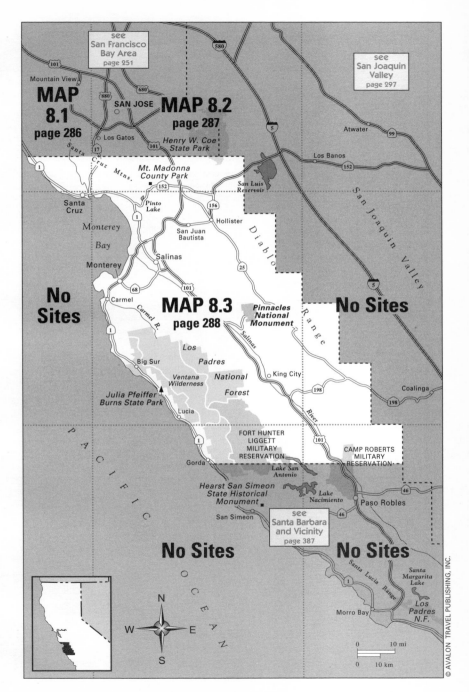

see
San Francisco
Bay Area
page 251

580

see
San Joaquin
Valley
page 297

101

Mountain View

MAP
8.1
page 286

880

680

SAN JOSE

MAP 8.2
page 287

Atwater

99

Los Gatos

101

Henry W. Coe
State Park

5

Los Banos

152

17

Santa Cruz Mtns.

152

Mt. Madonna
County Park

156

Santa
Cruz

Pinto
Lake

San Joaquin Valley

Monterey
Bay

1

San Juan
Bautista

Hollister

Salinas

No
Sites

Monterey

101

25

Diablo Range

Carmel

68

MAP 8.3
page 288

Pinnacles
National
Monument

No Sites

5

1

Carmel R.

Los
Padres

Salinas

Big Sur

Ventana
Wilderness

National

King City

Julia Pfeiffer
Burns State Park

Forest

198

Coalinga

Lucia

198

PACIFIC

1

FORT HUNTER
LIGGETT
MILITARY
RESERVATION

CAMP ROBERTS
MILITARY
RESERVATION

Gorda

Lake San
Antonio

101

Salinas River

46

Hearst San Simeon
State Historical
Monument

Lake
Nacimiento

Paso Robles

San Simeon

see
Santa Barbara
and Vicinity
page 387

46

No Sites

No Sites

OCEAN

N

W   E

S

Santa Lucia Range

1

Santa
Margarita
Lake

Los
Padres
N.F.

Morro Bay

0   10 mi

0   10 km

© AVALON TRAVEL PUBLISHING, INC.

Map 8.1

Site 1
Page 289

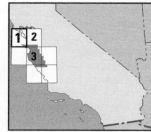

8.2

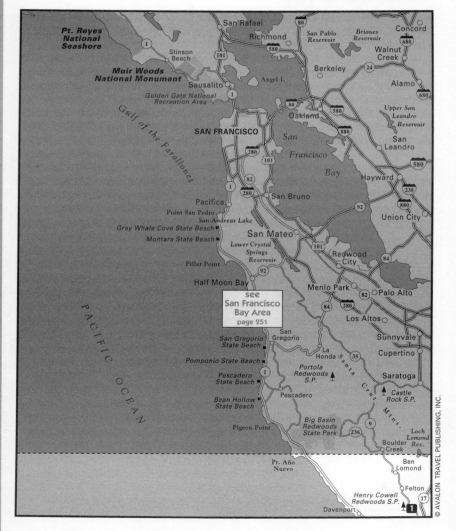

Pt. Reyes National Seashore

Muir Woods National Monument

Stinson Beach

San Rafael

Richmond

San Pablo Reservoir

Briones Reservoir

Concord

Walnut Creek

Berkeley

Angel I.

Sausalito

Golden Gate National Recreation Area

Alamo

Gulf of the Farallones

Oakland

Upper San Leandro Reservoir

SAN FRANCISCO

San Francisco Bay

San Leandro

Hayward

Pacifica

San Bruno

Point San Pedro

San Andreas Lake

Gray Whale Cove State Beach

Montara State Beach

San Mateo

Union City

Lower Crystal Springs Reservoir

Pillar Point

Redwood City

Half Moon Bay

Menlo Park

Palo Alto

see San Francisco Bay Area page 251

Los Altos

PACIFIC OCEAN

San Gregorio State Beach

San Gregorio

La Honda

Sunnyvale

Cupertino

Pomponio State Beach

Portola Redwoods S.P.

Saratoga

Pescadero State Beach

Pescadero

Castle Rock S.P.

Santa Cruz Mtns.

Bean Hollow State Beach

Pigeon Point

Big Basin Redwoods State Park

Boulder Creek

Loch Lomond Res.

Pt. Año Nuevo

Ben Lomond

Henry Cowell Redwoods S.P.

Felton

Davenport

© AVALON TRAVEL PUBLISHING, INC.

Map 8.2

Sites 2–4
Pages 289–292

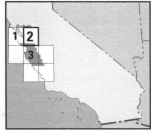

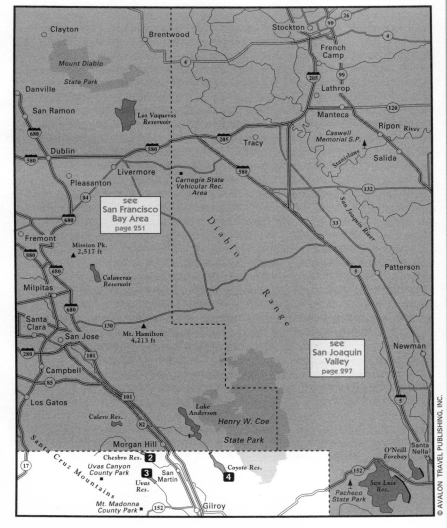

Map 8.3

Sites 5–8
Pages 292–294

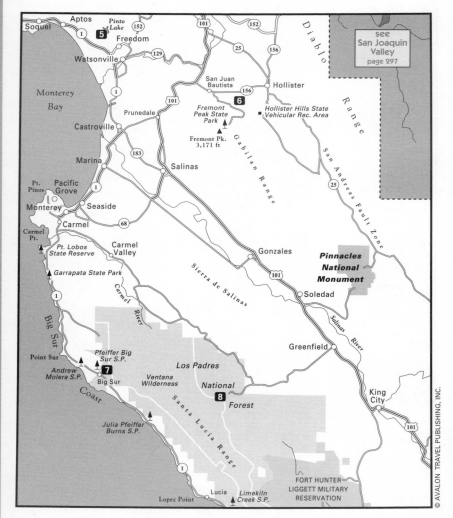

1 SAN LORENZO RIVER

Rating: 3

in Santa Cruz

Map 8.1, page 286

The San Lorenzo starts as a trickle in the Santa Cruz Mountains, then flows westward to the sea near Santa Cruz. Highway 9 parallels much of the route, and for most visitors, driving alongside the river in a car is as close as they get.

As with most short coastal streams, the recreational opportunities here are only fair. The most fun activity is actually not a water sport, but a ride aboard the Roaring Camp Big Trees Railroad, a slow-moving steam engine. It runs from Felton to Santa Cruz, much of the route along the San Lorenzo River. This is the best way to see the river and learn about the recreation it offers.

The first thing you may notice is that there are few prospects for swimming and water sports. The only good swimming hole is at the Garden of Eden near Henry Cowell State Park, a beautiful spot set in a picturesque redwood grove. Upstream there are no other spots suitable for swimming; the water is too shallow for anything but wading.

Downstream there is some potential at the seasonal lagoon, located just upstream from the river's mouth. In summer, the river is closed by a large sandbar, and though flows are reduced to a trickle, it creates a coastal lagoon. This small but pleasant area is ideal for youngsters to paddle around on rafts or float on inner tubes.

The river is narrow, and although shallow most of the year, it is subject to rapid rises during heavy rainstorms. That makes it extremely poor for kayaking. People occasionally attempt to inner tube or kayak here, but they rarely make it far.

Fishing (for steelhead) is permitted only on Wednesdays, weekends and holidays, during the season from mid-November through February. The fish are very difficult to catch, but anglers do enjoy one special perk: they can ride the train along the river, get dropped off at their chosen spot, and be retrieved later in the day. For information phone the Roaring Camp Big Trees Railroad, 408/335-4484.

Access: Swimming is permitted. There is no boat ramp. Rafting and boating are not recommended.

Facilities, fees: Henry Cowell Redwoods State Park provides a campground, restrooms with coin showers, drinking water, and picnic areas. There is an entrance fee at Henry Cowell Redwoods State Park.

Water sports, restrictions: A swimming hole is available at the Garden of Eden, which is accessible via Ox Road Trail in the park.

Directions: In Scotts Valley on Highway 17, take the Mount Hermon Road exit and drive west toward Felton to Lockwood Lane. Turn left on Lockwood Lane and drive about one mile to Graham Hill Road. Turn left on Graham Hill Road and drive .5 mile to the campground for Henry Cowell Redwoods State Park on the right. Access is available from the campground as well as at access points along Highway 9.

Contact: Henry Cowell Redwoods State Park, 831/335-4598, fax 831/649-2986.

2 CHESBRO RESERVOIR

Rating: 7

near Morgan Hill

Map 8.2, page 287

A series of lakes is set in the foothills on each side of the south Santa Clara Valley, including Chesbro, Calero, and Uvas on the west, and Coyote and Anderson on the east. Chesbro, which is most often referred to as Chesbro Dam, is known primarily as a bass fishing lake.

When full, the reservoir covers 269 acres. It was formed from the damming of Llagas Creek. It is surrounded by another 350 acres of parkland. No motors are permitted on the lake, so it is a much quieter scene than at nearby Calero.

You can't swim here, a shame since this would be a great place for swimming.

Sailboarding is permitted, but winds are typically light, making conditions fair at best, even for beginners who aren't seeking the challenge that comes with a gale. That pretty much leaves the reservoir free for anglers, some of whom take to the water in float tubes, casting into the lake's quiet coves.

While there are lots of small bass in this lake, there are also some absolute giants that are quite elusive. So you might see a monster bass swimming around and end up catching midgets, but you will be hooked on the place, just the same. Anglers often leave here in wonderment over a fish they glimpsed.

Anglers often call the lake "Chesbro Dam," and not Chesbro Reservoir, Chesbro Lake or its official name, Chesbro Reservoir County Park. Whatever you call it, it is certainly worth a look during the spring for a chance at the bass and crappie. In late winter and early spring, it is stocked with trout by the Department of Fish and Game in some years.

Access: A paved launch ramp is available on the lake's southeast side.

Facilities, fees: Picnic areas and restrooms are available. Fees are charged for day use and boat-launching.

Water sports, restrictions: Rowboats, boats with electric motors, canoes, kayaks, sailing, and sailboarding are permitted. No gas motors. Swimming is prohibited.

Directions: From San Jose, drive south on U.S. 101 for five miles to Coyote and Bernal Road. Take the Bernal Road exit west and drive a short distance to the Monterey Highway exit. Turn south on Monterey and drive a short way to Bailey Avenue. Turn right and drive to McKean Road. Turn left on McKean Road and drive about five miles (passing Calero; the road becomes Uvas Road) to Oak Glen Avenue. Turn left and drive to the lake entrance.

Contact: Santa Clara County Parks and Recreation, 408/355-2200, website: www.parkhere.org (click on Find a Park); fishing information: Coyote Discount Bait & Tackle, 408/463-0711.

3 UVAS RESERVOIR

Rating: 7

near Morgan Hill

Map 8.2, page 287

South of Chesbro Reservoir (see previous listing) is Uvas Reservoir, and conditions at the two are nearly identical.

Uvas gets slightly more use because there's a campground nearby, trout is stocked in late winter, and there are rare periods when bass fishing is excellent. For the most part, it is used primarily by anglers, with boating and water sports just an afterthought.

At times Uvas Reservoir can be the best bass lake in the Bay Area. When full to the brim with water, largemouth bass can be located in the coves in the spring. When Uvas has cool water temperatures from late winter through spring, Fish and Game adds to the bounty by stocking rainbow trout twice a month. Some say the big bass like to eat those hatchery-raised trout, and thus grow even bigger.

Access: A paved launch ramp is located on the lake's southeast side.

Facilities, fees: A picnic area is provided. A campground with restrooms and flush toilets is available four miles away at Uvas Canyon County Park. Fees are charged for day use and boat launching when the ramp is in use.

Water sports, restrictions: Rowboats, boats with electric motors, canoes, kayaks, sailing, and sailboarding are permitted. No gas motors. Swimming is prohibited.

Directions: From San Jose, drive south on U.S. 101 for five miles to Coyote and Bernal Road. Take the Bernal Road exit west and drive a short distance to the Monterey Highway exit. Turn south on Monterey and drive a short way to Bailey Avenue. Turn right and drive to McKean Road. Turn left on McKean Road and drive eight miles (passing Calero and Chesbro; the road becomes Uvas Road) to the park and reservoir. To reach Uvas Canyon County Park, continue to Croy Road. Turn right on Croy Road and drive 4.5 miles to the park.

Contact: Uvas Canyon County Park, 408/779-9232; Santa Clara County Parks and Recreation, 408/355-2200; website: www.parkhere.org (click on Find a Park); group picnic and camping reservations: 408/355-2201; fishing information: Coyote Discount Bait & Tackle, 408/463-0711.

⁴ COYOTE RESERVOIR

Rating: 8

near Gilroy

Map 8.2, page 287

Coyote Lake is a jewel among Bay Area parks and recreation lands. It is the No. 1 bass lake in the Bay Area, has an outstanding campground set within walking distance of the lake, and provides access for powerboating, canoeing and kayaking, and sailboarding.

Coyote Lake is a pretty surprise to newcomers, a long, narrow lake set in a canyon just over the ridge east of U.S. 101, about five miles upstream (south) of Lake Anderson. The lake covers 635 acres and is surrounded by an additional 796 acres of parkland. All boating is permitted, bass fishing is good during the summer, trout fishing is good in the spring, hiking trails are available along the shoreline, and the entire setting provides a pretty respite from the chaos of crowded San Jose to the north.

At one time Coyote Reservoir was considered simply an alternative to Lake Anderson, its big brother just to the north. Those days are over. The appeal of this lake has made it equally popular—maybe even better—and a visit here will quickly demonstrate why.

It is one of only a handful of lakes in the greater Bay Area with a nearby campground and the sites are filled on weekends

Its location is ideal for picking up strong, steady breezes as they sail down the canyon on afternoons in the spring and early summer, making this lake excellent for sailboarding and

sailing. The clear, warm waters would also be ideal for swimming, or at least bobbing around in a life jacket, but swimming is not permitted, a real shame.

Regardless, this lake is still a popular spot, one of the best in the Bay Area for campers and boaters.

Not only are more bass caught at this lake than any other Bay Area lake, but more big bass—the 8- to 12-pounders that have a way of getting inside your mind and realigning your senses.

There is an informal agreement here to release these fish to fight another day. That is one reason the fishery has stayed so strong, despite many big fish being caught. Instead of ending up dead, they are returned to propagate and then fill the lake with their progeny. In the winter and early spring, when the lake is cool, Coyote is also stocked with rainbow trout.

Access: A paved ramp is located on the reservoir's west side.

Facilities, fees: A campground, restrooms with flush toilets, and picnic areas are available. Fees are charged for day use and boat launching.

Water sports, restrictions: All boating is permitted. Owners of boats with gas motors are required to have proof of using MTBE-free gas. The boat ramp is often closed in the fall due to low water. A 35-mph speed limit is strictly enforced. A maximum of 40 personal watercraft per day is set for this reservoir. Only one powerboat per five surface acres is permitted. Sailboarding is permitted. Swimming is not allowed. Boats must follow a counterclockwise traffic pattern on busy days. Certain sections of the reservoir are designated environmental areas and are subject to a 5-mph speed limit.

Directions: From the Bay Area, drive south on U.S. 101 to Gilroy and the exit for Leavesley Road. Take that exit and drive east on Leavesley Road to New Avenue. Turn left on New Avenue and drive to Roop Road. Turn right on Roop Road and drive 3.5 miles (it becomes Gilroy Hot Springs Road) to Coyote Lake

Road. Turn left on Coyote Lake Road and drive to the park entrance.

Contact: Coyote Lake County Park, 408/842-7800; Santa Clara County Parks and Recreation, 408/355-2200, website: www.parkhere.org (click on Find a Park); camping reservations: 408/355-2201; fishing information: Coyote Discount Bait & Tackle, 408/463-0711.

5 PINTO LAKE

Rating: 6

near Watsonville

Map 8.3, page 288

Learning about Pinto Lake is a major surprise to many people, especially if they have been driving right by on nearby Highway 1 for years with nary a clue as to its existence.

Not only does this pretty spot offer good recreational opportunities, it is one of nine lakes in the greater Bay Area that has a campground (RVs only), with sites within proximity of the lake. With the state beach campgrounds typically jammed day after day, the campground at Pinto Lake provides an excellent alternative.

The lake is best known as a fishing lake, with trout stocks and a small resident population of crappie and bluegill. Rainbow trout are stocked twice weekly in season. The speed limit is strictly enforced; if park employees see a wake behind your boat, they'll call the cops out to give you a ticket. Gotcha!

Alas, swimming is no longer allowed at Pinto Lake. The rules were changed to ensure the safety of swimmers, who would be threatened by the accumulation of old fishing line, hooks, and gear; this underwater hazard is a testimonial to the habits of some of the inconsiderate slobs who think littering is their privilege. Oh well, the water is usually laden with algae by midsummer, anyway.

In the spring, sailboarding conditions are often excellent, providing that sailboarders can stick to the 5-mph speed limit. This is not a beginner's territory, though; the strong winds

can easily blow a sailboarder well out into the lake, leaving the inexperienced to face a long, exhausting paddle back to shore.

Want a great wild card suggestion for your visit to Pinto Lake? Try bird-watching from a canoe or a kayak.

Access: A paved ramp is available on the lake's south side.

Facilities, fees: A campground for RVs only, restrooms with flush toilets, drinking water, picnic areas, and a snack bar (in summer season) are provided. Rowboats and pedal boats are available for rent. A day-use fee is charged on weekends and a launch fee is charged at all times.

Water sports, restrictions: A 5-mph speed limit is strictly enforced. Sailing and sailboarding are allowed; note the speed limit. Swimming and wading are not permitted.

Directions: From Monterey, drive north on Highway 1 to the Green Valley Road exit. Take that exit and turn right at the Green Valley Road and drive 2.7 miles (.5 past the Holohan intersection) to the entrance for the lake and campground.

Contact: Pinto Lake Park, City of Watsonville, 831/722-8129, website: www.pintolake.com.

6 SAN JUSTO RESERVOIR

Rating: 5

near Hollister

Map 8.3, page 288

San Justo is open Wednesday through Sunday from February through August, and weekends only from September through June.

That known, note that the strong, steady winds that are predictable in the afternoon on most warm days make San Justo Reservoir an excellent spot for sailboarding and sailing.

A rule prohibiting gas motors means that there are no speedboats or personal watercraft rocketing around, another plus for enthusiasts of nonpowered water sports—except for people who want to take a dip, because swimming is not permitted.

San Justo Reservoir covers 200 surface acres. The surrounding landscape is sparse, with no facilities other than covered picnic areas. There are no trees, no grass, and no beach, just dirt and rocks. In late summer and early fall, water levels can fall significantly.

In addition to sailboarding and sailing, fishing is the other primary activity. The reservoir is stocked with rainbow trout when water temperatures are cool in winter and early spring. There are also prospects for bass and catfish in spring and summer, respectively. On hot days out Hollister way, it's still a decent enough spot to plunk a boat or sailboard, cool off, and have some fun.

Access: A paved launch ramp is available on the lake's northeast side.

Facilities, fees: Portable toilets, drinking water, picnic area, bait and tackle, and a snack bar are available. Fishing boat rentals are also available. No camping. Full facilities are available in Hollister. Fees are charged for day use and boat launching.

Water sports, restrictions: Electric motors are permitted on the lake, but gasoline motors are not. Sailing and sailboarding are permitted. Swimming is not allowed.

Directions: Take U.S. 101 to Highway 156 (north of Salinas). Turn east on Highway 156 and drive seven miles (through San Juan Bautista) to Union Road. Turn right (south) and continue a short distance to the reservoir.

Contact: San Justo Reservoir, 831/638-3300; San Benito County Parks Public Works, 831/636-4170.

7 BIG SUR RIVER

Rating: 6

near Big Sur in Los Padres National Forest

Map 8.3, page 288

Big Sur offers a unique opportunity to take a minor-league float trip through big-league surroundings. This stream is set amid a stand of coastal redwoods, a pretty spot known primarily as a summer vacation site and tourist destination.

Because this is a short coastal stream, rafting is possible only in late winter and spring, after the rainy season has provided sufficient runoff and stream flows. No commercial rafting trips are offered. Instead, most folks use inner tubes or kayaks. It is an easy float, with no drops or any sight of white water for seven miles. The standard run spans from Pfeiffer Big Sur State Park to Andrew Molera State Park, but many people just float on inner tubes between campgrounds along Highway 1. In the summer inner tubers can get away with short floats, but by then the river is generally too low for kayaks. The river is more of a creek than anything, and in spring, short portages are necessary in shallow spots.

The water is clear and cool, and swimming is excellent. Large, deep pools are found at all the campgrounds along the highway. For those who desire a more remote experience, you can hike to the headwaters of the Big Sur River in the Ventana Wilderness, where you'll discover some secret swimming holes.

Birdwatching is good with water ouzels and belted kingfishers among the year-round residents.

Access: There is no boat ramp. Rafters and kayakers may put in at Pfeiffer Big Sur State Park and float about seven miles to the river mouth at Andrew Molera State Park. Alternate take-outs are available at several campgrounds in between on Highway 1.

Facilities, fees: Campgrounds, lodging, picnic areas, and supplies are available along Highway 1. A day-use fee is charged for vehicles at Pfeiffer Big Sur State Park; walk-in access is free. Rafting permits are not required.

Water sports, restrictions: Deep pools for swimming are available at Andrew Molera State Park, Pfeiffer Big Sur State Park, Fernwood Park, Big Sur Campground, Riverside Campground, and at a few spots along the highway.

Directions: From Monterey, drive south on Highway 1 for 30 miles to Big Sur. Limited access is available off the highway; access is excellent at Pfeiffer Big Sur State Park (26 miles south of Carmel).

Contact: Pfeiffer Big Sur State Park and Andrew Molera State Park, 831/667-2315, fax 831/667-2886.

8 ABBOTT LAKES

Rating: 4

near Greenfield in Los Padres National Forest

Map 8.3, page 288

These two little reservoirs nestled in the Los Padres foothills are actually more like ponds, and upon first sight you might think this is the kind of place where on a hot summer day with nobody around, you'd like to get buck naked and take a quick dunk.

Wrong! First off, the rules prohibit you from swimming here. Second, you wouldn't want to anyway because these lakes are really a pair of mucky little ponds. The only thing swimming around and feeling any degree of happiness are the pint-size bluegill; fishing is mediocre.

There are days every year here when the temperatures hit 100-plus degrees, and the sur-rounding canyon traps heat, often making it 10 degrees hotter than down in the valley. You might feel as if you're sitting in a pizza oven, not a boat. If you hit it wrong, you can end up feeling something like a pepperoni pizza.

The rest of the year, you can have a quiet place virtually all to yourself, paddling around in a canoe, kayak, or raft.

Access: There is no boat ramp. Car-top boats may be hand launched.

Facilities, fees: A campground, restroom with flush toilets and coin showers, drinking water and a picnic area are available. A $5 day-use Adventure Pass (or $30 annual fee) is required.

Water sports, restrictions: Motors are not permitted on the lakes. They are too small for sailing and sailboarding. No swimming allowed.

Directions: Take U.S. 101 to the town of Greenfield and Greenfield-Arroyo Seco Road. Turn west on Greenfield-Arroyo Seco Road/County Roads G16 and 3050 and drive 19 miles to the campground and lake at the end of the road. The road runs right aside the northernmost of the two lakes; a short hike to the south brings you to the smaller lake.

Contact: Los Padres National Forest, Monterey Ranger District, 831/385-5434, fax 831/385-0628.

© ROBERT HOLMES/CALTOUR

FOGHORN OUTDOORS®

Chapter 9

San Joaquin Valley

Chapter 9—San Joaquin Valley

This section of the San Joaquin Valley is noted for its searing weather all summer long. But summer is also when the lakes in the foothills become something like a Garden of Eden for boating and water sports enthusiasts. The region also offers many settings in the Sierra foothills that can serve as launch points for short drives into the alpine beauty of Yosemite, Sequoia, and Kings Canyon National Parks.

The lakes are the primary recreation attraction, with the refreshing, clean water revered as a tonic against the valley heat all summer long.

When viewed from the air, the close proximity of these lakes to the Sierra Nevada mountain range is surprising to many. This proximity to the high country results in cool, high-quality water—the product of snowmelt sent down river canyons on the western slope.

Some of these lakes are among the best around for water-skiing and powerboat recreation, including Lake Don Pedro east of Modesto, Bass Lake near Oakhurst, Lake McClure near Merced, Pine Flat Reservoir east of Fresno, and Lake Kaweah near Visalia.

In addition, Lake Don Pedro, Pine Flat Reservoir, and Lake Kaweah are among the best fishing lakes in the entire San Joaquin Valley. Some anglers even rate Don Pedro as the number-one all-around fishing lake in the state.

The nearby Sierra rivers that feed these lakes (and others) also offer the opportunity for rafting, swimming and flyfishing for trout. In particular, the Kaweah and Kings Rivers provide outstanding white-water trips, and the rock-strewn beauty of the river canyons is exceptional.

Most of the destinations in this region are family-oriented. Many of them are on access roads to Yosemite. A bonus is that most have lower prices than their counterparts in the park, especially for camping and gear rentals.

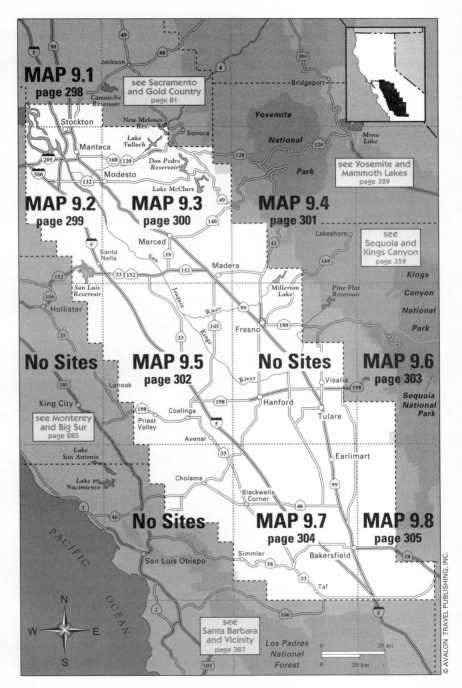

MAP 9.1
page 298

see Sacramento
and Gold Country
page 81

Yosemite

National

Park

see Yosemite and
Mammoth Lakes
page 329

MAP 9.2
page 299

MAP 9.3
page 300

MAP 9.4
page 301

see
Sequoia and
Kings Canyon
page 359

Kings

Canyon

National

Park

No Sites

MAP 9.5
page 302

No Sites

MAP 9.6
page 303

Sequoia
National
Park

see Monterey
and Big Sur
page 285

No Sites

MAP 9.7
page 304

MAP 9.8
page 305

see
Santa Barbara
and Vicinity
page 387

Los Padres
National
Forest

0   20 mi
0   20 km

© AVALON TRAVEL PUBLISHING, INC.

Jackson
Camanche
Reservoir
Stockton
New Melones Res.
Manteca
Lake Tulloch
Sonora
Don Pedro Reservoir
Modesto
Lake McClure
Bridgeport
Mono Lake
Merced
Madera
Lakeshore
Santa Nella
San
Joaquin
River
Millerton Lake
Pine Flat Reservoir
San Luis Reservoir
Hollister
Kings
Fresno
Lonoak
River
Visalia
King City
Coalinga
Hanford
Tulare
Priest Valley
Avenal
Earlimart
Lake San Antonio
Lake Nacimiento
Cholame
Blackwells Corner
Simmler
Bakersfield
San Luis Obispo
Taf

PACIFIC OCEAN

N
W   E
S

Map 9.1

Site 1
Pages 306–308

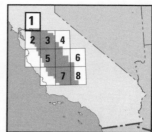

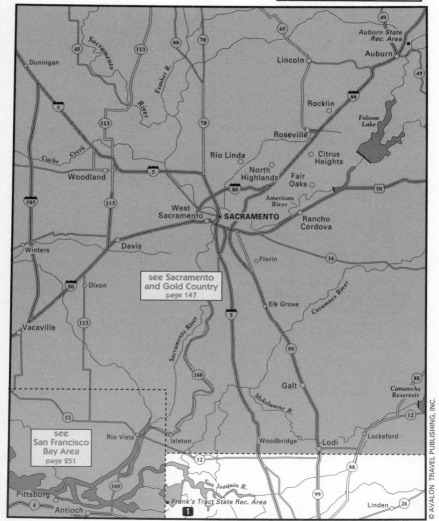

© AVALON TRAVEL PUBLISHING, INC.

Map 9.2

Sites 2–4
Pages 308–311

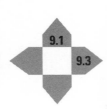

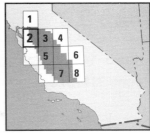

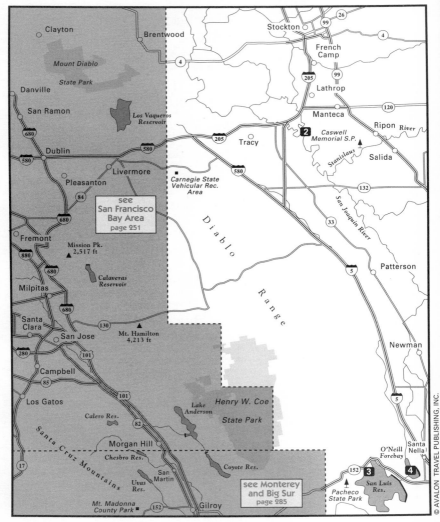

© AVALON TRAVEL PUBLISHING, INC.

Map 9.3

Sites 5–14
Pages 311–320

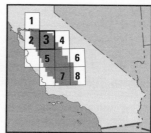

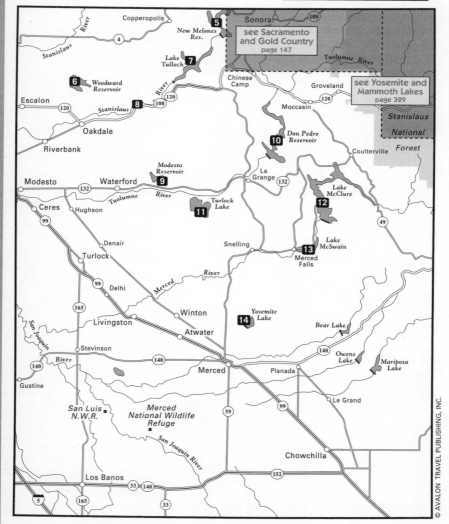

Map 9.4

Sites 15–17
Pages 320–322

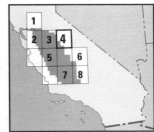

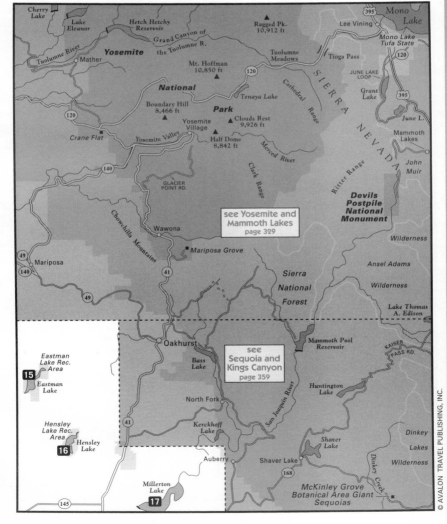

Map 9.5

Sites 18–20
Pages 322–324

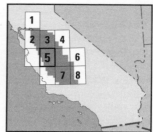

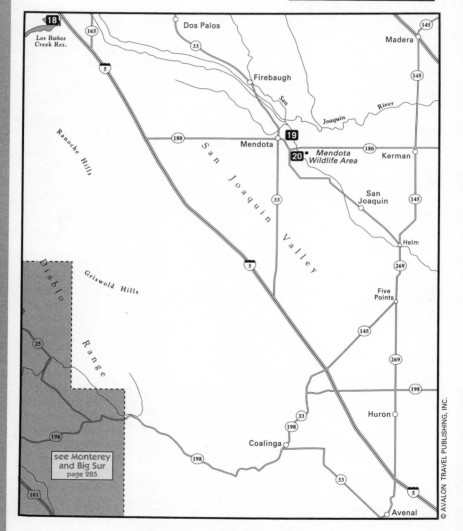

Map 9.6

Site 21
Page 324

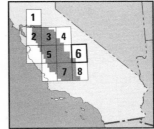

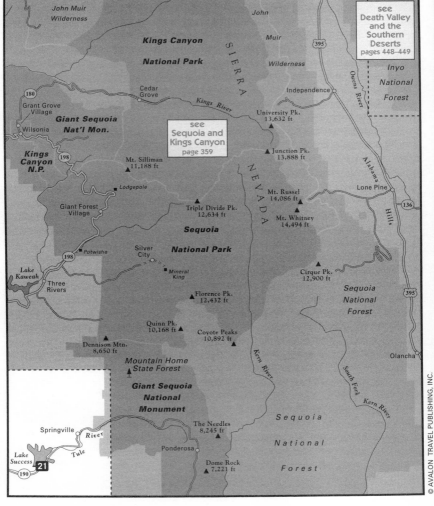

John Muir Wilderness

Kings Canyon

National Park

S I E R R A

John

Muir

Wilderness

Inyo

National

Forest

see
Death Valley
and the
Southern
Deserts
pages 448–449

395

Owens River

Cedar Grove

Kings River

Independence

180

Grant Grove Village

Giant Sequoia Nat'l Mon.

Wilsonia

see
Sequoia and
Kings Canyon
page 359

University Pk. 13,632 ft

Kings
Canyon
N.P.

198

Mt. Silliman 11,188 ft

Junction Pk. 13,888 ft

N E V A D A

Alabama Hills

Lone Pine

136

Lodgepole

Giant Forest Village

Triple Divide Pk. 12,634 ft

Mt. Russel 14,086 ft

Mt. Whitney 14,494 ft

Sequoia

198

Potwisha

Silver City

National Park

Mineral King

Lake Kaweah

Three Rivers

Cirque Pk. 12,900 ft

Sequoia

National

Forest

395

Florence Pk. 12,432 ft

Quinn Pk. 10,168 ft

Coyote Peaks 10,892 ft

Dennison Mtn. 8,650 ft

Kern River

Olancha

Mountain Home State Forest

*Giant Sequoia
National
Monument*

The Needles 8,245 ft

S e q u o i a

South Fork Kern River

Springville

River

Tule

Ponderosa

N a t i o n a l

Lake Success

190

21

Dome Rock 7,221 ft

F o r e s t

© AVALON TRAVEL PUBLISHING, INC.

Map 9.7

Sites 22–23
Pages 325–326

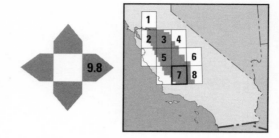

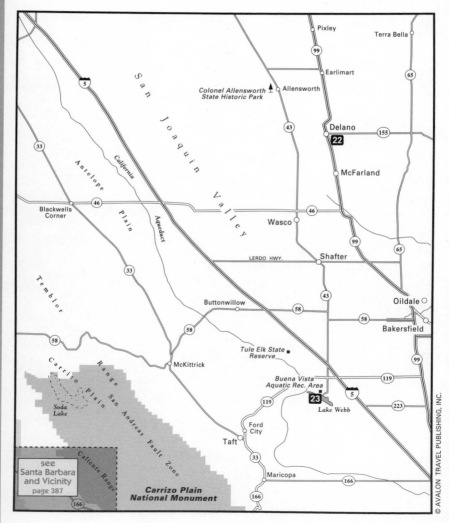

- Pixley
- Terra Bella
- 99
- Earlimart
- 65
- Colonel Allensworth State Historic Park
- Allensworth
- San Joaquin Valley
- 43
- Delano
- 22
- 155
- McFarland
- California Aqueduct
- Antelope Plain
- Blackwells Corner
- 46
- Wasco
- 46
- 33
- 99
- Shafter
- 65
- LERDO HWY.
- Temblor
- 33
- Buttonwillow
- 58
- 43
- Oildale
- 58
- 58
- Bakersfield
- 58
- Carrizo Plain
- Range
- McKittrick
- Tule Elk State Reserve
- 99
- Soda Lake
- San Andreas Fault Zone
- Buena Vista Aquatic Rec. Area
- 119
- 119
- 23
- 5
- 223
- Lake Webb
- see Santa Barbara and Vicinity page 387
- Caliente Range
- Ford City
- Taft
- 33
- Maricopa
- 166
- Carrizo Plain National Monument
- 166

© AVALON TRAVEL PUBLISHING, INC.

Map 9.8

Site 24
Page 326

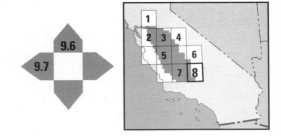

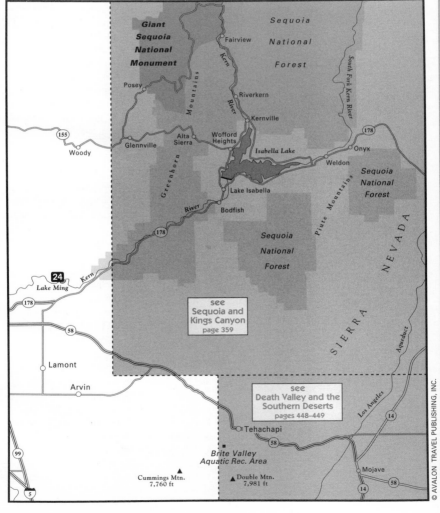

9.6

9.7

Giant
Sequoia
National
Monument

Sequoia

National

Forest

Fairview

Kern River

Mountains

South Fork Kern River

Posey

Riverkern

Kernville

155

Alta
Sierra

Wofford
Heights

Woody

Glennville

Isabella Lake

178

Onyx

Sequoia
National
Forest

Weldon

Greenborn

Piute Mountains

Lake Isabella

River

Bodfish

178

Sequoia

National

Forest

NEVADA

Kern

24

Lake Ming

see
Sequoia and
Kings Canyon
page 359

SIERRA

178

Aqueduct

58

Lamont

see
Death Valley and the
Southern Deserts
pages 448–449

Arvin

Los Angeles

14

99

Tehachapi

58

Brite Valley
Aquatic Rec. Area

Mojave

58

Cummings Mtn.
7,760 ft

Double Mtn.
7,981 ft

14

5

© AVALON TRAVEL PUBLISHING, INC.

1 SOUTH/EAST DELTA

⛴ ✕ 🛥 🎣 🛶 🏊 🏞 ⛺

Rating: 10

near Stockton

Map 9.1, page 298

Exploring the Delta can be like entering a vast human void—and a dreamland for boating, water sports, wildlife, and fishing. And yet just over the hills to the west are 6.8 million residents, where the nearby highways are jammed with angry people squeezing the life out of their steering wheels, pushing, pushing, pushing.

Here there is no push. It's the reward you've been waiting for. It gets rid of all the stress. Everybody comes out here to relax, to escape the hustle and bustle.

In many ways, the Delta provides the pinnacle of California water sports: The best waterskiing and wake boarding, the best bass fishing, and the fastest relief valve from the Bay Area pressure cooker. Out on the Delta, everybody suddenly acts nice to each other, even though just a few miles away on the highways, it is exactly the opposite.

The centerpiece of the South Delta is Discovery Bay and the nearby sites for water sports. This is a fantastic area for water-skiing and wake boarding, with water-skiing clubs, ski jumps, slalom courses and competitive events. Some of the top skiers in the world live here or train here.

Discovery Bay is the Delta's well-known development, a small pocket of luxury amid miles of marsh. It consists of a series of inlets with dozens of coves, where the shore is lined with waterfront homes and docks. Here at Lido Bay, dramatic estate homes are landscaped with palm trees. One waterfront house has docking with two $45,000 boats, a cruiser, and a ski boat, along with an airplane on floats. You turn the corner and a house with mansion-like frontage docked with five luxury boats. About 10,000 people with 3,000 boats live at Discovery Bay. Another 850 boats are kept in dry dock, that is, stacked on lifters on top of each other in a giant carport-like structure.

Elsewhere in the San Joaquin Delta, you can find occasional sites on the shores of islands and levees where small cabins have been built on pilings. All have bridged walkways from their cabins to their docks, just like Golden Pond. Instead of a car in the driveway, you have a boat out your porch.

Near the Riviera Marina, there is a leased settlement that looks like a scene out of Gilligan's Island. Tents are set amid lush, tall bamboo, palm trees, eucalyptus, and pine.

Because of narrowly focused media attention, some believe the Delta consists of a party scene with thong contests, lingerie shows, and heavy drinking. And on summer weekends at Lost Isle Resort, for instance, maybe that can seem the case. But that represents a tiny slice of Delta life, especially in the fall, when cool dawns are followed by warm, windless afternoons, my favorite time of the year, with few people and quiet water.

Since the South/East Delta is so close to Stockton and I-5, access is easy, and developed marinas get more traffic than any other delta areas. Campgrounds, lodgings, and boat rentals are booked solid, and at times some resorts refuse to allow boat owners to launch unless they have booked a room.

Houseboating is also popular on the South/East Delta, which is on the threshold of a thousand miles of waterways. Houseboats are sometimes the scene of floating parties.

There are many great boat-in beaches in the South Delta, but be wary of tides. It is unfortunately common for boaters to beach their boat for a few hours, have the tide run out, and then realize they are stuck until the incoming tide floats them off the bottom.

All of California's major rivers eventually feed into the Delta. The most notable are the Sacramento River, which starts from a spring at the base of Mt. Shasta, and the San Joaquin River, with its headwaters in the Ansel Adams Wilderness high in the Minarets of the Sierra

Nevada. In their course to the ocean, these two major rivers are fed by dozens of others, including the Mokelumne and Stanislaus rivers on the San Joaquin, and American and Feather Rivers on the Sacramento. Though large portions are diverted to points south, water eventually pours through the Delta and freshens San Francisco Bay.

Also check out the listings for other Delta locations in Chapter 7—San Francisco Bay Area.

Access: Boat launching facilities are available at the following locations:

• Discovery Bay Yacht Harbor, Byron: Take I-5 to Stockton and the exit for Highway 4 West. Drive west on Highway 4 to Discovery Bay Boulevard. Turn north (right if coming from the east) and drive about one mile to Willow Lake Road. Turn right and drive .5 mile to Marina Road. Turn right and drive .25 mile to the marina (well signed). Launching costs $20 for nonresidents. For more information call 925/634-5928, website: www.discovery-baymarina.com.

• Holland Riverside Marina, Brentwood: Take I-5 to Stockton and the exit for Highway 4 West. Take that exit and drive west on Highway 4 (past Discovery Bay Boulevard) to the Byron Highway (signed Knightsen). Turn right on the Byron Highway and drive six miles to Delta Road. Turn right on Delta Road and drive two miles to the marina at the end of the road. For more information call 925/684-3667.

• Lazy M Marina, Byron: Take Highway 205 to the exit for Grant Line Road (near Tracy). Take that exit, turn northwest and drive to the Byron Highway. Turn right on Byron Highway and drive approximately eight miles to Clifton Court Road. Turn right and drive .5 mile to the marina. For more information call 925/634-4555.

• Orwood Resort, Brentwood: Take I-5 to Stockton and the exit for Highway 4 West. Take that exit and drive west on Highway 4 to Bixler Road. Turn right and drive four miles to road's end at Orwood Road. Turn right and drive .25 mile to the resort on the right. For more information call 925/634-7181, website: www.orwoodresort.com.

• Herman & Helen's Marina, Stockton: Take I-5 to the exit for Eight Mile Road (located north of Stockton). Take that exit west and drive 7.5 miles to the marina at the end of the road. For more information call 209/951-4634.

• King Island Resort, Stockton: Take I-5 to the exit for Eight Mile Road (located north of Stockton). Take that exit west and drive four miles to Atherton Road. Turn left and drive a short distance to the resort. For more information call 209/951-2188.

• Paradise Point Marina, Stockton: Take I-5 to the exit for Eight Mile Road (located north of Stockton). Take that exit west and drive 2.5 miles to Rio Blanco Road. Turn left on Rio Blanco Road and drive 1.5 miles to the boat ramp. For more information call 209/952-1000 or 800/752-9669, website: www.paradise-point.com.

• Tiki Lagun Resort Marina, Stockton: Take I-5 to Stockton and the exit for Highway 4 West. Take that exit and drive west on Highway 4 for 5.5 miles to Inland Drive. Turn right and drive six miles (Inland Drive turns into McDonald Road) to the resort. For more information call 209/941-8975 or 800/338-7176.

• Turner Cut Resort, Stockton: Take I-5 to Stockton and the exit for Highway 4 West. Take that exit and drive west on Highway 4 for 5.5 miles to Inland Drive. Turn right and drive 6.5 miles (Inland Drive turns into McDonald Road) to the resort (located just past Tiki Lagun Resort). For more information call 209/465-4129.

• Village West Marina, Stockton: Take I-5 to Stockton and the exit for Benjamin Holt. Take that exit, turn west and drive one mile (Benjamin Holt turns into Embarcadero) to the entrance for the marina. For more information call 209/951-1551, website: www.villagewestmarina.com.

• Windmill Cove Marina, Stockton: Take I-5 to Stockton and the exit for Highway 4 West. Take that exit and drive west on Highway 4 for 5.5 miles to Inland Drive. Turn right and drive five miles (Inland Drive turns into McDonald Road) to Holt Road (one mile after the road becomes McDonald). Turn right and drive to the road's end at a T intersection with Windmill Cove Road. Turn right and drive .5 mile to the marina. For more information call 209/948-6995, website: www.windmillcove.com.

• Whiskey Slough Harbor, Holt: Take I-5 to Stockton and the exit for Highway 4 West. Take that exit and drive west on Highway 4 for six miles to Whiskey Slough Road. Turn right and drive about nine miles to Whiskey Slough Harbor. For more information call 209/942-4588.

• Tower Park Marina and Resort, Lodi: Take I-5 to Lodi and Highway 12. Take Highway 12 west and drive about five miles to Tower Park Way (before first bridge). Turn left and drive a short distance to the marina. For more information call 209/369-1041, website: www.westrec.com.

• Walnut Grove Marina, Walnut Grove: Take I-5 to the exit for Thornton-Walnut Grove/County Road J11 (located south of Sacramento and west of Galt). Take that exit, turn west and drive five miles to Old Walnut Grove/Thornton Road. Turn right and drive .3 mile to the marina. For more information call 916/776-1181, boat rentals at 916/776-4270 or 800/255-5561, website: www.walnutgrovemarina.com.

• New Hope Landing, Thornton: Take I-5 to the exit for Thornton-Walnut Grove/County Road J11 (located south of Sacramento and west of Galt). Take that exit, turn west and drive 3.3 miles to the campground entrance on the left. For more information call 209/794-2627, website: www.newhopelanding.com.

Facilities, fees: Lodging, cabins, campgrounds, houseboats, full-service marinas, and supplies are available at or near many of the boat ramps listed above. River access is free along roads. Fees are charged at parks and private marinas for day use, boat launching, and camping.

Water sports, restrictions: Powerboats, waterskiing, wake boarding, personal watercraft, sailing, and sailboarding are permitted. Swimming and sailboarding access is available in many of the sloughs. Some popular sandy beaches: Orwood Tract, north of Discovery Bay; the Mandeville (south) side of Venice Island, east of Frank's Tract; and Lost Isle, north of Holt.

Directions: Access is available from I-5 near Stockton and Lodi; on Highway 160 between Sacramento and Isleton; on Highway 12 between Lodi and Rio Vista; off Highway 4 between Brentwood and Stockton. See Access for specific directions.

Contact: Brannan Island State Recreation Area, 916/777-7701; Hal Schell's Delta Map and Guide, $2.99 at stores, $3.75 by mail at P.O. Box 9140, Stockton, CA 95208; California Delta Chamber & Visitor Bureau, 209/367-9840, website: www.californiadelta.org.

Boat rentals: Waterflies (will deliver), 916/777-6431; Herman & Helen's, Stockton, 209/951-4634. Kayaks: Big River Kayaks, Bethel Island, 925/684-3095; Tower Park Marina, Lodi, 209/368-3030, website: www.h2o rents.com; Paradise Point Marina, Stockton, 800/752-9669 or 209/952-1000, website: www.paradise-point.com; Walnut Grove Marina, Walnut Grove, 916/776-4270 or 800/255-5561. Houseboats: Delta Houseboat Rental Association, 209/477-1840.

Wake board and ski lessons: Discovery Bay Wakeboard & Ski Center, 925/634-0412, website: www.gowakeboard.com or www.gowater-ski.com.

Sailing instruction: Martin's Sailing School & Club, 916/369-7700, website: www.lovetosail.com.

Fishing guides: Fish Hooker Charters, 916/777-6498.

Boat charters: Delta Expeditions, 916/600-2420.

2 OAKWOOD LAKE

🚤 ✕ 🎿 🏊 ⛺

Rating: 7

near Manteca

Map 9.2, page 299

Oakwood Lake Resort is basically a big water

fun park. The attractions include the famous high-tech Manteca Water Slides, "river rapid" rides, video arcades, a roller skating rink, playgrounds, bungee jumping, a movie theater, bingo, and a softball field. This is one of the largest water-based theme parks in the country. And for those who want to spend more than one day here, there's a 400-site campground.

This site is adjacent to the San Joaquin River, with the park covering 375 acres of private land, including the 75-acre Oakwood Lake. Note that life jackets are required for all taking part in water sports on the lake. There are bass, bluegill, crappie, and catfish in the lake, but only resort campers are permitted to fish or use the lake.

Get the big picture? Right, this is the kind of place where you bring the youngsters on a hot summer day so they can have the time of their lives.

Access: There is no boat ramp.

Facilities, fees: A campground, restrooms, showers, RV dump station, store, coin laundry, propane gas, swimming lagoon, water slides, organized activities, and a stocked 75-acre lake are available. Children's kayaks are available for rent. A fee is charged for day use and fishing.

Water sports, restrictions: Rowboats, boats with electric motors, canoes, kayaks, inflatables, sailing, and sailboarding are permitted. No gas motors. No swimming. Life jackets are required at all times. Only campers are permitted to use the lake. Open weekends from May through September and daily from mid-June through Labor Day.

Directions: Drive on Highway 120 to Airport Way (two miles east of Manteca). Turn south on Airport Way and drive .5 mile to Woodward Way. Turn right and drive two miles to the park entrance.

Contact: Oakwood Lake Resort, 209/239-2500, website: www.oakwoodlake.com.

3 SAN LUIS RESERVOIR

Rating: 6

near Gilroy in San Luis Reservoir State Recreation Area

Map 9.2, page 299

San Luis Reservoir is literally a water hole, and it's one of the biggest water holes imaginable. The primarily stark, man-made reservoir was built on the edge of the San Joaquin Valley for the sole purpose of storing water on line with the California Aqueduct. When pumped full, usually by spring, it covers 13,800 acres and has 65 miles of shoreline. By fall the water gets drawn way down, and its vast, barren appearance can seem quite stark. The elevation is 575 feet.

Build a water-storage facility and you get an interesting by-product: opportunities for boating and recreation. In this area though, most boaters head instead to the adjoining O'Neill Forebay (see next listing), which has full facilities, boat rentals, and a large beach.

That leaves San Luis, which is largely undeveloped, to be used primarily by anglers, waterskiers, and sailboarders. The Department of Water Resources tries to fill this lake as early as possible in winter. When many reservoirs on the southwest slope of the Sierra are still largely empty, San Luis can be more than 90 percent full. This huge expanse of water can reach its highest levels from late March through mid-May.

In the spring and early summer, boaters should use extreme caution on San Luis. That is because the wind comes caterwauling out of the west, pounding the lake as it roars on its course from Monterey Bay to the San Joaquin Valley. Lights and horns have even been installed to alert boaters to get off the lake during dangerous wind warnings.

Most of the year the winds are tolerable enough to present a significant challenge to sailboarders. The stark, vast surroundings and choppy water don't add much ambience to the affair, however.

Summer temperatures can occasionally exceed 100 degrees, but evenings are usually pleasant.

San Pablo is well known for its striped bass fishing. This is best in the fall, when the stripers chase schools of baitfish on the lake surface. During the winter, tule fog is common.

Regardless, boater use is significant in the summer when the winds are down, and this enormous reservoir provides plenty of space compared to the oft-cramped quarters of O'Neill Forebay. After all, just combine a huge body of cool water and a hot climate, provide a boat, and this is where many people are apt to come.

Access: Two paved launch ramps are available.

Facilities, fees: Campgrounds, restrooms with flush toilets and coin showers, drinking water, RV dump station, and picnic areas are available. A store, coin laundry, gas station, restaurant, and propane gas are nearby. Supplies can be obtained in Gilroy and Los Baños. Fees are charged for day use, including for boat launching.

Water sports, restrictions: Water-skiing, wake boarding, and personal watercraft are permitted. Sailing, sailboarding, and swimming are allowed, although there are no developed beaches.

Directions: To San Luis Creek boat ramp: From Los Baños, drive west on Highway 152 for 14 miles to the park entrance (marked San Luis Creek State Recreation Area/O'Neill Forebay). Turn right and drive 1.5 miles to the boat ramp.

To Basalt boat ramp: From Los Baños, drive west on Highway 152 for 12 miles to Gonzaga Road (the park entrance road). Turn left and drive four miles to boat ramp.

To Dinosaur Point: Take Highway 152 to the west side of San Luis Reservoir and Dinosaur Point Road. Turn east on Dinosaur Point Road and continue to the boat ramp at the road's end.

Contact: San Luis Reservoir State Recreation Area, Four Rivers District, 209/826-1197, fax 209/826-0284.

4 O'NEILL FOREBAY

Rating: 8

near Los Baños in San Luis Reservoir State Recreation Area

Map 9.2, page 299

Sometimes bigger is not better, and that theory is proven at San Luis Reservoir State Recreation Area. O'Neill Forebay is the little brother of the adjacent and giant San Luis Reservoir, but even though it's by far the smaller of the pair, the opportunities for boating and water sports are far more attractive here.

O'Neill Forebay covers 2,000 surface acres with 14 miles of shoreline, providing the recreation for the recreation area. Whereas the main reservoir is used primarily for fishing, O'Neill Forebay caters to swimmers, water-skiers, and personal watercraft. Even anglers, however, will be pleased here, as there are some huge striped bass roaming these waters.

A large developed beach is available for swimmers, complete with outdoor showers for rinsing off. Boaters can dock at the beach to have lunch, go for a swim, and then head back out on the water to ski. Sailboarding is decent, but in the spring winds can get just as gusty as at San Luis, driving everybody off the water.

O'Neill Forebay is a very attractive recreation lake, but sometimes it can be too attractive. Weekends and holidays May through October can get so congested that some folks simply surrender and head over to San Luis Reservoir in order to avoid the crowds. Sailboarders, who like having some room to zoom, are the most likely to flee.

The Forebay is home of many of the biggest striped bass caught in California history, including the world record for landlocked striped bass.

Note that the Medeiros boat ramp has been closed since 9/11. It will not reopen. In addition to security concerns, there were problems with launching in low water here.

Access: A paved launch ramp is available.

Facilities, fees: Two campgrounds, chemical

toilets, drinking water, and showers are available. Fees are charged for day use, including for boat launching.

Water sports, restrictions: Water-skiing, wake boarding, and personal watercraft are permitted. All boaters must wear life jackets. Sailboarding and swimming are allowed; a large, sandy beach is available on the west side of the forebay.

Directions: From Los Baños, take Highway 152 west 12 miles to San Luis Reservoir and the signed Forebay entance road. Turn north and drive to the Forebay and beach area.

To San Luis Creek Boat Launch: Drive west on Highway 152 past San Luis Reservoir (12 miles west of Los Baños) to the signed campground entrance road (15 miles west of Los Baños). Turn and drive two miles to the campground on the left and continue to the boat ramp.

Contact: San Luis Reservoir State Recreation Area, Four Rivers District, 209/826-1197, fax 209/826-0284.

5 NEW MELONES RESERVOIR

Rating: 9

near Sonora

Map 9.3, page 300

New Melones is the fourth largest man-made lake in California, behind only Shasta, Oroville, and Trinity. When full, it is huge, covering 12,500 acres with more than 100 miles of shoreline, so there's plenty of room for all boating and water sports. There are countless hidden coves, inlets, and lake arms to fish and explore by boat, including the upper Stanislaus River Canyon. It is set in the valley foothills at an elevation of 1,085 feet, between the historic mining towns of Angels Camp and Sonora.

New Melones is established as one of California's top recreation lakes. One of the best things at New Melones is that day use is free, including boat launching and parking, as well as access for hiking or mountain biking. The lake rises significantly every spring as the Sierra snowpack starts melting on the western slopes below Sonora Pass.

A day on the lake here is nearly guaranteed with wildlife sightings. Osprey, blue herons, and bald eagles are common right now. So are turtles on rocks along the shore up the lake arms.

In summer, the place gets very crowded on weekends. On holiday weekends, the areas near boat ramps can resemble something like an aquatic zoo on parade. Once on the water, you can always find your own hideaway, since the lake is so big. In addition, weekdays are much more quiet.

Temperatures are warm in the summer, and the surface waters are perfect for water-skiing, personal watercraft, and swimming. The conditions are often excellent for water-skiing. A slalom course is available at Peoria Cove. The water-ski season doesn't usually get underway until Memorial Day Weekend.

Between fishing for bass or trout and wildlife watching, you might flip a three-sided die and have it land on its side, it's that good. Lake records: brown trout, 12.7 pounds; black bass, 12.98 pounds; spotted bass, seven pounds; catfish, 36 pounds.

There is so much water that low-speed anglers and high-speed boaters have room to stay out of each other's way. For the most part, fishermen stick to the lake's upper arms, while the high-speed boaters head to the more open, main lake body.

All water sports are permitted. Water-skiing and houseboating are particularly popular. When there are afternoon winds, common in the spring and early summer, it is possible to sailboard. Swimming is limited to the swimming beach; elsewhere the shoreline is fairly rocky or tree-lined.

Rafters may hate this lake, since it flooded the famed Camp Nine run on the Stanislaus River, but boaters love it.

Access: There are three paved boat ramps, two at Glory Hole Recreation Area and one at Tuttletown Recreation Area.

Facilities, fees: A full-service marina, rentals for fishing boats, pontoon boats, ski boats, personal watercraft and houseboats, moorings, bait and tackle, and boat storage are available at New Melones Lake Marina. Five campgrounds, restrooms with flush toilets, drinking water, showers, RV dump station, and picnic areas are available nearby. Supplies can be obtained in Sonora. Day use and boat launching are free. A fee is charged for camping.

Water sports, restrictions: Powerboats, waterskiing, wake boarding, personal watercraft, sailing, and sailboarding are permitted. A sandy swimming beach is available at Glory Hole Recreation Area, on the Angel Arm of the lake.

Directions: To Tutletown: From Sonora, drive north on Highway 49 to Reynolds Ferry Road. Turn left and drive about two miles to the entrance road for Tuttletown Recreation Area.

To Glory Hole: From Sonora, drive north on Highway 49 for about 15 miles (Glory Hole Market will be on the left side of the road) to Glory Hole Road. Turn left and drive five miles to Glory Hole Recreation Area.

Contact: New Melones Visitors Center 209/536-9094, website: www.recreation.gov/detail.cfm?ID=25; New Melones Lake Marina, 209/785-3300; Glory Hole Sports, 209/736-4333, website: www.gloryholesports.com.

6 WOODWARD RESERVOIR

Rating: 8

near Oakdale in Woodward Reservoir County Park

Map 9.3, page 300

This is one of the best sailing lakes in Northern California. Regattas are held through the year, and it is also very popular for sailboarding. Woodward's nickname, in fact, is "Windward Reservoir."

Woodward covers 2,900 acres with 23 miles of shoreline, set in the rolling foothills just north of Oakdale at an elevation of 210 feet.

A plus is that user conflicts have been solved here. The only solution to the water-skiing vs. fishing conflict is to separate the two groups. At Woodward Reservoir that is exactly what has happened. May each go thine own separate way and live in peace and happiness.

The two large coves on the lake's south and east ends, as well as the area behind Whale Island, are for low-speed boats only; no water-skiing or personal watercraft. Meanwhile, the jet boats have full run of the main lake, where they can make all the fun they want. This is an example of the correct way to organize a recreational lake.

All boating is allowed, but note the aforementioned restrictions designed to prevent user conflicts. The best area for sailboarding is at Office Point, located on the west side of the lake, near the marina. This is also the best place for swimming.

Trout are stocked here from October through March. By spring, bass fishing takes the top spot among anglers.

Because this is one of the largest reservoirs in the area near Modesto and Stockton, it gets lots of local traffic, especially on summer weekends. It can be extremely hot here in July and August, and by the end of summer, jumping in the lake may feel like stepping into a large hot tub.

Access: Three boat ramps are available: a paved, multi-lane ramp at the marina (at the entrance, turn left at the stop sign), a paved ramp at Area X (at the stop sign, turn right), and another paved ramp at Heron Point (at the stop sign, turn right).

Facilities, fees: Drinking water, flush toilets, showers, RV dump station, three boat ramps, a marina, mooring, dry boat storage, a store, bait, fishing licenses, and some equestrian facilities are available. Fees are charged for day use, including boat launching and camping.

Water sports, restrictions: Powerboats, waterskiing, wake boarding, personal watercraft, sailing, and sailboarding are permitted. Swimming is available at Office Point, near the marina; this is also the best spot for launching sailboards.

Directions: Take Highway 120 to Oakdale (the road becomes Highway 108/120) and the junction with County Road J14/26 Mile Road. Turn left on 26 Mile Road and drive four miles to the park entrance at Woodward Reservoir (14528 26 Mile Road).

Contact: Woodward Marina, 209/847-3129; Woodward Reservoir County Park, Stanislaus County, 209/847-3304 or 209/525-6750, website: www.co.stanislaus.ca.us.

7 LAKE TULLOCH

Rating: 7

near Jamestown

Map 9.3, page 300

Tulloch is set in two canyons that crisscross each other, like a giant X, and by boat you never see the other canyon. The lake is actually the afterbay for New Melones Lake, and the water that fills Lake Tulloch comes from the New Melones Dam on the northeastern end of the X. These extended lake arms give the reservoir a total of 55 miles of shoreline. The elevation is 500 feet.

The shape of the lake has an effect on boating. Because the water is basically set in filled canyons, the waterway is relatively narrow. Fishermen and powerboaters live in harmony for the most part due to the many coves and a six-mile long arm with an enforced 5-mph speed limit.

Unlike many reservoirs in the foothill country, Tulloch is nearly always filled with water.

If you pick your spots well, sailboarding and swimming can also be excellent. The best area for sailboarding is along the north shore, where the most predictable wind can be found. But because this lake lies in a deep canyon, winds can be erratic. In addition, sailboarding is not advised on summer weekends, when the narrow lake is swarming with speedboats and the danger factor is raised a few notches.

Both of the lake's resorts offer great swimming opportunities. Each has large, sandy

beaches complete with developed facilities. The only campground here is at South Shore.

Another surprise at this lake: It's one of the best for crawdad fishing.

Access: There are two paved boat ramps, at Lake Tulloch Marina on the south shore, and on the north shore (see Directions).

Facilities, fees: Marinas with boat launches, rentals, and docks are available at both the north shore and south shore. Lodging, a campground, picnic areas, drinking water, restrooms with showers, coin laundry, RV dump station, convenience stores, restaurant, and a bar are available. Fees are charged for day use, boat launching, and camping.

Water sports, restrictions: Powerboats, waterskiing, wake boarding, personal watercraft, sailing and sailboarding are permitted. Large, sandy swimming beaches are available at South Shore and North Shore. A 5-mph speed limit (signed) is enforced on a six-mile arm of the lake.

Directions: To the south shore: From Manteca, drive east on Highway 120 (it becomes Highway 108/120) to Oakdale. Continue east for 13 miles to Tulloch Road on the left. Turn left and drive 4.6 miles to the campground entrance and gatehouse at the south shore of Lake Tulloch. Or, continue for 10 more miles on Highway 108/120 to O'Byrnes Ferry Road. Turn left and drive to the north shore.

Contact: Lake Tulloch Campground and Marina (south shore), 209/881-0107, website: www.laketullochcampground.com; Lake Tulloch Resort (north shore), 209/785-2286 or 888/785-2286.

8 STANISLAUS RIVER

Rating: 10

below New Melones Lake to below
Knights Ferry

Map 9.3, page 300

You get everything from heaven to hell on the Stanislaus River, sometimes on the same day.

Two runs are available, the Goodwin Canyon

Run, which is exciting, even scary, and challenging, and the Knights Ferry Run, an easy float. Here are the details of both, followed by a synopsis of the Camp Nine Run.

As it pours through an untouched granite canyon in a wilderness setting, Goodwin Canyon Run is a stretch of water that can only be called beautiful. The Class V white water is exciting and difficult, winding through a narrow canyon with steep rapids and drops. The highlights are Mr. Toad's (Class IV+), Matterhorn (Class V-VI), Pinball (Class III), and Haunted House (Class IV+). Matterhorn is treated like an off-ramp by many rafters who choose to portage this scary and sometimes dangerous piece of white water.

Note that this river section can be run only when the water masters see fit to release enough water downstream to get it going. This means it can't be run every year. When it can be run, there is sometimes very short notice.

Knights Ferry Run: Not to worry, this is an easy float, all Class I water with one Class II rapid, Russian Rapid. Rafts and kayaks can be rented at Sunshine River Adventures and River Journey, which also provide shuttle services. The Knights Ferry Run is a great opportunity for newcomers, and most people adopt the do-it-yourself approach, alternating between paddling and floating, and stopping occasionally to jump in and swim. Half-day to multiday trips can be arranged, depending on one's schedule. Most people take out within 10 miles of Knights Ferry, but it is possible to float about 45 miles downstream, all the way to the San Joaquin River confluence.

This listing wouldn't be complete without a historical note. Before New Melones Dam was completed in 1982, the Camp Nine run on the Stanislaus above Melones Reservoir was considered one of the prime stretches of water in the state and was run more often than any other river. When the New Melones Dam was built, well, the dam backed up water so far that it covered the entire Camp Nine Run. Now it can only be run in drought conditions, that is,

when the lake is very low. This has occurred just a few times in the past 20 years. What you will find then is the deepest limestone canyon in the country: dramatic canyon beauty, plenty of excitement, one mind-bending rapid, seclusion, and great swimming.

Access: No boat ramp is available.

• Goodwin Canyon Run: To reach the put-in from Oakdale, drive east on Highway 108/120 for 17 miles to Tulloch Road. Turn left and drive north to the river. Put in .5 mile downstream from the dam. Take out four miles downstream at Knights Ferry, just down from the bridge. Note: This river section is rated Class V and is for experts only; people have drowned attempting this run. It can be run only when water is released from the dam upstream. Some years, low flows make it impossible to run. Call for conditions.

• Knights Ferry Run: From Oakdale, drive east on Highway 108/120 to the town of Knights Ferry. Put in at the new bridge. The standard take-out is eight miles downstream at Orange Blossom Park, although there are several other access points.

Facilities, fees: Campgrounds are available around New Melones Lake and at Knights Ferry. Rafts and kayaks can be rented at River Journey; kayaks and canoes can be rented from Sunshine Rafting Adventures. Supplies are available along Highway 4. Access is free. Rafting permits are not required.

Water sports, restrictions: Rafts and kayaks are permitted where appropriate. The river is generally too dangerous for swimming upstream of Knights Ferry, although there are some good swimming areas that can be accessed by boat. Downstream, swimming is available at several parks along Highway 108/120. A good one is Knights Ferry Resort in Knights Ferry.

Directions: Below New Melones, access is available near Knights Ferry off Highway 108/120. See Access above for specific directions.

Contact: All-Outdoors Whitewater Rafting, 925/932-8993 or 800/247-2387; Beyond Limits Adventures, 209/869-6060 or 800/234-7238;

River Journey, 209/847-4671 or 800/292-2938, website: www.riverjourney.com; Sunshine Rafting Adventures, 209/848-4800 or 800/829-7238, website: www.raftadventure.com; Knights Ferry Resort, 209/881-3349.

9 MODESTO RESERVOIR

Rating: 7

near Modesto

Map 9.3, page 300

Modesto Reservoir is a big lake, covering 2,800 acres with 31 miles of shoreline, set in the hot foothill country.

This is one of the first recreation lakes in the Central Valley to advertise "MTBE-free waters." To keep it that way, boaters must buy gas that does not contain MTBE. Some gas stations provide MBTE-free gas. You must show proof that the gas in your boat has been purchased from such a station. MTBE-free fuel is available at the lake.

Water-skiing is excellent in the main lake body. Anglers head to the southern shore of the lake, which is loaded with submerged trees and coves and is also protected by a 5-mph speed limit. Fishing for bass is good, though the fish are often small.

The reservoir is set at 200 feet on the edge of the Central Valley, where it gets very hot for days upon days in the summer. The proximity to, uh, (what's the name of that town? Oh yeah, Modesto, that's it) and the diverse recreation opportunities make it very popular, and it often gets extremely crowded in the summer months. On weekends the scene can be wild, with fast boats and lots of liquid refreshments and body oil flowing fast and furious.

In addition to good water-skiing and jet boating, the swimming in Modesto Reservoir is great. The best spots for swimming and playing in the water are near the day-use areas, where a 5-mph speed limit is in effect and boaters stay well clear of the near shore. That ensures calm water for non-boaters. Water levels fluctuate greatly.

One of the great things about the place is the boat-in camping. Many coves at the lake's southern end provide an opportunity to set up primitive self-made boat-in campsites. It's a good idea to bring a shovel in order to dig out a flat spot for sleeping, something that is often necessary when boat-in camping at a reservoir.

Access: Two paved boat ramps are available: one at the marina, located on the south shore just west of the campgrounds, and one on the reservoir's west side, off Rio Linda Drive.

Facilities, fees: Campgrounds, picnic areas, drinking water, restrooms with flush toilets, showers, RV dump station, marina, snack bar, store, and propane gas are available. Fees are charged for day use and boat launching.

Water sports, restrictions: Powerboats, water-skiing, wake boarding, personal watercraft, sailing, and sailboarding are permitted. Owners of boats with motors must have proof of purchase of MTBE-free gas. A 5-mph speed limit is enforced on the lake's southern arm and around the day-use areas. Water-skiing and personal watercraft are permitted in designated areas. Sandy swimming beaches are available at various spots around the shoreline; there's a designated swimming area next to the marina.

Directions: From Modesto, drive east on Highway 132 for 16 miles past Waterford to Reservoir Road. Turn left and drive to the lake and campground at 18143 Reservoir Road.

Contact: Modesto Reservoir, 209/874-9540, website: www.co.stanislaus.ca.us; Modesto Marina, 209/874-1340.

10 LAKE DON PEDRO

Rating: 8

northeast of Modesto

Map 9.3, page 300

Don Pedro is a giant lake with many extended lake arms and one of the best boating and recreation lakes in California.

Did I say giant? When full, it covers nearly 13,000 surface acres with 160 miles of shoreline. Not only do the lake arms extend far, but they harbor zillions of hidden coves and secret spots where you can park your boat, camp, swim, play in the water, and fish.

Temperatures soar here in the summer because the lake is set low, at an 800-foot elevation. To protect yourself from the sun, it is critical that you have a canvas canopy on your boat and bring along a light tarp with poles and rope. That done, prepare to have the time of your life on Don Pedro. The water is often lukewarm on top and cool a few feet down, perfect for water sports.

The best areas for water-skiing are just inside the lake arms, where the water is largely sheltered from wind, yet large enough for plenty of space. Because anglers tend to head well up the narrow lake arms and into coves, conflicts with water-skiers are less common than at many lakes. Personal watercraft can cause problems, however, if their riders zip into the coves and disrupt low-speed boaters.

Don Pedro has one designated swimming area at Fleming Meadows, located on the south shore. There is a fairly sandy beach here and a nearby concession stand. On the lake's northern end there are no beach areas, but people swim anyway, either from the shoreline or by jumping off their boats. Some shoreline areas have quick drop-offs, so children should always wear life jackets and be supervised.

Hey, newcomers, here's a great insider's note: The lake's northern, upper end sits in a deep, narrow canyon. It is ideal for fishing and other low-speed use, such as paddling a canoe or kayak, or floating about in a raft.

The lake gets sufficient wind in the afternoon to make sailing and sailboarding fairly popular. The best areas for these activities are at the lake's southern end, which is largely open and receives more predictable winds.

This is also one of the best fishing lakes in the foothill country. Bass, trout, salmon, redear

sunfish, catfish, crappie, and bluegill provide good fishing.

The big problem at Don Pedro is that it is subject to drawdowns from mid-summer through early fall. Low water also creates considerable boating hazards, and water-skiers should pay special attention at all times.

Access: There are three boat ramps.

• Moccasin Point: From Manteca, drive east on Highway 120 (it becomes Highway 108/120) for 30 miles to the Highway 120/Yosemite exit. Bear right on Highway 120 and drive 11 miles to Jacksonville Road. Turn left on Jacksonville Road and drive a short distance to the campground and lake on the right.

• Blue Oaks: From Manteca, take Highway 120 east to Oakdale (the road becomes Highway 120/108). Continue east on Highway 108 for 20 miles to La Grange Road/J59 (signed Don Pedro Reservoir). Turn right on La Grange Road and drive 10 miles to Bonds Flat Road. Turn left on Bonds Flat Road and drive .5 mile to the campground and boat ramp on the left.

• Fleming Meadows: From Manteca, take Highway 120 east to Oakdale (the road becomes Highway 120/108). Continue east on Highway 108 for 20 miles to La Grange Road/J59 (signed Don Pedro Reservoir). Turn right on La Grange Road and drive 10 miles to Bonds Flat Road. Turn left on Bonds Flat Road and drive 2.5 miles to the campground and boat ramp on the left.

Facilities, fees: Full-service marinas with fishing boat, houseboat, and pontoon boat rentals, mooring, boat storage, motor repairs, and bait and tackle are available at Lake Don Pedro Marina (south shore) and Moccasin Point Marina (north shore). Campgrounds, boat-in campsites, restrooms with flush toilets and showers, RV dump station, picnic areas, snack bars, café, convenience store, coin laundry, gas are available. Some facilities are wheelchair-accessible. Fees are charged for day use, boat launching and camping.

Water sports, restrictions: Powerboats, water-skiing, wake boarding, personal watercraft, sailing, and sailboarding are permitted. A sandy swimming beach is available on the south shore at Fleming Meadows Picnic Area.

Directions: See directions to ramps in Access, above.

Contact: Don Pedro Recreation Agency, 209/852-2396; Lake Don Pedro Marina, 209/852-2369, website: www.donpedrolake.com; Moccasin Point Marina, 209/989-2206.

11 TURLOCK LAKE

Rating: 7

east of Modesto in Turlock Lake State Recreation Area

Map 9.3, page 300

Turlock Lake covers 3,500 acres and has 26 miles of shoreline. New Melones Reservoir feeds Turlock Lake with cold, fresh water in the spring. Because this water comes from the bottom of New Melones, the lake is cooler than many San Joaquin Valley reservoirs, with surface temperatures usually ranging 65 to 74 degrees in late spring and summer, when other lakes in the region are 75 to 82 degrees. If you prefer cool water, the swimming is great and the excellent swimming beaches, big and sandy, are a special highlight.

But get this: The developed facilities—marina, grocery store, and gas station—are gone. That's right, the owner folded his tent and said adios. Lacking these facilities, Turlock Lake is one of the more primitive major recreation sites in the valley.

It does still get a lot of traffic. Turlock Lake has become far more family oriented than the old days when fast jet boats dominated the scene. One major factor in the personality change is that alcohol is no longer allowed on the lake or beaches, which keeps away the rowdiest folks.

When you arrive on the entrance road, note that the first beach you come to is the "family" beach, where people take their kids, and where the non-boaters hang out. Drive farther

down the road and you will arrive at another beach known as Ski Beach; this is where the recreational boaters tend to group.

In addition to water-skiing, wake boarding and personal watercraft are pretty popular at Turlock. Although permitted, sailing and sailboarding do not attract much traffic.

Access: A paved boat ramp and dock are located on the northwest shore, about one mile east of the Lake Road turnoff.

Facilities, fees: A campground is one mile away on the Tuolumne River. Picnic areas with drinking water and restrooms are provided. Some facilities are wheelchair-accessible. There is a day-use fee and boat launch fee.

Water sports, restrictions: Powerboats, water-skiing, wake boarding, personal watercraft, sailing, and sailboarding are permitted. You'll find large, sandy swimming beaches at the day-use area.

Directions: From Modesto, drive east on Highway 132 for 14 miles to Waterford, then continue eight miles on Highway 132 to Roberts Ferry Road. Turn right and drive one mile to Lake Road. Turn left and drive two miles to the campground on the left.

Contact: Turlock Lake State Recreation Area, 209/874-2008 or 209/874-2056, website: www .parks.ca.gov (click on Find A Park).

12 LAKE MCCLURE

Rating: 7

east of Modesto

Map 9.3, page 300

Some people think that Lake McClure and adjoining Lake McSwain (see next listing) appear to be the same lake. That will teach them to think. Even though McClure and McSwain are connected by the Merced River, they are two separate lakes, each with its own unique identity.

McClure is the giant, a huge H-shaped lake that covers more than 7,000 surface acres with 82 miles of shoreline. The water is warmer and there is more water sports activity here, including skiing, wake boarding and houseboating. The elevation is 900 feet.

This is a full-facility recreation area that offers developed campgrounds, picnic areas, and boating services. Water-skiing, personal watercraft, and houseboating are all very popular. In the summer the place can get crowded, but for the most part everybody seems to be having the time of their lives. In the off-season, it gets low to moderate use.

Swimming is pretty much limited to the lagoons in the campgrounds, which have sandy sunbathing areas. Although swimming is not prohibited in the lake, you'll rarely see people swimming or playing along the shore, mainly because of the typically steep drop-off. A more common sight is that of folks using their boats as swimming platforms, jumping in, treading water, floating around, and then scrambling back into the boat for a repeat performance.

Fishing for bass is best on the left half of the "H" near Cotton Creek. Fishing for trout is best on the right half of the "H." This is because of differences in water temperatures in these two areas.

Access: Paved ramps are located at Barrett Cove, McClure Point, Horseshoe Bend, and Bagby.

• Barrett Cove: From Modesto, drive east on Highway 132 for 31 miles to La Grange and then continue for about eight miles (toward Coulterville) to Merced Falls Road. Turn right and drive four miles to Bear Cove Road. Turn left and drive one mile to the kiosk.

• McClure Point Recreation Area: From Turlock, drive east on County Road J16 for 19 miles to the junction with Highway 59. Continue east on Highway 59/County Road J16 for 4.5 miles to Snelling and bear right at Lake McClure Road. Drive seven miles to Lake McSwain Dam and continue for seven miles to the end of the road to the campground and boat launch.

• Horseshoe Bend Recreation Area: From Modesto, drive east on Highway 132 for 31 miles to La Grange and then continue for about 17 miles (toward Coulterville) to the north end of Lake McClure and the campground entrance road on the right side of the road. Turn right and drive .5 mile to the campground and boat launch.

• Bagby: From Turlock, drive east on County Road J16 for 19 miles to the junction with Highway 59. Continue east on Highway 59/County Road J16 for 4.5 miles to Snelling and Merced Falls Road (continue straight, well signed). Drive .5 mile to Hornitos Road. Turn right and drive eight miles (drive over the bridge) to Hornitos to a Y. Bear left at the Y in Hornitos (signed to Highway 49) and drive 10 miles to Highway 49. Turn left on Highway 49 and drive eight miles the Bagby Bridge and entrance kiosk on the right.

Facilities, fees: Full-service marinas with mooring are available at McClure Point, Barrett Cove, and Bagby. Barrett Cove Marina rents fishing boats, ski boats, personal watercraft, houseboats, and pontoon boats. McClure Point rents fishing boats and pontoon boats. Campgrounds, fish-cleaning stations, picnic areas, restrooms with flush toilets and showers, convenience stores, snack bars, coin laundry, RV dump stations, and gas are available at all major access points. Fees are charged for day use and boat launching.

Water sports, restrictions: Powerboats, water-skiing, wake boarding, and personal watercraft are allowed. Sailing and sailboarding are permitted, but winds are usually light. The shoreline has no swimming beaches, but there are swimming lagoons at each recreation area.

Directions: See directions to ramps in Access, above.

Contact: McClure Point and Bagby Recreation Areas, Merced Irrigation District, 209/378-2521, website: www.lakeMcclure.com; Horseshoe Bend Recreation Area, 209/878-3452; Barrett Cove Marina, 209/378-2441; houseboat rentals, 209/378-2441, website: www.houseboats.com/mcclure.

13 LAKE MCSWAIN

Rating: 5

east of Modesto

> Map 9.3, page 300

If you find that adjacent Lake McClure is simply too large and filled with too many big, fast boats, then little Lake McSwain provides a perfect nearby alternative. You won't have to contend with the crowds that descend on McClure to the east because this lake is small, water-skiing is prohibited, and the water is much colder. If you have a canoe or car-top boat, this lake is preferable to Lake McClure.

McSwain may be like a puddle compared to McClure, but the water level is usually near full capacity here. That makes it the more attractive option, especially in low water years when McClure can look almost barren in comparison by late fall. McSwain, of course, is the afterbay for Lake McClure on the Merced River.

Although McSwain is developed, recreation is far more low-key than at big brother McClure. It is quite small, and the campground fills up fast on summer weekends, so reservations should be made in advance.

It is used primarily by fishermen. The lake is stocked with trout and fishing is often good. Several fishing derbies are held here each year.

Another bright spot is that much of the shoreline is favorable for swimming, and there's even a good, sandy beach. However, the lake is colder because the water that fills McSwain comes from the bottom of McClure Dam. But that cold water is what makes the trout fishing better here than at McClure.

Access: A paved boat ramp is available next to Lake McSwain Marina, located on Lake McClure Road.

Facilities, fees: A full-service marina is available with rentals for fishing boats and pedal boats. A campground, drinking water, restrooms with showers, RV dump station, coin laundry, playground, snack bar, and convenience store are nearby. Fees are charged for day use, boat launching, and camping.

Water sports, restrictions: Powerboats, canoes, kayaks, inflatables, and small sailboats are permitted. A 10-mph speed limit is strictly enforced. No water-skiing, wake boarding, personal watercraft, or houseboats permitted. The lake is too small and not windy enough for sailboarding and most sailboats. A sandy swimming beach is available adjacent to the marina.

Directions: From Turlock, drive east on County Road J16 for 19 miles to the junction with Highway 59. Continue east on Highway 59/County Road J16 for 4.5 miles to Snelling. Continue straight ahead to Lake McClure Road and drive seven miles to Lake McSwain Recreation Area on the right.

Contact: Lake McSwain Recreation Area, 209/378-2521 or 800/468-8889, website: www.LakeMcClure.com; Lake McSwain Marina, 209/378-2534.

14 YOSEMITE LAKE

Rating: 6

north of Merced in Lake Yosemite Park

> Map 9.3, page 300

Now don't get confused. Yosemite Lake is not in Yosemite National Park. In fact it has nothing to do with Yosemite National Park. It's more like a backyard lake for local residents. Unlike many lakes in the San Joaquin Valley, the water is cool, not warm. The lake is stocked with trout.

Yosemite Lake, on the outskirts of eastern Merced County, is a 25-acre lake where all water sports are permitted (outside of restricted areas). Unlike the national park with which it shares a name, it doesn't quite make the major leagues. Although not stellar in any way, this is still a nice spot, particularly for cooling off on a hot summer evening.

The best things going here are opportunities for swimming and sailboarding. Large swimming beaches are available, and lifeguards are posted during the summer. That's a winner. Another winner is sailboarding, with steady winds nearly every afternoon.

It is also popular with powerboaters and waterskiers, especially with the weather being so hot almost all summer long. Rate prospects good, but not great. One problem is that the water is usually too choppy for stellar water-skiing.

Access: A paved boat ramp is available just past the park entrance.

Facilities, fees: Picnic areas, restrooms, and drinking water are provided. A concessionaire with pedal boat and fishing boat rentals may be in business; check current status. Lodging and supplies can be found in Merced. Fees are charged for day use and boat launching.

Water sports, restrictions: Powerboats, water-skiing, wake boarding personal watercraft, sailing, and sailboarding are permitted in designated areas. Two large, sandy swimming beaches are available along the southern shore, off Lake Road.

Directions: From Modesto (or north of Merced), drive south on Highway 99 to Highway 59 near Merced. Take Highway 59 North and drive four miles to Bellevue Road. Turn right on Bellevue Road and drive five miles east to Lake Road. Turn left on Lake Road and drive to the lake.

From Fresno (or south of Merced), drive north on Highway 99 to Merced and 16th Street exit. Take that exit and drive a short distance to G Street. Turn right on G Street and drive five miles to Bellevue Road. Turn right and drive 2.5 miles to Lake Road. Turn left on Lake Road and drive to the lake.

Contact: Yosemite Lake Caretaker, 209/722-2568; Merced County Parks and Recreation, 209/385-7426.

15 EASTMAN LAKE

Rating: 7

southeast of Merced

Map 9.4, page 301

Tucked in the foothills of the San Joaquin Val-

ley at an elevation of 650 feet, Eastman Lake covers 1,800 surface acres. The reservoir was created when the federal government built a dam on the Chowchilla River. On your typical 100-degree summer day, it makes a nice tub to cool off in, ideal in early summer for water-skiing, swimming, or just taking a quick dunk.

All water sports have a place at this lake, including water-skiing and sailboarding, particularly early in the summer, and fishing for bass, which is best in late winter and spring. Swimming is best at the large beach on the west side, but boaters will discover a number of smaller, more private spots all along the shoreline. The lakeshore is edged with brush and oak trees, and the campgrounds and picnic areas are clean and well maintained.

A credit to operations here is a successful program that has largely eradicated and otherwise controlled the invasive aquatic weed hydrilla. Another bonus is a trophy bass program. Fishing can be good for not only bass, but for rainbow trout, catfish, bluegill, and redear sunfish, in season.

The lake is also designated as a "Watchable Wildlife" site, with 163 species of birds documented here. It is home to a nesting pair of bald eagles. A small area near the upper end of the lake is closed to boating to protect a bald eagle nesting site.

Access: Two paved ramps are available, one on the lake's east side, and one on the west side.

Facilities, fees: Campgrounds, picnic areas, restrooms with flush toilets, showers, and an RV dump station are available. Supplies can be obtained in Chowchilla. There is a fee for day use that includes boat launching.

Water sports, restrictions: Water-skiing, wake boarding, and personal watercraft are permitted. Sailing and sailboarding also are allowed. A swimming area is available along the northeast shoreline, where there is a buoy line prohibiting boating.

Directions: Drive on Highway 99 to Chowchilla and the Avenue 26 exit. Take that exit and drive east for 17 miles to County Road

29. Turn left (north) on County Road 29 and drive eight miles to the lake.

Contact: U.S. Army Corps of Engineers, Sacramento District, Eastman Lake, 559/689-3255, fax 559/689-3408.

16 HENSLEY LAKE

Rating: 6

north of Fresno

Map 9.4, page 301

Set in the foothills of Madera County at 540 feet in elevation, Hensley is one hot place. When full, it covers 1,500 surface acres and has 24 miles of shoreline. As long as water levels are sufficient, it is big enough to be a wonderful water playland. It was created by a dam on the Fresno River.

Popular with water-skiers and personal watercraft in spring and summer, it has prospects for bass fishing as well. Swimming is good, a swimming beach available. The best spot is at Buck Ridge on the lake's east side, where there are picnic tables and trees for shade.

In the spring, conditions for sailboarding can be decent, but they are inconsistent. One day the winds will be strong and steady, the next day gusty, followed by a day with no wind at all. Yeah, it drives everybody nuts, especially fishermen, who find the bass bite goes up and down like a yo-yo because of the fluctuating barometric pressure that drives winds.

By late spring the lake is at its fullest, the days are warm, and area boaters show in full strength, meaning heavy use through midsummer. That's typically when the water levels start to drop, as the water is shipped out for irrigation purposes to valley farmers. In low-rain years the lake level can fall way down and bear little resemblance to its appearance when full.

Access: Two paved launch ramps are available: one on the lake's east side, off County Road 400, and one on the west side, next to Hidden View Campground.

Facilities, fees: Campgrounds, restrooms with flush toilets and showers, RV dump station, and picnic areas are available. Supplies can be obtained in Madera. Day use and boat launching are free.

Water sports, restrictions: Water-skiing, wake boarding, personal watercraft, sailing, and sailboarding are permitted. Swimming beaches are available on each side of the lake, Buck Ridge on the east side and Hidden View on the west side.

Directions: From Madera, drive northeast on Highway 145 for about six miles to County Road 400. Bear left on County Road 400 and drive to County Road 603 below the dam. Turn left and drive about two miles on County Road 603 to County Road 407. Turn right on County Road 407 and drive .5 mile to the Hidden View campground and boat launch.

Contact: U.S. Army Corps of Engineers, Hensley Lake, 559/673-5151, fax 559/673-2044.

17 MILLERTON LAKE

Rating: 7

north of Fresno in Millerton Lake State Recreation Area

Map 9.4, page 301

Located at 578 feet elevation in the foothills of the San Joaquin Valley, Millerton gets very hot weather during midsummer. You can count on it. You can also count on this lake being a perennial victim of low water levels by the summer's end due to drawdowns that diminish the area's natural beauty.

Regardless, Millerton gets a lot of traffic because of its proximity to Fresno and Madera. In addition, the shape of the lake—a large lake body and a long, narrow inlet, with 43 miles of shoreline in all—helps to separate water-skiers from anglers. Fishermen head upstream, water-skiers downstream.

If you're just coming for the day, head to the lake's south side, which has a huge day-use area. If you'll be camping, head instead to the north side. There's a boat launch directly adjacent to the campgrounds. If the water is high enough and if you snare a shoreline site, you can even moor your boat right at the site, a great plus. These are premium sites and are highly coveted.

Water-skiing is popular here, as are sailing and sailboarding. Boat traffic is often heavy. The water-skiers and jet boats dominate the lake on most summer days to about 3 P.M. Then a strong, steady wind usually comes up, driving the water-skiers off the lake. Just like that, sailboarders and folks with small sailboats appear, ready to partake of the excellent prospects.

One of the quirks of Millerton Lake is that in the rare times when the lake is full (and quite pretty), the high water covers all the beaches. When the lake levels drop, the beaches become available, just right for swimming and wading, especially for kids who like horsing around in the water. So in the ideal situation, the lake is not quite full, but there's good lakeside access and swimming around most of the shore.

Fishing can be good for bass in the spring, catfish in summer. During winters, boat tours are available to view bald eagles.

Access: There are three paved boat ramps: two on the south side by the day-use areas, and one at the end of the campground entrance road, and three boat-in campsites.

Facilities, fees: Campgrounds, three boat-in campsites, picnic areas, restrooms with flush toilets and coin showers, drinking water, RV dump station, full-service marina, and a snack bar are provided. Fishing boats, ski boats, personal watercraft, pontoon boats, canoes, and kayas are available for rent at the marina. Supplies can be obtained in Friant. Fees are charged for day use and boat launching.

Water sports, restrictions: Water-skiing, wake boarding, personal watercraft, sailing, and sailboarding are permitted. Sandy swimming beaches are available on both sides of the lake.

Directions: Drive on Highway 99 to Madera at the exit for Highway 145 East. Take that exit east and drive on Highway 145 for 22 miles

(six miles past the intersection with Highway 41) to the park entrance on the right.

Contact: Millerton Lake State Recreation Area, 559/822-2332, fax 559/822-2319.

18 LOS BAÑOS CREEK RESERVOIR

Rating: 6

near Los Baños

Map 9.5, page 302

Set in a long, narrow valley, this lake covers 410 acres and has 12 miles of shoreline. The elevation is set at an elevation of 330 feet. The surrounding hills are often baked brown by late May, and on the typical summer day, it gets really hot out here.

Like nearby San Luis Reservoir, the wind can howl through this country in the early summer. That is why the number one activity has become sailboarding (the 5-mph speed limit is often exceeded) and sailing. Although not exactly paradise, it makes an excellent choice for an overnight stay, a quick respite from the grinding drive, or a couple hours of sailboarding for anybody making the long cruise up or down nearby I-5.

Sailboarders soon discover that the winds are less gusty and more predictable here than at San Luis Reservoir and O'Neill Forebay. In addition, the 5-mph speed limit keeps out personal watercraft and water-skiers, a bonus for sailboarders. Swimmers will find the best spots near the picnic area and campgrounds. Because of the speed limit, use at Los Baños Creek Reservoir is moderate.

Many anglers have discovered that the fishing here is often good for trout and bass. The lake is stocked with rainbow trout in winter and spring. Some large bass have been caught here.

Access: A paved launch ramp is available on the reservoir's northeast side.

Facilities, fees: A campground, chemical toilets, drinking water, and picnic areas are provided. Fees are charged for day use, including for boat launching.

Water sports, restrictions: A 5-mph speed limit is strictly enforced. Sailing, sailboarding, and swimming are permitted.

Directions: Drive on Highway 152 to Volta Road (five miles west of Los Baños). Turn south on Volta Road and drive about a mile to Pioneer Road. Turn left on Pioneer Road and drive a mile to Canyon Road. Turn south (right) onto Canyon Road and drive about five miles to the park.

Contact: San Luis Reservoir State Recreation Area, Four Rivers District, 209/826-1197, fax 209/826-0284.

19 MENDOTA POOL

Rating: 4

near Mendota

Map 9.5, page 302

Actually just the northern access point to Mendota Slough, Mendota Pool is the centerpiece of the surrounding county parkland.

This is basically little more than a boat-launching site for water-skiers. There is no beach and no developed facilities, and the water can be a bit too mucky for swimming. Water-ski boats may run down to the Highway 180/Whites Bridge Road overpass, then turn around, and make the run back; be sure not to water-ski past the overpass. For swimming and recreation better prospects are to be found at Jack's Resort at Mendota Slough (see next listing).

Access: A paved launch ramp is available.

Facilities, fees: Restrooms, picnic areas, drinking water, softball field, and barbecue pits are provided. Supplies can be obtained in Mendota. Access is free.

Water sports, restrictions: Water-skiing, wake boarding, and personal watercraft are permitted from Mendota Pool to the Highway 180/Whites Bridge Road overpass; you cannot ski south of this point. Sailboarding is not recommended. Swimming is permitted.

Directions: From Fresno, drive west on Highway 180/Whites Bridge Road for 11 miles

through the town of Kerman and continue 19 miles to the Mendota Wildlife Area entrance. Cross the bridge at the slough and drive five miles to Mendota and Bass Avenue. Turn right on Bass Avenue and drive 3.5 miles to a gravel road (past Mendota Pool Park). Turn right and drive .25 mile.

Contact: Contact: Mendota Pool Park, City of Mendota, 559/655-4298; Department of Fish and Game, 559/655-4645.

20 MENDOTA SLOUGH

Rating: 4

west of Fresno in Mendota Wildlife Area

Map 9.5, page 302

If you're planning a visit, make every effort to get here before dawn so you can see the surrounding marshland wake up with the rising sun. Mendota Slough is truly one of the highlights of the San Joaquin Valley. You get to watch all manner of waterfowl wake up, lift off, and fly past in huge flocks while the morning sun casts an orange hue over everything in sight.

The prime spot for boaters is Jack's Resort, a popular lunch break spot for boaters and swimmers. A swimming beach and day-use facilities are available. The boat launch at Jack's is more popular with anglers than with water-skiers. No water-skiing is permitted south of the Highway 180/Whites Bridge Road overpass to keep the waterfowl from being disturbed.

The Mendota Slough is the water source for the surrounding Mendota Wildlife Area, as well as a source of tranquility for anglers who want to fish for catfish amid a wetland vibrant with life. Striped bass and perch are also in these waters, but caught only rarely.

Access: A paved ramp is available at Jack's Resort on Highway 180/Whites Bridge Road.

Facilities, fees: A boat launch, restrooms, and dispersed camping are available at Mendota Wildlife Area. A boat launch, campground, restrooms with flush toilets and drinking water, restaurant, and bait and tackle are available at

Jack's Resort. There are fees for day use and boat launching at Jack's Resort. Access is free at the wildlife area.

Water sports, restrictions: Water-skiing, wake boarding, and personal watercraft are prohibited south of the Highway 180/Whites Bridge Road overpass. Sailboarding is not recommended. A swimming beach is available at Jack's Resort.

Directions: From Fresno, drive west on Highway 180 (Whites Bridge Road) for 11 miles, through the town of Kerman, and continue 19 miles to the wildlife area entrance (just before the bridge at the slough).

From I-5, take the Highway 33/Mendota exit to Derrick Avenue. Turn north on Derrick Avenue and drive to Mendota and Belmont Avenue. Turn right (south) on Belmont Avenue and drive one mile to Highway 180. Turn right and drive four miles to the wildlife area entrance.

Note: The entrance for Jack's Resort is directly across from the entrance to Mendota Wildlife Area.

Contact: Mendota Wildlife Area, DFG, 559/655-4645; Jack's Resort, 559/655-2335.

21 LAKE SUCCESS

Rating: 7

near Porterville

Map 9.6, page 303

Lake Success is a big lake with a series of major lake arms. When full, it covers nearly 2,500 acres and has 30 miles of shoreline, yet is much shallower than most reservoirs. It is set in the bare foothill country at an elevation of 650 feet. Those stark surroundings and the very hot temperatures that set in during the summer can make this lake look like a dream to boaters when they first arrive.

Water-skiing and personal watercraft are very big here, along with trout fishing in the winter and bass fishing in the spring. The latter includes a chance for very large bass. The water is quite warm by late May, and winds are typically light, so conditions are usually excellent for water-skiing.

The lack of wind, however, makes conditions poor for sailboarding most of the year. The exception is in late March and early April, or rarely, May, when this area can get some wind. This also happens to be the season when the lake is at its fullest, and the combination means outstanding opportunities for sailboarding.

The biggest problem with Lake Success is that the water levels can fluctuate from week to week, with major drawdowns during the summer. That is one reason why there are no beaches, although the day-use area does have a somewhat sloped stretch of shore that is good for swimming. There is a nature trail near the dam.

Lake use is moderate year-round, and there are lots of water-skiers in the summer. That's what you can expect.

Access: Three paved ramps are available: one on the west shore just north of the dam, and two on the east shore near the campgrounds.

Facilities, fees: A campground, restrooms with flush toilets, full-service marina, picnic areas, RV dump station, and convenience store with bait and tackle are available. You can rent fishing boats, pontoon boats, personal watercraft, and houseboats at Success Marina. Gas and a restaurant are nearby. There is a day-use fee that includes boat launching; fee for camping.

Water sports, restrictions: Water-skiing, wake boarding, personal watercraft, sailing, and sailboarding are permitted. There are no designated swimming beaches, but you can swim at the Tule Day-Use Area, just past the south parking area.

Directions: Drive on Highway 65 to Porterville and the junction with Highway 190. Turn east on Highway 190 and drive eight miles to Success Lake and the campground entrance on the left.

Contact: U.S. Army Corps of Engineers, Lake Success, 559/784-0215; Success Marina, 559/781-2078.

22 LAKE WOOLLOMES

Rating: 5

near Delano

Map 9.7, page 304

It's hard to believe that there is much of anything out in this country. This land is dry, hot, and flat. Little Lake Woollomes provides a respite, set in a small park, the kind that has lawns and even a few picnic spots. Woollomes covers about 300 acres, and in this part of the San Joaquin Valley, all lakes are considered something special.

This nice, quiet little spot is used mainly for picnicking, but it does attract a few anglers now and then. No motors are permitted, so people plop in a canoe and paddle around, a popular activity. Use is moderate year-round, mostly by families on picnics.

Access: An unimproved boat ramp for car-top boats is located next to the picnic areas.

Facilities, fees: Picnic areas, restrooms, drinking water, and boat docks are provided. An entrance fee is charged on weekends from March 15 to September 15.

Water sports, restrictions: Motors are not permitted on the lake. All boats are required to have a permit; boaters may purchase one at the park. Sailing is permitted. Sailboarding is not allowed. Swimming is available at a small lagoon area.

Directions: From Bakersfield, drive north on Highway 99 for 25 miles to Delano and Highway 155. Turn east on Highway 155 and drive one mile to Mast Avenue. Turn right (south) on Mast Avenue and drive one mile to Woollomes Avenue. Turn left (east) on Woollomes Avenue, and continue a short distance to the lake.

Contact: Kern County Parks and Recreation Department, 661/868-7000, website: www.co .kern.ca.us/parks.index.htm.

23 BUENA VISTA AQUATIC RECREATION AREA

Rating: 7

near Bakersfield

Map 9.7, page 304

This is the showpiece of Kern County recreation. In the desolate western San Joaquin Valley, any body of water is something of a haven. Buena Vista is actually two connected lakes fed by the West Side Canal: little Lake Evans to the west and larger Lake Webb to the east. It is set at an elevation of 330 feet. To get the most out of your visit, it is critical that you know the differences between the two.

Lake Webb, which covers 875 acres, is open to all boating (including personal watercraft), and jet boats towing skiers are a common sight in designated ski areas. On the other hand, Lake Evans is small, only 85 acres, quiet, and has a five mph speed limit.

The Buena Vista Aquatic Recreation Area is primarily a family-oriented park that offers full facilities. It attracts fairly heavy use in the summer; things slow down quite a bit in the fall.

Beaches are provided at Lake Webb for sailboarders and water-skiers, but no swimming is allowed. Although all boating is permitted (except for personal watercraft) at Lake Webb, the regulations are strict and enforced quickly here. Try to water-ski in the no-ski area, for instance, and you will be slapped immediately with a hefty ticket and told to leave the lake.

Sailing and sailboarding are permitted on both lakes, but are not popular.

Quotas are established of 300 boats and 125 personal watercraft per day. Lake Webb is a catfish lake, while Lake Evans is stocked in season with trout, and also has bass, bluegill, catfish and crappie.

Access: Paved boat ramps are available on the north side of Lake Webb and on the northeastern shore of Lake Evans. There is also a launch area for personal watercraft on the northern shore of Lake Webb.

Facilities, fees: A campground, restrooms with showers, RV dump station, picnic areas, marina, gas, snack bar, two swimming lagoons, and convenience store are available. Fees are charged for day use, boat launching, and camping.

Water sports, restrictions: Water-skiing, wake boarding, and personal watercraft are allowed at Lake Webb. The speed limit is 45 mph. One area on the lake's north side is off-limits to skiers; this is a designated area for personal watercraft only. Powerboating is allowed at Lake Evans, but a speed limit of 5 mph is strictly enforced. Swimming is prohibited at both lakes. Two special swimming lagoons are available.

Directions: From I-5 just south of Bakersfield, take Highway 119 West and drive two miles to Highway 43. Turn south (left) on Highway 43 and drive two miles to the campground at road's end.

Contact: Buena Vista Aquatic Recreation Area, Kern County parks, 661/868-7000, website: www.co.kern.ca.us/parks/index.htm; Buena Vista concessions, 661/763-1770.

24 LAKE MING

Rating: 5

near Bakersfield in Kern River County Park

Map 9.8, page 305

Squint your eyes just right in February when things have greened up a bit, and Lake Ming can be the prettiest sight for miles.

The lake is set near the Kern River at 450 feet in elevation and covers just 205 acres. Instead of scenic beauty, you will find that Lake Ming is mainly a big playground for speed boaters. Jet boat races are even held here, and sailing, sailboarding, and fishing can be restricted to a few days per month. As for swimming, forget it (and we'll get to that).

One weekend per month, the lake is closed to the public when private boat races and water-skiing events are scheduled. Always call ahead if you are planning a day trip.

Sailing and sailboarding are only permitted on the second weekend of every month and on Tuesday and Thursday afternoons, but they are very popular during those times.

All other boating is permitted on the remaining days; be aware that an annual boating permit is required for all craft. No permit is required for shoreline fishing.

You might ask why no swimming? Well, sailboarders and water-skiers should take note: There is a parasite in the lake that has been known to cause "swimmer's itch." Sounds like fun.

Access: A paved ramp is located on the lake's east side.

Facilities, fees: A campground is available approximately .25 mile west of the lake. A picnic area, restrooms with flush toilets and coin showers, drinking water, RV dump station, and a concession stand are available. Access is free.

Water sports, restrictions: Sailing and sailboarding are permitted on the second weekend of every month and on Tuesday and Thursday afternoons. All motorized boating, including water-skiing and personal watercraft, is permitted on the remaining days. All boats are required to have a permit; boaters may purchase one at the park. Swimming is not allowed. For alcohol consumption, a permit is required at the lake.

Directions: Take Highway 99 to Bakersfield and the exit for Highway 178. Turn east on Highway 178 and drive 11 miles to Alfred Harrell Highway. Turn north and drive four miles to Lake Ming Road. Turn right and drive .25 mile to the lake.

Contact: Kern County Parks and Recreation Department, 661/868-7000, website: www.co.kern.ca.us/parks/index.htm.

OGHORN OUTDOORS®

© ROBERT HOLMES/CALTOUR

Chapter 10

Yosemite and Mammoth Lakes

Chapter 10—Yosemite and Mammoth Lakes

Some of nature's most perfect artwork has been created in Yosemite and the adjoining eastern Sierra near Mammoth Lakes, as has some of the most profound natural phenomena imaginable.

Yosemite Valley is the world's greatest showpiece. It is also among the most highly visited and well-known destinations on earth, with 22,000 people squeezing into 2.5 square miles nearly every day of summer. Yet there are many stellar lakes and streams nearby that get far less use.

Many family recreation opportunities exist at lake-based settings. On the west slope of the Sierra, these include: Lake Alpine and Highlands Lakes off Highway 4, Beardsley and Pinecrest Lake on Highway 108, Cherry Lake off Highway 120, and Tenaya Lake in Yosemite.

On the east flank of the Sierra crest, the lake-based getaways are even more dramatic, with every canyon providing a lake, stream, and wilderness trailhead—and a paved road right to each. These include: Upper and Lower Twin Lakes, Trumbull Lake, and Lundy Lake southwest of Bridgeport; June Lake, Gull Lake, Silver Lake, and Grant Lake in the June Lake Loop; Lake Mary, Twin Lakes, Mamie Lake, Lake George of the Mammoth Lakes, Convict Lake, and Lake Crowley just south of Mammoth; and Rock Creek Lake, west of Toms Place on the edge of the John Muir Wilderness. In addition, there is Mono Lake near Lee Vining, a one-of-a-kind moonscape.

But that's still only scratching the surface. Over Tioga Pass, outside the park and just off Highway 120, are Tioga Lake, Ellery Lake, and Saddlebag Lake (10,087 feet). Saddlebag is the highest lake in California accessible by car.

The nearby June Lake Loop and Mammoth Lakes area is a launch point to another orbit. Both have small lakes with on-site cabin rentals, excellent fishing, and great hiking for all levels. In addition, just east of Mammoth Lakes airport is a series of hot springs, including a famous spot on Hot Creek, something of a legend in these parts.

If you didn't already know, many of California's best lakes for a chance to catch giant rainbow and brown trout are in this region. They include Bridgeport Reservoir, Twin Lakes, June Lake, Convict Lake, and Crowley Lake in the eastern Sierra, and Beardsley and Spicer Meadows in the western Sierra.

This region has it all. There is nothing else like it on earth.

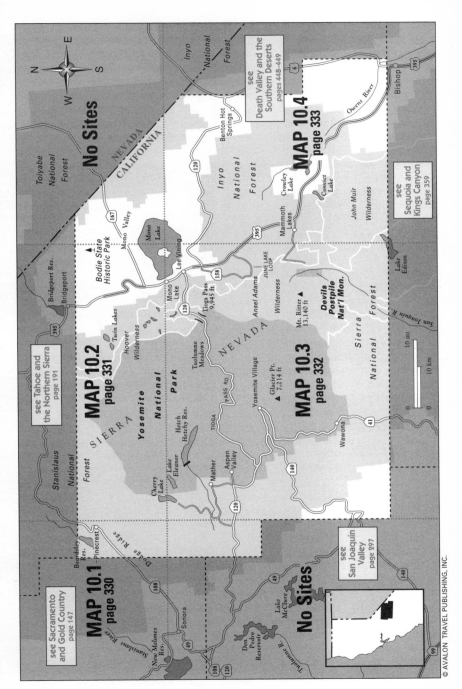

No Sites

see
Death Valley and the
Southern Deserts
pages 448–449

MAP 10.4
page 333

see
Sequoia and
Kings Canyon
page 359

see Tahoe and
the Northern Sierra
page 191

MAP 10.2
page 331

MAP 10.3
page 332

see
San Joaquin Valley
page 297

No Sites

see Sacramento
and Gold Country
page 147

MAP 10.1
page 330

Inyo National Forest

NEVADA
CALIFORNIA

Toiyabe National Forest

Benton Hot Springs

Bodie State Historic Park

Mono Valley

Mono Lake

Lee Vining

Bridgeport Res.

Bridgeport

Crowley Lake

Convict Lake

Mammoth Lakes

John Muir Wilderness

Lake Edison

Bishop

Owens River

Twin Lakes

Hoover Wilderness

Tioga Pass 9,945 ft

Tuolumne Meadows

Ansel Adams Wilderness

Mt. Ritter ▲ 13,140 ft

Devils Postpile Nat'l Mon.

Sierra National Forest

San Joaquin R.

Yosemite National Park

SIERRA NEVADA

Stanislaus National Forest

Hetch Hetchy Res.

Lake Eleanor

Cherry Lake

Mather

Aspen Valley

TIOGA PASS RD.

TIOGA

Yosemite Village

Glacier Pt. ▲ 7,214 ft

Wawona

Dodge Ridge

Beardsley Res.

Pinecrest

Sonora

New Melones Res.

Don Pedro Reservoir

Lake McClure

Stanislaus River

Tuolumne R.

10 mi
10 km
0

© AVALON TRAVEL PUBLISHING, INC.

Map 10.1

Site 1
Page 334

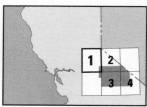

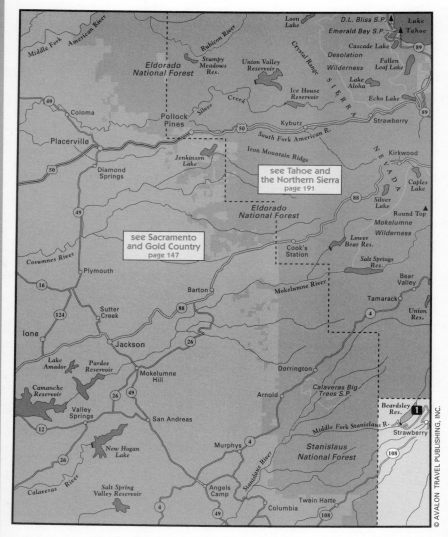

see Tahoe and
the Northern Sierra
page 191

see Sacramento
and Gold Country
page 147

© AVALON TRAVEL PUBLISHING, INC.

Map 10.2

Sites 2–6
Pages 334–338

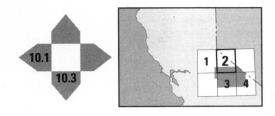

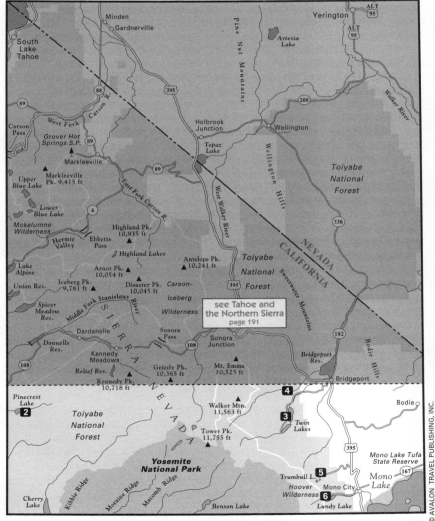

Minden
Gardnerville

South
Lake
Tahoe

Pine Nut Mountains

Yerington

Artesia
Lake

ALT 95

ALT 95

Carson Pass

West Fork

Carson R.

Holbrook
Junction

Wellington

208

Walker River

Grover Hot
Springs S.P.

Markleeville

Topaz
Lake

Toiyabe
National
Forest

Upper
Blue Lake

Markleeville
Pk. 9,415 ft

East Fork Carson R.

West Walker River

Wellington Hills

338

Lower
Blue Lake

Highland Pk.
10,935 ft

Mokelumne
Wilderness

Hermit
Valley

Ebbetts
Pass

Highland Lakes

Antelope Pk.
10,241 ft

NEVADA
CALIFORNIA

Lake
Alpine

Union Res.

Arnot Pk.
10,054 ft

Iceberg Pk.
9,781 ft

Disaster Pk.
10,045 ft

Carson-
Iceberg

Toiyabe

National

Sweetwater Mountains

Spicer
Meadow
Res.

Middle Fork Stanislaus River

Wilderness

395 Forest

**see Tahoe and
the Northern Sierra
page 191**

Dardanelle

Sonora
Pass

182

Donnells
Res.

Sonora
Junction

108

Kennedy
Meadows

Grizzly Pk.
10,365 ft

Mt. Emma
10,525 ft

Bridgeport
Res.

Relief Res.

Kennedy Pk.
10,718 ft

Bodie Hills

Bridgeport

4

Pinecrest
Lake

2

Toiyabe

National

Forest

Walker Mtn.
11,563 ft

3

Twin
Lakes

Bodie

395

Tower Pk.
11,755 ft

Mono Lake Tufa
State Reserve

**Yosemite
National Park**

167

Trumbull L.

5

Mono City

Mono
Lake

Cherry
Lake

Kibbie Ridge

Moraine Ridge

Macomb Ridge

Benson Lake

*Hoover
Wilderness*

6

Lundy Lake

SIERRA NEVADA

© AVALON TRAVEL PUBLISHING, INC.

Chapter 10 • Yosemite and Mammoth Lakes   331

Map 10.3

Sites 7–22
Pages 338–352

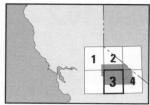

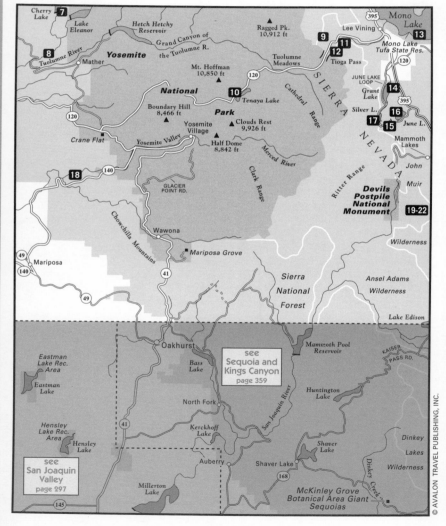

© AVALON TRAVEL PUBLISHING, INC.

Map 10.4

Sites 23–26
Pages 352–355

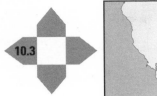

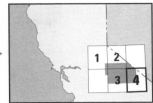

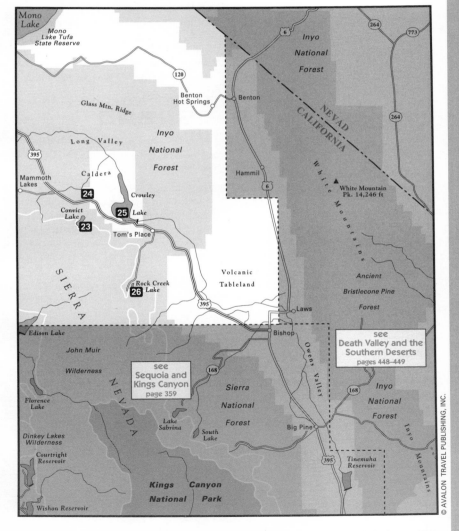

1 BEARDSLEY RESERVOIR

Rating: 7

near Strawberry in Stanislaus
National Forest

Map 10.1, page 330

Although best known as a good trout fishing lake, Beardsley Reservoir is also the only lake in the district that allows water sports with powerboats. The lake has a paved ramp, nice picnic area, and a fair beach, and all water sports are allowed.

The lake is set in a deep canyon on the Upper Stanislaus River. Although the setting is at an elevation of 3,400 feet, it actually feels as if it is much higher in the mountains, like about 6,000 feet. That's no accident.

From the turnoff on Highway 108, you drop nearly 2,000 feet on the eight-mile access road to reach the lake. The road is so long that the Forest Service keeps it gated during icy weather to prevent two-wheel-drive vehicles towing boats down to the bottom from getting stuck so far out there that their drivers are unable to get help.

The water is generally warm enough for swimming by midsummer. Aside from the beach area, the shoreline is steep, rocky in some places, and forested in others. Conditions for sailboarding are good in the early summer, but require high expertise due to gusty winds that come shooting up the canyon. You can count on them daily in the late afternoon and early evening. Fishing for trout is often excellent in early summer.

Beardsley can be subject to severe drawdowns, particularly in drought years, making it look something like the Grand Canyon. When the lake is low, you have to drive down on the dry lake bed to hand launch your boat. Believe it or not, that is often preferable to the situation during high water, when the walk up the boat ramp to the parking area is so long that some old-timers call it "Cardiac Hill."

Access: A paved ramp is located on the reservoir's entrance road; watch for the signed turnoff.

Facilities, fees: A campground, vault toilets, and a picnic area are available. No drinking water. Garbage must be packed out. Supplies are available in Strawberry. Access to the lake is free.

Water sports, restrictions: Powerboats, waterskiing, wake boarding, personal watercraft, sailing, and sailboarding are permitted. A swimming beach is available at the picnic area.

Directions: From Sonora, drive east on Highway 108 for about 25 miles to Strawberry and the turnoff for Beardsley Reservoir/Forest Road 52. Turn left and drive seven miles to Beardsley Dam.

Contact: Stanislaus National Forest, Summit Ranger District, 209/965-3434, fax 209/965-3372.

2 PINECREST LAKE

Rating: 7

near Strawberry in Stanislaus
National Forest

Map 10.2, page 331

No secrets here. The word is out about Pinecrest Lake, a family-oriented vacation center that is located near the Dodge Ridge Ski Resort. In the summer Pinecrest Lake provides what Dodge Ridge does in the winter: a fun spot with full amenities.

Pinecrest Lake is set at an elevation of 5,621 feet, covers 300 acres, and has 3.5 miles of shoreline. The water is clear and cold, but by midsummer it is good for swimming on a hot summer day.

This is the centerpiece of a fully developed family vacation resort, and it gets very heavy use throughout summer. The place is best suited for vacationing families who want to camp, boat, and fish.

The surrounding area is beautiful and heavily forested, with excellent hiking trails. Although it is pretty, don't expect the quiet wilderness. The campground usually has plenty of takers.

Sailboarding can be excellent; lessons and rentals are available.

A bonus is a small but excellent marina that rents all types of boats. Some families rent a pontoon boat so they can enjoy a picnic or barbecue on the water, then use the boat as a swimming platform.

The lake is stocked with rainbow trout, which join a small resident population of brown trout.

Access: A paved boat ramp is available at Pinecrest Lake Resort.

Facilities, fees: Cabins, campgrounds, lodging, picnic area, restrooms with flush toilets, groceries, gas, and a restaurant are available at the lake. Pinecrest Lake Resort rents fishing boats, pontoon boats, kayaks, and pedal boats, and has a full-service marina. Access is free.

Water sports, restrictions: Powerboats, inflatables, sailing, and sailboarding are permitted. No water-skiing, wake boarding, or personal watercraft. A 20-mph speed limit is strictly enforced. A sandy swimming beach is available next to the picnic area.

Directions: From Manteca at Highway 99, drive east on Highway 120 to Oakdale and Highway 108/120. Turn east on Highway 108/120 and drive to Sonora. Continue northeast on Highway 108 for 30 miles toward Sonora Pass to the Pinecrest Lake turnoff. Turn right and drive a short distance to the lake.

Contact: Pinecrest Marina, 209/965-3333; Pinecrest Lake Resort, 209/965-3411, website: www.pinecrestlakeresort.com; Stanislaus National Forest, Summit Ranger District, 209/965-3434.

❸ UPPER AND LOWER TWIN LAKES

🛥️ 🏕️ 🎿 🎣 〰️ ⛰️

Rating: 9

near Bridgeport in Humboldt-Toiyabe National Forest

Map 10.2, page 331

These are alpine lakes, set high in the eastern Sierra at an elevation of 7,000 feet. The water is quite cold, and the bordering landscape to the east is quite stark.

These are actually two lakes connected by a short stream. Boating and water sports prospects are unique at each.

Annett's Mono Village Resort is located on Upper Twin, a primary destination for boaters. Water-skiing and other water sports are permitted there. Swimming is especially popular at Upper Twin, where there is a sandy beach at the resort. Upper Twin is also the best spot for sailboarding; you can go as fast, or in some cases as slow, as you deem fit.

Lower Twin, on the other hand, is known as "the fishing lake" for its good catch rates of rainbow trout and a sprinkling of huge brown trout. The state-record brown trout, 26 pounds, 5 ounces, was caught here in 1985. A 5-mph speed limit here keeps this lake ideal for fishing, especially trolling, and prevents user conflicts between low-speed anglers and any high-speed boaters. Lower Twin also has a fine resort, Twin Lakes Resort.

These lakes have become very popular in the summer. An outstanding trailhead (and parking area) just upstream of Upper Twin Lake gives visitors the opportunity to hike into the adjacent Hoover Wilderness. In addition, there are Forest Service campgrounds set downstream of the lake along Twin Lakes Road.

Access: Each lake has a paved ramp: at Twin Lakes Resort on Lower Twin Lake, and at Annett's Mono Village Resort on Upper Twin Lake. Both are located off Twin Lakes Road.

Facilities, fees: Full-service marinas, mooring, and fishing boat rentals and pontoon boats are available at Twin Lakes Resort and Annett's Mono Village Resorts. Lodging, restaurants, and groceries are available at the lake. Campgrounds, vault toilets, and drinking water are available nearby on Twin Lakes Road. Access is free. Fees are charged for boat launching and camping.

Water sports, restrictions: Powerboats, inflatables, sailboats, and sailboarding are permitted. Water-skiing, wake boarding, and personal watercraft use are permitted from 10 A.M. to 3 P.M. on Upper Twin Lake only. A 5-mph speed limit is enforced on Lower Twin Lake. A beach is available next to the marina at Upper Twin; swimming is available all along the shoreline at Lower Twin.

Directions: On U.S. 395, drive to Bridgeport and the junction with Twin Lakes Road. Turn west and drive 12 miles to the lake entrance.

Contact: Twin Lakes Resort (Lower Twin Lake), 760/932-7751 or 877/932-7751, website: www.lowertwinlakesresort.com; Annett's Mono Village Resort (Upper Twin Lake), 760/932-7071, website: www.monovillage.com; Humboldt-Toiyabe National Forest, Bridgeport Ranger District, 760/932-7070, fax 760/932-1299.

4 BUCKEYE CREEK

Rating: 5
east of Bridgeport in Humboldt-Toiyabe National Forest

Map 10.2, page 331

The star attraction at Buckeye Creek is some little hot springs, and most vacationers don't even realize they exist (they are two miles from the campground).

Like nearby Robinson Creek, Buckeye Creek is better known for its brush-free grassy banks, with occasional pools and undercut shoreline where trout sometimes hide. Because there are few large pools and no sandy banks, this is not much of a destination for swimming, but rather for fishing for small trout. Brook trout are planted where Buckeye Road crosses the creek. In the course of trout fishing, some fishermen have stumbled upon the hot springs and turned their trip into a far greater success.

The hot springs come down from the canyon walls above the creek, and some people construct rock pools to capture the water on the creekside. During periods of high snowmelt and high flows, the hot springs can be drowned and impossible to find. Most of the summer they can be discovered easily enough, and making new pools is an ongoing effort here.

The hot springs get a fair amount of use, but because they are not publicized, you'll mostly find locals here. They add a great twist to a vacation in the eastern Sierra.

Access: Hike two miles to the hot springs.

Facilities, fees: A campground, flush toilets, and drinking water are available. Supplies can be obtained at Twin Lakes and Bridgeport. Access is free.

Water sports, restrictions: There are natural hot spring pools at the creek, near the parking area. Swimming is available near the hot springs and at various pools off Buckeye Creek Road.

Directions: On U.S. 395, drive to Bridgeport and the junction with Twin Lakes Road. Turn west and drive seven miles to Buckeye Road. Turn right (north) on Buckeye Road (dirt, often impassable when wet) and drive 3.5 miles to the campground.

Contact: Humboldt-Toiyabe National Forest, Bridgeport Ranger District, 760/932-7070; Doc & Al's Resort, 760/932-7051. For a map, send $6 to U.S. Forest Service, Attn: Map Sales, P.O. Box 587, Camino, CA 95709, 530/647-5390, fax 530/647-5389, website: www.fs.fed.us/r5/forests. Major credit cards accepted.

5 VIRGINIA LAKES

Rating: 5
near Bridgeport

Map 10.2, page 331

Big Virginia Lake and Little Virginia Lake are set at an elevation of 9,600 feet, between mountain peaks that rise 12,000 feet high. This canyon is the gateway to a beautiful high mountain basin where there are eight small alpine lakes within a two-mile circle.

The lakes are known for providing visitors with quiet solitude and trout fishing. They are stocked with rainbow trout. The speed limit allows canoeists to enjoy calm waters. No swimming or water sports are allowed.

Big Virginia gets the heaviest fishing traffic. Guests at Virginia Lakes Lodge usually stick to the lower lake.

A nearby trail is routed just north of Blue Lake, located inside the boundary for the Hoover Wilderness, then leads west to Frog Lake, Summit Lake, and beyond into a remote section of Yosemite National Park. This area has great natural beauty that is best seen on foot, exploring different lakes as you go.

Access: An unimproved boat ramp is available at Virginia Lakes Resort on Little Virginia Lake (also known as Lower Virginia Lake).

Facilities, fees: Boat rentals, lodging, café (open for breakfast and lunch only) and convenience store are available at Virginia. A campground, vault toilets, and drinking water is located nearby on Virginia Creek. Supplies can be obtained in Bridgeport. Access is free.

Water sports, restrictions: Rowboats, canoes, kayaks, inflatables, and small sailboats are permitted. A 10-mph speed limit is strictly enforced. No gas motors. Swimming and all water/body contact sports are prohibited.

Directions: From Bridgeport, drive south on U.S. 395 to Virginia Lakes Road. Turn west on Virginia Lakes Road and drive 6.5 miles to Little Virginia Lake.

Contact: Virginia Lakes Resort, 760/647-6484; Humboldt-Toiyabe National Forest, Bridgeport Ranger District, 760/932-7070.

⑥ LUNDY LAKE

Rating: 7

near Lee Vining

Map 10.2, page 331

Looking for good fishing, a campground, and a jumping-off point for hikes into the wilderness? Lundy Lake is one of the better answers. It is set in a high mountain canyon (at elevation 7,800 feet) in the stark eastern Sierra, just a short drive from U.S. 395.

This is a long, narrow lake that is surrounded by fantastic scenery. The lake is one mile long and .5 mile wide. Much of the shoreline is sprinkled with pine and aspen trees, and the old resort provides a rustic, New England–type feel, especially in the fall when the aspens turn color.

The water at Lundy Lake is clear and very cold, direct from snowmelt, even through the summer. Swimming is not recommended. Neither is sailboarding, not only because of the water temperature, but because there's usually just not enough wind.

That makes it an excellent choice for people with a canoe, rowboat, or small fishing boat. Fishing is good for rainbow trout and brown trout. The lake is calm on most summer mornings.

While use at the lake is moderate throughout the year, it's usually not too crowded, even on summer weekends. The resort, however, is a different story, and their cabins are often booked far in advance.

For a great side trip, hike up the trail that starts beyond the west end of Lundy Lake and is routed steeply up Mill Creek and into the Hoover Wilderness. The destination are several small, pretty lakes, passing two waterfalls en route, located two miles in. More ambitious hikers with two cars (one for a shuttle) will find an excellent short but steep trip by hiking from Lundy Lake, up over Lundy Pass, and then over to Saddlebag Lake.

Lundy Lake is sometimes overlooked because many travelers become fascinated instead with giant Mono Lake, located just to the east of the highway. The area is akin to a moonscape, the centerpiece of which is this giant saline lake. But hit it right at Lundy Lake and you'll have the opportunity to see colorful wildflower blooms in summer and beautiful aspens in the fall.

Access: An unimproved boat ramp is located at the lake's far west corner, near Lundy Lake Resort.

Facilities, fees: Cabins, hot showers, a small campground, and fishing boat rentals are available at Lundy Lake Resort. A picnic area and primitive campsites are provided near the lake's east side on Mill Creek. Limited groceries and supplies can be obtained at the lake. Supplies are available in Lee Vining. Access is free.

Water sports, restrictions: Powerboats, canoes, kayaks, inflatables, and sailing are permitted. The lake is usually too cold for swimming and sailboarding.

Directions: From the town of Lee Vining, drive north on U.S. 395 for seven miles to Lundy Lake Road. Turn left (west) on Lundy Lake Road and drive five miles to the lake at the road's end.

Contact: Inyo National Forest, Mono Basin Scenic Area Visitor Center, 760/647-3044; Lundy Lake Resort, 626/309-0415 (winter only). No phone is available at the resort.

7 CHERRY LAKE

Rating: 9

northwest of Yosemite National Park in Stanislaus National Forest

Map 10.3, page 332

Cherry Lake is set at an elevation of 4,700 feet, just outside the northwestern border of Yosemite National Park. It provides a base of operations for many activities, including camping, boating, swimming, sailboarding, and hiking. All water sports are allowed, yet because it takes a considerable drive to reach the lake, you won't find nearly the water-skiing traffic as at other regional lakes, such as Tulloch or Don Pedro in the foothills.

Most swimmers stick to the 200-yard stretch of rocky beach by the boat ramp, but that is pretty poor pluckings compared to what is available on the lake's far east side. You need a boat to get out there, but the ride is worth it, for you'll have access to a sandy stretch of shore in a far more private setting.

This lake is much larger and prettier than most people anticipate. It provides much better trout fishing than any lake in neighboring Yosemite National Park. The lake is bordered on the east by beautiful Kibbie Ridge (with gorgeous Eleanor Lake well hidden on the other side of the ridge).

Here's an insider's tip: During periods of campfire restrictions, which is often most of the summer in this national forest, the campground is the only one in the area where campfires are permitted. That makes the idea of camping here extremely compelling. A fire permit is required from the Forest Service.

Water levels can fluctuate, often dropping precipitously from mid-July through September.

Almost nobody sailboards here. Yet the water is cold and clear and afternoon winds that are predictable and strong.

At the dam at Cherry Lake is a trail that is routed north into the Emigrant Wilderness, or to the east to Lake Eleanor and farther into Yosemite National Park. Between the two wilderness areas, there are literally dozens and dozens of backcountry lakes. A Wilderness Permit is required from Yosemite.

Access: On Cherry Valley Road, take the signed turnoff on the right to reach the unpaved boat ramp. Note: The ramp may be unusable at low water levels. The gate across Cherry Lake Dam is closed the weekend following Labor Day and usually reopens Memorial Day Weekend, weather permitting.

Facilities, fees: Boat-in camping is permitted on the lake's east side. A campground, vault toilets, and drinking water are available .5 mile from the lake. Supplies can be obtained in Groveland. Access is free. A fee is charged for camping.

Water sports, restrictions: Powerboats, water-skiing, wake boarding, personal watercraft, sailing, and sailboarding are permitted. A rocky beach for swimming is located next to the boat launch. Sandy beaches are available on the lake's east side, and are accessible only by boat.

Directions: From Groveland, drive east on Highway 120 for about 15 miles to Forest Road 1N07/Cherry Lake Road on the left side of the road. Turn left and drive 18 miles to the south end of Cherry Lake and the campground access road on the right. Turn right and drive one mile to the campground.

Contact: Stanislaus National Forest, Groveland Ranger District, 209/962-7825. For a map, send

$6 to U.S. Forest Service, Attn: Map Sales, P.O. Box 587, Camino, CA 95709, 530/647-5390, fax 530/647-5389, website: www.fs.fed.us/r5/forests. Major credit cards accepted.

8 TUOLUMNE RIVER

Rating: 10

west of Yosemite National Park in Stanislaus National Forest

Map 10.3, page 332

Many rafters get baptized by the cool, clear, and pounding rapids of the Tuolumne. It is one of the most popular runs in California, and yes, that baptism usually includes a full dunking. It's a wildly exciting river with Class IV and Class IV+ water, enough to set the hearts of even the most experienced paddlers pounding. It's the classic pool-and-drop river.

There are two primary runs, and both are for experts only, usually in oar boats. Newcomers jumping into a raft had better make sure an expert is at the oars, or plan on sprouting gills. Both runs offer prime scenery and wilderness-like settings.

The water is clear and cold. Some people wear full dry suits or just the bottom or top of a dry suit or wet suit.

A great bonus is the long season, which can run from March to October. In wet years, however, both runs can be too high to attempt before May. Even when the river's levels are navigable, the runs will be high, turbulent, and dangerous.

Here are some specifics:

Upper Tuolumne: Pro rafters call this the Upper T for Upper Tuolumne. It peaks out at Class V+, just a half step from certain death. Perfect, eh? The run ranges nine miles from Cherry Creek to Meral Pool. Make absolutely sure that only experts are at the oars of a raft, and never, ever run at high flows.

From the put-in the trip starts with more than a mile of Class IV rapids, and just when you are getting accustomed to the thrills, the excitement is tweaked up a full notch. You then quickly run into several Class V drops, including Corkscrew, Jawbone, Mushroom, Catapult, and Miracle Mile. Any of these can popcorn you from the boat if you don't have a good hold, and even then, there are many times when you are so wet, literally submerged in the river, that you will not know when you are in the raft and when you are not.

At about mile seven you'll hit Flat Rock Falls, a Class V-VI drop that is often portaged. At high water you can buy the farm here. Same with Lumsden Falls, which is always portaged. After you get back in the boat, the run winds out with several more Class IV rapids over the course of 1.5 miles en route to the take-out at Meral Pool.

Main Tuolumne: The T, as it is affectionately known, includes one of the most fun rapids in California, Pinball, and one of the most terrorizing, Clavey Falls. It's an 18-mile run, starting at Meral Pool and running downstream to Ward's Ferry, and is rated Class IV.

From Meral Pool the first five miles feature encounters with several Class IV rapids and drops, including Nemesis, Sunderland's Chute, Hackamack Hole, Ram's Head, and Evangelist. While this may be exciting and enjoyable, the whole time in the back of your mind you will be anticipating the pending confrontation with Clavey Falls (Class V). You know it's coming, you know it's waiting, and finally, you round a bend and there it is. Before you even realize it, you are plunging down through the white water literally like a snowball in hell. This is the one nobody forgets. Some people surrender and portage.

From here the last nine miles are peppered with more Class IV rapids. Featured are Gray's Grindstone, Thread the Needle, Cabin, Hell's Kitchen, and .5 mile upstream of the take-out, Pinball, one of the most fun rapids on the run. So you end on an upbeat note, and with the knowledge that you have experienced firsthand one of life's most exhilarating adventures.

Access: There is no ramp. Two standard runs are available:

• Upper Tuolumne/Cherry Creek: The put-in for this run is on Cherry Creek (see Directions below). Some consider this the most challenging run in the United States. The Upper Tuolumne is comprised of long, nearly continuous rapids, with several Class V rapids, broken only by short pools, and virtually no spots to rest and catch your breath. Do not attempt it at high flows. Even during the river's low flows, this run is for experts only. Take out at Meral Pool.

• Main Tuolumne: Put in at Meral Pool, just downstream from the campground. At high flows (above 4,000 cubic feet per second) this run should be paddled only with expert guides.

Facilities, fees: Primitive campgrounds with vault toilets are available nearby. No drinking water. Access is free. Rafting permits are required; obtain forms through the Groveland Ranger District in Groveland.

Water sports, restrictions: Several excellent swimming holes are available along Lumsden Road/Forest Service Road 1N10. A good one is just downstream from Lumsden Campground.

Directions: To Cherry Valley put-in: From Groveland, drive east on Highway 120 for about 15 miles to Forest Road 1N07/Cherry Lake Road on the left side of the road. Turn left and drive to the bridge at the powerhouse. Cross the bridge and continue 1.5 miles to an unsigned paved road on the left. Turn left and continue to the put-in, located just downstream of the powerhouse. A Forest Service map is advised.

To Lumsden/Meral Pool: From Groveland, drive east on Highway 120 for about eight miles (just under a mile beyond County Road J132) to Ferretti Road. Turn left on Ferretti and drive to a Forest Service road intersection. Jog left, then right, and continue for four miles to Lumsden Camp. The take-out/put-in is at Meral Pool, just downstream from the campground. A Forest Service map is advised.

To Ward's Ferry take-out: From Groveland, drive west on Highway 120 for two miles to Deer Flat Road. Turn north and drive to Ward's Ferry Road. Turn north and drive to where the road crosses the river at the upper arm of Don Pedro Reservoir.

Contact: Stanislaus National Forest, Groveland Ranger District, 209/962-7825. For a map, send $6 to U.S. Forest Service, Attn: Map Sales, P.O. Box 587, Camino, CA 95709, 530/647-5390, fax 530/647-5389, website: www.fs.fed.us/r5/forests; major credit cards accepted.

Guided rafting trips: All-Outdoors Whitewater Rafting, 925/932-8993 or 800/247-2387, website: www.aorafting.com; ARTA River Trips, 209/962-7873 or 800/323-2782, website: www.arta.org; Outdoor Adventure River Specialists (OARS), 209/736-4677 or 800/346-6277, website: www.oars.com; Whitewater Voyages, 510/222-5994 or 800/488-7238, website: www.whitewatervoyages.com; Zephyr Whitewater Expeditions, 209/532-6249 or 800/431-3636, website: www.zraftng.com; ECHO, The Wilderness Company, 510/652-1600 or 800/654-3246, website: www.echotrips.com; Sierra Mac River trips, 209/532-1327 or 800/457-2580, website: www.sierramac.com.

9 SADDLEBAG LAKE

Rating: 6

near Yosemite in Inyo National Forest

Map 10.3, page 332

If you want to feel as if you are standing on top of the world, just take a trip here. Your vehicle may gasp for breath as it makes the climb (and maybe you will a bit, too), but when you finally arrive, you will be at the highest lake in California accessible by car, Saddlebag Lake, at elevation 10,087 feet.

If you like to camp, boat, and fish, this is an outstanding destination. It also makes a good jumping-off point for a wilderness backpacking trip.

Saddlebag Lake is by far the biggest lake in the region, and is set off by stark, pristine granite well above the treeline. Everything is granite, ice, or water, with only a few lodgepole pines managing precarious toeholds sprinkled across the landscape. It can be cold and windy here.

At this elevation don't even think about getting in the water without a wet suit. In the ideal situation you'll be high and dry in a fishing boat or canoe, enjoying the fantastic wilderness views and quiet water.

Most people who come here are interested in hiking and exploring the adjacent wilderness area, not the lake, so much of the traffic in the campground is generated by hikers, not boaters. This means that even when the campground is packed, the lake is often wide open. The campground is not at the lake, but about .25 mile up the access road. Some visitors find it difficult to catch their breaths on simple hikes. A hiker's shuttle boat, which will ferry you across the lake, is a nice plus.

The boat ramp is primitive, the air cool, the water always very cold. Because of the high elevation, the recreation season is short. In high snow years the place becomes accessible in late June, and sometimes not until after the Fourth of July. In low snow years access is often possible by Memorial Day weekend, rarely earlier in May. That makes late July and August the prime time, as the nights again become cold in September. The first big snow cuts off access again in the fall, often by Halloween.

Access: An unimproved boat launch is located at Saddlebag Lake Resort.

Facilities, fees: Boat rentals, hiker's shuttle boat, and convenience store are available at Saddlebag Lake Resort. A campground with vault toilets and drinking water is .25 mile away. Access is free. Fees are charged for boat launching and camping.

Water sports, restrictions: Powerboats, canoes, kayaks, sailing, and sailboarding are permitted. The water is too cold for swimming. A wet suit is needed for sailboarding.

Directions: From East Sierra on U.S. 395, drive .5 mile south of Lee Vining and the junction with Highway 120. Turn west and drive about 11 miles to Saddlebag Lake Road. Turn right and drive three miles to the lake.

From Merced, drive east on Highway 140 to the Arch Rock entrance station. Continue east to the Big Oak Flat Road junction (.5 mile before entering Yosemite Valley). Turn left and drive 14 miles to Tioga Road. Turn right and drive about 65 miles (past Tuolumne Meadows) and through the Tioga Pass entrance station. Continue two miles to Saddlebag Lake Road. Turn left and drive three miles to the lake.

Contact: Inyo National Forest, Mono Basin Scenic Area Visitor Center, 760/647-3044; Saddlebag Lake Resort, PO Box 303, Lee Vining, CA 93541.

10 TENAYA LAKE

Rating: 7

west of Lee Vining in Yosemite National Park

Map 10.3, page 332

There may be no prettier lake anywhere than Tenaya Lake on a warm, windless evening. It is set in a natural rock basin in the pristine, high granite country of Yosemite.

Tenaya sits at an elevation of 8,141 feet and covers 150 acres. The atmosphere feels almost sacred, like a mountain temple. The lake was named after Chief Tenaya of the Ahwahneechee tribe, who was Yosemite's last Native American chief and caretaker until a U.S. Army troop moved the entire tribe to a reservation.

Hiking is the most popular activity here. A very beautiful and easy trail loops around the lake's lower end to the far side. Another popular activity is watching the rock climbers on Polly Dome, a spectacular view from the lake.

It seems very few take advantage of this beautiful lake by paddling across in a canoe or kayak. Because of the sense that it is a sacred site, perhaps the parade of visitors in Yosemite believe that boating is banned here. Nope. Whereas there can be many people driving along adjacent Highway 120, or even stopping to picnic or hike, you often have the lake to yourself.

One reason is that the fishing is terrible. Trout have not been stocked for many years, and the lake is now fished out. So you'll see very few anglers and never a fishing boat. It is extremely rare even to see people paddling around in canoes or kayaks. If you see an old, beat-up green canoe, it's probably me doing the paddling.

Instead, Tenaya Lake attracts those who want to experience one of the most stunningly beautiful settings on the planet.

Access: There is no boat ramp. Car-top boats may be hand launched.

Facilities, fees: A picnic area is provided. A campground, flush toilets, café, and convenience store are available at Tuolumne Meadows. Fees are charged for park entrance and camping.

Water sports, restrictions: Canoes, kayaks, inflatables, sailing, and sailboarding are permitted. No motors. A swimming beach is available on the eastern shore.

Directions: From Merced, drive east on Highway 140 to the Arch Rock entrance station. Continue east to the Big Oak Flat Road junction (.5 mile before entering Yosemite Valley). Turn left and drive 14 miles to Tioga Road. Turn right and drive 31 miles to the lake on the right side of the road (15 miles west from Tioga entrance station).

From East Sierra, take U.S. 395 to the junction with Highway 120 (just south of Lee Vining). Turn west on Highway 120 and drive 11 miles to the Tioga Pass/Yosemite National Park entrance. Continue another 15 miles to the lake.

Contact: Yosemite National Park, 209/372-0200, website: www.nps.gov/yose.

11 ELLERY LAKE

Rating: 5

near Yosemite in Inyo National Forest

Map 10.3, page 332

Congress blew the deal when they set the borders for Yosemite National Park and failed to include Tioga and Ellery Lakes within park boundaries. Both are set just two miles outside the Highway 120 entrance on the eastern side of the park.

Ellery Lake offers spectacular deep-blue waters set in rock at 9,800 feet. Ellery and Tioga are among the most pristine lakes in national forest that you can reach by car in America. It looks like Yosemite, feels like Yosemite, but is not Yosemite. That means the lake is stocked with trout. As at nearby Tioga and Saddlebag lakes, the fishing is far better at Ellery Lake than at any lake in Yosemite.

This is a beautiful lake, although often freezing cold, and it is a popular spot for trout fishing and camping. Boats with small motors for trolling are allowed, but you almost never see them. Anglers usually fish from the shore and rarely bring car-top boats such as rowboats, canoes, or float tubes.

Use is heavy in the summertime. The lake is easily accessed off Highway 120, and the campgrounds get a lot of people who arrive late at Yosemite only to discover the camps there are full. Unfortunately, the camps at Ellery Lake are usually just as full.

Access: There is no boat ramp. Car-top boats may be hand launched.

Facilities, fees: A campground, vault toilets, and drinking water are available. Access is free. Fees are charged for boat launching and camping. Nearby Tioga Pass Resort offers cabins, café, and convenience store. If arriving through Yosemite, a fee is charged for park entrance.

Water sports, restrictions: Powerboats, canoes, and kayaks are permitted. The water is too cold for swimming. The lake is too small for sailboarding.

Directions: From East Sierra on U.S. 395, drive .5 mile south of Lee Vining and the junction with Highway 120. Turn west and drive about 10 miles to the campground and lake entrance on the left.

From Merced, drive east on Highway 140 to the Arch Rock entrance station. Continue east to the Big Oak Flat Road junction (.5 mile before entering Yosemite Valley). Turn left and drive 14 miles to Tioga Road. Turn right and drive about 65 miles (past Tuolumne Meadows) and through the Tioga Pass entrance station. Continue two miles to the campground and lake entrance on the right.

Contact: Inyo National Forest, Mono Basin Scenic Area Visitor Center, 760/647-3044.

12 TIOGA LAKE

Rating: 6

west of Lee Vining in Inyo National Forest

Map 10.3, page 332

Tioga, like nearby Ellery, is a drop-dead beautiful lake located just outside the borders of Yosemite National Park and set at an elevation of 9,700 feet.

Conditions here are much like those at neighboring Ellery, with one giant difference: Tioga has a boat ramp. Though small and primitive, the ramp makes the lake accessible for campers with trailered boats.

Most of those who do launch here are fishing for trout, trolling about slowly and enjoying the panoramic views of the many high granite peaks nearby. The lake is stocked with rainbow trout.

The only downer is that great expectations can make for disappointment. The camps fill quickly here, often from the overflow crowds that can't get a spot at Tuolumne Meadows. In addition, the wind often whistles down the canyon on summer afternoons.

At dawn, however, with most of the world asleep, this is a mountain shrine.

Note that the four major lakes in this region—Tioga, Ellery, Tenaya, and Saddleback—are usually locked up by snow and ice until late May, and in big snow years all the way into July. The 15 hike-to lakes in the vicinity don't usually become accessible until mid-June, with the high mountain spring arriving in July.

Access: A small, unimproved boat ramp is available near the campground.

Facilities, fees: A campground, vault toilets,

and drinking water are available. Access is free. Fees are charged for boat launching and camping. Nearby Tioga Pass Resort offers cabins, café, and convenience store. If arriving through Yosemite, a fee is charged for park entrance.

Water sports, restrictions: Powerboats, canoes, and kayaks are permitted. The water is too cold for swimming. The lake is too small for sailboarding.

Directions: From Merced, drive east on Highway 140 to the Arch Rock entrance station. Continue east to the Big Oak Flat Road junction (.5 mile before entering Yosemite Valley). Turn left and drive 14 miles to Tioga Road. Turn right and drive about 65 miles (past Tuolumne Meadows) and through the Tioga Pass entrance station. Continue one mile to the lake and campground entrance road on the right side of the road.

From East Sierra, take U.S. 395 to the junction with Highway 120 (just south of Lee Vining). Turn west on Highway 120 and drive about 11 miles (just past Ellery Lake) to the lake and campground on the left side of the road.

Contact: Inyo National Forest, Mono Basin Scenic Area Visitor Center, 760/647-3044.

13 MONO LAKE

Rating: 10

near Lee Vining

Map 10.3, page 332

There's no place on earth like Mono Lake. This lake is vast and stark, resembling a moonscape, and yet strangely beautiful. The unusual and remarkable tufa towers create one of the most extraordinary landscapes in California. Mono Lake covers 60 square miles. It is estimated to be more than 700,000 years old, making it one of the oldest lakes in North America.

Paddling a canoe across this lake on a calm dawn is one of the most awe-inspiring adventures in California. All types of boating are permitted on Mono Lake, although access is restricted near Negit and Paoha Islands from April 1 to August 1 each year to protect nesting gulls.

Canoes and kayaks are best launched near Navy Beach, located on the south shore. Larger craft should use the launch ramp near Lee Vining Creek on the western shore. Kayaks, canoes, and inflatables are advised to stay near shore. High winds have caused capsizings and drownings for boaters caught unprepared. Winds are strong and frequent in the afternoon.

There also are underwater obstacles, a hazard for powerboaters. Also note that boat motors need to be flushed with freshwater after boating here.

A swim in Mono Lake is a memorable experience. The lake's salty water is denser than ocean water so it provides a buoyant swim. Some people claim that a soak in the lake will cure almost anything. Be warned that the salty water will sting your eyes or any cuts or scratches. When you dry off, there is this weird whitish mineral residue on your skin, and your hair becomes stiff.

The tufa formations are formed when calcium-rich underwater springs are released from the lake bottom and mix with Mono Lake's saline water. That forms calcium carbonate, which builds in strange tower formations. It looks soft, but it feels as hard as a bowling ball. A one-mile loop trail is the best way to see these tufa formations. The trailhead is at the state reserve.

Day-use areas are available at Mono Lake County Park on the north end of the lake, and at Mono Lake Tufa State Reserve on the south side of the lake. In general, the south shore is sandier and less muddy than the north or west shores. Water temperature in the summer is about 75 degrees.

The Mono Basin Scene Area Visitors Center, located just off U.S. 395, is one of the better visitor's centers in California and features great views.

Access: Car-top boats can be launched from the Mono Lake Tufa State Reserve. A primi-tive boat ramp is available near Lee Vining Creek on the west shore.

Facilities, fees: Picnic areas with chemical toilets are available. No drinking water. Interpretive programs are available. Camping, lodging, and supplies are available in Lee Vining. A fee is charged for day use.

Water sports, restrictions: Powerboats, rowboats, canoes, kayaks, inflatables, sailing, sailboarding, and swimming are permitted. Two areas are closed to all boating from April through July to protect nesting birds. Another area near Navy Beach is closed year-round to protect nesting osprey.

Directions: From Lee Vining, drive south on U.S. 395 for five miles to Highway 120 (signed Mono lake South Tufa). Turn east (left) and drive 4.7 miles to an access road on the left. Turn left and drive one mile on a dirt road to the parking area.

Contact: Mono Lake Tufa State Reserve, 760/647-6331; Inyo National Forest, Mono Basin Scenic Area Visitor Center, 760/647-3044. For summer canoe and boating tours: Mono Lake Committee, 760/647-6595, website: www.monolake.org; Tioga Lodge, 760/647-6423 or 888/647-6423, website: www.tiogalodge.com.

14 GRANT LAKE

Rating: 7

near Lee Vining in Inyo National Forest

Map 10.3, page 332

The June Lakes Loop is highlighted by a series of quality lakes accessible by car along a loop road (Highway 158) off U.S. 395. These include Grant Lake, Silver Lake, Gull Lake, and June Lake.

Dramatic panoramic sunsets make Grant Lake a special place. This is the largest of the waters among the June Loop Lakes. The lake is shaped like an hourglass, is set at an elevation of 7,600 feet and covers 1,100 surface acres when full. Though the surroundings here are the most stark of all the lakes in the loop, it is still a very attractive destination for boaters and water sports enthusiasts. A great plus is the rule that sets a 10-mph speed limit each day until 10 A.M. That guarantees quiet water for trout anglers in the morning, and then the chance for wide-open water sports at mid-day. The lake is sometimes referred to as the home of the German brown trout.

Grant Lake is the only lake in the loop where water-skiing and personal watercraft are allowed. Because of that, it tends to attract more of a boater/party crowd, while the others get primarily anglers and campers.

The water can be cold, but it is still good for swimming and water-skiing. Sailboarding conditions are often excellent in late summer, even for experts, as the lake gets a west wind that really sends sailboarders across the lake at a fast clip. There is one large, fully developed campground that usually has some open sites, even on crowded summer weekends.

The lake is subject to drawdowns courtesy of the Los Angeles Department of Water & Power. In years with a light snowfall and a corresponding low snowpack, the water level can get low.

Access: A paved ramp is located at Grant Lake Marina.

Facilities, fees: A campground, flush toilets, drinking water, picnic area, store, and small marina are provided. Fishing boat and dock rentals are also available. Access is free. There is a fee for boat launching.

Water sports, restrictions: Powerboats, water-skiing, wake boarding, personal watercraft, sailing, and sailboarding are permitted. A 10-mph speed limit takes effect each day until 10 A.M. A sandy watercraft/swimming beach is available near the marina.

Directions: From Lee Vining on U.S. 395, drive south for six miles to the first Highway 158 North/June Lake Loop turnoff. Turn west (right) and drive five miles to the turnoff for Grant Lake.

Contact: Grant Lake Marina, 760/648-7964; Inyo National Forest, Mono Basin Scenic Area

Visitor Center, 760/647-3044; June Lake Chamber of Commerce, 760/648-7584.

15 GULL LAKE

Rating: 6

near Lee Vining in Inyo National Forest

Map 10.3, page 332

Little Gull Lake is the smallest of the June Loop Lakes, covering just 64 acres. It is set at an elevation of 7,600 feet below the peaks of the eastern Sierra, intimate yet dramatic, tiny yet beautiful. A boat ramp is located on the lake's southwest corner.

The lake is easily accessible, excellent for fishing and small boats. Swimming is not recommended near areas with steep shoreline. There is a rope swing at Gull Lake that youngsters love.

If this pretty lake were in the middle of nowhere, it would be treated like a slice of heaven. But with June Lake right down the road providing better fishing, boating, swimming, and camping, this place gets only moderate use throughout the summer.

The lake is stocked with nearly 50,000 trout each summer and provides good fishing.

Access: A paved boat ramp is located at Gull Lake Marina. Look for the turnoff on Highway 158 past June Lake.

Facilities, fees: A full-service marina, docks, and fishing boats, canoes, kayaks, and pedal boats are available at Gull Lake Marina. A campground, restrooms with flush toilets, drinking water, public park, coin laundry, store, and propane gas are nearby. Access is free. Fees are charged for camping and boat launching.

Water sports, restrictions: Powerboats, canoes, kayaks, and inflatables are permitted. A 10-mph speed limit is strictly enforced. No sailing or sailboarding is permitted. Swimming is permitted, although some of the shoreline is quite steep.

Directions: From Lee Vining, drive south on

U.S. 395 (past the first Highway 158/June Lake Loop turnoff) to June Lake Junction (a gas station/store is on the west side of the road) and Highway 158. Turn west on Highway 158 and drive three miles to the campground entrance on the right side of the road.

Contact: Gull Lake Marina, 760/648-7539; Inyo National Forest, Mono Basin Scenic Area Visitor Center, 760/647-3044; June Lake Chamber of Commerce, 760/648-7584.

16 JUNE LAKE

Rating: 8

near Lee Vining in Inyo National Forest

Map 10.3, page 332

This lake is the centerpiece of a beautiful and developed resort area. It has everything going for it—that is, except for solitude. Beauty? Try a 160-acre mountain lake set at 7,600 feet below awesome peaks that are often edged with snow. Accommodations? There are campsites near the water, nearby cabins, a good boat ramp, and stores within a mile. If you need something you can get it here.

June Lake is very beautiful and easily accessible off Highway 158. It gets the highest use by far of all the lakes in the June Lakes Loop for many reasons: It has the best fishing, best campground, best swimming, and best sailboarding. That's a lot of bests.

Even when the place is crowded, the 10-mph speed limit ensures a good deal of serenity. Most of the boaters you'll see are fishermen, and they are up early, getting their fishing done before the predictable afternoon wind comes up. June Lake receives stocks of nearly 100,000 trout per year.

The afternoon wind, along with the rules that prohibit water-skiing, makes sailboarding extremely popular here in mid-summer. Sailboarders enjoy clear, open water and brisk afternoon winds almost every day, and there are no water-skiers to get in the way.

This is also the best lake in the loop for swimming, as well as the only one with a developed beach.

Newcomers will need a little attitude adjustment when they arrive and discover two factors: the cold water and the number of other visitors. Sailboarders should wear wet suits, and swimmers should be prepared to turn into ice cubes. And even though it takes a long drive from almost anywhere to reach June Lake, the quality of the place is high enough that a number of people are willing to pay that price. Get the message? Right: Always have reservations for lodging.

Access: Two paved boat ramps are available: one at June Lake Marina and one at Big Rock Resort, both located off Highway 158.

Facilities, fees: A full-service marina, docks, and fishing boat, pontoon boat, and canoe rentals are available at June Lake Marina. Cabins, a small marina, and fishing boat and kayak rentals are available at Big Rock Resort. Campgrounds, restrooms with flush toilets, and drinking water are available. A store, propane gas, lodging, and cabins are available nearby. Access is free. Fees are charged for boat launching and camping.

Water sports, restrictions: Powerboats, canoes, kayaks, inflatables, and sailboarding are permitted. A 10-mph speed limit is strictly enforced. A large, developed swimming beach is available.

Directions: From Lee Vining, drive south on U.S. 395 (passing the Highway 158 North) for 20 miles (six miles past Highway 158 North) to June Lake Junction (a sign is posted for June Lake Village) and Highway 158 South. Turn west (right) on Highway 158 North and drive two miles to June Lake. Turn right (signed) and drive a short distance to the campground.

Contact: June Lake Marina, 760/648-7726; Big Rock Resort, 760/648-7717 or 800/769-9831; Pinecliff Resort, 760/648-7558; Inyo National Forest, Mono Basin Scenic Area Visitor Center, 760/647-3044; June Lake Chamber of Commerce, 760/648-7584.

17 SILVER LAKE

Rating: 6

near Lee Vining in Inyo National Forest

Map 10.3, page 332

Silver Lake was named for the way it looks when afternoon winds cause the surface waters to sparkle in refracted silvers—a beautiful sight against a background of several high but stark Sierra peaks. This lake is set at elevation 7,200 feet and covers just 80 acres. Yet all services are provided, including boat rentals, cabins, and a campground. There is an outstanding trailhead nearby that is routed up the beautiful Rush Creek drainage.

Silver Lake has a developed resort. Most visitors are campers/anglers who stay at the large, open campground just east of the lake at the adjacent RV park or in the resort's cabins. If you prefer fewer people, consider nearby Gull Lake instead, which gets far less use.

A 5-mph speed limit is designed to eliminate user conflict, as well as fast boats. That makes it ideal for fishing. The lake is stocked with trout.

Even with the speed limit, swimming is not recommended because the shoreline is rocky, the bottom is somewhat mucky, the water is cold, and by the afternoon, it's often windy.

Unlike Grant Lake, Silver Lake doesn't seem to have problems with water drawdowns. Snowmelt in spring and glacial water in summer flow into the lake, creating a pure setting that is usually full to the brim.

While the lake does not have a wilderness setting, you don't have to hike far to find that. The Ansel Adams Wilderness is only a two-hour hike from a signed trailhead located just south of the lake. From here, a trail is routed west from Silver Lake along the Rush Creek drainage and up to Agnew Lake, a great day hike that provides access not only to a pristine lake, but wonderful views of the June Lake Basin.

Access: Two paved boat ramps are located at the lake's south end near Silver Lake Resort.

Facilities, fees: A small marina with fishing boats for rent, RV park, cabins, store, coin laundry, RV supplies, gas, and a café are available at Silver Lake Resort. A campground, restrooms with flush toilets, and drinking water are nearby. Access is free. Fees are charged for boat launching and camping. Launching is free at the ramp next to the Forest Service campground.

Water sports, restrictions: Powerboats, canoes, kayaks, and inflatables are permitted. A 5-mph speed limit is strictly enforced. Swimming is not recommended due to the rocky shoreline. The lake is too small for sailboarding.

Directions: From Lee Vining on U.S. 395, drive south for six miles to the first Highway 158 North/June Lake Loop turnoff. Turn west (right) and drive nine miles (past Grant Lake) to Silver Lake. Just as you arrive at Silver Lake (a small store is on the right), turn left at the entrance for boat launch and campground.

Contact: Silver Lake Resort, 760/648-7525, website: www.silverlakeresort.net; Inyo National Forest, Mono Basin Scenic Area Visitor Center, 760/647-3044; June Lake Chamber of Commerce, 760/648-7584.

18 MERCED RIVER

Rating: 10

west of Yosemite National Park in Sierra National Forest

Map 10.3, page 332

So many vacationers drive right by this stream in their mad scramble to get to Yosemite National Park. It's a beautiful river, offering outstanding rafting and gorgeous scenery, and an opportunity to go swimming and fly-fishing for trout.

There are also several Bureau of Land Management campgrounds available along the Merced that have far fewer people in them than the camps in Yosemite, along with good river access. In the summer it is an ideal river to jump into during the daytime, with many deep holes and rocks perfectly situated for jumping platforms (always check the depth of the hole before jumping in and never dive head-first into a river, of course).

But the true attraction is rafting. An extraordinarily long stretch of river (29 miles) can be run from the put-in at Red Bud Day-Use Area to the take-out at Bagby. The first nine miles and the last 13 miles are rated Class IV+; the seven miles in between those two stretches are rated Class II.

The scenery and riparian zone is often beautiful. There are often spectacular blooms of redbud, poppies, and lupine. The run has a remote feel, even though much of it is paralleled by the highway. The water is cold and high early in the season, but becomes quite warm by the end of summer. In a year with average rainfall, the season lasts approximately from April to early July, with smaller boats capable of floating it from July to early August. In big snow years the ensuing snowmelt can turn this river into a torrent when the weather gets hot. In any case, always go with an experienced guide.

Within the first half hour after putting in at Red Bud, you will confront some of the river's nastiest rapids. The first 2.5 miles contain some Class IV white water, most notably Chipped Tooth and Nightmare Island. At high flows, in fact, it's often better to avoid these completely and put in farther downstream at Cranberry Gulch.

Five miles downstream of Cranberry Gulch, you come face-to-face with Ned's Gulch, another Class IV rapid. After that you can enjoy the scenery and relaxed Class II water for about seven miles.

Then prepare yourself for a series of more Class IV rapids that will spring you back to full attention. The guides call them Split Rock, Corner Pocket, and Quarter Mile. At mile 23, boaters encounter North Fork Falls, which must be portaged by all. It's a 25-foot vertical, rocky drop.

Afterwards it's easy going from here to the take-out, rated Class II. All in all, this is a beautiful, dramatic, and rewarding rafting trip.

Access: There is no boat ramp. The standard put-ins and take-outs:

• Put-ins: The standard put-in is at Red Bud, just across a bridge from Red Bud Picnic Area, located on Highway 140, 29 miles east of Mariposa. At high flows boaters can put in about three miles downstream at Cranberry Gulch in order to avoid the difficult rapids below Red Bud. An easy Class I float is also available in Yosemite National Park; enter at Arch Rock entrance station in El Portal on Highway 140.

• Take-out: The last possible take-out is at Bagby, near McClure Reservoir. To reach it, return to the junction of Highways 140 and 49 in Mariposa and then drive north on Highway 49 for 18 miles to a dirt road that heads toward Bagby Recreation Area at Lake McClure.

Facilities, fees: Indian Flat Day-Use Area is located on Highway 140, four miles south of El Portal. Lodging is available in El Portal. Campgrounds are available west of the national park entrance near El Portal. Supplies can be obtained in El Portal. Yosemite National Park rents small rafts. Fees are charged for entrance into Yosemite National Park and at the Bagby take-out. Rafting permits required for commercial outfitters only.

Water sports, restrictions: There are several great swimming holes along Highway 140. Look for turnouts and access points off the highway. Some of the most popular and easily accessible holes are near Indian Flat Day-Use Area.

Directions: From Merced, turn east on Highway 140 and drive 40 miles to Mariposa. Continue another 15 miles to Briceburg and the Briceburg Visitor Center on the left. Turn left at a road that is signed "BLM Camping Areas" (the road remains paved for about 150 yards). Drive over the Briceburg suspension bridge and turn left, traveling downstream on the road, parallel to the river. For camping, drive 2.5 miles to McCabe Flat, 3.8 miles to Willow Placer and 4.8 miles to Railroad Flat.

Contact: Bureau of Land Management, Folsom Field Office, 916/985-4474; Sierra National Forest, Bass Lake Ranger District, 559/877-2218; Yosemite National Park, 209/372-0200.

Guided rafting trips: All-Outdoors Whitewater Rafting, 925/932-8993 or 800/247-2387, website: www.aorafting.com; ARTA River Trips, 209/962-7873 or 800/323-2782, website: www.arta.org; Mariah Wilderness Expeditions, 510/233-2303 or 800/462-7424, website: www.mariahwe.com; American River Recreation, 530/622-6802 or 800/333-7238, website: www.arrafting.com; Outdoor Adventure River Specialists (OARS), 209/736-4677 or 800/346-6277, website: www.oars.com; Whitewater Excitement, 530/888-6515 or 800/750-2386, website: www.whitewaterexcitement.com; Whitewater Voyages, 510/222-5994 or 800/488-7238, website: www.whitewatervoyages.com; Zephyr Whitewater Expeditions, 209/532-6249 or 800/431-3636, website: www.zraftng.com.

19 TWIN LAKES

Rating: 5

near Mammoth Lakes in Inyo National Forest

Map 10.3, page 332

These Twin Lakes, located west of the town of Mammoth Lakes, are a pair of small lakes on little Mammoth Creek, high in Inyo National Forest at an elevation of 8,700 feet.

This linked pair of lakes is extremely pretty, a paradise for those with a canoe, rowboat, or float tube. That's about all you can do here water-wise, since powerboats, swimming, and sailboarding are not permitted. It is a beautiful setting, set amid Sierra granite and ringed by stands of old pines.

When you first drive here, go to the foot of the lake, where there is a perfect place to park, get out, and enjoy the view of this lake. From Twin Lakes, you can look west and take in pretty Twin Falls, a wide cascade that runs into the head of upper Twin Lake. Lower Twin Lake is a favorite for flyfishers in float tubes. The lake is stocked with rainbow trout.

Most people enjoy the view from this vantage point, then head on to one of the lakes with more developed boating facilities, such as Lake Mary.

There is a large Forest Service campground, with sites on each side of the access road, as well as excellent hiking trails in the area. Use is heavy at the campground, and for that reason, stays are limited to seven days. Often there will be people lined up, waiting for another family's weeklong vacation to end so theirs can start. Right: in the summer, when a campsite is vacated here, it is immediately filled.

The shuttle for Mammoth Mountain is nearby, and Mammoth Resort is three miles away.

By the way, don't get these Twin Lakes confused with the Upper and Lower Twin Lakes that are located farther north just west of Bridgeport (see listing in this chapter). They are two different animals.

Access: There is no boat ramp. Car-top boats may be hand launched.

Facilities, fees: Twin Lakes Store rents rowboats and canoes. Lodging and a restaurant are available at Tamarack Lodge. A campground with drinking water and flush toilets is available. Stores, coin laundry, coin showers, and propane gas are available nearby. Access is free.

Water sports, restrictions: Rowboats, canoes, kayaks, and inflatables are permitted. No motors. Swimming and sailboarding are not allowed.

Directions: Take U.S. 395 to Mammoth Junction and Highway 203. Turn west on Highway 203 and drive through the town of Mammoth Lakes to the junction of Minaret Road/Highway 203 and Lake Mary Road. Continue straight on Lake Mary Road and drive 2.3 miles to Twin Lakes Loop Road. Turn right and drive .5 mile to the lake and campground.

Contact: Tamarack Lodge and Resort, 760/934-2442 or 800/237-6879, website: www.tamaracklodge.com; Inyo National Forest, Mammoth Lakes Visitor Center, 760/924-5500.

20 LAKE MAMIE

Rating: 5

near Mammoth Lakes in Inyo
National Forest

Map 10.3, page 332

Little Lake Mamie is an idyllic site, a small, narrow lake set in the high Sierra, backed by gorgeous scenery, and filled with clear, cold water. For some, when they learn that cabins are available for rent, it's as if they have found their own Golden Pond.

And yet for others, the place scarcely elicits a pulse, because even though the scenic beauty here is fantastic, the opportunities for boating and water sports are quite scant. No motors are permitted, and the same goes for swimming and sailboarding. That leaves one

option for boaters: Rent or bring a car-top boat, such as a canoe or rowboat, and paddle about a bit, maybe fishing for trout. The lake is stocked with trout through summer.

Vacationers who rent cabins here often pick up a rowboat at the small marina and then spend some time oaring about the calm, serene waters. Lake use is lighter than elsewhere in the Mammoth Lakes Basin, primarily because there is no campground directly near the lake and motors are restricted.

Access: A boat ramp is available at Wildyrie Lodge.

Facilities, fees: Cabins, rowboat rentals, bait and tackle, and convenience store are available at Wildyrie Lodge. Campgrounds are available nearby. Access is free. A fee is charged for boat launching.

Water sports, restrictions: Rowboats, canoes,

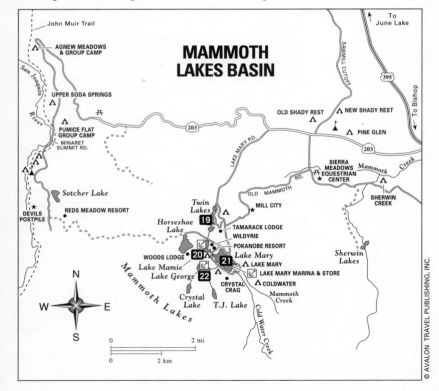

kayaks, and inflatables are permitted. No motors. Swimming and sailboarding are not allowed.

Directions: Take U.S. 395 to Mammoth Junction and Highway 203. Turn west on Highway 203 and drive through the town of Mammoth Lakes to the junction of Minaret Road/Highway 203 and Lake Mary Road. Continue straight on Lake Mary Road and drive 2.3 miles to Twin Lakes Loop Road. Turn right and drive past Twin Lakes and Lake Mary to Lake Mamie and the resort on the left.

Contact: Wildyrie Lodge, 760/934-2444; Mammoth Lakes Visitor Center, 760/924-5500.

21 LAKE MARY

Rating: 8

near Mammoth Lakes in Inyo
National Forest

Map 10.3, page 332

It only takes one look to see why this lake is so popular: The natural beauty is astounding. The lake is set high in the mountains at 8,900 feet, just below Crystal Crag, amid some of nature's most perfect artwork.

To campers, boaters, and anglers, Lake Mary is the headquarters for the Mammoth Lakes area. Of the 11 lakes in the immediate vicinity, Lake Mary is the largest and most developed. It provides a resort, boat launch, boat rentals, and a campground.

Like the other lakes in the basin, no water/body contact sports are permitted, including swimming and sailboarding. However, the rules at Lake Mary do permit motors, and boats with small motors are available at the resorts. Rentals are popular and, along with the number of vacationers who bring their own trailered boats, have made this the most-used lake in the Mammoth Lakes Basin.

Most of the visitors are here to fish for trout, which include some trophy-size rainbows. Fishing can be excellent. Lake Mary receives more trout stocks than any other lake in the Mammoth region.

The Forest Service campsites here are available on a first-come, first-served basis. In the summer, visitors should arrive as early as possible to secure a spot. Reservations are necessary to stay at one of the lodges, of course.

A great short walk starts at the back of Coldwater Camp, located just south of Lake Mary, and is routed up to Emerald Lake, about a mile away. A longer, more strenuous hike is accessed from the same trailhead. It runs along Mammoth Creek up to Arrowhead Lake, and then in turn up to Skeleton Lake, Barney Lake, and finally, up to Big Duck Lake. Duck Lake is even bigger than Lake Mary, always a surprise at first sight, and is just a mile from the Pacific Crest Trail.

Access: There are two paved ramps; one at Pokonobe Resort and one at Lake Mary Store and Marina. Both are located off Lake Mary Road.

Facilities, fees: Cabins and fishing boat rentals are available at Crystal Crag Lodge. A campground, store, and docks are available at Pokonobe Resort, along with pontoon boat, fishing boat, canoe, and pedal boat rentals. Lake Mary Marina has docks and rents out fishing boats, pontoon boats, canoes, and pedal boats. Campgrounds for tents and RVs are nearby. Drinking water, restrooms with flush toilets are available. Access is free. Fees are charged for boat launching and camping.

Water sports, restrictions: Powerboats, rowboats, canoes, kayaks, and inflatables are permitted. A 10-mph speed limit is strictly enforced. Swimming and sailboarding are not allowed.

Directions: Take U.S. 395 to Mammoth Junction and Highway 203. Turn west on Highway 203 and drive through the town of Mammoth Lakes to the junction of Minaret Road/Highway 203 and Lake Mary Road. Continue straight on Lake Mary Road and drive 2.3 miles to Twin Lakes Loop Road. Turn right and drive past Twin Lakes to Lake Mary. The road is well-signed and circles Lake Mary.

Contact: Crystal Crag Lodge, 760/934-2436; Pokonobe Resort, 760/934-2437; Lake Mary Store and Marina, 760/934-5353; Mammoth Lakes Visitor Center, 760/924-5500.

22 LAKE GEORGE

Rating: 7

near Mammoth Lakes in Inyo National Forest

Map 10.3, page 332

The backdrop for Lake George is an awesome granite mountain. It is a spectacular setting. This is a small, round lake set at the 9,000-foot range, fed by creeks coming from Crystal Lake and TJ Lake.

For some, this is the perfect place to camp (with lake-view sites) or stay in a cabin. You get outstanding hiking, fair fishing, and decent boating for a high mountain lake. Only small motors (six horsepower or less) are permitted; basically this rule allows trolling for trout in small boats, but nothing else. That's just fine because it keeps this small lake intimate as well as pristine.

Though Lake George is set just west of Lake Mary, it doesn't lure nearly as many people and has a completely different atmosphere—higher, more remote, and closer to wilderness.

Swimming and sailboarding are not permitted here, just boats with small motors that are perfect for going out on the water to fish for rainbow and brook trout. Although the campsites are in no way secluded, they do provide prime views of the lake. There are also two excellent short hikes, one to Crystal Lake and another to TJ Lake (separate trails). The trek to TJ Lake takes only about 20 to 25 minutes, and it's about a 45-minute romp to Crystal Lake, a beautiful lake set below giant Crystal Crag.

Access: A primitive boat launch is available at Woods Lodge.

Facilities, fees: Cabins, dock, fishing boats, and rowboats are available at Woods Lodge. A campground, restrooms with flush toilets, and drinking water are available. A convenience store, coin laundry, coin showers, and propane gas are available nearby. Access is free. Fees are charged for boat launching and camping.

Water sports, restrictions: Powerboats, rowboats, canoes, kayaks, and inflatables are permitted. No motors larger than 6 horsepower are permitted. Swimming and sailboarding are not allowed.

Directions: Take U.S. 395 to Mammoth Junction and Highway 203. Turn west on Highway 203 and drive through the town of Mammoth Lakes to the junction of Minaret Road/Highway 203 and Lake Mary Road. Continue straight on Lake Mary Road and drive .3 mile to Lake George Road. Turn right and drive a short distance to the lodge at the end of the road.

Contact: Woods Lodge, 760/934-2261 (summer) or 760/934-2342 (winter); Inyo National Forest, Mammoth Lakes Visitor Center, 760/924-5500.

23 CONVICT LAKE

Rating: 8

north of Bishop in Inyo National Forest

Map 10.4, page 333

People who love natural beauty can practice their religion at this mountain shrine. The lake is framed by a back wall of wilderness mountain peaks and fronted by a shore that's dotted with giant rocks and a few pines. All this is set at an elevation of 7,583 feet and bordered by a canyon leading into the John Muir Wilderness to the west, yet is very easily accessed off U.S. 395 to the east.

We're talking simply spectacular beauty. And even if that weren't enough, consider that the adjacent facilities include a boat ramp, boat rentals, cabin rentals, Forest Service campground, small store, fine restaurant, horse rentals, and a wilderness trailhead. Maps detailing the location of several hot springs in the area are available at the Convict Lake Store.

The lake is known primarily for fishing, particularly for having good catch rates of rainbow trout and rare but huge brown trout. What it's not ideal for is water sports. Although swimming is permitted, few try because the water is typically so cold that you'll freeze your little petunia off. Though winds are common here out of the west, it is also extremely rare to see somebody try to sailboard; the gusty winds can really howl, driving everybody off the lake.

Most mornings are extremely calm, so conditions are excellent for canoeing. However, most visitors have small boats that they've either hauled in or rented and use them to fish for trout. The water, which is fed at the upper end by Convict Creek, is extremely clear.

An outstanding trail circles the lake, providing a great day hike. If you walk (or ride horseback) along the southern shoreline, you discover that the trail branches off and heads up the canyon along Convict Creek. This is where you find seclusion and a perfect picnic spot along the creek, as well as picture-perfect views of the lake below on the return trip.

Access: A paved boat ramp is available at Convict Lake Resort.

Facilities, fees: Boat docks, small marina, and fishing boat, canoe, and rowboat rentals, fish-cleaning station, bait and tackle, RV dump station, convenience store, cabin rentals, and restaurant are available at Convict Lake Resort. A campground, restrooms with flush toilets, and drinking water are nearby. Access is free.

Water sports, restrictions: Powerboats, rowboats, canoes, kayaks, and inflatables are permitted. A 10-mph speed limit is strictly enforced. Swimming and sailboarding are not recommended.

Directions: From Bishop, drive north on U.S. 395 for 35 miles to Convict Lake Road (adjacent to Mammoth Lakes Airport). Turn left and drive two miles to the boat ramp.

From Lee Vining, drive south on U.S. 395 for 31 miles (five miles past Mammoth Junction) to Convict Lake Road (adjacent to Mammoth Lakes Airport). Turn west (right) on Convict Lake Road and drive two miles to the boat launch.

Contact: Convict Lake Resort & Cabins, 760/934-3800 or 800/992-2260, website: www.convict-lakeresort.com; Inyo National Forest, Mammoth Lakes Visitor Center, 760/924-5500.

24 HOT CREEK

Rating: 10

near Mammoth Lakes

Map 10.4, page 333

Hot Creek wanders through a meadow in the eastern Sierra on a course like a pretzel. Only two small pieces, totaling just three miles, are accessible. Below the Hot Creek Hatchery are two miles of stream bordered by private land, with access limited to flyfishers who book one of the nine cabins at Hot Creek Ranch. Downstream of that section is another piece of water, just under a mile long, that is accessible to the public.

At this latter stretch is a large parking area and paved trail down to a remarkable hot spring area. While the ice-cold stream is running past, it is fed by scalding-hot water at the far side of the stream. What results is a remarkable sensation in which the water temperatures are constantly changing as they swirl around you. Your first steps in the stream, for instance, can be shocking because the water is quite cold. But when you get shoulder deep, it is possible to feel very hot water at your chest and shoulders, cold water at your thighs, and warm water at your feet. You can then move a step in any direction and the mix will change completely.

It is advisable to bring some kind of wading shoes, either sandals or old tennis shoes, not only for walking to and from the parking lot, but for wading in the stream.

Hot Creek has become very popular, and that has inspired the Forest Service to develop an area where people can play in the hot springs and have a picnic. Despite this, the Forest Service has posted warning signs about the wildly fluctuating temperatures and high levels of arsenic that have been measured.

This is a classic meandering spring creek. Yet with the natural hot springs, waders are advised to watch their step and never look into river holes. They can turn into geysers without advance notice.

For an excellent hike, try the adjacent trail that fly fishers use to walk up and down the stream.

Access: Short walks are required to reach the hot springs areas.

Facilities, fees: A picnic area with restrooms is provided near the fish hatchery. Campgrounds, lodging, and supplies are available in the Mammoth Lakes area. Access is free.

Water sports, restrictions: This is a popular natural hot spring, although the Forest Service does not recommend swimming because of high levels of arsenic and rapid fluctuations of water temperatures.

Directions: From Lee Vining on U.S. 395, drive south for 31 miles (five miles past Mammoth Junction) to Hot Creek Hatchery Road. Turn left on Hot Creek Hatchery Road and look for the sign for Hot Creek Geologic Area. Continue for about three miles to the dirt parking areas and hike down to the creek.

From Bishop, drive north on U.S. 395 for 36 miles to Hot Creek Hatchery Road. Turn right on Hot Creek Hatchery Road and look for the sign for Hot Creek Geologic Area. Continue for about three miles to the dirt parking areas and hike down to the creek.

Contact: Inyo National Forest, Mammoth Lakes Visitor Center, 760/924-5500.

25 CROWLEY LAKE

Rating: 8

north of Bishop

Map 10.4, page 333

For many, Crowley is the trout fishing headquarters of the Eastern Sierra.

Crowley Lake is a huge lake with 45 miles of shoreline, set just east of U.S. 395 at elevation 6,720 feet. The surrounding landscape is high desert country, sparse and dry looking.

Crowley is known primarily for its fishing opportunities. At some point, every angler should experience a trout opener at Crowley Lake, the last Saturday every April. It is a wild scenario.

In the big years, thousands of anglers will arrive here on the Friday evening prior to the annual opener, the last Saturday in April every year, and convert the little nearby town of Tom's Place into an all-night cowboy rocker. The idea of "trout, trout, trout" mixed with favorite elixirs whips the place into a frenzy.

Before dawn, there can be so many anglers on the northwestern and southern shores of Crowley Lake that the Department of Fish and Game will sometimes even put up a rope barricade to keep people from fishing too early. When the legal opening time arrives, the DFG fires off a flare into the morning sky to signify the start of the trout season.

When the wind is down, the northwest corner is good for float-tubers. In peak season, they always seem to be bobbing around here.

Most water sports are permitted here. All types of boating are allowed from Memorial Day to Labor Day. Sailboarding, wake boarding, water-skiing, and personal watercraft are all doable, and of those sports, sailboarding can really shine. That is because the surface water of this lake warms considerably in the summer and the afternoon winds are often ideal. The most popular jumping-off point is at the beach next to the boat launch.

Swimming is prohibited because the lake is a domestic water source. The lake is operated by the Los Angeles Department of Water and Power.

Access: A paved ramp is available at the marina, located at the end of the access road.

Facilities, fees: Crowley Lake Fish Camp offers a full-service marina, docks, fishing boat and pontoon boat rentals, and a convenience store. Floating chemical toilets are on the lake. A campground is available with drinking water and flush toilets. On opening weekend of fishing season and on summer weekends, the campground is expanded to accommodate unlimited visitors. Fees are charged for day use, boat launching, and camping. All boats must be registered at the lake entrance.

Water sports, restrictions: Powerboats, waterskiing, wake boarding, personal watercraft, sailing, and sailboarding are permitted. Inflatables are permitted but swimming is not allowed.

Directions: From Bishop, drive north on U.S. 395 for 21 miles to the Crowley Lake Road exit. Take that exit and drive northwest on Crowley Lake Road for 5.5 miles (past Tom's Place) to the campground entrance on the left (well signed) or continue to the Crowley Lake Fish Camp.

Contact: Crowley Lake Fish Camp, 760/935-4301, website: www.crowleylakefishcamp.com; Tom's Place Resort, 760/935-4239, website: www.tomsplaceresort.com.

26 ROCK CREEK LAKE

Rating: 7

northwest of Bishop in Inyo National Forest

Map 10.4, page 333

This is a small lake that exudes great natural beauty. Rock Creek Lake is nestled in the Little Lakes Valley of Rock Creek Canyon, set in the high Sierra at an elevation of 9,682 feet. Located just north of the boundary to the John Muir Wilderness.

This is an excellent destination for a camping/hiking vacation. Some 35 other lakes are located nearby, many of which can be reached in a one-day round-trip hike. The trek out west to Mono Pass is a butt kicker, but you can stop on the way at Ruby Lake, named for its gemlike qualities.

You mainly see small fishing boats on the lake, rarely canoes. A 5-mph speed limit gives boaters a guarantee of quiet water. Note that at times, especially afternoons in the late spring, wind out of the west can be cold and frustrating. The lake is set in a slot in a high mountain canyon, and the wind can whip right on through. Though sailing in small boats would be ideal, as with sailboarding, few ever take advantage of the opportunity. The reason is because of the cold water, cold enough for sailboarders to need wet suits. This sport is best in the fall.

At just 63 surface acres, the lake is not big, but its beauty and resident rainbow trout make it popular for shoreline fishing. The lake is stocked with Alpers trout. In addition, resident brown trout in the 10-pound class are occasionally hooked, sometimes landed. The lake record brown trout weighed 15 pounds, 8 ounces.

Traffic is heavy in the summer months, with a lot of people using this as a base camp and jumping-off point for trips into the nearby John Muir Wilderness.

An excellent trailhead is available here for wilderness trips into the Little Lakes Valley. You can rent horses for pack trips at the Rock Creek Pack Station, 760/935-4493 (summers only).

Access: An unimproved launch ramp is available at Rock Creek Lakes Resort.

Facilities, fees: Lodging, campground, restrooms with flush toilets, drinking water, picnic area, café, and convenience store with bait and tackle are available. Fishing boats and rowboats can be rented at Rock Creek Lakes Resort. Access is free.

Water sports, restrictions: A 5-mph speed limit is strictly enforced. Sailing and sailboarding are permitted; note the speed limit. Swimming is allowed.

Directions: From the junction of U.S. 395 and Highway 203 (the Mammoth Lakes turnoff), drive 15 miles south on U.S. 395 to Tom's Place. Turn right (south) on Rock Creek Road and drive eight miles to the lodge on the left.

Contact: Inyo National Forest, White Mountain Ranger District, 760/873-2500, fax 760/873-2563; Rock Creek Lakes Resort, 760/935-4311, website: www.rockcreeklake.com; Rock Creek Lodge, 760/935-4170, website: www.rockcreeklodge.com.

© TOM STIENSTRA

Chapter 11

Sequoia and Kings Canyon

Chapter 11—Sequoia and
Kings Canyon

There is no place on earth like the high Sierra, from Mount Whitney north through Sequoia and Kings Canyon National Parks. This is a paradise filled with deep canyons, high peaks, and fantastic natural beauty, and sprinkled with groves of the largest living things in the history of the earth—giant sequoias.

Though the area is primarily known for the national parks, the campgrounds available span a great variety of settings. The most popular spots, though, are in the vicinity of Sequoia and Kings Canyon National Parks, or on the parks' access roads.

But this region also harbors many wonderful destinations that have nothing to do with the national parks.

On the western slopes of the Sierra, pretty lakes with good trout fishing include Edison, Florence, and Hume Lakes. Hidden spots in Sierra National Forest provide continual fortune hunts, especially up the Dinkey Creek drainage above Courtright Reservoir.

On the eastern slopes, a series of small streams offers good vehicle access; here, too, you'll encounter the beautiful Sabrina and South Lakes (west of Bishop), and great wilderness trailheads at the end of almost every road.

An example of what is possible is taking the trip up Highway 168 northeast of Fresno. In sequence, you pass Shaver Lake, Huntington Lake, and then if you continue, drive the twisty road over Kaiser Pass to the split, with Mono Hot Springs and Edison Lake to the left, Florence Lake to the right. You could spend a week or more on this trip, with a new destination every day.

The drive out of Sequoia and into Kings Canyon features rim-of-the-world views as you first enter the Kings River canyon. You then descend to the bottom of the canyon, right along the Kings River, and can gaze up at the high glacial-carved canyon walls, and drive all the way out to Cedar Grove, the end of the road. The canyon rises 8,000 feet from the river to Spanish Peak, the deepest canyon in the continental United States.

The Upper Kings River provides good flyfishing for small trout, and as the stream gains size as it runs downstream, it provides outstanding rafting opportunities.

This is only a start. Bears, marmot, and deer are abundant and are commonly seen in Sequoia, especially at Dorst Creek Campground. If you drive up to Mineral King and take a hike, it can seem like the marmot capital of the world.

In the Kernville area, there are a series of campgrounds along the Kern River, set upstream of popular Isabella Lake. Most choose this canyon for one reason: the outstanding white-water rafting and kayaking.

What else could you ask for?

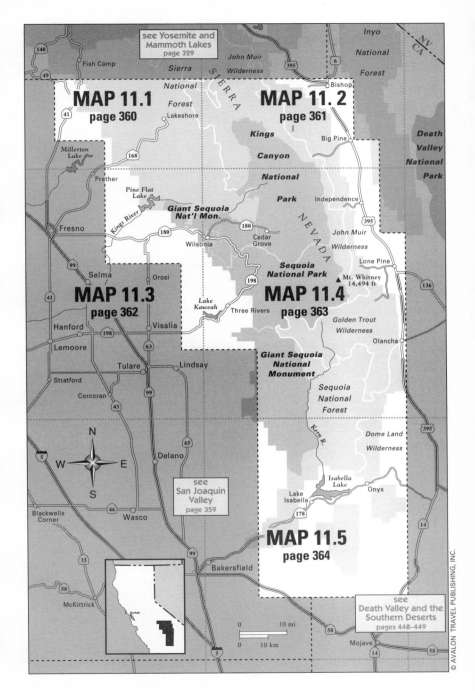

see Yosemite and
Mammoth Lakes
page 329

MAP 11.1
page 360

MAP 11.2
page 361

Inyo

National

Forest

Fish Camp

Sierra

John Muir

Wilderness

Bishop

SIERRA

National

Forest

Lakeshore

Kings

Canyon

Big Pine

National

Millerton
Lake

Prather

Pine Flat
Lake

Park

Giant Sequoia
Nat'l Mon.

Independence

NEVADA

John Muir

Wilderness

Death

Valley

National

Park

Kings River

Fresno

Wilsonia

Cedar
Grove

Lone Pine

Selma

Orosi

Sequoia
National Park

Mt. Whitney
14,494 ft

MAP 11.3
page 362

MAP 11.4
page 363

Hanford

Lake
Kaweah

Three Rivers

Golden Trout
Wilderness

Olancha

Lemoore

Visalia

Tulare

Lindsay

Giant Sequoia
National
Monument

Stratford

Sequoia
National
Forest

Corcoran

N

Delano

Dome Land

Wilderness

Kern R.

W   E

S

see
San Joaquin
Valley
page 359

Isabella
Lake

Onyx

Blackwells
Corner

Wasco

Lake
Isabella

MAP 11.5
page 364

McKittrick

Bakersfield

see
Death Valley and the
Southern Deserts
pages 448–449

© AVALON TRAVEL PUBLISHING, INC.

Mojave

0   10 mi

0   10 km

Chapter 11 • Sequoia and Kings Canyon   359

Map 11.1

Sites 1–6
Pages 365–369

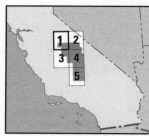

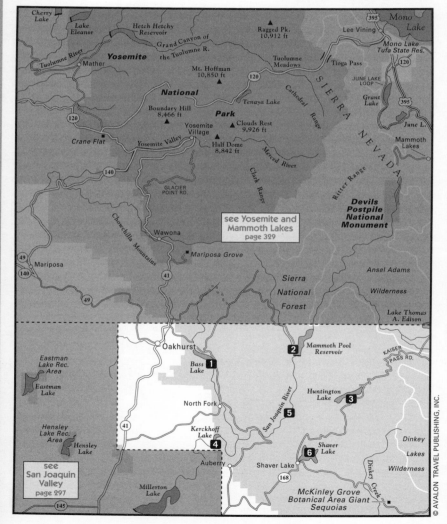

Map 11.2

Sites 7–13
Pages 369–373

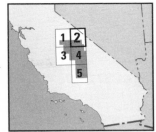

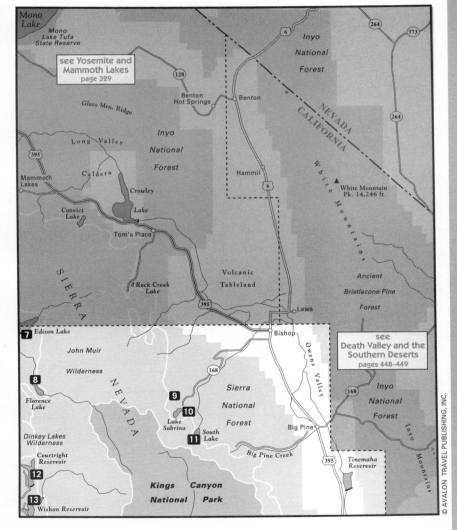

Map 11.3

Sites 14–15
Pages 373–376

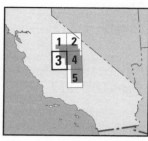

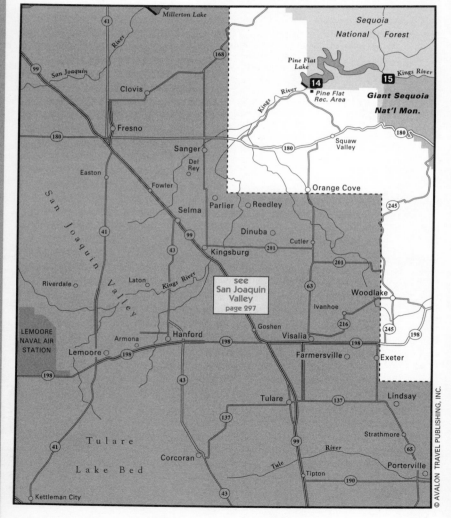

Map 11.4

Sites 16–19
Pages 376–378

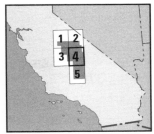

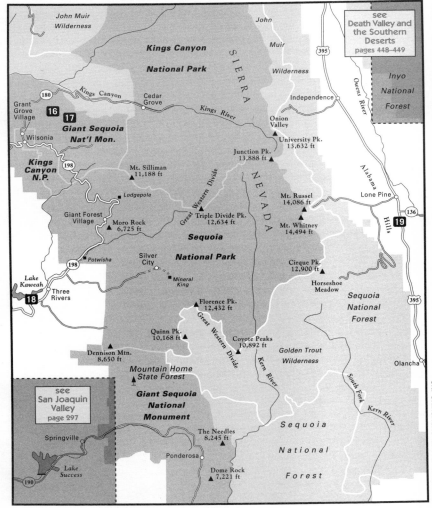

© AVALON TRAVEL PUBLISHING, INC.

Map 11.5

Sites 20–23
Pages 378–384

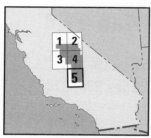

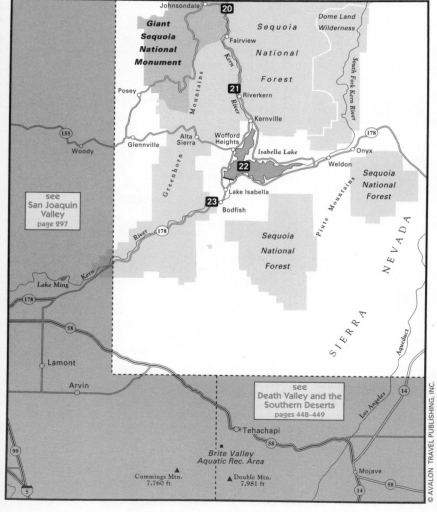

1 BASS LAKE

Rating: 8

northeast of Fresno in Sierra National Forest

Map 11.1, page 360

Bass Lake is popular with a diverse mix of people. That makes sense. This is a long, beautiful lake, set in a canyon at 3,400 feet and surrounded by national forestland. It covers nearly 1,200 acres when full, and has five campgrounds, four resorts, and two boat launches.

Water-skiing, personal watercraft riding, fishing, and swimming are all extremely popular here. On a hot summer day, you can always count on seeing jet boats zooming about, as the roar from their big V8 engines echoes down the lake.

A great plus is that the shoreline is quite sandy nearly all around the lake. So even though there are no designated swimming beaches, you can pull off the road almost anywhere and find a place to swim and sunbathe. In addition, larger beach areas are available near the campgrounds and resorts. Sailboarding prospects are poor because of inconsistent winds and boating traffic.

Bass Lake is hardly a quiet, pristine lake. In fact, it offers full facilities. It gets extremely crowded in the summer, especially in late summer, when temperatures are very hot and water levels creep down low enough to expose large expanses of beach. Although it's a family vacation destination within an hour's drive of the Yosemite National Park southern entrance, the lake also hosts bass fishermen and hotshot water-skiers. Fishing is best in the spring for rainbow trout and largemouth bass.

Access: Two paved boat ramps are available, one on the lake's northeast side, off Road 274 at The Pines Resort, and one on the southwest side, off County Road 222 near Miller's Landing.

Facilities, fees: Lodging, gas, snack bars, full-service marinas, picnic areas, coin laundry, and small stores are available. Campgrounds with flush toilets or vault toilets are available. Ski boats, personal watercraft, pontoon boats, fishing boats, kayaks, and canoes are available at Miller's Landing Resort and The Pines Marina. The Forks Resort rents fishing boats, pontoon boats, rowboats, and canoes. Access is free. There is a fee for boat launching, which includes a county fee based on engine horsepower.

Water sports, restrictions: After launching, boats must be registered at the Bass Lake observation tower. Water-skiing, wake boarding, sailing, and sailboarding are permitted. Personal watercraft are permitted in designated areas only. Swimming beaches are available all along the shoreline.

Directions: From Fresno, drive north on Highway 41 to Oakhurst and continue 2.5 miles to Yosemite Forks and Bass Lake Road/County Road 222. Turn right at Bass Lake Road and drive six miles (staying right at two forks) to the lakes's southern shore and access points.

Contact: Sierra National Forest, District Office, Bass Lake Ranger District, 559/877-2218, fax 559/877-3108; Bass Lake Chamber of Commerce, 559/642-3676. For boating information contact Miller's Landing Resort, 559/642-3633; The Pines Marina, 559/642-3200; The Forks Resort, 559/642-3737.

2 MAMMOTH POOL RESERVOIR

Rating: 7

northeast of Fresno in Sierra National Forest

Map 11.1, page 360

This lake was created by a dam in the San Joaquin River gorge, a steep canyon that drops nearly 3,000 feet, creating a long, narrow lake with steep, high walls. Mammoth Pool always seems to be much higher in elevation than its listed 3,330 feet. That is because of the surrounding high ridges.

One word of caution: If you'll be visiting from late August through November, always call ahead and ask about lake levels. Because the water is used to generate hydroelectric power at the dam, water levels can drop significantly late in the season. The lake covers 1,100 surface acres when full early in the season, but usually drops about 90 feet by the close of summer. This often renders the paved launch ramp useless.

All water sports are permitted at Mammoth Pool Reservoir, and water-skiing and personal watercraft riding are very popular. There are no designated beaches, but people swim all along the shoreline and the picnic areas and campgrounds. Even though strong winds do kick up most summer days in the late afternoon, it is rare to see people sailboarding at this lake. Trout fishing is far more popular, often good in early summer.

Access: A paved boat ramp is located on the reservoir's north side, next to Mammoth Pool Campground. A gravel launch is available on the south side, next to the picnic areas.

Facilities, fees: Campgrounds, drinking water, vault toilets, picnic areas, snack bar, and a grocery store are provided. A boat-in camp is located on the lake's upper reaches. Access to the lake is free.

Water sports, restrictions: The reservoir is closed to all boating from May 1 to June 15 for a deer migration (swimming) across the lake. During the rest of the year, water-skiing, wake boarding, and personal watercraft are permitted. A 35-mph speed limit is strictly enforced. Sailing and sailboarding are permitted. Swimming is available all along the shoreline.

Directions: From Fresno, drive north on Highway for about 25 miles to North Fork Road/County Road 200. Turn right and drive northeast for 17.5 miles to Auberry Road/County Road 222. Turn left (north) and drive one mile to the town of North Fork and Mammoth Pool Road. Turn right and drive 1.5 miles to County Road 225 (still Mammoth Pool Road.) Turn right and drive about 37 miles (the road becomes Minarets Road/Forest Road 81) to a junction. Bear right (still Mammoth Pool Road) and drive three miles to Mammoth Pool Reservoir and the camp-

ground. The drive from North Fork takes 1.5 to 2 hours.

Contact: Sierra National Forest, District Office, Bass Lake Ranger District, 559/877-2218, fax 559/877-3108.

3 HUNTINGTON LAKE

Rating: 10

northeast of Fresno in Sierra National Forest

Map 11.1, page 360

Huntington Lake is set at an elevation of 7,000 feet in the Sierra Nevada. The four-mile-long, half-mile-wide lake has 14 miles of shoreline, numerous campgrounds and resorts, and is a jumping-off point for a backpack trip into the nearby Kaiser Wilderness.

This is a great mountain lake for almost all boating and water sports. Sailing and sailboarding are particularly popular, and well-known regattas are held here during the summer every year. Although sailboarding conditions are excellent in early summer, there's no place at the lake to rent sailboards.

The lake water comes from snowmelt, so it is cold through the early summer and doesn't begin to get tolerably warm for swimming, about 65 degrees, until mid- to late July. A lot of people swim anyway, and many scouts earn a merit badge by completing a mile-long swim.

Lake use is heavy from May through September and diminishes greatly after Labor Day weekend. By mid-October, when the cold weather moves in for good, most operations shut down for winter.

The Rancheria Falls National Recreation Trail is located near the eastern end of the lake. It provides access to beautiful Rancheria Falls.

Access: A paved ramp is located on the northeast shore, near Lakeshore Resort, and a primitive launch is located on the northwest shore, at Huntington Lake Resort.

Facilities, fees: Campgrounds, restrooms, lodging, picnic areas, marina, boat slips, bait and tackle, propane gas, restaurants, and groceries are available. Fishing boats, pontoon boats, canoes, kayaks, personal watercraft, and sailboats can be rented at Huntington Lake Marina on the west shore. Horseback riding is available nearby. Access is free, but a parking fee is charged at some locations.

Water sports, restrictions: Water-skiing, wake boarding, personal watercraft, swimming, sailing, and sailboarding are permitted. A large, sandy swimming beach is available on the northeast shore at Lakeshore Resort.

Directions: From Fresno, drive east on Highway 168 to Shaver Lake, then continue 21 miles to Huntington Lake and Huntington Lake Road. Turn left on Huntington Lake Road and drive one mile. Continue on Huntington Lake Road to a series of several campgrounds and access points on the left.

Contact: Sierra National Forest, High Sierra Ranger District, 559/885-5360, fax 559/855-5375; Lakeshore Resort, 559/893-3193, website: www.lakeshoreresort.com; Huntington Lake Resort, 559/893-3226; Rancheria Marina, 559/893-3234.

4 KERCKHOFF RESERVOIR

Rating: 5

northeast of Fresno in Sierra National Forest

Map 11.1, page 360

It can seem hotter than the interior of Mount Vesuvius at Kerckhoff Reservoir, which is set in the foothill country east of Fresno at an elevation of 1,000 feet. If you camp here, be sure to bring a plastic tarp and some poles so you can rig a makeshift roof to provide some shelter from the sun.

Because the reservoir is remote and small and the use of motors more than 5 horsepower on boats is prohibited, it gets fairly light use, even in summer. Most of the visitors are anglers and folks out paddling canoes and other small boats. Swimming is permitted, and the best spot is the small beach next to the picnic area and campground.

The lake is something of a dud for fishing, with no trout and few largemouth bass.

Access: An unimproved boat ramp is located on the north shore.

Facilities, fees: A picnic area and small campground are provided. Drinking water and vault toilets are provided. Supplies can be obtained in Auberry and North Fork. Access is free.

Water sports, restrictions: No motors over 5 horsepower are permited. Sailboarding and swimming are allowed.

Directions: From Fresno, take Highway 41 north for three miles to the exit for Highway 168 East. Take that exit and drive east on Highway 168 for about 22 miles to Auberry Road. Turn left and drive 2.8 miles to Powerhouse Road. Turn left and drive 8.4 miles to the lake, campground and access points.

Contact: Sierra National Forest, District Office, Bass Lake Ranger District, 559/877-2218, fax 559/877-3108; PG&E Land Projects, 916/386-5164, fax 916/386-5388, website: www.pge.com/recreation.

5 REDINGER LAKE

Rating: 7

northeast of Fresno in Sierra National Forest

Map 11.1, page 360

Only about an hour's drive east from Fresno brings you to Redinger Lake, set at an elevation of 1,400 feet in the hot Sierra foothills. The lake is three miles long and .25 mile wide, and has a 35-mph speed limit that is tested by every jet boater who launches here.

Since it is so remote and undeveloped, Redinger Lake gets far lighter boating traffic than nearby Shaver and Huntington Lakes. Still, there's a fair number of water-skiers and personal watercraft riders plying the water throughout summer. After all, with hot weather, cool water, and a good boat ramp, you've got the recipe for fun.

From April through June, you can count on steady breezes out of the west. That makes this lake excellent for sailboarding, especially after winds force most water-skiers to shut down for the day.

While there are no designated swimming beaches, there are many sandy areas for sunbathing all around the lake's shoreline.

This area has high fire danger in summer and fall. No open fires are allowed year-round. Campfire permits are required for charcoal barbecues and camping stoves.

Fishing is normally poor, although there can be fair trout fishing at the headwaters of the lake.
Access: A paved ramp is located on the lake's south end.

Facilities, fees: A primitive campground with pit toilets and a picnic area are provided. No drinking water is available and garbage must be packed out. Supplies can be obtained in Auberry. Access to the lake is free.

Water sports, restrictions: Water-skiing and personal watercraft are permitted, but a 35-mph speed limit is enforced. Sailboarding, sailing, and swimming are allowed.

Directions: From Fresno, drive north on Highway for about 25 miles to North Fork Road/County Road 200. Turn right and drive northeast for 17.5 miles to Auberry Road/County Road 222. Turn left (north) and drive one mile to the town of North Fork and Mammoth Pool Road. Turn right and drive 1.5 miles to County Road 225 (still Mammoth Pool Road.) Turn right and drive about four miles to Italian Bar Road. Turn right and drive seven miles to the lake.

Contact: Sierra National Forest, District Office, Bass Lake Ranger District, 559/877-2218, fax 559/877-3108

6 SHAVER LAKE

Rating: 9

northeast of Fresno in Sierra National Forest

Map 11.1, page 360

You have to pass by Shaver Lake if you are heading to Huntington Lake, and a lot of folks can't stand the tease. They stop and check it out. Most like what they see, and considering the longer drive to Huntington, make this their lake of choice.

Though Shaver is not as high in elevation as Huntington (Shaver is set at 5,370 feet, while Huntington is at 7,000 feet), it is very pretty just the same. And as you might expect, by summer this becomes a very busy lake.

Water-skiing and wake boarding are extremely popular. Hey, there are usually tons of water-skiers, and personal watercraft, too, along with the family campers on their annual weeklong vacation. But let me tell you a little secret: there is one boat-in day-use area on the lake's back side for those who want to relax and at least have some semblance of privacy. The lake is also well stocked with trout and kokanee salmon.

A better-known secret is that the best area for swimming and playing in the water is on the lake's east side. Though more difficult to reach, this part of the lake offers sandy beaches rather than the rocky drop-offs so common on the west side. Fishing prospects at Shaver are better on the west side as well, so by making the effort to reach the lake's other side, you will be avoiding a potential user conflict.

Most sailboarders bypass Shaver Lake, which is well sheltered and rarely gets much wind.
Access: Paved boat ramps are located at Camp Edison (two miles from the town of Shaver Lake on the west shore) and Sierra Marina (seven miles north of the town of Shaver Lake) on Highway 168.

Facilities, fees: Campgrounds, lodging, restrooms, flush toilets, picnic areas, restaurant, bar, bait and tackle, and convenience store are available. Sierra Marina has full services and rents out fishing boats and pontoon boats. Fishing boat, pontoon boat, canoe, and kayak rentals are available at Shaver Lake Lodge. A fee is charged for day use. There is a fee for boat launching at Sierra Marina. Boat launching is free at the public boat ramp.

Water sports, restrictions: Water-skiing, wake boarding, personal watercraft, and sailboarding are permitted. Sailing is permitted, though winds are usually very light. Sandy swimming beaches are available at the day-use areas on Road 1 and Road 2 on the lake's east side.

Directions: From Fresno, take Highway 168 east and drive 50 miles to the town of Shaver Lake. Continue two to seven miles to access points on the west shore of the lake.

Contact: Sierra National Forest, High Sierra Ranger District, 559/855-5360, fax 559/855-5375; Sierra Marina, 559/841-3324, website: www.sierramarina.com; Shaver Lake Lodge, 559/841-3326; Camp Edison, 559/841-3134, website: www.sce.com/campedison.

7 EDISON LAKE

Rating: 10

northeast of Fresno in Sierra National Forest

Map 11.2, page 361

Edison Lake offers nearby campgrounds, a rustic mountain lodge, boat launch, boat rentals, horse rentals, nearby trailhead to the John Muir Trail, and good fishing. A 15-mph speed limit keeps the lake quiet, and there's a hiker's ferry boat that runs across the lake and back twice a day to a wilderness trailhead.

Edison Lake is set at an elevation of 7,650 feet and is fed by Mono Creek, a cold, pure, and pristine trout stream. It is one of the most remote lakes you can drive to in California. Camping and fishing are the main draws, with people either renting small fishing boats or bringing their own trailered boats. Because many people start their backpacking trips here, lake use is high in the summer. Hang out here for long and you are bound to see John Muir Trail hikers taking a break, eating everything in sight at the small restaurant.

All along the shoreline there are areas for swimming, but the water is quite cold. If you're looking for the kind of water that won't chill your bones, nearby Mono Hot Springs offers mineral baths and access to hot springs.

This is a well-known stopping point for hik-ers on the John Muir Trail (JMT). Day-hikers can take advantage of the setting as well. A day-trip option is to hike the trail from the camp out along the north shore of Lake Edison for five miles to Quail Meadows where it intersects with the JMT. This provides excellent stream fishing access along Mono Creek.

Another option is to take the hiker's boat shuttle to the head of the lake in the morning, and then spend the day tromping around in the wilderness—and catch the return boat trip in late afternoon. It's an easy hike up to the JMT. From there, if you don't mind a steep climb, head south up Bear Mountain. It takes about 40 minutes to reach an absolutely wondrous aspen grove that is pretty year-round.

Note that the drive to Edison Lake is extremely twisty on a narrow road. If you want a near-death experience, try driving it on a Friday or Sunday afternoon where you get a guarantee of the chance of a head-on collision with idiots trying to race to and from Mono Hot Springs. If you are towing a boat, it is extremely precarious. What to do? Drive slowly, take your time, and enjoy the Sierra views. My personal preference is to make the trip at night, when you can more easily spot oncoming vehicles from the headlight beams boring holes in the darkness, so there are no surprises on all the blind turns.

Access: A paved boat ramp is located on the west shore; Kaiser Pass Road leads directly to it.

Facilities, fees: Lodging, restrooms, showers, convenience store, flush toilets, primitive launch ramp, fishing boat and canoe rentals, bait and tackle, and a hiker's water taxi are available at Vermillion Valley Resort. A campground with drinking water and vault toilets is nearby. Access to the lake is free.

Water sports, restrictions: A 15-mph speed limit is strictly enforced on the lake. Sailing, sailboarding, and swimming are permitted.

Directions: From the town of Shaver Lake, drive north on Highway 168 for 21 miles to Kaiser Pass Road/Forest Road 80. Turn right and drive 16 (narrow and twisting) miles to a fork in the road. Bear left onto Edison Lake Road and drive approximately six miles to the resort at the end of the road.

Contact: Sierra National Forest, High Sierra Ranger District, 559/855-5360, fax 559/855-5375; Vermilion Valley Resort, 559-259-4000 (summer), 619/668-8711 (winter), website: www.edisonlake.com.

8 FLORENCE LAKE

Rating: 10

northeast of Fresno in Sierra National Forest

Map 11.2, page 361

Like nearby Edison Lake to the north, Florence Lake is a great vacation destination with excellent hiking opportunities. Located at an elevation of 7,327 feet, the lake features a beautiful mountain setting (just as pretty as Edison), with the awesome Glacier Divide country providing a backdrop to the east. A 15-mph speed limit maintains a degree of serenity. A hiker's water taxi makes two trips per day across the lake and back.

Most years the lake becomes ice-free around Memorial Day weekend. The resort is usually open from June through September, sometimes later. Water levels can fluctuate, with the lake often quite low in late summer and fall.

Although Florence is smaller and less developed than its northerly neighbor Edison, conditions are much the same. Fewer people know about this place, however; it does not get the amount of camping traffic that Edison does. Canoeing, rafting, and float-tubing are good here, high-Sierra style.

If you like hiking, this is a great place to start your trip. From the lake inlet a trail is routed up the South Fork San Joaquin River to the Pacific Crest Trail (about five miles in). From there you can continue southeast along the San Joaquin, turning into Evolution Valley, one of the prettiest meadow/woodlands in the entire high Sierra.

This lake is very remote and on the edge of wilderness, one of the most remote lakes you can reach by car in California. The drive in is long and circuitous. See details about tricks for handling the road in the trip notes for Edison Lake (see previous listing).

Access: A paved boat ramp is available at Florence Lake Resort on the lake's northwest side.

Facilities, fees: A campground, picnic area, vault toilets, drinking water, water taxi, and small store are available. Fishing boat rentals and water taxis are available at Florence Lake Resort. There is a wheelchair-accessible pier. Access is free; fee for water taxi and camping.

Water sports, restrictions: A 15-mph speed limit is strictly enforced. Sailing, sailboarding and swimming are permitted.

Directions: From the town of Shaver Lake, drive east on Highway 168 for 21 miles to Kaiser Pass Road. Bear northeast on Kaiser Pass Road/Forest Road 80 (slow and curvy) to a junction (left goes to Mono Hot Springs and Lake Edison) with Florence Lake Road. Bear right at the junction and drive five miles to the campground.

Contact: Sierra National Forest, High Sierra Ranger District, 559/855-5360, fax 559/855-5375; Florence Lake Resort, 209/966-3195 (winter only).

9 NORTH LAKE

Rating: 4

southwest of Bishop in Inyo National Forest

Map 11.2, page 361

If you prefer a tiny, intimate setting in the high country, then little North Lake might work for you. The lake sits at an elevation of 9,500 feet, and the surface area is just 13 acres, more the size of a high mountain pond.

Some visitors bring car-top boats for improved access, but the lake is too small and too shallow for anything but canoes; boats with motors are not permitted. This is not a good choice for swimming because the water is often mucky and very cold. Hence the place gets light use year-round.

North Lake is best used as a layover spot before heading off on a backpacking expedition. Just west of the lake is a trailhead for a route that follows the North Fork of Bishop Creek up to a remarkable granite basin loaded with similar small mountain lakes. Loch Leven and Plute Lake are just a three-mile hike away; and if you head over the pass into Hu-mphreys Basin, you can venture cross-country to your choice of 25 lakes, many filled with golden trout.

If you don't want to hike, nearby Lake Sabrina and South Lake provide better prospects for boating and water recreation.

This is a beautiful spot for trout fishing. It is surrounded by aspens and is gorgeous year-round, especially in early fall when each side of the canyon comes alive in golds and yellows.
Access: There is no boat ramp. Car-top boats may be hand launched.
Facilities, fees: A campground, drinking water, and vault toilets are available. Supplies can be obtained in Bishop. Access is free.
Water sports, restrictions: Motors are not permitted on the lake. The lake is too small for sailing and sailboarding. Swimming is not recommended.
Directions: Take U.S. 395 to Bishop and Highway 168. Turn northwest (toward the Sierra) on Highway 168 and drive 17 miles to Forest Road 8S02 (signed North Lake). Turn right (north) on Forest Road 8S02 and drive for two miles to the campground.
Contact: Inyo National Forest, White Mountain Ranger Station, 760/873-2500, fax 760/873-2563.

10 LAKE SABRINA

Rating: 7

southwest of Bishop in Inyo National Forest

Map 11.2, page 361

The largest of the three lakes in the Bishop Creek drainage, Lake Sabrina is also the most popular. It is set at an elevation of 9,130 feet and covers nearly 200 acres, yet it is only a 20-mile ride out of Bishop.

Sound good? It is. Sabrina provides a boat ramp, enforces a 10-mph speed limit to guarantee quiet water, and has good hiking destinations nearby, with two lakes within a 2.5-mile hike from here.

Camping, trout fishing, and low-speed boating are the major attractions. A small concession operation offers boat rentals, but there are no other facilities at the lake. Use is moderate, primarily by anglers. That is because it is stocked with rainbow trout, including some big Alpers trout and big browns. Large trout are not unusual at Sabrina.

The water in the lake comes from glacier runoff, so it is freezing cold. Swimming is out of the question for most people, but hey, sometimes you'll see visitors having contests to see who can keep their feet in the water the longest. Some last less than 10 seconds.

If you want solitude, the trail on the lake's southeast side provides an ideal opportunity to strike out on your own. Shortly after leaving the lake's shore, the trail forks; head to the left and you can hike to Lake George; head to the right and you will hit Blue Donkey, and Baboon Lakes. All are excellent day-hike destinations.

Insider's note: It's pronounced "Sa-bry-na," not "Sa-bree-na."
Access: A boat ramp is located on the lake's north end.
Facilities, fees: A campground with drinking water and vault toilets is available nearby. Fishing boats, canoes, and pontoon boats are rented out at Sabrina Lake Boat Landing. Supplies can be obtained in Bishop. Access is free.
Water sports, restrictions: A 10-mph speed limit is strictly enforced. Sailing, sailboarding and swimming are not recommended.
Directions: Take U.S. 395 to Bishop and Highway 168. Turn northwest (toward the Sierra) on Highway 168 and drive 17 miles to a signed fork (signed Lake Sabrina). Take that fork and drive .5 mile to the lake.

Contact: Inyo National Forest, White Mountain Ranger Station, 760/873-2500, fax 760/873-2563; Sabrina Lake Boat Landing, 760/873-7425.

11 SOUTH LAKE

Rating: 7

southwest of Bishop in Inyo National Forest

Map 11.2, page 361

When a small dam was built on the South Fork of Bishop Creek, South Lake was created. This 166-acre lake is set in the high country at 9,755 feet. There's a good boat ramp, which makes it popular among owners of trailered aluminum boats. A 5-mph speed limit is in effect, allowing trolling for trout and not much more.

South Lake is the most developed of the three lakes in the area (the others are North and Sabrina), but doesn't offer anything more in the way of water sports. You still get the ice-cold glacial runoff, which prohibits swimming and sailboarding, and the 5-mph speed limit restricts all boating save for fishing. Of course, canoeing and kayaking are always possible.

This is a beautiful setting, in a deep Sierra canyon filled with aspen and peppered with conifers. The lake is used primarily by anglers. It is stocked with rainbow trout, including Alpers, and also is home for some large resident browns.

A trailhead at the lake provides access to Bishop Pass and Dusy Basin. A great day hike from this launch point is to head up the canyon toward Bishop Pass, then take the cutoff trail on the left to Ruwau Lake. The final stretch is short but steep, and rewards hikers with the chance for large brook trout in a gorgeous rock-bowl setting.

Access: An unimproved boat ramp is located on the lake's north end.

Facilities, fees: Several campgrounds are provided on South Lake Road. Picnic areas are available at the lake. A convenience store, bait and tackle, moorings, café, and fishing boat rentals are available at South Lake Boat Landing. Access is free.

Water sports, restrictions: A 5-mph speed limit is strictly enforced. Sailboarding, sailing, and swimming are not recommended.

Directions: Drive on U.S. 395 to Bishop and Highway 168. Turn northwest (toward the Sierra) on Highway 168 and drive 15 miles to South Lake Road on the left. Turn and drive seven miles south to the lake.

Contact: Inyo National Forest, White Mountain Ranger Station, 760/873-2500, fax 760/873-2563; South Lake Boat Landing, 760/873-4177, website: www.bishopcreekresorts.com.

12 COURTRIGHT RESERVOIR

Rating: 7

northeast of Fresno in Sierra National Forest

Map 11.2, page 361

Courtright Reservoir is one great recreation destination. You can camp, boat, and fish, or you can park at the nearby trailhead and head off into the John Muir Wilderness.

Courtright is set in the high Sierra at an elevation of 8,200 feet. If you plan to stick around, the early summer is the best time to visit. That is when the lake level is the highest by far. It can drop quickly from mid-August on through fall.

The surrounding scenery is very pretty, and this is a good choice for a picnic site, typically very peaceful and quiet. With a 15-mph speed limit, all the fast boats, water-skiers, and personal watercraft head elsewhere. What you get here is the ideal lake for fishing, camping, and low-speed boat use, especially paddling about in a canoe or kayak. Trout fishing can be good here.

In fact, much of the visitor traffic is not from boaters, but from wilderness backpackers. They use the lake's campground as home base before heading off into the John Muir Wilderness.

And by the way, if you hope to swim while you're at Courtright, plan on joining the Polar Bear Club. Yow! This water is cold!

Access: A paved boat ramp is located on the lake's south side.

Facilities, fees: Campgrounds, drinking water, vault toilets and picnic areas are available. Supplies can be obtained in Fresno and the town of Shaver Lake. Access to the lake is free.

Water sports, restrictions: A 15-mph speed limit is strictly enforced. Water-skiing, wake boarding, and personal watercraft are not permitted. Swimming is allowed, but the water is generally too cold. Sailing and sailboarding are permitted, but are not popular.

Directions: From Fresno, drive east on Highway 168 to Dinkey Creek Road (on the right just as entering the town of Shaver Lake). Turn right and drive 13 miles to McKinley Grove Road (Forest Road 40). Turn right and drive 14 miles to Courtright Road. Turn left (north) and drive 12 miles to the campground entrance road on the right. Note: This route is slow and twisty.

Contact: Sierra National Forest, High Sierra Ranger District, 559/855-5360, fax 559/855-5375; PG&E Land Projects, 916/386-5164, fax 916/386-5388, website: www.pge.com/recreation.

13 WISHON RESERVOIR

Rating: 7

northeast of Fresno in Sierra National Forest

Map 11.2, page 361

When full, Wishon is an attractive lake surrounded by national forest land and filled with snowmelt poured from the North Fork Kings River. The hitch is that Wishon Reservoir doesn't ever seem to be full.

This PG&E-managed lake is set at elevation 6,500 feet, and conditions are much the same as at nearby Courtright Reservoir, with a campground and a 15-mph speed limit. However, Wishon is easier to reach and more developed than Courtright.

This is the kind of place where a family might take a short vacation, a pretty spot that promotes a sense of tranquility. The 15-mph speed limit keeps it that way.

Sometimes, just paddling a canoe at Wishon

Reservoir and trailing a fishing line out the back can make for a memorable and relaxing evening.

Access: A paved ramp is available on the lake's west side.

Facilities, fees: Campgrounds, restrooms with coin showers, a picnic area, coin laundry, bar, bait and tackle, gas, and convenience store are available. Fishing boats can be rented at Wishon Village. Access to the lake is free.

Water sports, restrictions: A 15-mph speed limit is strictly enforced. Water-skiing, wake boarding, and personal watercraft are not permitted. Sailing and sailboarding are permitted, but winds are usually light. Swimming is allowed, but the water is generally too cold.

Directions: From Fresno, drive east on Highway 168 to Dinkey Creek Road (on the right just as entering the town of Shaver Lake). Turn right and drive 13 miles to McKinley Grove Road (Forest Road 40). Turn right and drive to the Wishon Dam. To reach the boat ramp, continue for about three miles to the boat ramp on the southeast shore. Note: This route is slow and twisty.

Contact: Sierra National Forest, High Sierra Ranger District, 559/855-5360, fax 559/855-5375; PG&E Land Projects, 916/386-5164, fax 916/386-5388, website: www.pge.com/recreation; Wishon Village RV Resort, 559/865-5361, website: www.wishonvillage.com.

14 PINE FLAT LAKE

Rating: 7

east of Fresno

Map 11.3, page 362

When Pine Flat Lake is full or close to full, it is surprisingly pretty. It is set in the foothills east of Fresno at an elevation of 970 feet, is 20 miles long with 67 miles of shoreline and 4,912 surface acres—a big lake with seemingly unlimited recreation potential. It fills in years with high snowpack in the Sierra and the ensuing melt-off in the spring and summer.

That is when Pine Flat becomes one of the most popular lakes in the entire region. This is a highly developed, commercial destination that includes a resort and numerous private campgrounds and RV parks that offer full facilities, even boat rentals.

Fresno is such a short drive away that boater and camper traffic is extremely heavy from the first warm days of spring on through Labor Day. Reservations are advised for anybody who plans on camping.

Pine Flat features hot summer days and warm water, a combination that often results in large amounts of liquid refreshments being consumed, oil being applied to bodies, and fast boats zooming around. Water-skiing, powerboating, swimming, and fishing for white bass can be quite good here. There are also largemouth bass, smallmouth bass, bluegill, white catfish, and black crappie.

Most people who jump in the water to cool off and maybe swim around a bit do so from houseboats and pontoon boats on the main lake body. The problem is that there aren't many sandy spots on the shoreline. The few good areas are located near the resorts, where you can hike on steep trails that are routed down to little sandy patches.

Because the water is warm even in the spring, this lake is excellent for all water/body contact sports. That includes sailboarding, though the winds are very inconsistent. Call ahead for conditions before heading out here.

One crazy element about Pine Flat is that the conditions are actually best in the fall, when the weather is cooler and much more bearable, yet during that season the lake can be empty.

That is because the lake has a terrible reputation for being extremely low. How low? Would you believe about 80 percent empty? Happens way too many years.

Access: Four boat ramps are located on the north shore off Trimmer Springs Road, Lakeview Resort, Deer Creek, and Island Park.

Facilities, fees: Lodging, campgrounds, restrooms with coin showers, RV dump station, fish-cleaning station, picnic areas, full-service marinas, snack bars, and convenience store are available. Fishing boats, pontoon boats, and houseboats can be rented at Lakeridge Marina. Fees are charged for day use and boat launching.

Water sports, restrictions: Water-skiing, wake boarding, personal watercraft, sailing, and sailboarding are permitted. There are no sandy swimming beaches, but swimming is available along the shoreline.

Directions: From Fresno, drive east on Highway 180 for 17.5 miles to Trimmer Springs Road. Turn left and drive eight miles to the town of Piedra. Continue on Trimmer Springs Road for one mile to Pine Flat Road. Turn right and drive .25 mile to the park entrance (signed Island Park).

Contact: U.S. Army Corps of Engineers, Sacramento District, Pine Flat Field Office, 559/787-2589; Lakeridge Resort, 559/787-2260; Lakeridge Marina, 559/787-2506; Trimmer Marina, 559/855-2039; Lakeview Resort, 559/787-2207.

15 KINGS RIVER

Rating: 10

northeast of Fresno

Map 11.3, page 362

The Kings is well known for providing some of the best rafting and kayaking water in California. There are three primary runs, but the one that is ideal for most is the Main Kings, a great Class III run that spans just under 10 miles. The other two are quite different. The Upper Kings is a scintillating stretch of water for daredevil experts only, rated Class V+, with incredible views and death-defying drops. Because the water is so cold, wet suits or dry suits are recommended and are usually required by commercial rafting companies through June. The Lower Kings, on the other hand, is pretty much an easy float that has only fair scenic value.

Here are more precise descriptions of all three runs:

• Main Kings: 9.5 miles; Class III. This is a very popular run for commercial outfitters, with daily trips from spring through midsummer. The scenery is excellent; the river winds through a pretty canyon, and there's little auto traffic to disturb the wild river ambience. Highlights include white-water rapids named Banzai (the most difficult rapid on the run), Mule Rock, Fang Tooth, Sidewinder, and Rooster Tail. Kayak races are held here every year. The season usually runs from April through July.

• Upper Kings: 10 miles; Class V+. This stretch of the river is very, very, very difficult (got that?), practically untouched by humankind. Even experts rarely try it. Getting to the put-in requires a long, steep hike, and you must carry in your gear and your boat.

Still with us? The first three miles are Class IV-V, which include several possible portages. After that it's Class V+ all the way, with many portages, huge drops, and terrifying rapids.

The reward is unequaled wilderness scenery, including a spectacular view of Garlic Falls (on the right at mile five), 650 feet high in four dramatic tiers. Nonboaters must hike in five miles to get a glimpse.

In addition, no trails access this river stretch, save for the trail to the put-in. This means that rafters and kayakers must be confident about their skills, because there is no turning back and no chance of being rescued here. The season is short, usually from July 1 to August 1. Expert kayakers, not rafters, are the primary groups who attempt this run during low flows.

• Lower Kings: 15 miles; Class I-II. This run is basically advertised as a scenic float, except that it is not all that scenic. But it does make for an easy canoe or inner tube float. Note that Pierce's Park on Highway 180 has the monopoly on canoe rentals because it's the only place around for miles. Numerous roads and highways cross the river along the way. So even though this is technically the same river as the Upper Kings, it is a world apart

in character. The season runs from June through August.

Access: No boat ramp is available. There are three rafting runs:

• Upper Kings: To reach the put-in from Fresno, drive east on Highway 180 for 55 miles to the Big Stump Entrance Station at Sequoia-Kings Canyon National Park. Continue 1.5 miles to a junction (signed left for Grant Grove). Turn left and drive to Grant Grove, and then continue 15 miles to Yucca Point. Park and hike two steep miles down to the river. Do not attempt to put in farther upstream where the highway crosses the river; the section above Yucca Point should not be run. Take out 10 miles downstream at Garnet Dike Campground.

Note: The Upper Kings is an extremely difficult Class V+ stretch that is rarely run; only experts should attempt it.

• Main Kings: From Fresno, take Highway 180 and drive east for 17.5 miles to Trimmer Springs Road. Turn left on Trimmer Springs Road and drive 26 miles (past Pine Flat Lake). Continue east on Trimmer Springs Road for seven miles to the put-in at Garnet Dike Campground. The take-out is 9.5 miles downstream (at Kirch Flat Campground, also on Trimmer Springs Road).

• Lower Kings: From Fresno, take Highway 180 and drive east for 17.5 miles to the small town of Centerville. Continue a short distance east to Pierce's Park (located where Highway 180 crosses the river). Canoeists may put in here and make a 15-mile run to the takeout at Cricket Hollow.

Facilities, fees: Several campgrounds are available along Trimmer Springs Road. Supplies can be obtained in Piedra. Canoe rentals and camping are available at Pierce's. River access is free. Rafting permits are not required. An access fee is charged per vehicle when entering Sequoia-Kings Canyon National Park.

Water sports, restrictions: No swimming access is available on the Upper Kings. A few swimming holes are located on the Main Kings, but swimming is not recommended due to the swift current and cold water. There is a beach at the take-out at Cricket Hollow on the Lower Kings.

Directions: To the Kings River south of Pine Flat Lake: From Fresno, take Highway 180 east and drive 17.5 miles to Trimmer Springs Road. Turn left (north) on Trimmer Springs Road (which parallels the west side of the river). Or continue a few miles east to Minkler and Piedra Road. Turn left (north) on Piedra Road (which borders the river's east side). Access is available here all the way upstream to the bridge at Piedra and downstream off numerous county roads.

To the Kings River north of Pine Flat Lake: From Fresno, take Highway 180 east for 17.5 miles to Trimmer Springs Road. Turn left (north) on Trimmer Springs Road and drive 26 miles (past Pine Flat Lake). Continue east on Trimmer Springs Road for seven miles. Access is available off the road and off unimproved roads that parallel both sides of the river.

Contact: Sequoia National Forest, Hume Lake Ranger District, 559/338-2251; Pierce's Park, 559/787-3450.

Guided rafting trips: Kings River Expeditions, 559/233-4881 or 800/846-3674, website: www.kingsriver.com; Zephyr Whitewater Expeditions, 209/532-6249 or 800/431-3636, website: www.zrafting.com; Whitewater Voyagers, 510/222-5994 or 800/400-7238, website: www.whitewatervoyages.com.

16 HUME LAKE

Rating: 6

east of Fresno in Giant Sequoia National Monument

Map 11.4, page 363

This gorgeous lake is set at 5,200 feet in elevation and is bordered by Kings Canyon National Park, Sequoia National Forest, and the Hume Lake Christian Camp (we'll get to that later).

The lake covers 85 acres and is filled with emerald green water. Swimmers will find an excellent spot for jumping in at Sandy Cove Beach, a large day-use area surrounded by pine

trees. This is a very peaceful, pretty place, and the 5-mph speed limit ensures that things stay that way. Canoeing and kayaking are excellent. So is the trout fishing, often best near the dam. In addition to swimming, other activities include low-speed boating (electric motors only) and paddling, trout fishing, and Bible study.

Right: Hume Lake Christian Camp has jurisdiction over the lake's south side, and they are friendly folks who are more than happy to rent you a boat. They also rent bicycles. In the summer, there are often youth camps here, tons of happy kids enjoying this beautiful spot to the max.

Access: A primitive launch ramp is located on the lake's south side.

Facilities, fees: A campground, restrooms with flush toilets, drinking water, and picnic area are provided. Convenience store, bait and tackle, gas, and a cafe are also available. Boats can be rented at Hume Lake Christian Camp. Access is free.

Water sports, restrictions: A 5-mph speed limit is enforced. Gas-powered motors are not permitted. Sailing and sailboarding are allowed. Swimming is available at Sandy Cove Beach on the lake's east side.

Directions: From Fresno, drive east on Highway 180 for 55 miles to the Big Stump Entrance Station at Sequoia-Kings Canyon National Park. Continue 1.5 miles to a junction (signed left for Grant Grove). Turn left and drive six miles to the Hume Lake Road junction. Turn right and drive three miles to Hume Lake and the campground entrance road. Turn right and drive .25 mile to the campground on the left.

Contact: Sequoia National Forest, Hume Lake Ranger District, 559/338-2251; Hume Lake Christian Camp, 559/335-2000.

17 TEN MILE CREEK

Rating: 4

east of Fresno

Map 11.4, page 363

Vacationers and campers who want to alleviate

the intense summer heat by taking a quick dunk have made Ten Mile Creek a popular place.

The trout fishing can be good here during the evening rise, and swimming can be good on hot days. The best fishing areas are found off pullouts on Ten Mile Road, close to Hume Lake. All of these spots are do-it-yourself specials, undeveloped, and difficult to find; keep a close eye out for the little parking pullouts along the road.

Beautiful forest land surrounds the creek-side campgrounds, which get quite a bit of traffic. Swimming conditions are poor directly adjacent to the campgrounds. Instead, you need to drive a bit and find those secret little swimming holes. It's like a fortune hunt.

Access: There is no boat ramp.

Facilities, fees: Several campgrounds are available on Ten Mile Road. Campgrounds have drinking water and vault toilets. Limited supplies can be obtained at Hume Lake and the town of Wilsonia. Access is free.

Water sports, restrictions: Several swimming holes are available near pullouts off of Ten Mile Road, near the campgrounds.

Directions: From Fresno, drive east on Highway 180 for 55 miles to the Big Stump Entrance Station at Sequoia-Kings Canyon National Park. Continue 1.5 miles to a junction (signed left for Grant Grove). Turn left and drive six miles to the Hume Lake Road junction. Turn right and drive three miles to Hume Lake. Continue one mile to Ten Mile Road. Turn and drive along Ten Mile Road. Access is available in several places along the road.

Contact: Sequoia National Forest, Hume Lake Ranger District, 559/338-2251.

18 LAKE KAWEAH

Rating: 8

east of Visalia

Map 11.4, page 363

If you visit Kaweah in late March, April, or early May, you can discover a big, pretty reser-voir set in the foothill country. When full, the lake covers nearly 2,000 acres, with 22 miles of shoreline. It is set at an elevation of 694 feet in the Sierra foothills on the highway that is routed to the southern entrance of Sequoia National Park. You may even think you have found paradise. The bass fishing, in particular, can be excellent at Kaweah.

But if you visit Kaweah in late summer or fall, you can often be greeted by a pit of a water hole and weather so hot you may expect the lake to start boiling at any minute. Heavy use of personal watercraft and high-speed power-boats is pretty typical in summer.

Many people do visit in late summer and fall, thinking the late summer heat is the perfect excuse to head to the lake to cool off. Not always. The annual water drawdown here shrinks the lake and makes it look like a dust bowl.

In the spring, however, this is a boater's heaven. Bass fishing is good in the coves, and there is plenty of room for personal watercraft riders and water-skiers to steer clear of those who are fishing. Some people even roam around in pontoon boats and enjoy the warm temperatures and cool water. There are some huge bass in this lake, and they inspire a lot of fishermen.

When the lake is full, prospects for swimming are decent in two spots: the lake's west side near the boat docks, and the east side at Slick Rock Day-Use Area. Over the years the fluctuating water levels have killed any prospects for developed beaches for swimming and wading.

Winds are erratic, coming and going far too unpredictably to make this a reliable destination for sailboarding or sailing. Then comes summer and out goes the water. In late summer and fall, when Kaweah starts to get low, unmarked rocks just beneath the surface can create boating hazards, and boaters should be sure to stay in deep water.

Access: Two boat ramps are available on the lake's west end at Kaweah Recreation Area and Lemon Hill Recreation Area.

Facilities, fees: A campground, restrooms with flush toilets and showers, RV dump station, picnic areas, full-service marina, bait and tackle, and a concession stand are provided at the lake. Fishing boats, pontoon boats, and personal watercraft can be rented at the marina. A store, coin laundry, snack bar, restaurant, gas station, and propane gas are available nearby. Access is free. There is a fee for boat launching and camping.

Water sports, restrictions: Water-skiing, wake boarding, personal watercraft, sailing, and sailboarding are permitted. Swimming is available on the lake's west side near the boat docks, and on the east side at Slick Rock Day-Use Area.

Directions: From Visalia drive east on Highway 198 for 20 miles to the lake.

Contact: U.S. Army Corps of Engineers, Lake Kaweah, 559/597-2301; Kaweah Marina, 559/597-2526.

19 DIAZ LAKE

Rating: 7

south of Lone Pine

Map 11.4, page 363

Little Diaz Lake is set at 3,650 feet in the Owens Valley, where it gets overshadowed by nearby Mount Whitney and the Sierra range to the west. The lake has three camping areas along the western shore, making it a decent spot for campers/boaters.

Covering 85 acres, the lake is small enough to provide a degree of intimacy, yet just large enough for water-skiing, and is close enough to Mount Whitney to have a looming sense of grandeur. Those features make Diaz Lake extremely popular for water-skiing and swimming, and often good for sailboarding.

A 15-mph speed limit during the prime fishing season, November through April, makes this an ideal setting for fishing. The lake is stocked with Alpers trout. By May, most anglers head north on U.S. 395 to find better prospects in the eastern Sierra; the speed limit is bumped up to 35 mph here, warm weather sets in, and

in come the water-skiers. For swimmers there is an excellent beach area.

One sidelight here is hang gliding, which is very popular from May through July on the leeward side of Mount Whitney. On the rare day you might even see hang gliders along the Whitney face as high as 14,000 feet, an extraordinary sight.

Access: A paved boat ramp is located on the lake's east side.

Facilities, fees: Campgrounds, restrooms with flush toilets, solar showers, picnic area, and boat dock are available. A 9-hole golf course is available nearby. Supplies can be obtained in Lone Pine. Access is free. There is a fee for boat launching and camping.

Water sports, restrictions: Water-skiing, wake boarding, personal watercraft, sailing, and sailboarding are permitted. Boats over 20 feet long are prohibited. The speed limit is 35 mph from May through October, and 15 mph from November through April. Swimming is available at the day-use area on the west shore.

Directions: Take U.S. 395 to Diaz Lake entrance (located two miles south of Lone Pine) on the west side of the road.

Contact: Diaz Lake Campground, 760/876-5656; Inyo County Parks Department, 760/873-5577.

20 FORKS OF THE KERN RIVER

Rating: 10

northeast of Bakersfield in Sequoia National Forest

Map 11.5, page 364

You have to be a little crazy to raft the Forks of the Kern, and that's exactly why we like it.

This river stretch is famous for having one heart-pumping rapid after another set in a beautiful wilderness canyon that is extremely difficult to access. The run is rated Class V—and just a notch below a Class VI, which is unrunnable (with risk of death). Only experts with at least Class IV paddling experience should consider attempting the run, and even for them it can be a death-defying act.

The run is 17 miles long, most of it amid complete wilderness, all of it on clear, icy water that's fed primarily by Whitney snowmelt from May through July. There are no access roads anywhere, a factor that is of paramount importance. It means that if an accident should occur, a timely rescue would be virtually impossible. It also means that once you start downriver, there is no turning back, because the only way out is down the river to the take-out.

Getting to the put-in requires a three-mile descent into a canyon. That's why most parties hire horses or pack mules to cart in their gear. Even then it is wise to pack light, as portages are common on this run and you'll end up carrying your gear anyway. Still with us?

If so then note that the run starts in the Golden Trout Wilderness near the confluence with the Little Kern River. This is an absolutely beautiful river canyon, but few rafters have time to admire it because right off the bat you hit Class V water, a river section considered a world-class rafting run for its series of sensational miniature falls.

Highlights include Upper (Class IV+) and Lower (Class V) Freeman Creek Falls, Needlerock Falls (Class IV+), Slalom (Class IV+), Vortex (Class V-VI), Rincon Aisle (Class IV+), Westwall (Class V), and Carson Falls (Class V-VI).

Even experts often portage Vortex and Carson Falls. The longest successive piece of white water is Rincon Aisle, which features three consecutive rapids over the course of .75 mile.

This is considered the most popular expert white-water rafting run in the state.

Note: A permit is required for camping in the Golden Trout Wilderness.

Access: There is no boat ramp. To reach the put-in see the directions above. Take out 17 miles downstream at the Johnsondale Bridge, located 20 miles north of Kernville.

Facilities, fees: Boat-in campsites are provid-ed along the river. Access is free. Rafting permits are required from May 15 to September 15; contact the Sequoia National Forest, Cannell Ranger District office, for information.

Water sports, restrictions: Swimming is not recommended. Rafters are advised to wear wet suits.

Directions: From Bakersfield, drive east on Highway 178 for about 40 miles to the town of Lake Isabella and Highway 155/Burlando Way. Turn left (north) and drive 10 miles to Kernville and the Kern River Highway/Sierra Way. Turn left on the Kern River Highway and drive 25 miles to the abandoned town of Johnsondale. Continue .5 mile to Lloyd Meadow Road/Forest Road 22S82. Turn right and drive 15 miles to Forest Road 20S67 (signed Forks of the Kern). Turn right and drive three miles to the trailhead for the Forks. Hike three miles down to the river. This trail offers the only developed access to this river section.

Contact: Sequoia National Forest, Cannell Meadow Ranger District, 760/376-3781, fax 760/376-3795; for pack animals, Golden Trout Wilderness Pack Trains, 559/542-2816 (summer) and 559/539-2744 (winter).

Guided rafting trips: Kern River Outfitters, 760/376-3370 or 800/323-4234, website: www.kernrafting.com; Kern River Tours, 760/379-4616 or 800/844-7238, website: www.kernrivertours.com; Chuck Richards' Whitewater, 760/379-4444 or 800/624-5950, website: www.chuckrichards.com; Whitewater Voyages, 510/222-5994 or 800/488-7238, website: www.whitewatervoyages.com.

21 UPPER KERN RIVER

Rating: 10

northeast of Bakersfield in Sequoia National Forest

Map 11.5, page 364

Merle Haggard, who grew up in Bakersfield, vowed, "I'll never swim the Kern River again," in one of his favorite songs. Why not? Because

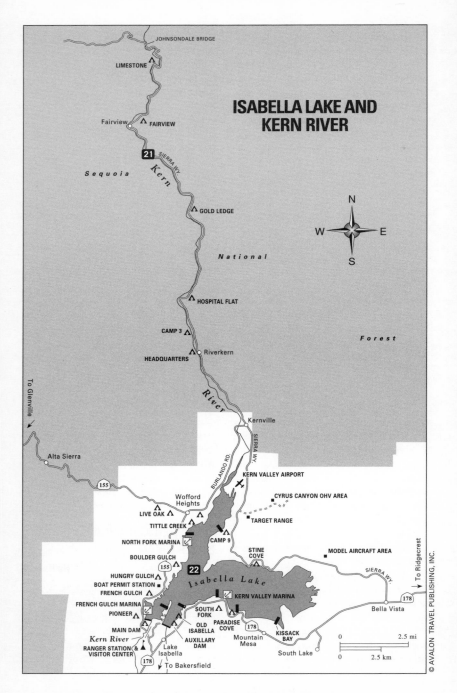

ISABELLA LAKE AND KERN RIVER

JOHNSONDALE BRIDGE

LIMESTONE

Fairview   FAIRVIEW

SIERRA WY.   21

Kern

Sequoia

GOLD LEDGE

National

HOSPITAL FLAT

CAMP 3

HEADQUARTERS   Riverkern

Forest

River

To Glenville

Kernville

Alta Sierra

BURLANDO RD.

SIERRA WY.

KERN VALLEY AIRPORT

155

Wofford
Heights

CYRUS CANYON OHV AREA

LIVE OAK

TITTLE CREEK

TARGET RANGE

NORTH FORK MARINA   CAMP 9

MODEL AIRCRAFT AREA

BOULDER GULCH

STINE
COVE

HUNGRY GULCH

155   22

Isabella Lake

BOAT PERMIT STATION

FRENCH GULCH

SIERRA WY.

To Ridgecrest

FRENCH GULCH MARINA

KERN VALLEY MARINA

178

PIONEER

SOUTH
FORK

Bella Vista

MAIN DAM

PARADISE
COVE

178

0   2.5 mi

Kern River

OLD
ISABELLA

KISSACK
BAY

RANGER STATION &
VISITOR CENTER

AUXILLARY
DAM

Mountain
Mesa

South Lake

0   2.5 km

178

Lake
Isabella

To Bakersfield

© AVALON TRAVEL PUBLISHING, INC.

he lost his "little darlin'" on the Kern when the "swiftness took her life away." And as Haggard sums it up, "It's not deep or wide, but it's a mean piece of water, my friend."

There is some truth to that. The Upper Kern has some of the better stretches of white water for rafting, and it can be dangerous for the inexperienced.

Great white water, beautiful canyon, easy access, and numerous commercial rafting trips have made this run one of the most popular in California. The season typically lasts from April to June, even later in big snow years. The water is always clear and very cold, fresh from snowmelt. The road parallels most of the river, but from the water, you can't see any traffic for the most part. There are few downers, that is, besides the fate of Merle's little darlin'.

The run spans 21 miles, but few people float the entire length. Most rafting companies will break it down into shorter runs because there's a wide range of difficulty over the course of the river. For instance, some stretches are Class III, a good exciting run for beginners, yet others are Class V, where even seasoned professionals can find their hearts pounding like pile drivers. Private boaters without guides should note that there are two mandatory take-out points, Fairview Dam and Salmon Falls, which provide natural break points. Even for experts, the best suggestion is to always run this river with an experienced professional before trying it on your own. Remember what Merle said.

Here are the run's highlights, starting at the Johnsondale Bridge put-in:

• Miles 0–2.5: This section is rated Class IV and features Limestone (Class IV) and Joe's Diner (IV).

• Miles 2.5–6: Rated Class III, with the exception of Bombs Away, a Class V cataract followed by a hydraulic suckhole that'll scare you out of your britches.

• Miles 6–8: Rated Class IV+ and featuring Entrance and Satan's Slot, both Class IV+ white water.

• Miles 9.5–16.5: Yeah, this is a pulse-pounder, with three Class V rapids and two Class IVs. In sequence, they are Squashed Paddler (Class V), Sock-em-Dog (Class V), The Flume (Class IV+), Fender Bender (Class V), and The Cable (Class IV).

• Miles 16.5–19: A great piece of water rated at Class IV. Highlights, as you encounter them heading downriver, are The Wall (Class IV), Tombstone (Class IV), Buzzard's Perch (Class III+), Tequila Chute (Class IV), and Powerhouse (Class III+).

• Miles 19–21: The last stretch is a Class III run through private property, highlighted by Big Daddy (Class III-) and Ewing's (Class III-). Do not take out until you reach the town of Kernville, provided you are still in one piece.

Access: There is no boat ramp. To reach the put-in once you are in Kernville, turn north on Sierra Way and drive 20 miles to the Johnsondale Bridge. There are several good take-outs along the way; the final take-out is 18 miles downstream at Riverside Park in Kernville. Note: Sections of the river are unrunnable; be sure to take out above Fairview Dam (mile 2.5) and above Salmon Falls (mile eight).

Facilities, fees: Campgrounds are provided on Highway 178 and Sierra Way, as well as at Isabella Lake. Supplies can be obtained in Lake Isabella, Kernville, and River Kern. Access is free. Rafting permits are required year-round; contact the Sequoia National Forest, Cannell Ranger District, for information.

Water sports, restrictions: Swimming is available at several holes along Sierra Way, north of Kernville. The best are near the Forest Service campgrounds. But note that the Forest Service does not recommend swimming in the river; see notes about Merle Haggard's experience above, ha!

Directions: From Bakersfield, drive east on Highway 178 for about 40 miles to the town of Lake Isabella and Highway 155/Burlando Way. Turn left (north) and drive 10 miles to Kernville and the Kern River Highway/Sierra Way. Turn left on the Kern River Highway and drive seven miles to the campground (access is available here and elsewhere along the road; see Access above).

Contact: Sequoia National Forest, Cannell Meadow Ranger District, 760/376-3781.

Guided rafting trips: Kern River Outfitters, 760/376-3370 or 800/323-4234, website: www .kernrafting.com; Kern River Tours, 760/379-4616 or 800/844-7238, website: www.kern-rivertours.com; Chuck Richards' Whitewater, 760/379-4444 or 800/624-5950, website: www.chuckrichards.com; Whitewater Voyages, 510/222-5994 or 800/488-7238, website: www.whitewatervoyages.com.

22 ISABELLA LAKE

Rating: 9

east of Bakersfield

Map 11.5, page 364

The largest freshwater lake in Southern California is Isabella, covering 38,400 acres when full. Here you will find what is among the most complete and dynamic array of facilities available anywhere. The largest of the three marinas is French Gulch Marina, with 104 boat slips.

The lake, which is set at an elevation of 2,600 feet in the foothills east of Bakersfield, is the centerpiece for a wide variety of activities, namely water-skiing and camping. The majority of visitors are boater/campers who dominate much of the lake, water-skiing on most summer days. There are two major lake arms, each wide and long, and campgrounds are situated along the western shoreline. The weather is hot, the water temperate, and with lots of boats and bodies, this is the kind of place where the suntan oil and various liquid refreshments can flow faster than the nearby Kern River.

Sailboarding is extremely popular at Isabella Lake. The best spot is east of Auxiliary Dam, where the winds come up and sail right over the dam; it's quite ideal, usually a steady breeze in the afternoon, not gusty. The boat ramp between the auxiliary dam and the main dam

is by far the most used and busiest boat ramp at the lake.

The cool, clear Kern River waters feed into the lake and make for excellent swimming conditions. Although there are no designated beaches, there are some beachlike areas. The shoreline is mostly hard-packed dirt and sagebrush.

Boater/camper traffic is heavy well into fall. After that, when the cool weather arrives, anglers show up in significant numbers. There is good bird-watching in the area, and of course with the nearby Kern River feeding the lake, there are excellent opportunities for white-water rafting (see previous and next listings).

Birdwatching is good at the South Fork Wildlife Area along the northeast corner of the lake. Fishing for trout and bass is good in early summer, and there is a major fishing tournament held every May. The lake is stocked with trout in late winter. In summer, there is fishing for bluegill, catfish, and crappie.

Access: Ramps are available at several points around the lake.

• Ponderosa Drive: From the town of Lake Isabella, drive east on Highway 178 for a short distance to Ponderosa Drive. Turn left and drive a short distance to the boat ramp (located between the auxiliary dam and the main dam).

• Paradise Cove Campground: From the town of Lake Isabella, drive east on Highway 178 for six miles to Paradise Cove Campground and the boat ramp. This ramp is closed during low lake levels.

• Kissack Bay: From the town of Lake Isabella, drive east on Highway 178 for nine miles to Kissack Bay and the boat ramp. This ramp is closed during low lake levels.

• Camp 9: From the town of Lake Isabella and Highway 155/Burlando Way, turn right (south) and drive six miles to Camp 9.

• French Gulch: From the town of Lake Isabella and Highway 155/Burlando Way, turn left (north) and drive three miles to French Gulch Campground.

• North Fork Marina: From the town of Lake Isabella, turn west on Highway 155 and drive approximately four miles around the lake's west side. The ramp is located between North Fork Marina and Tillie Creek Campground. Note: This ramp may be unusable when water levels are low.

• Old Isabella Road: From the town of Lake Isabella, drive east on Highway 178 for approximately two miles to Old Isabella Road. Turn left and continue to the ramp.

• South Fork Recreation Area: From the town of Lake Isabella, continue east on Highway 178 for approximately four miles to the sign for South Fork Recreation Area. Turn left and continue to the ramp, located between Paradise Cove and Kern Valley Marina.

Facilities, fees: Several campgrounds are available. Full-service marinas, RV dump station, restaurants, gas, lodging, and convenience stores are also available. Fishing boats, pontoon boats, ski boats, and personal watercraft can be rented at Dean's North Fork Marina, 760/376-1812, and at French Gulch Marina, 760/379-8774, website: www.frenchgulchmarina.com. All boaters must purchase a 3-day or an annual permit to boat on the lake; obtain one at any of the marinas or local businesses. Permit includes launching privileges.

Water sports, restrictions: Water-skiing, wake boarding, and personal watercraft are permitted. Sailing and sailboarding are allowed; the best spot is on Auxiliary Dam's east side, off Old Isabella Road. Swimming is available all along the shoreline; a popular site is at French Gulch Bridge on the west shore.

Directions: From Bakersfield, take Highway 178 east and drive 40 miles to the town of Lake Isabella. Continue two miles to the lake (see Access above for directions to specific boat ramps).

Contact: Sequoia National Forest, Greenhorn Ranger District, 760/379-5646, fax 760/379-8597; Sierra South Mountain Sports and Kayak Tours, 760/376-3745 or 800/457-2082, website: wwwsierrasouth.com; Mountain and River Adventures and Kayak Tours, 760/376-6553 or 800/861-6553, website: www.mtnriver.com.

23 LOWER KERN RIVER

Rating: 10

east of Bakersfield

Map 11.5, page 364

While not as rambunctious as the Upper Kern, this stretch of river can provide rafters with plenty of thrills and chills. There are a few caveats about safety, however, but we'll get to that in a bit.

This 12-mile-long run is rated Class IV, best for intermediate to advanced rafters. The white-water season is a long one, from Memorial Day weekend through August. One reason is that the Lower Kern is set below Isabella Lake, so water releases from the dam for farmers keep this river pumping well through summer. It also means that the water is far warmer than at the stretches of the Kern located upriver of the lake, which are fed by snowmelt.

Access is excellent because the highway parallels the river. And despite the proximity of the road, the steep canyon provides great scenery and has wilderness-like feel.

There are calm stretches between rapids where you can catch your breath. The water is far warmer than the icy flows of the Upper Kern, far better for swimming. Stay in the river eddies, and do not try to swim in moving current.

A challenging intermediate-advanced section is the run's star attraction. Most of the white water is rated Class III+, though a few Class IVs are sprinkled along the route, including White Maiden's Walkway, Powerful Possum, Hari-Kari, Horseshoe Falls, and Pinball.

Anybody without a guide should note that there is one Class V rapid called Royal Flush that is nearly always a mandatory portage. Do not attempt to run this piece, and if you are unfamiliar with its location, then you should not be on the river without a guide.

Another option is to make this a two-day trip by rafting or kayaking from below the dam to Miracle Springs, an eight-mile run—and then continuing the next day from Miracle Springs to the take out. This first stretch is easier, nothing over Class III. Some also use this upper stretch as a one-day run.

Here's an insider's tip: There are hot springs at the Miracle Hot Springs camping area. Since the old hotel there burned down, this area is no longer developed. Some visitors keep trying to install tubs for the hot springs, and the Forest Service keeps tearing them out.

Access: There is no boat ramp. To reach the put-in: From the town of Lake Isabella, turn north on Highway 155 and drive just under a mile and look for the sign for Keysville. Turn left and drive about .5 mile to a paved parking area. Put in on the left bank. Take out 18 miles downstream at Delonegha Picnic Area (reached by taking a signed dirt road off Highway 178).

Facilities, fees: A primitive camping area is provided at Miracle Hot Springs, located on Kern River Canyon Road off Highway 178. More developed drive-to campgrounds are available at Lake Isabella. Supplies can be obtained in Kernvale. Access is free. Rafting permits are required from May 15 to September 15; contact the Cannell Meadow or Greenhorn Ranger District offices for information. **Water sports, restrictions:** Swimming is not recommended.

Directions: From Bakersfield, take Highway 178 east and drive 40 miles to the town of Lake Isabella. Access to the lower river is available directly off the highway from 10 miles east of Bakersfield all the way to Kernvale (see directions below to put-in).

Contact: Sequoia National Forest, Cannell Meadow Ranger District, 760/376-3781, or Greenhorn Ranger District, 760/379-5646.

Guided rafting trips: Kern River Outfitters, 760/376-3370 or 800/323-4234, website: www.kernrafting.com; Kern River Tours, 760/379-4616 or 800/844-7238, website: www.kernrivertours.com; Chuck Richards' Whitewater, 760/379-4444 or 800/624-5950, website: www.chuckrichards.com; Whitewater Voyages, 510/222-5994 or 800/488-7238, website: www.whitewatervoyages.com; Mountain & River Adventures, 760/376-6553 or 800/861-6553, website: www.mtnriver.com; Sierra South Mountain Sports, 760/376-3745 or 800/457-2082, website: www.sierrasouth.com.

FOGHORN OUTDOORS®

PLASTIC WORLD MEDIA // ©2002

Chapter 12

Santa Barbara and Vicinity

Chapter 12—Santa Barbara and Vicinity

For many, this region of California coast is like a dream, the best place to live on earth. The region is a unique mix of sun-swept sand beaches that stretch 200 miles and surprise inland coastal forests.

Yet as popular as the coast can seem, just inland lie many remote, hidden campsites and destinations, and some of California's best recreation lake destinations, such as Lake Nacimiento and San Antonio Reservoir.

To the north, it is Lake Nacimiento that provides the most for the most, that is, boating of all types, outstanding wake boarding and water-skiing opportunities, excellent swimming, and often great catch rates when fishing for white bass. Nacimiento is one of the top family-oriented lakes in California for water sports. San Antonio Reservoir is also outstanding, with the bonus of excellent fishing for largemouth bass and bald eagle tours by boat (best in winter). Santa Margarita is also a very good lake for bass fishing.

To the south of this region, Lake Cachuma and Lake Casitas near Santa Barbara have produced some of the largest bass caught in history.

Los Padres National Forest spans a matrix of canyons with small streams, mountaintop lookouts, and wilderness trailheads. The landscape is a mix of pine, deep canyons, chaparral, and foothills. Some spots are so primitive and difficult to reach the rangers asked me to delete a hike-in campground from my camping book because nearly nobody was able to reach it.

The ocean is dramatic here, the backdrop for every trip on the Coast Highway, and it seems to stretch to forever-land. Maybe it does. For many visiting here, forever is how long they wish to stay.

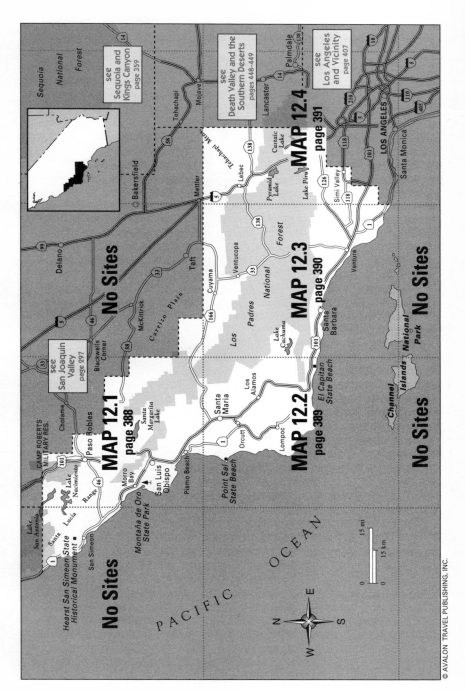

© AVALON TRAVEL PUBLISHING, INC.

Map 12.1

Sites 1–6
Pages 392–396

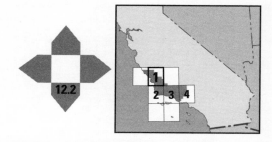

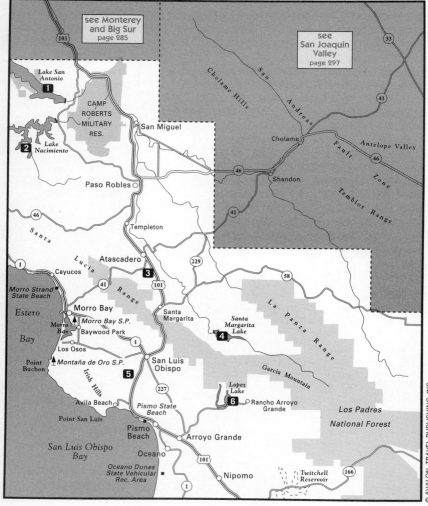

© AVALON TRAVEL PUBLISHING, INC.

Map 12.2

Site 7
Pages 396–397

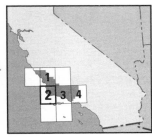

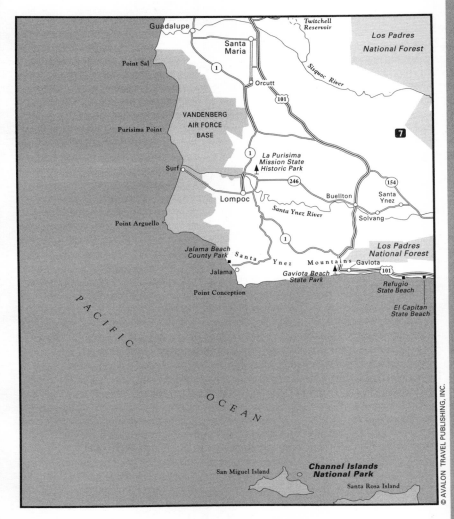

© AVALON TRAVEL PUBLISHING, INC.

Map 12.3

**Sites 8–10
Pages 397–399**

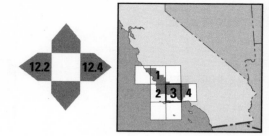

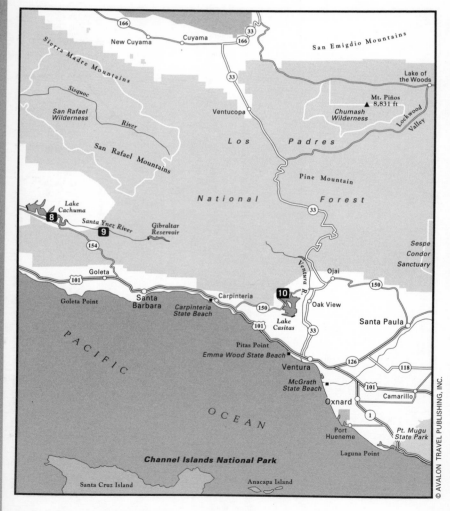

© AVALON TRAVEL PUBLISHING, INC.

Map 12.4

Sites 11–13
Pages 400–403

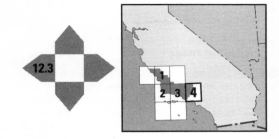

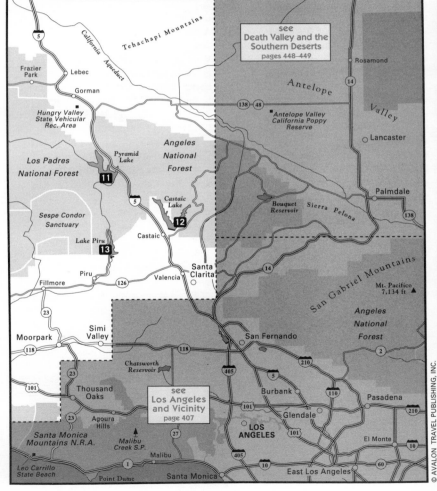

see
**Death Valley and the
Southern Deserts**
pages 448–449

see
**Los Angeles
and Vicinity**
page 407

© AVALON TRAVEL PUBLISHING, INC.

1 LAKE SAN ANTONIO

🚤 🍴 ♿ ⛴ 🚣 ⛵ 💺 〰 ⛺

Rating: 8

north of San Luis Obispo

Map 12.1, page 388

Have you ever felt like someone or something was watching you? At Lake San Antonio—which has the largest population of bald eagles in central California—that perception is usually accurate.

That's just one of the special things about the San Antonio experience. This is a big lake, long and narrow, covering 5,500 surface acres with 60 miles of shoreline. The lake is 16 miles long. The setting is at an elevation of 780 feet in the southern Monterey County foothills. The average temperature in the summer is in the 70s, courtesy of its location 20 miles from the coast.

Lake San Antonio, thanks to its large size and warm water, is the most popular water-skiing lake in the region. In the winter, eagle-watching tours are the main attraction, and the chances of seeing both bald and golden eagles by boat are excellent. But no matter when you come, keep an eye out to the skies. The eagles are always watching. Eagle tours are available out of South Shore.

In addition to four boat ramps and several campgrounds, the lake offers full facilities. With all these attractions, it gets significant use and can be extremely crowded on holiday weekends as well as on summer weekends when the weather is good.

Surface temperatures are warm and comfortable, making water-skiing and personal watercraft riding very popular year-round. And providing you can avoid all the fast action, swimming is also excellent. The best spot for swimming is at the sandy beach on the south shore.

Prospects for sailboarding are decent in the spring, but are generally only fair; most sailboarders head to the other side of the hill to Lake Nacimiento (see next listing), which tends to get steadier winds than at San Antonio. Boat rentals are available out of South Shore only.

This is one of the top lakes in California for bass fishing, best in spring and early summer. It is also good for striped bass, catfish, crappie, redear sunfish, and bluegill.

Access: Four paved ramps are available.

Facilities, fees: Campgrounds, restrooms with showers, mobile home rentals, picnic areas, a full-service marina, mooring and slips, snack bar, restaurant, gas station, coin laundry, RV dump station, and convenience store are available. Fishing boats, pontoon boats, ski boats, canoes, and kayaks can be rented at Lake San Antonio Marina. Fees are charged for day use, boat launching, and camping.

Water sports, restrictions: Water-skiing, wake boarding, personal watercraft, sailing, and sailboarding are permitted. A sandy swimming beach is available on the south shore between the marina and Harris Creek Day-Use Area.

Directions: To North Shore: On U.S. 101, drive to Jolon Road/G-14 exit (just north of King City). Take that exit and turn south on Jolon Road and drive 27 miles to Pleyto Road (curvy road). Turn right and drive three miles to the North Shore entrance of the lake. Note: When arriving from the south or east on U.S. 101 near Paso Robles, it is faster to take G-18/Jolon Road exit.

To South Shore: From the south, drive on U.S. 101 to Paso Robles and the 24th Street exit (G-14 West). Take that exit and drive 14 miles to Lake Nacimiento Drive. Turn right and drive across Lake Nacimiento Dam to Interlake Road. Turn left and drive seven miles to Lake San Antonio Road. Turn right and drive three miles to South Shore entrance.

From the north on U.S. 101 (just north of King City), take the Jolon Road/G-14 exit. Turn south on Jolon Road and drive 20 miles to Lockwood and Interlake Road (G-14). Turn right and drive 13 miles to San Antonio Lake Road. Turn left and drive three miles to the South Shore entrance of the lake.

Contact: Lake San Antonio, 805/472-2311, web-

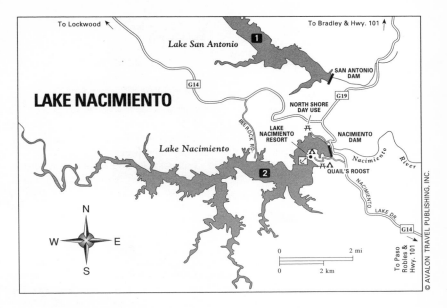

site: www.co.monterey.ca.us/parks; Lake San Antonio Marina and boat rentals, 805/472-2818; boat tours, 888/588-2267.

2 LAKE NACIMIENTO

Rating: 9

north of San Luis Obispo

Map 12.1, page 388

A remarkable number of lake arms and coves add to the boundary of Lake Nacimiento, a big lake set in the coastal foothill country of the southern edge of Monterey County. When full, the lake covers more than 5,000 acres and has 165 miles of shoreline.

That combination—a huge surface area with many private coves—provides the ideal conditions for high-speed boating, water-skiing, and personal watercraft riding, as well as low-speed boating, canoeing, and fishing. The lake is a favorite for many, and provides some of the best water-skiing in California.

In the main lake body, water-skiers and personal watercraft riders often dominate the scene. There is even a slalom course on the lake for expert water-skiers. If you have a fast boat, you will feel right at home. But if you don't, well, don't despair.

That is because you can explore the rest of the lake and hunt down a quiet, private spot for fishing or swimming in one of the coves. Fishing is often excellent for white bass and largemouth bass, with high catch rates common in the spring and early summer. About 25 fishing tournaments are held each year here. There are also opportunities for bluegill and catfish in summer.

While there is no drive-to swimming beach, with a boat you can access any number of private little beaches in the coves. Swimming is very pleasant here, as the water temperature hovers in the 67- to 72-degree range most of the summer.

Nacimiento is also good for sailboarding in the spring, when coastal winds whip in from the ocean and through the lake canyons en route to the valley. However, the main lake is big enough to get quite choppy and provide a rough riding surface, often making it difficult for novices.

This is a fully developed resort destination that is popular with families. Use is highest in the summer, of course, but holds steady year-round. Its location near U.S. 101 in central California puts it within reach of residents to the south in Santa Barbara as well as those from up north in San Jose—a rarity.

The restaurant at Nacimiento is a good one, with the bonus of a lake view.

Access: A paved boat ramp is located on the southeast shore, next to Lake Nacimiento Resort. Another boat ramp is available intermittently during the summer season on the north shore.

Facilities, fees: Campgrounds, picnic area, lodging, restrooms with showers, restaurant, gas, full-service marina, boat docks, coin laundry, RV dump station, and grocery store are available. Fishing boats, pontoon boats, ski boats, personal watercraft, canoes, and kayaks can be rented at the Lake Nacimiento Marina. Swimming beaches and swimming pool are available. Fees are charged for day use, boat launching, and camping.

Water sports, restrictions: Water-skiing, wake boarding, personal watercraft, sailing, and sailboarding are permitted. Swimming is available all along the shoreline (you need a boat to reach the best spots). Some areas are designated and signed with speed limits and skiing restrictions.

Directions: On U.S. 101, drive to Paso Robles and the 24th Street/Lake Nacimiento exit. Take that exit, turn west on 24th Street (becomes Lake Nacimiento Road/G-14) and drive for nine miles. Bear right on Lake Nacimiento Road and continue for seven miles to the resort entrance on the left. Note: If you cross the Lake Nacimiento dam, you've gone too far.

Contact: Lake Nacimiento Resort, 805/238-3256 or 800/323-3839; Lake Nacimiento Marina, 805/238-1056, website: www.nacimientoresort.com.

3 ATASCADERO LAKE

Rating: 4

north of San Luis Obispo in Atascadero Memorial Park

Map 12.1, page 388

This 30-acre lake is the centerpiece of a friendly city park that provides the chance to enjoy a variety of activities.

Unfortunately, those activities do not include most water sports. There are lots of nos: no gas motors, no boat ramp, no water-skiing, no sailboarding, no swimming, no wading. The lake is occasionally stocked with rainbow trout and largemouth bass.

What that leaves is the opportunity for kids to play, usually pedaling around the lake in a pedal boat. Visitors can hand launch a car-top boat, such as a canoe or a rowboat, and then paddle about, but that's about it. That leaves fishing, and the prospects for that are practically zilch since the occasional trout and bass plants are so light.

Most of the folks you'll see at Atascadero Lake are just out for a lakeside picnic.

Access: There is no boat ramp. Car-top boats may be hand launched.

Facilities, fees: Restrooms, a café, and pedal boat and kayak rentals are available. A zoo is nearby. Access is free.

Water sports, restrictions: Gas-powered motors are not permitted on the lake. Sailing is permitted. A 5-mph speed limit is strictly enforced. Sailboarding is not allowed. Swimming is limited to a children's wading pool at the park.

Directions: From San Luis Obispo, drive north on U.S. 101 to Atascadero and the Morro Road/Highway 41 exit. Take that exit onto El Camino Real. Drive a short distance to the stoplight at Morro Road. Turn left on Morro Road and drive 1.5 miles to the park entrance on the left.

Contact: City of Atascadero, Parks & Recreation Department, 805/461-5000, fax 805/461-7612.

4 SANTA MARGARITA LAKE

Rating: 5

east of San Luis Obispo

Map 12.1, page 388

This lake should have a sign that declares, "Fishing only!" because the rules here do not allow water-skiing or any water contact: no swimming, wading, sailboarding, or anything else, just fishing.

The lake covers nearly 800 acres, most of it long and narrow. It is set at an elevation of 1,300 feet in a dammed-up valley in the foothill country five miles southeast of the town of Santa Margarita. It is set just below the Santa Lucia Mountains, and is fed by the Salinas River.

Anglers from near and far are enamored with the idea of a fishing-only lake, as well as being equally fascinated with the fine bass prospects here. Expect heavy fishing traffic on weekends virtually year-round.

Note that some users, primarily owners of small craft, must get approval prior to launching. **Access:** A paved boat ramp is located on the southwest shore and another ramp is on the south shore.

Facilities, fees: Several campgrounds are in the vicinity. Picnic areas, a full-service marina with launch ramp, and convenience store are available. Fishing boats, kayaks, water bikes, and pontoon boats can be rented. There are fees for day use, boat launching, and camping.

Water sports, restrictions: The speed limit is 30 mph. Water-skiing, personal watercraft, sailboarding, swimming, and water/body contact are not allowed. Boaters with craft under 10 feet long or inflatables must get approval prior to launching. Float tubes are allowed providing the user wears waders.

Directions: From San Luis Obispo, drive north on U.S. 101 for eight miles to the Highway 58/Santa Margarita exit. Take that exit, drive through the town of Santa Margarita to Entrada. Turn right on Entrada and drive seven miles (Entrada becomes Pozo Road) to Santa

Margarita Lake Road. Turn left and drive to the lake.

Contact: Santa Margarita Lake Recreation Area, 805/788-2397; Santa Margarita Lake Marina, 805/438-3754, website: www.slocountyparks.com.

5 LAGUNA LAKE

Rating: 5

near San Luis Obispo

Map 12.1, page 388

Basically a big neighborhood lake, this is the kind of place where locals unwind on the weekends and on summer evenings. Most fish a little, jog a bit, or have a picnic. The lake is very small, just 60 acres.

What most people don't realize is that Laguna Lake is a great spot for sailboarding. The winds come up nearly every day in the afternoon, and by 4 P.M. they are usually whipping sailboarders at a fast clip. Conditions can be ideal because, unlike at larger lakes, the surface here doesn't get choppy when pushed by strong winds. Still, be forewarned that this is no place for a novice sailboarder.

The best thing about Laguna is that sailboarders practically have the lake to themselves. You see, swimming and motorized boats are not allowed.

The lake is far more popular with picnickers and joggers, however. There is even a fitness trail in the park. Big events, including weddings, are often held in the park, which is also the starting point for some running and walking races. There is also fishing for bass, catfish, and carp.

Access: An unimproved boat ramp is available.

Facilities, fees: Restrooms, flush toilets, drinking water, picnic area, and a playground are provided. Access is free.

Water sports, restrictions: Gas motors are not permitted on the lake. Sailing and sailboarding are allowed. No swimming is permitted.

Directions: From San Luis Obispo drive south

on U.S. 101 for approximately two miles to Madonna Road. Turn west (left) on Madonna Road and drive 1.5 miles to the park entrance on the right.

Contact: City of San Luis Obispo, Parks & Recreation Department, 805/781-7300, fax 805/781-7292.

6 LOPEZ LAKE

Rating: 9

east of San Luis Obispo

Map 12.1, page 388

They've got it right at Lopez Lake. This lake can be ideal for water-skiing, personal watercraft riding, sailboarding, and fishing. Bass fishing takes center stage in the spring, and then when the water temperatures heat up, water sports tend to take over.

A great plus is that special marked areas are devoted exclusively to water-skiing, personal watercraft, and sailboarding, and the rest of the lake designated for fishing and low speed boating. That keeps everybody happy and out of each other's way—a perfect example of the best way to manage a recreational lake.

There are also full facilities for swimming, with a big swimming beach and two giant water slides, a children's wading pool, along with a nice picnic area. Another bonus is the scenic boat tours, available on Saturdays, which get plenty of takers.

So it will come as no surprise to hear that visitor use is extremely high in the summer.

All these activities and special-use rules work so well because Lopez Lake is a decent-sized lake, 940 surface acres when full, with 22 miles of shoreline, and it gets excellent summer weather in the foothills southeast of San Luis Obispo. The lake is set amid oak woodlands, and is shaped somewhat like a horseshoe.

One word of caution: In the spring, this isn't the place to bring a canoe or, for that matter, any boat that can't handle wind. Why? You guessed it. It gets very windy here in the spring,

especially in the afternoon, making it great for sailboarders and sailboaters. The best spot is the main channel of the Wittenberg arm. You can avoid the wind in the Arroyo Grande or Lopez arms.

The lake is stocked with trout, and also provides fishing for largemouth bass, bluegill, crappie, and catfish. A 25-mile trail system provides opportunities for biking, hiking, and horseback riding.

Access: A paved boat ramp is located at the marina, just past the lake entrance on the left.
Facilities, fees: A campground, restroom with showers, full-service marina, mooring, gas, coin laundry, snack bar, and convenience store are available. Fishing boats, personal watercraft, kayaks, and pontoon boats can be rented at Lopez Lake Marina. Fees are charged for day use, boat launching, and camping.
Water sports, restrictions: There is a 40-mph speed limit. Water-skiing, wake boarding, personal watercraft, sailing, and sailboarding are allowed. A swimming area is available on the lake's east side.
Directions: Take U.S. 101 to Arroyo Grande and the exit for Grand Avenue. Take that exit, turn east and drive through Arroyo Grande to Lopez Drive. Turn northeast on Lopez Drive and drive 10 miles to the park.
Contact: Lopez Lake Marina, 805/489-1006; Lopez Lake, Recreation Area, 805/788-2381, website: www.slocountyparks.com.

7 ZACA LAKE

Rating: 7

south of Santa Maria

Map 12.2, page 389

Little Zaca Lake is the perfect retreat for the boater whose ideal vacation wouldn't be complete without a cabin to bed down in.

This small lake, covering just 25 acres, is set at a 2,400-foot elevation on privately-owned land, about 40 miles north of Santa Barbara. Boating is restricted to nonmotorized craft, which keeps the mood nice and quiet here. A full-service lodge has canoes and rowboats.

The few people who have learned about the charms of Zaca Lake have been pretty successful at keeping the place a secret. That hasn't been too difficult because fishing is not permitted, which keeps it out of the loop of most mainstream boaters/campers/anglers.

Swimming is popular, and a buoy line marks a swimming area and rocky beach at the lake's south end. Because of the lake's proximity to the coast, there are steady afternoon winds almost daily, meaning conditions for sailboarding are often excellent. Amazingly, rarely does one see sailboarders taking advantage of it—perhaps they simply haven't heard the word on Zaca.

Side trip options include hiking and horseback riding. Some good trails are routed into the national forestland located north of the lake.

The region features the Santa Ynez wine country, with 20 wineries located within a 30-minute drive.

Access: An unimproved launch ramp is located on the lake's northern side.

Facilities, fees: Primitive campsites, cabins, and picnic areas are provided. The lodge has sailboats, kayaks, canoes, rowboats, and sailboards. Day use is available to the public only on Sundays. Fees are charged for day use, and includes boat launching.

Water sports, restrictions: Motors are not permitted on the lake. Sailing, sailboarding, and swimming are allowed. The lake is closed to fishing.

Directions: From the junction of U.S. 101 and Highway 154 south of Santa Maria, turn east on Highway 154 and drive 200 yards to Zaca Station Road. Turn left on Zaca Station Road and drive about 10 miles to the lake entrance.

Contact: Zaca Lake Retreat and Mineral Springs, 805/688-5699, fax 805/688-9839, website: www.zacalakeretreat.com.

8 LAKE CACHUMA

Rating: 6

north of Santa Barbara

Map 12.3, page 390

Here's a place that can be transformed from hell to heaven in one fell swoop.

Hell? Because water levels at Cachuma depend solely on rain runoff, it takes only one winter with sub-par rains for this lake to become a relative puddle edged by miles of barren, exposed lake bottom.

High water has meant heaven for anglers, and as the bass population has boomed, with lots of big fish, Cachuma has become one of the best bass lakes in America. Furthermore, boating restrictions have made this lake perfect for fishing. The often ideal climate makes this a winner for camping as well.

Very little water recreation is permitted because this is a reservoir used to store drinking water (at least that's the excuse that's provided). No water-skiing, personal watercraft use, swimming, or sailboarding is allowed. Canoes and kayaks are prohibited from the lake, as are boats under 10 feet long. That leaves it all to the fishing boats, and with a speed limit of 5 mph in the coves, 10 mph elsewhere, and 40 mph in the center of the lake. It's the perfect setup for high-speed bass boats.

Cachuma is set at an elevation of 750 feet in the foothills northeast of Santa Barbara. When the lake is full, it is big and beautiful, covering 3,200 acres. In low rain years the drawdowns are so significant that you'd hardly recognize the place.

After fishing, picnicking and camping come in a distant second and third in popularity, respectively. Use is steady year-round, but in summers when the lake is full, the camping traffic skyrockets.

Access: Three boat ramps, located for access at different lake levels, are on the south shore. The primary ramp is a multi-lane paved ramp.

Facilities, fees: A campground, yurts, picnic

areas, full-service marina, moorings, fishing piers, bait and tackle, restrooms with flush toilets, showers, snack bar, coin laundry, and general store are available. Fishing boats, pontoon boats, rowboats, and water bikes are available for rent. Fees are charged for day use and boat launching. Lake tours are available year-round. **Water sports, restrictions:** Powerboating and sailing are permitted. Water-skiing, personal watercraft, sailboarding, canoes, kayaks, or water/body contact are not permitted. The speed limit is 40 mph in the middle of Lake Cachuma, 5 mph in the coves. Craft under 10 feet long are prohibited and inflatables must be at least 12 feet. Catamarans with trampoline decks must be at least 14 feet long. Swimming pools are available just outside the lake. Leashed pets must be kept at least 50 feet from the lake.

Directions: From Santa Barbara, take Highway 154 north and drive 20 miles to the lake on the right.

Contact: Lake Cachuma Recreation Area, Santa Barbara County, 805/686-5054; Cachuma Marina and Boat Rentals, 805/688-4040; Cachuma Boat Tours, 805/686-5050, website: www.cachuma.com.

🟧 SANTA YNEZ RIVER

Rating: 4

north of Santa Barbara in Los Padres National Forest

Map 12.3, page 390

This river is at the mercy of water releases out of Lake Cachuma, and in dry years these can be pretty sparse. The flow is sometimes reduced to a mere trickle in the summer. But when it's right, there are some great swimming holes in this stream—in fact, some of the best in any river in Southern California.

Swimming holes are available at campgrounds and picnic areas along Paradise Road; the best spots are at Fremont Campground, White Rock Picnic Area, Sage Hill Group Campground,

Lower Oso Picnic Area, Falls Picnic Area, and Santa Ynez Campground. Red Rock Campground has the best swimming and fishing, and is located just downstream from Lake Cachuma on Paradise Road. Fishing can be decent for rainbow trout and bass at Red Rock.

But it seems to be either feast or famine here, with extremely high stream flows in spring that can taper off to nothing by late summer. When the water level is reasonably high, swimming is excellent. It gets very hot down here and the river provides the perfect respite, especially at the developed recreation spots along Paradise Road, which come complete with shady sites for picnicking and camping. The best spots typically get heavy use in the summer.

Rafting and boating are not recommended because the river becomes quite brushy in places and can be difficult to navigate.

Access: There is no boat ramp. Rafting is not recommended.

Facilities, fees: Several campgrounds are located on the river. A convenience store and restaurant are available on Paradise Road. Supplies can be obtained in Santa Barbara or at Lake Cachuma. Access is free.

Water sports, restrictions: Swimming is permitted.

Directions: Take U.S. 101 to the junction with Highway 154 (at the north end of Santa Barbara). Turn northeast on Highway 154 and drive 10 miles to Paradise Road/FR 5N18. Turn right on Paradise Road and drive east for .25 mile to the first campground (Fremont Campground). Access is available at the campground, as well as elsewhere off Paradise Road. Note: Paradise Road is sometimes closed due to high water. In winter, phone the ranger station before making your trip, 805/967-3481.

Contact: Los Padres National Forest, Santa Barbara Ranger District, 805/967-3481, fax 805/967-7312. For a map of Los Padres National Forest, send $6 to U.S. Forest Service, Attn: Map Sales, P.O. Box 587, Camino, CA 95709, 530/647-5390, fax 530/647-5389, website: www.fs.fed.us/r5/forests. Major credit cards accepted.

10 LAKE CASITAS

Rating: 6

north of Ventura

Map 12.3, page 390

To bass fishermen, Lake Casitas is something of a legend, but to other boaters and water users, it is just something.

The legend grew from the fact that there are so many huge bass here, as many in the 10-pound-plus class as you'll find anywhere. One of the largest bass in history was caught here: 21 pounds, 3 ounces. Some say that if the next world-record bass isn't landed at Lake Casitic, it will be here. Hopes for that prize often have anglers lining up at the entrance gate before dawn, and even if they don't catch the world record, the prospect of a legendary 10-pounder tends to keeps things exciting just the same. Hey, it could be you! The lake is also stocked with trout, which are like growing pills for the giant bass.

Casitas is located north of Ventura, set at an elevation of 285 feet in the foothill country bordering Los Padres National Forest. The lake has 32 miles of shoreline with a remarkable number of sheltered coves. When full of water, it covers 2,700 acres. The Casitas Municipal Water District administers the lake.

But remember, the regulations prohibit water-skiing, personal watercraft, and all water/body contact sports. That means no swimming and no sailboarding. In addition, there are strict rules about what size of boat you can use, with no craft under 11 feet or over 25 feet long permitted. These restrictions are very similar to those at Lake Cachuma.

The boating regulations are so stringently enforced that you shouldn't even try to sneak in with a kayak or anything else you have in mind that doesn't meet the standards. Note that the entire shoreline, except for the developed north shore, is closed to the public.

The park holds many special events, including the Ojai Wine Festival, the Ojai Renaissance Festival, and the Native American Indian Pow-Wow. At the 1984 Olympics, the canoeing and rowing events were held here.

Fishing at night is permitted on selected weekends. Other fish species include catfish, crappie, and sunfish.

Access: Two paved boat ramps are located on the lake's north side.

Facilities, fees: Campgrounds, trailer rentals, full-service marina, fishing docks, floating restrooms, bait and tackle, slip rentals, picnic areas, showers, snack bar, and convenience store are available. Fishing boats, canoes, kayaks, pedal boats, rowboats, and pontoon boats can be rented at the marina, 805/649-2043. Fees are charged for day use, boat launching, and camping.

Water sports, restrictions: Powerboating and sailing are permitted. The speed limit is 35 mph except in designated areas, where it is 15 mph, plus 5 mph in coves and 3 mph in vicinity of marina. Craft under 11 feet long or over 26 feet long are prohibited. Water-skiing, personal watercraft, and inflatables are not allowed. No sailboarding, swimming, or water/body contact is permitted.

Directions: Take U.S. 101 to the junction of Highway 33 (located at the north end of Ventura). Turn north on Highway 33 and drive 10.5 miles to Highway 150/Baldwin Road. Turn left (west) and drive three miles to Santa Ana Road. Turn left and drive 100 yards to the lake entrance on the right.

From Santa Barbara, drive south on U.S. 101 for 11 miles to Highway 150/Baldwin Road. Turn left (east) and drive three miles to Santa Ana Road. Turn left and drive 100 yards to the lake entrance on the right.

Contact: Lake Casitas Recreation Area, 805/649-2233; Lake Casitas Marina, 805/649-2043; Nature Cruises, 805/649-3535.

11 PYRAMID LAKE

Rating: 9

**north of Los Angeles in Angeles
National Forest**

Map 12.4, page 391

Pyramid Lake is one of the most heavily used recreation lakes in California. One of the cornerstones of California's Central Valley Project, Pyramid Lake is a major storage facility for water as it is moved from north to south.

Pyramid Lake is set at an elevation of 2,600 feet. Although the lake is surrounded by Angeles National Forest, I-5 is routed right past several lake arms, making it one of the more easily accessible bodies of water in California. It is

a favorite destination for powerboaters; note that a 35-mph speed limit is enforced.

The lake covers 1,300 acres and has 20 miles of shoreline. Because it's a showpiece, the water masters tend to keep it fuller than other lakes on line with the California Aqueduct. The primary activities are water-skiing and fishing, though the two are not always compatible.

Sailboarding is best from the northern launch ramp. Swimming is best at the boat-in picnic sites or the designated swimming area.

Several pretty boat-in picnic sites with nice sandy beaches are located along the shoreline. Since most of the shoreline is inaccessible by car, these spots offer that rarity—a chance for seclusion. This is one great bonus for boaters.

Sailboarding can be excellent here as well, and the sport seems to be gaining in popular-

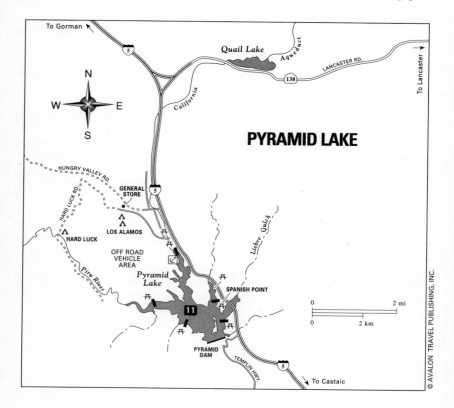

ity each year. The best jump-off spot is at the northern launching area, where you can sail off to access any of Pyramid Lake's more private arms.

A large off-road-vehicle area is located three miles from the lake.

Some anglers feel that the water-skiers are trying to drive them off the lake, and the situation would be greatly improved if the powers that be would set aside special areas for low-speed boating. You typically see anglers here in the spring and fall, when prospects are best for striped bass, largemouth bass, catfish, crappie, and bluegill; then the water-skiers take over the lake during the summer months.

Access: A paved launch ramp is located on the lake's north side.

Facilities, fees: Picnic areas, restrooms with flush toilets, a convenience store, and a concession stand are provided. Fishing boats can be rented at Pyramid Lake Marina. A campground is available two miles away. There is a fee for day use and a fee for boat launching.

Water sports, restrictions: Water-skiing, wake boarding, personal watercraft riding, sailing, and sailboarding are allowed. Swimming is available at a sandy beach near the marina and at several boat-in sites around the lake. A quota is set of 75 personal watercraft per day.

Directions: From Los Angeles, drive north on I-50 for about 60 miles to the exit for Smokey Bear Road (about eight miles south of Gorman). Take that exit west and drive 1.7 miles to the lake.

Contact: Pyramid Lake Marina, 661/257-2892; Pyramid Enterprises, 661/295-1245.

12 CASTAIC LAKE

Rating: 9

north of Los Angeles

Map 12.4, page 391

Castaic Lake is known the world over as the lake most likely to produce the next world-record bass. After all, this is where, in 1991, Bob Crupi

caught, weighed, photographed, and released a 22-pound largemouth bass, just four ounces shy of the world record. Who knows where that fish is swimming around now. Or how big it might be—or its many cousins.

But the lake is famous for more than fish. It's a boater's paradise, an outstanding choice for all water sports, with even a specially designated area for personal watercraft.

Castaic is easy to reach, just a short hop from the junction of I-5 and Highway 126. It is set at 1,535 feet in the foothills adjoining Angeles National Forest to the north. Shaped like a giant V, it covers nearly 2,400 acres when full. That's right: it's huge. There is also an adjacent lagoon, which provides additional facilities. Locals call Castaic the upper lake, and the afterbay is referred to as the lower lake or the lagoon.

Of course it is the big brother, the upper lake, that attracts most of the attention. This is where the giant bass roam and where water-skiing is most popular. In general, people who are fishing for bass stick to the coves, while the water-skiers run in a counterclockwise direction from the dam on up the northern lake arm. Note that a buoy line marks the boundary of a restricted area on the far end of the northern lake arm. The area closest to the dam is for personal watercraft.

If you prefer quiet water, try the nearby afterbay, commonly known as the Castaic Lagoon. It is located just below the Castaic Dam. No gas motors are permitted here (electric motors are permitted), and even though a few rental watercraft are allowed, for the most part the place is very low-key compared to the main lake. A bonus is that fishing is allowed 24 hours a day at the lagoon. Rainbow trout are stocked, and there are also catfish and crappie.

Sailboarding is quite popular. The best areas are the upper lake's west arm and all over the lagoon. Swimming is prohibited at Lake Castaic, but is permitted at Castaic Lagoon from mid-June through September. Use is quite heavy into fall.

Access: Paved boat ramps are located on the main lake's east and west arms (near the dam) and on the lagoon's south shore; follow the ramp signs from the lake entrance.

Facilities, fees: A primitive campground is available .5 mile west of the lagoon. Picnic areas are provided at both the lake and the lagoon; drinking water and flush toilets are available. Castaic Boat Rentals (on the main lake) rents out fishing boats and personal watercraft. Rowboats, water bikes, canoes, and kayaks are available for rent at the lagoon. Bait and tackle are available at the marina. Fees are charged for day use and boat launching.

Water sports, restrictions: The speed limit on the main lake is 35 mph. Water-skiing, wake boarding, personal watercraft riding, and sailing are allowed. No motorized boats are allowed on the lagoon, except for electric motors. Sailboarding is allowing on the upper lake on weekdays only. Swimming is allowed in the lagoon, but prohibited on the main lake.

Directions: From Los Angeles drive north on I-5 for 40 miles to Castaic and Lake Hughes Road. Turn north on Lake Hughes Road and drive .5 mile to Ridge Route Road. Turn left and drive .75 mile to Castaic Lake Drive. Turn right and drive a short distance to the lake entrance.

Contact: Castaic Lake, Los Angeles County, 661/257-4050; Castaic Boat Marina and Rentals, 661/775-6232; personal watercraft rentals, 661/775-3800.

13 LAKE PIRU

Rating: 7

northwest of Los Angeles

Map 12.4, page 391

Things can get crazy at Piru. Luckily, it's usually a happy crazy, not an insane crazy.

You see, this lake is within a pretty quick drive from the Los Angeles Basin, and it's no secret either, so quite a lot of people come here for boating, water-skiing, fishing, swimming, and sunbathing. The weather is warm, and the water often seems to be the perfect temperature.

Water-skiing is restricted to a designated area, roughly the middle of the lake, where there's a 35-mph speed limit. The wind can really kick up here in the spring and early summer. At times, conditions are excellent for sailing, but then the winds can make the lake look something like a washing machine in full spin—enough to scare everybody off the water.

The lake covers 1,200 acres when full and is set at an elevation of 1,055 feet. Most summer mornings are quite beautiful here, with the warm temperatures, pretty scenery, and emerald green water adding to the charm. If you're looking for a good spot for swimming and picnicking, head to the west shore, where there is a large sandy beach.

Fishing is often very good here, best in spring, of course, for both bass and trout.

Most boaters come here in the summer to go water-skiing or sailing. Afternoon winds are predictable on most days, and fishing is popular from fall through spring. Use is quite heavy from May through mid-September, as you might figure. Because the place is so popular, especially with boaters on summer weekends, all boating rules are strictly enforced.

Access: A multi-lane paved launch ramp is located on the lake's western side.

Facilities, fees: A campground, restrooms with showers, picnic areas, full-service marina, temporary mooring, snack bar, RV dump station, and convenience store are available. Fishing boats and pontoon boats can be rented at the marina. There is a fee for day use, boat launching, and camping.

Water sports, restrictions: Motorized boats under 12 feet long or over 26 feet long are prohibited. Canoes and kayaks over eight feet long are permitted in a special use area; anything smaller is prohibited. Water-skiing is permitted. Sailing is allowed. Personal watercraft and sailboards are not allowed. Swimming is allowed only in designated areas during the summer season; a beach is available on the west shore, past the gatehouse.

Directions: From Ventura, drive east on Highway 126 for about 30 miles to the Piru Canyon Road exit. Take that exit and drive northeast on Piru Canyon Road for about six miles to the campground at the end of the road.

Contact: Lake Piru Recreation Area, 805/521-1500; Lake Piru Marina, 805/521-1231, website: www.lake-piru.org.

FOGHORN OUTDOORS®

© ROBERT HOLMES/CALTOUR

Chapter 13

Los Angeles and Vicinity

Chapter 13—Los Angeles and Vicinity

The L.A. image you see on TV—the blond in a convertible, the surfer with the movie-star jaw line—is so flawed as to be ridiculous, pathetic, and laughable. And while there is some classic beach, lifeguards and all, the surrounding area for recreation spans some of the best opportunities in California.

It stuns some to learn that Angeles and its nearby forests provide more campgrounds than even the Yosemite area, and three times as many as the San Francisco Bay Area and its 1.2 million acres of greenbelt.

The water-sports highlight for many is the region's top recreation lake, Big Bear, with fishing and boating available. The region is known for its high population, and Big Bear is no exception on weekends. Yet even here, many are stunned to discover how relatively few people visit on weekdays, especially Monday to Thursday mornings, pre–July 4th and post–Labor Day.

Other top lakes in the area include Arrowhead, Castaic, and several smaller reservoirs, many with developed trophy fishing programs for trout and catfish.

For those of us who know this landscape, the stellar opportunities do not come as a surprise. The area has a tremendous range of national forests, canyons, mountains, lakes, coast, and islands. In fact, there are so many hidden gems that it is like a giant fortune hunt for those who love the outdoors.

Angeles National Forest and San Bernardino National Forest provide more than 1 million acres, a thousand miles of trails, and dozens of hidden campgrounds, including remote sites set along the Pacific Crest Trail that make perfect launch points for weekend trips, many to small streams for swimming and searching out waterfalls.

One quiz I occasionally prescribe is to write down every lake and stream you can think of, and then compare it to the listings in this chapter. Despite the yearnings of many for exactly such spots, most people do not get passing grades.

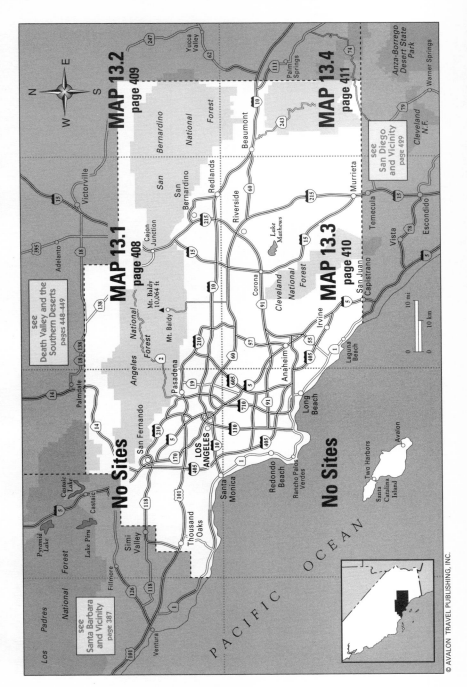

Map 13.1

Sites 1–7
Pages 412–416

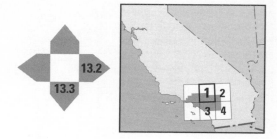

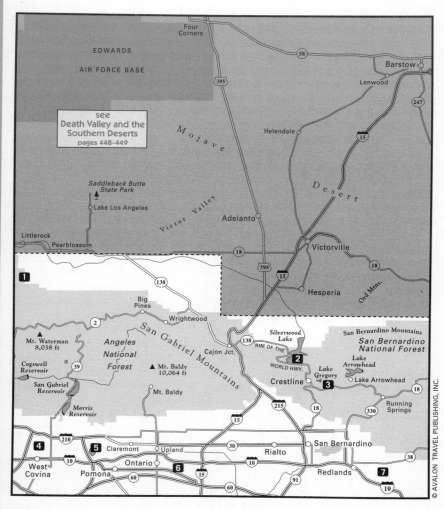

© AVALON TRAVEL PUBLISHING, INC.

Map 13.2

Site 8
Pages 416–419

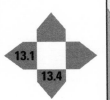

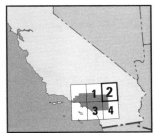

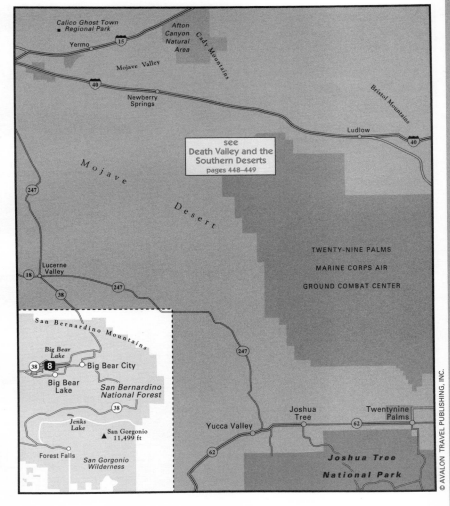

see
**Death Valley and the
Southern Deserts**
pages 448–449

© AVALON TRAVEL PUBLISHING, INC.

Map 13.3

Sites 9–17
Pages 419–425

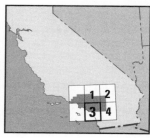

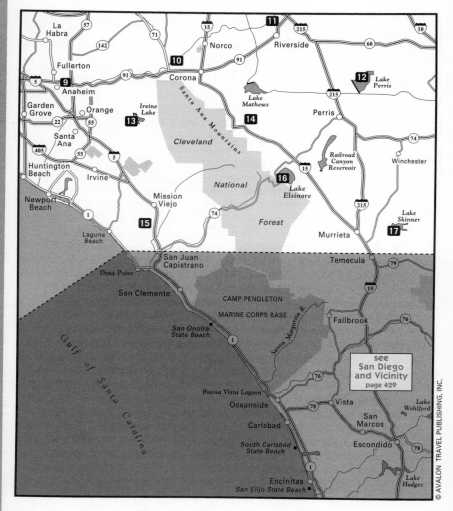

13.1

13.4

1 2
3 4

La Habra
57
Fullerton
142
91
9
Anaheim
Garden Grove
22
Orange
55
Santa Ana
405
55
5
Huntington Beach
Irvine
Newport Beach
1
Laguna Beach

71
15
Norco
10
Corona
91

Santa Ana Mountains

Irvine Lake
13

Cleveland

National

Forest

Mission Viejo
74
15

Dana Point
San Clemente

San Onofre State Beach
1

Gulf of Santa Catalina

11
215
Riverside
60
10

Lake Mathews
14
Perris
215

74
Winchester

Railroad Canyon Reservoir
15

16
Lake Elsinore

Lake Skinner
17

Murrieta

Temecula
79
15

CAMP PENDLETON
MARINE CORPS BASE

Santa Margarita R.

Fallbrook
76

see
San Diego
and Vicinity
page 429

76

Buena Vista Lagoon
Oceanside
78
Vista
San Marcos
Lake Wohlford

Carlsbad
Escondido
78

South Carlsbad State Beach
1

Encinitas
San Elijo State Beach

Lake Hodges

12
Lake Perris

© AVALON TRAVEL PUBLISHING, INC.

Map 13.4

Site 18
Pages 425–426

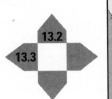

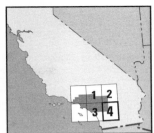

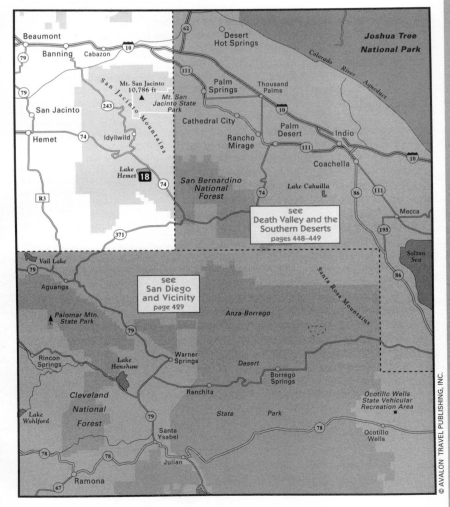

Beaumont

Banning Cabazon

San Jacinto

Hemet

San Jacinto Mountains

Mt. San Jacinto
10,786 ft

Mt. San
Jacinto State
Park

Idyllwild

Lake
Hemet **18**

San Bernardino
National
Forest

Desert
Hot Springs

Joshua Tree
National Park

Colorado River Aqueduct

Palm
Springs

Thousand
Palms

Cathedral City

Rancho
Mirage

Palm
Desert

Indio

Coachella

Lake Cahuilla

Mecca

see
Death Valley and the
Southern Deserts
pages 448–449

Salton
Sea

Vail Lake

Aguanga

Palomar Mtn.
State Park

Rincon
Springs

Lake
Henshaw

Lake
Wohlford

Cleveland
National
Forest

see
San Diego
and Vicinity
page 429

Anza-Borrego

Santa Rosa Mountains

Warner
Springs

Desert

Ranchita

Borrego
Springs

State Park

Ocotillo Wells
State Vehicular
Recreation Area

Santa
Ysabel

Julian

Ramona

Ocotillo
Wells

© AVALON TRAVEL PUBLISHING, INC.

1 LITTLEROCK RESERVOIR
🛶 🏊 ⛵ ♿ ⛰

Rating: 5

near Palmdale in Angeles National Forest

Map 13.1, page 408

In the summer when Littlerock Reservoir is the only cool place around for miles, this is quite a popular spot.

This small lake is set at an elevation of 3,258 feet in Angeles National Forest and covers just 150 acres. It's open year-round, and although fishing is the number one activity most of the time, in the summer, camping and swimming attract their fair share of attention.

The 5-mph speed limit keeps things quiet, eliminating most powerboating, personal watercraft riding, and sailboarding. Note, however, that the wind can really whip through here in the late afternoon.

From late winter to spring and early summer, Littlerock Reservoir is a pretty little mountain lake. But when the water starts to be drained down the Palmdale Ditch and into the California Aqueduct to the north, the lake can be turned into a miniature Grand Canyon. In low water years it might even resemble a moonscape by late fall. When that happens, boaters might as well see when the next spaceship is departing.

At that time, the lake is used for OHV use, and the campground is taken over by off-road enthusiasts.

Access: A primitive launching area is located on the lake's northwest shore.

Facilities, fees: A wheelchair-accessible boat ramp, campground, picnic areas, and store with groceries, bait, and tackle are available. Littlerock Lake Resort rents fishing boats. Adventure Pass ($30 annual fee) or $5 daily fee per parked vehicle is required.

Water sports, restrictions: Gas motors up to 10 horsepower are permitted. A 5-mph speed limit is strictly enforced. Personal watercraft and water-skiing are not allowed. Swimming is permitted.

Directions: From Los Angeles, drive north on I-5 to the Highway 14/Lancaster/Palmdale exit. Turn east and continue to Palmdale and Highway 138/Pearlblossom Highway. Turn east on Highway 138/Pearlblossom Highway and drive about five miles (through the stoplight at the four-way intersection) to Cheseboro Road. Turn right on Cheseboro Road and continue for four miles to the reservoir.

Contact: Angeles National Forest, Santa Clara/Mojave Rivers Ranger District, 661/296-9710; Littlerock Lake Resort, 661/533-1923.

2 SILVERWOOD LAKE
🛶 🏕 🎣 🚣 🛥 ⛵ ⛰

Rating: 9

north of San Bernardino in Silverwood Lake State Recreation Area

Map 13.1, page 408

Silverwood Lake is bordered by San Bernardino National Forest to the south and high desert to the north, and its proximity to San Bernardino makes it very popular with boaters, especially on hot summer days. It is set at an elevation of 3,350 feet, and when full to the brim, covers 1,000 acres and has 13 miles of shoreline.

The speed limit is 5-mph in all of the major coves, and there are several other boating rules that keep the place relatively sane. The main lake area south of the dam is the hot spot for water-skiing, with a 35-mph speed limit. There is a 175-boat quota per day. Boat launch reservations are required on summer weekends and holidays.

Tourists of every kind are attracted to the clear and cool water in the summer. All boating is allowed, as well as water-skiing, personal watercraft riding, fishing, and sailboarding, though the latter is restricted to designated areas. This lake is quite good for sailboarding, with afternoon winds usually strong in the spring and early summer.

The lake facilities are fully developed and include an excellent marina, boat rentals, and a small store. Some people make a great day of it by renting a pontoon boat, having a floating barbecue or picnic, then parking in a cove and using the boat as a swimming platform. In addition to drive-in campsites, there are some hike-in and bike-in campsites—a rare treat. The lake also has a modest trail system for hiking and biking.

Fishing varies dramatically according to season, with trout planted in the cool months, largemouth bass coming to life in the spring, and striped bass and bluegill occasionally caught the rest of the year.

Because of its location on the edge of the high desert, there are times when the winds can really kick up here, making boating potentially hazardous. Aside from that, Silverwood Lake is a great spot.

Access: A paved boat ramp is located on the lake's south shore. There is an unimproved ramp for car-top boats on the northwest shore.

Facilities, fees: Campgrounds, restrooms with flush toilets and showers, a full-service marina, picnic areas, RV dump station, and convenience store are available at the lake. Fishing boats and pontoon boats can be rented at the marina. Supplies can be obtained nearby. Fees are charged for day use, boat launching, and camping.

Water sports, restrictions: There is a 35-mph speed limit (5-mph in the major coves). Waterskiing, wake boarding, sailing, sailboarding, and personal watercraft are permitted. There are designated areas for boating, water-skiing, fishing, and sailboarding. Boats must be off the water by sundown. A large, sandy swimming beach is available on the lake's southeast side at the Sawpit Recreation Area.

Directions: Drive on I-15 to Cajon Junction (north of San Bernardino) and the exit for Highway 138 East. Take that exit and drive east on Highway 138 for 13 miles to the park entrance on the right.

Contact: Silverwood Lake State Recreation Area, 760/389-2303 or 760/389-2281; Silverwood Lake Marina, 760/389-2299.

3 LAKE GREGORY

Rating: 6

north of San Bernardino in Lake Gregory Regional Park

Map 13.1, page 408

Little Lake Gregory (120 acres) is set at an elevation of 4,520 feet, just north of San Bernardino on the edge of San Bernardino National Forest. An adjacent regional park, good swimming (no gas-powered motors permitted on boats), and an opportunity to paddle a canoe or kayak in a family setting make Lake Gregory a winner.

While no privately owned boats are permitted here, a real downer, boats can be rented at the marina. Beauty, intimacy, and cool waters make this a very popular destination, and it is often packed to capacity on summer weekends.

The setup is family oriented, and rules that forbid motors keep the lake quiet and safe for swimming. There is a large swimming beach on the south shore that even has a water slide, along with restrooms.

The lake is stocked with rainbow trout, and starting in 2003, steelhead. No brown trout have been stocked here since 1993. The lake also has catfish and crappie.

It is also one of the relatively few lakes in California where you can buy property near a lake. The trip here is a pleasant one, too, on Rim of the World Drive, a winding but pretty road that builds up a bit of anticipation before your arrival. Nearby Silverwood Lake to the northwest is an alternative choice.

Access: Private boats may not be launched here; only boats rented at Lake Gregory may be used.

Facilities, fees: A campground, restrooms with flush toilets, drinking water, picnic area, and a snack bar are available. Rowboats, pedal boats, sailboards, sailboats, and water bikes can be rented at the boathouse in summer. Cabins are available nearby at Camp Switzerland. Supplies are available neaby. A fee is charged for day use.

Water sports, restrictions: No private boats are permitted, but you may bring your own electric motor to use with a rental boat. No gas motors. Sailing and sailboarding are permitted. A large, sandy swimming beach on the northwest shore is open from Memorial Day Weekend to Labor Day Weekend.

Directions: Drive on Highway 30 to San Bernardino and Highway 18 (located two miles east of the junction of Highway 30 and Highway 259). Turn north on Highway 18/Rim of the World Highway and drive 14 miles to Crestline/Highway 138. Turn north (left) on Highway 138 and drive two miles to Lake Drive. Turn right and drive three miles to the lake.

Contact: Lake Gregory Regional Park, San Bernardino County, 909/338-2233; Camp Switzerland, 909/338-2731.

4 SANTA FE RESERVOIR

Rating: 6

east of Los Angeles in Irwindale

Map 13.1, page 408

This is a 70-acre lake that is used primarily by local fishermen.

It was built as a flood-control area for the San Gabriel River. Flood? What's a flood? It's rare when anybody around here ever speaks that word. Given a fair shot of rainfall in the San Gabriel Mountains, then decent water releases from San Gabriel and Morris Reservoirs, the Santa Fe Dam will have enough water to provide a viable urban trout fishery.

It is stocked from late fall through early spring with rainbow trout and with catfish in summer. Other species are largemouth bass, bluegill, and carp.

There is no powerboating permitted on the lake. That makes it popular for swimming and human-powered craft, even pedal boats. Canoes, kayaks, and inflatables are permitted and popular. There is also a swimming beach, rated high in summer months.

Although sailing and sailboarding are permitted, these sports are rarely practiced because wind is typically low here, and the lake is very small.

Access: A paved boat ramp is located on the south side of the lake.

Facilities, fees: Rowboats and pedal boats are available for rent. Restrooms, a picnic area, swimming beach, concession stand, and bait are available. Supplies can be obtained nearby. Fees are charged for day use and boat launching.

Water sports, restrictions: Rowboats, boats with electric motors, canoes, kayaks, inflatables including float tubes, sailing, and sailboarding are allowed. A swimming beach is available. No gas motors permitted. No boats under eight feet or over 18 feet long. Open year-round, sunrise to sunset.

Directions: From Los Angeles, drive east on I-10 to I-605. Turn north and drive to the Live Oak exit. Turn right on Live Oak Avenue and drive east for about 1.5 miles to the park entrance on the left.

Contact: Santa Fe Reservoir Recreation Area, Los Angeles County, 626/334-1065.

5 PUDDINGSTONE LAKE

Rating: 8

in San Dimas

Map 13.1, page 408

Puddingstone Lake provides a good chance to catch bass and trout during the morning and evening, and a place to water-ski during the day. That's not too shabby considering the lake is in such close proximity to millions of people. It's set just south of Raging Waters in San Dimas, bordered on its southern side by Bonnelli Regional Park.

When full, the lake covers 250 acres, and is an excellent destination during the winter and spring months. As soon as the weather turns cold, the general public abandons the place—water-skiers included. Yet that is when the trout plants start up, and they are generous: the lake gets large numbers of rainbow trout from fall through spring. In addition, there are some big catfish, and the lake record is 45 pounds. Other species include largemouth bass, bluegill, and crappie.

This is an excellent recreation facility for water sports, with all craft permitted, and rules set up (see Water sports, restrictions information below) to keep the place fun and sane, with a minimum of conflicts.

A ski beach is available on the north shore, and there is a large, sandy swimming beach on the southwest shore, about a mile away.

As the warm weather begins to arrive, usually in late February here, the bass fishing gets quite good. The water is still too cool for water-skiers, but not too cool for the bass to bite.

The nickname of the lake is the "old mud puddle." Why? Because after particularly intense rains, runoff from the southern slopes of the San Gabriel Mountains muddies up the lake significantly. When that occurs, the fishing turns off. But how often does it rain enough around here for runoff to be a factor? Not very often. The ideal situation is a moderate rain, which clears the air, allows fishermen and boaters an excellent view of the mountains to the north, and freshens the lake. During the summer it gets so smoggy in this area that the mountains are often not even visible.

Note that all vessels must obtain a boat inspection before launching. In addition, in order to separate personal watercraft riders from other users, an even-odd system is in effect; no personal watercraft on even-numbered days.

Access: A boat ramp is located on the north side of the lake. Another ramp for nonpowered boats is located on the west side of the lake.

Facilities, fees: Powerboats, personal watercraft, and pedal boats are available for rent at a marina. A campground, restrooms, showers, convenience store, coin laundry, concession stand (summers only), and picnic areas are available. Raging Waters (water theme park), equestrian facilities, a golf course, and hot tub

rentals are nearby. Fees are charged for day use, boat launching, and camping.

Water sports, restrictions: Powerboats, water-skiing, wake boarding, personal watercraft, swimming, sailing, and sailboarding are permitted. The speed is 35-mph. The minimum length for powerboats is 12 feet and the maximum length is 26 feet. Personal watercraft are allowed on odd-numbered days, 10 A.M. to sunset. Fishing, sailing, and sailboarding are allowed daily. Canoes, kayaks, and inflatables are permitted. Fast powerboats for water-skiing, wake boarding, and kneeboarding are allowed on even-numbered days, 10 A.M. to sunset. Boat inspections are required before launching. The lake is open from sunrise to 10 P.M., March through October, and sunrise to 7 P.M., November through February.

Directions: From Pomona, drive west on I-10 for five miles to the Fairplex exit. Take the Fairplex exit north to the first traffic light and Via Verde. Turn left on Via Verde and drive to the first stop sign. Drive straight to enter the park, or turn right at Campers View and drive to the RV park.

Contact: Frank G. Bonelli Regional Park, 909/599-841; East Shore RV Park, 909/599-8355 or 800/809-3778.

6 CUCAMONGA-GUASTI REGIONAL PARK

Rating: 6

northeast of Ontario

Map 13.1, page 408

This is a 150-acre day-use park that is especially popular with local residents because of its swimming lagoon and water slide. These are open from Memorial Day Weekend through Labor Day Weekend.

Although no water/body contact is permitted in the two small lakes, visitors still have the opportunity to cool off on hot summer days in the lagoon.

No private boats are allowed, but pedal boats

and water bikes can be rented at the smaller lake during the summer months. Shorefishing is available year-round at the largest lake—still just 10 acres—and fishing is allowed at the smaller lake in the winter months. The lakes are stocked with trout and catfish in the 10-acre lake only. Other species include bass and bluegill. Fishing is prohibited on Thursdays.

Access: A swimming lagoon and waterslide area are available.

Facilities, fees: Pedalboat and water bike rentals are available. Water slide, swimming lagoon, picnic areas, and a snack bar are available. Fees are charged for day use, fishing, swimming, and waterslide.

Water sports, restrictions: Rental pedalboats and water bikes are permitted. A separate swimming lagoon and water slide area are available. No private boats including inflatables. No sailboarding, swimming, or water/body contact in the lakes. Open daily from Memorial Day Weekend through Labor Day Weekend, 7:30 A.M. to 7 P.M., and daily the rest of the year from 7:30 A.M. to 5 P.M. No fishing permitted on Thursdays.

Directions: From Ontario, take I-10 east for 3.5 miles to the exit for Archibald Avenue. Take that exit and drive north on Archibald Avenue for about .25 mile to the park entrance on the right.

Contact: Cucamonga-Guasti Regional Park, 909/481-4205, website: www.co.san-bernardino.ca.us/parks.

7 YUCAIPA REGIONAL PARK

Rating: 7

near Redlands

Map 13.1, page 408

This is a great family-oriented county park, complete with water slides and pedal boats for the kids and fishing access and hiking trails for adults.

A one-acre swimming lagoon and two 350-foot water slides make this a favorite for young-

sters. Three lakes are stocked weekly with catfish in the summer and trout in the winter, the closest thing around to an insurance policy for anglers.

Spectacular scenic views of the Yucaipa Valley, the San Bernardino Mountains, and Mount San Gorgonio are highlights from the park. The park covers 885 acres in the foothills of the San Bernardino Mountains. The Yucaipa Adobe and Mousley Museum of Natural History is nearby.

Access: A rental boat dock is available.

Facilities, fees: A swimming lagoon, fishing ponds, water slides, and pedal boat and water bike rentals are available. A campground, restrooms, drinking water, flush toilets, showers, pay phone, snack bar (summer only), picnic shelter, playground with volleyball and horseshoes, and RV dump station are available nearby. The water slide is open Memorial Day weekend through Labor Day weekend. Fees are charged for day use, use of the water slide, swimming, and fishing.

Water sports, restrictions: Rentals are available for pedal boats and water bikes (summer only). A water slide and swimming lagoon are available Memorial Day weekend to Labor Day weekend. No private boats permitted. No canoes, kayaks, or inflatables. No water/body contact permitted at main lake.

Directions: Drive on I-10 to Redlands and the exit for Yucaipa Boulevard. Take that exit and drive east on Yucaipa Boulevard to Oak Glen Road. Turn left and continue two miles to the park on the left.

Contact: Yucaipa Regional Park, 909/790-3127, website: www.co.san-bernardino.ca.us/parks.

8 BIG BEAR LAKE

Rating: 10

northeast of San Bernardino in San Bernardino National Forest

Map 13.2, page 409

Here is a lake that's got everything: It is big

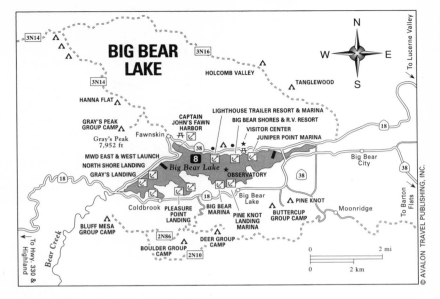

and beautiful. The lake has good trout fishing, quality boating opportunities, many campgrounds, and a few resorts. And it is located near the highest regions of San Bernardino National Forest, set at 6,743 feet in elevation. Alas, it often has a lot of people, too. Like I said, this place has got everything.

Among the waters in the region, Big Bear is unmatched for beauty, particularly in the spring when the snow is melting. The deep-blue water contrasts strikingly with the surrounding white mountaintops. The lake covers over 3,000 acres, offers 22 miles of shoreline, and has a faithful vacation following, something like the Lake Tahoe of Southern California.

This is a great choice for trout fishing as well as water-skiing, and for the most part skiers and anglers manage to stay out of each other's way. Trout fishing is best during the spring and summer in the morning and the evening, when the water is cool; water-skiers tend to be out in force on warm summer afternoons. Personal watercraft are also very popular in the summer.

If you're renting a boat, note the restric-

tions on water-skiing (see Water sports, restrictions information below); no one and nothing (not even inner tubes) can be pulled behind a rental boat unless a designated driver is hired. In addition, while all types of boating are allowed (as long as your craft is less than 26 feet long), all private motorized boats are required to have a permit; these are available at most of the marinas.

Swimming is excellent at Big Bear Lake, with large, sandy beaches all around the shoreline. However, the water, fresh from snowmelt, can be cold until late spring, and in big snow years, even into early summer. During most of the vacation season, the water is clear and cool. The most popular swimming spot is Meadow Park Swim Beach on the south shore, where there is not only a good stretch of beach but a large swimming raft as well.

Sailboarding and sailing conditions are erratic at Big Bear, but overall this is a good site. The best advice for sailboarders is to stick to the more open north shore, which tends to have a bit more wind and fewer anglers. The south shore, in contrast, has many small coves that are favorites of people looking for a quiet spot to fish.

The lake is a favorite for trout fishing. The lake is stocked with trout and catfish, and also has largemouth bass, smallmouth bass, crappie, bluegill, and sunfish.

The Pacific Crest Trail passes just a few miles north of here. Easy trailhead access is available, so if you want to break away from the crowds for awhile, you can.

Access: A boating permit, available at most marinas, must be obtained for all private boats with motors. Boats over 26 feet long are prohibited. Paved boat ramps (or boat rentals) are provided at the following locations:

• Big Bear Marina: Take Highway 18 (on the lake's south shore) toward Big Bear Lake Village to Paine Road/Highway 18 (look for the big wooden arch that goes across the road). Turn left on Paine Road and continue about two blocks to the marina. Fishing boats, pontoon boats, personal watercraft, pedal boats, canoes, and kayaks are available for rent. Storage docks, moorings, boat ramp, tackle, and driver service are available. For more information call 909/866-3218.

• Holloway's Marina & RV Park: Take Highway 18 (on the lake's south shore) toward Big Bear Lake Village. Continue over the dam and drive three miles to Edgemore Street (look for the Log Cabin Restaurant). Turn left on Edgemore Street and drive about .5 mile to the marina. Fishing boats, pontoon boats, sailboats, pedal boats, and personal watercraft are available for rent. Docks, moorings, boat ramp, gas, bait and tackle, and groceries are available. For more information call 909/866-5706 or 800/448-5335.

• Municipal Water District East Launch: Take Highway 18 (on the lake's south shore) toward Big Bear Lake Village. Continue to the dam and the junction with Highway 38. Turn east on Highway 38 and drive nine miles to the public launch (well signed) on the northeast shore. For more information call 909/866-5200.

• Municipal Water District West Launch: Take Highway 18 (on the lake's south shore) toward Big Bear Lake Village. Continue to the dam and the junction with Highway 38. Turn east on Highway 38 and drive 2.5 miles to the public launch (well signed) on the northwest shore. For more information call 909/866-2917.

• Pine Knot Landing: Take Highway 18 (on the lake's south shore) toward Big Bear Lake Village to Pine Knot Road (the first stop sign after the wooden arch that goes across the road). Turn left on Pine Knot Avenue and drive to the marina at the road's end. Fishing boats, pontoon boats, speedboats, personal watercraft, sailboats, kayaks, and canoes are available for rent; docks, mooring, slips, storage, bait and tackle, small store, boat tours, parasailing and lessons for water-skiing, wake boarding, and kneeboarding available. For more information call 909/866-2628.

• Pleasure Point Marina: Take Highway 18 (on the lake's south shore) toward Big Bear Lake Village. Continue over the dam and drive two miles to Cienega Way. Turn left on Cienega Way and drive .5 mile to Landlock Landing Road. Turn right and drive into the marina. Docks, moorings, boat storage, bait and tackle, snack bar, and rentals for fishing boats, pontoon boats, pedal boats, and canoes are available. For more information call 909/866-2455.

• North Shore Landing: Take Highway 18 (on the lake's south shore) toward Big Bear Lake Village. Continue to the dam and the junction with Highway 38. Turn east on Highway 38 and drive two miles to the marina. Fishing boats, sailboats, personal watercraft, speedboats, pontoon boats, canoes, and kayaks are available. Driver service, pirate ship cruises (summer only), docks, moorings, bait and tackle, snack bar, and lessons for sailing, water-skiing, wake boarding, and kneeboarding are also available. For more information call 909/878-4386, website: www.bigbearboating.com.

• Big Bear Shores & RV Resort: Take Highway 18 (on the lake's south shore) toward Big Bear Lake Village. Continue to the dam and the junction with Highway 38. Turn east on

Highway 38 and drive 6.5 miles to the resort. Fishing boats and pontoon boats are available for rent. Docks and moorings are available. For more information call 909/878-4386.

Facilities, fees: Campgrounds, lodging, cabins, picnic areas, full-service marinas, restaurants, and stores are available. Most campgrounds have restrooms with flush toilets and drinking water. Full facilities are provided in Big Bear Lake Village. There are fees for boat launching at all private marinas; the Municipal Water District launches are free.

Water sports, restrictions: Water-skiing and wake boarding are allowed if you bring your own boat, but you may not be towed with any rental boat unless you hire a driver. Drivers and equipment are available at North Shore Landing, Pine Knot Marina, and Holloway's Marina. Personal watercraft, sailing, and sailboarding are allowed. Much of the shoreline is sandy and suitable for swimming; developed beaches are available at the Municipal Water District Day-Use Areas on the north shore and at Meadow Park Swim Beach on the south shore.

Directions: From San Bernardino, turn north on Highway 18. Drive 15 miles to the Arrowhead Ranger Station. Continue east for about 15 more miles to Big Bear Lake.

Contact: Big Bear Discovery Center, 909/866-3437; San Bernardino National Forest, Mountaintop Ranger District, 909/337-2444; Big Bear Municipal Water District, 909/866-5796, website: www.bbmwd.org; Big Bear Lake Resort Association, 909/866-6190 or 800/244-2327 (BIG-BEAR). For specific boating information or conditions, contact any of the marinas listed above.

9 SANTA ANA RIVER LAKES

Rating: 6

in Anaheim

Map 13.3, page 410

Want to know what lake gets the most fishermen in Southern California? Here it is, Santa Ana River Lakes in Anaheim, which attracts 2,000 to 5,000 fishermen per week.

The reason is simple: Giant trout and catfish, for a fee in the $20 range. So if you are not interested in fishing for trophies, check the other listings in the book or perhaps head to Disneyland, located just a short distance away.

No water/body contact is permitted, although float tubes are permitted, and the anglers using them must wear waders.

So how does it work? You pay a hefty access/fishing fee, which in turn, goes to purchase the giant trout and catfish, and then you fish away, hoping to catch a big one. Your odds are good here. The state record for lake-caught rainbow trout was caught here, 26.08 pounds, as well as the record for channel catfish, 52 pounds, 10 ounces. There are also bass, crappie, sturgeon, wiper (a hybridized striped bass), and bluegill.

There are three lakes here: a main fishing lake, a catfish lake, and a children's fishing pond.

Access: A boat launch is located on the northeast side of Big Lake. A rowboat dock is located on the west side of Catfish Lake.

Facilities, fees: Rowboat and powerboat rentals, rod rentals, tackle, picnic area, and convenience store are available. Open 6 A.M. to 11 P.M. Supplies can be obtained nearby. Fees are charged for day use/fishing, float tubes, and boat launching. No fishing license required.

Water sports, restrictions: Powerboats, rowboats, and inflatables are permitted. No two-stroke motors. Only 4-cycle motors are allowed. No personal watercraft, sailboarding, swimming, or other water contact. Signed speed limits are enforced. This fish factory is open daily, year-round, from 6 A.M. to 11 P.M., and is occasionally kept open during full moons for all-night fishing.

Directions: Take Highway 91 to Anaheim and the exit for Tustin Avenue. Take that exit and drive north on Tustin Avenue for .25 mile to La Palma Avenue. Turn right and drive .5 mile to the lake entrance on the right.

Contact: Santa Ana River Lakes, 714/632-7830, website: www.fishinglakes.com.

10 PRADO PARK LAKE

Rating: 6

at Prado Regional Park near Corona

Map 13.3, page 410

Prado Park Lake is the centerpiece of a 2,280-acre, recreation-oriented park that features an equestrian center, athletic fields, shooting range, and a golf course.

The lake is small and used primarily for paddling small boats. It is also popular for fishing in the winter and early spring when trout are planted, and then in early summer for catfish and bass. The shooting facility is outstanding; it was the 1984 Olympic shooting venue.

Access: A paved boat ramp is available on the lake's north shore.

Facilities, fees: Rowboat and pedal boat rentals are available at a small marina. A campground, restrooms, coin laundry, showers, pay phone, snack bar, picnic area, playing fields, boat ramp, bait shop, and boat rentals are available. A playing field with softball, soccer, and horseshoes is on site. Supplies can be obtained nearby. Fees are charged for day use, boat launching, fishing, and camping.

Water sports, restrictions: Rowboats, boats with electric motors, canoes, kayaks, and sailing are allowed. No gas motors, inflatables, sailboarding, swimming, or water/body contact. Open year-round, 7:30 A.M. to sunset.

Directions: Drive on Highway 91 to Highway 71 (west of Norco and Riverside). Take Highway 71 north and drive four miles to Highway 83/Euclid Avenue. Turn right on Euclid Avenue and drive a mile to the park entrance on the right.

Contact: Prado Regional Park, 909/597-4260, website: www.san-bernardino.ca.us/parks/prado.

11 LAKE EVANS

Rating: 4

in Riverside at Fairmount Park

Map 13.3, page 410

Quit your yelpin'. Sure Lake Evans is a far cry from Big Bear Lake (see listing earlier in this chapter), but considering how hot it can be out here, and how few lakes there are in the area, this little lake is one of the few places that can provide a respite from the sweltering summer heat.

Evans is a good spot to bring a small rowboat or canoe, go fishing for a bit, or have a picnic. Rules prohibit most boats and water sports. What you usually see here are fishermen out to catch some small rainbow trout, which are planted when the water is cool enough, plus a few folks just paddling canoes.

The surrounding park is grassy and pleasant, and a golf course and a bowling green are located nearby. Lake use is relatively light. There are several fishing derbies for catfish each year. The lake is stocked with channel catfish, and there's also bluegill, bass, and carp.

Access: A primitive launching area is provided. Boats under eight feet or over 15 feet long are prohibited, with the exception of canoes and kayaks. A free boating permit must be obtained at the park.

Facilities, fees: Rowboats and pedal boats are available for rent. Restrooms and picnic areas are provided. Supplies are available in Riverside. A campground is available at Jurupa Regional Park. Access is free.

Water sports, restrictions: Motorized boats and inflatables are not permitted. No swimming, sailing, or sailboarding is allowed. The lake is open from 10 A.M. to 7 P.M., Thursdays through Tuesdays, Memorial Day Weekend through Labor Day Weekend; then 10 A.M. to sunset in the offseason.

Directions: Take Highway 60 to the north end of Riverside to the exit for Market Street. Take that exit. Turn left (south) and continue to the park entrance on your right.

Contact: Riverside County Department of Parks and Recreation, 909/715-3440, website: www.riversidecountyparks.org; boat rentals, 909/715-3406.

12 LAKE PERRIS

Rating: 8

southeast of Riverside at Lake Perris State Recreation Area

Map 13.3, page 410

The weather out here in the summer and fall can make you feel like you're standing in a fire pit, and that's why water-skiing and swimming are such big hits at Lake Perris.

The lake is set in Moreno Valley, just southwest of the Badlands foothills, at an elevation of 1,500 feet. It has a roundish shape, covering 2,200 acres, with an island that provides a unique boat-in picnic site.

The recreation area covers 8,300 acres and includes 11 miles of paved bike trails, including a great route that circles the lake. There are also 15 miles of equestrian trails and five miles of hiking trails.

Although known primarily for fishing (many records for spotted bass have been set here), Lake Perris is an extremely popular vacation destination for all types of boating and water recreation in the summer. In addition to fishing, favorite activities are water-skiing, sailboarding, sailing, and swimming. There is also a special area for scuba diving.

With large ski beaches on the northeast and southeast shores, the lake can be great for water-skiing and riding personal watercraft. There is a designated sailing cove on the northwest side, an ideal spot for sailboarding and sailing.

Swimming is also excellent, but note that it is only allowed at the developed beaches, a short distance from the campground.

For an out-of-the-ordinary picnic site, steer your boat over to the island, where you can hike up 200 feet to get a unique view of the surrounding country. In addition, there are many trails near the lake that are ideal for mountain biking, horseback riding, and hiking. On the lake's south side, there is even a rock climbing area. Note that no swimming or scuba diving is permitted at the island.

As you might figure, visitor traffic at Perris is extremely high in the summer. Crowds are considerably smaller in the spring and fall, but the attractions are just as compelling then.

The lake also provides fishing for spotted bass, trout, largemouth bass, bluegill, catfish, and sunfish.

Access: A large, multilane paved launching area is located on the lake's north shore, just east of the marina, and a personal watercraft launching area is on the northeast shore.

Facilities, fees: Campgrounds, restrooms with flush toilets, coin showers, RV dump station, picnic areas, a full-service marina, moorings, two swimming beaches, snack bar, and convenience store are available. Fishing boats and pontoon boats are available for rent. Fees are charged for day use and boat launching.

Water sports, restrictions: The speed limit is 35-mph, except in a few areas where it is reduced to 5-mph. Water-skiing, wake boarding, personal watercraft, sailing, and sailboarding are permitted. No towing of inflatables is permitted. Ski beaches are available on the lake's north and south shores. A large, sandy swimming beach is available on the north shore, east of the boat ramps.

Directions: From Riverside, drive east on I-215/Highway 60 for about five miles to the I-215/60 split. Bear south on I-215 at the split and drive six miles to Ramona Expressway. Turn left (east) and drive 3.5 miles to Lake Perris Drive. Turn left and drive .75 mile to the park entrance. Boat ramps are located on the north shore of the lake.

Contact: Lake Perris State Recreation Area, 909/940-5603, or 909/657-0676. Lake Perris Marina, 909/657-2179.

13 IRVINE LAKE

Rating: 6

southeast of Los Angeles

Map 13.3, page 410

This is a quiet, 700-acre lake nestled at the base of Cleveland National Forest. The lake is fed by Santiago Creek. The lake has steep, rocky cliffs, shallow coves, deep creek channels, submerged high spots, overhanging trees, and is well known as a producer of giant trout.

Instead of searching across miles and miles of country to catch a fish, at Irvine Lake, you get the opposite approach: they bring the fish to you. The fishing fee is turned around and used in part to purchase stocks of huge trout in the winter and huge catfish in the summer. How big? Well, it is kind of mind-boggling, with rainbow trout in the 10-pound class, and occasionally even 20 pounds, and a lake-record catfish of 89.6 pounds.

Bluegill, crappie, and largemouth bass are also in the lake. For bass, fishing is strictly catch-and-release. In addition, a five-acre fishing pond for children is also available.

Although no water/body contact is permitted, the Cutting Edge Water Ski School provides lessons for water-skiing and wake boarding after 4 P.M. It is allowed because participants wear dry suits.

The rental boat fleet here numbers 100 boats. They are very popular among fishermen.

The fish species are dependent on water temperature, with the trout plants going in from mid-November through March when the water is cool, and the big catfish the rest of the year when the water is warm. Almost never is a trout under a foot stocked in the lake; they leave the dinkers to the Department of Fish and Game. Most of the fish are caught on bait. The top spots are Sierra Cove and the buoy line.

Access: A paved boat ramp is located on the south side of the lake.

Facilities, fees: Powerboats, rowboats, pontoon boats, and fishing rods are available for rent.

A children's fishing pond, picnic area, campground, restrooms, café, bait and tackle, and RV and boat storage are available. Fees are charged for day use, fishing, boat launching, and camping.

Water sports, restrictions: Powerboats, canoes, kayaks, sailing, and inflatables are allowed. No sailboarding, swimming, or water/body contact. A 5-mph speed limit is enforced from sunrise to 4 P.M. Water-skiing and wake boarding are permitted after 4 P.M. through the water-ski school only. Skiers and boarders must wear dry suits. All boats, including inflatables, must be at least eight feet long. For fishing, a state license is not required. Open daily from 6 A.M. to 4 P.M. Night fishing is available June through August on Fridays and Saturdays until 11 P.M.

Directions: From I-5 (east of Los Angeles), drive to the Highway 91 exit east and drive about nine miles to Highway 55. Turn south on Highway 55 and drive four miles to Chapman Avenue. Turn east and drive nine miles (Chapman Avenue will become Santiago Canyon Road) and look for the lake entrance on the left side of the road.

Contact: Irvine Lake, 714/649-9111 or 714/649-2168; water-skiing and wake boarding lessons: Cutting Edge Wakeboard and Water Ski School, 714/532-5379 or 800/797-7791, website: www.waterski-school.com.

14 CORONA LAKE

Rating: 6

southeast of Corona

Map 13.3, page 410

If you're looking for fishing action, this is the place. If not, you're advised to look elsewhere.

This is one of the Southern California lakes where the concept of pay-to-fish has turned the lake into a winner. Corona Lake is heavily stocked at least twice per week with trout and catfish, and it receives heavy fishing pressure. Corona has held state records for catfish, while the lake record for rainbow trout is 21.7 pounds.

Other species include hybridized striped bass, sturgeon, largemouth bass, crappie, and bluegill.

Corona Lake is located in the foothills of Corona and is surrounded by oak canyons and meadows. No water/body contact is permitted, but float tubing is allowed, providing anglers wear waders. Powerboats are allowed, but a 5-mph speed limit is strictly enforced.

Access: A primitive boat ramp is located on the west side of the lake.

Facilities, fees: Powerboats, rowboats, and fishing rods are available for rent. A picnic area, convenience store, and tackle are available. In 2003, a campground was being constructed. Supplies can be obtained nearby. Fees are charged for day use and fishing, float tubes, and boat launching.

Water sports, restrictions: Powerboats, rowboats, and inflatables, including float tubes, are permitted. A 5-mph speed limit is strictly enforced. No personal watercraft, sailboarding, swimming or other water contact. Open 6 A.M. to 11 P.M.

Directions: From Corona, take I-15 south for about nine miles to the exit for Indian Truck Trail. Take that exit and drive (under the freeway) to Temescal Canyon Road. Turn right and drive .25 mile to the lake entrance on the left.

Contact: Corona Lakes, 909/277-4489, website: www.fishinglakes.com.

15 LAGUNA NIGUEL LAKE

Rating: 6

in South Laguna

Map 13.3, page 410

Laguna Niguel is a very pretty 44-acre lake, set in a canyon in the coastal foothills south of the L.A. Basin. It is the centerpiece for a regional park, a nice spot for picnics and walks, and a great place for folks who might want to toss out a fishing line and see what bites.

Who knows, maybe little Laguna Niguel will shock the world. Some say the lake has become a world-class bass fishery. It has become the site of catch-and-release bass events, and the chance of giant bass appears inevitable. The lake record for blue catfish is 68 pounds.

Trout, bass, and catfish are stocked, and the lake also has bluegill and black crappie. Fishing on Laguna Niguel Lake is catch-and-release only for largemouth bass and trout; other species can be kept. No private boats are permitted, but float tubes are allowed, and it's become quite a spectacle to get out in a float tube and cast for these big bass.

A bonus for pet owners is that dogs are permitted at the lake on the rental boats.

Access: A rental boat dock is located on the west side of the lake.

Facilities, fees: Rowboats, boats with electric motors, and fishing rods are available for rent. A fish-cleaning station, concession stand, picnic areas, and bait and tackle are available. Supplies can be obtained nearby. Fees are charged for day use, fishing, float tubes, and boat launching.

Water sports, restrictions: Float tubes are permitted. No private boats, swimming, sailboarding, or water/body contact sports. Fishing is catch-and-release only for trout and bass. No state fishing license required.

Directions: From I-5 near Mission Viejo, take the La Paz exit. Turn south on La Paz Road and drive four miles to the park on the right.

Contact: Laguna Niguel Regional Park, 949/362-3885 (recorded message) or 949/831-2791, website: www.lagunaniguellake.com.

16 LAKE ELSINORE

Rating: 8

south of Riverside at Lake Elsinore

Map 13.3, page 410

Whoosh! Whoosh! What's faster than a speeding bullet? Whoosh! Whoosh! If it's at Lake Elsinore, then the answer is a water-skier being towed by a jet boat. The place is loaded with them. You can't blame them though, not with day after day of barn-burner weather all summer and into the fall, and few anglers to get in their way.

Lake Elsinore is set at 1,239 feet in an area hot enough to make the water here more valuable to boaters than gold. The lake is big enough to accommodate all kinds of boats, covering 3,300 acres when full. It's a winner, and a lot of people take advantage of its offerings.

Most of the developed recreation areas are situated on the northern shore along Highway 74, and that's where the adventure usually starts. Elsinore is extremely popular, and here you will find anglers, water-skiers, personal watercraft, and sailboarders. But get this: If you like to go the daredevil route, there are a few more activities you can participate in, namely hang gliding and parachuting. As you are coursing across the lake, you can often look up and see these adventurers soaring overhead, an incredible sight.

Swimming access is good at Elsinore, but you should stick to the developed beaches. It is prohibited elsewhere. The best swimming spots are at private resorts, with marked swimming areas, and a fairly gentle sloping lake bottom.

There are also several trails for hiking, biking, and horseback riding. In addition, if you drive up the Ortega Highway to Glen Ivy, you will find some hot springs.

Fishing is something of a legend here regarding the pursuit of a giant catfish named "Whiskers." It was planted in 2000, and as of 2003, had yet to be caught. The lake is stocked with catfish and trout and it also has bullhead, crappie, and bluegill.

One word of caution: In low rain years Elsinore's water level can be subject to extreme and erratic fluctuations, and it is advisable to call ahead for lake conditions before planning a trip. In high rain years the problem isn't nearly as extreme.

Access: Eight boat ramps are provided at the following locations:

• West Shore: Take I-15 to the Bundy Canyon Road exit. Take that exit and turn west (driving under the freeway) and drive to where the road deadends at Mission Trail. Turn right and drive .75 mile to Corydon Road. Turn left and drive one mile to its end at Grand Avenue. Turn right and drive four miles to the Playland RV Park and boat launch on the right. Or continue on Grand Avenue to Weekend Paradise and Crane Lakeside Park & Resort (if you reach the Ortega Highway—Highway 74—you have gone too far. Playland RV Park, 909/678-4663; Weekend Paradise, 909/678-3715; Crane Lakeside Park & Resort, 909/678-2112.

• East Shore: Take I-15 to the exit for Main Street. Take that exit and turn west on Main Street and drive one mile to Lakeshore Drive. Turn right and drive a short distance to Lake Elsinore City Public Launch Ramp on the left (this ramp is not useable when lake levels are low). For more information call 909/245-9308.

• North Shore: Take I-15 to the exit for Central Avenue/Highway 74. Take that exit and turn west on Highway 74 and drive west for three miles to the entrance for the ramp on the left. Or continue a short distance on Highway 74 to reach boat ramps at The Outhouse, Roadrunner RV Park, and Elsinore West Marina. The ramp at The Outhouse is suitable for personal watercraft and small boats only. The ramp at Roadrunner is not useable when the lake level is low. Lake Elsinore Recreation Area, 909/471-1212; The Outhouse, 909/674-2766; Roadrunner RV Park, 909/674-4900; Lake Elsinore West Marina, 909/678-1300 or 800/328-6844.

Facilities, fees: Campgrounds, lodging, marina, boat rentals, picnic areas, RV dump station, snack bar, bait and tackle, and small stores are available. Fishing boats and pedal boats can be rented at Lake Elsinore West Marina, 909/678-1300. Fees are charged for day use and boating; the boating fee includes a lake permit.

Water sports, restrictions: The speed limit is 35-mph, except in designated high-speed areas. Water-skiing, personal watercraft, sailing, and sailboarding are allowed. Swimming beaches are available at Lake Park Resort, The Outhouse Campground, and Crane Lakeside Park.

Directions: Take I-15 to the town of Lake Elsinore and the junction with Highway 74. Turn west on Highway 74 and drive three miles to a primary launch ramp.

Contact: City of Lake Elsinore, 909/674-3124, ext. 265; for boating information phone any of the resorts listed above.

17 LAKE SKINNER

Rating: 7

near Temecula in Lake Skinner County Park

Map 13.3, page 410

Don't like water-skiers? Don't like personal watercraft? Don't like fast boats of any kind? Well, you've come to the right place. Whereas Lake Elsinore to the nearby west is dominated by water-skiers, Skinner is dominated by anglers.

Lake Skinner is set within a county park at an elevation of 1,470 feet in sparse foothill country. When full, it covers 1,200 surface acres.

No sports that involve body contact with water are permitted here, and you know what that means. Right: no water-skiing. It also means no other contact sports, including swimming and sailboarding. A large swimming pool is available at the park, however, and considering how hot it can get, taking a dip here can feel like you are being submerged in magic waters.

It's a shame that sailboarding is not permitted, because winds are fairly consistent and it would be a great site for sailboarders. Instead, only folks with small sailboats can take advantage of the wind, and right, it makes a great sailing lake. Consistent winds arrive about mid-day.

But the predominant users are anglers who come to fish for trout or striped bass. Many fish are stocked at this lake, including trophy-sized bass and trout, along with catfish, crappie and bluegill. Lake records here feature a 39-pound, 8-ounce striped bass, 33-pound catfish and 14-pound, 8-ounce largemouth bass.

Hiking and horseback riding trails are available at the park, and they provide a good option for day trips.

Access: Paved launch ramps are available on the lake's northeast and southeast arms. Boats less than 10 feet long and 42 inches wide are prohibited. Sailboats must be a minimum of 12 feet long and have at least 12 inches of freeboard.

Facilities, fees: Campgrounds, restrooms with flush toilets and coin showers, RV dump station, picnic area, swimming pool (in summer), coin laundry, snack bar, moorings, and convenience store are available. Fishing boats and pontoon boats can be rented. There are fees for day use, fishing, and boat launching.

Water sports, restrictions: A 10-mph speed limit is strictly enforced. Sailing is permitted. Water-skiing and personal watercraft are not allowed. No sailboarding, swimming, or other water/body contact is permitted.

Directions: Take I-15 to Temecula and the exit for Rancho California. Take that exit and drive 9.5 miles northeast to the entrance for Lake Skinner Recreation Area on the right.

Contact: Lake Skinner Recreation Area, Riverside County, 909/926-1541; Lake Skinner Marina, 909/926-1505, website: www.riverside countyparks.org.

18 LAKE HEMET

Rating: 7

near Hemet

Map 13.4, page 411

Lake Hemet covers 420 acres, is set at 4,340 feet, and sits near San Bernardino National Forest just west of Garner Valley. Many campsites have lake views.

This lake provides a good camping/fishing destination, with stocks of 75,000 trout each year (a lot for a lake this size) and yep, catch rates are good. The lake also has bass, bluegill, and catfish. If catch rates weren't good, the fish would have to be planted vertically in order to fit. Every now and then, Hemet can really turn on, and when that happens, don't wait—you have to be here right away to get in on it. At other times, things can be very tough.

Boating rules prohibit boats under 10 feet,

canoes, sailboats, inflatables, and swimming. No swimming or wading at Lake Hemet.

Lake Hemet is quiet. It has full facilities, including a campground and boat ramp, with a 10-mph speed limit on the lake that keeps it intimate.

The lake is under the jurisdiction of the Lake Hemet Municipal Water District.

Access: A paved boat ramp is located on the east shore of the lake.

Facilities, fees: Powerboats and rowboats are available for rent. A campground, restrooms, flush toilets, drinking water, coin showers, RV dump station, playground, pond, convenience store, coin laundry, and propane gas are available. Supplies can be obtained nearby. Fees are charged for day use, boat launching, and camping.

Water sports, restrictions: Powerboats and rowboats are permitted; minimum boat length is 10 feet. A 10-mph speed limit is enforced. No canoes, kayaks, inflatables, sailboats, sailboarding, swimming, or water/body contact is permitted. Open April through September from 6 A.M. to 10 P.M., open October through March from 7 A.M. to 8 P.M., and Fridays to 10 P.M.

Directions: From Palm Desert, drive southwest on Highway 74 for 32 miles to the lake entrance on the left.

Contact: Lake Hemet, 909/659-2680, website: www.lakehemet.com.

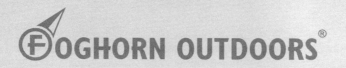

FOGHORN OUTDOORS®

© SAN DIEGO COUNTY PARKS AND RECREATION DEPARTMENT

Chapter 14

San Diego and Vicinity

Chapter 14—San Diego and Vicinity

San Diego was picked as one of the best regions to live in in America in an unofficial vote at a national conference for the Outdoors Writers Association of America. The reasons? The weather, the ocean and beaches, the lakes and the fishing, Cleveland National Forest, the state parks, the Palomar Mountains, and the hiking, biking, and water sports. What more could you ask for? For many, the answer is you don't ask for more, because it does not get any better than this.

The weather is near perfect. It fits a warm, coastal environment with an azure-tinted sea that borders foothills and mountains. In other words, in a relatively small geographic spread, you get it all.

The foothills provide canyon settings for many lakes, including Lower Otay, Morena, Barrett, El Capitan, Cuyamaca, San Vicente, Hodges, and Henshaw . . . and several more—with some of the biggest lake-record bass ever caught in the world. Many of these lakes are a testimonial to the best-run fishing programs in America.

Yet there are also some surprise hidden streams. Cleveland National Forest provides, remote mountains with canyons and hidden streams, often with small campgrounds nearby. The terrain features forest of fir, cedar, and hardwoods.

Everywhere you go, you will find campgrounds and parks, from primitive to deluxe. Some of the more remote sections of Cleveland National Forest, as well as Cuyamaca Rancho State Park, provide access to wild lands and primitive campsites.

The region is one of the few that provides year-round recreation at a stellar level.

If you could live anywhere in America, where would it be? Well, just as long as you have a boat of some type, any boat—a kayak on the roof of an SUV, an inflatable pram folded up in the back, a powerboat on a trailer being towed—you can unlock this water sports paradise.

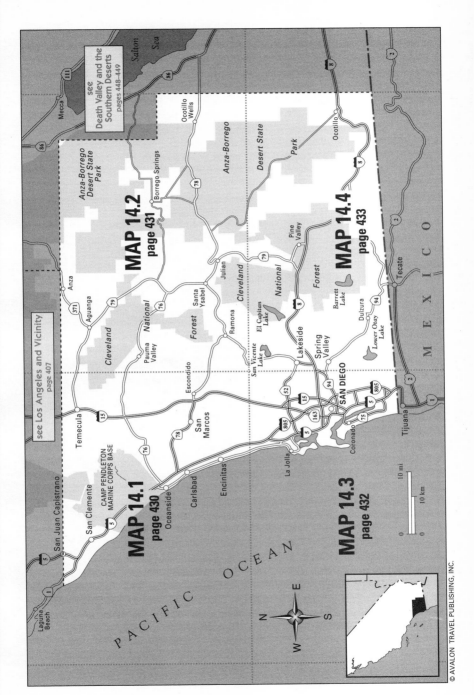

see Death Valley and the Southern Deserts
pages 448-449

Salton Sea

Mecca

Anza-Borrego Desert State Park

Ocotillo Wells

Anza-Borrego Desert State Park

Borrego Springs

MAP 14.2
page 431

Ocotillo

see Los Angeles and Vicinity
page 407

Anza

Aguanga

Julian

Cleveland

National

Forest

Santa Ysabel

Pine Valley

MAP 14.4
page 433

Tecate

M E X I C O

Pauma Valley

Ramona

Cleveland

National

Forest

Barrett Lake

Dulzura

Escondido

San Vicente Lake

El Capitan Lake

Lakeside

Spring Valley

Lower Otay Lake

Temecula

San Marcos

SAN DIEGO

CAMP PENDLETON MARINE CORPS BASE

Coronado

Tijuana

San Juan Capistrano

San Clemente

Oceanside

Carlsbad

Encinitas

La Jolla

MAP 14.1
page 430

MAP 14.3
page 432

Laguna Beach

P A C I F I C   O C E A N

10 mi

10 km

N E W S

© AVALON TRAVEL PUBLISHING, INC.

Map 14.1

Sites 1–4
Pages 434–436

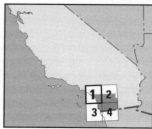

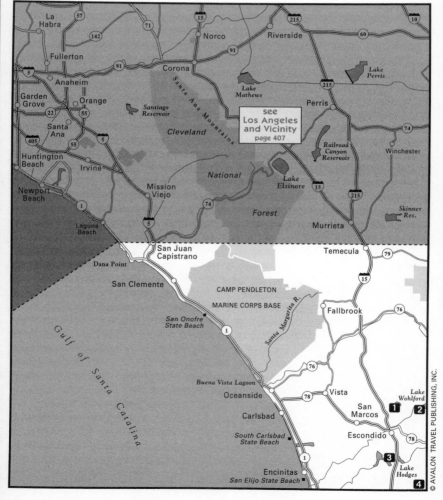

Map 14.2

Sites 5–6
Pages 436–437

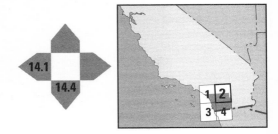

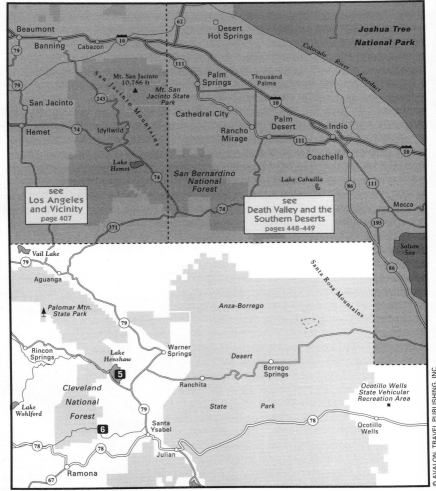

Beaumont

Banning   Cabazon

San Jacinto

Hemet

Idyllwild

San Jacinto Mountains

Mt. San Jacinto
10,786 ft

Mt. San
Jacinto State
Park

Lake
Hemet

**see
Los Angeles
and Vicinity
page 407**

Desert
Hot Springs

Palm
Springs

Thousand
Palms

Cathedral City

Rancho
Mirage

Palm
Desert

Indio

Coachella

Lake Cahuilla

**see
Death Valley and the
Southern Deserts
pages 448–449**

*Joshua Tree
National Park*

Colorado River Aqueduct

San Bernardino
National
Forest

Mecca

*Salton
Sea*

Vail Lake

Aguanga

Palomar Mtn.
State Park

Rincon
Springs

Lake
Henshaw

5

Warner
Springs

Ranchita

Anza-Borrego

Desert

Borrego
Springs

Santa Rosa Mountains

Cleveland

National

Forest

Lake
Wohlford

6

Santa
Ysabel

Julian

Ramona

State   *Park*

Ocotillo Wells
State Vehicular
Recreation Area

Ocotillo
Wells

© AVALON TRAVEL PUBLISHING, INC.

Map 14.3

Sites 7–8
Pages 437–438

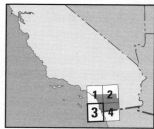

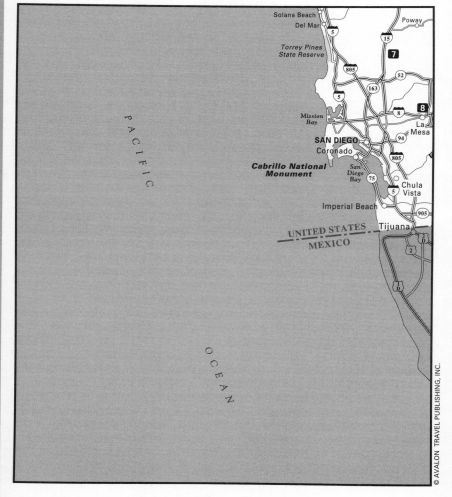

Map 14.4

Sites 9–16
Pages 439–445

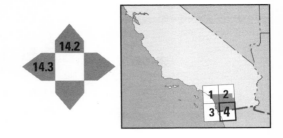

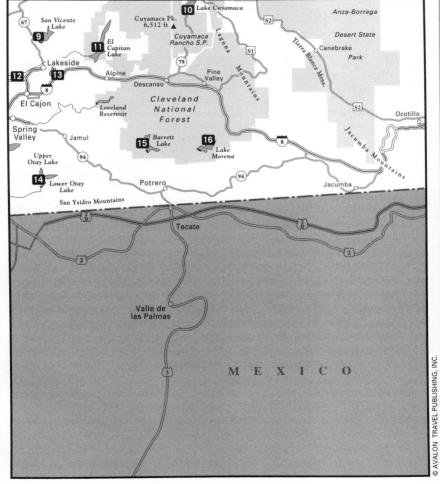

San Vicente Lake

67 **9**

11 El Capitan Lake

Lakeside

12 **13**

Alpine

8

El Cajon

Loveland Reservoir

Spring Valley

Jamul

94

Upper Otay Lake

14 Lower Otay Lake

San Ysidro Mountains

Cuyamaca Pk. 6,512 ft ▲

10 Lake Cuyamaca

Cuyamaca Rancho S.P.

79

Pine Valley

Descanso

Cleveland National Forest

15 Barrett Lake

16 Lake Morena

Potrero

94

Laguna Mountains

S2

S1

Tierra Blanca Mtns.

Anza-Borrego Desert State Park

Canebrake Park

S2

Ocotillo

Jacumba Mountains

8

Jacumba

Tecate

2 D

2 D

2

2

Valle de las Palmas

3

M E X I C O

© AVALON TRAVEL PUBLISHING, INC.

1 DIXON LAKE

Rating: 6

near Escondido

Map 14.1, page 430

Little Dixon Lake is the centerpiece of a regional park in the Escondido foothills. The campground is set at an elevation of 1,405 feet, about 400 feet above the lake's shoreline.

No private boats are permitted, and a 5-mph speed limit for rental boats keeps things quiet. The water is clear, with fair bass fishing in the spring, and trout fishing in the winter and early spring. Catfish are stocked in the summer, trout in winter and spring. In the summer, the lake is open at night for fishing for catfish.

A pretty and easy hike is available on the Jack Creek Nature Trail, a one-mile walk to a 20-foot waterfall.

The saving grace: Powerboats, rowboats, and pedal boats can be rented at a small marina.

Access: A boat rental dock is located on the west shore of the lake.

Facilities, fees: Rental powerboats, pedal boats, and rowboats are available. A campground, restrooms, drinking water, flush toilets, showers, wheelchair-accessible fishing pier, bait, ice, snack bar, picnic area, and a playground are available. Supplies available in Escondido.

Water sports, restrictions: Only rental boats are permitted. No boat ramp. No privately-owned boats, including canoes, kayaks, inflatables, or sailboarding are allowed. No swimming or water/body contact. No pets. A 5-mph speed limit is enforced. Fees are charged for day use (weekends only), fishing, and camping. Open sunrise to sunset. Night fishing permitted from mid-June through Labor Day Weekend, Wednesdays through Saturdays.

Directions: Drive on I-15 to the exit for El Norte Parkway (located four miles north of Escondido). Take that exit northeast and drive four miles to La Honda Drive. Turn left and drive to Dixon Lake.

Contact: Dixon Lake Recreation Area, 760/839-4680; camping reservations, 760/741-3328, website: www.dixonlake.com.

2 LAKE WOHLFORD

Rating: 5

near Escondido

Map 14.1, page 430

It's no secret that Lake Wohlford is set up for one thing—fishing—and that all other water sports fall by the wayside.

The lake covers 190 acres and is set at 1,500 feet in elevation, and that's right, it gets scorching hot out here in the summer. That is why the prime time to visit is in spring and fall, when the campground gets a fair amount of use. Even though fishing is the lone activity possible here, the prospects are only fair for bass, bluegill, and crappie.

The lake is stocked with rainbow trout, brown trout, steelhead, channel catfish, and blue catfish. Catfishing is good in winter, and trout fishing is good in spring.

A bald eagle winters here. The best place to spot it is at Lusardi Point, its favorite perching area.

The "no-nos" really add up: No swimming, no canoeing, and no sailboarding, and that's not to mention the regulations governing boat size. But that's typical; many lakes in the greater San Diego area enforce similar restrictions.

Access: A paved boat ramp is located on the north shore.

Facilities, fees: Fishing boats, rowboats, and pedalboats are available for rent at a small marina. Cabins, RV park, picnic areas, bait, snack bar, restaurant, and limited supplies are available. Fees are charged for day use, boat launching, daily fishing permits, and camping.

Water sports, restrictions: Powerboats and rowboats are permitted. A 5-mph speed limit is strictly enforced. No canoes, inflatables, sailboats, or boats that are under 10 feet or over 20 feet long. No swimming, sailboarding, or other water/body contact sports. No glass containers, alcoholic beverages, or pets. The lake is open daily, 6 A.M. to dusk, from mid-December through early September (the weekend after Labor Day); open weekends only from early September to mid-December.

Directions: From Escondido on I-15, take the Via Rancho Parkway exit and turn east on Valley Parkway/County Road S6. Drive five miles to Lake Wohlford Road. Turn right and continue about two miles to the lake.

Contact: Lake Wohlford Resort, 760/749-2755; Lake Wohlford, City of Escodido, 760/839-4346, website: www.wohlfordlake.com; Oakvale RV Park, 760/749-2895.

3 LAKE HODGES

Rating: 6

south of Escondido

Map 14.1, page 430

How you feel about Lake Hodges depends entirely on your perspective. If you like to catch big bass and you are lucky enough to get a few, you might think that this is the best lake in America. If you are a boater looking for some excitement, you will probably be frustrated by the strict rules prohibiting high-speed water sports, as well as the fact that the high number of anglers can turn this lake into the aquatic version of the San Diego Zoo.

Lake Hodges is set at an elevation of 314 feet in the coastal foothills just west of I-15. The long, narrow, snakelike reservoir is shaped like an inverted V and covers 1,234 acres. The lake has 27 miles of shoreline, with a maximum water depth of 115 feet. It is located in a coastal canyon on the San Dieguito River. Hiking and equestrian trails are routed around much of the lake.

Hodges is a fantastic producer of big bass, including the monster-size lake record, 20 pounds, 4 ounces. Typically, all the good spots have been hit by 10 A.M. Fishing is most popular for largemouth bass, but the lake also has crappie, bluegill, channel catfish, bullhead,

and carp. A 35-pound channel catfish was caught here.

During the spring, early summer, and fall, there are usually good afternoon winds, and prospects for sailboarding are better than at any lake in the region. What? You say Hodges is the only lake in the region that even allows sailboarding? Yeah? Well, yeah, that's true.

This lake is notorious for low water levels, which can close it to boating or limit the activities. In addition, while this lake has been open for years on Wednesdays and weekends, as well as holidays, March through October (water levels permitting), as of 2003, this status was being debated. The lake could be closed Wednesdays, yet open on Fridays. Check for status.

Access: A boat launch is located at the beach at Hidden Cove.

Facilities, fees: Fishing boats and rowboats are available for rent from a small marina. A picnic area, snack bar, bait and tackle, and a wheelchair-accessible fishing float are available. Full facilities in Escondido to the north or San Diego to the south. Access is free. Fees are charged for boat launching and fishing.

Water sports, restrictions: Powerboats, canoes, kayaks, inflatables, sailing, and sailboarding are permitted. A 35-mph speed limit is strictly enforced. No swimming or water/body contact sports are permitted. No glass containers or pets.

Directions: From I-15 at Escondido, turn west on Via Rancho Parkway and drive to Lake Drive. Turn left on Lake Drive and continue to the lake entrance. From the entrance, continue one mile to the boat ramp.

Contact: San Diego City Lakes, 619/465-3474 (recorded message) or 619/668-2050, website: www.sandiego.gov/water/recreation; boat rentals, 760/735-8088.

4 LAKE POWAY

Rating: 7

south of Escondido

Map 14.1, page 430

Lake Poway is set in the coastal foothills, about 20 miles northeast of San Diego. The lakeshore setting includes groves of eucalyptus and chaparral. A walk-in (one mile) campground is located at the base of the dam.

The lake covers just 60 acres and provides rental boats, but privately owned boats, even canoes, are not permitted.

This lake has gained a reputation for trophy trout fishing and now holds the San Diego County record for trout at 17 pounds, 14 ounces, with many fish at over 10 pounds. And with all the fishing records in this county, that isn't bad. The lake is stocked weekly with rainbow trout during the winter and catfish in summer. In 2003, steelhead and brown trout were also added.

The bass fishing here is no longer a secret either. Summer catfishing and night fishing are popular, and anglers can add bluegill, bass, sunfish, and panfish to the list of possibilities here.

The lake is surrounded by 400-acre Clyde E. Rexrode Wilderness Area. This features several trails, including a three-mile loop around Lake Poway.

Access: A paved boat ramp is available on the west side of the lake.

Facilities, fees: Powerboats, rowboats, pedal boats, sailboats, and canoes are available for rent at a marina. Privately-owned float tubes are allowed. A hike-in campground, picnic area, bait and tackle, and snack bar are available. Supplies are available in Rancho Bernardo or Poway. Fees are charged for day use on weekends and holidays (excluding residents of Poway), fishing, and camping.

Water sports, restrictions: Rentals boats, electric motors, and privately-owned float tubes are permitted. No privately-owned boats. No gas motors. No swimming or water/body contact sports. Open sunrise to sunset Wednes-

day through Sunday year-round. Night fishing permitted on Fridays and Saturdays from late May to early September.

Directions: From Escondido, drive south on I-15 to Rancho Bernardo Road. Turn east and drive four miles to Lake Poway Road. Turn left and drive a short distance to the park entrance.

Contact: Lake Poway Recreation Area, 858/679-5470 or 858/679-5466 (recorded information); facilities reservations: City of Poway, 858/679-4342; Lake Poway Concession, 858/486-1234, website: www.ci.poway.ca.us/lakepowa.html.

5 LAKE HENSHAW

Rating: 5

east of Escondido

Map 14.2, page 431

This is the biggest lake in San Diego County, covering 1,100 acres with 25 miles of shoreline. Henshaw is designed for fishing and not much else. The lake's record bass weighed 14 pounds, 4 ounces. There is also fishing for crappie, bluegill, and catfish.

Lake Henshaw is set at an elevation of 2,727 feet at the foot of the Palomar Mountains near Cleveland National Forest. Don't expect to find yourself out in the wilderness, though; you see, the lake is bordered by a permanent-residence mobile home park. A large developed campground is also available.

Like many reservoirs, Lake Henshaw is sometimes plagued by low water levels. In big rain years, of course, that is never a problem.

Access: A paved boat ramp is located along the access road.

Facilities, fees: Fishing boats are available for rent. Cabins, campground, picnic areas, flush toilets, showers, swimming pool, whirlpool, clubhouse, convenience store, café, coin laundry, playground, and RV dump station are available. Fees are charged for day use, boat launching, and camping.

Water sports, restrictions: Powerboats and rowboats are permitted. A 10-mph speed limit is strictly enforced. No canoes, inflatables, sailboats, or boats that are under 10 feet long. No swimming, sailboarding, or other water/body contact sports.

Directions: From Santa Ysabel, drive seven miles north on Highway 79 to Highway 76. Turn east on Highway 76 and drive four miles to the campground and lake access on the left.

Contact: Lake Henshaw Resort, 760/782-3501; for lodging or camping, 760/782-3487, website: www.lakehenshawca.com.

6 LAKE SUTHERLAND

Rating: 5

near Ramona

Map 14.2, page 431

The intense number of anglers that hammer away at Hodges, El Capitan, San Vicente, and Lower Otay don't seem to make it out here. The lake is just distant enough from the San Diego metropolitan area and just small enough (only 557 acres) that many of the go-getters do their go-getting elsewhere.

The lake is set at an elevation of 2,059 feet in the foothills near Cleveland National Forest. It was created from the dammed flows of Santa Ysabel Creek and Bloomdale Creek; its deepest point is 145 feet, and there are five miles of shoreline.

A bonus is that anglers can rent small fishing boats at the lake. Fishing is popular for largemouth bass, bluegill, crappie, redear sunfish, channel and blue catfish, and bullhead. Strict rules prohibit most water sports.

A few notes: The west shore and Santa Ysabel arm of the lake are accessible on foot, just under two miles of shore. From November through January, waterfowl hunting is permitted, usually only on Wednesdays and weekends. There is no camping at the lake; the nearest campground is 12 miles away at Dos Picos County Park.

Access: A paved boat ramp is located on the west shore.

Facilities, fees: Rowboat, powerboats, and canoe rentals are available from a small marina. Picnic areas, snack bar, and bait and tackle are available. Supplies can be obtained in Ramona. Fees are charged for boat launching and fishing; no day-use fee.

Water sports, restrictions: Powerboats, inflatables, and sailboats are permitted. A 20-mph speed limit is strictly enforced. No water/body contact sports are permitted, including sailboarding. From mid-March through September, the lake is open only on Fridays, weekends, and holidays from sunrise to sunset.

Directions: From I-15 at Escondido, turn east on Highway 78 and drive about 30 miles to Sutherland Dam Road (located about eight miles past Ramona). Turn left and drive north to the lake entrance. Continue .7 mile to launch ramp.

Contact: Boat rentals, 619/698-3474; San Diego City Lakes, 619/465-3474 (recorded message) or 619/668-2050, website: www.sandiego.gov/water/recreation.

7 LAKE MIRAMAR

Rating: 5

north of San Diego

Map 14.3, page 432

Little Lake Miramar, covering 160 acres with four miles of shoreline, is a pretty spot in the San Diego foothills at an elevation of 700 feet. It is located 18 miles from San Diego.

This tiny lake is a great one for producing fish stories. It is best known as the place where someone caught a 21-pound, 10-ounce bass that was later discovered to have a lead diving weight in its stomach! The official lake record bass actually weighed 20 pounds, 15 ounces. In the cool months the lake is stocked with trout, which seem to work like growing pills for the big bass. The lake also has bluegill, catfish, and sunfish. The lake record catfish weighed 26 pounds, 12 ounces.

Float tubes are allowed at Miramar, a bonus

for anglers. The rental canoes at Miramar are a real treat, and paddling around in one of them for a bit is the only possible activity besides fishing.

Miramar is really more of a large pond, with little underwater structure and clear water, and is small enough that anglers can pick over the same spots day after day. That has a way of smartening up the bass. There are days when you can see the fish but not catch them, and believe me, it will drive you crazy. But hey, you can always just give up and paddle around in a canoe, maybe throw your paddles at them.

Access: A paved boat ramp is located on the lake's south end.

Facilities, fees: Fishing boats, rowboats, and canoes are available for rent at a small marina. A picnic area, snack bar, and bait and tackle are available. No camping. Nearest campground is 25 miles away at Lake Dixon. Supplies can be obtained in Mira Mesa. Access is free. Fees are charged for boat launching and fishing.

Water sports, restrictions: A 5-mph speed limit is strictly enforced. No water/body contact sports are permitted. Float tubes are allowed. The lake is open Saturday through Tuesday from early November through September.

Directions: From San Diego, turn north on I-15 and drive about 10 miles to Mira Mesa. Take the Mira Mesa Boulevard exit and turn east. Continue to Scripps Ranch Boulevard. Turn right (south) and drive to Scripps Lake Drive. Turn east (left) on Scripps Lake Drive and drive to the lake entrance.

Contact: San Diego City Lakes, 619/465-3474 (recorded message) or 619/668-2050, website: www.sandiego.gov/water/recreation.

8 LAKE MURRAY

Rating: 6

northeast of San Diego

Map 14.3, page 432

Lake Murray covers 171 surface acres and has 3.2 miles of shoreline and a maximum water depth of 95 feet. The facilities were refurbished in 2003, and the lake now has a two-lane boat ramp, docks, restrooms, parking lot, and landscaping.

This is primarily a lake for fishing. That is because no water/body contact sports are allowed. Since water levels can fluctuate greatly, check the status before making a trip.

This reservoir is part of Mission Trails Regional Park, located a few miles east of San Diego. The park is popular for bicycling, jogging, walking, in-line skating and picnicking. A 6.4-mile roundtrip walk is available to the dam gate.

Fishing is popular for largemouth bass, bluegill, channel catfish, black crappie, and trout (stocked November through early May).

The nearest campground is at Lake Jennings County Park, located about 20 miles east.

Access: A paved boat ramp is located on the south shore of the lake.

Facilities, fees: Fishing boats, rowboats, and canoes are available for rent at a small marina. A boat dock, picnic area, snack bar, restrooms, and bait are available. Supplies can be obtained in La Mesa. Access is free. Fees are charged for boat launching and fishing.

Water sports, restrictions: Powerboats, canoes, kayaks, sailing, and float tubes are permitted A 5-mph speed limit is enforced. Boaters can bring their own small outboard motors for use on rental boats. No water-skiing, wake boarding, personal watercraft, swimming, sailboarding, or water/body contact sports allowed. No alcohol. Open sunrise to sunset, Wednesdays, weekends, and some holidays, November through Labor Day weekend.

Directions: From San Diego, take I-8 east and drive to La Mesa and Lake Murray Boulevard. Turn north and drive about three-quarters of a mile to Kiowa Drive. Turn left and continue to the lake.

Contact: San Diego City Lakes, 619/465-3474 (recorded message) or 619/668-2050, website: www.sandiego.gov/water/recreation.

9 SAN VICENTE LAKE

Rating: 8

northeast of San Diego

Map 14.4, page 433

This lake looks different than the other lakes in the San Diego area. The shoreline includes some steep, rocky banks, which provide ideal structure for the aquatic food chain. The underwater habitat fosters the growth of zoo-plankton and insects, which in turn attract minnows, then trout and bass. That is why the fishing here is often so good and trout are stocked in winter.

San Vicente is located in arid foothills at an elevation of 659 feet and comes complete with an island. When full, the lake has 14 miles of shoreline and covers 1,069 acres, with a maximum depth of 190 feet. It is located about 25 miles north of San Diego. Like most lakes in the San Diego area, the rules here are designed primarily to cater to anglers. On weekends, however, San Vicente is a rare breed: It's one of the few lakes around where water-skiing is allowed.

To prevent conflicts, a special use schedule has been established (see Water sports, restrictions). However, even these are subject to change during periods of low water levels.

The state record blue catfish, 101 pounds, was caught here in March of 2000, by Roger Rohrbouck, who was actually fishing for bass with a small shiner. This record catfish was just over 15 years old and stocked in the lake in 1985, when it probably weighed about two pounds, according to the Department of Fish and Game.

What you get here is good fishing in the late winter, spring, and fall, and good water-skiing in the summer. But the highlight, of course, is the bass fishing. More than 500 bass weighing five pounds or more are caught here every year. Other species include black crappie, bluegill, channel catfish, white catfish, and green sunfish.

Access: A paved boat ramp is located on the lake's south side.

Facilities, fees: Fishing boats and rowboats are available for rent at a small marina. A water-ski slalom course is available in four-hour shifts. A picnic area, snack bar, and bait and tackle are available. Supplies can be obtained in Lakeside. Access is free most of the year. Fees are charged for day use Friday through Sunday during summer, for boat launching, for fishing, and for access to the slalom course.

Water sports, restrictions: The lake is open Thursdays through Sundays, sunrise to sunset, year-round. Powerboats, water-skiing, and wake boarding are permitted Thursdays through Sundays and holidays from mid-May to mid-October. Fishing, sailing, and low-speed boating are permitted only Thursdays through Sundays, from mid-October to mid-May, and Tuesdays through Thursdays from mid-May to mid-October. All user groups are permitted on Thursdays only in summer. A 35-mph speed limit is strictly enforced, and a 10-mph speed limit is in effect on low-speed boating days. No camping (the nearest campground is seven miles away at Lake Jennings). No swimming, personal watercraft use, or sailboarding.

Directions: From San Diego turn east on I-8 and drive to El Cajon and Highway 67. Turn north on Highway 67 and drive about 10 miles to Vigilante Road. Turn right on Vigilante Road and drive to Morena Drive. Turn left on Morena Drive and drive to the lake.

Contact: San Diego City Lakes, 619/465-3474 (recorded message) or 619/668-2050, website: www.sandiego.gov/water/recreation; boat rentals, 619/390-0222.

10 LAKE CUYAMACA

Rating: 6

northeast of San Diego near Cuyamaca Rancho State Park

Map 14.4, page 433

This lake is just far enough away from the San Diego area to make a trip here something special, and many visitors are rewarded appropriately for their efforts.

Lake Cuyamaca is a small lake covering just 110 acres, and is set at 4,620 feet in elevation on the Cuyamaca Mountains' eastern slopes. Cuyamaca Rancho State Park surrounds the lake on three sides and offers a network of pretty hiking and horseback riding trails amid an oak and pine forest.

First and foremost, Lake Cuyamaca is a fishing lake, and it gets relatively high use by anglers year-round. Fishing boats usually are rented out by 8:30 or 9 A.M. on weekends. The rest of the visitors are pretty much hikers and backpackers who come to explore the adjacent park in the summer months.

Fishing prospects are often good. Many trout are stocked by the Department of Fish and Game, and there are sizable resident populations of crappie, bluegill, and bass, along with bonus channel catfish and sturgeon. The lake is stocked with more than 44,000 pounds of fish per year.

Cabins and campgrounds are available at the state park. That makes Cuyamaca a good choice for the boater/angler/camper. In addition, fishing boats, canoes, and pedal boats can be rented at the lake, a plus. The lake is just the right size and has a low enough speed limit (10 mph) to make paddling around quite fun for families in the summer. A youth fishing program is offered. Free fishing classes are held each Saturday at 10 A.M., and free guided nature walks are offered at 1 P.M. the first Sunday of the month.

Access: A paved boat ramp is located on the lake's west shore, off Highway 79.

Facilities, fees: Fishing boats, canoes, and pedal boats are available for rent (arrive by 8 A.M. on Saturdays and Sundays for fishing boats). Cabins, a campground, restrooms, drinking water, flush toilets, coin-operated showers, and RV dump station are available at the state recreation area. Free fishing classes are offered at 10 A.M. on Saturdays. A convenience store and café are nearby. Get supplies in Julian. Fees

are charged for day use, boat launching, fishing permits, and camping.

Water sports, restrictions: Powerboats, pedal boats, and canoes are permitted. No sailboats, sailboards, inflatables, rafts (except for Zodiac-type rafts), or boats under 10 feet. A 10-mph speed limit is strictly enforced. No water/body contact sports are permitted. The lake is open daily 6 A.M. to sunset.

Directions: From El Cajon, drive east on I-8 to Highway 79 (near Descanso Junction). Turn north (left) and drive nine miles to the park entrance on the left.

Contact: Lake Cuyamaca, 760/765-0515 or 877/581-9904, website: www.lakecuyamaca.org; Cuyamaca Rancho State Park, 760/765-0755.

11 EL CAPITAN LAKE

Rating: 6

northeast of San Diego

Map 14.4, page 433

The bassers call this place "El Cap" and rarely without a touch of reverence. Although you may hear stories about the bass at other lakes, El Cap is the one that produces them. The lake is set in a long canyon at an elevation of 750 feet, with 22 miles of shoreline and a maximum water depth of 197 feet. It is the biggest of the lakes managed by the City of San Diego, covering 1,562 acres when full.

Although this place is primarily set up for fishing, a few quirks have been thrown in. First, this is the only reservoir in the City of San Diego's system where personal watercraft are permitted, though only on certain days; call headquarters for the schedule. It is extremely popular when permitted. But read on:

Second, the water level fluctuates. It was so low in 2003, for instance, that water-skiing and wake boarding were prohibited for the year.

Fluctuating water levels can throw off the fishing. In rainy years, runoff causes the lake to be somewhat murky in the spring. The latter is actually a boon for anglers because the

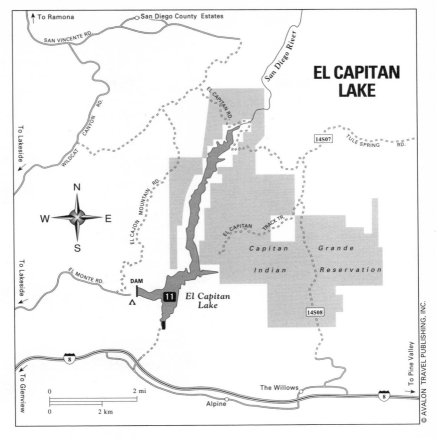

EL CAPITAN LAKE

To Ramona
San Diego County Estates
SAN VINCENTE RD.
San Diego River
EL CAPITAN RD.
WILDCAT CANYON RD.
To Lakeside
14S07
TULE SPRING RD.
N
W E
S
EL CAJON MOUNTAIN RD.
To Lakeside
EL CAPITAN TRACK TR.
Capitan Grande
Indian Reservation
EL MONTE RD.
DAM
To Lakeside
11 El Capitan Lake
14S08
8
To Glenview
0 2 mi
0 2 km
The Willows
Alpine
To Pine Valley
8

© AVALON TRAVEL PUBLISHING, INC.

fish are far less skittish than those at lakes with high water clarity, such as Miramar. The lake has bass, crappie, bluegill, catfish, sunfish, and carp.

As you might have figured, this place is special and gets a lot of use in the summer months; it attracts a moderately sized crowd the rest of the time. When the lake is opened to the public (usually in February), anglers get delirious, even jittery, at the prospects of casting a line to fish that have had four months of downtime to forget all about hooks and lures.

Access: The boat ramp is located on the south shore, 2.5 miles from the entrance.

Facilities, fees: Fishing boats and rowboats are available for rent. Picnic areas, snack bar, and bait and tackle are available. No camping (nearest camping is at Lake Jennings). Fees are charged for day use, boat launching, and fishing. Access is free in winter.

Water sports, restrictions: Powerboats and rowboats are permitted. Water sports depend on lake levels. Under normal conditions, water-skiing, wake boarding, and personal watercraft use are permitted on select days; phone San Diego Water Utilities for a current schedule. (In 2003, water-skiing and wake boarding were prohibited because of low water levels.) A 35-mph speed limit is strictly enforced. No swimming or sailboarding. The lake is open Fridays through Sundays from mid-

February to mid-October (dates can vary depending on water levels).

Directions: From San Diego, turn east on I-8 and drive 16 miles to Lake Jennings Park Road. Turn north and drive about two miles to the town of Lakeside and El Monte Road. Turn right on El Monte Road and drive about eight miles to the entrance for El Capitan Lake.

Contact: San Diego City Lakes, 619/465-3474 (recorded message) or 619/668-2050, website: www.sandiego.gov/water/recreation.

12 SANTEE LAKES

Rating: 6

near Santee

Map 14.4, page 433

This is a 190-acre park built around a complex of seven lakes.

So how many lakes can you boat on? Answer: Only one, Lake 5. Float tubing is allowed on Lake 1, if you're fishing.

Most campsites are lakefront and the park is best known for its fishing. The lakes are stocked with 44,000 pounds of trout and catfish annually, with fantastic lake records including a 39-pound catfish, 16-pound rainbow trout, 12-pound largemouth bass, and 2.5-pound bluegill.

Quiet, low-key boating is the name of the game here. Rowboats, pedal boats, and canoes are available for rent. This small regional park is 20 miles east of San Diego. It receives more than 100,000 visitors per year. The camp is set at 400 feet in elevation.

Access: Rental boats are available on Lake 5. Fishermen are allowed in float tubes on Lake 1.

Facilities, fees: Rental rowboats, canoes, kayaks, and pedalboats are available at a small marina at Lake 5. A campground, restrooms, drinking water, flush toilets, showers, RV dump station, playground, swimming pool, convenience store, snack bar, recreation center, pay phone, propane, and coin laundry are available. Fees are charged for access, fishing, and camping.

Water sports, restrictions: Rental boats allowed only at Lake 5. Float tubes permitted on Lake 1, but only if used for fishing. No private boats. No motors. No sailing, sailboarding, swimming or water/contact sports. No state fishing license required. Open sunrise to sunset.

Directions: Drive on I-8 to El Cajon and Highway 67. Turn north on Highway 67 and drive two miles to Santee and the Prospect Avenue exit. Take that exit and turn left and drive to Magnolia. Turn right on Magnolia and drive to Mission Gorge Road. Turn left on Mission Gorge Road and drive 2.5 miles to Carlton Hills Drive. Turn right and drive to Carlton Oaks Drive. Turn left and drive a mile to the park on the right.

Contact: Santee Lakes Regional Park, 619/596-3141, website: www.santeelakes.com.

13 LAKE JENNINGS

Rating: 6

northeast of El Cajon at Lake Jennings County Park

Map 14.4, page 433

Lake Jennings is a nice little backyard fishing hole and recreation area just five miles east of El Cajon at an elevation of 700 feet. The lake covers 108 surfaces with a maximum depth of 160 feet. The surrounding landscape is chaparral-covered hills.

This is the kind of place where you would come for an evening weekend picnic to enjoy yourself and maybe toss out a fishing line for catfish. A big bonus here is the campground with hot showers and concessionaire. The 100-acre park (not including the lake) includes a nature trail, playground, and enclosed clubhouse.

All water/body contact sports are prohibited. You know what that means? Of course you do: No swimming, water-skiing, sailboarding, or float tubing.

It's your basic catfish hole, thanks to a summer stocking program. But surprises happen here. You could be enjoying a summer evening for catfish and have one of the giant blue catfish decided to grab your bait. The lake record blue catfish at Lake Jennings is 60 pounds.

Trout fishing in the winter is good, too, with plentiful stocking. From June through August, night fishing is permitted. Bluegill and sunfish can be caught from shore and the lake is also home to largemouth bass.

Access: A paved boat ramp is located on the south side of the lake.

Facilities, fees: Rowboats and boats with electric motors are available for rent. A campground, restrooms, showers, snack bar, picnic areas, RV dump station, bait and tackle, fishing float, fish-cleaning station, and convenience store are available at the lake. Supplies available in El Cajon. Fees are charged for day use, boat launching, fishing, and camping.

Water sports, restrictions: Powerboats, canoes, kayaks, and some inflatables are permitted. No water-skiing, wake boarding, personal watercraft, sailing, sailboarding, float tubes, swimming, or water/body contact sports allowed. A 10-mph speed limit is enforced. Open for boating from November through August, Fridays through Sundays. Open daily for day use and shore fishing if camping. Open for night fishing on Fridays through Sundays from June through August.

Directions: From San Diego, turn east on I-8 and drive 16 miles to Lake Jennings Park Road. Turn north and continue one mile to the lake.

Contact: Lake Jennings Entrance Station, 619/443-2510; boat rentals, 619/443-9503; San Diego County Parks, 858/694-3049; camping reservations, 858/565-3600, website: www.sdparks.org; Helix Irrigation District, 619/466-0585.

14 LOWER OTAY LAKE

Rating: 5

southeast of San Diego

Map 14.4, page 433
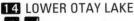

Otay is set at an elevation of 490 feet in the foothills near Chula Vista, just north of the California/Mexico border. It's about 20 miles from San Diego. When full, the lake covers 1,100 acres with 25 miles of shoreline and a maximum depth of 137.5 feet. There is a variety of aquatic habitat, including submerged trees, tules, underwater holes, and ledges.

It could make your brain gears squeak trying to imagine a five-bass limit that weighs in at 53 pounds, 14 ounces. But that is what the scales read when Jack Neu of San Diego weighed the five bass he caught at Otay, the largest single bass limit ever documented on the planet. I fished with Jack on that record day, and if by now you have figured that Otay is set up mainly for fishing, well, you got that right.

What occurs here are long periods of slow to fair fishing results despite intense fishing, followed by short periods of unbelievable snaps with giant bass. Other fish include bluegill, crappie, catfish, and bullhead. The lake record bass weighed 18 pounds, 12 ounces, and the lake record catfish 85.9 pounds. Lower Otay also held the state record for bluegill (3.5 pounds) from 1991 to 2002.

Otay is the home of the U.S. Olympic Training Center for rowing sports. Note that water sports involving water/body contact are prohibited, including water-skiing, wake boarding, and personal watercraft use.

Also note that Upper Otay Lake is not listed because boating and water sports are prohibited. Fishing is catch-and-release only from shore or float tubes at Upper Otay.

Otay is surrounded by rolling foothills, and if you're interested in a side trip, there are some places where you can hike. But most people are here for one reason: the bass. And the dream of catching a stringer of fish just like the one Jack Neu did.

Access: A paved boat ramp is located off Wueste Road on the west shore.

Facilities, fees: Fishing boats and rowboats are available for rent. Picnic areas, a snack bar, and bait and tackle are available. Access is free. Fees are charged for boat launching and fishing.

Water sports, restrictions: Powerboats, rowboats, sailboats, and inflatables are permitted. No water-skiing, wake boarding, sailboarding, or personal watercraft. A 35-mph speed limit is strictly enforced. No water/body contact sports are permitted. The lake is open from sunrise to sunset on Wednesdays, Saturdays, and Sundays and certain holidays from February through September. Waterfowl hunting is permitted November through January.

Directions: From San Diego, drive south on I-805 to Chula Vista and Telegraph Canyon Road. Turn east on Telegraph Canyon Road and drive five miles to Wueste Road. Turn right and drive to the lake access road on the left.

Contact: San Diego City Lakes, 619/465-3474 (recorded message) or 619/668-2050, website: www.sandiego.gov/water/recreation.

15 LAKE BARRETT

Rating: 7

near Tecate, east of San Diego

Map 14.4, page 433

Located behind locked gates in a remote area of San Diego County, Lake Barrett has become a special fishing paradise. You cannot see the lake from the road.

Lake Barrett was closed to the public starting in 1969, then reopened in the summer of 1994 with a genius-level fishing program where entrance is by permit only, with a quota.

Access is controlled through a reservation system (see Contact information) and special fishing rules. All lake users must be escorted through private property to the lake. Along with Upper Otay Lake, this is one of only two reservoirs in the region operating under highly restrictive rules. One of the reasons for this is to protect the last significant local population of northern strain largemouth bass. The Florida strain bass has replaced these fish in almost all of Southern California.

Other species at Lake Barrett include bluegill, bullhead, and both black and white crappie.

In addition, threadfin shad and silverside minnows have been planted for forage. They are reproducing successfully, resulting in healthier and bigger bass.

When you arrive, you will discover a beautiful, 811-acre lake set in a remote valley. Except for one gated road, which crosses private property, there is no public access. According to the San Diego City Lakes Department, access will be permitted as long as there is no abuse of private property, such as littering, trespassing, or petty damage. If you witness any wrongdoing, immediately try to correct the situation.

Lake Barrett is located at the confluence of Cottonwood and Pine Valley Creeks, about 35 miles east of San Diego.

Though the lake is hampered in some years by low water levels, I ranked it as the state's No. 1 fishing lake in my book *Foghorn Outdoors California Fishing.*

Access: A paved boat ramp is located on the south side of the lake.

Facilities, fees: Rental boats with 4-horsepower motors are provided. Visitors are allowed to bring their own outboard motors up to 25 horsepower. Vault toilets are available. No drinking water. Garbage must be packed out. No glass containers and no pets. No more than two vehicles per group and no more than 100 persons per day. No RVs permitted. Access is by reservation only through Ticketmaster at 619/220-TIXS. Fees are charged for reservations and day use.

Water sports, restrictions: Powerboats, rowboats, canoes, kayaks, and inflatables are permitted. A 20-mph speed limit is permitted. No sailboarding, swimming, or water/body contact. Waterfowl hunting is permitted in season. Fishing is catch-and-release only with barbless, artificial hooks. Open from spring to fall, one to three days per week, by reservation only.

Directions: From San Diego take I-8 east about 30 miles to Japatul Road. Turn south (right) on Japatul Road and drive 5.6 miles to Lyons Valley Road. Bear left on Lyons Valley Road and drive six miles (just past milepost 12) to Barrett Lake Road and an unsigned entrance gate. A ranger will be waiting to check your entrance pass. The lake is approximately 2.5 miles beyond the gate.

Contact: San Diego City Lakes, 619/465-3474 (recorded message) or 619/668-2050, website: www.sandiego.gov/water/recreation; electric motor rentals, Stoney's Marine, El Cajon, 619/449-9459.

16 LAKE MORENA

Rating: 6

east of San Diego in Lake Morena County Park

Map 14.4, page 433

Lake Morena is located out in the boondocks, but it's well worth the trip. If you like bass, this is a must-do lake.

The lake is set at an elevation of 3,200 feet just south of Cleveland National Forest, and only seven or eight miles from the California/Mexico border. When full, the lake covers 1,500 surface acres. It's about a 45-minute drive from San Diego.

Because the elevation is much higher than the other lakes in the greater San Diego area, everything gets going a little later, with the best fishing in April, May, and June. The landscape is chaparral, oak woodlands, and grasslands.

Lake use is limited to fishing only. No other water sports are permitted, and a 10-mph speed limit keeps even the fastest boats at a reasonable pace.

Catch rates are often excellent, and some bass are quite big. The lake record here is 19 pounds, 3 ounces. The lake record for trout is nine pounds, six ounces.

Water levels can fluctuate wildly, which can have a tremendous impact on the quality of your visit. In low-rain years it is advisable to call ahead before planning a trip to the lake.

When the lake is full, lakeside camping is a major bonus, and because of it, visitor use is heavy in late spring and summer. In addition, the surrounding national forest offers the chance for lots of other activities, including hiking and horseback riding.

Access: A paved launch ramp is available on the lake's south side.

Facilities, fees: Campgrounds, cabins, restrooms with flush toilets, showers, propane gas, coin laundry, and picnic areas are available. Developed facilities are available at Morena Village to the east. Fees are charged for day use and boat launching.

Water sports, restrictions: Powerboats, rowboats, canoes, kayaks, inflatables, sailing, and sailboarding are permitted. A 10-mph speed limit is strictly enforced. No swimming, waterskiing, wake boarding, or personal watercraft are permitted. Open daily from 30 minutes before sunrise to 30 minutes after sunset.

Directions: From El Cajon, drive east on I-8 to Pine Valley, then continue east for four miles to Buckman Springs Road/County Road S1. Take the Buckman Springs off ramp, turn right (south) on Buckman Springs Road and drive 5.5 miles to Oak Drive. Turn right on Oak Drive and drive 1.5 miles to Lake Morena Drive. Turn left on Lake Morena Drive and drive to the lake (RV park on right at 2330 Lake Morena Drive).

Contact: Lake Morena, San Diego County Parks, 858/694-3049, website: www.sdparks.org.

FOGHORN OUTDOORS®

© TOM STIENSTRA

Chapter 15

Death Valley and the Southern Deserts

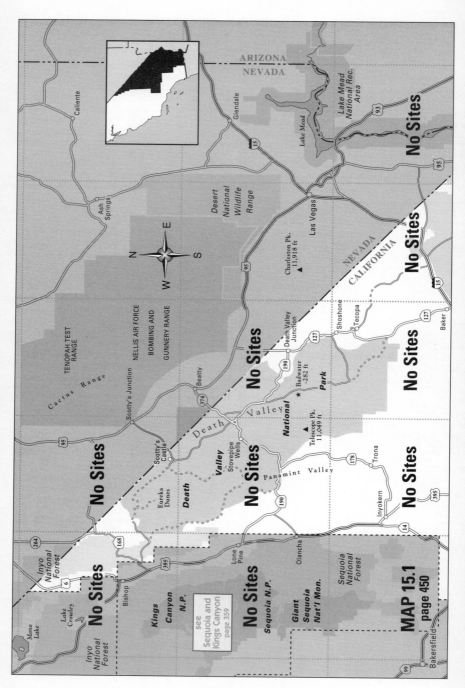

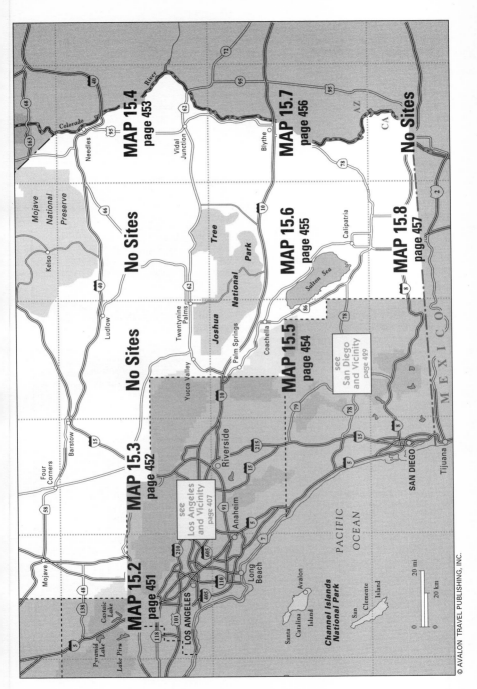

MAP 15.4
page 453

MAP 15.7
page 456

No Sites

MAP 15.6
page 455

MAP 15.8
page 457

No Sites

No Sites

MAP 15.5
page 454

see
San Diego
and Vicinity
page 429

MAP 15.3
page 452

see
Los Angeles
and Vicinity
page 407

MAP 15.2
page 451

Mojave
National
Preserve

Joshua   Tree   National   Park

Salton Sea

PACIFIC
OCEAN

Channel Islands
National Park

MEXICO

Colorado

Needles

Vidal
Junction

Blythe

Calipatria

Kelso

Twentynine
Palms

Palm Springs

Coachella

Yucca Valley

Ludlow

Barstow

Four
Corners

Riverside

Anaheim

Long
Beach

Avalon

San
Clemente
Island

Santa
Catalina
Island

Mojave

Castaic
Lake

Pyramid
Lake

Lake Piru

LOS ANGELES

SAN DIEGO

Tijuana

River

Colorado

AZ
CA

0   20 mi
0   20 km

© AVALON TRAVEL PUBLISHING, INC.

Map 15.1

Site 1
Page 459

15.2

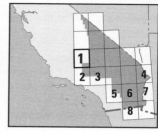

1
2 3
5 6 7
8
4

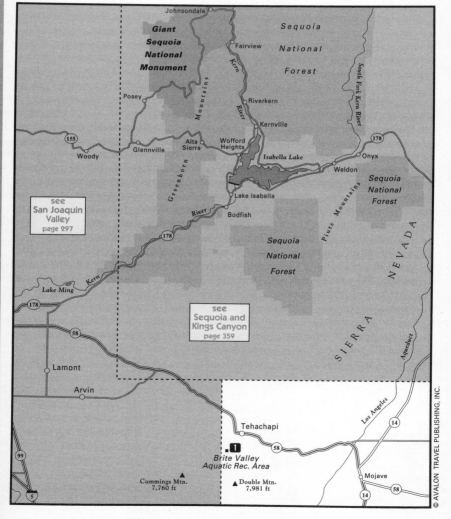

Johnsondale

Giant Sequoia National Monument

Fairview

Sequoia National Forest

Posey

Kern River

Riverkern

Kernville

South Fork Kern River

155

Woody

Glennville

Alta Sierra

Wofford Heights

Isabella Lake

178

Onyx

Sequoia National Forest

Weldon

see San Joaquin Valley page 297

Greenhorn Mountains

River

178

Bodfish

Lake Isabella

Piute Mountains

Lake Ming

Kern

178

Sequoia National Forest

see Sequoia and Kings Canyon page 359

SIERRA NEVADA

Aqueduct

58

Lamont

Arvin

Los Angeles

14

99

Tehachapi

58

1

Brite Valley Aquatic Rec. Area

▲ Cummings Mtn. 7,760 ft

▲ Double Mtn. 7,981 ft

Mojave

14

58

5

© AVALON TRAVEL PUBLISHING, INC.

Map 15.2

Site 2
Pages 459–460

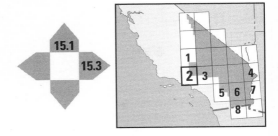

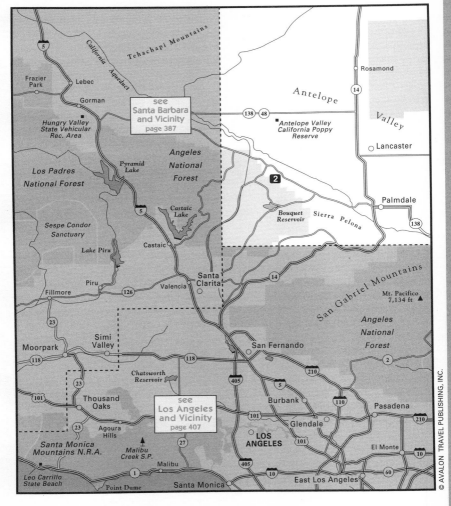

© AVALON TRAVEL PUBLISHING, INC.

Map 15.3

Site 3
Page 460

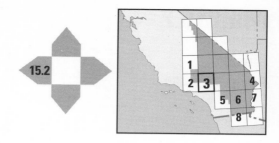

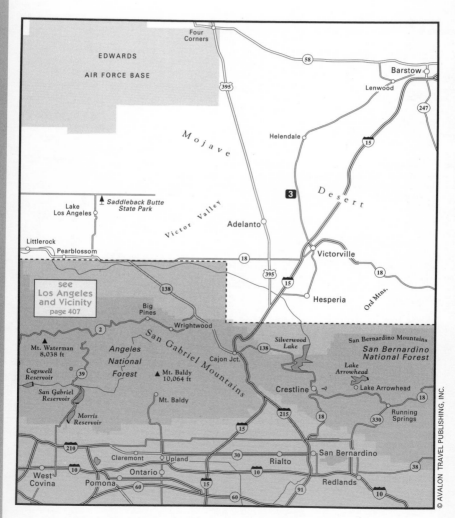

Map 15.4

Sites 4–6
Pages 460–466

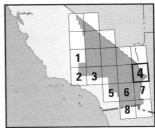

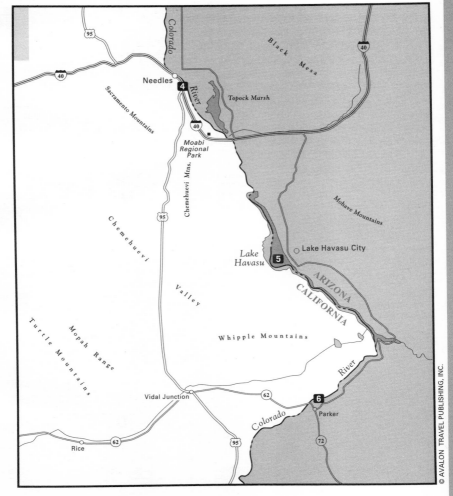

© AVALON TRAVEL PUBLISHING, INC.

Map 15.5

Site 7
Page 466

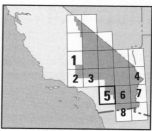

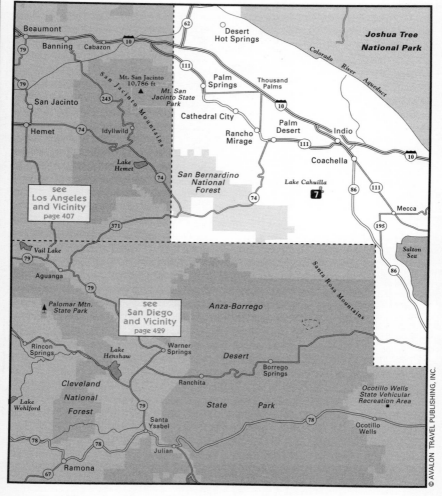

Map 15.6

Sites 8–10
Pages 466–469

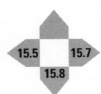

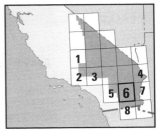

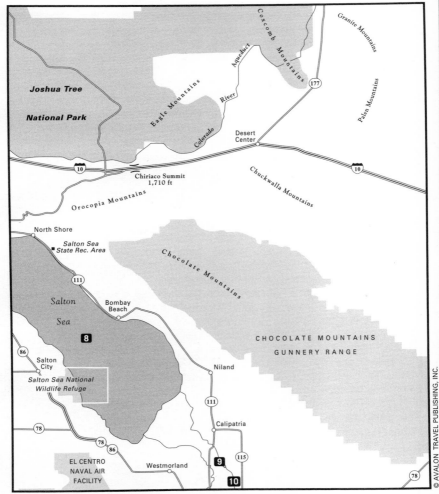

Map 15.7

Site 11
Pages 469–471

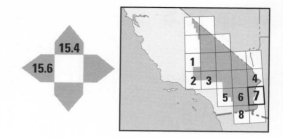

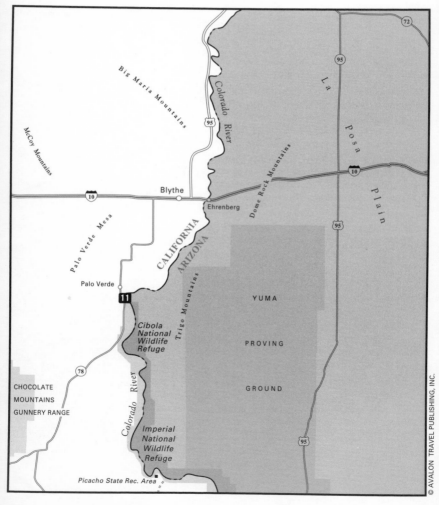

© AVALON TRAVEL PUBLISHING, INC.

Map 15.8

Site 12
Page 471

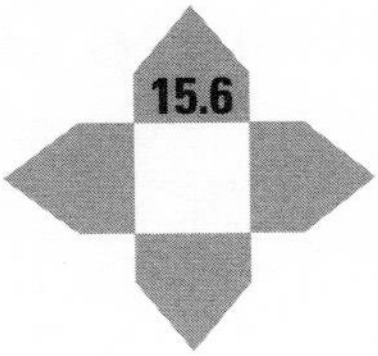
15.6

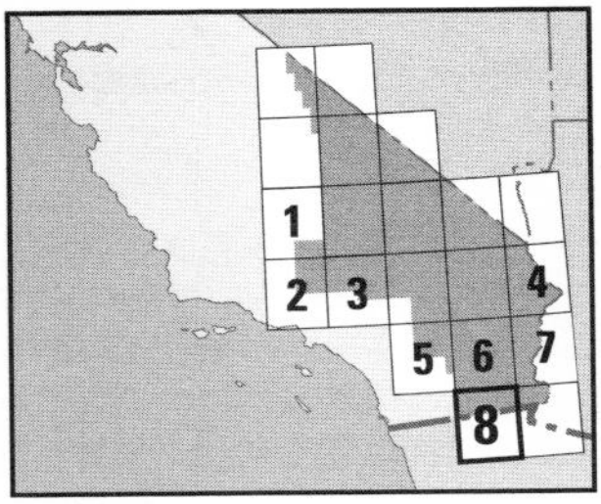
1
2
3
4
5
6
7
8

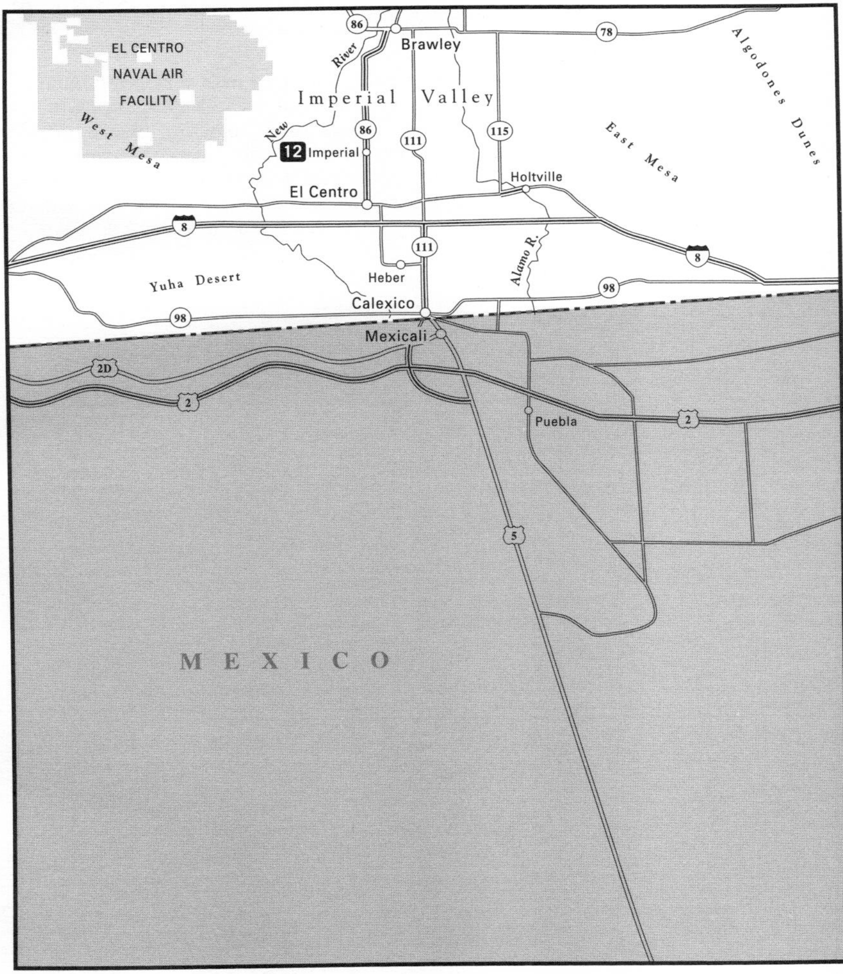
EL CENTRO NAVAL AIR FACILITY
West Mesa
86
New River
Brawley
78
Algodones Dunes
Imperial Valley
111
115
East Mesa
12
Imperial
Holtville
El Centro
8
Alamo R.
Yuha Desert
Heber
98
Calexico
Mexicali
2D
2
Puebla
5
MEXICO

© AVALON TRAVEL PUBLISHING, INC.

Chapter 15—Death Valley and the Southern Deserts

There is no region so vast in California—yet with fewer people—than this broad expanse of Anza-Borrego State Desert, Joshua Tree National Park, Mojave National Preserve, Salton Sea, and endless BLM land. And yet the area is best-loved not for the desert, but for the boating, water sports, and recreation of the Colorado River—it's often a party on the Colorado that attracts people for the first time.

On big weekends, it can even seem as if there is a party within close vicinity of every boat ramp on the river. The weather is hot, the boats are fast, and the body oil can flow as fast as the liquid refreshments. For many, the experiences are electric and sensational.

Each section of the Colorado River offers a different type of experience. Check out the following pages and see which is one is for you.

The rest of the area is far different.

Salton Sea and the endless BLM desert land provides one of the most distinct (and strange) lakes and terrain on earth. The Salton Sea, created by accident from a broken dike, is one of the largest inland seas in the world. The BLM desert land (BLM stands for Bureau of Land Management, of course) is under BLM control only because no other agency wanted it.

Most of the other highlights of this region have nothing to do with boating and water sports. Anza-Borrego is so big that it seems to stretch to forever. Joshua Tree National Park features a sweeping desert landscape edged by mountains, and peppered with the peculiar Joshua Tree and strange rock formations. The Mojave National Preserve features the Kelso Dunes.

Somewhere amid all this, you will likely be able to find a match for your own personal desires.

⬛ BRITE VALLEY LAKE
🛥️ ✖️ 🎣 ⛺

Rating: 5

near Tehachapi at Brite Valley
Recreation Area

Map 15.1, page 450

Here's a hidden spot that is often overlooked.
Brite Valley Lake is a small water hole (90
acres) set in the northern flank of the
Tehachapi Mountains at an elevation of 4,000
feet. Gas motors are prohibited, but that
makes this a good lake for hand-powered craft
such as canoes or rafts, or small boats with
electric motors.

Fishing prospects are fair for trout in the
spring (trout are stocked here), and catfish in
the summer. Instead, the lake is best used for
picnicking, canoeing, or kayaking. Right—this
is the kind of place where you have a picnic,
then plunk in a canoe and paddle around a
bit, maybe casting a line for small trout without any delusions of grandeur. Use is moderate, primarily picnickers and anglers enjoying
the warm temperatures and cool water. A nearby golf course is a popular attraction.

Note: The lake is closed to the public from
late October through late April.

Access: A primitive boat ramp is located on
the lake's south shore.

Facilities, fees: A campground, restrooms with
showers, picnic areas, RV dump station, and
fish-cleaning station are available. Supplies
are available eight miles away in Tehachapi.
Fees are charged for day use, boat launching,
and camping.

Water sports, restrictions: Sailing is permitted.
Gas motors are not permitted on the lake. Sailboarding and swimming are not allowed.

Directions: From Bakersfield, drive east on
Highway 58 and for 40 miles toward the town
of Tehachapi. Take the Highway 202 exit and
drive three miles west to Banducci Road. Turn
left and head south to the park.

Contact: Tehachapi Valley Recreation and Parks
Department, 661/822-3228, fax 661/823-8529.

⬛ ELIZABETH LAKE
🛥️ 🏊 🎣 🏊

Rating: 6

west of Lancaster in Angeles National Forest

Map 15.2, page 451

It might be wise to bring in some Mi-Wok
medicine men to conduct a rain dance here
every winter because Elizabeth Lake is often
extremely low. It is a prisoner of rainfall; so
is nearby Lake Hughes to the west, which is
privately owned.

A pretty lake, Elizabeth is set at 3,300 feet
in elevation in the northern outskirts of Angeles National Forest below Portal Ridge. There's
a good picnic area and a nice, sandy shoreline.
Sailboarding can be excellent, although conditions tend to be inconsistent. Use is light
year-round, slightly heavier in summer.

The lake provides fair trout fishing in the
cool months and bass fishing in the spring
and summer.

For an exceptional side trip, head over to the
Antelope Valley California Poppy State Reserve,
located a few miles to the north. In the spring
it can be blanketed wall-to-wall with blooming
poppies, best usually in late March or very early
April. When late rains are followed by warm
temperatures, there can be nine square miles
of golden poppies—a fantastic sight.

Special note: Newcomers should pay special
attention to the fact that the lake's eastern half
is private and is off limits to the public.

Access: A primitive boat ramp is located on
the lake's northwestern shore.

Facilities, fees: Picnic areas, drinking water,
and vault toilets are available. Access to the
lake is free. Adventure Pass ($30 annual fee)
or $5 daily fee per parked vehicle is required.

Water sports, restrictions: Water-skiing, wake
boarding, and personal watercraft are not
allowed. Motors are restricted to a maximum
of 10 horsepower. Sailing, sailboarding, and
swimming are allowed.

Directions: From Los Angeles, drive north on
I-5 for about 40 miles to Castaic and Lake

Hughes Road. Turn north on Lake Hughes Road and then drive to Elizabeth Lake Road. Turn right and drive about three miles east (past Lake Hughes and Munz Lake) to Elizabeth Lake.

Contact: Angeles National Forest, Santa Clara/Mojave Rivers Ranger District, 661/296-9710, fax 661/296-5847.

3 MOJAVE NARROWS REGIONAL PARK

🛥 🐟 🏕 ♿ 🚐 ⛰

Rating: 6

on the Mojave River

Map 15.3, page 452

Almost no one except the locals knows about this little county park. It is like an oasis in the Mojave Desert.

There are actually two small lakes here: The larger Horseshoe Lake and Pelican Lake. For water sports, rental rowboats and pedal boats are provided on weekends. No private boats.

The park is set at 2,000 feet and provides a few recreation options, including a pond stocked in season with trout and catfish for fishing, horseback riding facilities, and equestrian trails. Hiking includes a wheelchair-accessible trail.

The Mojave River level fluctuates here, almost disappearing in some years in summer and early fall. One of the big events of the year here is on Father's Day in June, the Huck Finn Jubilee.

Access: A boat rental dock is located on the east side of Horseshoe Lake.

Facilities, fees: A campground, restrooms, drinking water, flush toilets, showers, RV dump station, picnic area, snack bar, pay phone, playground, archery range, bait, boat rentals, horse rentals, and horseback riding facilities are available. A store, propane gas, and coin laundry are available three miles from the campground. Fees are charged for day use, fishing, and camping.

Water sports, restrictions: Rental rowboats and pedal boats are permitted on weekends. No private boats permitted, including canoes,

kayaks, and inflatables. No swimming or any water/body contact sports. Open daily from mid-October to mid-April from 7:30 A.M. to 5 P.M. Open mid-April to mid-October from 7:30 A.M. to 6 P.M. Sundays through Thursdays, and from 7:30 A.M. to 7 P.M. on Fridays and Saturdays. Note: The gate closes each evening.

Directions: Drive on I-15 to Victorville and the exit for Bear Valley Road. Take that exit and drive east on Bear Valley Road for six miles to Ridgecrest. Turn left on Ridgecrest, drive three miles, and make a left into the park.

Contact: Mojave Narrows Regional Park, 760/245-2226, website: www.co.san-bernardino.ca.us/parks/mojave.htm.

4 COLORADO RIVER (ABOVE LAKE HAVASU)

🛥 ✗ 🏕 🛶 🐟 🌊 ⛰

Rating: 8

in the Mojave Desert

Map 15.4, page 453

Bring your suntan lotion and a beach towel. This section of the Colorado River is a big tourist spot where the body oil and beer can flow faster than the river. There are a lot of hot bodies and hot boats, and water-skiing is the dominant activity in the summer. But it's not all craziness; there are also some relatively private beaches and a chance for canoeing and kayaking.

Water-skiing, wake boarding, and personal watercraft riding are, of course, the most popular boating activities. Because the river current averages 4 to 8 mph, it causes wakes to disappear quickly, leaving glass conditions that skiers love. It can get crowded.

The only designated swimming beach is at Park Moabi Marina, but as mentioned above, there are several out-of-the-way beaches that offer a little more privacy. Boat speed is restricted at these no-wake areas, better suited for families, especially those with small children who are either wading or floating in the water.

Canoeists and kayakers can paddle anywhere

from Bullhead City, Arizona, down to Lake Havasu, but the best bet is the Needles-Castle Rock Run, the most scenic run in these parts. A two-day affair, the Needles-Castle Rock Run is about 29 miles long and flows through the scenic Topock Gorge, a steep, narrow canyon. This canyon features rock formations, lava rock pinnacles, arches, and a chance to see Native American petroglyphs. Water-skiing is prohibited here. Alas, if only watercraft were also banned, this easy run would have a good chance at attaining canoeing acclaim. If you're interested in this run, an Arizona company called Jerkwater Canoe & Kayak (see Contact, below) will provide equipment, tours and shuttle service for reasonable rates. Jerkwater also offers tours of Topock Marsh in the Havasu National Wildlife Refuge. WACKO also provides kayak and canoe tours from Topock Gorge to Castle Rock, and boat tours and charters of the Topock Gorge.

Upstream of the Needles put-in, canoeing and kayaking are possible, but the scenery is, well, blah, and canoeists should be wary in that area of water-skiers and personal watercraft.

About 30 miles of the Colorado River, from Needles to Lake Havasu City (Arizona), is part of the Havasu National Wildlife Refuge. One of the last remaining natural stretches of the lower Colorado River flows through the Topock Gorge.

Access: Paved launch ramps are available at the following locations:

• Needles Marina Park and Jack Smith Memorial Park: Drive on I-40 to Needles and the exit for J Street. Take that exit and drive to Broadway. Turn left on Broadway and drive .75 mile to Needles Highway. Turn right on Needles Highway, and drive .5 mile to Needles Marina Park on the left. Continue .5 mile to Jack Smith Memorial Park.

• Moabi Regional Park: From Needles, drive east on I-40 for 11 miles to Park Moabi Road. Turn left on Park Moabi Road and continue .5 mile to Moabi Regional Park entrance at the end of the road.

• Rainbo Beach Resort: Drive on I-40 to Needles and River Road. Turn north on River Road and drive 1.5 miles to Rainbo resort on the right.

Canoeists and kayakers may put in at any of the launch ramps listed above. For those who desire a longer trip, a popular put-in is located farther north, at Bullhead City, Arizona. To reach the launching area, take I-40 east to the Needles Highway/West Broadway exit. Take the exit and turn left. Stay in the left-hand lane; when the road splits, continue straight on Needles Highway (Broadway heads to the right into town). When you reach the four-way stop, turn left on Harbor Avenue. The road crosses the California/Arizona border and becomes Highway 95. Continue north for about 25 miles to Bullhead City. Turn left on Riverview Drive and proceed down to the launching area.

Boaters may take out downstream at one of several river access sites in Needles or continue all the way to Lake Havasu. The last take-out before Lake Havasu is at the town of Topock, Arizona, where I-40 intersects with the river. If you miss it, you will have to float approximately 17 more miles to the next take-out at Lake Havasu.

Facilities, fees: Lodging, cabins, campgrounds, full-service marinas, picnic areas, restaurants, tackle, and groceries are available in the Needles area. Fees are charged for day use and/or boat launching at private marinas and parks.

Water sports, restrictions: No-wake restrictions are enforced at marina areas. Water-skiing is prohibited in the Topock Gorge and Havasu Wildlife Refuge, but is allowed everywhere else. Personal watercraft are permitted everywhere. River currents make sailboarding impractical. The only designated swimming beach is located at Park Moabi Marina, but there are numerous undeveloped sandy beaches all along the river.

Directions: From Southern California, take I-15 north to I-40 at Barstow. Turn east on I-40 and drive approximately 150 miles to Needles.

From Northern California, drive south on
U.S. 395 to Highway 58 at Kramer Junction.
Turn east on Highway 58, then cross over on
I-15 to I-40. Turn east on I-40 and drive approx-
imately 150 miles to Needles.

Contact: Needles Chamber of Commerce,
760/326-2050; Lake Havasu Tourism Bureau,
website: www.golakehavasu.com; Lake Havasu Area Chamber of Commerce, website:
www.havasuchamber.com.

Boating information: Park Moabi Marina,
San Bernardino County, 760/326-4777, website:
www.moabi.com; Rainbo Beach Resort, 760/326-
3101; Needles Marina Park, 760/326-2197;
Topock Gorge Marina (Topock, Arizona),
928/768-2325, website: www.topockmarina.com.

Boat rentals: Paradise Boat Rentals, 928/854-
4214 or 877/736-6131, website: www.paradise-
boatrentals.com; Nautical Sports Center,
928/855-7000, website: www.boatrentallake-
havasu.com; Park Moabi Marina, 760/326-
3831, website: www.moabi.com; Jerkwater
Canoe & Kayak, 928/768-7753 or 800/421-
7803, website: www.jerkwater.com; Western
Arizona Canoe & Kayak Outfitter (WACKO),
928/855-6414 or 888/881-5038, website:
www.azwacko.com.

Houseboat rentals: Havasu Springs Resort,
928/667-3361, website: www.havasusprings.com;
Sandpoint Marina & RV Park, 928/855-0549,
website: www.sandpointresort.com; Nautical
Sports Center, 928/855-7000, website: www.boa-
trentallakehavasu.com.

Boat tours and charters: Bluewater Jet Boat
Tours, 928/855-7171 or 888/855-7171, website:
www.coloradoriverjetboattours.com; London
Bridge Jet Boat Tours (boat and personal watercraft tours), 702/298-5498 or 888/505-3545,
website: www.jetboattour.com; Capt. Doyle's
River Excursions, 928/768-2664, website:
www.captdoyle.com; Dixie Belle River Party
Boat, 928/453-6776.

Scuba diving: Aquastrophics Dive & Travel,
928/680-3483, website: www.aquastrophics.com.

5 LAKE HAVASU

Rating: 10

from Topock to Parker Dam on the
Colorado River

Map 15.4, page 453

Giant Lake Havasu is like a lone sapphire in
a vast coal field. Only the mighty Colorado
River breaks up a measureless expanse of desert.
Havasu was created when the Parker Dam was
built across the river, and it is currently one
of the most popular boating areas in the southwestern United States.

The lake is 45 miles long, covers 19,300 acres,
and is located at the low elevation of 482 feet.
Size, hot weather, warm water, and proximity
to Las Vegas make this one of the top vacation and water-skiing hot spots in the West.
The lake is used year-round, although fewer
people use it in the late winter months.

During spring, summer, and fall, it's considered a boating wonderland. Much of the
boating activity is located around Pittsburgh
Point, the big island across from Lake Havasu City. To get there, you must cross the famous
London Bridge, and that alone gives people
quite a charge.

Water-skiing and personal watercraft riding
are very popular activities. Competitions are
held here yearly, but most boaters do their own
thing, heading off on this great expanse of
water in search of wild fun and frolic. Most
find it. Over the course of a year, enough suntan oil is poured at Lake Havasu to fill many
small lakes, and enough liquid refreshment is
poured to fill the California Aqueduct.

The hot weather and lukewarm surface waters
make this lake ideal for swimming. Many
boaters search out relatively private beaches,
then set up shop to have picnics, swim a little,
play a little, and then maybe water-ski or tow
somebody around on a wake board.

Southern California is well known for being
home to a vast amount of people, and Lake
Havasu definitely attracts many of them. How-

ever, this lake is big enough to handle all of the people who throng here, and big enough for all of them to have the time of their lives.

Access: Paved ramps are available at the following locations:

• Lake Havasu State Park, Arizona: From Parker Dam, drive north on Arizona Highway 95 for 40 miles (two miles north of London Bridge) to the park entrance. There are three multi-lane ramps; one is for personal watercraft only. Facilities include a campground, restrooms with showers, and a swimming beach. For more information call 928/855-2784.

• Site Six Ramp, Arizona: Take Arizona Highway 95 north to Lake Havasu City and to Swanson Boulevard. Turn left on Swanson Boulevard and drive a short distance to Lake Havasu Boulevard. Turn left and drive one block to McCulloch Boulevard. Turn left and cross the London Bridge and continue for two miles to the far end of the island and the ramp on the left. A wheelchair-accessible fishing pier is available. For more information call 928/453-8686.

• Cattail Cove State Park, Arizona: Drive north on Arizona Highway 95 to milepost 168 (located 15 miles north of Parker Dam) and the park entrance road. For more information call 928/855-1223.

• Crazy Horse Campground, Arizona: Take Arizona Highway 95 north to Lake Havasu City and to Swanson Boulevard. Turn right on Swanson Boulevard and drive a short distance to Lake Havasu Boulevard. Turn left and drive one block to McCulloch Boulevard. Turn left and cross the London Bridge and continue .25 mile to the entrance on the right. For more information call 928/855-4033.

• Havasu Landing Resort & Casino, California: From Vidal Junction, drive north on U.S. 95 toward Needles to 17 Mile Road (about halfway between Vidal Junction and Needles). Turn right and drive 13 miles to the resort. Campground, restaurant, convenience store, and deli are available. For more information call 760/858-4593 or 800/307-3610.

• Lake Havasu Marina, Arizona: Take Ari-

zona Highway 95 north to Lake Havasu City and to Swanson Boulevard. Turn right on Swanson Boulevard and drive a short distance to Lake Havasu Boulevard. Turn left and drive one block to McCulloch Boulevard. Turn left and cross the London Bridge and continue to the marina on the left at 1100 McCulloch Boulevard. For more information call 928/855-2159.

• Sandpoint Marina & RV Park, Arizona: Take Arizona Highway 95 north and drive 15 miles north to Milepost 168 and the exit for Cattail Cove/Sandpoint Marina. Turn left and drive to the park entrance. Fishing boats, pontoon boats, personal watercraft, and houseboats for rent. Full service marina and boat repair are available. For more information call 928/855-0549, website: www.sandpointresort.com.

Facilities, fees: Campgrounds, resorts, full-service marinas, and supplies are available off Arizona Highway 95 in the vicinity of Lake Havasu City, and on the west shore on the California side along Highway 95. There are 40 shoreline miles of boat-access camping on the lake's Arizona side between the dam and Lake Havasu City. (See Contact, below.) A fee is charged at most resorts and marinas for day use and/or boat launching.

Water sports, restrictions: Water-skiing, wake boarding, personal watercraft, sailing, and sailboarding are permitted. Swimming beaches are available at the following locations: Cattail Cove State Park, Havasu Landing Resort, Sandpoint Marina, Lake Havasu State Park, and Crazy Horse Campground. There are numerous undesignated beaches all along the shoreline.

Directions: From Southern California take I-10 east to Blythe and turn north on U.S. 95. Continue to Vidal Junction at the intersection of U.S. 95 and Highway 62. Or take Highway 62 directly east to Vidal Junction. To access the west side of the lake, turn north on U.S. 95 and drive about 28 miles to Havasu Lake Road. Turn right (east) and continue to the lake. To reach the east side of the lake, drive east on Highway 62 to Parker, then turn north on Arizona Highway 95 (the Arizona side) or Parker Dam Road (the California side) and drive to Parker Dam. Continue north on Highway 95 to Lake Havasu City.

From Northern California drive south on U.S. 395 to Highway 58. Turn east and drive to Barstow and I-40. Turn east on I-40 and drive to Arizona Highway 95. Turn right (south) on Highway 95 and continue 20 miles to Lake Havasu City on the east side of the lake. To access the west side of the lake, turn south on California U.S. 95 (south of Needles) and drive about 17 miles to Havasu Lake Road. Turn left (east) and continue to the lake.

Contact: Lake Havasu Tourism Bureau, 800/2-HAVASU (242-8278) or 928/453-3444, website:golakehavasu.com; Lake Havasu Area Chamber of Commerce, 928/855-4115, website: www.havasuchamber.com.

Boat rentals: Havasu Lake Service 928/858-4392; Champion Rentals, 928/855-8088; Arizona Watersports, 928/453-5558; Paradise Boat Rentals, 977/736-6131 or 928/854-4214, website: www.paradiseboatrentals.com; Nautical Sports Center, 928/855-7000, website: www.boatrentallakehavasu.com.

Houseboat rentals: Havasu Springs Resort, 928/667-3361, website: www.havasusprings.com; Sandpoint Marina & RV Park, 928/855-0549, website: www.sandpointresort.com; Nautical Sports Center, 928/855-7000, website: www.boatrentallakehavasu.com.

Canoe and kayak rentals and tours: Jerkwater Canoe & Kayak, 928/768-7753 or 800/421-7803, website: www.jerkwater.com; Western Arizona Canoe & Kayak Outfitters (WACKO), 928/855-6414 or 888/881-5038, website: www.azwacko.com.

Boat tours and charters: Bluewater Jet Boat Tours, 928/855-7171 or 888/855-7171, website: www.coloradoriverjetboattours.com; London Bridge Jet Boat Tours (boat and personal watercraft tours), 702/298-5498 or 888/505-3545, website: www.jetboattour.com; Capt. Doyle's River Excursions, 928/768-2664, website:

www.captdoyle.com; Dixie Belle River Party Boat, 928/453-6776.

Scuba diving: Aquastrophics Dive & Travel, 928/680-3483, website: www.aquastrophics.com.

6 COLORADO RIVER (PARKER DAM TO PALO VERDE DAM)

🚤 🍴 🛥 🎣 🏊 🏄 🚐 🏔

Rating: 8

in the Mojave Desert

Map 15.4, page 453

Whoa, look at all the water-skiers. On hot summer days the Colorado River is about the only thing liquid around these parts that isn't in a can or bottle. One way or another the natural response is to get in the water, then boat, water-ski, swim, float around on an inner tube, anything—just get on the river. If this sounds like a prime place for water recreation, that's because it is.

The boating season here is a long one, courtesy of that wonderful desert climate. Day after day this place is turned into one of the water-skiing capitals of America. Some days it can seem like a competition to determine who has the loudest boat. No matter where you access the river, you will share in the happy/wild/nutso romance with the water, where hot sun and speedboats make this a water-ski winner.

Families with youngsters who desire a more quiet pace, perhaps a calm spot where they can play in the water or swim, should head to one of the La Paz county parks.

One of the best spots for big catfish is below Parker Dam, including large flathead catfish and channel catfish. If you catch a razorback sucker, a very rare event, it must released. It is an endangered species.

This place is popular year-round. In the winter, even though temperatures can get pretty cold (around 40 degrees at night) the campgrounds fill because of the yearly migration of snowbirds, retired folks with RVs and trailers who leave the snow country (or the rain country in Oregon and Washington) and spend much of their winter here every year.

Access: Paved boat ramps are provided at the following locations:

• Rockhouse, Arizona: From Vidal Junction turn east on Highway 62 and drive to Earp. Continue straight on Parker Dam Road for nine miles to the BLM ramp. For more information call 928/505-1200.

• Buckskin Mountain State Park, Arizona: From Vidal Junction turn east on Highway 62 and drive to Parker and Arizona Highway 95. Turn north on Arizona Highway 95 and drive approximately 12 miles to the state park entrance. Campground, restrooms with showers, restaurant, convenience store, gas, and swimming beach are available. For more information call 928/667-3231.

• River Island State Park, Arizona: From Vidal Junction turn east on Highway 62 and drive to Parker and Arizona Highway 95. Turn north on Arizona Highway 95 and drive approximately 13.5 miles to the state park entrance. A tent campground and swimming beach are provided. For more information call 928/667-3386.

• La Paz County Park, Arizona: From Vidal Junction turn east on Highway 62 and drive to Parker and Arizona Highway 95. Turn north on Arizona Highway 95 and drive approximately seven miles to Golf Course Drive. Turn left on Golf Course Drive and drive .25 mile to Riverside Drive. Turn right and drive .5 mile to the park entrance on the left. A campground is available. For more information call 928/667-2069.

• Cienega Springs Public Ramp, Arizona: From Vidal Junction, take Highway 62 east to Parker, Arizona, and Business 95. Turn north on Business 95 and drive approximately five miles to Cienega Springs and boat ramp.

• Patria Flats County Park, Arizona: From Vidal Junction, take Highway 62 east to Parker, Arizona, and Business 95. Turn north on Business 95 and drive approximately seven miles to Golf Road. Turn left and drive .25 mile to Riverside Drive. Turn left and drive .5

mile to the park on the right. For more information call 928/667-2069.

• River Land Resort, California: From Vidal Junction, take Highway 62 east to Earp. Continue straight on Parker Dam Road and continue five miles to the resort. A campground, cabins, gas, and convenience store are available. For more information call 760/663-3733, fax 760/663-3203.

Facilities, fees: Campgrounds, resorts, marinas, and supplies are available off Highway 95 near Parker, Arizona. Boats may be rented at resorts on Lake Havasu (see previous listing). A fee is charged for boat launching at resorts and most parks (Rockhouse is an exception).

Water sports, restrictions: Water-skiing, wake boarding, and personal watercraft are permitted. Sailboarding is not recommended. Swimming is available at La Paz County Park, Patria Flats County Park, Buckskin Mountain State Park, and River Island State Park (all in Arizona) and at several undesignated areas along the riverbanks. Canoeists can put in at any of the boat ramps listed.

Note: The Parker Valley portion of the river is part of the Colorado River Indian Reservation, and the tribe requires that all anglers obtain a permit. Permits are available at the tribe's Fish and Game Department in Parker, Arizona, 928/669-9285. Fishing permits can also be obtained at retail outlets and marinas in Ehrenberg, Arizona, and Poston, Arizona, and at two resorts near Blythe, California: Aha Quin Resort, 760/922-3604; Lost Lake Resort, 760/664-4413.

Directions: From Southern California take I-10 east to Blythe and turn north on U.S. 95. Or take Highway 62 east to Vidal Junction at the intersection of U.S. 95 and Highway 62 and turn south on U.S. 95. There are numerous access points off U.S. 95 between Blythe and Vidal Junction in the Parker Valley area. To reach the Parker Dam section of the river, drive about 20 miles east of Vidal Junction on Highway 62 (crossing the Colorado River) to the town of Parker. From Parker, Arizona, turn north on either U.S. 95 or Parker Dam Road (in California, before crossing the California side of the river). Numerous access points are available off these roads.

From Northern California, drive south on U.S. 395 to I-15. Turn south on I-15 and drive to I-10. Turn east on I-10 and drive to Blythe. Turn north on U.S. 95 or turn north off I-10 on Highway 62 near Palm Springs and continue northeast to Vidal Junction at the intersection of U.S. 95 and Highway 62. Turn south on U.S. 95. There are numerous access points off U.S. 95 between Blythe and Vidal Junction in the Parker Valley area. To reach the Parker Dam section of the river, drive about 20 miles east of Vidal Junction on Highway 62 to the town of Parker, Arizona. From Parker, turn north on either U.S. 95 or Parker Dam Road (in California). Numerous access points are available off these roads.

Contact: Parker Area Chamber of Commerce, 928/669-2174; Bureau of Land Management, Lake Havasu Field Office, 928/505-1200, La Paz County, Arizona, 928/669-6115.

7 LAKE CAHUILLA

Rating: 5

near Indio in Lake Cahuilla County Park

Map 15.5, page 454

What a place. If it weren't for this little patch of water, there would be times when it would be quite appropriate to put up a sign on I-10 that says, "You are now entering hell."

Temperatures are commonly in the 100-degree range, and the desert winds can blow at gale force.

Lake Cahuilla covers just 135 acres, but those are the most important acres in the entire region. The park here—complete with large, shady palm trees—offers a bit of relief from the heat. The lake has 3.5 miles of shoreline. No swimming is permitted.

Boating is strictly small-time. Only car-top boats may be used, and the 10-mph speed limit keeps things quiet.

Sailboarding conditions can be good in the late fall, but the wind is often too strong in the spring for decent sailboard prospects.

In the winter, the lake is stocked with trout. In summer, it is stocked with catfish. A resident bass population manages to sustain itself. If you find yourself out this way during the winter, a good side trip is to Joshua Tree National Park to the northeast.

The place gets a lot of use in the winter season, but because of very hot weather, is very quiet in summer and early fall.

Access: A primitive hand-launch ramp is located on the west shore.

Facilities, fees: A campground, picnic areas, restrooms with showers, and flush toilets, RV dump station, and swimming pool are available. Supplies can be obtained in Indio. A fee is charged for day use and camping.

Water sports, restrictions: Gas-powered motors are not permitted on the lake. A 10-mph speed limit is strictly enforced. Sailing and sailboarding are permitted. No swimming.

Directions: Drive on I-10 to Indio and the exit for Monroe Street. Take that exit and drive south on Monroe Street to Avenue 58. Turn right and drive three miles to the park at the end of the road.

Contact: Lake Cahuilla County Park, 760/564-4712, fax 760/564-2506, website: www.riversidecountyparks.org; camping reservations at 800/234-7275.

8 SALTON SEA

Rating: 7

east of San Diego

Map 15.6, page 455

Some people pray for love. Some people pray for riches. At the Salton Sea you pray for the wind not to blow in the spring, and for it not to be too hot in the summer and fall.

This vast water covering 360 square miles is set at 228 feet below sea level. The nearby mountain range is stark and reaches up to 10,000 feet, creating an eerie backdrop.

When you first arrive at the Salton Sea, it appears to be a desolate, godforsaken wasteland. The lake is 35 miles long but has an average depth of just 15 feet. Nothingness surrounds you for miles in all directions. When the wind blows, there's no obstacle to slow it down, and it can howl across the water, whipping up large waves that are dangerous to boaters. To help alert boaters when hazardous winds are in the offing, local authorities have posted a flashing red light on the northeast shore that warns boaters to get off the lake. Sailing and sailboarding are not popular because the winds can be too powerful, even dangerous.

Damn, it's hot—terrible at times. But the climate is balmy in winter, spring, and fall. In addition to the weird setting, scorching temperatures, and occasional frothing winds, this lake is known for being a good place to fish for corvina, a warmish spot for camping in the winter, and an odd place to go swimming.

Since the water is, for the most part, quite shallow, boaters who aren't used to the place should be aware of unmarked underwater obstacles located at the lake's far north and south ends, which can pose navigational hazards.

Most of the boaters here are fishermen casting about for corvina, and they rarely have any unusual problems. Other species include tilapia, sargo, and croaker. Fishing is often good for corvina and croaker.

This is also one of Southern California's most popular boating areas. Because of the low elevation, the corresponding barometric pressure allows high performance for powerboats.

Salton Sea is not only visually unique, it is an extremely unusual place to swim. Because of the water's high salinity level, swimmers kind of bob around effortlessly, their buoyancy obviously boosted by all the salt. It is possible to swim pretty much anywhere on the east and west shores, but note that some areas on the west shore tend to be more mud than sand. Yeah, right, very ugly.

Use is moderate at Salton Sea year-round, but is lowest in the summer and highest in the winter, when quite a few retirees make the trip in order to take advantage of the temperate off-season climate. Other activities in the area include golfing, bird-watching, and hiking.

The Salton Sea was created in 1905 when a dike broke and the basin was flooded with saltwater. This is one of the world's true inland seas. It is about a three hour drive from the Los Angeles Basin.

When it gets really hot here in the summer, with the mercury hovering in the 110-degree range for days in a row, you may think you are in hell—and you might be right.

Access: Boat ramps are available at the following locations:

• Desert Shores Trailer Park (west shore): From Indio, take Highway 86 Expressway south and drive 30 miles to Desert Shores. For more information call 760/395-5280.

• Red Hill County Park (east shore): From Mecca, drive south on Highway 111 to Niland, and continue to Sinclair Road. Turn right and drive 3.5 miles to Garst Road. Turn right and drive 1.5 miles to the end of Garst Road at Red Hill Road. Turn left on Red Hill Road and drive to the park at the end of the road. For more information call 760/348-2310 or Imperial County, 760/482-4384.

• Salton Sea Beach Marina (east shore): From Indio, take Highway 86 Expressway south and drive to Salton Sea Beach and Brawley Avenue. Turn right and drive to Santa Rosa Street. Turn left and drive two blocks to Coachella. Turn right and drive one block to the marina. For more information call 760/395-1066.

• Salton Sea State Recreation Area (west shore): From Mecca, drive south on Highway 111 for about 12 miles to the headquarters campground. A boat ramp is available. For more information call 760/393-3052 or 760/393-3059.

• West Shores RV Park (west shore): From Indio, take Highway 86 Expressway south and drive to Salton City and North Marina Drive. Turn left and drive two miles to Sea Garden and the sign for Johnson's Landing. Turn left and drive .3 mile to the resort at the end of the road. For more information call 760/394-4755.

• Bombay Beach Marina (east shore): From Mecca, drive south on Highway 111 for about 25 miles to the exit for Bombay Beach campground (in Salton Sea State Recreation Area) and the Bombay Beach Marina (located next to the rec area). Turn right and drive a short distance to the boat launch. For more information call 760/354-4049.

Facilities, fees: Campgrounds, marinas, picnic areas, lodging, bait and tackle, restaurants, and groceries are available. No boat rentals. Fees are charged for day use, boat launching, and camping.

Water sports, restrictions: Powerboats, waterskiing, wake boarding, personal watercraft, sailing, and sailboarding are permitted. Swimming is available anywhere around the lake; a good spot is Mecca Beach in Salton Sea State Recreation Area.

Directions: From the Los Angeles area, take I-10 east to Indio and the exit for the Highway 86 Expressway. Take that exit and drive south for 12 miles to 66th Avenue. Turn left and drive less than one mile to Mecca and Highway 111. Turn right (south) and drive 12 miles to the Salton Sea.

Contact: Salton Sea State Recreation Area, 760/393-3052 or 760/393-3059; Salton Sea West Shore Chamber of Commerce, 760/394-4112 (or resorts listed above).

9 RAMER LAKE

Rating: 4

near Calipatria in the Imperial Wildlife Area

Map 15.6, page 455

Almost nobody knows about little Ramer Lake—nobody, that is, except for a few duck hunters. The lake is located in the Imperial Wildlife Area, which provides waterfowl habitat and duck-hunting grounds during the winter. The rest of the year it is largely ignored, attracting only a handful of folks who fish the lake for bass, catfish, and carp.

Set in the Imperial Valley, Ramer is sur-

rounded by farmland and is overshadowed by the massive Salton Sea to the near north. You must register at the entrance station, then leave a written record of anything you've caught because it is part of the wildlife area.

There is not much in the area except for this little fishing pond. Wildlife lovers are welcome to toss in a canoe and paddle around, using their binoculars to look for birds. Hiking trails and nature-study sites are available in the wildlife area.

Access: A paved ramp is located on the east shore of the lake.

Facilities, fees: Chemical toilets are provided. No drinking water is available. A campground is available to the south at Wiest Lake. Supplies can be obtained in Calipatria and Brawley. Access to the lake is free.

Water sports, restrictions: Motorized boats are not permitted. All water/body contact sports are prohibited.

Directions: From Brawley, drive north on Highway 111 toward Calipatria and the signed turn on the right for Imperial Wildlife Area (five miles before reaching Calipatria). Turn right and continue to the lake.

Contact: Department of Fish & Game, Imperial Wildlife Area, 760/359-0577 or 760/348-2493.

10 WIEST LAKE

Rating: 6

south of Calipatria in Wiest Lake County Park

Map 15.6, page 455

Wiest Lake is a little lake, just 50 acres, about .3 mile across. It is set at 110 feet below sea level amid desolate country that is scorching hot much of the year. Because there is not much else around, this place can seem almost like an oasis. The Salton sea is about a 20-minute drive to the northwest.

The lake is filled by the All American Canal (via the Colorado River), and despite its small size it is actually a pretty fair setting for water-skiing. Sailboarding conditions can be excellent, though relatively few sailboarders take advantage of it.

Use is moderate in spring, fall, and winter, and very light in summer when scorching temperatures keep away all but the most desperate vacationers. Arrive then and you'll begin to feel kind of like an iguana. Arrive in the spring and you'll get the chance to have some good times.

The Department of Fish and Game plants trout here in winter and catfish in summer. The lake also has bass and bluegill.

Access: A paved boat ramp is located on the lake's east side.

Facilities, fees: A campground, restroom with flush toilets and showers, picnic areas, and RV dump station are available. A store, coin laundry, and propane gas are nearby. A fee is charged for day use and includes boat launching.

Water sports, restrictions: Water-skiing, wake boarding, personal watercraft, sailing, sailboarding, and swimming are allowed. A beach with a designated swimming area is located on the southeast shore, near the campground. No alcoholic beverages are permitted.

Directions: From El Centro, drive north on Highway 111 to Brawley and Highway 78/Main Street. Turn west (left) on Highway 78/Main Street and drive a short distance to Highway 111. Turn right (north) on Highway 111 and drive four miles to Rutherford Road (well signed). Turn right (east) and drive two miles to the park entrance on the right.

Contact: Wiest Lake County Park, 760/344-3712; Imperial County, 760/482-4384.

11 COLORADO RIVER (PALO VERDE DAM TO YUMA, ARIZONA)

Rating: 9

near Yuma, Arizona

Map 15.7, page 456

This region of the Colorado River is way out in the middle of nowhere, and to get here you have to want it. And plenty of people want it. Despite the limited services in many areas, the campgrounds and boat launches are packed on summer and holiday weekends, and there are an impressive number of winter vacationers who flock here. You should always carry a good supply of water with you when visiting this area.

The main activities here are powerboating and fishing and the conditions are good for both. Water-skiing and personal watercraft are allowed on most portions of the Colorado River, with exceptions in some of the national wildlife refuges. These refuges, in turn, are ideal for fishing, canoeing, kayaking, and solitude. Note that hunting is allowed in the refuges during season. Swimming conditions are generally not good in this lower stretch of the Colorado River because so many of the banks have been cut to force the river in one direction or another. This raping of the land created a landscape and conditions nothing like that of a hundred years ago. To see what the river looked like long ago, visit the refuges where work is ongoing to restore habitat. Here you'll find mass wintering grounds for waterfowl traveling along the Pacific Flyway, along with a few bighorn sheep, wild burros, coyotes, and reptiles.

In the Blythe-Palo Verde area, this span of water is flanked by agricultural areas, although several developed recreation areas and county parks are on the California side of the river near Palo Verde. Most visitor accommodations are found in the Blythe area. The fishing is fair, with striped bass, largemouth bass, bluegill, crappie, and catfish roaming the area.

On the Yuma-Winterhaven stretch of river, located farther south, of course, it is less developed than the Palo Verde area. Some areas are marshy. For anglers, there are some big catfish roaming these water, along with small largemouth bass and a sprinkling of bluegill. Martinez Lake, created by the construction of the Imperial Dam, is the best spot for catfish. By canoe, you can gain access to several small backwater lakes here.

Access: Paved boat ramps are provided at the following locations:

• Oxbow Campground, California: Drive on I-10 to Highway 78 (two miles west of Blythe). Take Highway 78 south and drive to Palo Verde. Continue three miles south to a gravel road signed "Colorado River." Turn east (left) and drive .75 mile to the campground and boat launch. Boat launch, boat trailer parking, campground, and vault toilets. A bridge crosses the river. Off-channel boat ramp with access to the Colorado River. Bureau of Land Management, Yuma Field Office, 520/317-3200.

• Palo Verde County Park, California: Drive on I-10 to Highway 78 (two miles west of Blythe). Take Highway 78 south and drive about 20 miles (past Palo Verde) to the park entrance road. Boat ramp, restrooms with flush toilets, and campground are available. No drinking water. Imperial County, 760/482-4384.

• Picacho State Recreation Area, California: From El Centro, drive east on I-8 to Winterhaven and the exit for Winterhaven/4th Avenue. Take that exit to 4th Avenue. Turn left and drive .5 mile to County Road S24/Picacho Road. Turn right and drive 18 miles (crossing rail tracks, a railroad bridge, and the American Canal, the road becoming dirt) to the campground. The road is not suitable for large RVs. The drive takes one hour from Winterhaven. In summer, thunderstorms can cause flash flooding, making short sections of the road impassable. Two boat ramps, a campground, three boat-in campsites, drinking water, pit toilets, solar showers, RV dump station, and camp store are available. Picacho State Recreation Area, c/o Salton Sea State Recreation Area, 760/393-3059 or 760/996-2963 (reservations); California State Parks, Colorado Desert District, 760/767-5311.

• Imperial National Wildlife Refuge, Arizona: From Yuma, Arizona, drive north on Highway 95 for 25 miles to Martinez Lake Road. Turn west (left) and drive 13 miles to the lake and visitor center. The boat launch is located on the north side of the lake at Meers Point. Direct access to the Colorado River is available. A boat launch, day-use area, and toilets are available. For more information call 928/783-3371.

• Senator Wash Recreation Area, California: Drive on I-8 to Yuma, Arizona, and the exit for 4th Avenue. Take that exit and drive to Imperial Highway/County Road S24. Turn north and drive 22 miles to Senator Wash Road. Turn left and drive four miles to the day-use boat launch area. Day-use area provides restrooms with flush toilets, outdoor showers, drinking water, buoyed swimming area, and boat-in access to campgrounds at North Shore and South Shore. No direct boat access to the Colorado River. Bureau of Land Management, Yuma Field Office, 520/317-3200.

• Squaw Lake, California: Drive on I-8 to Yuma, Arizona, and the exit for 4th Avenue. Take that exit and drive to Imperial Highway/County Road S24. Turn north and drive 22 miles to Senator Wash Road. Turn left and drive about four miles (well signed) to the lake. Two boat ramps, boat trailer parking, two buoyed swimming area, campgrounds, restrooms with flush toilets, outdoor showers, drinking water at central location, RV dump station, and hiking trail. Direct access to the Colorado River with a 5-mph speed limit (no wake zone) at Squaw Lake.

Facilities, fees: Campgrounds, resorts, marinas, and supplies are available near Palo Verde, Picacho State Recreation Area, and Senator Wash Recreation Area in California, and near Yuma, Arizona. A fee is charged for day use and/or boat launching at resorts and most parks.

Water sports, restrictions: Sailboarding is not recommended. Water-skiing, wake boarding, and personal watercraft are permitted in many areas of this stretch of the Colorado River, including the Picacho State Recreation Area. Water-skiing and personal watercraft are prohibited below the Imperial Dam and in the Imperial National Wildlife Refuge and certain portions of the Cibola National Wildlife Refuge (the Old River Channel, Cibola Lake, Three Fingers Lake, and all backwaters). Portions of the Cibola National Wildlife Refuge are closed from Labor Day to March 15 to protect wintering waterfowl. A 5-mph speed limit is enforced at Squaw Lake. Swimming beaches are available at Squaw Lake, Senator Wash Recreation Area, Picacho State Recreation Area, and at undesignated areas along the riverbanks.

Directions: From Southern California take I-10 east to the Blythe area and turn south on Highway 78. There are access points off Highway 78 between Blythe and the Palo Verde area. You can also take I-8 east to Highway 78 North or Highway 267 North, or continue past the town of Winterhaven on I-8 to Yuma, Arizona, and river access there. See Access for details.

Contact: Bureau of Land Management, Yuma Field Office, 520/317-3200, or any of the parks and refuges listed under Access above.

12 SUNBEAM LAKE/LAGOON

Rating: 6

near El Centro

Map 15.8, page 457

Sunbeam Lake is an oasis in desert-like country—the lake is even surrounded by palm trees. This popular little lake has three miles of shoreline and a lagoon that is about half the size of the lake.

It is operated by Imperial County and open year-round. The lagoon is primarily for fishing, while recreational boaters and swimmers use Sunbeam Lake. All water sports are allowed at the lake, including swimming (when lifeguards are present).

The lagoon is stocked with rainbow trout in the winter months and catfish during the summer. Other species occasionally caught are largemouth bass, bluegill, crappie, and carp.

Temperatures are pleasant in the fall, winter, and spring. But in the summer, the average temperature is over 100 degrees—and everybody heads to Sunbeam to take a dunk and try to cool off. The lake is below sea level.

Access: Paved boat ramps are available on the south side of the lake at the Imperial County Park and at the northwest end of the lagoon (adjacent to Sunbeam Lake).

Facilities, fees: Picnic areas, restrooms with flush toilets, drinking water, and swimming beach are available at Imperial County Park. An RV resort is nearby. Supplies available in El Centro. Fees are charged for day use and boat launching.

Water sports, restrictions: Powerboats, water-skiing, wake boarding, personal watercraft, canoes, kayaks, inflatables, sailing, and sailboarding are permitted at Sunbeam Lake (powerboats and personal watercraft are permitted only on the east side of the lake). Sailing, sailboarding, canoes, kayaks, and inflatables are permitted at the lagoon (no gas motors). Swimming is permitted when lifeguards are on duty. No alcoholic beverages. The lake is open year-round from sunrise to 10 P.M.; the lagoon is open from sunrise to sunset.

Directions: From El Centro, drive west on I-8 for seven miles to the exit for Drew Road. Take that exit and drive north on Drew Road for .5 mile to the county park entrance on the left.

Contact: Imperial County Parks & Recreation, El Centro, 760/482-4384; Sunbeam Lake RV Resort, 760/352-7154 or 800/900-7154.

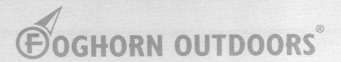
FOGHORN OUTDOORS®

© ROBERT HOLMES/CALTOUR

Resources

Resources

National Forests

The Forest Service provides many secluded camps and allows camping anywhere except where it is specifically prohibited. A permit is required when camping in designated wilderness areas; this permit doubles as a campfire permit. If you ever want to clear the cobwebs from your head and get away from it all, this is the way to go.

Many Forest Service campgrounds are quite remote and have no drinking water. You usually don't need to check in or make reservations, and sometimes, there is no fee. At many Forest Service campgrounds that provide drinking water, the camping fee is often only a few dollars, with payment made on the honor system. Because most of these camps are in mountain areas, they are subject to winter closure because of snow or mud.

Dogs are usually permitted in national forests with no extra charge and no hassle. Leashes are required for all dogs in some places. Always carry documentation of current vaccinations.

National Forest Adventure Pass

Angeles, Cleveland, Los Padres, and San Bernardino National Forests require an Adventure Pass for each parked vehicle. Daily passes cost $5; annual passes are available for $30. Adventure Passes can be purchased at national forest offices in Southern California and dozens of retail outlets and online vendors. The new charges are use fees, not entrance fees. Holders of Golden Age, Golden Access, and Golden Eagle passports can use these cards in lieu of purchasing an Adventure Pass.

When you purchase an annual Adventure Pass, you can also buy a secondary annual Adventure Pass for $5. Major credit cards are accepted at most retail and online outlets, but not at Forest Service offices. Adventure Passes can be purchased by telephone at 909/382-2622, or by mail at San Bernardino National Forest, Fee Project Headquarters, 1824 S. Commercenter Circle, San Bernardino, CA 92408-3430. Checks should be made payable to USDA Forest Service.

You will not need an Adventure Pass while traveling through these forests nor when you've paid other types of fees such as camping or ski pass fees. However, if you are camping in these forests and you leave the campground in your vehicle and park outside of the campground for recreation purposes, such as at a trailhead, day-use area, near a fishing stream, etc., you will need an Adventure Pass for your vehicle. You also need an Adventure Pass if camping at a no-fee campground. More information about the Adventure Pass program, including a listing of retail and online vendors, can be obtained by checking the website www.fsadventurepass.org.

National Forest Maps

National Forest maps are among the best you can get for the price. They detail all backcountry streams, lakes, hiking trails, and logging roads for access. They typically cost $6, sometimes more for wilderness maps, and can be obtained in person at Forest Service offices, or by contacting U.S. Forest Service, Attn: Map Sales, P.O. Box 9035, Prescott, AZ 86313, tel. 928/443-8285, fax 928/443-8207, or website: www.fs.fed.us/recreation/nationalforeststore. Major credit cards are accepted if ordering by telephone.

Forest Service Information

Forest Service personnel are most helpful for obtaining camping, hiking, boating, or fishing information. Unless you are buying a map or Adventure Pass, it is advisable to phone to get the best service. For specific information on a national forest, contact the following offices:

USDA Forest Service
Pacific Southwest Region
1323 Club Drive
Vallejo, CA 94592
707/562-USFS (707/562-8737)
website: www.fs.fed.us/r5

Angeles National Forest
701 N. Santa Anita Avenue
Arcadia, CA 91006
626/574-1613
fax 626/574-5233
website: www.fs.fed.us/r5/angeles

Cleveland National Forest
10845 Rancho Bernardo Road, Ste. 200
San Diego, CA 92127-2107
858/673-6180
fax 858/673-6192
website: www.fs.fed.us/r5/cleveland

Eldorado National Forest
100 Forni Road
Placerville, CA 95667
530/622-5061 or 530/644-6048
fax 530/621-5297
website: www.fs.fed.us/r5/eldorado

Humboldt-Toiyabe National Forest
1200 Franklin Way
Sparks, NV 89431
775/331-6444
fax 775/355-5399
website: www.fs.fed.us/htnf

Inyo National Forest
351 Pacu Lane, Ste. 200
Bishop, CA 93514
760/873-2400
fax 760/873-2458
website: www.fs.fed.us/r5/inyo

Klamath National Forest
1312 Fairlane Road
Yreka, CA 96097-9549
530/842-6131
fax 530/841-4571
website: www.fs.fed.us/r5/klamath

Lake Tahoe Basin Management Unit
35 College Drive
South Lake Tahoe, CA 96150
530/543-2600
fax 530/543-2693
website: www.fs.fed.us/r5/ltbmu

Lassen National Forest
2550 Riverside Drive
Susanville, CA 96130
530/257-2151
fax 530/ 252-6428
website: www.fs.fed.us/r5/lassen

Los Padres National Forest
6755 Hollister Avenue, Suite 150
Goleta, CA 93117
805/968-6640
fax 805/961-5729
website: www.fs.fed.us/r5/lospadres

Mendocino National Forest
825 N. Humboldt Avenue
Willows, CA 95988
530/934-3316
fax 530/934-7384
website: www.fs.fed.us/r5/mendocino

Modoc National Forest
800 W. 12th Street
Alturas, CA 96101
530/233-5811
fax 530/233-8709
website: www.fs.fed.us/r5/modoc

Plumas National Forest
P.O. Box 11500
159 Lawrence Street
Quincy, CA 95971
530/283-2050
fax 530/283-7746
website: www.fs.fed.us/r5/plumas

San Bernardino National Forest
1824 Commercenter Circle
San Bernardino, CA 92408-3430
909/383-5588
fax 909/383-5770
website: www.fs.fed.us/r5/sanbernardino

Sequoia National Forest
Giant Sequoia National Monument
900 W. Grand Avenue
Porterville, CA 93257
559/784-1500
fax 559/781-4744
website: www.fs.fed.us/r5/sequoia

Shasta-Trinity National Forest
2400 Washington Avenue
Redding, CA 96001
530/244-2978
fax 530/242-2233
website: www.fs.fed.us/r5/shastatrinity

Sierra National Forest
1600 Tollhouse Road
Clovis, CA 93611-0532
559/297-0706
fax 559/294-4809
website: www.fs.fed.us/r5/sierra

Six Rivers National Forest
1330 Bayshore Way
Eureka, CA 95501
707/442-1721
fax 707/442-9242
website: www.fs.fed.us/r5/sixrivers

Stanislaus National Forest
19777 Greenley Road
Sonora, CA 95370
209/532-3671
fax 209/533-1890
website: www.fs.fed.us/r5/stanislaus

Tahoe National Forest
631 Coyote Street
Nevada City, CA 95959
530/265-4531
fax 530/478-6109
website: www.fs.fed.us/r5/tahoe
or
Big Bend Visitor Center
49685 Hampshire Rocks Road
Soda Springs, CA 95728
530/426-3609
fax 530/426-1744

State Parks

The California State Parks system provides many popular camping spots in spectacular settings. These campgrounds include drive-in numbered sites, tent spaces, and picnic tables, with showers and restrooms provided nearby. Reservations are often necessary during the summer months. Although many parks are well known, there are still some little-known gems in the state parks system where campers can enjoy seclusion, even in the summer.

California Department of Parks and Recreation
Communications Office
P.O. Box 942896
Sacramento, CA 94296
800/777-0369 or 916/653-6995
fax 916/654-6374
website: www.parks.ca.gov

National Parks

California's national parks are natural wonders, ranging from the spectacular yet crowded Yosemite Valley to the remote and rugged Lava Beds National Monument. Reservations for campsites are available five months in advance for many of the national parks in California. In addition to campground fees, expect to pay a park entrance fee ranging from $5 to $20 per vehicle (you can buy a National Parks Pass or Golden Eagle annual pass that waives entrance fees). This entrance fee is valid for seven days. Various discounts are available for holders of Golden Age and Golden Access passports, including a 50 percent reduction of camping (group camps not included), parking, boating, and swimming fees and a waiver of park entrance fees. For information about the National Parks Pass, telephone 888/467-2757 (GO-PARKS) or visit the website: www.nationalparks.org.

National Park Service
Pacific West Region
One Jackson Center
111 Jackson Street, Suite 700
Oakland, CA 94607
510/817-1300
website: www.nps.gov

Cabrillo National Monument
1800 Cabrillo Memorial Drive
San Diego, CA 92106-3601
619/557-5450 or 619/222-8211
fax 619/557-5469
website: www.nps.gov/cabr

Channel Islands National Park
1901 Spinnaker Drive
Ventura, CA 93001

805/658-5730
fax 805/658-5799
website: www.nps.gov/chis

Death Valley National Park
P.O. Box 579
Death Valley, CA 92328-0579
760/786-3200
fax 760/786-3283
website: www.nps.gov/deva

Devils Postpile National Monument
P.O. Box 3999
Mammoth Lakes, CA 93546
760/934-2289 in summer only
559/565-3341 year-round
website: www.nps.gov/depo

Golden Gate National Recreation Area
Fort Mason, Building 201
San Francisco, CA 94123-0022
415/561-4700
fax 415/561-4750
website: www.nps.gov/goga

Joshua Tree National Park
74485 National Park Drive
Twentynine Palms, CA 92277-3597
760/367-5500
fax 760/367-6392
website: www.nps.gov/jotr

Lassen Volcanic National Park
P.O. Box 100
Mineral, CA 96063-0100
530/595-4444
fax 530/595-3262
website: www.nps.gov/lavo

Lava Beds National Monument
1 Indian Well Headquarters
Tulelake, CA 96134
530/667-2282
fax 530/667-2737
website: www.nps.gov/labe

Mojave National Preserve
222 E. Main St., Ste. 202
Barstow, CA 92311
760/255-8800 or 760/733-4040
fax 760/255-8809
website: www.nps.gov/moja

Pinnacles National Monument
5000 Highway 146
Paicines, CA 95043
831/389-4485
fax 831/389-4489
website: www.nps.gov/pinn

Point Reyes National Seashore
Point Reyes, CA 94956-9799
415/464-5100
fax 415/663-8132
website: www.nps.gov/pore

Redwood National and State Parks
1111 Second Street
Crescent City, CA 95531
707/464-6101
fax 707/464-1812
website: www.nps.gov/redw

Santa Monica Mountains National Recreation Area
401 W. Hillcrest Drive
Thousand Oaks, CA 91360
805/370-2300 or 805/370-2301
fax 805/370-1850
website: www.nps.gov/samo

Sequoia and Kings Canyon National Parks
47050 Generals Highway
Three Rivers, CA 93271-9651
559/565-3341 or 559/335-2856
fax 559/565-3730
website: www.nps.gov/seki

Smith River National Recreation Area
P.O. Box 228
10600 Highway 199 North
Gasquet, CA 95543
707/457-3131
fax 707/457-3794

Whiskeytown National Recreation Area
P.O. Box 188
14412 Kennedy Memorial Drive
Whiskeytown, CA 96095
530/246-1225 or 530/242-3400
fax 530/246-5154
website: www.nps.gov/whis

Yosemite National Park
P.O. Box 577
Yosemite National Park, CA 95389
209/372-0200 for 24-hour recorded message
fax 209/372-0220
website: www.nps.gov/yose

Bureau of Land Management

Most of the areas managed by the BLM are primitive and in remote areas. Parking and access are usually free. Often there is also no fee charged for camping. Holders of Golden Age or Golden Access passports receive a 50 percent discount, except for group camps, at BLM fee campgrounds.

Bureau of Land Management
California State Office
2800 Cottage Way, Room W-1834
Sacramento, CA 95825-1886
916/978-4400
website: www.ca.blm.gov

Alturas Field Office
708 W. 12th Street
Alturas, CA 96101
530/233-4666
fax 530/233-5696
website: www.ca.blm.gov/alturas

Arcata Field Office
1695 Heindon Road
Arcata, CA 95521-4573
707/825-2300
fax 707/825-2301
website: www.ca.blm.gov/arcata

Bakersfield Field Office
3801 Pegasus Drive
Bakersfield, CA 93308
661/391-6000
fax 661/391-6040
website: www.ca.blm.gov/bakersfield

Barstow Field Office
2601 Barstow Road
Barstow, CA 92311
760/252-6000
fax 760/252-6098
website: www.ca.blm.gov/barstow

Bishop Field Office
351 Pacu Ln., Ste. 100
Bishop, CA 93514
760/872-5000
fax 760/872-5050
website: www.ca.blm.gov/bishop

California Desert District Office
22835 Calle San Juan De Los Lagos
Moreno Valley, CA 92553
909/697-5200
fax 909/697-5296
website: www.ca.blm.gov/cdd

Eagle Lake Field Office
2950 Riverside Drive
Susanville, CA 96130
530/257-0456
fax 530/257-4831
website: www.ca.blm.gov/eaglelake

El Centro Field Office
1661 S. 4th Street
El Centro, CA 92243
760/337-4400
fax 760/337-4490
website: www.ca.blm.gov/elcentro

Folsom Field Office
63 Natoma Street
Folsom, CA 95630
916/985-4474
fax 916/985-3259
website: www.ca.blm.gov/folsom

Hollister Field Office
20 Hamilton Court
Hollister, CA 95023
831/630-5000
fax 831/630-5055
website: www.ca.blm.gov/hollister

Palm Springs/South Coast Field Office
690 W. Garnet Avenue
North Palm Springs, CA 92258-1260
760/251-4800
fax 760/251-4899
website: ca.blm.gov/palmsprings

Redding Field Office
355 Hemsted Drive
Redding, CA 96002
530/224-2100
fax 530/224-2172
website: www.ca.blm.gov/redding

Ridgecrest Field Office
300 S. Richmond Road
Ridgecrest, CA 93555

760/384-5400
fax 760/384-5499
website: www.ca.blm.gov/ridgecrest

Ukiah Field Office
2550 N. State Street
Ukiah, CA 95482
707/468-4000
fax 707/468-4027
website: www.ca.blm.gov/ukiah

U.S. Army Corps of Engineers

Some of the family camps and most of the group camps operated by the U.S. Army Corps of Engineers are on a reservation system. Reservations can be made up to 240 days in advance, and up to 360 days in advance for groups. To reserve a site, call 877/444-6777 or visit the website: www.reserveusa.com. Major credit cards are accepted. Holders of Golden Age or Golden Access passports receive a 50 percent discount on campground fees, except for group sites.

U.S. Army Corps of Engineers
Los Angeles District
911 Wilshire Boulevard
Los Angeles, CA 90017-3401
213/452-3908
website: www.spl.usace.army.mil

U.S. Army Corps of Engineers
Sacramento District
1325 J Street

Sacramento, CA 95814-2922
916/557-5100
website: www.spk.usace.army.mil

U.S. Army Corps of Engineers
South Pacific Division/San Francisco District
333 Market Street
San Francisco, CA 94105
415/977-8272
website: www.spn.usace.army.mil

Other Valuable Resources

State Forests
Jackson Demonstration State Forest
802 N. Main Street
Fort Bragg, CA 95437
707/964-5674
fax 707/964-0941

Mountain Home Demonstration State Forest
P.O. Box 517
Springville, CA 93265
559/539-2321 (summer) or
 559/539-2855 (winter)

County/Regional Park Departments
Del Norte County Parks
840 9th Street, Suite 11
Crescent City, CA 95531
707/464-7230
fax 707/464-5824

East Bay Regional Park District
2950 Peralta Oaks Court
P.O. Box 5381
Oakland, CA 94605-0381
510/562-PARK (562-7275) or 510/544-2200
fax 510/635-3478
website: www.ebparks.org

Humboldt County Parks
1106 2nd Street
Eureka, CA 95501
707/445-7651
fax 707/445-7409

Marin Municipal Water District
220 Nellen Avenue
Corte Madera, CA 94925
415/945-1455
website: www.marinwater.org

Midpeninsula Regional Open Space District
330 Distel Circle
Los Altos, CA 94022-1404
650/691-1200
fax 650/691-0485
website: www.openspace.org

Monterey County Parks Department
855 E. Laurel, Bldg. G
P.O. Box 5249
Salinas, CA 93915
831/755-4895
fax 831/755-4914
website: www.co.monterey.ca.us/parks

Orange County Harbors, Beaches, and Parks
1 Irvine Park Road
Orange, CA 92869
866/627-2757
website: www.ocparks.com

Pacific Gas and Electric Company
FERC/Land Projects
2730 Gateway Oaks, Ste. 220
Sacramento, CA 95833
916/386-5164
fax 916/923-7044
website: www.pge.com/recreation

Sacramento County Parks and Recreation Division
4040 Bradshaw Road
Sacramento, CA 95827
916/875-6961
website: www.sacparks.org

San Diego County Parks and Recreation Department
5201 Ruffin Road, Ste. P
San Diego, CA 92123
858/694-3049
website: www.sdparks.org

San Luis Obispo County Parks
1087 Santa Rosa Street
San Luis Obispo, CA 93408
805/781-5930
fax 805/781-1102
website: www.slocountyparks.com

San Mateo County Parks and Recreation
455 County Center, 4th Floor
Redwood City, CA 94063-1646
650/363-4020
fax 650/599-1721
website: www.eparks.net

Santa Barbara County Parks
610 Mission Canyon Rd.
Santa Barbara, CA 93105
805/568-2461
fax 805/568-2459
website: www.sbparks.com

Santa Clara County Parks and Recreation Department
298 Garden Hill Drive
Los Gatos, CA 95032-7669
408/355-2200
fax 408/355-2290
website: www.parkhere.org

Sonoma County Regional Parks
2300 County Center Drive, Ste. 120A
Santa Rosa, CA 95403
707/565-2041
fax 707/579-8247
website: www.sonoma-county.org/parks

State and Federal Offices

**California Department of
Boating and Waterways**
2000 Evergreen Street, Ste. 100
Sacramento, CA 95815-3888
916/263-1331
website: http://dbw.ca.gov

California Department of Fish and Game
1416 Ninth Street, 12th Floor
Sacramento, CA 95814
916/445-0411
fax 916/653-1856
website: www.dfg.ca.gov

California Department of Water Resources
1416 9th Street
P.O. Box 942836
Sacramento, CA 94236
916/653-6192
website: http://wwwdwr.water.ca.gov

U.S. Fish and Wildlife Service
1849 C Street NW
Washington, D.C. 20240
202/208-4131 or 800/344-WILD (344-9453)
website: www.fws.gov

U.S. Geological Survey
Branch of Information Services
P.O. Box 25286, Federal Center
Denver, CO 80225
303/202-4700 or 888/ASK-USGS
(888/275-8747)
website: www.usgs.gov

Information Services

Lake County Visitor Information Center
6110 East Highway 20
P.O. Box 1025
Lucerne, CA 95458
707/274-5652 or 800/525-3743
fax 707/263-9564
website: www.lakecounty.com

Mammoth Lakes Visitors Bureau
437 Old Mammoth Road, Ste. Y
P.O. Box 48
Mammoth Lakes, CA 93546
760/934-2712 or 888/GO-MAMMOTH
(888/466-2666)
fax 760/934-7066
website: www.visitmammoth.com

**Mount Shasta Chamber of Commerce
and Visitors Bureau**
300 Pine Street
Mount Shasta, CA 96067
530/397-1519 or 800/397-1519
website: www.mtshastachamber.com

The Nature Conservancy
California Chapter
201 Mission Street, 4th Floor
San Francisco, CA 94105-1832
415/777-0487
fax 415/777-0244
website: www.tnccalifornia.org

Plumas County Visitors Bureau
550 Crescent St.
P.O. Box 4120
Quincy, CA 95971
530/283-6345 or 800/326-2247
website: www.plumascounty.org

Shasta-Cascade Wonderland Association
1699 Highway 273
Anderson, CA 96007
530/365-7500 or 800/474-2782
website: www.shastacascade.org

Map Resources

Earthwalk Press
5432 La Jolla Hermosa Avenue
La Jolla, CA 92037
800/828-MAPS (800/828-6277)

Map Center
1995 University Ave., Ste. 117
Berkeley, CA 94704
510/841-6277
fax 510/841-0858

Map Link
30 South La Patera Lane, Unit 5
Santa Barbara, CA 93117
805/692-6777 or 800/962-1394
fax 805/692-6787 or 800/627-7768
website: www.maplink.com

Olmstead Maps
P.O. Box 5351
Berkeley, CA 94705
tel./fax 510/658-6534

Tom Harrison Maps
2 Falmouth Cove
San Rafael, CA 94901-4465
tel./fax 415/456-7940 or 800/265-9090
website: www.tomharrisonmaps.com

U.S. Forest Service
Attn: Map Sales
P.O. Box 9035
Prescott, AZ 86313
928/443-8285
fax 928/443-8207
website: fs.fed.us/recreation/nationalforeststore

U.S. Geological Survey
Branch of Information Services
P.O. Box 25286, Federal Center
Denver, CO 80225
303/202-4700 or 888/ASK-USGS
   (888/275-8747)
fax 303/202-4693
website: www.usgs.gov

ABCs of the California Boating Law

Adapted from a Department of Boating and Waterways booklet.

PREPARATION

EDUCATION

The Department of Boating and Waterways recommends taking a boating safety class offered by the U.S. Coast Guard Auxiliary, the U.S. Power Squadrons, or certain chapters of the American Red Cross. For more information on Coast Guard Auxiliary and Power Squadron classes call:

> Toll-Free:
> U.S. Coast Guard Auxiliary: (800) 869-SAIL(7245)
> U.S. Power Squadrons: (800) SEA-SKIL (732-7545)
> U.S. Coast Guard Customer Infoline: (800) 368-5647

The Department of Boating and Waterways offers a home study guide, California Boating Safety Course. In addition, Aquatic Centers, operated by colleges, universities, and nonprofit organizations throughout California, offer on the water boating safety courses for a number of different boating activities, including sailing, canoeing, kayaking, water skiing, and the use of personal watercraft. Please see our website www.dbw.ca.gov under "education" for more information.

WEATHER

Before you begin a cruise, check the local "weather and sea" conditions. Detailed information can be obtained by tuning in to local radio stations or the National Weather Radio broadcasts on frequencies of 162.400, 162.475, and 162.550 MHz in areas where available, or by consulting local newspapers.

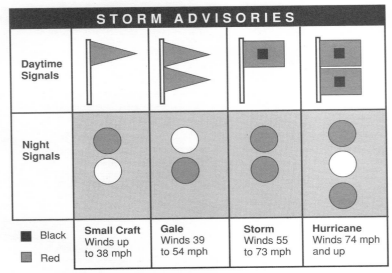

STORM ADVISORIES				
Daytime Signals				
Night Signals				
■ Black ■ Red	**Small Craft** Winds up to 38 mph	**Gale** Winds 39 to 54 mph	**Storm** Winds 55 to 73 mph	**Hurricane** Winds 74 mph and up

NOTE: In some areas, the display of storm advisory flags has been discontinued. Boaters should check current weather conditions before getting under way.

At selected locations in and near boating areas, storm advisories are displayed by flag hoists or lights. Coast Guard stations and many marinas no longer display storm advisory flags. Remaining display points are located at some park ranger stations, marinas, or municipal piers. A boater should become familiar with the display stations in the area and the meanings of the signals.

EPIRB OR VHF MARINE RADIO LICENSING INFORMATION

For information on getting a license for a VHF marine radio or Emergency Position Indicating Radio Beacon (EPIRB), contact the U.S. Federal Communications Commission (FCC) at (800) 418-3676 for forms, or (888) CALL-FCC for assistance.

FUELING

Most fires happen after fueling. To prevent fires, follow these rules:
- Don't smoke or strike matches.
- Shut off motors. Turn off electric equipment.
- Close all windows, doors and openings.
- Take portable tanks out of the boat and fill them on the dock.
- Keep the filling nozzle in contact with the tank.
- Wipe up any spilled gas with petroleum-absorbent pads. Discard the pads in a safe manner.
- Ventilate for at least five minutes. Make sure there is no odor of gasoline anywhere in the boat.
- Periodically check the system for fuel leaks.
- Visually check for leaks, or fuel in the bilges.

BOAT CAPACITY

Single-hull motorboats less than 20 feet in length which are manufactured after 1972 must display capacity and safe horsepower information. The maximum weight in persons, gear and motors is offered as a guide to boaters, and should not be exceeded. It is not a violation of federal or California state law to exceed recommended maximums. However, other states may cite an operator who exceeds capacity and horsepower limitations. Some insurance companies will not insure craft exceeding horsepower maximums and some boat manufacturers will void any applicable warranties for the same reasons.

LOADING

It's the operator's responsibility that supplies be carefully loaded and all passengers be properly seated. Remember:
- Spread weight evenly.
- Fasten gear to prevent shifting.
- Keep passengers seated.
- Don't overload.

CHECK LIST AND FLOAT PLAN

CHECK LIST

Before embarking on a cruise:

1. File a float plan (see below)
2. Give consideration to basic safety items, including the following:

   ☐ Vessel in good condition   ☐ Tools

   ☐ Vessel properly loaded   ☐ Extra starting battery

   ☐ Ample supply of fuel   ☐ Personal flotation devices
        (Coast Guard-approved)

   ☐ Check weather reports

   ☐ Compass and charts   ☐ Fire extinguishers
        (Coast Guard-approved)

   ☐ Good anchoring equipment

   ☐ Bailing Device   ☐ Visual distress signals

   ☐ Spare parts   ☐ Oars or paddles

   ☐ First-aid kit   ☐ Marine VHF radio

   ☐ Flashlight

3. Cancel your "Float Plan" when you return

FLOAT PLAN

Operator _____

     Name and address of operator   Phone number

Search for an overdue boat has a much greater chance of being successful if the Coast Guard or other rescue agencies have certain facts. For your own safety and before leaving on a cruise, complete this form and leave it with a reliable person who will notify authorities if necessary.

If Overdue, Contact _____

     Name and phone number or rescue agency near point of departure

Vessel _____

Name	CF Number	Length
Power, Inboard - Outboard	Rig, If Sail	Hull Color
Type/Style	Range	Speed

Persons _____   **Radio** _____

     Number Persons Aboard   Frequencies

Departure From _____

     Place   Date/Time Depart

Car Parked License #	Trailer Parked License #	Where parked

Destination _____

IMPORTANT: DON'T FORGET TO CANCEL FLOAT PLAN WHEN YOU RETURN

AIDS TO NAVIGATION
LATERAL SYSTEM (FEDERAL)

The waters of the United States are marked for safe navigation by the lateral system of buoyage. The system employs a simple arrangement of colors, shapes, numbers, and light characteristics to show the side on which a buoy should be passed when proceeding in a given direction. The characteristics are determined by the position of the buoy with respect to the navigable channels as the channels are entered from seaward.

The expression "red right returning" has long been used by the seafarer as a reminder that the red buoys are kept to the starboard (right) side when proceeding from the open sea into port (upstream). Likewise, green buoys are kept to the port (left) side, (see page 491). Conversely, when proceeding toward the sea or leaving port, red buoys are kept to port side and green buoys to the starboard side. Red buoys are always even numbered. Green buoys are odd numbered. Red and white vertically striped buoys mark the center of the channel.

UNIFORM STATE WATERWAY MARKING SYSTEM

Most waterways used by boaters are located entirely within the boundaries of the state. The California Uniform State Waterway Marking System has been devised for these waters. Examples of such aids are found on page 490.

The waterway marking system employs buoys and signs with distinctive standard shapes to show regulatory or advisory information. These markers are white with black letters and have orange borders. They signify speed zones, restricted areas, danger areas, and general information.

Aids to navigation on state waters use red and green buoys to mark channel limits. Red and green buoys are generally used in pairs. The boat should pass between the red buoy and its companion green buoy.

MOORING TO BUOYS

Tying up to or hanging on to any navigation buoy (except a mooring buoy) or beacon is prohibited.

AIDS TO NAVIGATION

In recent years, modifications to certain aids to navigation located on coastal and inland waters have been completed. These changes apply to aids used in both the lateral and state waterway marking systems. (See charts which follow.)

- Port-hand buoys are painted green, with green fixed or flashing lights.
- Starboard-hand buoys are painted red, with red fixed or flashing lights.
- Safe water buoys, also called midchannel or fairway buoys, and approach buoys are painted with red and white vertical stripes, with flashing lights.
- Preferred channel, or junction buoys, are painted with red and green horizontal bands, with flashing lights.
- Special marks (traffic separation, anchorage areas, dredging, fishnet areas, etc.) are painted yellow. If lighted, the light may be fixed or flashing.

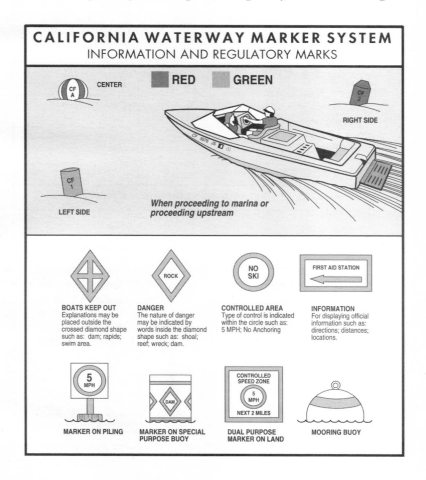

CALIFORNIA WATERWAY MARKER SYSTEM
INFORMATION AND REGULATORY MARKS

RED GREEN

CENTER

CF A

RIGHT SIDE

CF 2

CF 1

LEFT SIDE

CF 5576 JS

When proceeding to marina or proceeding upstream

BOATS KEEP OUT
Explanations may be placed outside the crossed diamond shape such as: dam; rapids; swim area.

DANGER
The nature of danger may be indicated by words inside the diamond shape such as: shoal; reef; wreck; dam.

ROCK

CONTROLLED AREA
Type of control is indicated within the circle such as: 5 MPH; No Anchoring

NO SKI

INFORMATION
For displaying official information such as: directions; distances; locations.

FIRST AID STATION

MARKER ON PILING

5 MPH

MARKER ON SPECIAL PURPOSE BUOY

DAM

DUAL PURPOSE MARKER ON LAND

CONTROLLED SPEED ZONE
5 MPH
NEXT 2 MILES

MOORING BUOY

FEDERAL CHANNEL MARKING SYSTEM
LATERAL SYSTEM AS SEEN ENTERING FROM SEAWARD

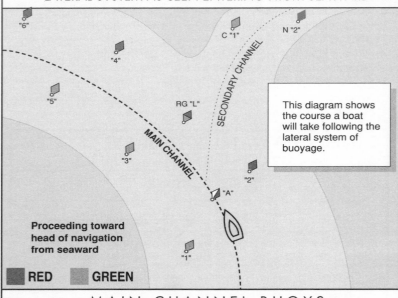

This diagram shows the course a boat will take following the lateral system of buoyage.

Proceeding toward head of navigation from seaward

RED   GREEN

MAIN CHANNEL BUOYS

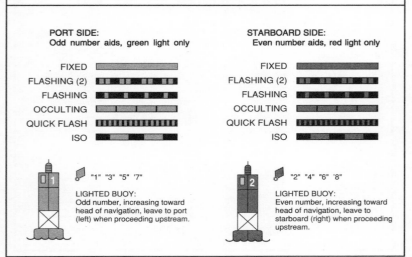

PORT SIDE:
Odd number aids, green light only

FIXED
FLASHING (2)
FLASHING
OCCULTING
QUICK FLASH
ISO

STARBOARD SIDE:
Even number aids, red light only

FIXED
FLASHING (2)
FLASHING
OCCULTING
QUICK FLASH
ISO

"1" "3" "5" '7'

LIGHTED BUOY:
Odd number, increasing toward head of navigation, leave to port (left) when proceeding upstream.

"2" "4" "6" '8'

LIGHTED BUOY:
Even number, increasing toward head of navigation, leave to starboard (right) when proceeding upstream.

RED GREEN

SAFE WATER BUOY - MARKS MIDCHANNEL:
No numbers - may be lettered, white light only

MORSE CODE (A)

"A"

LIGHTED AND/OR SOUND:
Marks midchannel, pass on either side. Not numbered, may be lettered. Letter has no lateral significance, used for identification and location purposes.

UNLIGHTED

SPHERICAL

MR

PREFERRED CHANNEL BUOY: No numbers, may be lettered

Topmost band denotes preferred channel. Letter has no lateral significance, used for identification and location purposes.

COMPOSITE GROUP FLASHING (2 + 1)

STARBOARD

LIGHTED BUOY "L"

UNLIGHTED CAN "L"

PORT

LIGHTED BUOY "L"

UNLIGHTED NUN "L"

DAYMARK

DAYMARK

PORT

C "1"

UNLIGHTED CAN BUOY:
Odd number, leave to port.

DAYMARK

STARBOARD

N "2"

UNLIGHTED NUN BUOY:
Even number, leave to starboard.

DAYMARK

INLAND RULES OF THE ROAD
NAVIGATION RULES

The inland navigational rules, commonly called the *"Rules of the Road,"* govern the operation of boats and specify light and sound signals on inland waters in order to prevent collisions.

Existing law requires that a complete copy of the new inland navigational rules must be kept for reference on board all boats of 39 feet 4 inches (12 meters) or more in length operating on inland waters. A copy of the *Navigation Rules International - Inland* booklet, which is published by the Coast Guard, may be ordered from: Superintendent of Documents, U.S. Government Printing Office, Attn: Customer Service, Washington, DC 20402.

There is a charge for this booklet. Please call (202) 783-3238 for availability and price.

RESPONSIBILITY

Nothing in the rules of the road shall exonerate the operator of a vessel from the consequences of neglecting to comply with the inland rules of the road, or from neglecting any precaution which may be required by the ordinary practice of seamen, or by the special circumstances of the case.

In construing and complying with the inland rules of the road, due regard shall be had to all dangers of navigation and collision and to any special circumstances, including the limitations of the vessels involved, which may make a departure from the rules of the road necessary to avoid immediate danger.

NAVIGATION SIGNALS

The law prescribes signals for vessels in sight of each other to indicate the intended course of a vessel when necessary for safe navigation.

- One short blast (1 second) of the horn or whistle will show an intention to direct course of vessel to own starboard (right).
- Two short blasts will show intention to direct course of vessel to own port (left).
- Three short blasts will indicate the vessel's engines are going astern (in reverse).
- Five or more short and rapid blasts is a danger signal used when the other vessel's intentions are not understood or where the other vessel's indicated course is dangerous.
- Prolonged blast (4 to 6 seconds) will indicate situations of restricted visibility (see Fog Signals, page 495).

Motorboats should not use cross signals, that is, answering one blast with two blasts or two blasts with one blast.

MEETING OR CROSSING SITUATIONS

When motorboats are in sight of one another and meeting or crossing at a distance within half a mile of each other, each vessel shall indicate its intended maneuver with the following signals: one short blast – *I intend to leave you on my port side*, or two short blasts – *I intend to leave you on my starboard side,* or three short blasts – *I am operating astern propulsion.* Upon hearing the one- or two-blast signal, the other vessel shall, if in agreement, sound the same signal and take steps to effect a safe passing. If the proposed maneuver is unsafe, the danger signal (five or more short and rapid blasts) should be sounded and each vessel shall take appropriate action until a safe passing agreement is made.

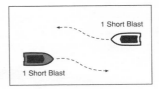

When meeting head-on, or nearly so, either vessel shall signal its intention with one short blast which the other vessel shall answer promptly. Both vessels should alter their course to starboard (right) so that each will pass to the port (left) side of each other.

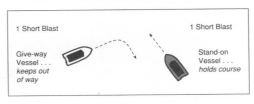

When crossing, the vessel which has the other on the starboard (right) side shall keep out of the way and avoid crossing ahead of the other vessel. The give-way vessel, the vessel directed to keep out of the way, shall take early and substantial action to keep well clear of the other vessel (stand-on vessel). This latter vessel should hold course and speed. However, it may, as the stand-on vessel, take action to avoid collision by maneuvering as soon as it becomes apparent that the vessel required to keep out of the way is not taking appropriate action.

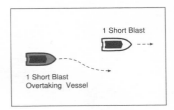

OVERTAKING SITUATIONS

When two motorboats are running in the same direction and the vessel astern desires to pass, it shall give one short blast to indicate a desire to pass on the overtaken vessel's starboard. The vessel ahead shall answer with one blast if the course is safe.

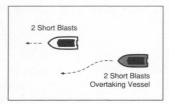

2 Short Blasts

2 Short Blasts
Overtaking Vessel

If the vessel astern desires to pass to port of the overtaken vessel, it shall give two short blasts. The vessel ahead shall answer with two short blasts if the course is safe. If it is unsafe to pass, the vessel being overtaken should answer with the danger signal (five or more short and rapid blasts).

A vessel approaching another vessel from the stern and overtaking it shall keep out of the way of the overtaken vessel. The vessel being overtaken shall hold its course and speed.

OTHER SITUATIONS

- A boat nearing a bend in a channel where vessels approaching from the other direction cannot be seen shall signal with a prolonged blast (four to six seconds), which shall be answered with the same signal by an approaching boat within hearing. Should such signal be answered by a boat on the farther side of the bend, then usual signals for meeting and passing shall be given upon sighting. If the signal is unanswered, the channel may be considered clear.
- Boats shall keep to the starboard side of narrow channels whenever safe and practicable.
- Motorboats leaving a dock or berth shall sound one prolonged blast.
- Motorboats shall keep out of the way of sailing vessels where courses involve the risk of collision.
- In narrow channels, do not hamper the safe passage of vessels, such as deep-draft liners and freighters, which can navigate only inside such channels.

RULES FOR SAILING VESSELS

When two sailing vessels are approaching one another, so as to involve risk of collision, one of them shall keep out of the way of the other as follows:

- When each has the wind on a different side, the vessel which has the wind on the port side shall keep out of the way of the other.
- When both have the wind on the same side, the vessel which is to windward shall keep out of the way of the vessel which is to leeward.
- If a vessel with the wind on the port side sees a vessel to windward and cannot determine with certainty whether the other vessel has the wind on the port or on the starboard side, she shall keep out of the way of the other.

The windward side shall be deemed to be the side opposite to that on which the mainsail is carried or, in the case of a square-rigged vessel, the side opposite to that on which the largest fore-and-aft sail is carried. The international rules for sailing are the same as the above.

FOG SIGNALS

The law also prescribes signals to identify vessels navigating in or near areas of restricted visibility.

Upon hearing a fog signal apparently forward of the beam, the operator should reduce speed to the minimum at which the boat can be kept on course, unless it has been determined by radar or other means that the risk of collision does not exist. If necessary, the operator should use reverse propulsion. In any event, navigate with extreme caution until any danger is over.

Motorboats:
- Making way through the water, sound, at intervals of not more than two minutes, one prolonged blast.
- Under way but stopped and making no way through the water, sound, at intervals of not more than two minutes, two prolonged blasts in succession, with an interval of about two seconds between them.

Sailboats or Vessels Not Under Command, Restricted in Ability to Maneuver, Towing or Pushing Another Vessel, or Engaged in Fishing with Nets or Trawling:
- Sound at intervals of not more than two minutes, one prolonged followed by two short blasts.

Boats at Anchor:
- Ring, at intervals of not more than one minute, a bell rapidly for about five seconds. In addition, one short blast followed by one prolonged and one short blast may be sounded to give warning of position and of the possibility of collision to an approaching vessel.
- Boats less than 39 feet 4 inches (12 meters) in length may, instead of the above, make an efficient sound signal at intervals of not more than two minutes.
- Boats less than 65 feet 7 inches (20 meters) are not required to sound signals when anchored in a federally designated anchorage area.

OPERATIONAL LAW
PEACE OFFICERS

Every peace officer of the state, city, county, harbor district, or other political subdivision of the state is empowered to enforce California Boating Law. Such officers have the authority to stop and board any vessel where the peace officer has probable cause to believe that a violation of law exists.

Peace officers are also authorized to order the operator of an unsafe vessel to shore. A vessel can be ordered to the nearest safe moorage if an unsafe condition is found that cannot be corrected on the spot and where, in the judgment of the officer, the continued operation of the vessel would be especially hazardous.

Any vessel approaching, overtaking, being approached, or being overtaken by, a moving law enforcement vessel operating with a siren or an illuminated blue light, or any vessel approaching a stationary law enforcement vessel displaying an illuminated blue light, shall immediately slow to a speed sufficient to maintain steerage only, shall alter its course, within its ability, so as not to inhibit or interfere with the operation of the law enforcement vessel, and shall proceed, unless otherwise directed by the operator of the law enforcement vessel, at the reduced speed until beyond the area of operation of the law enforcement vessel.

TRAILERING

It is against the law to tow a trailered vessel containing a passenger, except when engaged in launching or retrieving a vessel.

STOLEN VESSELS

If a numbered vessel is stolen, the owner or legal owner should notify the local law enforcement agency as soon as possible. The owner shall also notify the local law enforcement agency if the vessel reported stolen is recovered.

COUNTY AND CITY LAWS

In addition to state law, many counties, cities, and districts have special laws or ordinances which restrict activities in certain areas, prohibit certain acts at certain times, or establish additional requirements. These ordinances may regulate speed, set aside certain areas or hours for special purposes and prohibit acts which would be contrary to public interest. Boaters must comply with these local rules as well as with the state laws. Check with your local waterway operator for special laws or ordinances in your area.

AGE RESTRICTIONS

No person under 16 years of age may operate a motorboat of more than 15 horsepower, except for a sailboat that does not exceed 30 feet in length or a dinghy used directly between a moored boat and the shore, or between two moored boats. The law allows persons 12-15 years of age to operate motorboats of more than 15 horsepower or sailboats over 30 feet if supervised on board by a person at least 18 years of age. A violation of these provisions is an infraction.

SPEED

Speed is limited by law for certain conditions and areas. The maximum speed for motorboats within 100 feet of a bather (but not a water skier) and within 200 feet of a bathing beach, swimming float, diving platform or life line, passenger landing being used, or landing where boats are tied up is five miles per hour.

A safe speed should be maintained at all times so that: a) action can be taken to avoid collision and b) the boat can stop within a distance appropriate to the prevailing circumstances and conditions.

In restricted visibility, motorboats should have the engines ready for immediate maneuvering. An operator should be prepared to stop the vessel within the space of half the distance of forward visibility.

RECKLESS OR NEGLIGENT BOAT OPERATION

No person shall operate any vessel or manipulate any water skis, aquaplane, or similar device in a reckless or negligent manner so as to endanger the life, limb, or property of any person. Examples of such operation include, but are not limited to:

1. Riding on the bow, gunwale, or transom of a vessel under way, propelled by machinery, when such position is not protected by railing or other reasonable deterrent to falling overboard; or riding in a position or manner which is obviously dangerous. These provisions shall not apply to a vessel's crew in the act of anchoring, mooring or making fast to a dock or another vessel, or in the necessary management of a sail.

2. Maneuvering towed skiers, or devices, so as to pass the towline over another vessel or its skier.

3. Navigating a vessel, skis, or other devices between a towing vessel and its tow or tows.

4.   Operating under the influence of intoxicants or narcotics.

Other actions, such as speeding in confined or restricted areas, "buzzing" or "wetting down" others, or skiing at prohibited times or in restricted areas can also be construed to be reckless or negligent operation.

"Hit and run" - Any person involved in a boating accident resulting in injury, death or disappearance, who is convicted of leaving the scene without furnishing appropriate information to others involved or to any peace officer at the scene and/or rendering any reasonable assistance to any injured person, is liable for a fine of up to $10,000 or imprisonment for up to one year, or both.

INTOXICATED BOAT OPERATION

Alcohol is a factor in 39 percent of all fatal motorboat accidents in California. Please do not drink and operate a boat! State law specifies that:

1.   No person shall operate any vessel, water skis or similar device while under the influence of intoxicating liquor or drugs, or who is addicted to any drug.

2.   No person 21 years of age or older shall operate any vessel, water skis or similar device who has .08% or more, by weight, of alcohol in their blood. A level of at least .05% but less than .08% may be used with other evidence in determining whether the person was under the influence of alcohol. No person under 21 years of age may operate a vessel, water skis or similar device who has .01% or more, by weight, of alcohol in their blood.

3.   A person who has been arrested for operating a mechanically propelled vessel "under the influence" may be requested to submit to a chemical test to determine blood alcohol content. Refusal may result in increased penalties upon conviction. A person convicted of intoxicated boat operation could receive up to a $1,000 fine and six months in jail.

4.   If you are convicted of operating a vessel while intoxicated, the Department of Motor Vehicles may suspend or revoke your vehicle driver's license. Depending upon the number and type of vehicle and/or vessel violations accumulated, this suspension or revocation could be for up to 5 years, and could also result in fines of up to $1,000.

COURT-ORDERED BOATING EDUCATION

A person convicted of a moving violation, such as reckless or negligent operation or speeding may be ordered by the court upon a first conviction, and *must* be ordered by the court upon a subsequent conviction within seven years of a previous conviction, to complete and pass a boating safety course.

Any person convicted of operating a motorboat under the influence of drugs or alcohol must be ordered by the court to take a boating safety course approved by the Department of Boating and Waterways.

PERSONAL WATERCRAFT OPERATION

"Personal watercraft" means a vessel 13 feet in length or less, propelled by machinery, that is designed to be operated by a person sitting, standing, or kneeling on the vessel rather than in the conventional manner of sitting or standing inside the vessel.

Personal watercraft (PWC) are subject to the same laws governing the operation of motorboats of the same size. For proper display of registration numbers and stickers, see the Registration section of this booklet. For more information, see the Department of Boating and Waterways publication, Safe Boating Hints for Personal Watercraft.

Every person on board a personal watercraft (PWC) and any person towed behind a vessel *must wear* a Coast Guard-approved Type I, II, III, or V life jacket. Exceptions: a person aboard a personal watercraft or being towed behind a vessel on water skis if that person is a performer in a professional exhibition, or preparing to participate or participating in an official regatta, marine parade, tournament or exhibition. In lieu of wearing a Type I, II, III, or V Coast Guard-approved personal flotation device, any person engaged in slalom skiing on a marked course, or any person engaged in barefoot, jump, or trick water skiing may elect to wear a wetsuit designed for the activity and labeled by the manufacturer as a water ski wetsuit. A Coast Guard-approved Type I, II, III, or V life jacket must be carried in the tow vessel for each skier electing to wear a wetsuit.

Lanyard/Self-Circling Device - The law requires a person operating a personal watercraft equipped with a lanyard cutoff switch to attach the lanyard to his or her person. Operating a personal watercraft equipped with a self-circling device is prohibited if the self-circling device has been altered.

Nighttime Operation Prohibited - The law prohibits the operation of personal watercraft at any time between the hours from one-half hour after sunset to one-half hour before sunrise, even if the PWC is equipped with the proper navigational lights.

Operator Age - It is an infraction for a person under 16 years of age to operate a motorboat of more than 15 horsepower, including personal watercraft. Any person who permits a person under the age of 16 to do so is also guilty of an infraction. A person 12-15 may operate a motorboat of more than 15 horsepower if supervised by a person on board who is at least 18 years of age.

Reasonable and Prudent Operation - California law holds that no person shall operate any craft in a reckless or negligent manner so as to endanger the life, limb or property of any person. Some examples are:

Navigating a vessel, skis, or other devices between a towing vessel and its tow or tows.

Operating under the influence of intoxicants or narcotics.

Jumping or attempting to jump the wake of another vessel within 100 feet of the other vessel constitutes unsafe operation. Other actions which constitute unsafe operation are operating a PWC toward any person or vessel in the water and turning sharply so as to spray the person or vessel; and operating at a rate of speed and proximity to another vessel so that either operator is required to swerve at the last minute to avoid collision.

WATER-SKIING

When using a boat to tow a person on water skis or an aquaplane, there must be in the boat, in addition to the operator, one other person who can observe the person being towed. The observer must be at least 12 years of age.

Effective January 1, 2001, California law provides that any person being towed behind a vessel *must wear* a Coast Guard-approved Type I, II, III, or V life jacket. Exceptions: the law does not apply to performers engaged in professional exhibitions, official regattas, marine parades, or tournaments. Any person engaged in slalom skiing on a marked course, or barefoot, jump or trick water skiing, may instead wear a wetsuit designed for the activity and labeled by the manufacturer as a water ski wetsuit. However, for each skier who elects to wear a wetsuit, a Type I, II, III, or V life jacket still must be carried on board. Note: Inflatable personal flotation devices are not approved for use while water-skiing.

The towing of water-skiers from sunset to sunrise is prohibited by state law. Local laws may also restrict skiing at certain times during the day and in certain areas.

Water skis and aquaplanes must not be operated in a manner to endanger the safety of persons or property. Passing the towline over another vessel or skier is prohibited. Towing a skier or navigating between a vessel and its tow is prohibited. Towing a skier does not give the operator of the vessel any special privileges. The rules of the road must be observed.

Skiers being towed are considered to be persons on board for personal flotation device requirements. For more information on water-skiing, send for the free pamphlet titled "Safety Hints for Water-Skiing" from the Department of Boating and Waterways.

WATER-SKI FLAG

It is mandatory for the operator of a vessel involved in towing a skier to display, or cause to be displayed, a red or orange water-ski flag, to indicate:

- A downed skier
- A skier in the water preparing to ski
- A ski line extended for the vessel
- A ski in the water in the vicinity of the vessel

The flag must be no less than 12 inches on each side and be in the shape of a square or rectangle. The display of the ski flag does not in itself restrict the use of the water, but when operating in the area, boaters should exercise caution.

DIVING

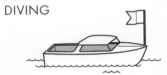

Required for use by vessels engaged in diving operations and restricted in their ability to maneuver.

ALPHA FLAG

Whenever the size of a vessel engaged in diving operations during daytime hours makes it impracticable to exhibit the daytime shapes required of a vessel restricted in its ability to maneuver, a rigid replica of the international blue-and-white code flag (Alpha) is required to be displayed. The flag must measure not less than 1 meter (3 ft. 3 in.) in height and must be visible all round the horizon.

For boats tending free-swimming divers where the diving does not interfere with the maneuverability of the boat, the alpha flag is not required and they may display the "divers down" flag.

Recognized for use by persons engaged in diving.

DIVERS DOWN FLAG

State law recognizes that a red flag with a white diagonal stripe – commonly called the divers down flag – indicates a person engaged in diving in the immediate area. Displaying the divers down flag is not required by law and does not in itself restrict the use of the water. When operating in an area where this flag is displayed, boaters should exercise caution.

For more information

about the legal requirements for emergency equipment and safe operation of recreational vessels, contact the Department of Boating and Waterways at **1-888-326-2822** (toll free), and on the Web at **www.dbw.ca.gov** or contact the local sheriff's marine patrol.

ACCIDENT REPORTING

Boat operators involved in an accident must provide their name, address and vessel registration number to other involved parties, provide assistance to any injured persons and, in case of a death or disappearance, report the accident without delay to law enforcement officials.

Boat operators or owners must also make a written report of a boating accident to the Department of Boating and Waterways when:
- A person dies, disappears, or is injured and requires medical treatment beyond first aid.
- Total damage to all vessels involved and other property is more than $500 or there is complete loss of a vessel.

This report must be made within 48 hours of the accident in cases involving a disappearance, death that occurs within 24 hours of the accident, or injury that requires medical treatment beyond first aid. In all other incidents where a written accident report is required, the report must be made within 10 days of the accident.

An accident report form is contained in this booklet and may be used for such reports. Forms are available through most sheriff's and harbormaster's offices and many police departments. They may also be obtained by writing to the Department of Boating and Waterways. Failure to comply with the above requirements is punishable by a fine of up to $1,000 or imprisonment up to six months, or both.

RADIO PROCEDURES - MARINE AND EMERGENCY DISTRESS

SPEAK SLOWLY AND CLEARLY - CALL:
A. If you are in distress (i.e., when threatened by grave and imminent danger) or are observing another vessel in distress, transmit the International Distress Call on Channel 16 "MAYDAY MAYDAY MAYDAY THIS IS (state vessel's name and assigned call letters, repeated 3 times)".

If aboard a vessel in trouble--state:
1. WHO you are (your vessel's call letters and name).
2. WHERE you are (your vessel's position in latitude/longitude or true bearing and distance in nautical miles from a widely known geographical point; local names known only in the immediate vicinity are confusing).
3. WHAT is wrong.
4. Kind of assistance desired.
5. Number of persons aboard and the condition of any injured.
6. Present seaworthiness of your vessel.
7. Description of your vessel--length, type, cabin, masts, power, color of hull, superstructure, and trim.
8. Your listening frequency and schedule.

If observing another vessel in distress--give:
1. Your position and, if possible, the bearing and distance of the vessel in difficulty.
2. Nature of distress.
3. Description of the vessel in distress (see Item 7 above).
4. Your intentions, course, and speed, etc.
5. Your radio call sign, name of your vessel, listening frequency, and schedule.

NOTE: The international sign for an aircraft that wants to direct a surface craft to a vessel in distress is: Circling the surface craft, opening and closing the throttle or changing propeller pitch (noticeable by change in sound) while crossing ahead of the surface craft, and proceeding in the direction of the vessel in distress. If you receive such a signal, you should follow the aircraft. If you cannot do so, try to inform the aircraft by any available means. If your assistance is no longer needed, the aircraft will cross your wake, opening and closing the throttle or changing the propeller pitch. If you are radio equipped, you should attempt to communicate with the aircraft on Channel 16 when the aircraft makes the above signals or makes any obvious attempt to attract your attention. In the event you cannot communicate by radio, be alert for a message block dropped from the aircraft.

B. If you need INFORMATION OR ASSISTANCE FROM THE COAST GUARD (other than in a distress), call COAST GUARD on Channel 16 (The Distress and Calling Frequency). In this situation you will normally be shifted to a common working frequency (21, 22, or 23) allowing the DISTRESS frequency to remain open.

RADIO CHECKS:
Do not use Channel 16 to call the Coast Guard merely for a radio check. Such use is prohibited by the Federal Communications Commission.

NOTIFY THE COAST GUARD PROMPTLY AS SOON AS THE EMERGENCY TERMINATES

BOATING ACCIDENT REPORT

CALIFORNIA DEPARTMENT OF BOATING AND WATERWAYS

The operator of every recreational vessel is required by Section 656 of the Harbors and Navigation Code to file a written report whenever a boating accident occurs which results in death, disappearance, injury that requires medical attention beyond first aid, total property damage in excess of $500, or complete loss of a vessel. Reports must be submitted within 48 hours in case of death occurring within 24 hours of an accident, disappearance, or injury beyond first aid. All other reports must be submitted within 10 days of the accident. Reports are to be submitted to the California Department of Boating and Waterways at 2000 Evergreen Street, Suite 100, Sacramento, California 95815-3888, (916) 263-8189. Failure to submit this report as required is a misdemeanor and is punishable by a fine not to exceed $1000 or imprisonment not to exceed 6 months or both.

DATE OF ACCIDENT (M/D/Y)	TIME OF ACCIDENT	COUNTY	BODY OF WATER		LOCATION ON WATER
	□ AM □ PM				

# INJURED	# DEAD	TOTAL $$	LAW ENFORCEMENT ON ACCIDENT SCENE?	AGENCY NAME
			□ YES □ NO	

WEATHER (CHECK ALL THAT APPLY):

□ CLEAR □ RAIN
□ CLOUDY □ SNOW
□ FOG □ HAZY

WATER CONDITIONS

□ CALM (waves less than 6")
□ CHOPPY (waves 6"-2')
□ ROUGH (waves 2'-6')
□ VERY ROUGH (waves >6')

WIND CONDITIONS

□ NONE
□ LIGHT (0-6 mph)
□ MODERATE (7-14 mph)
□ STRONG (15-25 mph)
□ STORM (over 25 mph)

TEMPERATURE

WATER _____   AIR _____

VISIBILITY
□ GOOD
□ FAIR
□ POOR

STRONG CURRENT
□ YES □ NO

TYPE OF ACCIDENT (CHECK ALL THAT APPLY):

□ CAPSIZING
□ COLLISION WITH VESSEL
□ COLLISION WITH FIXED OBJECT
□ COLLISION WITH FLOATING OBJECT
□ FALL OVERBOARD
□ FALL IN BOAT
□ OTHER _____

□ FIRE / EXPLOSION (fuel)
□ FIRE / EXPLOSION (other than fuel)
□ FLOODING / SWAMPING
□ SINKING
□ STRUCK BY BOAT / PROPELLER
□ SKIER MISHAP

CAUSE OF ACCIDENT (CHECK ALL THAT APPLY):

□ IMPROPER LOOKOUT / INATTENTION
□ OPERATOR INEXPERIENCE
□ EXCESSIVE SPEED
□ MACHINERY FAILURE
□ EQUIPMENT FAILURE
□ IMPROPER LOADING
□ OVERLOADING

□ HAZARDOUS WEATHER / WATER
□ RESTRICTED VISION
□ IGNITION OF SPILLED FUEL / VAPOR
□ IMPROPER ANCHORING
□ ALCOHOL USE
□ FAILURE TO VENT
□ OTHER _____

DESCRIBE WHAT HAPPENED AND WHAT YOU COULD HAVE DONE TO PREVENT THIS ACCIDENT
(Explain the cause of death or injury, medical treatment, etc. Use sketch if helpful. If needed, continue description on additional paper.)

VICTIM OR WITNESS INFORMATION

VICTIM / WITNESS NAME & ADDRESS	VICTIM / WITNESS STATUS	RIDING IN VESSEL #	AGE	INJURY DESCRIPTION	CAUSE OF DEATH	COULD VICTIM SWIM?	LIFE JACKET WORN?
	☐ INJURED ☐ DEAD ☐ WITNESS ONLY				☐ DROWNING ☐ TRAUMA ☐ OTHER	☐ YES ☐ NO	☐ YES ☐ NO
	☐ INJURED ☐ DEAD ☐ WITNESS ONLY				☐ DROWNING ☐ TRAUMA ☐ OTHER	☐ YES ☐ NO	☐ YES ☐ NO
	☐ INJURED ☐ DEAD ☐ WITNESS ONLY				☐ DROWNING ☐ TRAUMA ☐ OTHER	☐ YES ☐ NO	☐ YES ☐ NO
	☐ INJURED ☐ DEAD ☐ WITNESS ONLY				☐ DROWNING ☐ TRAUMA ☐ OTHER	☐ YES ☐ NO	☐ YES ☐ NO

THIS CONFIDENTIAL REPORT IS USED IN RESEARCH FOR THE PREVENTION OF ACCIDENTS AND A COPY IS FORWARDED TO THE UNITED STATES COAST GUARD

DBW FORM BAR-1 (1/00)

BOATING ACCIDENT REPORT

CALIFORNIA DEPARTMENT OF BOATING AND WATERWAYS

INFORMATION: OPERATOR #1

OPERATOR NAME AND ADDRESS	IS OWNER DIFFERENT THAN OPERATOR? ☐ YES ☐ NO	OPERATOR EXPERIENCE	OPERATOR EDUCATION
	OWNER NAME AND ADDRESS	☐ UNDER 10 HOURS ☐ 10 TO 100 HOURS ☐ OVER 100 HOURS	☐ AMERICAN RED CROSS ☐ USCG AUXILIARY ☐ US POWER SQUADRON ☐ STATE COURSE ☐ INFORMAL ☐ NONE
AGE			

INFORMATION: VESSEL #1

THIS VESSEL ONLY	# INJURED	# DEAD	ESTIMATED DAMAGE	RENTED BOAT ☐ YES ☐ NO	BOAT NAME	# OF PERSONS ON BOARD	# OF PERSONS TOWED

BOAT NUMBER (CF OR DOC #)	MFR. HULL ID #		LENGTH

BOAT MANUFACTURER	BOAT MODEL	YEAR BUILT	TYPE OF FUEL	# OF ENGINES	HORSEPOWER

ACTIVITY ☐ RECREATIONAL ☐ COMMERCIAL ☐ OTHER _____

HULL MATERIAL	FIRE EXTINGUISHER ON BOARD ☐ YES ☐ NO	PROPULSION	FIRE EXTINGUISHER USED ☐ YES ☐ NO	OPERATION AT TIME OF ACCIDENT	LIFE JACKETS ON BOARD ☐ YES ☐ NO	LIFE JACKETS ACCESSIBLE ☐ YES ☐ NO	LIFE JACKETS WORN ☐ YES ☐ NO

TYPE OF BOAT
☐ OPEN MOTORBOAT
☐ CABIN MOTORBOAT
☐ PERSONAL WATERCRAFT
☐ HOUSEBOAT
☐ SAILBOAT (aux. engine)
☐ SAILBOAT (sail only)
☐ CANOE / KAYAK
☐ RAFT
☐ ROWBOAT
☐ OTHER (specify) _____

HULL MATERIAL
☐ WOOD
☐ ALUMINUM
☐ FIBERGLASS
☐ PLASTIC
☐ RUBBER / VINYL
☐ OTHER (specify) _____

PROPULSION
☐ OUTBOARD
☐ INBOARD
☐ INBOARD / OUTBOARD
☐ JET
☐ SAIL ONLY
☐ PADDLE / OARS
☐ OTHER (specify) _____

OPERATION AT TIME OF ACCIDENT
☐ CRUISING
☐ CHANGING DIRECTION
☐ CHANGING SPEED
☐ TOWING SKIER / TUBER
☐ TOWING SKIER- SKIER DOWN
☐ TOWING ANOTHER VESSEL
☐ BEING TOWED BY ANOTHER VESSEL
☐ DRIFTING
☐ AT ANCHOR
☐ TIED TO DOCK
☐ LAUNCHING
☐ DOCKING / LEAVING DOCK
☐ SAILING
☐ OTHER (specify) _____

SPEED _____ MPH

INFORMATION: OPERATOR #2

OPERATOR NAME AND ADDRESS	IS OWNER DIFFERENT THAN OPERATOR? ☐ YES ☐ NO	OPERATOR EXPERIENCE	OPERATOR EDUCATION

INFORMATION: VESSEL #2

AGE

THIS VESSEL ONLY	# INJURED	# DEAD	ESTIMATED DAMAGE $$

OWNER NAME AND ADDRESS

RENTED BOAT
☐ YES ☐ NO

OF PERSONS ON BOARD
☐ UNDER 10 HOURS
☐ 10 TO 100 HOURS
☐ OVER 100 HOURS

OF PERSONS TOWED
☐ AMERICAN RED CROSS
☐ USCG AUXILIARY
☐ US POWER SQUADRON
☐ STATE COURSE
☐ INFORMAL
☐ NONE

BOAT NUMBER (CF OR DOC #)

MFR. HULL ID#

BOAT NAME

LENGTH

BOAT MANUFACTURER

BOAT MODEL

YEAR BUILT

TYPE OF FUEL

OF ENGINES

HORSEPOWER

ACTIVITY
☐ RECREATIONAL ☐ COMMERCIAL ☐ OTHER _____

FIRE EXTINGUISHER ON BOARD
☐ YES ☐ NO

FIRE EXTINGUISHER USED
☐ YES ☐ NO

LIFE JACKETS ON BOARD
☐ YES ☐ NO

LIFE JACKETS ACCESSIBLE
☐ YES ☐ NO

LIFE JACKETS WORN
☐ YES ☐ NO

TYPE OF BOAT
☐ OPEN MOTORBOAT
☐ CABIN MOTORBOAT
☐ PERSONAL WATERCRAFT
☐ HOUSEBOAT
☐ SAILBOAT (aux. engine)
☐ SAILBOAT (sail only)
☐ CANOE / KAYAK
☐ RAFT
☐ ROWBOAT
☐ OTHER (specify) _____

HULL MATERIAL
☐ WOOD
☐ ALUMINUM
☐ FIBERGLASS
☐ PLASTIC
☐ RUBBER / VINYL
☐ OTHER (specify) _____

PROPULSION
☐ OUTBOARD
☐ INBOARD
☐ INBOARD / OUTBOARD
☐ JET
☐ SAIL ONLY
☐ PADDLE / OARS
☐ OTHER (specify) _____

OPERATION AT TIME OF ACCIDENT
☐ CRUISING
☐ CHANGING DIRECTION
☐ CHANGING SPEED
☐ TOWING SKIER / TUBER
☐ TOWING SKIER- SKIER DOWN
☐ TOWING ANOTHER VESSEL
☐ BEING TOWED BY ANOTHER VESSEL

SPEED _____ MPH

☐ DRIFTING
☐ AT ANCHOR
☐ TIED TO DOCK
☐ LAUNCHING
☐ DOCKING / LEAVING DOCK
☐ SAILING
☐ OTHER (specify) _____

QUALIFICATION OF PERSON COMPLETING REPORT
☐ OPERATOR ☐ OWNER ☐ OTHER (specify)

NAME OF PERSON COMPLETING THE REPORT _____

SIGNATURE OF PERSON COMPLETING THE REPORT _____

THIS CONFIDENTIAL REPORT IS USED IN RESEARCH FOR THE PREVENTION OF ACCIDENTS AND A COPY IS FORWARDED TO THE UNITED STATES COAST GUARD

DBW FORM BAR-1 (1/00)

REQUIRED EQUIPMENT

Recreational vessels are required to carry specified safety equipment which may vary according to type of propulsion, type of construction, area and time of use, and number of people aboard. Unless otherwise noted, all required equipment must be Coast Guard approved and must be kept in good, serviceable condition, be readily accessible, and be of the proper type and/or size. Recreational vessels may carry extra equipment that is not Coast Guard approved—provided that the minimum requirements for approved equipment are satisfied. For equipment purposes, sailboats, canoes, rowboats, and inflatable rafts equipped with motors are considered to be "motorboats". Requirements vary considerably for commercial vessels and vessels engaged in racing.

SAILBOATS AND MANUALLY PROPELLED VESSELS

Personal Flotation Devices: Vessels less than 16 feet in length, and all canoes and kayaks, regardless of length, must carry one Type I, II, III, or V Coast Guard-approved personal flotation device for each person on board. They must be readily accessible and of a suitable size for the intended wearer.

Vessels 16 feet and over, except canoes and kayaks, must have one Type I, II, III, or V Coast Guard-approved wearable device for each person aboard, plus at least one Type IV throwable device. The throwable device must be kept where it is immediately available. Wearable devices must be of a suitable size for the intended wearer.

Navigation Lights: All vessels are required to display navigation lights between sunset and sunrise and during times of restricted visibility. In inland and international waters, sailing vessels under sail alone shall exhibit navigation lights shown on page 521. The tricolored lantern and the all-round green and red lights should *never* be used together.

A sailing vessel of less than 23 feet (7 meters) in length shall, if practicable, exhibit those lights prescribed, or have ready at hand an electric torch or lighted lantern showing a white light which shall be exhibited in sufficient time to prevent collision. A vessel under oars may display those lights prescribed for sailing vessels or have ready at hand an electric torch or lighted lantern showing a white light which shall be exhibited in sufficient time to prevent collision.

Sound Signaling Devices: A vessel of less than 39 feet 4 inches (12 meters) is not required to carry a whistle or bell, but must be able to provide some other means of making an efficient sound signal.

Visual Distress Signals (Coastal Waters Only): Boats less than 16 feet, manually propelled craft of any size, sailboats under 26 feet — of completely open construction and not equipped with propulsion machinery, and boats competing in an organized marine parade, regatta, race, or similar event are only required between sunset and sunrise to carry aboard devices that are suitable for night use (see page 520).

MOTORBOATS LESS THAN 16 FEET IN LENGTH

Personal Flotation Device: One Type I, II, III, or V Coast Guard-approved personal flotation device must be carried for each person on board. They must be readily accessible and of a suitable size for the intended wearer.

Fire Extinguisher: One Type B-I Coast Guard-approved fire extinguisher must be carried when no fixed fire extinguishing system is installed in machinery spaces. Extinguishers are not required for outboard motorboats less than 26 feet in length and of open construction. No portable extinguishers are required if an approved, fixed fire extinguishing system is installed in machinery spaces.

Backfire Flame Arrestor: A Coast Guard-approved backfire flame arrestor is required for inboard gasoline motors which are not exposed to the atmosphere above the level of the gunwale.

Muffling System: An effective muffling system is required for the exhaust of each internal combustion engine. Unmodified outboards usually meet legal requirements (see page 516).

Ventilation System: See page 516.

Sound Signaling Devices: A vessel of less than 39 feet 4 inches (12 meters) must be able to provide a means of making an efficient sound signal but is not required to carry a whistle or bell.

Visual Distress Signals (Coastal Waters Only): Boats less than 16 feet of completely open construction and not equipped with propulsion machinery, and boats competing in an organized marine parade, regatta, race, or similar event are only required between sunset and sunrise to carry aboard devices that are suitable for night use (see page 523).

Navigation Lights: Navigation lights must be kept in serviceable condition and displayed between sunset and sunrise and at times of restricted visibility. For motorboats operating during these times, see page 520.

16 FEET TO LESS THAN 26 FEET

Personal Flotation Devices: One Type I, II, III, or V Coast Guard-approved wearable personal flotation device must be carried for each person aboard. They must be readily accessible and of a suitable size for the intended wearer. In addition, the vessel must carry an approved Type IV throwable device which should be immediately available.

Fire Extinguisher: One Type B-I Coast Guard-approved fire extinguisher must be carried when no fixed fire extinguishing system is installed in machinery spaces. Extinguishers are not required for outboard motorboats less than 26 feet in length and of open construction. No portable extinguishers are required if an approved fixed fire extinguishing system is installed in machinery spaces.

Backfire Flame Arrestor: A Coast Guard-approved backfire flame arrestor is required for inboard gasoline motors which are not exposed to the atmosphere above the level of the gunwale.

Muffling System: An effective muffling system is required for the exhaust of each internal combustion engine. Unmodified outboards usually meet legal requirements (see page 516).

Ventilation System: See page 516.

Sound Signaling Devices: A vessel of less than 39 feet 4 inches (12 meters) must be able to provide a means of making an efficient sound signal but is not required to carry a whistle or bell.

Visual Distress Signals (Coastal Waters Only): All boats 16 feet or more in length must carry devices aboard at all times. Boaters must carry: EITHER a) devices that are suitable for day use and devices suitable for night use, OR b) devices that can be used for both day and night use (see page 522).

Navigation Lights: Navigation lights must be kept in serviceable condition and be displayed between sunset and sunrise and at times of restricted visibility. For motorboats operating during these times, see page 520.

MOTORBOATS 26 FEET TO LESS THAN 40 FEET

Personal Flotation Devices: One Type I, II, III, or V Coast Guard-approved wearable personal flotation device must be carried for each person aboard. They must be readily accessible and of a suitable size for the intended wearer. In addition, the vessel must carry an approved Type IV throwable device which should be immediately available.

Fire Extinguisher: Two Type B-I or one Type B-II Coast Guard-approved fire extinguisher must be carried when no fixed fire extinguishing system is installed in machinery spaces. With a fixed system in the machinery space, one Type B-I fire extinguisher must be carried.

Backfire Flame Arrestor: A Coast Guard-approved backfire flame arrestor is required for inboard gasoline motors which are not exposed to the atmosphere above the level of the gunwale.

Muffling System: An effective muffling system is required for the exhaust of each internal combustion engine. Unmodified outboards usually meet legal requirements (see page 516).

Ventilation System: See page 516.

Sound Signaling Devices: A vessel of less than 39 feet 4 inches (12 meters) must be able to provide a means of making an efficient sound signal but is not required to carry a whistle or bell. (See page 512 for vessels over 12 meters.)

Visual Distress Signals (Coastal Waters Only): All boats 16 feet or more in length must carry devices aboard at all times. Boaters must carry: EITHER a) devices that are suitable for day use and devices suitable for night use, OR b) devices that can be used for both day and night use (see page 522).

Navigation Lights: Navigation lights must be kept in serviceable condition and be displayed between sunset and sunrise and at times of restricted visibility. For motorboats operating during these times, see page 520.

MOTORBOATS 40 FEET TO 65 FEET IN LENGTH

Personal Flotation Devices: One Type I, II, III, or V Coast Guard-approved wearable personal flotation device must be carried for each person aboard. They must be readily accessible and of a suitable size for the intended wearer. In addition, the vessel must carry an approved Type IV throwable device which should be immediately available.

Fire Extinguisher: Three B-I or one B-I and one B-II Type Coast Guard-approved fire extinguishers must be carried when no fixed fire extinguishing system is installed in machinery spaces. With a fixed system in the machinery space, two Type B-I or one Type B-II extinguisher must be carried.

Backfire Flame Arrestor: A Coast Guard-approved backfire flame arrestor is required for inboard gasoline motors which are not exposed to the atmosphere above the level of the gunwale.

Muffling System: An effective muffling system is required for the exhaust of each internal combustion engine. Unmodified outboards usually meet legal requirements (see page 516).

Ventilation System: See page 516.

Sound Signaling Devices: Vessels 39 feet 4 inches (12 meters) or more in length are required to carry a whistle and a bell.

Visual Distress Signals (Coastal Waters Only): All boats 16 feet or more in length must carry devices aboard at all times. Boaters must carry: EITHER a) devices that are suitable for day use and devices suitable for night, OR b) devices that can be used for both day and night use (see page 522).

Navigation Lights: Navigation lights must be kept in serviceable condition and displayed between sunset and sunrise and at times of restricted visibility. For motorboats operating during these times, see page 520.

PERSONAL FLOTATION DEVICES (PFDS)
The minimum requirements are:
- Except canoes and kayaks, all boats 16 feet or more in length: One wearable life jacket (Type I, II, III, or V) for each person on board and one throwable (Type IV) in each boat.
- Canoes and kayaks of any length and all other boats less than 16 feet in length: One I, II, III, or V PFD for each person on board.

Under state law, it is an infraction, punishable by a fine of up to $250, to operate a vessel that is 26 feet or less in length unless *every child 11 years of age or younger on board is wearing a Type I, II, or III Coast Guard-approved personal flotation device (life jacket).* The law does not apply to:
- the operator of a sailboat on which every child under age 12 is restrained by a harness tethered to the sailboat, OR
- the operator of a vessel on which every child under age 12 is in an enclosed cabin.

Inflatable PFDs - The U.S. Coast Guard approved inflatable PFDs in 1996. Only certain brands are U.S. Coast Guard approved, so check the label. While activation upon impact is not a required feature, inflatables must be equipped, at a minimum, with both manual (pull) and oral inflation systems. They must be wearable, not throwable-type PFDs. Inflatables are not recommended for non-swimmers and are not intended for use while water-skiing or on personal watercraft.

PERSONAL FLOTATION DEVICES (PFDS)

Off-Shore Life Jacket
(Type I PFD)

Best in open, rough or remote water where rescue may be slow. Type I's float you best, turn most unconscious wearers face up in the water, and are highly visible.

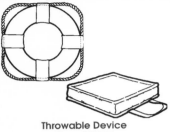

Throwable Device
(Type IV PFD)

Use in calm inland water with heavy boat traffic where help is always nearby. Type IV's do not help unconscious persons, and are not designed for non-swimmers or children. Type IV's are not suitable for many hours in rough water.

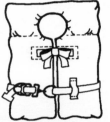

Near-Shore Buoyant Vest
(Type II PFD)

Good in calm, inland water, or where there is a good chance of fast rescue. Less bulk. Type II's will turn many, but not all, unconscious wearers face up in the water, but Type II's are not suitable for long hours in rough water.

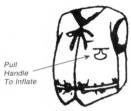

Pull
Handle
To Inflate

Hybrid Device
(Type V PFD)

High flotation when inflated. Good for continuous wear. However, may not adequately float some wearers unless this PFD is partially inflated. Type V's must be worn and require care of inflation chamber.

Flotation Aid (Type III PFD)

Good in calm, inland water or where there is a good chance of fast rescue. Generally the most comfortable PFD, Type III's are not good for use in rough water and the wearer may have to tilt head back to avoid face-down position in water.

In addition to the above requirements, all boats, powered or nonpowered, must carry at least one wearable Coast Guard-approved personal flotation device for every person aboard. PFDs bearing Coast Guard approval are identified by Types I, II, III, IV, or V. Coast Guard approval is shown by a stencil marking or tag on the PFD. This tag or marking shows the name and address of the manufacturer and the Coast Guard approval number. It also shows the amount of flotation in the device and the PFD Type (I, II, III, IV, V). Failure to have a sufficient number of approved devices aboard constitutes a violation of state and federal law.

California Boating Law requires that all Type I, II, and III PFDs must be readily accessible and all Type IV (throwable) PFDs must be immediately available. All PFDs must be kept in serviceable condition. If the PFD is badly torn, damaged, rotted, punctured or otherwise unserviceable, it no longer meets legal requirements and should be replaced.

Every person on board a personal watercraft (PWC) and any person being towed behind a vessel must wear a Coast Guard-approved Type I, II, III, or V life jacket, with exceptions (see "Water Skiing.") Except for these requirements, the requirements for some Type V PFDs, and the requirements for children under age 12, California boating law does not require wearing life jackets while under way. However, it is highly recommended that all persons, especially non-swimmers, wear life jackets. All wearable life jackets must be of suitable size.

Non-approved devices such as ski belts may be carried aboard as excess equipment only. Buoyant cushions should never be worn on the back when in use. For further details concerning the types and designs of PFDs, send for the free pamphlet titled "Safe Boating Hints For Personal Flotation Devices" from the Department of Boating and Waterways.

FIRE EXTINGUISHERS

Motorboats are required to carry readily accessible fire extinguishers accepted for marine use by the Coast Guard. The size and number of extinguishers accepted for use on motorboats depend on the size of the boat and whether or not there is a fixed extinguishing system installed

CARBON DIOXIDE
EXTINGUISHER

HALON
EXTINGUISHER

DRY CHEMICAL
EXTINGUISHER

aboard your boat. Fire extinguishers are not required for outboard pleasure boats less than 26 feet in length, not carrying passengers for hire, without permanently installed fuel tanks and which do not have spaces in which explosive or flammable gases or vapors can collect. (See Table A for specific requirements.) The minimum size approved for use aboard pleasure boats is the B-I size extinguisher.

All extinguishers must be readily accessible (preferably not stowed next to common fire sources), and they must be kept in a serviceable condition.

REMEMBER, the number required by law is only the minimum. Extra extinguishers provide additional safety.

An extinguisher is suitable for marine use when it bears either:
■   A label that includes Coast Guard approval numbers, "Marine Type USCG," or both markings.
■   A label that states the extinguisher is listed with Underwriters Laboratories (UL) and is suitable for marine use. It must be of the type and size described in Table B. UL-listed extinguishers must bear a UL rating of 5-B:C or higher. (All recently manufactured UL marine-type extinguishers will bear both the UL and Coast Guard label markings.)

All carbon tetrachloride extinguishers and others of the TOXIC vaporizing-liquid type, such as chlorobromomethane, are not approved and are not accepted as required fire extinguishers on any motorboats.

For further details concerning the types and designs for approved fire extinguishers, send for the free pamphlet titled "Safe Boating Hints for Fire Extinguishers" from the Department of Boating and Waterways.

TABLE A - FIRE EXTINGUISHER REQUIREMENTS

Boat Length	Without fixed extinguishing system in machinery space	With fixed extinguishing system in machinery space
Less than 26 ft.	1 B-I	None
26 ft. to under 40 ft.	2 B-I or 1 B-II	1 B-I
40 ft. to 65 ft.	3 B-I or 1 B-II and 1 B-I	2 B-I or 1 B-II

TABLE B - FIRE EXTINGUISHER CHARACTERISTICS

UL Listed extinguishers of the type and weight shown below may be selected to meet the type and size requirements for the corresponding Coast Guard classification (see Table A). For example, if a Coast Guard Type B, Size II extinguisher is required, a 10 lb. dry chemical extinguisher would be one of the equivalents. The following specifies only the minimum net agent weight. A larger extinguisher would be acceptable.

Coast Guard Classes	UL-Listed Equivalent	Dry Chemical lb.	Carbon Dioxide lb.	Halon 1211 / 1301 lb.
B-I	5-B:C	2	4	2 1/2
B-II	0-B:C	10	15	10

MUFFLING SYSTEMS

Any motorboat operated on the inland waters of this state must be muffled or otherwise prevented from exceeding the following noise levels when recorded at a distance of 50 feet:

- 82 dB (A) for engines manufactured on or after January 1, 1978.
- 84 dB (A) for engines manufactured on or after January 1, 1976 and before January 1, 1978.
- 86 dB (A) for engines manufactured before January 1, 1976.

Authorities generally agree that unbaffled exhaust pipes (stacks) and most water-injected pipes do not meet any of the above noise level requirements.

VENTILATION SYSTEMS

All motorboats or motor vessels, except open boats, made after 1940 and using gasoline as a fuel must have at least two ventilator ducts fitted with cowls or their equivalent for the efficient removal of explosive or flammable gases from the bilges of every engine and fuel tank compartment. If engine and fuel tank compartments are closed and separated, two such ventilation systems are required.

There must be at least one exhaust duct installed so as to extend from the open atmosphere to the lower portion of the bilge and at least one intake duct installed so as to extend to a point at least midway to the bilge or at least below the level of the carburetor air intake. The cowls must be located and trimmed for maximum effectiveness so as to prevent displaced fumes from being recirculated.

Boats built after July 31, 1980 that have a gasoline engine for electrical generation, mechanical power, or propulsion must be equipped with an operable ventilation system. A compartment containing a permanently installed gasoline engine must either be open to the atmosphere or ventilated by an exhaust blower system. The intake duct for an exhaust blower must be in the lower one-third of the compartment and above the normal level of accumulated bilge water. A combination of more than one exhaust blower may be used to meet specified requirements.

Boats equipped with outboard motors or inboard motors, not enclosed and of "open" construction, are exempt from ventilation requirements.

BACKFIRE FLAME CONTROL DEVICES

Backfire flame control devices are designed to prevent open flame from leaving the carburetion system in the event of a backfire.

Vessels equipped with gasoline engines, except outboard motors, must have a backfire flame control device installed on the engine. These can be either:

- a Coast Guard-approved backfire flame arrestor, suitably secured to the air intake with flame-tight connection,
- a backfire flame arrestor marked "SAEJ-1928" or "UL 1111", and suitably secured to the air intake with a flame-tight connection,
- an approved engine air and fuel induction system which provides adequate protection from propagation of backfire flame to the atmosphere, equivalent to that provided by an acceptable backfire flame arrestor, or
- a flame-tight metallic carburetor air intake attachment, located or positioned so backfire flames would be dispersed to the atmosphere outside the vessel. This latter device must be acceptable to the Coast Guard and be such that the flames will not endanger the vessel, persons on board, or nearby vessels and structures.

MARINE SANITATION DEVICES

Federal law forbids the dumping of sewage, treated or untreated, or any waste derived from sewage, into the lakes, reservoirs, or fresh water impoundments of this state.

Federal regulations and equipment standards established jointly by the Federal Environmental Protection Agency and the Coast Guard govern the use of marine sanitation devices (MSDs). For a pamphlet on the federal

MSD regulations, including a list of those coastal harbors whose waters have been declared as "no-discharge" areas, write to the Department of Boating and Waterways.

State law provides that it is a misdemeanor to disconnect, bypass, or operate an MSD so as to discharge sewage into the waters of this state, unless expressly authorized or permitted by law. In no-discharge areas, a) no person shall disconnect, bypass, or operate an MSD so as to potentially discharge sewage, and b) no person shall occupy or operate a vessel in which an MSD is installed unless the MSD is properly secured. A first violation is an infraction and any subsequent violation is a misdemeanor. State and local peace officers may enforce state laws relating to MSDs and may inspect vessels if there is reasonable cause to suspect noncompliance with those laws.

OILY WASTE DISCHARGE PLACARD
Federal law requires all boats 26 feet or longer to display an Oily Waste Discharge Placard in the engine compartment or near the fuel tank. For more information, call the U.S. Coast Guard toll-free boating safety information line, (800) 368-5647.

MARINE POLLUTION PLACARD
Federal law now requires all boats 26 feet or more in length, when operating in waters under federal jurisdiction, to display an informational placard on the subject of the federal marine pollution prevention laws. Under the Marine Pollution (MARPOL) International Convention To Prevent Pollution From Ships, the discharge into the navigable waters of the U.S. of the following is prohibited:

- plastic, paper, rags, glass, metal, crockery, dunnage, or food in U.S. lakes, rivers, bays, sounds, and up to 3 miles from shore.
- any plastic, or any of the above items if not ground to less than an inch in size, between 3 and 12 miles from shore.
- plastic or dunnage 12 to 25 miles from shore.
- plastic outside 25 miles from shore.

The required placard details these prohibitions. The placard must be displayed in a prominent location where the crew and passengers can read it, must be at least 9 inches wide by 4 inches high, and must be made of durable material bearing letters at least 1/8 inch high. The placards can be purchased at marine supply dealers, or a free placard can be obtained by writing to the Department of Boating and Waterways, or by calling tollfree (888) 326-2822.

MARINE POLLUTION
(MARPOL)
REGULATIONS

LAKES, RIVERS, BAYS, SOUNDS AND 3 MILES FROM SHORE

NOT LEGAL
Plastic and any garbage other than Graywater or Dishwater

LEGAL
Graywater (drainage from shower, laundry, bath and wash basin drains), Dishwater (liquid drainage from manual or automatic washing of cooking utensils)

3 TO 12 MILES FROM SHORE

NOT LEGAL
Plastic and if 1 square inch or larger: Food Waste, Paper, Rags, Glass, Crockery, Metal, Dunnage (lining & packing materials that float)

LEGAL
Graywater, Dishwater, if ground to pieces smaller than 1 sq. inch: Food Waste, Paper, Rags, Glass, Crockery, Metal

12 TO 25 MILES FROM SHORE

NOT LEGAL
Plastic and Dunnage (lining & packing materials that float)

LEGAL
Graywater, Dishwater, Food Waste, Paper, Rags, Glass, Crockery, Metal

OUTSIDE 25 MILES FROM SHORE

NOT LEGAL
Plastic

LEGAL
Graywater, Dishwater, Food Waste, Crockery, Metal, Dunnage (lining & packing materials that float)

WASTE MANAGEMENT PLAN

All U.S. vessels 40 feet or more in length and equipped with a galley and berthing must, in addition, carry a Waste Management Plan, if the vessel operates beyond 3 miles from shore. The Waste Management Plan must be in writing, must designate the person who is in charge of carrying out the plan, and must describe procedures for collecting, processing, storing and properly disposing of garbage in keeping with the prohibitions described above.

RUNNING LIGHTS - INLAND AND INTERNATIONAL

Operating a boat at night without lights is not only dangerous, it is against the law. Running lights make it possible for boat operators to properly interpret and react to the movements of other boats in darkness. *If a boat is used exclusively in the daylight hours, and not during periods of restricted visibility, running lights are not required.*

All vessels must show required running lights between sunset and sunrise and during periods of restricted visibility. Light requirements vary, based on vessel length and propulsion type. In most cases, requirements for a particular vessel are the same under both inland and international rules.

Power-Driven Vessels: A recreational powerboat under way is required to display a masthead light forward, red and green sidelights and a sternlight, as indicated in Figure 1. A recreational powerboat under 39 feet 4 inches (12 meters) may instead display a 360° all-round sternlight and combination red and green sidelights (Figure 2).

Sailing Vessels and Vessels Under Oar: A sailing vessel operating under power of sail only must exhibit sidelights and a sternlight (Figure 3). A sailing vessel of less than 23 feet (7 meters) in length must, if practicable, exhibit sidelights and a sternlight or a lighted lantern showing a white light which must be exhibited in sufficient time to prevent collision (Figure 4). *A sailing vessel operating under machinery power only, or under power and sails, is considered a power-driven vessel, and must display the proper lights for a powerboat (Figure 5).*

A vessel under oars may: a) display those lights prescribed for sailing vessels, or b) have ready at hand an electric torch or lighted lantern showing a white light which must be exhibited in sufficient time to prevent collision (Figure 6).

Boaters operating at night should be aware that there are other possible combinations of lights; the ones presented above are the most common.

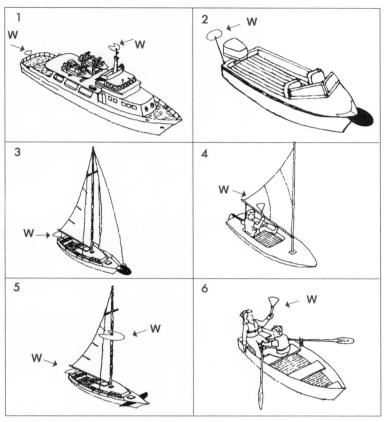

W=WHITE

ANCHOR LIGHTS

An anchor light is an all-round white light exhibited where it can best be seen and is visible for two miles.

Power-driven vessels and sailing vessels at anchor must display anchor lights. Exceptions are: a) vessels less than 23 feet (7 meters) in length are not required to display anchor lights unless anchored in or near a narrow channel, fairway or anchorage, or where other vessels normally navigate, and b) vessels less than 65 feet 7 inches (20 meters) in inland waters when at anchor in a special anchorage area designated by the Secretary of Transportation are not required to exhibit an anchor light.

VISUAL DISTRESS-SIGNALING DEVICES

Vessels operating on coastal waters must carry the required number of approved visual distress-signaling devices selected from Table C.

Coastal waters include: a) territorial seas and b) those waters directly connected to the territorial seas (bays, sounds, harbors, rivers, inlets, etc.) where any entrance exceeds 2 nautical miles between opposite shorelines to the first point where the largest distance between shorelines narrows to two miles. The carriage requirements for vessels operating on coastal waters are:

1. All boats 16 feet or more in length must carry devices aboard at all times. Boaters must carry: EITHER a) devices that are suitable for day use and devices suitable for night use OR b) devices that can be used for both day and night use.

2. Boats less than 16 feet; manually propelled craft of any size; sailboats under 26 feet of completely open construction and not equipped with propulsion machinery; and boats competing in any organized marine parade, regatta, race, or similar event are only required between sunset and sunrise to carry aboard devices that are suitable for night use.

TABLE C - VISUAL DISTRESS REQUIREMENTS

Boaters may select a group or any combination as long as it meets the specific requirement for their boat.

Number on Device	Device Description	Accepted use for	Number required to be carried
160.021	Hand red flare, distress signals	Day and night[1]	3
160.022	Floating orange smoke distress signals	Day only	3
160.024	Pistol-projected parachute red flare distress signals	Day and night[2]	3
160.036	Hand-held rocket-propelled parachute red	Day and night	3
160.037	Hand-held orange smoke distress signals	Day only	3
160.057	Floating orange smoke distress signals	Day only	3
160.066	Distress signal for boats, red aerial pyrotechnic flare	Day and night[3]	3
160.072	Distress signal for boats, orange flag	Day only	1
160.013	Electric distress light for boat	Night only	1

[1] These signals must have a date of manufacture of October 1, 1980 or later to be acceptable.
[2] These signals require use in combination with a suitable launching device approved under 46 CFR 160.028.
[3] These devices may be either self-contained or pistol launched, and either meteor or parachute assisted type. Some of these signals may require use in combination with a suitable launching device approved under 46 CFR 160.028.

All visual distress-signaling devices must be Coast Guard-approved, be readily accessible, and in serviceable condition. Devices carried aboard beyond the date stamped on each device will not meet legal minimum requirements.

RECOGNIZED DISTRESS SIGNALS

The following are some of the signals that are recognized as indicating distress and need of assistance. On coastal waters, boaters must carry Coast Guard-approved visual distress-signaling devices (see page 522).

Items E = essential D = desirable	Less than 16 ft.			16 ft. to under 26 ft.			26 ft. to under 40 ft.			40 ft. to 65 ft.		
	Open waters	Semi-protected	Protected	Open waters	Semi-protected	Protected	Open waters	Semi-protected	Protected	Open waters	Semi-protected	Protected
Anchor, cable (line, chain, etc.)	E	E	E	E	E	E	E	E	E	E	E	E
Bailing device (pump, etc.)	E	E	E	E	E	E	E	E	E	E	E	E
Boat hook	–	–	–	D	D	D	E	E	E	E	E	E
Bucket (fire fighting/bailing)	E	E	E	E	E	E	E	E	E	E	E	E
Compass	E	E	D	E	E	D	E	E	E	E	E	E
Distress signals *	E	E	E	E	E	E	E	E	E	E	E	E
Emergency drinking water	E	D	–	E	D	–	E	D	–	E	D	–
Fenders	D	D	D	D	D	D	D	D	D	D	D	D
First-aid kit and manual (10- to 20-unit)	E	E	E	E	E	E	E	E	E	E	E	E
Flashlight	E	E	E	E	E	E	E	E	E	E	E	E
Heaving line	–	–	–	–	–	–	D	D	D	D	D	D
Light list	D	D	–	E	E	D	E	E	E	E	E	E
Local chart(s)	E	D	–	E	E	E	E	E	E	E	E	E
Mirror (for signaling)	D	D	–	D	D	–	D	D	–	D	D	–
Mooring lines	E	E	E	E	E	E	E	E	E	E	E	E
Motor oil and grease (extra supply)	–	–	–	D	D	D	D	D	D	D	D	D
Oars, spare	E	E	E	E	E	E	–	–	–	–	–	–
Radio direction finder	–	–	–	D	–	–	D	–	–	D	–	–
Radio, telephone	D	–	–	D	D	–	D	D	–	D	D	–
Ring buoy(s) (additional)	D	D	D	D	D	D	D	D	D	D	D	D
Shear pins (if used)	E	E	D	E	E	D	–	–	–	–	–	–
Depth sounding device (lead line, etc.)	D	D	–	D	D	D	E	E	E	E	E	E
Spare batteries	D	D	D	D	D	D	D	D	D	D	D	D
Spare parts	E	D	–	E	E	D	E	E	D	E	E	D
Tables, current	–	–	–	–	–	–	–	D	D	–	E	E
Tables, tide	–	–	D	–	–	D	–	D	D	–	E	E
Tools	E	D	–	E	E	D	E	E	D	E	E	D

* Distress signal devices are required on coastal waters on certain sized boats or during certain times.

REGISTRATION

California law requires current registration of most vessels. This includes vessels that are moored, whether or not they are used. All vessels must be registered and numbered except:

1. Boats propelled manually.

2. Boats eight feet or less in length propelled solely by sail.

3. Certain vessels owned by public agencies.

4. Vessels documented by the Coast Guard.

5. Foreign vessels.

6. Ship's lifeboats used solely for lifesaving purposes.

7. Vessels having valid registration in the state of principal use and not remaining in California over 90 consecutive days.

8. Sailboards.

HOW TO REGISTER

Application to register a vessel may be made at any office of the Department of Motor Vehicles (DMV). Upon receipt of the required information and fees, DMV will issue a Certificate of Number, a Certificate of Ownership, and a set of registration stickers. The boat registration number is the number (beginning with CF) shown on the certificates.

Upon registration, your vessel may be subject to Use Tax based on the purchase price if it is acquired out-of-state or from a private party. For additional information regarding Use Tax, contact your local Board of Equalization or DMV office.

The Certificate of Ownership is your evidence of title to the vessel and, therefore, should be kept in a safe place. Certificates issued will also contain the boat's identifying number (known as the hull identification number), which is the number permanently marked on the transom by the manufacturer or builder, or the number assigned by DMV and marked on the transom by the owner. The reverse side of the Certificate of Ownership is an application for transfer of ownership.

The Certificate of Number, or temporary Certificate of Number, must be available for inspection on the vessel whenever it is being used on the water. Proper display of the current registration stickers on the vessel next to the CF number is required to permit enforcement officers to determine, without boarding, that the vessel is currently registered.

REGISTRATION FEES

Original Registration (including stickers)	$	9.00
Penalty, Late Original Registration	$	4.00
Renewal of Registration (two-year)	$	10.00
Renewal of Registration	$	5.00
Penalty, Late Renewal	$	2.00
Non-resident Original Registration	$	37.00
Penalty, Late NR Original Registration	$	18.00
Boat Trailer Registration	$	30.00 + VLF*
Transfer of Ownership, Single	$	15.00
For each additional Transfer	$	15.00
Penalty, Late Transfer	$	7.00
Duplicate Certificate of Number	$	15.00
Duplicate Certificate of Ownership	$	15.00
Duplicate Set of Stickers	$	15.00
Repossession	$	15.00
Historical Vessel Plaque	$	20.00

*The VLF or Vehicle License Fee is part of the annual fee due upon initial registration and registration renewal. The formula for VLF assessment is established by the legislature and is based upon the vehicle's purchase price. An eleven-year depreciation schedule is used to calculate the VLF.

Although DMV is responsible for collection of biennial vessel registration fees, boat owners may still be subject to annual local county taxes. Boats are subject to personal property taxes assessed by the assessor in the county where your boat is principally located. Failure to pay personal property taxes assessed on a boat may result in the nonrenewal of the boat's registration. Questions concerning taxes on boats should be directed to the assessor of that particular county.

DISPLAY OF NUMBERS AND STICKERS

Numbers and stickers issued at the time of registration must be placed on each side of the forward half of the vessel, usually on the bow, in the manner indicated below. If placement of a number on a flared bow would result in difficult reading, the number should be placed on some other part of the forward half of the vessel where it can be easily read.

For personal watercraft, the numbers and stickers must also be affixed on each side of the forward half of the vessel on a non-removable portion of the hull.

On inflatable boats or vessels so configured that a number will not properly adhere or cannot be clearly seen, the number should be painted on or attached to a backing plate along with the registration sticker. The number must be visible from each side of the vessel. No other numbers, letters, or devices may be placed in the vicinity of the state-assigned number.

To separate the numerals from the letters, spaces the width of the letter "C" or hyphens may be used between the prefix and the number, and between the number and the suffix. Letters and numerals must be at least three inches high, of block character, and of a color which will form a good contrast with the color of the hull or backing plate. In determining height and contrast, any border, trim, outlining, or shading around the number shall not be considered.

CORRECT DISPLAY OF NUMBER
REGISTRATION STICKER

STARBOARD SIDE   PORT SIDE

NOTIFICATION REQUIREMENTS

The owner is required to notify DMV in writing whenever any of the following takes place:

1. The vessel has been destroyed or abandoned. This notice must be given within 15 days and be accompanied by the Certificate of Number and Certificate of Ownership.

2. The owner's address has been changed. This notice must be given within 15 days.

3. The vessel is sold. This notice must be provided within five calendar days and must include date of sale, a description of the vessel and name and address of the new owner.

Registration forms may be obtained from any local DMV office or authorized registration agent or by writing:

Department of Motor Vehicles
Registration Processing Units
P.O. Box 942869
Sacramento, CA 94269-0001

California Department of Boating and Waterways

recommends that boaters *always*:

- Check the weather before heading out.

- Wear their life jackets while under way.

- Abstain from alcohol consumption while boating.

Thank you for keeping California's waterways safe!

Index

Silver Lake (Tahoe National Forest): **200**
Silverwood Lake: **408,** 412–413
Silverwood Lake State Recreation Area: 412
Simi Valley: **391**
Sinkyone Wilderness State Park: **21**
Siskiyou National Forest: **42**
Siskiyou Wilderness: **41, 42**
Sisquoc River: **389, 390**
Six Rivers National Forest: **23,** 27, 31–33, **41, 42, 44,** 46, 48, 65
Sly Creek Reservoir: **149**
Sly Park: 181–182
Sly Park Recreation Area: 181
Smith River: **22,** 27–28
Snag Lake (Lassen Volcanic National Park): **84**
Snag Lake (Tahoe National Forest): 199–**200**
Snow Mountain Wilderness: **115, 117**
Sonoma: **119**
Sonora: 311
Sotcher Lake: **350**
South Carlsbad State Beach: **430**
South Cow Mountain Recreation Area: **116**
South/East Delta: 306–308
South Fork American River: 179–181, **191, 193**
South Fork Battle Creek: **84**
South Fork Eel River: **25,** 36–37, **116**
South Fork Feather River: **149, 156**
South Fork Gualala River: **118**
South Fork Kern River: **363, 364**
South Fork Pit River: **83**
South Fork Rubicon River: **227**
South Fork Smith River: **23,** 32–33
South Fork Yuba River: 161–162

South Laguna: 422
South Lake: **361,** 372
South Lake Tahoe: **194, 222,** 231
South Warner Wilderness: **81, 83**
Spanish Creek: 195
Spenceville Wildlife Area: **149**
Spicer Meadow Reservoir: **194,** 247–248
Spring Lake: 141–142
Spring Lake County Park: 141
Spring Valley: **429, 433**
Stampede Reservoir: **192, 212,** 213–214
Stanislaus National Forest: **152,** 186, **191,** 242–245, 247, **300, 329,** 334, 338–339
Stanislaus River: **152, 299, 300,** 313–315
Stateline: **222**
Stevens Creek Reservoir: 268
Stillwater Cove Regional Park: **118**
Stockton: 182–185, **297, 299,** 306
Stone Lagoon: **22,** 29–30
Stony Creek: **117**
Stony Gorge Reservoir: **115, 117,** 127–128
Stumpy Meadows Lake: **193**
Stumpy Meadows Reservoir: 226–227
Sugar Pine Point State Park: **192**
Sugar Pine Reservoir: **150,** 169–170
Suisun Bay: **251, 252**
Summit Lake: 99–100
Sunbeam Lake/Lagoon: 471
Sunnyvale: **254**
Sunol Regional Wilderness: **255**
Susanville: **85**
Sutter National Wildlife Refuge: **149**

T

Taft: **304**
Tahoe City: **192, 222**

Tahoe National Forest: 160–161, 166, 169, 172, **191, 192,** 198–211, 213–215, 217, **222**
Tahoe State Recreation Area: **222**
Tamarack Lake: 62
Taylor Lake (Plumas National Forest): 111
Taylor Lake (Russian Wilderness): 50–51
Tecate: 444
Tehachapi: **450**
Tehama State Wildlife Area: **81**
Tehama Wildlife Area: **84**
Temecula: **429, 430**
Tenaya Lake: **332,** 341–342
Ten Mile Creek: 376–377
Ten Mile River: 120
Thermalito Afterbay: **149, 156**
Thermalito Forebay: **149,** 155, **156,** 157
Thermalito North Forebay Recreation Area: **156**
Thomes Creek: **117**
Thousand Lakes Wilderness: **81, 84**
Thousand Oaks: **407**
Thurston Lake: **131**
Tilden Regional Park: **254,** 264
Tinemaha Reservoir: **361**
Tioga Lake: 343
T.J. Lake: **350**
Toad Lake: 57–58
Toiyabe National Forest: **194, 331**
Tomales Bay: **251, 252**
Topaz Lake: **194,** 241–242
Topock: 462
Torrey Pines State Reserve: **432**
Tracy: **299**
Trinity Alps Wilderness: **41, 42, 43, 44**
Trinity Lake: **41, 43,** 66–67
Trinity River: **41, 42, 44,** 64–65
Truckee: **192,** 217
Truckee Creek: **212**

ALSO FROM
AVALON TRAVEL PUBLISHING

MOON HANDBOOKS®
THE CURE FOR THE COMMON TRIP

For a more personal, entirely uncommon,
and ultimately more satisfying travel
experience, MOON HANDBOOKS has
guides to destinations throughout the
Americas, Asia, and the Pacific.

www.moon.com/handbooks

MOON METRO
UNFOLD THE CITY

Perfect for the city traveler or urban dweller,
these innovative guides feature laminated
foldout maps and listings of the hottest sights,
restaurants, hotels, shops, and entertainment.

www.moon.com/metro

More Savvy. More Surprising. More Fun.

Experience everything Europe has to offer with RICK
STEVES' best-selling guidebooks, phrase books, videos,
and DVDs. As the #1 authority on European
travel, Rick gives you inside information on
what to visit, where to stay, and how to get
there—economically and hassle-free.

www.ricksteves.com

www.travelmatters.com

AVALON TRAVEL PUBLISHING GUIDES ARE AVAILABLE
AT YOUR FAVORITE BOOK OR TRAVEL STORE

ⒻOGHORN OUTDOORS®

YOUR ADVENTURE STARTS HERE

Ready for your next outdoor adventure?
FOGHORN OUTDOORS has guides for
camping, hiking, biking, fishing, and more.

www.foghorn.com

ROAD TRIP USA

OPEN ROAD. ENDLESS POSSIBILITIES.

See what the interstates have left behind.
ROAD TRIP USA takes you off the beaten path,
onto classic blacktop, and into the soul of America.

www.roadtripusa.com

THE INSIDE SCOOP ON WHERE TO TAKE YOUR DOG

A special breed of guidebook for travelers and residents
who don't want to leave their canine pals behind.

WWW.DOGLOVERSCOMPANION.COM